MODERN THEORIES *of* MOTIVATION

K. B. MADSEN

Modern Theories *of* Motivation

A Comparative Metascientific Study

MUNKSGAARD

Modern Theories of Motivation. 1st edition, 1st printing

© 1974 by K. B. Madsen and Munksgaard, Copenhagen, Denmark

Cover and design by Poul Jeppesen

No part of this publication may by reproduced, stored in a retrieval system, or transmitted in any form of by any means, electronic, mechanical photocopying, recording or otherwise without prior permission by the copyright owner and the publishers.

Published simultaneously in the USA by Halsted Press, a Division of John Wiley & Sons, Inc., New York

Printed in Denmark by Andelsbogtrykkeriet, Odense

ISBN 87 16 01322 0

Contents

Meta-Introduction 9
Introduction 13

Part I

BACKGROUND: THEORY OF SCIENCE

Chapter 1: *Metascience* 17
  The Philosophy of Science 17
  The History of Science 20
  The Psychology of Science 21
  The Sociology of Science 22
  A Systematic Integration of Metascientific Disciplines 23
  What is Science? 26

Chapter 2: *Systematology* 31
  Some Basic Definitions 31
  The Strata of a Theory 35
  The Strata of Psychological Theories 42
  The Theory as a Whole 62
  A Systematological Questionnaire 72

Chapter 3: *An Historical Introduction to Motivational Psychology* 78
  The Instinct Theories 78
  Motivation in Learning 80
  Motivation in Personality Theory 84

Part II

ANALYTICAL STUDIES

Chapter 4: Duffy's Theory 95
Chapter 5: Bindra's Theory 104
Chapter 6: Berlyne's Theory 115

Chapter 7: Konorski's Theory	129
Chapter 8: Pribram's Theory	150
Chapter 9: Miller's Theory	174
Chapter 10: Brown's Theory	198
Chapter 11: Woodworth's Theory	211
Chapter 12: Festinger's Theory	223
Chapter 13: Cattell's Theory	243
Chapter 14: Atkinson's and Birch's Theory	268
Chapter 15: Maslow's Theory	289
Chapter 16: Other Important Theories	314
Bolles's Theory	314
Bühler's Theory	318
Eysenck's Theory	327
Irwin's Theory	337
Fowler's Theory	347
Luria's Theory	349
Nuttin's Theory	354
Reventlow's Theory	358
Schultz's Theory	367
Sokolov's Theory	372
Reviews of other Theories: Berkowitz, Cofer and Appley, Heckhausen, Logan, Mowrer, Murray, Schachter, Thomae	375

Part III

COMPARATIVE STUDY

Chapter 17: *The Metastrata of the Theories*	389
The Philosophicual Propositions	389
The Metatheoretical Propositions	394
The Methodological Propositions	399
Chapter 18: *The Hypothetical Strata of the Theories*	404
The Hypothetical Terms	404
The Hypotheses of the Theories	420
Chapter 19: *The Descriptive Strata of the Theories*	431
The Abstract D-levels	431
The Concrete D-levels	432
The Descriptive Units	439

Chapter 20: *The Theories as Wholes* 440
   The Formal Properties 440
   The Epistemological Properties 443
   The Theory? Empiry Ratios 445
   Patterns of Preferences 451
   Computer-Assisted Theory Analysis 453

Meta-Introduction

Purpose, Scope and Background of this Book

The Purposes of this Book

The present book is written with two purposes in mind.

First: to contribute to the development of *metascience* by establishing a new metascientific discipline: *the comparative study of theories,* which I suggest calling *"systematology"*. The metascientific frame of reference for conducting such a systematological study of psychological theories is presented in the first two chapters. And the results of this comparative, metascientific study are presented in the last four chapters, which for metascientific purposes, are the most important.

Second: to contribute to the *education of psychologists* – students, professional psychologists and research workers – through the presentation of *the systematic analyses of several important theories of motivation*. These analytical studies of theories are presented in the Chapters 4 to 16, which are the most important for educational purposes. I have had such well known books as Hilgard and Bower's *Theories of Learning* and Hall and Lindzey's *Theories of Personality* in mind as ideals for educational purposes. But I am aware of how difficult it is to attain the same educational standards as in the two above mentioned works – especially as I simultaneously attempt to make a contribution to metascience. I hope that I have attained an optimal combination of these two purposes by concentrating mainly on the *educational* purpose in the middle part of the book (Chapters 4–16) and mainly on the *metascientific* purpose in the last part of the book (Chapters 17–20). The three introductory chapters are concerned with both purposes.

Even if I have not succeeded in writing a book which is satisfactory from both the educational and metascientific points of view I believe that there is an increasing need for books of this kind. The accelerating growth of all sciences creates the need for such a "higher-order science" or *metascience*; and if this metascience is to be of any utility for basic science and society, it requires literature which contributes to the *education of scientists*.

I feel that psychology needs such a metascientific education more than most other sciences.

The Scope of this Book

As indicated in the above section, this book is aimed at psychology students, professional psychologists and research workers. I hope that the level of difficulty is not such that it prevents the book from being used as a textbook for advanced undergraduate students or graduate students. I have used stencilled chapters of the book in my own teaching of psychology students at the Royal Danish School of Educational Studies. These students have in advance graduated from a teachers' college and, in addition, have had one year of psychological studies before starting with "theoretical psychology", as I call my subject.

The Background of this Book

The present book can be regarded as a supplement to my *"Theories of Motivation"* (1st ed., 1959; 4th ed., 1968. Spanish and Czech translations). But the present book can be read as a completely independent volume. My first book, "Theories of Motivation", presented a comparative metascientific study of 20 theories of motivation from the period 1930–1957, while the present book deals with 22 theories from the period 1957–1971.

As most of the authors of the theories studied in this book are contemporaries, I have had the opportunity of checking with them. Thus all the authors have received a stencilled copy of the analysis of their theory, and have been kind enough to read it critically and suggest improvements. These improvements have been incorporated in the present version. In addition, I feel that the book has gained something by including material about developments in the philosophy of science and metascience during the last two decades.

Finally, this book has profited – compared to my "Theories of Motivation" – from the educational improvements suggested by the try-out of the manuscript in my own teaching.

Acknowledgments

First: I wish to acknowledge the feedback I have received from the authors whose theories I have studied. It has been both a scientifically and socially important form of contact for me.

Second: I wish to acknowledge the inspiration I have received from the publications of and the personal contact I have had with Dr. *Håkan Törnebohm*, Professor of "the Theory of Science" at the University of Gothenburg, Sweden. The contact I have had with Törnebohm and his co-workers – especially *Gerard Radnitzky* and *Carl Lesche*– has been of great intellectual and motivational value to me.

Third: I wish to acknowledge the inspiration I have received from the exchange of ideas I have had with my students. In those instances where a student has made a direct contribution I have noted this in the text.

Fourth: I wish to acknowledge the contribution of *Mr. John T. Bruce, M.A.* with whom I have worked closely on this book since 1966. Mr. Bruce is language consultant at our school and is responsible for correcting my manuscripts. But, in addition, he has improved the whole presentation and style to such an extent that the book has gained considerably in educational utility.

Fifth, I wish to acknowledge the contribution of *Mr. H. Amnitsby,* who is draughtsman and photographer at our school and is responsible for all the diagrams which illustrate the analyses of the various theories, and thus has constributed to the educational value of the book.

Finally, I should like to explain the delay in publication of this book which I promised to have finished in 1969. This delay was mainly caused by the fact that most of the writing had to be done during week-ends and vacations, as I had no pause from my teaching and other duties.

Copenhagen October 1972

K. B. Madsen, dr. phil.
Professor of General Psychology
The Royal Danish School of
Educational Studies
101 Emdrupvej
DK-2400 Copenhagen NV.

Introduction

The problem of dealing with many theories

There are many theories of motivation, and besides parts of many learning and personality theories also deal with motivation.

This fact demonstrates that "motivation" is an important concept in modern psychology. It is not possible to understand, explain or predict human behavior without some knowledge of "motivation" – the "driving force" behind behavior. Consequently, a psychologist cannot construct a general psychological theory or a theory about personality, learning or the cognitive processes without having some explanatory concepts and hypotheses about motivation or the activation of behavior. For the same reasons a student of psychology also has to know something about motivation.

But the importance of motivation coupled with the existence of many different theories of motivation created a major problem for psychologists. How can a psychologist utilize all these theories of motivation as they are expressed in divergent and confusing "languages" or terminologies.

Psychologists react in different ways to this problem of multiple theories.

A few psychologists are *"anti-theoretical"*: they avoid and reject *all* theories. This "solution" is the easiest, but also unfruitful and unscientific, as theories are the products of advanced sciences.

Some psychologists are *"mono-theorists"*: they select one theory – e. g., *Freud*'s theory – and all other theories are either avoided or are "translated" into the terms of the favorite theory. This last version of mono-theorism is the most fruitful of the two solutions, but to be fruitful such a "translation" requires a deeper insight into theories in general and also a "neutral" conceptual frame-of-reference.

Many psychologists are *"eclectics"*: they try to select something from many theories, and they apply these fragments of theories where they find them useful. But they don't combine them into an integrated whole.

Some psychologists are *"integrative theorists"*: they try to integrate many or all theories into one big synthesis, which may be just as original, creative and fruitful as any of the theories on which it is based. But such integrative theorizing also requires a "neutral" conceptual frame-of-reference, a sort of "higher-level-language", which can be used as the medium for "translation" from one theory to another. Without such a "higher-level-language" it is difficult to discriminate between *"apparent"* (i. e., only terminological) similarities and differences on the one hand, and the *"real"* (i. e., theoretical) similarities and differences on the other hand.

Thus we can conclude that mono-theorists, eclectics and integrative theorists all need a "higher-level-language", in which different theories can be described and discussed.

But this "higher-level-language" must be created on a *scientific* basis in order to be really fruitful. This scientific basis consists of a *comparative study of theories*, which has to be done in the most *scientific* manner possible: systematically, objectively and precisely.

It is the purpose of this book to present the results of such a scientific comparative study of theories of motivation.

In addition, it is our purpose to present these results in such a manner that psychologists may gain a deeper understanding and systematic overview not only of theories of motivation – but also of psychological – and perhaps scientific theories in general.

In order to attain these goals we have to follow a systematic disposition, and therefore in the next section we shall draw up an outline of this disposition.

The outline of this book

As this book presents a *scientific* study of theories of motivation, we shall present – in the *first part* of the book – the *conceptual frame-of-reference,* which consists of three parts:
1. An outline of *"metascience"* – the science of sciences – to which belongs the study of theories. This general outline is presented in the first chapter.
2. A more systematic and detailed exposition of the necessary "higher-level-language" or *taxonomy* for the comparative study of theories is presented in Chapter 2 under the title *"systematology"*. This term includes the taxonomy necessary for scientific descriptions and classifications of scientific theories.
3. A brief *historical* introduction to modern theories of motivation is presented in Chapter 3, which deals with the development of the conception of motivation in psychology in the last century.

After the exposition of our conceptual frame-of-reference, we shall, in the *second part* of this book, present an analysis of 12 modern theories of motivation, devoting a chapter to each theory. Additional modern theories are more briefly dealt with in one chapter.

After the analytical part of the book follows, in the *third* part, a presentation of the main results of the *comparative* study of the theories analyzed. These results are then related to other comparative studies of psychological theories, including those made by this author.

PART I

BACKGROUND: THEORY OF SCIENCE

In the first part of this book we present the necessary background or frame of reference for our study of motivational theories.

The first chapter is concerned with an overview of the whole field of *metascience*, the science of sciences, to which our study belongs.

The second chapter deals in detail with the conceptual frame of reference for the metascientific, *comparative study of theories*, which we call *Systematology*.

The third chapter comprises an *historical introduction* to motivational psychology.

1 : Metascience

*– The Science of Science –
and its application to psychology*

*Introduction**

Everything can be the object of a scientific study – even science itself. This book is a contribution to such a scientific study of one science, psychology. Therefore, we shall devote the first Chapter to a general discussion of the science of science or *"meta-science"*.

Meta-science has not yet evolved into a systematically organized science. It exists only as separate disciplines inside several sciences. The disciplines are:

1. The philosophy of science.
2. The history of science.
3. The psychology of science.
4. The sociology of science.

We shall discuss these disciplines separately, and, finally try to organize them into a systematic science of science.

The Philosophy of Science

General. The oldest science of science is the 'motherscience', *philosophy*. But not all philosophy is about science. There are: 'a philosophy of morality', 'a philosophy of religion', 'a philosophy of the arts', 'a philosophy of education', and so on. But a main part of modern philosophy can be called *'the philosophy of science'*. This is a part of meta-science, and is well established with its own journals and several textbooks, handbooks and monographs. The philosophy of science can be divided further inth three subdisciplines:

The philosophy of science
1. Epistemology
2. Methodology
3. Metatheory

Epistemology. Among these disciplines 'epistemology' – or the 'theory of knowledge' – is the oldest and most fundamental. It deals with the fundamental prob-

---

* The main part of this chapter is identical with Chapter 1 of my "Theories of Motivation" (4th ed. 1968).

lems of all knowledge – pre-scientific as well as scientific. It tries to answer questions such as: What is knowledge? What is truth? What are the conditions for obtaining true knowledge? and so on. In the course of time several schools of philosophy have tried to answer these questions with their peculiar theories of knowledge, such as 'rationalism,', 'empiricism', 'positivism', 'pragmatism', 'operationism', 'logical empiricism', 'Oxford philosophy', etc. Many of the modern philosophies of science can be united under the label '*analytical philosophy*', as they see the task of philosophy as *analyzing* concepts, propositions and theories (in opposition to the older philosophy, which saw the task of philosophy mainly as *synthesizing* all available knowledge into a comprehensive 'world system').

Methodology. This subdiscipline deals with the *empirical methods* of science. It describes and analyzes the problems about such methods as general observation, experimentation, case-studies, testing, measuring, etc. There are several papers and books about this subject matter in general – and about the methods of psychology in particular. Among these the works of *Andrews* (1948), *Bjørkman* (1962), *Brown and Ghiselli* (1955) and *Hyman* (1964) may be noted. Sometimes 'methodology' is used in a comprehensive way including the next discipline, too. But the difference is, that methodology deals with *empirical* methods, while meta-theory deals with *theoretical* methods: the methods of constructing theories.

Meta-theory. From what has already been said you can understand that 'meta-theory' is 'the theory of theories'[1]). This sub-discipline deals with the 'products of science': scientific theories, which perhaps are the most complex products of the most complex organisms on the earth. As theories are complex systems of words and sentences it could also be said, that meta-theory deals with the vocabulary (concepts) and language (theories) of science (cf. Mandler and Kessen, 1959).

The role of theory in science is in modern times stressed by the philosophical school named: '*Logical Empiricism*'. As the name of this school indicates, they hold that theory is second only to empirical observation. The role of theory in science can also be illustrated by the sequence:

Observation → theory → observation.

The first arrow indicates what is called 'induction': a generalization from empirical observation to general formulations of 'hypotheses', which explain the observation. The second arrow indicates the so-called 'deduction': logical specification from general formulations to specific descriptions of observations. These observations are said to be 'predicted' from the theory. This theory of theories is based for the most part on works of philosophers who could be united under the broad label 'analytical philosophers': *Ayer, Bergman, Braithwaite, Brod-*

1. The author should here like to introduce a new term as a substitute for 'meta-theory' namely the term: '*systematology*'; the study of scientific systems ('theories', 'models', etc.).

beck, Campel, Carnap, Feigl, Hempel, Jørgensen, Kaila, Ness, Neurath, Popper, Reichenback, Russel, Ryle, Scriven* and many others who are indicated in the list of references.

The philosophers belonging to logical empiricism have been most interested in studying theories within mathematics and physics. And they are more or less implicitly of the opinion, that all scientific theories ought to be like mathematical-physical theories. In other words: their concepts, definitions and theories about theories can be described as 'normative'.

A more purely descriptive approach to meta-theory is found in a Scandinavian meta-theory called *'discourse analysis'*. It was formulated by *H. Törnebohm* (1952, 1955, 1957) and applied to psychology by *Carl Lesche* (1960).

While the logical empiricists study scientific theories by comparing them with logical or mathematical systems, the discourse analysts make 'case-studies' of theories and describe them in their own ways.

A similar purely descriptive approach to meta-theory was independently formulated by another Scandinavian philosopher, *Arne Ness* (1936, 1962).

The approach to meta-theory in this book is a combination of the different analytical approaches. The author has combined the ideas of Logical Empiricism and discourse analysis with ideas of certain psychologists – especially *Tolman, Lewin, Spence*, and *S. Koch*.

The comparison of theories in the last part of this book is completely the author's own work – for better or for worse.

The Philosophy of Psychology. We have now discussed the philosophy of science in general. But this book is devoted especially to the *'philosophy of psychology'* which is the application of the philosophy of science to psychology. Besides this application there are of course similar applications of the philosophy of science to other sciences, and so we have 'the philosophy of mathematics', 'the philosophy of physics', etc.

Perhaps physics and psychology are the two sciences which have attracted most philosophical attention. Many philosophers and psychologists are engaged in the study of the philosophy of psychology. The American Psychological Association has now a division for 'philosophical psychology' which is more or less identical with 'the philosophy of psychology'.

The same division of the philosophy of science into three subdisciplines can be made with the philosophy of psychology, and we then have the following subdisciplines:

The philosophy of psychology =
1. Epistemology of psychology
2. Methodology of psychology
3. Meta-theory of psychology.

Among these subdisciplines the third has our special interest as this book belongs to *'the meta-theory of psychology'* or *'meta-theoretical psychology'* as it also could be designated[2]). It is here formally defined as *'the meta-theoretical*

---

2. Or in accordance with our new term: 'systematology of psychology'.

study of psychological theories'. This meta-theoretical study is made as a *purely empirical or descriptive study: an analysis and comparison of (psychological) theories, which results in a description and classification of the theories.*

The frame of reference or tools for the analysis are presented in the first part of this book. In the second part we present results of the analysis of 22 theories, while in the third part we describe the comparison of the theories. We have chosen theories of motivation as the special object for our meta-theoretical study, because motivation plays a central role in modern psychology. Many of the theories could as well be characterized as theories of learning or theories of personality, as they in fact are comprehensive and general psychological theories. But we have especially analyzed their concepts and hypotheses about motivation.

As mentioned earlier many philosophers and psychologists are interested in the philosophy of psychology. Perhaps it is because some philosophers are mainly interested in the epistemology of psychology. Among these are *Bergman, Feigl, Jørgensen, Kaila, Ness, Peters, Russel, Ryle* and *Scriven*. Many psychologists are interested in the methodology of psychology and the meta-theory of psychology. We can mention only a few, who are indicted in the list of references: *Brunswik, Griffith, Hebb, Hilgard, Hull, Kantor, Koch, Lewin, Marx, Pratt, Rosenthal, Spence, Stevens, Tolman, Turner* and *Wolman*.

It is of course difficult to draw a sharp boundary between these subdisciplines, as well as between the whole philosophy of science and the other discipline, the history of science, to which we now turn.

The History of Science

General. The second discipline belonging to meta-science is *'the history of science'*. It is the only discipline which is developed to a degree comparable to the philosophy of science. History is almost as old as philosophy, and these two disciplines dealing with science are the oldest disciplines constituting meta-science.

It is difficult to draw a sharp boundary between these two disciplines, as between the other disciplines. It is most difficult to distinguish methodology and meta-theory on the one side and the history of science on the other side, especially if the meta-theory is of the purely descriptive sort – as it is in this book. The difference lies mainly in the fact that the history of science describes the chronological order of the scientific production, and tries to *explain* the scientific development. In other words, it is especially the (historical) *explanations* which make the difference between the history of science, which is both descriptive and explanatory, and the philosophy of science, which is purely descriptive.

The history of science can be divided into subdisciplines in accordance with the sciences the history deals with. Thus we have 'the history of philosophy', 'the history of physics', and so on. Among these subdisciplines belongs the history of psychology.

The History of Psychology. There has in the last decade been a growing interest in the history of psychology. It is perhaps a symptom of psychology's growing to a mature state that psychologists are interested in the past development of their science.

The 'grand old man' in the history of psychology is *E. G. Boring*, who also has dealt with the other meta-scientific disciplines. Besides his books you can find in the list of references the books of *Esper* (1965), *Garrett* (1941), *Murphy* (1951), *Peters* (1953), *Postman* (1962), *Razran* (1965), *Tegen* (1949), *Watson* (1963), *Woodworth* (1964), *Wolman* (1960), and *Misiak and Sexton* (1966).

There are many works which belong both to the history of psychology and the next discipline, we are going to discuss, 'the psychology of science'. This is specially the case with biographical studies of famous scientists. The most well-known case of an historical and psychological study of a scientist is perhaps *Ernest Jones's* (1962) biography of *Sigmund Freud*.

The Psychology of Science

General. A complete science of science or meta-science must include a discipline called '*the psychology of science*', because science is a result of human behavior. This discipline for the moment only exists in the form of scattered investigations. But in its full development it must come to include the same disciplines as psychology does – all applied to science as the object. We then have the following subdisciplines:

'The psychology of science' =
1. The general psychology of science.
2. The differential psychology of science.
3. The social psychology of science.

We will discuss the content of these subdisciplines and mention some of the investigations already made.

The General Psychology of Science. Scientific *activity* is mainly observation and creative thinking. Therefore, the general psychology of science must be a special part of the general psychology of *perception* and *thinking*. In recent years there has been a growing interest in creative thinking – artistic, technical, and scientific. But many of the investigations have been more with the creative personality which belongs to the next subdiscipline. A bibliography on 'creativity in research in the physical sciences' was compiled by *Benton* (1961).

Scientific activity must, just as all behavior, be motivated. The special motivation for scientific activity is, therefore, a possible object of study for the general psychology of science[3]).

The Differential Psychology of Science. This is the psychological study of the special scientific *personality* (and intelligence-structure). There have been some studies in this field. They are of two slightly different types:

3. A book which is 'a critical examination of the psychology of science and scientists' is: Abraham H. Maslow: 'The Psychology of Science' (N. Y. 1966).

a. *'Case studies'* of single – often famous – scientists. This type of study has much in common with general *biographical* studies. Besides the biography of Freud by Ernest Jones, we can mention *Amon's* (1962) and *Hays's* (1962) studies of Hull's 'Notebooks'.
b. *'Group studies'* of a group of scientists often employing tests and other objective methods. While the first mentioned type often are longitudinal studies, this type is often 'cross-sectional'. One of these group studies is that of *Anna Roe* (1953). Also *Terman* (1959) has among his approximately 1500 intelligent children compared those who became scientists with those who did not.

The Social Psychology of Science. Much modern scientific research is accomplished as teamwork, and, therefore, the group-conditions and group-relationships and the leadership in the group are important for the research work. As group-behavior is the object for social psychology, there must be a *'social psychology of science'*. This subdiscipline of the psychology of science has been cultivated by the American psychologist *Donald C. Pelz* (see Pelz, 1958, 1964). He has studied the different kinds of leadership and the different form of contact in research team-work, and found what its influence was on the productivity of group-members.

With the social psychology of science we are in the border area of the last meta-scientific discipline, but we must first deal with a special application of the psychology of science.

The Psychology of Psychology. As is the case with the other meta-scientific disciplines the psychology of science also can be divided into subdisciplines according to the special science – or group of scientists, which are the object of the psychological study. We thus get:

'the psychology of mathematics'
'the psychology of physics'
'the psychology of biology'
'the psychology of psychology'.
etc.

The examples of research in the psychology of science mentioned have been concerned with almost all areas of science. But E. Jones's biography of Freud is a good example of a piece of 'psychology of psychologists'. Other examples are *David P. Campell's* (1965) investigation of the vocational interests of presidents of the American Psychological Association and *P. H. Kriedl's* (1949) investigation of the vocational interests of psychologists in general.

The Sociology of Science

General. The development of modern science depends much on the society to which it belongs: it depends on financial facilitation or inhibition, etc. Besides, this modern science is organized into institutions and professions, and the scientific development is dependent on information and communication in the society in general and in the professional organization in particular. There is a Scandinavian investigation of the co-operation between scientists (Valpola and Törnudd, 1963).

All these phenomena are the object for a *'sociology of science'*. This metascientific discipline is of course connected with the other meta-scientific disciplines, and there are border-zones between them. We have just mentioned that the social psychology of science must have a border-zone in common with the sociology of science. And there is also a border-zone between the sociology of science and the history of science. This border-zone comprises the description of the contemporary condition of science in a special country or area. It could perhaps be called *'the geography of science'*.

The Sociology of Psychology. As the other meta-scientific disciplines the sociology of science can be divided into subdisciplines according to the science studied. Thus we have: 'the sociology of mathematics', 'the sociology of physics' and so on. And among these of course *'the sociology of psychology'*. Some research has been done within this discipline. The American Psychology Association has taken the initiative and sponsored two research projects. One is reported on in *K. E. Clark's:* America's Psychologists: A survey of a growing profession' (1957). The other is an as yet unfinished project on scientific information exchange among psychologists. (See the preliminary report from 1964).

A systematic integration of meta-scientific disciplines

General. We have now analyzed the different existing meta-scientific disciplines. There are not any other disciplines developed at the moment – at least not any known to the author.

But now we come to the problem: what are the systematic relationships between the disciplines? We will try to draw a model for an integration of the diciplines into a *systematic meta-science*. We will make this integration on the basis of a conception of the *tasks of sciences*. In accordance with the general opinion among contemporary scientists the tasks of sciences are: *description, explanation* and *prediction*[4]). We will now see how these tasks are distributed among the meta-disciplines.

1. '*The philosophy of science* has the task of analyzing and *describing* the sciences. This task is further divided between the subdisciplines in the following way:

a. *Epistemology* has the task of analyzing the fundamental problems of all scientific knowledge and *describing* the solutions of these problems by formulations of the *basic propositions* (principles, axioms, working hypotheses, etc.), which are the more or less explicit starting points for the sciences.

---

4. Prediction is logical, identical with explanation; it is only the time perspective which is different and makes prediction more difficult.

b. *Methodology* has the task of analyzing and *describing* the *empirical methods* of the sciences.
c. *Meta-theory*[5]) has the task of analyzing and *describing* the *theories* of the sciences.

Summarizing we could say, that the philosophy of science has the task of giving a *systematic description* of the sciences, which can form the basis for the description given in the other disciplines.

2. *The history of science* also has the task of describing the sciences. But this description must be a description of the development of the sciences, in other words: a *chronological or historical description*. But besides this, the history of science has the task of explaining (and perhaps predicting) the historical development of the sciences. Perhaps one could roughly characterize historical explanations as *ideographic*' or 'single case explanations'. This is different from the *'nomothetic'* or general law explanations, which we find in the remaining two meta-scientific disciplines.

3. *The psychology of science* also has the task of *describing* and *explaining* (perhaps predicting) sciences. But the psychological description must, of course, be a description of scientific *activity* as a kind of *behavior*. And the description of the men of science, must be a description of the *scientific personality*.

Besides these descriptions there can be *explanations* of the scientific *activity* in accordance with *general* psychological concepts, hypotheses and theories; and there can be explanations of the *development* of the scientific personality in accordance with the concepts, hypotheses and theories in *differential* psychology (of personality and intelligence).

As mentioned earlier a *combination* of historical and psychological descriptions and explanations can be *made* in the *biographical* studies of famous scientists.

4. *The sociology of science* also has the tasks of *describing* and *explaining* sciences. But the description must, of course, be a sociological description, which is a description in accordance with sociological concepts (group, organisation, institution, society, profession, class, communication, etc); and explanations (and perhaps predictions) are made in accordance with sociological hypotheses as theories.

As mentioned earlier there are also border-zones between sociology and the psychology of science (*the social psychology* of sciences) and between sociology and the history of sciences (the 'geography' of science).

We can illustrate this systematic integration of meta-scientific disciplines by a diagram (Fig. 1.1).

Meta-scientific Psychology. We have now analyzed and integrated the whole of meta-science. As the meta-scientific disciplines are so intimately interrelated, it is possible to combine them in one study of a particular science – or of a part of a science. We then get the following *'combined meta-scientific disciplines'*:

---

5. or rather 'systematology'.

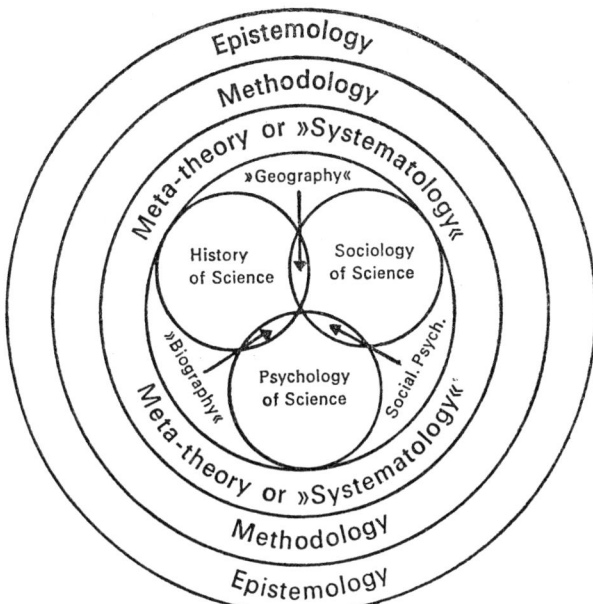

Fig. 1.1. A diagram representing the systematic organisation of the different disciplines constituting the *Meta-science*.

'Meta-scientific mathematics', 'meta-scientific physics', meta-scientific chemistry', 'meta-scientific biology', 'meta-scientific psychology', etc.

We can make an explication of the content of the combined meta-scientific disciplines applied to psychology:

Meta-scientific Psychology' =
1. The philosophy of psychology.
   a. The epistemology of psychology.
   b. The methodology of psychology.
   c. The meta-theory of psychology.
2. The history of psychology.
3. The psychology of psychology.
4. The sociology of psychology.

'*Meta-scientific psychology*' can formally be defined as *the combined meta-scientific* (philosophical, historical, psychological and sociological) *study of psychology*. The term 'meta- scientific psychology' could perhaps be shortened to 'meta-psychology', and similarly in the other sciences: 'meta-methematics', 'meta-physics', etc. Unfortunately, the term meta-physics' is still in use with an outdated meaning: 'a speculative philosophy of nature', which supplements the physics for a world-system. And the term 'meta-psychology' was used in yet another way by Freud. In other words: the old meaning of 'meta-' is 'philosophical supplements to a science', while the modern meaning of 'meta-' is 'science dealing with'. In order to prevent confusing these two meanings of 'meta-' we recommend always using 'meta-scientific' when the meaning is 'science dealing with'.

There have of course been some combined meta-scientific studies of psychology. One of the 'grand old men' in this science is *E.G. Boring*, who not only has made historical studies of psychology, but has also contributed many philosophical, psychological and sociological studies (see Boring 1961 and 1963). Another all-round meta-scientific psychologist is *Sigmund Koch*. Besides several papers and sections of books, he has been the editor of the great work sponsored by the American Psychological Association: 'Psychology – A study of a science' (see *Koch* 1959–63). This latter work, which is not yet finished, is based upon a questionnaire sent to all the contributing psychologists. In this questionnaire they are asked to answer meta-scientific questions about philosophical matters (especially, methodological and meta-theoretical) as well as about historical, psychological and sociological subjects. Koch has analyzed the questionnaire and made preliminary summaries in six volumes. He is at the moment writing the 7th volume, which is designed to be a comprehensive exposition of this extensive and intensive meta-scientific study of psychology. This volume will be the first comprehensive all-round and systematic exposition of 'meta-scientific psychology' – and perhaps of any meta-science.

Scattered through this monumental work there are many contributions related to the subject matter of this book. One might single out a meta-scientific study of 'motivation in learning' by E. R. Hilgard (see S. Koch, vol V, 1963) for particular praise.

Another meta-scientific book is 'Allgemeine Psychologie' – '2. Band: Motivation' edited by *H. Thomae* (1965). There are many systematic and thorough meta-scientific analyses of several concepts and theories (but no overall comparison).

What is 'Science'?

We conclude this chapter about metascience with a section defining the basic term 'science'.

It is very difficult to define such a term as "science", because it is used in many different ways and covers a very complex set of phenomena.

Firstly, we should like to make it clear that we prefer a *broad* application of the term, one which includes both the *natural* sciences (= "science" in the narrow sense) as well as the *social* and *humanistic* sciences (= "Geisteswissenschaften").

Secondly, we wish to point out that "science" refers to both 1) a *process or activity* (= "research"), and to 2) the *products* of this activity (= "theories"). We shall devote the entire following chapter to these scientific *products*, or *theories*. In this section we shall concentrate on the scientific process, the *research*.

This activity belongs to a class of human and animal behavior called *"exploratory behavior"*. This type of behavior includes the primitive "orientation reflexes" discovered by Pavlov, as well as more complex locomotory and manipulative investigations of the environment. Human beings also perform all these kinds of exploratory behavior. But, in addition, we find a special kind of human exploratory behavior which includes the use of *symbolic processes* – ordinary language as well as mathematical and other special sets of symbols. This symbolic, exploratory behavior is called *epistemic* behavior by D. E. Berlyne (Berlyne, 1960, 1963). This specific type of human behavior, like animal exploratory behavior, is motivated by *curiosity* – a special need or drive for *information* about the world. The difference between epistemic and other types of exploratory behavior is found in the use of symbolic processes.

We thus have classified scientific research as a sort of *information-seeking behavior*, more specifically as *epistemic* behavior, but not all epistemic behavior constitutes scientific research. To qualify as "scientific" the epistemic behavior must follow certain established *social* "norms, "rules" or "principles". These "rules" prescribe how research must be conducted in order to qualify as being "scientific". There are rules about methods of *acquiring* information and methods of *checking* the "truth-value" of the information. *The purpose of these socially established rules or principles of research is first and foremost to improve and guarantee the truth-value* of the information product (i. e., its "truthfulness", "falsity", "probability").

It is these research-method principles which characterize scientific research as a *socially organized activity*, and which differentiate research from non-scientific epistemic behavior.

The social background of the norms, rules or principles of research consists of the community of scientific workers. Much scientific research is accomplished by *teamwork*, and thus is primarily a group-activity. But even in the cases where a scientist works individually – perhaps in a remote place – he has to follow the rules if he wants his results to be *accepted* by other scientists. And being accepted by one's associates is a very strong kind of motivation – also among scientists. The individual scientist is always inclined to regard himself as belonging to a larger group composed of co-workers in "his" science. Perhaps he also regards himself as belonging to a special *"school"*, which is defined by the principles of research that are accepted as *the* principles. In contemporary science there is also the possibility that a scientist is a formal *member* of one or more *organizations* (e. g., American Psychological Association) which also have principles. Furthermore, many scientists work in *academic institutions* (universities, "academies", research institutions, etc.), which also have their special norms or rules.

The rules of all these organizations – the "team", the "school", the professional groups, the academic institution – may vary somewhat and even be in conflict to some extent. But *the common core of these rules involves defining the quality required of epistemic behavior so that it can be counted as scientific research.*

The rules or principles of research may change from place to place and from time to time. Most of the principles belong to the *historical tradition* of the various sciences. This tradition has helped to establish some continuity in the evolution of science, but sometimes new principles are established by one or more creative scientist, the result being *"scientific revolutions"*, which, according to *Th. Kuhn* are important factors in the development of all the sciences (see Kuhn, 1962).

We conclude this explication of the term "science" with a summarizing diagram (Fig. 1.2).

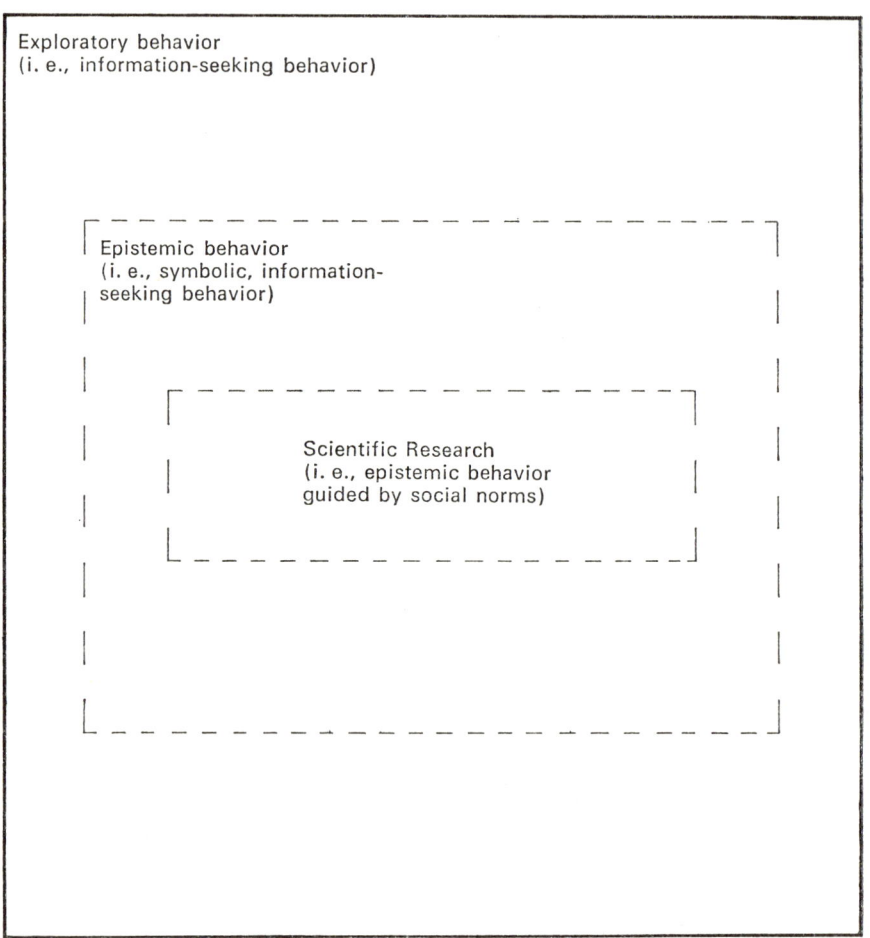

Fig. 1.2. Diagram illustrating the classification of scientific research as a sort of information-seeking behavior.

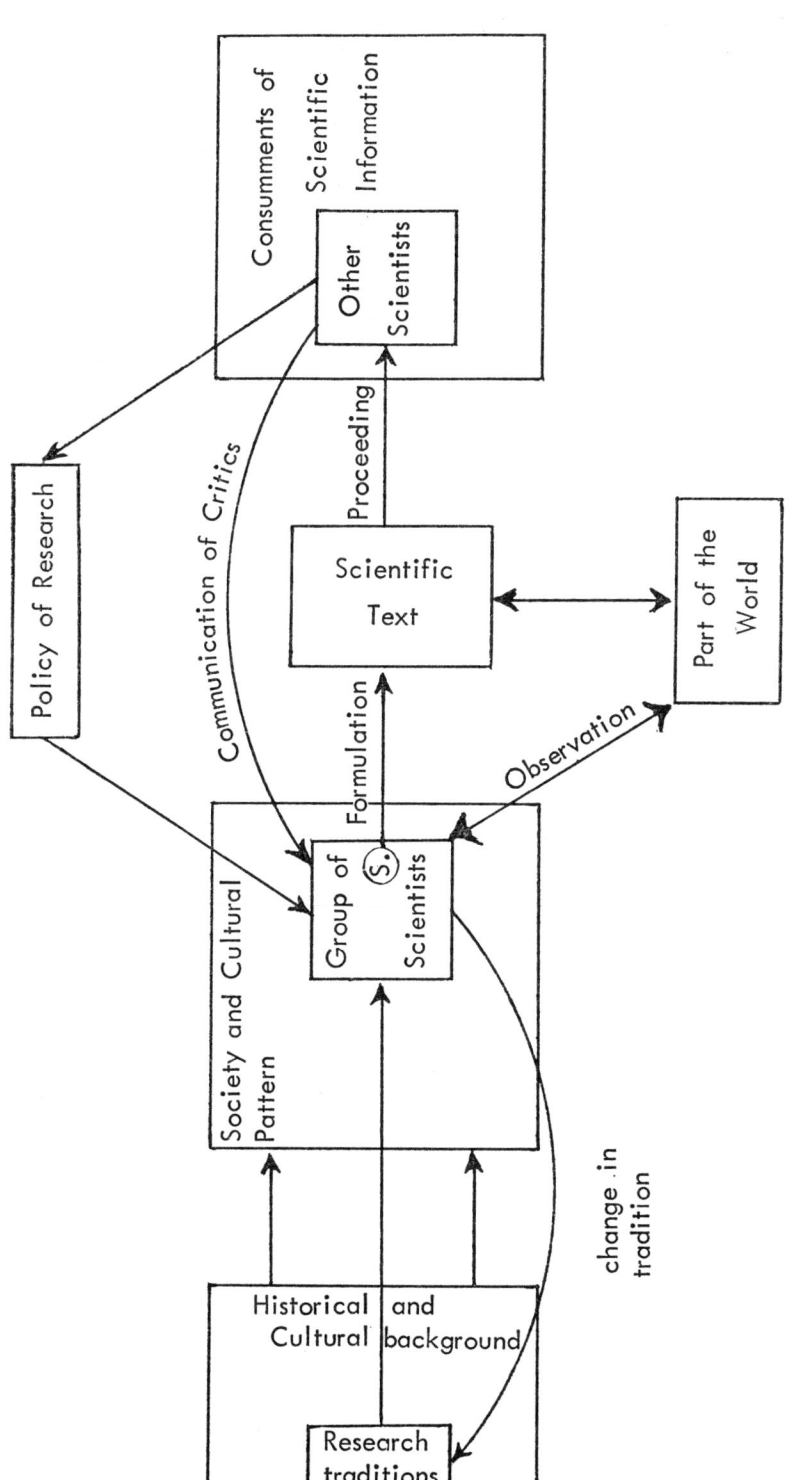

Fig. 1.3. Diagram representing the world of science.

30 . *Metascience*

As this diagram (Fig. 1.2) demonstrates, it is not easy to draw a sharp boundary between scientific research and other epistemic behavior as there is only a degree of difference and this should be kept in mind while reading the following *basic definition No. 1:*

"Science" is socially organized information-producing activity (= "research") as well as the products of this activity (= "theories").

We can illustrate this social organization of scientific research with the help of a diagram (Fig. 1.3).

2 : Systematology

The Comparative Study of Theories

1. Some Basic Definitions

In the first chapter of this book we presented a survey of the whole field of metascience. From among the various disciplines constituting metascience we shall concentrate on the philosophy (or theory) of science. The main reason for dealing with other disciplines as well was to present the systematic relationships between all different metascientific disciplines.

In this chapter we shall further concentrate on one of the sub-disciplines within the philosophy of science. This sub-discipline is traditionally called *"metatheory"*, but we have suggested confining this term to *products* of the *metascientific* comparative study of theories. These products are more or less *general* in scope.

The broader metatheories are those dealing with *scientific theories-in-general* – including the natural, the social and the humanistic sciences. An example of such a general metatheory is that proposed by the philosophers belonging to the school of "Logical Empiricism" (e. g., Bertrand Russell, R. Carnap, C. G. Hempel, R. B. Braithwaite and many others.) This logical empirical theory has the short-coming, however, that it was based solely upon the study of *mathematical* theories. Nevertheless, it was generalized and supposed to be valid for all sciences.

A less general metatheory is one about theories in *one science* only. An example of this is the metatheory set forth in this chapter. This metatheory is – contrary to the logical-empirical theory – based upon "case studies" of more than 20 theories of motivation (Madsen, 1968).

The most specific metatheories are theories about *one theory* only. Examples may be found in the most developed psychological theories – e. g., those of Freud, Lewin, Hull and Tolman – each of which contains a part which deals with the rest of that theory. Such a specific metatheory may be called the "meta-part", the "meta-level" or the "meta-stratum" of the theory under consideration. We shall later return to this topic.

In accordance with our wish to make a general distinction between scientific *products* (i. e., theories) and scientific processes (i. e., research), we have previously proposed the term *"systematology"*[1]), and we shall here repeat the definition as our *basic definition No. 2:*

"Systematology" is that metascientific research which is concerned with the comparative study of scientific theories, and which may produce a metatheory."

It might also be convenient at this point to define the term "theory" which until now we have used in a rather loose fashion without any formal definition.

We feel that it will be the most fruitful to start with a very broad and inclusive definition of "theory" and then later to introduce some qualitative discriminations btween "theories". Thus we suggest defining the term *"theory"* as being equivalent to *" a scientific text or discourse"*. This definition is borrowed from the Swedish metascientist, *Hakon Törnebohm*, who has created a so-called "discourse-analytic metatheory" (i. e., a metatheory which is based upon so-called "case-studies" of real, existing scientific discourses). *"Discourse"* includes oral as well as written (or printed) expositions, and therefore we prefer the term *"text"*, which refers exclusively to written or printed discourses, which are more convenient objects for a scientific study than the oral expositions.

As we have just defined a "theory" as a "scientific text", we only lack a definition of the phrase "scientific text". It is of course very difficult to define the word "scientific". We defined it in Chapter 1 in connection with "research" and found that it was the *social organization* which discriminated scientific research from other epistemic behavior. This social organization is established in accordance with some accepted "norms", "rules" or "principles", and we may use the same principles to discriminate between "scientific texts" and "non-scientific texts". The problem is that these principles are not all "eternal and universal", but may vary from time to time and from society to society. (As so convincingly demonstrated by Thomas Kuhn, 1962). But as we also wish to start with a broad and inclusive definition of "scientific texts", we only need "the least common denominator" of these principles. But what is that? The present author is inclined to follow *Sigmund Koch*, who in his great systematological work (see Koch, 1959) used the phrase: *"systematic formulations"* as including everything normally included by terms like "theory", "model", explanatory system", "frame-of-reference", etc.

Thus we may conclude that a *"text"* has as a minimum to be a *"systematic* formulation" to be counted or regarded as a *"scientific* text".

This definition creates two problems. The least significant problem is that "systematic" is a property which varies in terms of degree. But this problem can be solved by using this very dimension as one possible classification of scientific texts or theories[2]).

The other problem created by this definition is more serious: "Systematic"

1. After suggesting this name (in Madsen, 1959) the author has discovered that *J. R. Kantor* had earlier suggested the name "systemology" for what he also calls the "Logic of Science" (see Kantor, 1953 and 1958).
2. The same problem would have been raised if we had chosen other properties – such as "objective" or "exact" – to define scientific texts. And the present author thinks that "systematic" is basic to being "objective" and "exact".

is a *formal* property which is necessary but not sufficient to discriminate scientific from non-scientific texts. There exist many political, ideological, religious and technical texts which are systematic discourses without being regarded as scientific. We therefore have to look for another property which can be used to discriminate and define scientific texts.

The present author thinks that by going back to our definition of "scientific research" we may get some valuable hints. We defined "scientific research" as "socially organized *information-producing* activity". Thus the products of this activity – theories or scientific texts – must contain *information* in order to be counted as "scientific". This discriminates a scientific text from the earlier mentioned examples of systematic discourses, which are *not* scientific, as they are not informative texts. Of course there may be some information in a pamphlet dealing with political ideology or in a religious doctrine, but for the most part such material is non-informative (rather it is evaluative, prescriptive, etc.).

On the other hand we have texts which are for the most part informative which are not regarded as scientific, as they are not sufficiently systematic. Examples can be found in folklore as well as in other popular "explanations" of all the world's problems to be found in the daily newspaper. Of course we also have textbooks and popular scientific books which are on the borderline to being scientific texts, but this creates no real problem for our study[3]).

Therefore, we may now conclude our search for criteria to help us define "theories" or "scientific texts" with our *basic definition No. 3a:*

A *"theory" or "scientific text" is a text which is exclusively informative and systematically organized.*

We can illustrate the basic classification implicit in this definition by a classification table (Fig. 2.0.).

It only remains to explicate the key-term "informative". All readers will agree, we think, that an "informative" text contains *descriptive* statements or sentences. This is regarded as necessary – and by some people also as sufficient – for a text to be regarded as informative (and scientific). But many scientists – as well as non-scientists – also believe that *explanatory* sentences or propositions are "informative", and are needed to supplement the purely descriptive sentences. Furthermore, some scientists – and especially metascientists – think that a scientific text also may – or even ought to – contain some *philosophical argumentation* about basic terms, empirical methods and types of explanation. Besides there may be statements about fundamental philosophical problems (e. g., the Mind-Body Problem). As these philosophical argumentations refer to the rest of the text or theory we could call them "meta-theoretical propositions", or, more succinctly: *"meta-propositions".*

We are now able to elaborate our definition of "theory" into our *basic definition No. 3b:*

---

3. We need only supplement the other criteria ("systematic" and "informative") with a *social* criterion. We select for study those texts which are regarded by other scientists as very valuable as they often refer to or quote favorably from them.

34 . *Systematology*

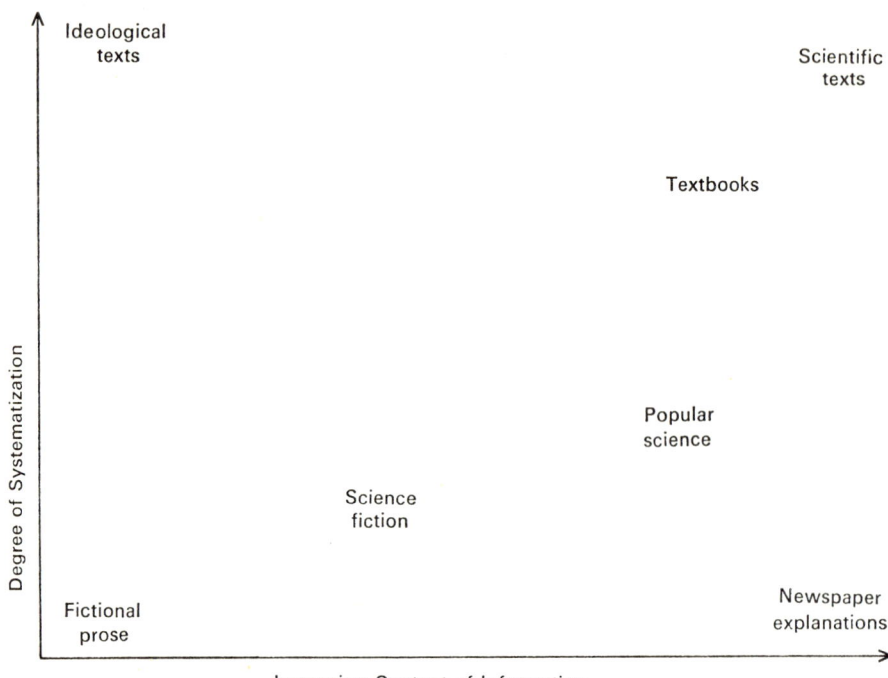

Fig. 2.0. A diagram illustrating the difference of degree between scientific texts and other texts. The differences consist of degrees of systematization and content of information.

A "theory" or "scientific text" is a systematic, informative text which contains descriptive, explanatory and metatheoretical propositions[4]).

This final version of our definition of "theory" leads logically to the next task: a more detailed analysis of the three basic components of a scientific text. These basic components constitute three "parts" of the same text, or three "levels of abstraction", or *"strata of the discourse"*: The *descriptive stratum*, the explanatory or *hypothetical stratum*, and the *metastratum*.

Not all theories contain all three strata, but a fully developed theory usually does. Those theories which do *not* include all three levels often *implicitly* presuppose certain propositions. In some theories these strata are mixed together or confused with one another in the text (e. g., descriptions and explanations may be mixed together or explanatory and metatheoretical propositions may be confused with one another). However, many theories are systematically organized

---

4. Some readers wonder why we have *not* included any requirements regarding the *truth-value* of the text in order to determine whether or not it can be designated as being scientific. But the truth-value of a scientific text is an extremely complicated matter and very difficult to determine. Consequently, we decided not to include it in our definition of a scientific text.

into three strata[5]), but the sequence of the discourse may be from the descriptive via the hypothetical to the metatheoretical stratum as well as in any other sequence.

In the following section about the scientific theory in general we shall use the sequence from "the bottom" (the descriptive stratum) to "the top" (the metatheoretical stratum). In the next section about psychological theories we shall go from "the top" to "the bottom".

2. The Strata of a Theory

2.1. *The descriptive stratum*

This is a part of a scientific text which contains *descriptions* of observed events or objects. These descriptions can be more or less abstract and more or less general.

The most concrete and specific descriptions of single events or objects are called *"data"*. A datum is not identical with what is ordinarily called "a fact", because "a fact" is an intersubjectively observed event or object, while "a datum" is the *description* of this "fact" in linguistic or other symbolic form. Even in the description of the most concrete and simple event a certain qualified selection is made of what it is possible to describe in that language, and therefore a certain interaction occurs between the observing and describing subject and the observed object. The *"data" are thus the result of this interaction between subject, language and object.*

But of course there are some concrete single events or objects which are so easy to observe and describe that some subjects can reach a rather high degree of intersubjective consistency in their descriptions. Such concrete, intersubjective descriptions are the *data* in a scientific text. They are often expressed in the so-called *"protocol-sentences"*, that is, the sentences used in the experimental protocols. E. g., a psychologist may write in his experimental protocol: "Rat No. 2 on the first trial turned left at the first choice-point in the maze, then right at the next point, etc."

But we also find more abstract and general descriptions in the descriptive stratum of the text. E. g., a psychologist may write about the actions of a rat in a maze, that "the rat performed the "V. T. E." ("Vicarious Trial-and-Error") at a certain choice-point". "V.T.E." is a more abstract term than turning right, etc., and the intersubjective agreement may not be so pronounced. There may be even more abstract terms in the descriptive stratum. Thus a psychologist may use the term "goal-directed behavior". Later in this chapter we shall show how such *highly abstract descriptive terms* can be defined in such a way that intersubjective agreement in descriptions can be attained.

---

5. Perhaps a minimum condition should be imposed in order that a text can be classified as being scientific, i.e., that it is organized into three strata.

36 . *Systematology*

In the descriptive stratum there may also be descriptions of *regularly* observed relationships between events and objects. Such *descriptions of relationships between observed "facts"* are often called *"laws"*.

If a description of a single event – a datum – is subsumed under a "law" then it is sometimes called an "explanation" of the datum. But "explanations" of "laws" are often found in another stratum of the scientific text, to which we now turn.

2.2. *The hypothetical stratum*

By an *"explanation"* we mean, both in everyday language and in scientific language, *the formulation of a causal or "functional" relationship between two or more observed facts*[6]). All the "links" in such functional relationships are not always observable. Perhaps it may only be possible to directly *observe* the first event – "the cause" or *"independent variable"* – and the last event – "the effect" or *"dependent variable"*. In order to "explain" functional relationships we have to postulate the existence of "mediating" or *"intervening variables"*. The *terms* in a scientific text which stand for or *represent these intervening variables* are called *"explanatory terms"*.

In the following section we shall deal with explanatory terms as they are found in scientific theories generally. In a later section of the chapter, we shall deal in more detail with explanatory terms especially found in *psychological* theories.

2.2.1. *Explanatory terms and propositions*

As the intervening variables are not observed or even observable directly, these "explanatory terms" are often called *"hypothetical constructs"*.

But there may be differences between explanatory terms in their "hypothetical loading".

Some explanatory terms are easier to define by connecting them directly to the *descriptive* stratum by a so-called *"operational or reductive definition"*. This kind of definition *"reduces"* the hypothetical loading by connecting the explanatory terms to descriptions of experimental or other observational *"operations"*. There may only be a *slight difference in degree of abstraction* between these *operationally* defined *explanatory terms* and the most *highly abstract descriptive terms*.

Other explanatory terms are not so easy to define operationally because they are more heavily loaded with hypothetical meaning. As this meaning is not directly defined by operational definitions, it is sometimes called *"surplus meaning"*. This surplus meaning is often "borrowed" or "imported" from another

---

6. As "causal" refers to a special conception of determinism, we prefer the broader term "functional". Later in this chapter we shall return to the problem of "causality".

field or research. In psychology the "surplus meaning" of explanatory terms may be imported from such different fields as brain-physiology and cybernetics. We shall return to this point later in the chapter.

The term *"hypothetical constructs"* is often confined to those *explanatory terms with "surplus meaning"* which are not directly definable by reference to observational operations.

The sentences or propositions which contain *formulations of the functional relationships* between independent variables and intervening variables, and between intervening variables and dependent variables, are called *"explanatory propositions"*. As the *intervening variables* are often postulated or *hypothetical*, such explanatory propositions must contain explanatory terms with hypothetical surplus meaning. Therefore, the term *"hypothesis"* in this book is covered by the broader term *explanatory propositions*.

The causal or functional relationships between the independent variable ("cause") and the dependent variable ("effect") frequently include several intervening variables. Therefore, an explanation of the functional relationship often requires *a formulation into several explanatory propositions or hypotheses*.

When a text contains several explanatory propositions they may be connected or interrelated in a more or less *systematic organization:* from loose *"sketches"* via *"systematic theories"* to *"deductive systems"*. Later in this chapter we shall go into more detail concerning these differences.

2.2.2. Types of Explanations

At this point we shall focus our attention on the most systematically organized theories, the deductive systems, because we are now interested in an analysis of the more basic problems concerning "explanation", and these features are more easily demonstrated in connection with deductive systems.

There are two main types of scientific explanations:

1. Deductive explanations are explanations by means of logical deductions (or inferences). Such an explanation is best made by using a deductive system.

A *"deductive system"* is a logically organized system of propositions. It consists of a few *basic propositions* – often called *"axioms"* or *"postulates"* – and of some *derived propositions* – often called *"theorems"*. These theorems are derived by "deduction" (i. e., logical inference) from the axioms. If the theorems are already derived or formulated it can be "demonstrated logically" that they are formally correct consequences of the axioms.

The first and most well-known deductive system is that found in *Euclid's* geometry. But later deductive systems came to be used outside the field of mathematics in the empirical sciences. In such instances the basic propositions are frequently called *"postulates"* as they are conceived of as *basic hypotheses* postulating something about the world. They can then be used in the explanation of the "theorems" which are possibly identical with observed "laws".

A purely mathematical system of formulas – a so-called *"calculus"*, which can be used for calculating purposes – may be connected to an explanatory system[7]). The reason for using such a mathematical calculus is often based upon the necessity of making calculations of quantitative estimates of measurable aspects of observations. In this way it is possible to *predict* new data. From these predictions it is possible to test the "truth-value" and fruitfulness of our explanatory formulations. Besides, these predictions can be used for *practical purposes* when we apply these scientific explanations.

2. Model-explanations are explanations by means of different kinds of "models".

In recent years the term *mathematical "model"* has often been used to denote a mathematical calculus. This terminology is a bit confusing, as the term *"model"* was originally used to denote more *concrete representations* in the form of two dimensional diagrams (e. g., geographical maps) and three-dimensional objects (e. g., globes).

From the beginning the natural sciences have used concrete (often mechanical) models to explain observed phenomena. Many classical physicists thought that they had not really understood or explained a thing until they had constructed a concrete model of "hidden mechanisms" behind the observed phenomena. The use of (concrete) models in explanations in psychology has increased in recent years under the influence of *cybernetics* – the science of self-regulating systems. In this science it was common to make use of an electronic computer as a concrete model of the brain. It is now more popular to use a computer program as a *simulation* of the working of the brain (e. g., in learning and problem-solving).

Thus we find two different types of explanations in modern science: the deductive explanation through a deductive system and the model-explanation by means of a concrete model. The feature common to both types of explanations is that the explanation consists of a "representation" of the observable phenomena by a "system" – abstract or concrete.

The *similarity* between the two types of explanations is further stressed by the fact that a concrete model – e. g., a computer – may be represented by a set of formulas which outline the functioning of the concrete model. Therefore, it is also understandable that a mathematical calculus is called a "model".

But there are also, of course, some *differences* between the deductive explanations and the model-explanations.

Thus the deductive explanation has the great advantage that it makes *predictions* easy. And predictions have – as already mentioned – a double function:

---

7. The term "calculus" is used in this way by *R. B. Braithwaite* in his book "Scientific Explanations" (1953).

1) Predictions may be used for *testing* – or checking – the *"truth-value"* or *"probability"* of the theory and
2) predictions may be used for *practical purposes* (application of the theory in praxis).

The *model-explanation* has, on the other hand, special *"heuristic"* and *pedagogical* advantages:

1) A concrete model may facilitate the scientist's problem-solving so that he can more easily "understand" the phenomena and therefore may *discover* new phenomena and *invent* new hypotheses. This facilitation of scientific research is called the *"heuristic"* function of the model.
2) A concrete model may also facilitate the scientist's communication with other people – scientists, students and the lay consumers of scientific production. It is easier for the reader to "understand" a scientific discourse if it is connected to a concrete model which for practical reasons often must be in the form of two-dimensional diagrams printed in books). This is the *pedagogical* function of the model.

The heuristic and the pedagogical functions of models are perhaps two sides of the same "coin": the scientist makes the model in order to better communicate, the result being that he himself "understands" better and discovers new relationships.

If a theory explains something by the use of a concrete model, then the exposition of the structure and functioning of the model – as well as diagrams – belong to the hypothetical stratum of the text.

Some scientific texts contain *both a deductive explanation and a model-explanation*. Besides, a mathematical calculus – or "model" – may be employed for the purpose of calculating predictions. Such complicated theories must contain *rules* for the co-ordination of the formal and the material explanations (and of the calculus).

We have now finished our discussion of the two main types of explanations, but in addition to these we should mention a few others. One category is *inductive-statistical explanations*. They differ from deductive explanations by the degree of probability they transfer to the explained "laws" or data. The deductive explanations transfer a 100 % probability by logical necessity from the premises (postulates) to the conclusions (theorems). On the other hand, *inductive-statistical* explanations transfer only with a probability just under 100 % a certain truth-value from the premises to the conclusions. But, as we have indicated, this difference is only a difference of degree. Therefore, one of the leading philosophers of science, C. G. *Hempel*, subsumes the deductive and the inductive-statistical explanations under the common term: *"the covering-law-explanation"* (see Hempel, 1964). Therefore, in this book we shall continue to use the term *"deductive* explanation" as a common term for both inductive-statistical explanations and deductive explanations proper.

Another category of explanations is *functional or teleological explanations*.

These are explanations using terms like "function", "effect", "goal" or "purpose" instead of "cause", "conditions" or "independent variable". This category of explanations was formerly regarded as a special basic type of explanation in the fields of biology and psychology. But in 1859 *Darwin* demonstrated that biological evolution can be explained deductively by causal-deterministic hypotheses, and in 1932 *Tolman* demonstrated that purposive behavior can be explained by a causal-deterministic model (including both motivational and cognitive hypothetical variables). Therefore, there is no longer any reason to regard functional or teleological explanations as representing basic types.

As a last category of explanations we shall mention the *historical (or genetic)*. This type is regarded as basic by some philosophers of history, but Hempel has also argued for the idea that historical explanations can be subsumed under his "covering-law-explanation".

If this argumentation is accepted we can classify all explanations as belonging to one or the other of our two main categories: the deductive explanations and the model-explanations.

Finally, we shall discuss the possibility of reducing these two types to *one* basic category of explanation.

One group of philosophers of science who belong to the empiristic tradition argues for the thesis that *all* scientific explanations are *deductive*. This was proposed as early as 1843 by *J. S. Mill* and later by *Braithwaite* (1953), *Hempel* (1964), and *Nagel* (1961).

Another group of philosophers of science maintains that the model-explanation is a basically independent type of explanation which cannot be reduced to the deductive category of explanations. This was originally proposed by *N. R. Campbell* in 1920, and later by *Bunge* (1964, 1969), *Deutsch* (1960), *Harré* (1961), *Hesse* (1963), *Hutten* (1962), *Kaplan* (1964) and *Tørnebohm* (1957).

Norwood R. Hanson has presented very convincing historical evidence in support of the thesis which maintains that significant reasoning in a developing science is neither inductive nor deductive but what he (based on *C. S. Peirce*) calls *abduction*. This is reasoning which, on the basis of a *pattern* of empirical and theoretical evidence, proposes an hypothesis. Thus abduction is a part of the construction of a new theory, while *deduction* can only be applied when a scientific theory is already established. As a supplement to these types of reasoning we can add *induction* which can be used when we are formulating empirical laws (generalizations).

Although not formulating explicit statements about the problem, *Hanson's* thesis may be interpreted as an argument for *model-explanation as the basic type of explanation* – or at least as the historically and psychologically primary type.

In psychology we can find both types of explanation. Thus *Hull*'s theory is the first example of a formally developed deductive theory in psychology. On the other hand, we may regard *Tolman*'s theory as one of the earlier developed model-explanations.

The theorist's arguments for his type of explanation belong to the next level of abstraction in the scientific text, to which we now turn.

2.3. *The Meta-Stratum*

This stratum of a scientific discourse is what may be called the *"metatheory"* of that special instance of a "theory" or scientific text, because it refers to the rest of the discourse, and *not* to the observable events or objects which are described and explained in the two strata of the text already discussed. In the meta-stratum we may find several different kinds of propositions.

The most concrete or least abstract level of the metastratum contains propositions about the *empirical methods* used in the research which have produced the *data* and perhaps *"laws"* in the descriptive stratum of *that* scientific text. Perhaps these are some arguments for choosing one special empirical method instead of another. All these *propositions about empirical methods* may be designated by the term *"methodological propositions"*.

At the next level of the meta-stratum we find propositions about the hypothetical stratum. Besides the already mentioned "rules of coordination" between the system of hypotheses and the model(s), we may find other propositions which formulate the scientist's conception of scientific explanations in general. We may also find his arguments for selecting his special model or using a particular category of explanatory terms with special surplus meaning. All these *propositions about the hypothetical stratum* may be designated by the term *"metatheoretical propositions"*.

Finally, at the highest level of abstraction we may find some propositions about fundamental, philosophical, especially epistemological problems. They may be propositions about the possibility and the conditions for obtaining "true" knowledge or information. There may also be propositions about the relationship between scientific information and some sort of "ultimate reality". Furthermore, there may be propositions about other controversial ontological problems peculiar to that particular science (e. g., in psychology the "mind-body" problem). All these *propositions about fundamental epistemological and ontological problems* may be designated *"philosophical propositions"*.

2.4. *The Relationships between the Strata*

We have now finished the description of a scientific text in general and seen that it is composed of several strata or "levels of abstraction". We started with the most *concrete* descriptions of *data*, then took up the more *abstract descriptions* and concluded with the hypothetical stratum. In the latter we started with the least abstract level containing *explanatory terms* which may be *operationally* defined and went on to explanatory terms with *hypothetical* surplus meaning. From the hypothetical stratum we went to the *meta-stratum*. In this we first mentioned the least abstract *methodological* propositions, after which we took up the more abstract metatheoretical propositions. Finally, we looked at the most abstract philosophical propositions.

But instead of going "up" from the most concrete level to the most abstract level, we could just as well have gone in the *other direction through the "continuum of abstraction"*: from the "top" level of abstraction (the philosophical propositions) to the bottom level (the description of data).

One way is probably as good as the other from a *pedagogical* point-of-view. But which way is the correct one from a *systematological* point-of-view? How are scientific texts usually composed? We must realize that there is no general or final answer to this question.

Some scientific texts (perhaps mostly *books*) start with the *meta-stratum*. If there is any meta-stratum, it is often contained in the introductory chapters of the book. Then the author normally proceeds to the *hypothetical* and *descriptive* strata.

Other scientific texts – especially the shorter experimental reports – start with the *descriptive* stratum and go on to the *hypothetical* and *meta*-strata.

We also find many scientific texts (especially experimental reports) which start with a brief *meta-stratum* (mostly methodological propositions), proceed to the *descriptive* stratum, and conclude with a *hypothetical* stratum (the section devoted to "discussions and conclusions" in the experimental reports in journals).

Finally, we may find scientific texts which mix together propositions from all the strata in a very unsystematic and confusing fashion. If such a text is *too* unsystematic it is a matter of definition whether we decide to count it as a *scientific* text or not (cf. Koch's "systematic formulations").

From these general descriptions of scientific texts we now turn to more special descriptions of *psychological* texts.

In the following part of the chapter we shall "go down" through the "continuum of abstraction": beginning with the meta-stratum and concluding with the descriptive stratum.

Before we do this it might be convenient to summarize our analysis of a scientific text in general by means of a diagram (see Fig. 2.1.) which illustrates the levels or strata of a theory.

3. The Strata of Psychological Theories

3.1. *Meta-Stratum*

In this part of the chapter we shall make a detailed study of the special problems arising in connection with "theories", i. e., scientific texts appearing in psychology. We begin with the "top level" of abstraction at the meta-stratum.

3.1.1. *Philosophical propositions*. The most fundamental philosophical problem in psychology is the "mind-body problem" or, in more modern terms, the *"psycho-somatic problem"*. This problem is as old as philosophy, and since the

Systematology . 43

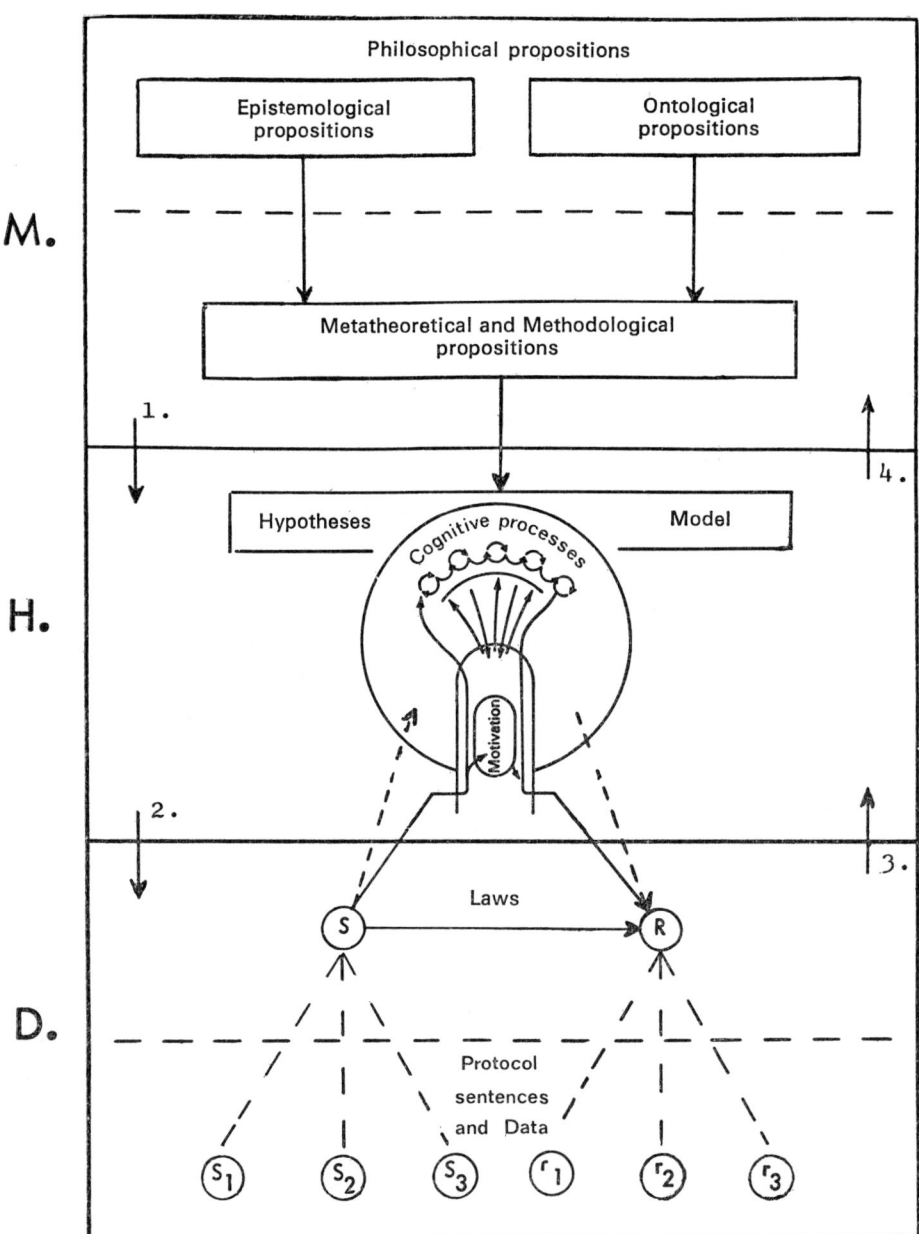

A Scientific Text.

Fig. 2.1. The hierarchical structure of a theory. This diagram illustrates the three strata of a scientific text: "M" = "M-level" or "Meta-stratum"; "H" = "H-level" or "Hypothetical stratum"; "D" = "D-level" or "Descriptive stratum". The four arrows (1, 2, 3, 4) indicate that the top level influences the formation of he next level, which in turn influences the bottom level. But there is also a "feed-back" of influence from the D-level to the H-level and the M-level. (otherwise it would *not* be a *scientific* theory).

time of *Plato* and *Aristotle* many possible solutions to it have been advanced. Contemporary psychologists have seldom been explicit in their formulations regarding this problem, perhaps because they think that it belongs to philosophy, and that psychology should be an independent science. But *no* science can be completely independent of philosophy (at least not of epistemology). Every science has its special epistemological problems, and it is much more fruitful when explicit epistemological and other philosophical propositions are formulated, as they probably influence formulations about other problems placed lower in the "hierarchy" of abstraction. And it is much easier to make a critical test of the scientist's important conceptions, if they are formulated in explicit propositions. Therefore, psychologists should also make explicit propositions about their special philosophical problem, the psychosomatic problem. The present author thinks that behind many discussions among psychologists about problems both in the hypothetical stratum and the descriptive stratum there is hidden disagreement about the solution of the psychosomatic problem.

Over the years various philosophers have advanced different propositions concerning the psychosomatic problem. For our purposes we shall make a simplified survey of these different propositions. The various philosophical propositions or "theories" about the psychosomatic problem may be divided into *two main categories:* the *"dualistic"* and the *"monistic"* theories.

The *dualistic* theories about the psychosomatic problem postulate that "behind" all phenomena in the world there are two different kinds of "ultimate reality" (or two "substances" as they were designated in ancient philosophical terminology).

One basic kind of reality is the "psychical" or "mental" and the other is the "physical" or "material". They manifest themselves in "minds" and "bodies" respectively. As these two kinds of reality are so different it has been a great problem when composing the dualistic theories to adequately explain their interaction. One solution to this problem was advanced by *Plato*. Centuries later a similar solution, clearer and more soundly based, was presented by *Descartes*. The latter theory states that the "psychical" and "material" substances *interact* in the *brain*. It has been difficult for this theory to survive in light of the constantly increasing knowledge we have about the physical and physiological worlds. Therefore, another version of the dualistic theory about the psychosomatic problem was needed. This theory also conceived of the world as consisting of two "substances", but these "substances" do not interact; they exist independently of each other. To be more concrete it was postulated that psychical processes and physiological (brain-)processes run *"parallel"* to one another. This version of the dualistic theory was advanced by *Leibnitz* and had many followers among the first experimental psychologists (e. g., *Wundt*).

The other *main* category of theories concerning the psychosomatic problem involves *the monistic theories*. These theories postulate only *one* kind of reality. There are three possible versions of these monistic theories.

One version is called *"spiritualism"* (or sometimes "idealism") as it postulates that all phenomena in the world can be "reduced" to the psychical. This version was very consistently formulated by *George Berkeley*.

Another version of the monistic theories tries to do the opposite: to reduce all phenomena in the world to a physical or material kind of reality. Such a theory of *"materialism"* was very clearly and consistently formulated by the ancient Greek philosopher, *Democritus*.

There is a third version of monistic theories. This version does *not* try to "reduce" all phenomena to one or the other of the two kinds of reality, but rather postulates that there is only *one kind of "neutral" reality*. This version was very consistently formulated by *Spinoza*, who said that psychical and physical phenomena were two aspects of the same, identical reality observed from two different points-of-view. From one point-of-view (the "inside") the neutral reality appeared as psychical phenomena, but from the other point-of-view (the "outside"), the neutral reality appeared as physical phenomena. This *"neutral monism"* has appeared in many contemporary versions including those of the "Logical Empiricists", the "Oxford philosophers" and other partisans of so-called *"analytical philosophy"*.

In summing up then we have *the following two main theories concerning the psychosomatic problem:*

1. *"Dualism"*, in two versions:
    a. "Interactionism".
    b. "Parallelism".
2. *"Monism"*, in three versions:
    a. "Spiritualism".
    b. "Materialism".
    c. "Neutral monism".

The present author believes that *all possible logical formulations about the psychosomatic problem are encompassed by these main theories which may be found in many different versions*[7a]).

In the whole history of modern psychology (as an independent science) psychologists have formulated (implicitly or explicitly) only three of the five possible theories about the psychosomatic problem:

1. Dualism (especially in the form of parallelism),
2. Materialism, and
3. Neutral monism.

7a. Perhaps we should mention a third psychosomatic theory in addition to *monism* and *dualism,* namely *"pluralism"*. According to this philosophy there are three or even more kinds of "realities". Thus *Karl Popper* proposes the existence of the "physical", the "mental" and the "cultural" worlds (see Popper, 1968). And *Karl H. Pribram* presupposes as many kinds of realities as we have different kinds of scientific discourses: the atomic, the molecular, the cellular, the organic, the organismic, the personalistic, the social and the cultural (see Pribram, 1971).

In the following pages we shall discuss how these psychosomatic formulations influence other levels of the psychological texts[8]).

3.1.2. *Metatheoretical propositions.* In a psychological text the metatheoretical propositions are especially concerned with the problem of the meaning of *explanatory terms.*

Many psychologists use explanatory terms that represent *Hypothetical Constructs* (= "H.C.") containing some kind of "surplus meaning". But there is much disagreement and discussion about what kind of surplus meaning the H.C. should have. Some psychologists prefer to use the H.C. which possesses *physiological* surplus meaning. That is, a surplus meaning which is borrowed or imported from neurophysiology. Sometimes this kind of explanation is called *"reductive"* as it is supposed to *"reduce" psychology – or psychological explanations – to physiological data and laws.* Many psychologists (e. g., *Pavlov*) regard this as their purpose or "program". But this "program" has never been realized. Modern psychologists who – like *Hebb* – use such explanatory terms with physiological surplus meaning know that they are *not* using physiological *data,* but rather (hypothetical) *constructs,* which bridge the gaps in our physiological data about the intervening processes in the brain[9]).

Other psychologists use explanatory terms which possess a *mentalistic* surplus meaning. This surplus meaning is imported from the psychologist's own introspection or the phenomenological analysis of consciousness. But the explanatory terms are used to explain other peoples' – and even animals' – behavior. Thus they really *are* (hypothetical) *constructs* (while the psychologist's description of his *own* consciousness is *data*).

A third group of psychologists uses explanatory terms with a surplus meaning which is imported from fields other than physiology or introspection. It may, e. g., be drawn from cybernetics, as one can use the computer as a *concrete model.* Freud's "lenze-model" may be cited as an early example of this. The present author suggests using the term *"neutral"* surplus meaning about these H.C. because their use often presupposes a neutral monistic formulation about the psychosomatic problem. On the other hand, the use of H.C. with *physiological* surplus meaning often – but not always – presupposes a *materialistic* theory, and the use of H.C. with *mentalistic* surplus meaning usually presupposes a *dualistic* theory. But as mentioned earlier modern psychologists very seldom construct explicit propositions about the psychosomatic problem. There remains thus only the possibility of *inferring* their implicit conception of the problem,

---

8. The present author believes that the selection of one psychosomatic theory from among the various possible versions of theories is determined mainly by the personality of the psychologist. And this choice influences the construction of the whole theory. We thus have an example of the important connection between the psychology of scientists and systematology.
9. In the following discussion we prefer to confine *"reductive"* to explanations which only use physiological *data* as intervening variables. But such explanations do *not* exist yet – as far as I know.

and this can be accomplished not only by their use of explanatory terms with surplus meaning, but also from their arguments about methods and descriptive language to which we shall return later in the section dealing with methodological propositions.

Before we leave this topic of metatheoretical propositions we should mention that some psychologists prefer using explanatory terms *without any* surplus meaning. Such explanatory terms are completely defined operationally by their connections with descriptions of specific observations. It has been suggested by *Meehl* and *MacCorquodale*[10]) that psychologists ought to distinguish between "intervening variables" and H.C. (with surplus meaning). As good examples of such *"intervening variables" (= I.V.)* we could mention *mathematical* or other purely *formal terms* taken from a mathematical *"model"* used in the explanatory formulations. But it is not easy to find other examples of I.V. which can be clearly distinguished from H.C., as almost always there is some more or less explicit surplus meaning connected with all explanatory terms. The psychologist who "invented" the term "intervening variable", *Tolman*, did *not* accept this distinction between H.C. and I.V., and particularly objected to the suggestion from Meehl and MacCorquodale that psychologists should give preference to I.V. and restrict the use of H.C. as much as possible.

As it is difficult to draw a sharp distinction between I.V. and H.C. the present author has suggested (in Madsen, 1959) using the term *"Hypothetical variable"* (H.V.) as a common term for both "Intervening variable" (I.V.) and "Hypothetical construct" (H.C.).

In connection with the lively discussion among psychologists regarding I.V. and H.C. we should mention that a very influential modern psychologist, *B. F. Skinner*, has argued very strongly against the use of *any* kind of explanatory terms, whether I.V. or H.C. He prefers confining the psychologist's task to *descriptions* of data and laws. And *the establishment of relationships between independent or "Stimulus-variables" and dependent or "Reaction-variables"* should be the only kind of "explanation" which psychologists should use.

In recent years Skinner has gained many adherents for his arguments against "intervening variables", which he regards as completely useless – even dangerous. The best counterargument to Skinner's has been set forth by the American psychologist, *N. E. Miller* (see Miller, 1959). He proposes that *the induction of intervening variables is justified and even useful when there are 3 or more S-variables in functional relationship with 3 or more R-variables. We can illustrate this by using Miller's own very instructive examples.*

If we consider an experiment about the functional relationship between "Hours of Deprivation" ("S_D") and "Rate of Bar-pressing" ("R_B"), no gain is made by introducing an intervening variable (e. g., "Thirst"). On the contrary: the number of functional relationships would be doubled as is shown in this figure:

---

10. K. MacCorquodale and P. E. Meehl: On a distinction between hypothetical constructs and intervening variables. Psychological Review, 1948, *55*, 95–107.

48 . *Systematology*

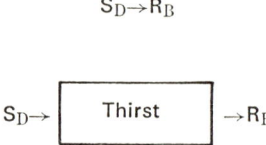

Fig. 2.2.

If we consider an extension of the experiment to include a functional relationship between the variables "Feeding of dry food" (S_F) and "Volume of water drunk" (R_V), the introduction of an intervening variable ("thirst") would be neither a gain nor a loss, as this figure shows:

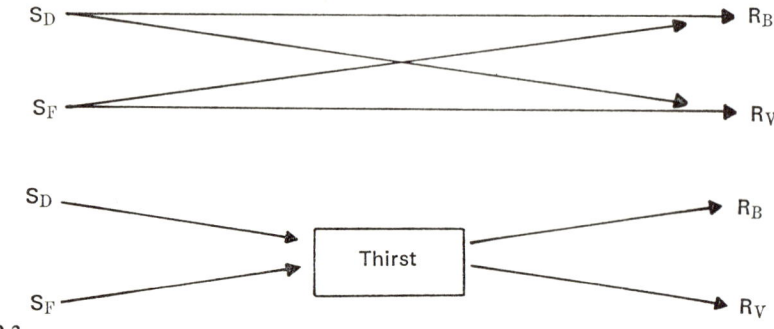

Fig. 2.3.

If we make a further extension of the experiment to include both the relationship between the variable "Saline-injection" (S_{S-I}) and "Quinine required to stop drinking" (R_Q) and introduce an intervening variable ("thirst"), we make a real gain (a reduction of the number of functional relationships from 9 to 6) as this figure shows:

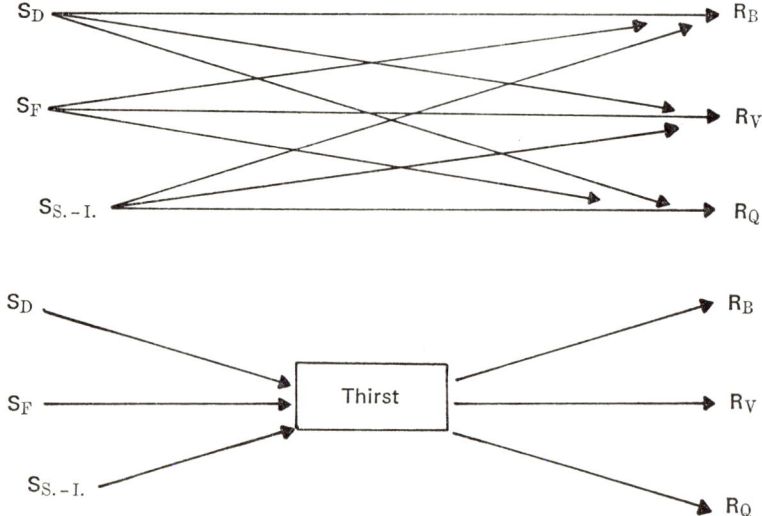

Fig. 2.4.

Miller further points out the fact that Skinner has always worked with but *one* dependent variable ("response-rate") and therefore has not had the possibility of estimating the usefulness of intervening variables.

Summing up this discussion of *metatheoretical propositions* contained in psychological texts we can construct the following Classification of Types of Explanatory Terms:

1. Explanatory terms *with* surplus meaning (H.C.) of different kinds:
   a. H.C. with *physiological* surplus meaning designated by "H.C.(O.)" (where "O" stands for "organic processes").
   b. H.C. with *mentalistic* surplus meaning designated by "H.C.(M.)" *(where* "M" stands for "mental processes" or "mind").
   c. H.C. with *neutral* surplus meaning designated by "H.C.(N.)" (where "N" stands for "neutral processes").
2. Explanatory terms *without any* surplus meaning designated by the term *"Intervening Variables"* (I.V.).
3. Explanatory terms with *unclear* surplus meaning designated by the term *"Hypothetical Variables"* (H.V.), which is also used as a *common term for both H.C. and I.V.*

After this analysis of the metatheoretical level of a psychological discourse, we turn to the next level.

3.1.3. *Methodological Propositions.* In psychology the most discussed methodological problem has been that of the choice between *behavioristic* methods and introspective or *phenomenological* methods. In the history of psychology all possible points-of-view have been presented.

The first experimental psychologists used only – or mainly – the *introspective* method. They required that their subjects should describe the content of their consciousness, which they thought to be composed of mental "elements": sensations, images, feelings, etc.

Later the Gestalt-psychologists changed the method to the so-called *phenomenological* method. They required that their subjects should describe their conscious experiences as wholes or "Gestalts", without making an analysis into arbitrary elements.

At about the same time *John B. Watson* proposed the use of *behavioristic* methods. That is, methods which involve the observation of the behavior of the experimental subject, which may be an animal or an infant without language or an adult man.

After the first two decades of controversy about methods, there were many psychologists who argued for a *liberal use of all methods*.

But in connection with this methodological proposition another problem emerged: the question of which data-language should be used, i. e., the language to be used when describing the "facts" observed. There are two possible data-languages which van be used in the protocol sentences of any science: the *phenomenological* data-language and the *physicalistic, behavioristic* – or, better, *behavioral* data-language.

The *"phenomenological"* data-language is a language which uses protocol sentences about the *phenomena which are experienced by a subject*. These protocol sentences may be illustrated by such examples as: "I see something green", or, "I feel pain", etc. It was natural to use this data-language in connection with introspective or phenomenological *methods*.

The *"behavioral"* data-language[11]) is a language which makes use of protocol sentences about the *observed behavior of an organism*. These protocol sentences may be illustrated by such examples as: "The child cries when he is shown a rat", or "The rat turns left at the first choice-point in a maze". It is natural to use this data-language in connection with behavioristic *methods*.

Many of the psychologists who exclusively used *behavioristic* methods and data-language also preferred to use explanatory terms with *physiological* surplus meaning (if they did not prefer confining the task to descriptions – as, e. g., Skinner did). They have also explicitly formulated *materialistic* propositions of the psychosomatic problem in many cases.

On the other hand, there were many psychologists who made exclusive use of *phenomenological* methods and data-language and preferred using explanatory terms (if any) with *mentalistic* surplus meaning. They also often explicitly formulated a *dualistic* conception of the psychosomatic problem.

And between them we have the psychologists who have formulated a *neutral-monistic* conception of the psychosomatic problem, and expressed preference for the use of explanatory terms with *neutral* surplus meaning (or perhaps formal "intervening variables"). These psychologists have also frequently expressed a *liberal* attitude toward the use of both *methods*. But as far as *data-language* is concerned many of these psychologists have followed the lead of *Tolman* and adopted an exclusively *behavioral* data-language.

Many reasons have been put forth to explain preference for a behavioral data-language.

Behavioral data-languge is more like the *"thing-language"* of daily life, which has evolved through generations into a medium which is well-adapted for communication between people[12]). Behavioral data-language is also more like the languages in *other sciences*, which have developed their own descriptive terminology as refinements of everyday-language. Furthermore, it is *always possible to "translate" from the phenomenological data-language to the behavioral data-language, but not vice versa*. A subject's expression of his conscious ex-

---

11. We prefer to use the term "behavioral" instead of "behavioristic", because the first term is more neutral and does *not* – as the latter may – imply that we should accept the behavioristic metatheory and methodology as they are proposed by Watson – and later by Skinner.
12. This is convincingly stressed by G. Mandler and W. Kessen in "The Language of Psychology". N. Y.: Wiley, 1959).

periences may be treated as a kind of behavior, especially a kind of *verbal behavior*.

We can sum up this section about *methodological propositions* by stating that all the arguments for using *exclusively behavioral* methods and data-language as well as *exclusively phenomenological* methods and data-language have been set forth. And we can also find all possible *combinations* of methods and data-languages, perhaps in the last three decades mostly the *behavioral* data-language.

With this we have finished the treatment of the metastratum in psychological texts and turn now to the next one.

3.2. The Hypothetical Stratum

We have already dealt with many of the fundamental problems about this particular part of a psychological text (especially in connection with the analysis of the metatheoretical propositions). But there remain some specific problems about classifications of *psychological terms* and *hypotheses*.

3.2.1. *Classifications of Psychological Terms*. Before we discuss this topic we must clarify a terminological problem: The words "term", "concept" and "variable" have often – also in the preceding pages – been used interchangeably, but we sometimes need a more precise and consistent usage of the terms. We therefore suggest the following distinctions:

1. *"Term"* should be used exclusively about the *words* in the texts (e. g., the word "need" is a term).
2. *"Variable"* should be used exclusively about the *processes, states or factors* in the organism which the term refers to (e. g., "need" refers in Murray's theory (1938) to both states of imbalance or disequilibrium in an organism as well as to personality factors).
3. *"Concept"* should be used exclusively about the *cognitive structures* which function in the head of both the writer and the reader when certain terms are used (e. g., Murray had a very special conception of the variable "need", when he used that term in 1938).

By using this terminology it is possible for us to clearly describe the similarities and differences between different psychologists' terms (and concepts). E. g., we can state that (in 1951) Tolman and Hull both used the terms "need" and "drive", but they used them in such divergent ways that the meaning was almost "opposite": Tolman's "drive" represents the same variable as Hull's "need" and vice versa. We should also add that Murray's concept of "need" (1938) was much broader than Hull's, as Murray's "need" included both Hull's "need" and "drive" as well as some personality factors which are not included at all in Hull's theory.

In order to formulate the results of this comparative study of theories, it is useful to have some *systematological classifications of psychological terms* (and of the variables they represent). Thus in this section we shall introduce some classifications of *explanatory* terms – while in a later section we shall deal with *descriptive* terms.

We have already introduced one classification which we shall consequently treat very briefly here:

3.2.1.1. *Classification of Explanatory Terms According to "Surplus Meaning"*:
1. Terms *without* surplus meaning
   ("Intervening Variables" in the narrow sense).
2. Terms *with* surplus meaning
   ("Hypothetical Constructs" in the narrow sense) which includes three subclasses:
   1. Terms with *physiological* surplus meaning ("H.C.O.").
   2. Terms with *mentalistic* surplus meaning ("H.C.M.").
   3. Terms with *neutral* surplus meaning (H.C.N.").

In cases of doubt we use the all-inclusive designation *"H-term"*, which represents all *explanatory* terms representing *H-variables*.

This classification is based upon suggestions made by *E. C. Tolman* (see especially Tolman 1951 and 1959). The same is true concerning the next classification.

3.2.1.2. *Classification of Terms According to Duration of the Existence of the Variables*. While the former classification was a classification primarily of terms, this classification is primarily concerned with variables and only secondarily – or indirectly – with terms. Psychological variables have different durations of existence: some last only for a few seconds and others for years. There is, of course, a whole possible continuum of duration between these extreme cases, but we can roughly divide it into 2–3 categories:

1. *"Disposition variables"* are comparatively long-lived *"factors"* in the organism, which it brings along into a given situation, and which determine *individual differences* among various organisms in their reactions to the same situation. These "disposition variables" include both *heredity* determined, congenital dispositions as well as later *acquired* ones. If we attribute to disposition variables a *physiological* "surplus meaning", they can be conceived of as comparatively permanent *structures* in the central nervous system (which perhaps are biochemically determined). In different psychological theories these disposition variables are variously designated as "intelligence factors", "personality factors", "habits", etc.
2. *"Function variables"* are comparatively short-lived processes and states in the organism which are determined by contemporaneous external or internal stimuli which together with the disposition variables present determine the actual behavior. If we bestow a *physiological* "surplus meaning" on these

function variables, they can be regarded as *brain processes* or, in any case, processes of the central nervous system.

As intimated there is a possibility for middle cases between disposition and function variables; namely comparatively *long-lived states* in the organism which influence the behavior. As examples we can cite protracted fatigue resulting from illness, or the result of prolonged malnutrition, etc.

We should add that there is another difference between disposition variables and function variables (including processes and states); namely, that *functions directly mediate* in the "causal link" or functional relationship between independent and dependent variables (behavior), while *dispositions only indirectly influence* the functional relationship[13]).

We shall, for the sake of consistency, conclude this classification of variables by adding that the corresponding *terms* can be called *"disposition terms"* and *"function terms"*.

3.2.1.3. *Classification of Terms According to the Effect of the Variables on Behavior.* We shall now introduce one more classification of explanatory terms which is not based upon Tolman, but upon the present author's comparative study of theories of motivation (see Madsen, 1968). This classification is especially important when studying different terms, conceptions and theories of motivation. As in the case of the last classification it is primarily a classification of *variables* and only *secondarily* and *indirectly* a classification of the corresponding *terms*. This classification is based upon the important conceptual analyses made concurrently and independently (in the 1930's) by *Elisabeth Duffy* (see Duffy, 1962) and *Kurt Lewin* (see Lewin, 1938). According to this analysis psychological variables may produce two different *effects* on behavior – a *directive* and a *dynamic* effect. In addition, some variables have both effects simultaneously. Therefore, we have three categories:

1. *Directive variables* are variables whose function is to direct, organize, steer, guide or "regulate" behavior. Thus these variables determine the *direction* of the behavior towards specific goals. To this category belong all *cognitive* processes. A variable such as Hull's "habit" (sHr) is also a good example. But it is a matter for discussion if any *motivational* variable belongs to this category.
2. *Dynamic variables* are variables whose effect is to *activate* the behavior or, in other words, to mobilize the necessary energy. These variables determine the intensity of the behavior. This category includes many *motivational* variables. One of the clearest examples is Hull's "drive" (D).
3. *Vector-variables* are variables which have *both* a dynamic and a directing effect. They are called by this name because K. Lewin pointed to (psycholo-

---

13. This distinction was pointed out to the author by *W. Rozeboom* in a personal discussion at the Center for Advanced Study in Theoretical Psychology, University of Alberta.

gical) *forces* as variables which could be represented mathematically by a vector. In addition to Lewin's "force" we could mention Hull's "reaction-evocation-potential" (sEr) as a variable which is *defined* as a combined variable. Many variables in the older motivational theories also belong to this category (e. g., McDougall's "instinct") either because they are defined as such or more often because they are vaguely defined.

The terms representing these variables can thus be classified as *"direction terms"*, *"dynamic terms"* and *"vector terms"*.

In conclusion we should mention that the three classifications of terms (and variables) can be *combined*, and this *combined classification of terms* is a very useful tool for our forthcoming analyses and comparisons of motivational theories.

3.2.2. *Classifications of Explanatory Propositions or "Hypotheses"*. Before introducing some useful systematological classifications of propositions we should clarify our terminology. In the preceding pages we have used "explanatory propositions" and "hypotheses" synonymously. But logically speaking "explanatory propositions" is a broader term including both "hypotheses" and "laws". All three kinds of propositions are explanatory as they refer to "causal" or other "functional relationships". We thus suggest the following definitions:

1. *"Functional relationships"* will be used about the *actual relationships between variables which are observed* (discovered or found by empirical methods). The functional relationships thus belong to that part of "reality" which the text deals with.
2. *"Law"* will be used about *symbolic formulations* – in propositions or mathematical formulas – which represent the *observed* functional relationships. They can also be called "empirical generalizations" and thus would belong to the "descriptive stratum" of the scientific text.
3. *"Hypotheses"* will be used about the *symbolic formulations* (propositions or mathematical symbols) *about unobserved – and perhaps unobservable – functional relationships*. Thus in our terminology a hypothesis always must contain at least one *hypothetical term* (representing an H-variable)[14]. Thus "hypotheses" always belong to the hypothetical stratum of a scientific text.

Many scientists conceive of a "deeper" and fully "satisfactory" (or sufficient) explanation as one which goes "beyond" the observable level of phenomena. Thus a "law" cannot offer a sufficient explanation as it only explains the single phenomenon "covered" by the law, not the observed functional relationship. Therefore, a fully sufficient explanation requires one or

---

14. The reader should be warned that in general usage "hypotheses" may also be used to designate not-yet-fully-verified "laws". But we prefer not to take into account the degree of verification of the propositions – but only concern ourselves with *formal* structure.

more hypotheses. It can thus be said that it is not incorrect to regard "explanatory propositions" as being equal to "hypotheses".

We are now ready for the introduction of some classifications of hypotheses.

3.2.2.1. *Classification of Hypotheses According to their Constituent Terms.* As a consequence of our definition of "hypotheses", we must deal with two main categories of hypotheses:

1. *"Theoretical hypotheses"* or better: "completely hypothetical, explanatory propositions", which denotes hypotheses containing exclusively hypothetical terms (besides the necessary syntactical words). These hypotheses formulate the functional relationships between two (or more) H-variables. Thus we could use the abbreviation *"H-H-hypotheses"* for these theoretical hypotheses.
2. *"Partly empirical hypotheses"*, i. e., explanatory propositions which contain *both hypothetical* terms and *descriptive* terms. These *descriptive* terms represent *observed (or empirical)* variables which can be divided into *independent* and *dependent* empirical variables. In psychology it is convenient to represent the *independent* variables with "S" (standing for "stimuli" og "situation") and the *dependent* variables with "R" (standing for "reaction" or "behavior"). We thus have two subclasses of partly empirical hypotheses:

    1) *"S-H-hypotheses"*, i. e., hypotheses containing a *descriptive* term representing an *S-variable* and a *hypothetical* term representing an *H-variable*. Thus the S-H-hypotheses are explanatory propositions about functional relationships between S-variables and H-variables.
    2) *"H-R-hypotheses"*, i. e., hypotheses containing a *hypothetical* term representing an *H-variable* and a *descriptive* term representing an *R-variable*. Thus H-R-hypotheses are explanatory propositions about functional relationships between H-variables and R-variables.

Consequently, a complete "causal link" or functional relationship in psychology is represented by an S-H-R-hypothesis as a minimum of complexity.

We shall deal with the more complex cases in the next classification.

Before leaving this classification we should emphasize that this is the most basic systematological classification of psychological hypotheses. It is based upon a more detailed classification constructed by *K. W. Spence*, which is discussed in Madsen (1968)[15]).

15. Some readers possibly believe that logic requires the existence of *completely* empirical hypotheses in addition to *"partly* empirical hypotheses". But we prefer calling the completely empirical hypotheses "laws" or "S–R propositions" and not hypotheses.

3.2.2.2. *Classification of Hypotheses According to Degree of Complexity.* In some instances we have hypotheses concerning rather complicated reciprocal functional relationships between several H-variables. Thus we have the basis for a new classification of hypotheses according to *degree of complexity:*

1. *"One-dimensional"* hypotheses, i. e., formulations of fairly simple functional relationships such as, e. g., S-H-hypotheses, H-H-hypotheses, H-R-hypotheses and possibly S-H-R-hypotheses.
2. *"Multi-dimensional"* hypotheses, i. e., formulations of fairly complicated functional relationships, in which *several* variables by interaction determine another variable. This can be formulated thusly:

$$(H_1 \times H_2 \times \ldots H_n) \to R.$$

As a concrete example we can cite one of Hull's major hypotheses, which a little simplified, reads as follows:

$$sEr = f(sHr \times D \times K \times I_r).$$

All the symbols used here stand for H-variables. "sEr" represents "reaction-potential", which is a function of "habit" (sHr), "drive" (D), as well as "incentive-motivation" (K) and "inhibition" (I_R).

The classification presented here was introduced and discussed in the history of psychology in connection with the Gestalt-psychologists criticism of the Behaviorists, the Reflexologists and the early Associationists. The Gestalt-psychologists have described all these kinds of psychological theories as *"mechanistic"*, by which they have alluded to a comparison between human beings and machines, whose functions can be explained "mechanistically". The Gestalt-psychologists have described their own theory as "dynamic", which is a slightly unfortunate use of the word. This designation could better be applied to Freud's theory, which actually introduced the dynamic terms in their more precise and original meanings. Later K. Lewin borrowed a better term from physics for this kind of theory: *"field theory"*. Lewin defined a "field" as a totality of interacting variables which determine behavior. Thus it is possible to retain the term *"mechanistic theory"* to designate a theory containing mainly *one-dimensional* hypotheses, and *"field theory"* for a theory containing mainly *multi-dimensional* hypotheses.

We now turn to our last classification of hypotheses.

3.2.2.3. *Classification of Hypotheses According to the Type of Functional Relationships.* In the preceding pages we have chiefly used the term "functional relationships" in connection with hypotheses, but sometimes we have used the term "causal link". It is now time to clarify the problem "causality" versus functional relationships. In psychology it is common to *substitute the terms "cause"* and *"effect"* with *"independent variable"* and *"dependent variable"*. This originally mathematical usage has, among other things, the advantage that it is neutral regarding the disputed philosophical problem concerning "strict causal relationship" or *causality*, which we shall return to at a later point. We thus say in psychology that a factor in a particular situation (e. g., a stimulus) is an "independent variable", and that a particular type of behavior, reaction or performance is the "dependent variable". We have with these words simply indicated that the independent and the dependent variables appear *regularly* together or successively after each other. *This regular relationship between independent and dependent variables is called a "functional relationships"*. It can include "strictly causal relationships" (causality), in which the independent variable ("the cause"), with the "absolute necessity of natural law", is *always* followed by the dependent variable ("the effect"). But the term "functional relationship" also includes those cases in which the independent variable is *not always*, but more or less frequently, followed by the dependent variable. The relative frequency can be expressed by a number representing a *probability*. Functional relationships between independent and dependent variables can thus be of the causality type or the probability type.

We shall briefly sum up that discussion which has been carried on in the sciences (especially in physics, but also in psychology) concerning the problem of causality. Two main theories in particular have been advanced: "determinism" and "indeterminism".

"Determinism" is that theory which maintains that in nature we find *absolute causal* connections in such a way that it is, *in principle*, possible to formulate causal or *deterministic laws*, from which it is possible both to *explain* and also, with a 100 % degree of probability, to *predict* "the effect" when "the cause" is known.

"Indeterminism" is that theory which maintains that in nature we do *not* find absolute causality, but that things happen *by chance*, so that *in principle* we can only formulate *statistical laws*, from which we can explain and predict with a certain degree of *probability*.

In physics the chief representatives for the two major theories under discussion here were *Albert Einstein* and *Niels Bohr*. It was Einstein's opinion that the present lack of deterministic laws in atomic physics was only the fault of temporary and practical difficulties, and that they were not of a fundamental nature, while Bohr felt that we must always accept statistical laws as fundamental laws in atomic physics.

In psychology we have had representatives for the same opposing points of view. Psychologists such as *Freud, Pavlov* and *K. Lewin* maintained the existence of a *fundamental determinism* in psychology, even though they – just as Einstein in the case of physics – realized that for practical reasons it was not possible, for the time being, to advance a completely deterministic theory.

In the last few decades in psychology – especially in the psychology of the learning process – there have also been representatives of a *fundamental inde-*

terminism, in which *statistical* or *"stochastic theories"* (as they are also called) are formulated.

Finally, we have in the field of psychology a leading representative for a *"practical* indeterminism", B. F. Skinner. He formulates all of his laws as probabilities, because that is in practice the only thing we can do today — and the fundamental problems and possibilities do not interest him.

The designation "indeterminism" is of course negative and very indefinite, so from now on we shall use the *designation "probabilistic" concerning these theories which contain statistical or stochastic, explanatory propositions; whilst we shall use the designation "causal-deterministic" concerning those theories which contain strictly causal explanatory propositions.*

The reason for introducing this new term, "probabilism", is that in psychology other *indeterministic* theories have been set forth.

There has thus been asserted a fundamental indeterminism in psychology which is based on the hypothesis that human beings should possess a so-called *"free will"*. This conception was, in relation to the philosophical opinions in question, a vague and half-mystical concept which was in all probability sustained on religious and moral-philosophical grounds. This "free will" should thus be a cause of actions (the "arbitrary" actions) which are themselves without cause. This old, humanistic conception of Man as possessing a "free will" and having the ability to think rationally has, in the 1960's, been re-adopted by the so-called *"humanistic psychologists"*. Influenced by *existentialistic philosophy* they propose that Man is able to emancipiate himself from causal determinism, to make free choices independent of heredity and environment. We can call this *"humanistic indeterminism"*.

As already mentioned in this chapter (see 2.2) another type of explanation has been advanced in psychology as well as in biology, the *"teleological"* or *"finalistic"*. According to this viewpoint behavior should — especially human actions — be *"purpose determined"* rather than "cause determined". There is a certain inconsistency between the deterministic and the teleological points of view, because causes are always perceived as relating to *the past or the contemporary* with their "effects", whereas an action's "purpose" is in some respects prospective. In modern motivational psychology, however, the essential points in the teleological viewpoint have been reformulated into a deterministic formulation. It has consequently been asserted that it is not the prospective purpose but the *actual "purpose-consciousness"* that is the cause of the action and its purposive character. "Purposive consciousness" is at the same time a concept which chiefly has its origin and application in an "introspective consciousness psychology", that is to say a psychology which has chosen a phenomenological data-language. But *Tolman* demonstrated in 1932 that it is possible to deal with "purposive behavior in animals and men" in an intersubjective behavioral data-language.

But this problem belongs to the next stratum of a psychological text to which we now turn.

3.3. The Descriptive Stratum

We have already dealt with many problems related to the descriptive stratum of a psychological text, but there are a few left.

3.3.1. Levels of Abstraction.
The relationship between the three strata of a scientific text can be conceived of as a *dimension of abstraction* which we have divided somewhat arbitrarily into *three levels of abstraction*, in which the meta-stratum is the most abstract and the descriptive stratum the most concrete. But as these levels *are* arbitrary "cuts" in a continuum, it is sometimes difficult to decide to which stratum of the text a certain term or proposition belongs.

This conception of a continuum of abstraction can also be applied to a single stratum. We have previously mentioned that among the hypothetical terms those representing Hypothetical Constructs are more abstract than those representing the Intervening Variables. And the same applies to the descriptive stratum, which also may be conceived of as a continuum of abstraction in the text.

The most *concrete descriptions* are the *protocol sentences,* which describe *data.*

As we already have dealt in detail with the problems of two *data-languages: the behavioral and the phenomenological,* we shall leave this concrete stratum and investigate the more *abstract descriptive terms and propositions.*

As an instructive example of a very abstract descriptive term we can take Tolman's "purposive behavior", which has already been touched upon. It was one of Tolman's many contributions to psychology that he convincingly demonstrated that *"purposive"* can be conceived of as a *descriptive* term, albeit a rather *abstract* descriptive term, which has to be related to more *concrete* descriptive terms by "reductive" or "operational" definitions. We shall illustrate this by reconstructing Tolman's discussion in the light of a more recent analysis of the same problem made by *Dalbir Bindra* (see Bindra, 1959). Bindra uses the term "goal-directed" as a substitute for "purposive" – but the logic of the reasoning is the same:

"Purposive" or *"goal-directed behavior"* is a highly abstract term with which different observers may agree to describe the observed behavior of an organism if it manifests certain properties. These properties can be reduced to three essential ones, each of which can be represented by the following descriptive terms:

1. *"spontaneity",* which is ascribed to behavior which is independent of external stimuli. When it is not possible to observe any change in the external situation, and the behavior of an organism changes – we say that this behavior is spontaneous. As an example: a cat is sleeping, but suddenly it wakes up and walks to its feeding-place (without any external stimuli having been perceived by the psychologist).
2. *"docility",* a property ascribed to behavior which is flexible and adjusts to changes in the external situation. Thus we may say that a cat demonstrates

60 . *Systematology*

docility if it finds no food at the feeding-place and then walks to another possible feeding-place. While doing this the cat may notice a mouse and follow it in a "well-adjusted" way.

3. *"persistence"*, which is a property ascribed to behavior which continues or lasts until a certain end, which the psychologist may later designate as *"the goal"* of the behavior. Thus our cat may continue following the mouse until he catches it and eats it (or perhaps until he is exhausted).

Thus the highly abstract term "goal-directed behavior" is defined by at least three less abstract descriptive terms, each of which is used as a generalized description of a particular type of behavior. We may illustrate this by means of a diagram which traces the highly abstract term down to the most concrete terms (see Fig. 2.5.):

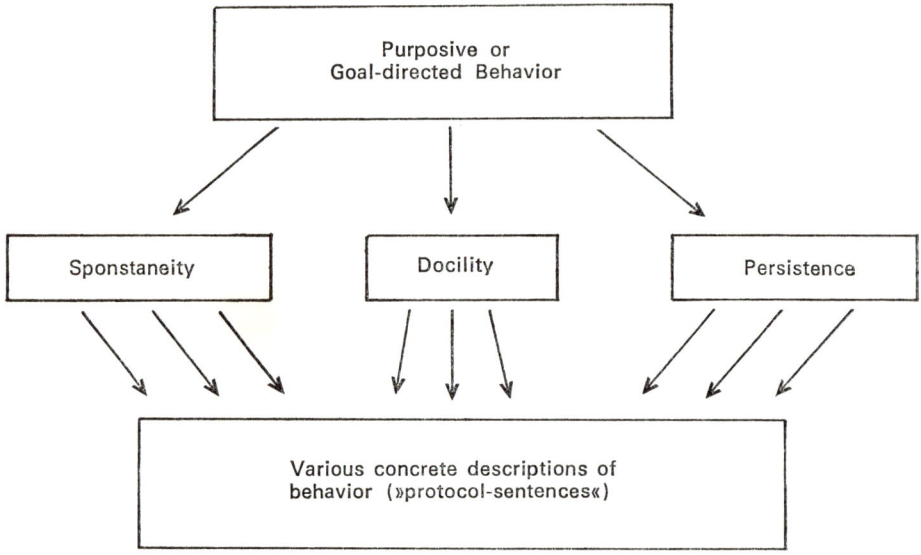

Fig. 2.5. This diagram illustrates the relationships between a highly abstract, descriptive term, "purposive", which is defined by three less abstract, descriptive terms (spontaneity", "docility" and "persistence"), which are furhter operationally defined by some very concrete protocol sentences containing data.

In this example we can analyse and classify the descriptive terms according to three levels of abstraction. But the reader must not generalize from this figure as it is not possible to find three different levels of abstraction in the descriptive stratum of every psychological theory. Sometimes we may only find two levels of abstraction (concrete and abstract descriptive terms), and other times we may find more than three levels. This fact reinforces our conception of a scientific text as being constituted of a whole continuum of abstraction from the most concrete descriptions via the more abstract descriptions to the hypothetical stratum and, finally, to the meta-stratum – the most abstract level.

The reader should also be warned against making another generalization from our example. This would seem to indicate that all the descriptive terms were behavioral because Tolman presupposed a behavioral data-language. Although *most* modern psychologists accept and make use of a behavioral data-language, it is well to bear in mind that this is not always the case. But our *metatheory is not bound to a behavioral data-language, as it can be applied to theories with a phenomenological data-language as well*.

When a behavioral data-language is applied, which is the case generally, then the *descriptive terms* refer to:

1. *S-variables:* i. e., external and (observable) internal *stimuli or other independent variables* in the actual situation in which the behavior occurs. The reader should bear in mind that we also regard *internal* stimuli as independent variables – but only when they are in principle observable and manipulative by an experimenter.
2. *R-variables:* i. e., reactions, performances, behavior acts or other *observable activity of the whole organism* in relation to its environment. This also comprises *verbal* activity, oral as well as written, spontaneously emitted as well as responses to questions from psychologists.

    It is this extension of "behavior" to include verbal activity which makes behavioral data-language *broader* than phenomenological data-language, as behavioral data-language can describe (indirectly) both *conscious* (i. e., verbally reportable) as well as *unconscious* behavior[16]).

When a theory contains a behavioral data-language representing S- and R-variables, then a *"law"* – or empirical explanatory proposition – is called *an S-R-proposition*.

Thus it is easier to classify the descriptive *sentences* than the terms – because they may be divided into *two levels of abstraction:* the concrete *protocol sentences* and the abstract *empirical explanatory propositions*.

We now turn to our last classification:

3.3.2. *Classification According to the Units of Description*. The descriptive terms of scientific theories represent different *"descriptive units"*. Thus some terms refer to "small-scale" or "microscopic" units, while others refer to "large-scale" or "macroscopic" units. The "microscopic" units need not literally be based upon observation via a microscope, but on any observational method which presupposes a detailed analysis. While, on the other hand, the macro-

---

16. There is, of course, the possibility that something may be experienced consciously by an organism without any possibility existing of expressing it verbally. Even adult people may under certain circumstances – e.g., narcotic states – experience something which they are unable to express verbally. But the present author believes that such experiences cannot be objects for scientific research – they should rather be expressed through the arts.

scopic units are based upon observable methods which presuppose analyses which are less detailed. Thus in psychology we can describe behavior either in terms of microscopic units such as "stimulus" and muscular "response" or in terms of macroscopic units such as "situation" and "behavior-act".

It was *Tolman* who introduced this metascientific distinction into psychology. Tolman used the terms *"molar"* and *"molecular"* instead of "macroscopic" and "microscopic", and he used these terms to *classify psychological theories* according to the preferred scale of descriptive unit:

1. *"Molar* theories" are psychological theories which for the most part employ "large-scale", "macroscopic" descriptive units (e. g., Tolman regarded his own theory as molar).
2. *"Molecular* theories" are psychological theories which largely employ small-scale", "microscopic" descriptive units (e. g., Tolman regarded Watson's Classical Behaviorism as a molecular theory).

Of course there are also theories which employ descriptive units of both "scale sizes". Thus this classification – like many other systematological classifications – is based upon an arbitrary division of a *continuum* varying – in this case – from the most molar to the most molecular.

We shall in our last section return to the problems involved in classifications of a scientific theory as a whole, but first let us summarize our metatheory of psychological theories in a diagram (Fig. 2.6) which represents the three strata of a psychological text.

4. The Theory as a Whole

While in the preceding sections we have analyzed the details of a scientific text, we shall now describe and classify the psychological theories as wholes. In other words: while our *descriptive units* in the preceding sections have been terms, propositions and strata of the scientific text, we *shall now take "a theory" as our descriptive unit*. In doing this we introduce some new systematological classifications of psychological theories, but these classifications are mainly based upon analyses previously made, so this section acts as a kind of overall review.

4.1. *The Formal Properties of Theories*

In several connections we have touched upon the problems of differences in formal properties of theories, but it remains to make a more detailed analysis of these problems. The formal development of a theory includes at least three different aspects, which we now shall discuss one by one.

4.1.1. *The Systematic Organization of Theories.* A scientific text has been defined as a *systematic*, informative discourse, and this formal property is a very

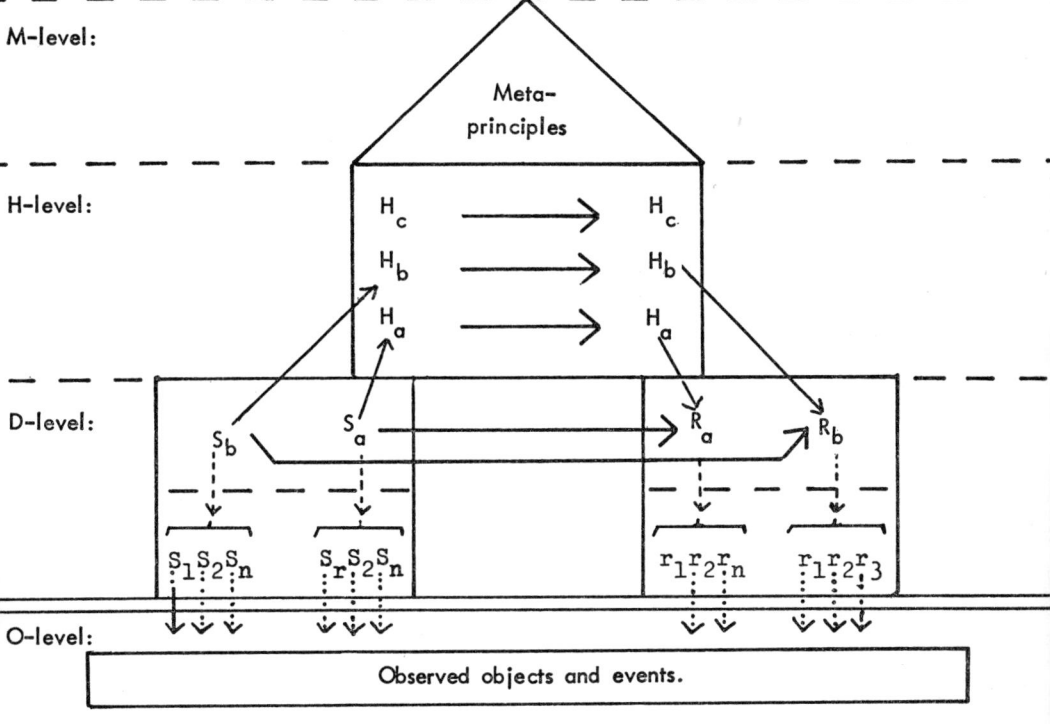

Fig. 2.6. Diagram Representing a Psychological Theory.

There are four levels (from below):

"*O-level*": "*Ob*ject-level": Observed objects and events.

"D-level": "Descriptive level": Descriptions of the observations. $S_1 \ldots S_n$ and $r_1 \ldots r_n$ represent basic terms constituting protocol statements. S_a, S_b and R_a, R_b represent generalized terms and empirical generalizations ($S_a \to R_a$, $S_b \to R_b$).

"H-level": "Hypothetical level": The explanatory system containing explanatory terms (or H-variables) and explanatory sentences ("hypotheses": H → H-relations). $H_c \to H_c$ represents variables and hypotheses without direct connection with the descriptive level.

"M-level": "Meta-level": Meta-principles about philosophical, methodological, and meta-theoretical problems.

important factor, but it is one which theories have in different *degrees*. There is possibly a whole *continuum* of differences in systematic organization, but we have found it useful to make a classification which divides this possible continuum into roughly *three categories:*

1. *"Explanatory sketches":* i. e., loosely organized texts where the discourse is much like an informative discourse in daily life, without any "stratification" into the three levels of abstraction and without explicit, formalized explanatory propositions (laws and hypotheses). It is of course a matter of definition how much systematic organization should be required of a text for it to be regarded as scientific. But some of the mest important, fruitful and inspiring theories in psychology – e. g., Freud's and Pavlov's theories – have been explanatory sketches.
2. *"Systematic theories":* i. e., theories with "stratification" in the descriptive, hypothetical and metatheoretical strata and some important propositions explicitly formulated in each stratum (as "principles", "postulates", "hypotheses", "theorems", "laws", etc.). Besides, there may be some order in these propositions (a sequence or a hierarchy: basic and derived propositions). Most psychological theories – e. g., Murray's, Tolman's, Hebb's, etc. – belong to this category.
3. *"Deductive theories":* i. e., theories organized as a deductive system: a logical hierarchy of axioms or postulates and derived theorems. Such a system is often formulated (at least partly) through the use of logical or mathematical symbols. But this is not necessary in order to have the system regarded as a deductive system, as such a system can also be formulated verbally.
   Some psychological theories are deductive systems – e. g., *Hull*'s theory and some modern learning theories.

With these last remarks concerning verbal contra mathematical formulation we have touched upon another classification.

4.1.2. *The Preciseness of Representation.* This is another formal property of theories which often – but not always – is connected to the systematic organization. As these properties are not always related, it should be useful to make a separate classification according to the *preciseness of representation:*

1. *Purely verbal theories,* i. e., theories formulated exclusively in words and sentences from everyday language – perhaps supplemented with some precisely defined scientific terms.
2. *Partly symbolized theories,* i. e., theories which to some extent make use of logical, mathematical and other *symbols* as substitutes for words. Such a substitution has the advantage that the many kinds of "surplus meaning" words may carry with them from use in ordinary language is avoided, and the

writer's concepts are therefore more precisely communicated to the reader. *Hull*'s and *K. Lewin*'s theories are partly symbolized theories.
3. *Mathematical theories*, i. e., theories containing a complete system of mathematical formulas – a "calculus" – as a parallel to a verbal formulation. Such a system of mathematical formulas has the advantage of the possibility of a *quantitative representation*, which is the most precise representation of information. In the years following the Second World War some modern learning theories were mathematized.

Intimately related to the last classification is a classification of the *explanatory models* used in the theories.

4.1.3. Classification of Models According to Formal Properties.

We can classify the models into four categories:

1. *Verbal analogies*, i. e., verbal formulation using a metaphor or an analogy in the explanations without any precise representation of this analogy. E. g., *Freud* used many of these analogies in his theory.
2. *Two-dimensional models*, i. e., diagrams, maps and other two-dimensional representations used in explanations. E. g., *Freud's* "lenze-model", and *Lewin's* and *Tolman's* diagrams.
3. *Three-dimensional models*, i. e., a globe or another three-dimensional structure. The structure may be a "working model" – a mechanical or electronic system used for explanations. Several of these working models have been constructed by psychologists (see Deutsch, 1960).
4. *Computer simulation programs*. This is a type of model which is being used with increased frequency in psychological theories. In this case it is the logical structure and sequences of the program which "simulate" or represent the phenomena to be explained.

The last category of models is quite similar to a mathematical calculus which provides good grounds for equating a calculus with a mathematical "model". But even though we admit the similarity, we prefer distinguishing between the *deductive explanations* (e. g., with a deductive, mathematized theory) and *model-explanations* with concrete models (e. g., computer programs).

It is now time to turn to the next classification.

4.2. An Epistemological Classification of Theories

This classification of theories is very important, as it is a classification based upon the *data-language* and the category of *hypothetical terms* used in a theory. As previously indicated the psychologist's preference for these may be influenced by his whole *philosophy of science*. We thus have the following epistemological classification of theories:

1. *Purely descriptive theories*, i. e., psychological texts without any hypothetical stratum or explicit metastratum. They can be subdivided into the following sub-classes:

   1. *Behavioral descriptive or S-R-theories* (in the narrow sense). E. g., Skinner's theory.
   2. *Phenomenological descriptive theories*. This category is not represented in modern psychology as far as the present author knows, but some philosophers have produced such theories, e. g., David Hume, E. Husserl and the Danish philosopher, Herbert Iversen.
   3. *Physiological descriptive or "reductive theories"* (in the strict sense). Some psychologists have had such theories as "programs", but they have never been fully carried out.

2. *Explanatory theories*, i. e., psychological texts with both a descriptive and a hypothetical stratum – as well as a metastratum. They can be subdivided according to the category of hypothetical terms used in the explanations:

   1. *Physiological explanatory or S-O-R-theories*, i. e., theories applying hypothetical terms with a *physiological* surplus meaning. E. g., Pavlov's Hebb's, Berlyne's, and others' theories.
   2. *Neutral explanatory or S-H_N-R-theories,* i. e., theories applying hypothetical terms with a *neutral* surpuls meaning or perhaps terms representing purely "intervening variables" (in the narrow sense). E.g., Freud's Tolman's Lewin's, Hull's and many other theories.
   3. *Mentalistic explanatory or S-M-R-theories,* i. e., theories applying hypothetical terms with a *mentalistic* surplus meaning. E. g., many of the classical psychological theories (Wundt's, Titchener's, W. James's and other's theories).

3. *Interpreting or M-theories*. This is a type of theory which we have not earlier touched upon. They are theories which do *not* explain or predict behavior by using a deductive explanation or a model-explanation. These theories rather represent a more *intuitive "understanding"* or "Verstehen" of other peoples' "minds". This category encompasses some of the earlier German "Geisteswissenschaftliche Psychologie" (e. g., Dilthey and Spranger) and possibly some of the modern existentialistic or "humanistic" psychological theories.

We can summarize this epistemological classification into types of theories by means of a diagram (Fig. 2.7.):

Systematology . 67

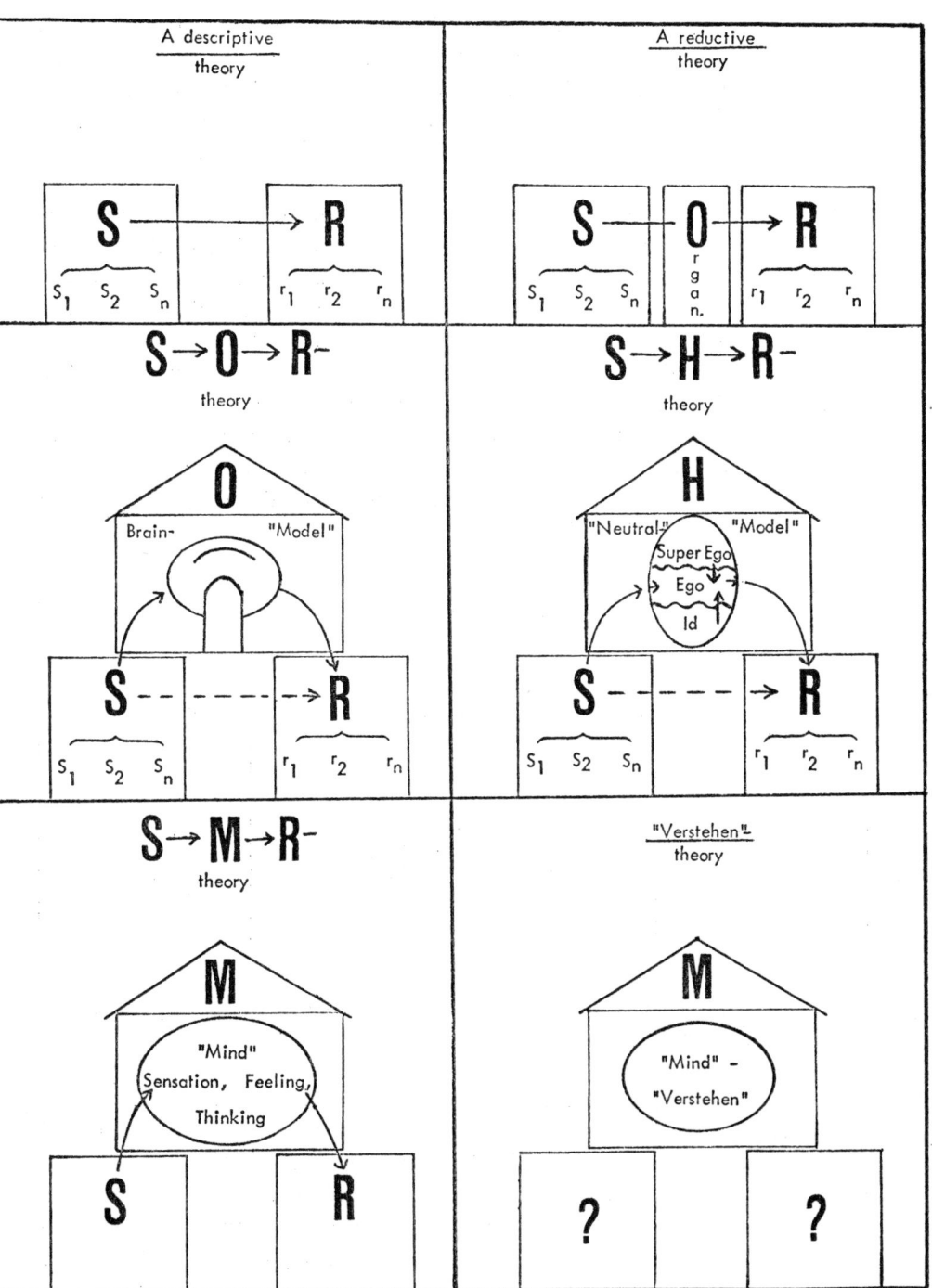

Fig. 2.7.
Types of theories.

68 . *Systematology*

The three main types of theories (descriptive, explanatory and interpretative) may be conceived of as corresponding to the three main epistemological theories according to *Joseph Royce*'s "psycho-epistemology" (see Royce, 1970). In this work he presents three types of epistemological theories: *empirical, rationalistic* and *metaphorical*. These three philosophies represent a one-sided emphasis of three cognitive *processes: perception, thinking* and *intuition*.

Thus it is easy to conceive of the *purely descriptive* theories as the products of radical *empiricism* relying mainly upon *perception*, and it is also easy to conceive of *interpretative "Verstehen"-psychology* as the product of *"metaphorism"* relying mainly upon *inutition*. But it is possible that the *explanatory* theories do *not* all represent a one-sided rationalism which mainly relies upon thinking. Most of them rather represent a balanced *"empirical rationalism"* or *"rational empiricism"* (cf. logical empiricism), which relies upon both perception and thinking. Metaphorism and intuition are perhaps also represented to some degree in the explanatory theories, as the surplus meaning of the hypothetical terms is based upon the metaphorical use of the language. We can summarize this in a table (Table 2.2.):

Basic Epistemology	Empiricism	Rationalism	Metaphorism
Preferred cognitive processes	Perception	Thinking	Intuition
Type of theory produced	Purely descriptive theories	Explanatory theories	Interpretative »Vestehen« - theories

Table 2.2. Represents the supposed relationship between Joseph Royce's psychoepistemology and various types af theories.

Another important philosophical aspect of theories is included in the epistemological classification of types of theories. Thus the theorist's conception of the "mind-body" problem is implicitly or explicitly revealed in his choice of hypothetical terms according to their surplus meaning. We have already mentioned in an earlier section that psychologists with a *materialistic* conception of the psychosomatic problem will probably show a preference for a purely descriptive theory of the behavioral type or perhaps for an explanatory theory with *physiological* surplus meaning in its terms. On the other hand, a psychologist with a *dualistic* conception of the psychosomatic problem will probably show a preference for an explanatory theory with mentalistic surplus meaning in its terms or for a "Verstehen"-theory. Perhaps they might instead prefer a purely descriptive phenomenological theory. And those psychologists with a *neutral-monistic* theory would probably prefer an explanatory theory with neutral surplus meaning in its terms – but of course these theorists might prefer a physiological or a mentalistic explanatory theory instead. We can summarize the above in a table (Table 2.3.):

Basic psycho-somatic theory / Epistemological type of theory	Materialistic theory	Neutral-monistic theory	Dualistic theory
Epistemological type of theory	S-R theory or S-O-R theory	S-H_N-R-theory or S-O-R-theory or S-M-R-theory	S-M-R theory and M theory

Table 2.3.

4.3. *Classification According to the t/e-ratio or the H.Q.*

In the preceding classification we touched upon the fact that explanatory theories may differ according to the balance between rational thinking and empirical perception. This balance is manifested in *the relationship between the hypothetical stratum and the descriptive stratum*. Some theories have a rather large hypothetical stratum based upon a rather small descriptive stratum, while other theories may have a large descriptive stratum upon which a smaller hypothetical stratum is based. This relationship can be called the "theory-empiry ratio" (or "t/e-ratio"). Psychological theories can be *classified according to the t/e-ratio* into two classes:

1. *Mainly "speculative" theories,* i. e., theories with a high t/e-ratio.
2. *Mainly "empirical" theories,* i. e., theories with a low t/e-ratio.

Of course there are many psychological theories in which the two strata are so well-balanced that it is difficult to put them into either category.

Some readers are perhaps tired of all these difficult systematological classifications of theories along continuous dimensions, where the theories have to be placed according to the estimation or judgment of the metascientist. But these are the necessary conditions for many sciences which are in their early phases of development – also psychology, which must still rely on many "scales" of judgment.

All sciences are developed by the increasing production of intersubjective, reliable and precise information, and the present author believes that meta-science can also be developed in this direction.

As a contribution to a more precise classification of theories, the author has in an earlier book substituted the t/e-ratio with a so-called *"Hypotheses-Quotient"*, which is defined in this way:

$$H.Q. = \frac{\Sigma(H-H)}{\Sigma(S-H)+(H-R)}$$

Thus, to calculate the H.Q. for a given theory, you have to count all the purely theoretical hypotheses (H-H-hypotheses) and all the partly empirical hypotheses (S-H and H-R hypotheses) and then calculate the quotient by division. We have done this for 10 important psychological theories (in Madsen, 1959). The H.Q.'s for these theories are:

Tinbergen's theory:	0.11
Hebb's theory:	0.13
McClelland's theory:	0.14
Hull's theory:	0.30
McDougall's theory:	0.43
Lewin's theory:	0.50
Murray's theory:	0.71
Young's theory:	0.82
Allport's theory:	1.00
Tolman's theory:	1.43

Thus Tinbergen's, McClelland's and Hebb's theories are among the most empirical while Allport's and Tolman's are the most speculative.

However, there is one great problem in calculating these H.Q.s: the theory must be rather *systematically organized* with explicit formulations of explanatory (and other important) propositions. And many psychological theories are not developed formally to such an extent that it is possible to count the theoretical and the partly empirical hypotheses. Therefore, it is necessary to make a systematic *reconstruction* of the theory before calculating the H.Q. And this reconstruction opens the possibility for a *source of error:* the skill of the metascientist to make this reconstruction in a reliable and objective way without distorting the theory. But *it is possible to eliminate this subjective factor by the construction of a computer program* which guides an electronic computer to do the work of classifying propositions as H-H, S-H and H-R hypotheses. This program is in the process of being developed by one of my graduate students, *Svend Jørgensen.* The program is founded on, developed and inspired by the content-analyses program, *"The General Inquirer"* (see Philip J. Stone et al., 1966), which has been developed to make content-analyses of psychological, humanistic and social texts.

It is important for two reasons that such a *systematological computer program* be developed.

The *first* reason is that *the H.Q. is an estimation of an important property of a theory: its "explanatory power"*. Since the late Middle Ages when *Occam* used his famous "razor" to cut all superfluous hypothetical terms and propositions from theories, it has been a generally accepted rule or principle that theories ought to be "parsimonious" or "economical" in their use of hypothetical terms and propositions. This *epistemological "parsimony principle"* is, according to *Thomas Kuhn,* one of the most important guiding principles when scientists have to make a choice among several theories (see Kuhn, 1962). And according to Kuhn scientists have such a need for a theory to guide their research that even when they know that a theory is contradicted by certain facts, they continue to use it until a better one is created. Kuhn maintains that the history of science demonstrates that the *process of verification of theories is always a comparison between two or more theories on one side and the sum of data on the other side. Therefore, comparative studies of theories are so important.*

The *second* reason for our emphasizing the development of a computer program for calculating the H.Q. is that the success of such a program may reinforce our expectations concerning more computer programs for the analyses of theories. In principle such programs should be possible for all tasks which consist of counting the sum of certain elements – terms or propositions – in a scientific text. It should also be possible to calculate to what degree a theory is a "field-theory" by calculating the ratio between "multi-dimensional" and "one-dimensional" hypotheses. And other programs may be invented. *Thus we hope that by using computer-assisted analysis it will be possible to make systematology a more exact metascience.* But that depends on future research, and in the present book we must be satisfied with the use of our more qualitative methods in our analyses of theories of motivation.

We therefore summarize the entire second chapter by formulating an *outline for systematological analyses.*

Appendix to Chapter 2

A Systematological Questionnaire

We present here a summary of our metatheory presented in Chapter 2 in the form of a systematological questionnaire which can be used in a comparative study of psychological theories.

The first and most important question about a given book or paper is:
Is this text a scientific text ("theory")?

The criteria are that it be a *systematic, informative* text containing descriptive, explanatory and metapropositions. If these criteria are fulfilled we may proceed with our analysis:

1. The Metastratum

We analyse the explicit metapropositions – or *reconstruct* the implicit metapropositions according to the following classification:

1.1. *Philosophical propositions:*

1.1.1. What are the main propositions concerning "knowledge", "science", "truth", etc.?

1.1.2. What are the main propositions concerning the psychosomatic problem (materialistic, neutral-monistic, dualistic or perhaps other propositions)?

1.2. *Metatheoretical propositions:*

What are the main propositions concerning "theory", "explanation", "models", etc.?

1.3. *Methodological propositions:*

1.3.1. What are the main propositions concerning *empirical* methods?

1.3.2. What are the main propositions concerning *data-language* (phenomenological or behavioral)?

2. The Hypothetical Stratum

2.0. What is the main content of the explanations in the theory? (a short summarizing reconstruction).

2.1. *Hypothetical terms*

What are the main explanatory or *hypothetical terms?*

2.1.1. What *surplus meaning* is contained in the terms?: They may be classified as:

2.1.1.1. *"Intervening Variables":* terms without surplus meaning or:
2.1.1.2. *"Hypothetical Constructs":* terms with surplus meaning, including:
2.1.1.2.1. "H.C.O."-terms with *physiological* surplus meaning.
2.1.1.2.2. "H.C.M."-terms with *mentalistic* surplus meaning.
2.1.1.2.3. "H.C.N."-terms with *neutral* surplus meaning.

2.1.2. What is the *duration of the existence of the variables* to which the terms refer? They may be classified as:

2.1.2.1. *"Disposition terms"*, representing variables with a long duration (years), "structures" and "factors", etc.
2.1.2.2. *"Function terms"*, representing variables of shorter duration, either:
2.1.2.2.1. *"States"* (lasting hours or days) or
2.1.2.2.2. *"Processes"* (lasting seconds or minutes).

2.1.3. What is the *effect of the variables* to which the terms refer? They may be classified as:

2.1.3.1. *"Directive terms"*, representing variables which determine the *direction*, organization, regulation or steering of behavior.
2.1.3.2. *"Dynamic terms"*, representing variables which determine the *activation* or energy-mobilizing of behavior.
2.1.3.3. *"Vector-terms"*, representing variables defined as having a combination of directive and dynamic effects. In addition, the vague, undefined terms may be classified as vector-terms.

2.2. *Classifications of the Hypotheses*

What are the main *explanatory propositions or hypotheses?* They may be classified in different categories.

2.2.1. *Basic Classification:* What are the *constituent terms* in the hypotheses? They may be classified as:

2.2.1.1. *Theoretical hypotheses or H-H hypotheses,* containing exclusively H terms.
2.2.1.2. *Partly empirical hypotheses,* containing both descriptive and hypothetical terms. They may be divided into:
2.2.1.2.1. *S-H hypotheses,* which contain terms representing *"S variables"* (observable situation- or stimuli-variables) and H terms.
2.2.1.2.2. *H-R hypotheses,* which contain H terms and terms representing *"R variables"* (observable behavior-variables).

2.2.2. What is the *degree of complexity of the hypotheses?* They may be classified as follows:

2.2.2.1. *One-dimensional* hypotheses, containing only two terms: S-H, H-H, or H-R hypotheses.
2.2.2.2. *Multi-dimensional* hypotheses, containing more than two terms referring to interacting variables (e. g., $(H_1 \times H_2 \times H_3) \rightarrow R$).

2.2.3. What is the *functional relationship* assumed by the hypotheses? They may be classified as follows:

2.2.3.1. *Causal-deterministic* hypotheses, which assume completely invariant, functional relationships between variables (occuring with 100 % probability).
2.2.3.2. *Stochastic or probability-deterministic* hypotheses, which assume functional relationships occuring with less than 100 % probability.
2.2.3.3. *Teleological or finalistic* hypotheses, which assume relationships determined by "ends", "goals" or "purposes".
2.2.3.4. *Indeterministic* hypotheses, which assume completely unpredictable variable relationships (free will, etc.).

3. The Descriptive Stratum

What is the main content of descriptions in the theory? The descriptive content may be classified in at least two *levels of abstraction:*

3.1. The *abstract* D-level:

What is contained in the most *abstract descriptive level?*
3.1.1. Abstract *descriptive terms,* which may be classified into:

3.1.1.1. *S-terms* representing S-variables (external and internal stimuli).
3.1.1.2. *R-terms* representing R-variables (behavior).
3.1.2. Abstract, *general, descriptive propositions:* "laws" or S-R-propositions.

3.2. The *concrete* D-level:

What is contained in the most *concrete descriptive level?*

    3.2.1. *Protocol-sentences* describing intersubjectively observed events and objects.

    3.2.2. *Data-terms* representing fragments of information. They may be classified as follows:

        3.2.2.1. *Behavioral* data-terms, or
        3.2.2.2. *Phenomenological* data-terms.

3.3. What types of *descriptive units* are applied in the theory? There may be:
    3.3.1. *"Molar terms,* which refer to relatively "large-scale", "macroscopic" units of description.
    3.3.2. "Molecular" terms, which refer to relatively "small-scale", "microscopic" units of description.

4. The Theory as a Whole

After an analysis of the terms, propositions and strata of which a theory is composed, we shall continue with some classifications of the theory as a whole.

    4.1. *What are the formal properties of the theory?* There are several formal properties to be noted:

        4.1.1. *The systematic organization of the theory*, which may be classified into three categories:

            4.1.1.1. *"Sketches"*, i. e., loosely organized texts with very little systematic organization.
            4.1.1.2. *"Explanatory systems"*, i. e., more systematically organized texts (e. g., with stratification of the text and explicit definitions of terms and formulations of hypotheses.
            4.1.1.3. *"Deductive theories"*, i. e., scientific texts in which the propositions are organized into a deductive system.

4.1.2. *The preciseness of representation*, which may be classified into:

> 4.1.2.1 *Purely verbal theories,* i. e., scientific texts formulated in ordinary language which may possibly contain some scientific terms.
>
> 4.1.2.2. *Partly symbolized theories*, i. e., scientific texts partly formulated with mathematical, logical or other special symbols.
>
> 4.1.2.3. *Mathematical theories*, i. e., scientific texts containing a complete system of mathematical formulas – a so-called "calculus", which supplements the verbal formulation.

4.1.3. *Classification of the properties of models*. If a *model-explanation* is applied alongside the deductive explanation, it may be classified into:

> 4.1.3.1. *Verbal analogies*, i. e., verbal formulations using metaphors or analogies in the explanation.
>
> 4.1.3.2. *Two-dimensional models*, i. e., diagrams, maps or other two-dimensional representations of the phenomena to be explained.
>
> 4.1.3.3. *Three-dimensional models*, i. e., three-dimensional structures or mechanisms which represent the phenomena to be explained.
>
> 4.1.3.4. *Computer-simulation programs*, i. e., programs for computers which, by means of their function, "simulate" the logical structure and sequence of the phenomena to be explained.

4.2. *What are the epistemological properties of the theory?*
Theories may be classified into several categories or "types" according to certain important *epistemological* properties:

> 4.2.1. *Purely descriptive theories*, i. e., scientific texts containing explicit descriptive propositions as well as some implicit or explicit metapropositions. This category may be subdivided into:
>
> > 4.2.1.1. *Behavioral,* descriptive theories (or purely "S-R theories").
> > 4.2.1.2. *Phenomenological*, descriptive theories.
> > 4.2.1.3. *Physiological*, descriptive theories (or "reductive" theories in the narrow sense).

4.2.2. *Explanatory theories*, i. e., scientific texts which contain both explicit descriptive and explanatory propositions as well as some implicit or explicit metapropositions. This category may be further subdivided into:

> 4.2.2.1. *S-O-R theories* or physiological, explanatory theories (using explanatory terms with physiological surplus meaning).

4.2.2.2. *S-H_N-R theories* or neutral explanatory theories (using explanatory terms with neutral surplus meaning).

4.2.2.3. *S-M-R theories* or mentalistic explanatory theories (using explanatory terms with mentalistic surplus meaning).

4.2.3. *M theories*, i. e., interpretative or intuitive "Verstehen" theories.

4.3. *What is the $^t/e$-ratio (or the H.Q.) of the theory?* The theories may be roughly classified according to the proportion or ratio between hypothetical and descriptive strata as follows:

4.3.1. *Speculative theories*, i. e., theories with a high $^t/e$-ratio.

4.3.2. *Empirical theories*, i. e., theories with a low $^t/e$-ratio.

This rough classification may be replaced by the calculation of the "Hypotheses-Quotient":

$$H.Q. = \frac{\Sigma (H-H)}{\Sigma [(S-H)+(H-R)]}$$

This calculation can be made by means of a *computer program* which may be the beginning of *a development of systematology into a more exact metascience*.

3 : An Historical Introduction to Motivational Psychology

Introduction

This book is *not* a history of the psychology of motivation, but a short historical introduction may contribute to a deeper insight into the problems dealt with in modern theories of motivation. Therefore, we shall try to trace the main trends in the evolution of motivational psychology[1]), which can trace its origins back to the old conception of "instinct".

1. The Instinct Theories

1.1. *"Instinct" before Darwin*

Before Darwin philosophers proposed widely divergent theories to explain human and animal behavior.

Human behavior was explained by referring to the special human "power" for *rational reasoning* and the "power" of decision or *will*. These human "powers" or "faculties" were often supposed to be "free" or *non-determined*. Thus an explanation of human behavior was conceived of as being complete when an act had been traced back to rational reasoning and free will, or rather: *a rational act was intuitively understood* or interpreted without any explanation. Sometimes human behavior was *not* conceived of as rational but determined by the "lower" feelings, emotions, sentiments or passions which made it more animal-like.

Animal behavior was often explained by referring to the age-old instinct concept. Animals were supposed to have a certain number of inbuilt instincts which were conceived of as the "ability to act rationally without the faculty of reasoning". Thus instincts explained the almost *rational* adjustment of animals, which were *not* supposed to possess faculties for reasoning or thinking. But instincts were also supposed to have inbuilt "driving forces" of their own. Thus the old instinct concept conceived of instincts as having both dynamic and directive effects, and consequently, instinct may be classified as a *vector*-term in accor-

---

1. The present author has presented a more detailed historical description of motivational theories in his chapter in *Benjamin B. Wolman* (Ed.): Handbook of General Psychology (New Jersey: Prentice-Hall, 1973).

dance with the classification we introduced in Chapter 2. But it must be added that the old instinct concept was usually very vaguely defined.

1.2. "Instinct" after Darwin

The theory proposed by Darwin in *"The Origin of Species"* in 1859 postulated no principal differences between Man and other animals – only differences of degree, which could be explained as the result of a continuous biological evolution. This biological or *naturalistic conception of Man* made it possible or even logically consistent to explain human behavior through the medium of instinct. Psychologists postulated many instincts in human beings – especially in the Anglo-Saxon world. One of the most elaborated and widely accepted theories of instinct was proposed by the British-American psychologist, *William McDougall*. His most read and influential book was "Introduction to Social Psychology", first published in 1908 (and later appearing in more than 30 editions). In this book he defines instinct in this way (p. 29):

"We may then define an instinct as an inherited or innate psycho-physical disposition which determines its possessor to perceive, and to pay attention to, objects of a certain kind, and to experience an emotional excitement of a particular quality upon perceiving such an object, and to act in regard to it in a particular manner, or at least, to experience an impulse to such action".

The reader may recognize this definition as a definition of a very all-inclusive *vector-term*, referring both to directive variables (perception and attention) as well as to dynamic variables (emotion and impulse to action). Besides, we can see that instinct is explicitly defined *indirectly* by referring to several *functions* ("perceiving", "paying attention", "experiencing an emotion", and "impulse to action").

Thus instinct referred to a very complicated set of variables, and this fact determined both the strength and the weakness of the instinct concept: its "explanatory power" and its vagueness, with the risk for pseudo-explanations. This risk multiplied with the growing number of instincts. McDougall only postulated a few instincts (12 in 1908, later increased to 18)[2]. But other psychologists postulated even more instincts, and there was very little agreement between them. Thus it was pointed out during the very critical debate about instinct theories in the early twenties that several thousand instincts were to be found in psychological literature. This "instinct controversy" left the instinct concept with a very bad scientific reputation. Even McDougall himself gave up. In his last book – "The Energies of Men", which appeared in 1932 – he substituted other words for the term instinct: *"propensity"* is a *disposition* and *"tendency"* is the corre-

---

2. A more detailed analysis of McDougall's theory and its development is presented in Chapter 5 in my book "Theories of Motivation" (Copnhagen: Munksgaard, 4th ed., 1968).

sponding *function*, but both terms were defined as (mainly) *dynamic* terms. The *directive* effect was ascribed to *"abilities"*. Thus the vague, complicated term instinct was replaced by several more precise terms, each referring to an aspect of the old instinct concept. This proved to be an advantage for psychological theorizing.

1.3. *"Instinct" after McDougall*

At the time when the instinct controversy was at its height other terms had already been suggested and new theories formulated to explain behavior. We shall return to these theories later in this chapter, but before doing that let us trace the history of the term instinct, from its first use to the present day.

As a result of the instinct controversy the term instinct was almost abandoned by psychologists in the nineteen-thirties and forties.

But in the meantime the term was used with another meaning in another science. The European zoologist, *Konrad Lorenz*, proposed a new instinct concept and theory in the thirties.

This theory attracted many followers among zoologists, who called themselves *"Ethologists"*. They studied instinctive behavior in animals – mainly through field-observations under natural conditions, rather than by means of artificial experiments in the laboratory. The results of this research have been systematized by *N. Tinbergen* in his book "The Study of Instinct", 1951[3]). In this book he proposes a theory of instinct, which is defined as *an hierarchically organized system of hypothetical Innate Releasing Mechanisms (IRM)*. Thus instinct is clearly defined as a *directive disposition term*. These steering and regulating mechanisms (IRM) are assumed to be activated by so-called *"motivational factors"*, which is Tinbergen's term for hormones and internal stimuli which have a dynamic effect on the IRMs and indirectly on behavior.

Thus we see once more that the theoretical development has produced a clear conceptual differentiation between the *dynamic* and the *directive* variables as well as between *dispositions* and *functions*.

We shall now leave the instinct theories and turn to the other two branches of psychology in which theories of motivation were created: *Learning psychology* and *personality psychology*.

2. Motivation in Learning

2.1. *Woodworth's drive concept*

At about the same time that the instinct controversy began some alternatives for the instinct concept were proposed.

---

3. Tinbergen's theory is analyzed in Chapter 13 of my book "Theories of Motivation" (Copenhagen: Munksgaard, 4th ed., 1968).

One of these new proposals was set forth in a book by *Robert S. Woodworth:* "Dynamic Psychology" (1918). In his book Woodworth proposed a conceptual distinction between *"drives"* and *"mechanisms"*. This was the first time that the term "drive" was introduced into Anglo-Saxon psychological terminology. This term mainly referred to *dynamic functions,* while "mechanisms" mainly referred to *directive dispositions.* Woodworth also suggested the term *"Motivology"* as the name for a whole new pyschological discipline, which should deal with drives and related variables. Thus Woodworth may be regarded as the formal founder of motivational psychology. Forty years later he formulated a new and very modern theory of motivation, which is analyzed in a later chapter in this book.

2.2. Tolman's theory

Woodworth's drive concept was introduced into the psychology of learning by *Edward Tolman* —especially in his main work, "Purposive Behavior in Animals and Men" (1932).

As already indicated in Chapter 2, Tolman regarded "purposive" as a *descriptive* term, which can be objectively (or rather: inter-subjectively) defined. And furthermore, he proposed a theory to *explain* purposive behavior. The main explanatory terms – or "intervening variables", as Tolman later called them – were *"drive"* and *"cognition"*. He employed the term drive to denote variables with mainly dynamic effects, and cognition to denote variables with mainly directive effects. But he did *not* distinguish so clearly between dynamic and directive effects as this summary of his theory might suggest, and he later created a rather confusing terminology, which he changed several times[4]). His most important influence on learning theory was made via C. L. Hull.

2.3. Hull's theory

The most important theory of learning in the whole history of psychology was constructed by *Clark L. Hull.* Hull adopted Tolman's conception of "intervening variables" – "theoretical constructs" as he preferred to call them. He then combined these theoretical constructs with the metatheory of the logical empiricists, who conceive of a "theory" as a deductive system. He created a theory consisting of 17 postulates and 133 derived theorems. This theory was presented in his two main books: "Principles of Behavior" (1943) and "A Behavior System" (1952). In these 17 postulates he defined – implicitly – some hypothetical terms, among which we find "drive" and "habit". These terms referred to two clearly separated variables. Thus *"drive" (D)* in Hull's theory represents a *general activating state* (i. e., a purely dynamic function in our terminology),

---

4. A more thorough analysis of Tolman's theory is presented in Chapter 6 of my book "Theories of Motivation" (Copenhagen: Munksgaard, 4th ed., 1968).

while *"habit" (sHr)* represents an "associative" directive mechanism (i. e., a purely *directive disposition* in our terminology). Thus Hull clearly distinguishes between the effects of variables (dynamic and directive), but *not* so clearly between disposition and function.

Hull also introduced a combined *vector term*, called "reaction-evocation-potential (sEr), which is defined in one of the postulates by this formula:

$$sEr = f(sHr \times D \times K \times I_r \times V).$$

In this formula we meet three other symbols which also stand for hypothetical terms of great interest for motivational psychology:

"K" stands for *"incentive-motivation"*, which is a dynamic function determined by "incentives" (stimulus-objects like food, water, etc.).

"I_r" stands for *"reactive inhibition"*, which is a *negative* dynamic function created by the amount of work done.

"V" stands for *"stimulus dynamism"*, which is a dynamic function of the intensity of external stimuli.

While we have made mention of the independent S-variables which determine the three last mentioned H-variables, we have not mentioned the S-variables, which determine the two first mentioned H-variables. "sHr" or "habit" is determined by the number of reinforcements (at least in the last version of Hull's theory), and *"reinforcement"* is defined as *"drive-reduction"*. *"Drive" (D)* is determined by *"needs"*, which are states of lack or disequilibrium in peripherical organs or tissues. *Thus "need" is a descriptive term* in Hull's theory, as these states of peripherical organs can be observed – in principle at least.

Let us *summarize* this very brief presentation of Hull's theory[5]) by saying that according to Hull behavior is determined by a complex product (sEr) of learned mechanisms (sHr) and states of motivation (D, K, I_r and V).

In spite of the fact that Hull's theory is the most precise and systematically organized general behavior theory, there are some weak points, which have been corrected by several of Hull's co-workers and followers, to whom we now turn.

2.4. *Hull's co-workers and followers*

Among the many important co-workers around Hull the most influential was *Kenneth W. Spence*. His influence was, in fact, so great that it is not incorrect to call the theory "the Hull-Spence theory". Among other things it was Spence who postulated the important function of *incentive motivation*[6]). An-

---

5. The interested reader is feferred to a more thorough analysis of Hull's theory presented in Chapter 11 in my book "Theories of Motivation" (Copenhagen: Munksgaard, 4th ed., 1968).
6. Hull has acknowledged Spence's influence by using the symbol "K" for incentive motivation, thus honoring Kenneth W. Spence.

other of Hull's co-workers was *Judson S. Brown,* who has concentrated his efforts on developing the *motivational* content included in Hull's general behavior theory. We shall deal with Brown's theory in a later chapter in this book.

A third important co-worker was *Neal E. Miller,* who has conducted many experiments and formulated a theory of *learned* drives and rewards. Besides, he has created a theory of *conflicts* based upon animal experiments which he has applied to personality theory and psychotherapy. Miller's theory is treated in a later chapter in this book.

Both Brown and Miller have worked with *O. H. Mowrer,* who has elaborated some parts of Hull's theory and applied the results to psychotherapy and other fields (see Chapter 16 in this book).

2.5. Other Learning Theorists

Despite Hull's great influence on learning theory, there were other influential learning theorists who disagreed with him on important questions.

One of the most distinguished contemporary learning psychologists is *B. F. Skinner,* who has profoundly influenced experimental learning psychology as well as its practical application in programmed instruction and behavior therapy. But Skinner has *not* been interested in motivation as he takes a rather negative position towards explanatory theories. Thus he has substituted the *descriptive* terms "deprivation" and "reinforcement" for the hypothetical explanatory terms "drive" and "incentive".

In spite of this Skinner has had some influence on motivational theory. Thus *Bolles* has presented (in Bolles, 1967) a very detailed analysis of the historical development of the drive concept and presented a lot of experimental evidence for an incentive theory which is rather close to Skinner's reinforcement theory (see Chapter 16 in this book).

Another motivational theorist influenced by Skinner is *Dalbir Bindra*, who has formulated a theory of motivation which is analyzed in a later chapter of this book. This theory is based upon Skinner and Hebb, to whom we now turn.

The Canadian psychologist *Donald O. Hebb*, is one of the most influential psychologists in the fields of both learning and motivation.

While Hull proposed a "neutral", explanatory theory, and Skinner argued for a purely descriptive theory, Hebb produced evidence illustrating the utility of a "neuropsychological" or physiological, explanatory theory. Thus Hebb followed the same approach to psychology earlier started by *Pavlov* and later contioned in America by *K. Lashley*, with whom he studied before proposing his neuropsychological theory. This theory was presented in his book "Organization of Behavior" (1949). In a later paper (Hebb, 1955) he revised his hypotheses about motivation. In this new version of the theory he introduced the explanatory concept *"arousal"*, which is a hypothetical term referring to the function of the brain stem reticular formation. It was discovered in 1949 by the neurophysiologists *Guiseppe Moruzzi* and *H. W. Magoun* that the reticular formation was a general, non-specific activating system. Thus the "arousal" of this system was postulated – by Hebb and others – to possess the function of a general "drive"[7]).

The conception of arousal has played an important role in motivational theory during the last decade. Thus it is the main explanatory concept in a theory about "curiosity", which has been formulated by one of Hebb's followers, *D. E. Berlyne*, whose theory is analyzed in a later chapter of this book.

Close to the conception of "arousal" is the concept *"activation"*. A theory of activation was proposed by *Elisabeth Duffy* as early as the thirties. She later independently developed this theory and presented it in her book "Activation and Behavior" (1962), which is analyzed in a later chapter of this book.

Still another "independent" theorist must be mentioned in this historical survey: *P. T. Young*. He is a pioneer in the field of motivation because as early as the mid-thirties he wrote a book about the "Motivation of Behavior" (1936). In this book he presented a drive theory which integrated physiological and psychological observations. Later – in the forties – he developed a theory of *"hedonic or affective arousal"*, which was meant to supplement drive theories. "Affective arousal" is supposedly determined by external stimuli and to influence both learning and behavior. Thus the affective arousal concept was a forerunner of incentive motivation, already mentioned in connection with Hull.

Young's theory is so all-embracing that it could have been mentioned in connection with the other branch of psychology which has also developed theories of motivation and to which he now turn[8]).

3. Motivation in Personality Theory

3.1. *Freud's Theory*

At the time Woodworth proposed the drive concept in American psychology, it had already been introduced into the German language by *Sigmund Freud*. In a paper published in 1915 (Freud, 1915) he used the term "Trieb", which should have been translated into English as "drive". But unfortunately the word was translated as meaning "instinct", and this was just before the "instinct controversy" got started. But in more recent years psychoanalytical theorists like *D. Rapaport* (see Rapaport, 1959) have suggested using the term "drive" – or perhaps "instinctual drive" – in order to distinguish Freud's drive concept from Hull's. Therefore, in the following quotations from the English translation of Freud's 1915 paper we have substituted "drive" for "instinct":

7. A more detailed analysis of Hebb's theory is presented in Chapter 12 of my book "Theories of Motivation" (Copenhagen: Munksgaard, 1959, 4th ed., 1968).
8. A more detailed analysis of Young's theory is presented in Chapter 7 of "Theories of Motivation" (Copenhagen: Munksgaard, 1959, 4th ed., 1968).

"we may probably conclude that drive and not external stimuli are the true motive forces - - -"

"We are now in a position to discuss certain terms used in reference to the concept of a drive, for example, its impetus, its aim, its object and its source.

By the *impetus* of a drive we understand its motor element, the amount of force or the demand upon energy which it represents.

The *aim* of a drive is in every instance satsfaction, which can only be obtained by abolishing the condition of stimulation in the source of the drive.

The *object* of a drive is that in or through which it can achieve its aim. It is the most variable thing about a drive and is not originally connected with it, but becomes attached to it only in consequence of being peculiarly fitted to provide satisfaction.

By the *source* of a drive is meant that somatic process in an organ or part of the body from which there results a stimulus represented in mental life by a drive". (Freud, 1915).

Thus Freud's drive concept referred to a *vector variable* while Hull's drive was a purely dynamic variable. There was also the difference that Hull took for granted the existence of only *one* general drive plus many drive conditions or needs, while in his later years Freud postulated the existence of *two* broad drives: *Eros*, or the "life drive", and *Thanatos*, or the "death drive".

Freud's theory has had a tremendous influence on psychology – especially on the psychology of motivation and the psychology of personality, but it would take us too far afield to go more deeply into it at this point[9]).

3.2. *Lewin's Theory*

Another important psychologist who was to some extent influenced by Freud, but more by classical experimental psychology and Gestalt theory, was the German-American psychologist, *Kurt Lewin*. As early as during the First World War he carried out some experiments which resulted in a critical revision of *N. Ach*'s theory of *"determining tendencies"*. In Lewin's theory this term referred to *dynamic* variables, which in company with the directive variables, *"associations"*, determined the cognitive processes and behavior. Later Lewin developed a conception of *"need"* ("Bedürfnisse"), which included both the "real" *biological needs* (such as hunger, thirst, etc.) as well as the so-called *"quasi-needs"* (or "determining tendencies") like decision making, task acceptances, expectations, etc. Still later, after coming to America – he developed a so-called *"field theory"* of the social sciences which was presented in his main books: "Principles of Topological Psychology" (1936) and "Psychological

---

9. The reader is referred to the following books which specifically deal with Freud's theory of motivation, of which we can mention: K. M. Colby: "Energy and Structure in Psychoanalysis" (N. Y.: Ronald Press, 1965); W. Toman: "An Introduction to Psychoanalytic Theory of Motivation" (N. Y.: Pergamon Press, 1960); and D. Rapaport: "On the Psychoanalytic Theory of Motivation" (in M. R. Jones (Ed.): Nebraska Symposium on Motivation, Lincoln, Nebr. Univ. Press, 1960).

Forces" (1938). This was a Gestalt-inspired theory which explained behavior as a function of the *total* situation (the so-called "Life-space"), which included both the environment (E) and the person (P). Thus Lewin's basic formula was:

$$B = f(P,E).$$

The most important variable in Lewin's last theory was *"psychological force"*. This was a *vector variable* defined as having both strength and direction which were functions of two other variables, *"tension"* and *"valence"*. Thus we have:

$$B = f(Force) = f(tension, valence).$$

Tension was defined as a state in a system of the hypothetical person representing – or rather determined by – a need in the empirical organism. Valence was defined as the qualities of goal objects which determine behavior toward or away from the goal object. Thus the *dynamic strength* of the psychological force is determined by both tension and valence, while the direction of the force is determined by the perception of the location of the goal object in relation to the organism.

Kurt Lewin's theory has influenced later theories both in the fields of motivation and personality theory as well as in social psychology[10]).

3.3. *Murray's Theory*

One of those who was influenced by both Lewin and Freud (especially by the later) was *Henry A. Murray*. Murray and his many co-workers at Harvard's Psychological Clinic made a clinical *and* experimental study of 50 college students and presented the results in the now famous book: "Explorations in Personality" (1938).

In this work Murray presented his theory of *needs*, which he regarded as the most important personality factors. This important variable in modern "dynamic" personality theory was defined in this way (in Murray, 1938, pp. 123–24):

"A need is a construct (a convenient fiction or hypothetical concept) which stands for a force (the physico-chemical nature of which is unknown) in the brain region, a force which organizes perception, apperception, intellection, conation and action in such a way as to transform in a certain direction an existing, unsatisfying situation. A need is sometimes provoked directly by internal processes of a certain kind (viscerogenic, endocrinogenic, thalamicogenic) arising in the course of vital sequences, but, more frequently (when in a state of readiness) by the occurrence of one of a few commonly effective press (or by anticipatory images of such press). Thus, it manifests itself by leading the organism to search for or to avoid encountering or, when encountered, to attend and respond to certain kinds of press. It may even engender illusory perceptions and delusory apperceptions (projections of its imaged press into unsuitable objects). Each

---

10. The reader is referred to a more detailed analysis of Lewin's theory in Chapter 9 of my book "Theoies of Motivation" (Copenhagen: Munksgaard, 4th ed., 1968).

need is characteristically accompanied by a particular feeling or emotion and tends to use certain modes (sub-needs and actones) to further its trend. It may be weak or intense, momentary or enduring. But usually it persists and gives rise to a certain course of overt behavior (or fantasy), which (if the organism is competent and external opposition not insurmountable) changes the initiating circumstances in such a way as to bring about an end situation which stills (appeases or satisfies) the organism."

It is obvious from this definition that Murray's need concept is very different from the need of Hull and other learning theorists. Hull uses need as a *descriptive* term referring to an experimental controllable variable, a state in a "pericherical" organ outside the brain and therefore in principle observable (or at least controllable). But Murray used the term need explicitly as a *hypothetical term* which can be said to be parallel to Hull's drive, from which it, however, differs in several respects: Murray's need is defined as a *vector term*, while Hull's drive is a dynamic term. Besides, Murray's need includes both *dispositions* (enduring personality factors) and *functions* (states or processes), which are determined by the personality factors, internal stimuli, and external stimuli – the so-called "press" situation. Murray's need is thus more like Freud's drive, but there is a great difference in the number of variables postulated. While Freud only assumed the existence of *two* basic drives, Murray postulated about 40 needs, which were divided into two categories:

1. *viscerogenic needs*, which are inborn and determined primary by the states of or processes in peripherical organs (the viscera) such as hunger, thirst, pain, etc.
2. *psychogenic needs*, which are acquired and determined by external *"press" situations*, such as affiliation, achievement, dominance, etc.

Murray's theory has influenced more recent personality theories enormously. In addition, Murray created an important tool for research in human motivation and personality, the so-called *"Thematic Apperception Test"*. This test is a projective test which is used almost as much as the Rorschach Test. By his combination of clinical and experimental methods he facilitated the integration of psychoanalytic theory with other sorts of personality theories[11]).

3.4. *McClelland's and Atkinson's Theory*

Following close behind Murray is *David McClelland*, who has continued empirical research with the TAT and the development of a theory of motivation. Thus he has made a group-test-version of the TAT, which he and his co-workers have tried out in validation experiments. They "measure" the content of phan-

---

11. The reader is referred to a more detailed analysis of Murray's theory in Chapter 10 in my book "Theories of Motivation" (Copenhagen: Munksgaard, 1959, 4th ed., 1968).

tasies in the TAT-stories made by subjects in several different situations, where different motivations may be created (motivations such as hunger, sex, aggressions, fear, affiliation, power and achievement). In this work he and his co-workers have exhibited very imaginative inventiveness in combining experimental and field-observational methods. McClelland and his co-workers have also made a sort of standardization of the procedure of "content-analysis" of the TAT-stories, which has been developed to such an extent that it can be done by an electronic computer. It is also symptomatic for modern psychology that McClelland's group has concentrated its research and theoretical development mainly on one motivational variable, the so-called *"achievement-motive"* (see McClelland et al., 1953). Through this research they have demonstrated that individual differences in the strength of the achievement-motive as measured by the TAT are dependent on the environment – especially when child-rearing practices favor independence and self-reliance. In later works McClelland's group has also demonstrated the value of the TAT in measuring other motives (see McClelland, 1955 and Atkinson, 1958). McClelland himself has investigated the achievement-motive's influence on economical growth in contemporary and ancient societies (McClelland, 1961).

On the *theoretical* side, McClelland has made a significant contribution by shifting from a "need-determined" to a *"hedonistic, expectation-determined" conception of motivation* (which is influenced by – or at least parallel to – Young's and Tolman's theories). This is apparent from McClelland's first formulation of his theory (in McClelland, 1951, p. 466) where he writes:

"A motive becomes a strong affective association, characterized by an anticipatory goal reaction and based on past association of certain cues with pleasure and pain."

Thus a "motive" in McClelland's theory is an expectation of an affective change. The primary variables are called "affective changes", which are mainly *dynamic* variables. The acquired, more cognitive and *directive* variable is called "expectation". Thus motive is a combined or *vector* variable in McClelland's theory[12]).

This "cognitive trend" in motivational theory have been further developed by McClelland's closest associate, *John W. Atkinson*, who has developed a more systematic version of what he calls an "Expectation x Value" theory, which is also very much inspired by Lewin and Tolman. Atkinson's theory is analyzed in a later chapter of this book.

Achievement motivation has also been investigated outside America. One of the leading non-American psychologists in this field is *H. Heckhausen* in Germany. He has made an intensive study of achievement motivation to which

---

12. The reader is referred to a more detailed analysis of McClelland's theory in Chapter 14 in my book "Theories of Motivation" (Copenhagen: Munksgaard, 1959, 4th ed., 1968).

he has contributed an improved method of measuring motivation, and an independent theory of achievement motivation (see, e. g., Heckhausen, 1963 and Chapter 16 of this book).

3.5. *Other Personality Theorists*

In personality psychology outside the "Murray tradition" many valuable contributions to motivational research and theory have been made.

One of the most outstanding personality theorists of today is the British-American psychologist, *Raymond B. Cattell*. He has been one of the leaders in the development of the *factor-analytical method* applied to personality research. This method is a mathematically statistical technique, which consists of the construction of *"factors"* on the basis of correlations between test matter. These factors must according to our systematological taxonomy be described as *dispositional hypothetical variables with neutral surplus meaning.* They may be *dynamic* or *directive* as well as combined *vector variables*. The purely directive factors belong to the realm of *"intelligence factors"*, while the dynamic and vectorial factors belong to the realm of *"personality factors"*.

Cattell and his co-workers have developed several tests, and they have "discovered" – or rather constructed several dynamic or motivational factors. Cattell's theory is therefore analyzed in a later chapter of this book.

Another factor-analytical group is working under the leadership of the British psychologist, *H. J. Eysenck*, who, however, has been more interested in the application of this approach to clinical practice, than in the development of a theory (see Eysenck, 1964 and Chapter 16 of this book).

Quite another tradition in the psychology of personality is associated with the group of theorists characterized by the common label *"humanistic psychologists"*. One of the pioneers in this approach was *Gordon W. Allport*. With his well known book about "Personality" (1937) he transplanted to America a "personalistic philosophy" created by the German psychologist *W. Stern*. Allport advocated an *idiographic* approach to personality, i. e., a *descriptive* approach, which treats the individual person at a unique phenomenon. This approach is opposed to the *nomothetic* approach, which is the search for general laws and theories to *explain* personality. These two approaches could be renamed the *"humanistic"* and the *"naturalistic"* approaches. Allport's contribution to motivational psychology was his theory of *functional autonomy*. This theory postulates that adult people's motivation is *independent* of the primary motivation found in infants and animals. Therefore, Allport was antagonistic to both psychoanalytic as well as behavioristic theories[13]).

---

13. The reader is referred to a more detailed analysis of Allport's theory in Chapter 8 in my book "Theories of Motivation" (Copenhagen: Munksgaard, 1959, 4th ed., 1968).

90 . *Historical Introduction*

From the middle of the nineteen fifties Allport was joined by some American psychologists who were inspired by the *existentialistic philosophy* as it is presented by such European philosophers and psychiatrists as *Ludwig Binswanger, Karl Jaspers* and *Victor Frankel*. One of the leaders of these *humanistic psychologists* is the American psychologist, *Abraham H. Maslow,* who was especially interested in the development of a theory of motivation. His theory is analyzed in a later chapter in this book. Another leader is Charlotte Bühler. Her theory is analyzed in Chapter 16 of this book.

3.6. *Concluding Remarks*

We have now finished our brief survey of the history of motivational psychology. As a sort of summary the reader may wish to consult Fig. 3.1., which is a diagram representing the main trends in motivational psychology.

Historical Introduction . 91

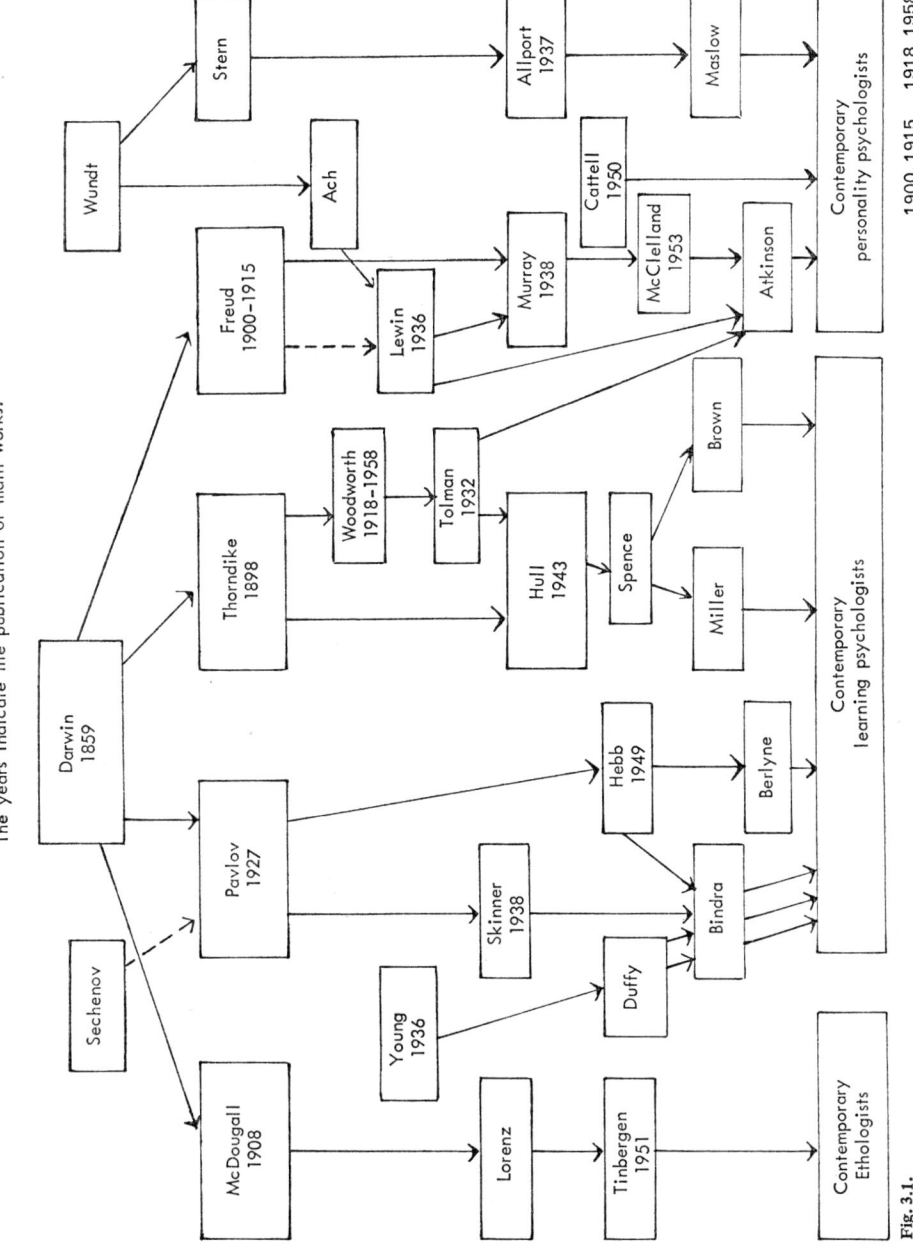

Fig. 3.1.

PART II

ANALYTIC STUDIES

In this part of the book we present the results of our analytic studies of the single theories. We have studied 12 theories and devote a chapter to each. In addition, there is a chapter containing brief studies of some other theories.

The order of presentation of the theories follows the historical overview in Chapter 3:

First, the theories belonging to the *"Pavlov-Hebb-tradition"*: Duffy, Bindra, Berlyne, Konorski and Pribram.

Next, the theories belonging to the *"Thorndike-Hull tradition"*: Miller, Brown and Woodworth.

Finally, the theories belonging to the *"Freud-Lewin-Murray tradition"*: Festinger, Cattell, Atkinson and Maslow.

4: Duffy's Theory

Introduction

The American psychologist *Elisabeth Duffy* as early as in the 1930's[1]) laid the foundation for a theory which she has elaborated in her book, *"Activation and Behavior"* (1962). In this book she formulates an "activation theory" of motivation and emotion, which is in accordance with one of the main trends in modern motivational psychology. If we look at this theory in historical perspective, we cannot escape the conclusion that Elisabeth Duffy was the first to see the fruitfulness in the concept of "activation" or "arousal". Duffy's theory therefore deserves to be analyzed in this book.

The metastratum

1.1. *Philosophical propositions*

We have not found any explicit formulations of philosophical propositions in Duffy's book. But this is not unusual, as the reader will clearly see from the following chapters in this book. We must therefore reconstruct the propositions from inferences based on the context, and have concluded from this that Duffy presupposes a *neutral monistic* thesis about the psychosomatic problem. We are also of the opinion that she presupposes the biological Darwinian philosophy of Man, which is a common disposition among American psychologists.

1.2. *Metatheoretical propositions*

Duffy writes about the necessity of *theory construction* in science (p. 13):

"For my own part, I should like to see poor concepts replaced by better ones, with the conviction that as our knowledge increases these better concepts will in turn be modified or replaced as new information may indicate. We must not shrink from theoretical ventures, for if we do so, we shall be handicapped in the assimiliation and interpretation of empirical data."

We shall later see what sort of theory Duffy has constructed.

---

1. Especially in a series of articles in *Psychological Review*.

1.3. *Methodological propositions*

She does not explicitly formulate any methodological principles about the basic "protocol language" of psychology. The most explicit is the following (p.IX):

"A basic purpose of the present volume (strayed from many times because of the necessity of using the language employed by others in describing their experiments) is to present psychological phenomena in terms which will harmonize with those of the other sciences, and to show the relationship of psychology to the foundation sciences upon which it rests."

It is rather clear from this quotation, and it is obvious while reading through the book, that Duffy prefers a *behavioral* protocol language rather than a phenomenological one.

The present author has not found other methodological principles explicitly formulated, but the book is replete with descriptions of *experiments* where *physiological* measuring techniques are employed.

The hypothetical stratum

2.0. *Summary of the hypotheses*

Before going to an analysis of the *content* of Duffy's explanatory system, we shall present a very short summary of the system. It can best be accomplished by quoting from her own summary in "General Conclusions" (p. 112):

"1. All behavior is describable in terms of (a) its direction (approach or withdrawal) and (b) its intensity (internal arousal), though subheads of these basic categories are no doubt needed."

"2. These descriptive categories referring to functional and measurable behavior, might advantageously be substituted for the traditional descriptive categories of psychology, many of which cannot be defined operationally."

"3. When the intensity of behavior or the degree of activation of the organism is the subject of investigation, it is observed that a large number of measures of autonomic functioning, of skeletal-muscle functioning, and of cortical functioning vary with considerable consistency *in one direction with increased stimulation* of the organism and *in the opposite direction with decreased stimulation* of the organism."

"4. These changes are not specific to sleep or to "emotion" or to any other particular condition. On the contrary, they may be found, not only during sleep on the one hand, and intense excitement on the other hand, but also during such intermediate conditions as waking relaxation, work on easy tasks, or work on more difficult tasks. They apparently vary in a continuum."

It is apparent from this extensive quotation of four of Duffy's 13 "conclusions", that she is suggesting a completely new system of psychological variables. In accordance with this suggestion all variables should be divided into two main categories:

1. *intensity* (or activation) variables, and
2. *direction* variables.

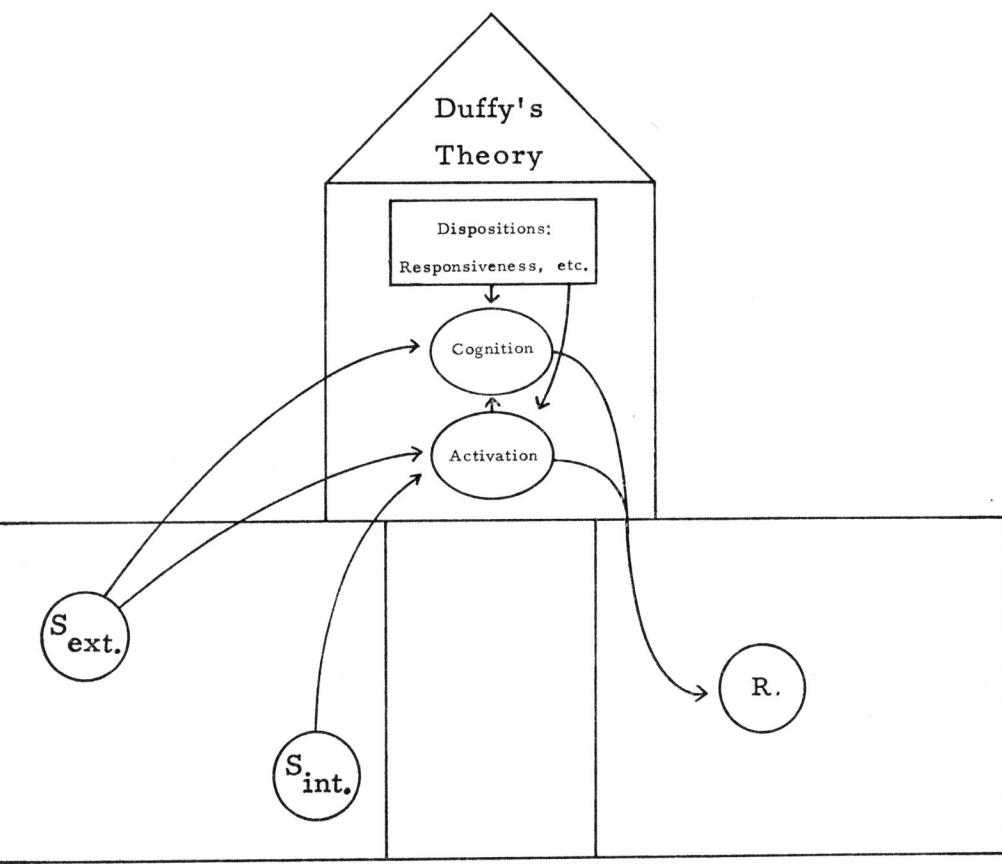

Fig. 4.1. Diagram illustrating the main variables and their functional relationships in Elisabeth Duffy's theory.

The old psychological concepts often confuse these two descriptive and conceptual dimensions. This is also the case with "motivation" and "emotion". Duffy writes about these concepts (p. 11):

"The concept of "motivation" incorporates a description of both the direction taken by behavior (selectivity of response) and the intensity or "drive level" of behavior. . . . The concept of "emotion" affords a particularly striking example of the failure to differentiate clearly between the degree of activation and the direction of behavior. Both aspects of response are included in a single concept."

Duffy argues very convincingly for separating these two conceptual dimensions. She does not redefine all the old concepts ("motivation", "emotion", "perception", "thinking" and "learning"), she simply drops them and starts afresh. For practical reasons she confines her book to the activation variables.

The present author regards Duffy as a pioneer in dealing with this problem. The rest of motivational psychology has moved in the suggested direction, which can be seen from the fact that many newer definitions of motivation stress "activation" as the main aspect[2]).

We have made a diagram summarizing the main features of Duffy's theory (see Fig. 4.1.).

2.1. *The hypothetical terms (H-terms)*

First, we shall look at one of Duffy's formal definitions (p. 17):

> "The level of activation of the organism may be defined, then, as the extent of *release of potential energy, stored in the tissues of the organism,* as this is shown in activity or response." (Italics mine).

From this formal definition it should be rather easy to classify "activation" as a *neuro-physiological* variable. But sometimes one is in doubt, because Duffy uses the term "activation" as if it were only a very general *descriptive* or empirical term, not an *explanatory* term at all. Thus she writes (on p. 5):

> ". . . activation, like any psychological concept, represents an abstraction from the total behavior of the organism."

In this quotation "activation" resembles a very general behavior variable, not an intervening hypothetical variable. That is also the case when Duffy discusses measuring activation level. She occasionally gives the reader the impression that "activation" is only a measurable aspect of behavior. Thus she writes (p. 20):

> "The choice of definition depends perhaps upon whether one feels there is more security in speaking in neural terms or more in being *strictly operational. Preference is given to the latter type of definition in this book,* that is, to a definition of activation closer to actual measurements with full recognition accorded the fact that all activity of the organism has a neurohumoral basis, and that further investigation will no doubt make clearer the relationship between peripheral and central events." (Italics mine).

But Duffy continues:

> "As the term "activation" is employed in the present discussion, it refers, as mentioned, to *organismic arousal,* not merely to the activation pattern of the EEG." (Italics mine).

Thus we think that it is correct to classify "activation" as an H-term.

2.1.1. *The surplus meaning of the H-terms.* As we have decided that "activation" is an H-term – not a highly abstract descriptive term – we can rather easily classify it as an H_0-term, a hypothetical term with neurophysiological surplus meaning.

2. The reader should compare Duffy's theory with E. G. Berlyne's. (Cf. Chapter 6).

2.1.2. *Dispositional or functional terms?* It is easiest to describe Duffy's "activation" variable in accordance with our second classification as a *functional* variable. But she also deals with the corresponding *disposition* variable, which causes individual differences in activation or "responsiveness" (as it is called in this connection). She devotes more than a third of her book to the problems of individual differences. She summarized several studies about individual differences in this way (p. 276):

"The studies reviewed in the present chapter give support to the conclusion that differences between individuals in activation are basically differences in responsiveness or exitability."

Thus "responsiveness" is the dispositional variable corresponding to the functional variable "activation".

About the causes of the responsiveness Duffy writes (p. 227):

"A considerable degree of consistency in the extent of activation appears, however, to be provided by such constitutional factors as type of nervous system and endocrine system, and by established habits of meeting a situation in one way or in another. Genetic and environmental factors are thus seen to interact in producing the differences in the degree of activation."

From this it is seen that the *dispositional* variable "responsiveness" is also of the neurophysiological type.

2.1.3. *Dynamic, directive or vectorial terms?* It is very easy to place the terms "activation" and "responsiveness" in the third classification, because Elisabeth Duffy herself contributed to establishing this classification by her clear distinction between "direction" and "intensity". Thus "intensity" is the descriptive label denoting the effect of *dynamic variables*, to which "activation" and "responsiveness" clearly belong, while "direction" is the descriptive label denoting the effect of directive variables, which she does not deal with in her book.

2.2. *Classifications of the hypotheses*

We shall present a summary of the main hypotheses in combination with the basic classification (2.2.1.) into S-H, H-H, and H-R-hypotheses.

First, we shall look at the *S-H-hypotheses*. They are summarized by Duffy in her "General Conclusions" (p. 112):

"5. Changes in the level of activation may be produced by any type of stimulus, physical and symbolic. They may be brought about by drugs, by hormones, by the chemical products of fatigue, by simple sensory stimuli, or by complex situational stimuli, present, past or anticipated."

There are really many S-H-hypotheses concentrated in the above quotation. The reader, who is interested in the individual hypotheses and their experimental bases is referred to Duffy's book.

Her theory also contains several *H-H-hypotheses*. They are dealt with in part II of her book under the title: "The effects of variations in activation". The first chapter in this part (Chapter 7) deals with "sensory sensitivity and the level of activation". In the beginning of this chapter she formulates the general H-H-hypotheses (p. 119):

"Evidence from many sources suggests the possibility that, at least up to a certain point, *sensory sensitivity is increased (i.e., faint stimuli are more easily perceived) when the level of activation is higher.*"

Later Duffy specifies the relationship in this way (p. 138):

"It seems probable that the relationship is curvilinear – i.e., that sensory sensitivity is somewhat less when there is either a very low or a very high level of activation, and that an intermediate degree of activation is most facilitative to sensory functioning."

As far as the present author can see, there are no other H-H-hypotheses in Duffy's theory.

But there is a very extensive Chapter 8 devoted to "activation and performance". The contents of this chapter can be summarized in an *H-R-hypothesis*, which in Duffy's own words reads (p. 194):

"The degree of activation of the individual appears to affect the speed, intensity, and co-ordination of responses, and thus to affect the quality of performance. In general the optimal degree of activation appears to be a moderate degree, with the curve expressing the relationship between activation and performance taking the form of an inverted U."

We thus see the inverted U both in the relation between activation and sensitivity and between activation and performance.

2.2.1. *The basic classification of the hypotheses.* After this brief presentation of Duffy's hypotheses we shall make our basic classification of them into S-H, H-H, and H-R-hypotheses. Before we do that let us *reformulate* the hypotheses into partially symbolic formulas, which facilitates the classification as well as the later calculation of the H.Q. Our reformulations consist of abbreviating the main terms in the purely verbal formulations quoted above. To these abbreviations of main terms we add the letters "S", "H", and "R" in order to indicate which of the terms, we regard as S-,H- or R-terms.

Applying this general procedure to Duffy's hypotheses results in the following *systematic reconstruction* of hypotheses:

1. hypothesis: S(simple stimuli) → H(activation)
2. hypothesis: S(complex stimuli → H(activation)
3. hypothesis: S(symbolic stimuli) → H(activation)
4. hypothesis: S(drugs) → H(activation)
5. hypothesis: S(hormones) → H(activation)
6. hypothesis: S(humorals) → H(activation)

7. hypothesis: H(optimal activation) → H(optimal percpetual sensitivity)
8. hypothesis: H(optimal activation) → R(optimal performance)

Having made this partially symbolic reformulation of the hypotheses, we conclude this section with the final classification:

1. *Purely theoretical hypotheses (H-H):*
   One hypothesis (No. 7 in our reconstruction).
2. *Partly empirical hypotheses:*
   a. S-H-hypotheses: 6 hypotheses (No. 1 to No. 6 in our reconstruction).
   b. H-R-hypotheses: One hypothesis (No. 8 in our reconstruction).

2.2.2. *The complexity of the hypotheses.* It remains to describe the hypothesis according to the *degree of complexity*. It is not easy because the explicitly formulated hypotheses are very condensed summaries (as the reader may have realized from the quotations). In this condensed form they appear as rather simple "mechanistic hypotheses". But on reading the book one gets the impression of a more complicated "dynamic" or "field-theoretical" theory. Thus there is a whole chapter (chapter 5) dealing with "the patterning of activation". The contents are summarized in "General Conclusions" (p. 113):

> "8. *There is a patterning of activation.* The organism is not activated as an undifferentiated whole. Nevertheless, it is the organism, not relatively autonomous part-systems, which is activated. This is shown by the fact that measures of activation in one part of the organism are usually, but not always, related in the expected direction to measures of activation in other parts of the organism."

We are perhaps most correct if we classify the hypotheses in Duffy's theory as being *rather dynamic*.

2.2.3. *The functional relationships in the hypotheses.* Concerning the last problem: "kind of determinism", Duffy is not explicit. But it seems most correct to describe the hypotheses in her theory as *"causal deterministic"*.

The descriptive stratum

3.1. *The abstract D-level*

In connection with the analysis of the variable "activation", we mentioned that Duffy sometimes uses the term as though it were a descriptive and not an explanatory term. However, as it is mainly used as an explanatory term, we decided to classify it as an explanatory, neurophysiological variable. But she sometimes uses the word "intensity" about behavior[3]). This word is the descriptive term corresponding to the explanatory term "activation". Duffy's theory would be a little more consistent, if she always had made this distinction. We therefore

---

3. The reader is referred to the above quotation of the first of Duffy's "conclusions".

suggest that "activation" should always be used as an explanatory term (referring to a neurophysiological H-variable), while "intensity" should always be used as a descriptive term. "Intensity" is a very general empirical ("high-level") term, which summarizes several measurable aspects of behavior.

Before we set out to analyze these measurable aspects, we should point to the fact that Duffy has not formulated any "higher-level", empirical generalizations (S-R-sentences). All relations between S-variables and R-variables are formulated (at least explicitly) with "activation" as the intervening variable.

3.2. The concrete D-level

If we move to the more "basic level" of the descriptive stratum, we find the previously noted measurable aspects of behavior. Perhaps it is not correct to use the term "behavior" in this connection, as some of the measurements deal with inner organical processes.

The most used measures of activation (according to Duffy) are:

1. EMG: the electromyogram (and other measures of the tension of skeletal muscles).
2. GSR: the galvanic skin response (or the electrical resistance of the skin).
3. EEG: the electroencephalogram (the recording of the electrical potentials of the brain).

Besides these three electro-physiological measures of the level and change of activation, Duffy also mentions investigations using measures of respiration, blood pressure, pulse, body temperature, skin temperature and the volume of various parts of the body.

She summarizes the knowledge about the interrelations between all these measures in one of her "general conclusions" (p. 113):

"*9. The level of activation is measurable.* Measures of individual physiological processes which participate in the activation of the organism bear significant relationships to stimulus situations and, in general, to each other. Some type of summation of these measures should provide a more adequate indicator of the general level of activation than any individual measure. Such a composite measure would no doubt show closer relationships to stimulus situations and to measurable aspects of response. However, investigations based upon a single indicator of activation are in no sense meaningless. The consistent relationships which some of them have shown, both to stimulus situations and to other aspects of response, proclaim their relative adequacy as indicators of the average degree of activation of groups, if not as reliable measures of individual responses."

3.3. The descriptive units

The above quotation about measuring indicates what a reading of the whole book clearly shows: the level of description used in the basic protocol statements of Duffy's theory is rather *molecular*.

The theory as a whole

4.1. *The formal properties*

4.1.1. The systematic organization of Duffy's theory is on the level of an *explanatory system*. There are many explicit formulations of hypotheses in the "conclusions" to every chapter. But no attempt is made to construct a deductive system, although this would have been an easy matter.

4.1.2. The preciseness of representation in Duffy's theory is that of a *purely verbal theory*.

4.1.3. No use is made of any kind of models, except perhaps for a few verbal analogies.

4.2. *The epistemological properties*

We have in an earlier section (2.1.) discussed the main variable in Duffy's theory – "activation"–, and we came to the conclusion that it was not an abstract, descriptive term, but an H-term. Therefore, the theory as a whole must be classified as an *explanatory theory*. As "activation" is classified as an H_0-term, we must classify the theory as a whole as a *physiological* explanatory theory, an S-O-R-theory.

4.3. *The theory-empiry ratio*

The general impression one receives from reading Duffy's book is that her theory should undoubtedly be classified as an *empiristic* theory. On the basis of our reconstruction of the hypotheses we can calculate the Hypotheses Quotient by means of the formula:

$$H.Q. = \frac{\Sigma(H-H)}{\Sigma[(S-H)+(H-R)]} \frac{1}{6+1} = \frac{1}{7} = 0.14$$

This is a rather low H.Q. which confirms our general impression of Duffy's theory as being very empiristic.

Concluding remarks

We wish once again to emphasize, that Elisabeth Duffy's theory has been a pioneer work on two counts: It is one of the first physiological approaches to motivation, and it is the first theory introducing a clear distinction between activation and direction of behavior.

5: Bindra's Theory

Introduction

In 1959 a book was published entitled "Motivation – A Systematic Reinterpretation", by *Dalbir Bindra*, who was at that time Associate Professor of Psychology at McGill University in Montreal. This fact is mentioned because *Hebb* at the same time was (and still is) Professor of Psychology at the same university, and Bindra confesses himself that:

"The general point of view adopted in the writing of this book lies somewhere between the positions of Skinner and Hebb" (p. 289).

The present author thinks that it is a fruitful approach to try to make a synthesis between the two most outstanding contemporary learning theorists, and therefore has decided to analyze Bindra's theory.

The metastratum

1.1. *Philosophical propositions*

Bindra makes no explicit formulations of philosophical propositions. But from the context it is not incorrect to infer that Bindra presupposes a *neutral monistic* thesis about the psychosomatic problem. In addition, he presupposes a biological, Darwinian philosophy of Man.

1.2. *Metatheoretical propositions*

The most explicit metaprinciple is concerned with theory construction (p. 22):

"Now, in the present context, the refinement and elaboration of concepts means nothing more than ascribing precise properties to the hypothetical neural constructs and then changing these properties so that deductions from them would better correspond to the observed behavioral relations. Such refinement and elaboration must be based either on advances in neurophysiology . . . or on the observed new functional relations between behavior and various internal and external conditions (independent variables). Clearly, then, the approaches of Skinner and Hebb overlap with each other at a crucial point."

In the above quotation Bindra states how he has tried to combine Skinner's non-theoretical approach with Hebb's neurophysiological approach.

He also presents a very sharp analysis of the two sorts of "mediation" variables: the *"transformation concepts"* which are pure intervening variables without surplus meaning, and the *"hypothetical* constructs" with surplus or excess meaning, which is perhaps intuitively defined. Bindra concludes his analysis with these words (pp. 288–289):

"In between the two extremes of transformation variables and intuitively derived hypothetical constructs lie most of the mediation variables employed in psychology. ... Thus, in deciding upon an approach to the study of behavior, the question is not whether mediation concepts should have any excess meaning at all, but rather how much excess meaning a hypothetical construct can have and still be useful."

We have quoted these formulations so extensively because they contain more insight than any formulations we have found about the problem: intervening variables contra hypothetical constructs.

1.3. *Methodological propositions*

In accordance with this program Bindra's theory must be said to build firmly on a *behavioristic* protocol language. The theory also is based solely on "some sort of *experimental analysis* of the phenomena" (p. 20)[1]) as the only accepted methodological principle.

The hypothetical stratum

2.0. *Summary of the hypotheses*

Before we turn to the analyses of the *contents* of the explanatory system, let us make a very short *summary* of the theory:

The book deals with "motivational phenomena" or "motivational activities", which include the behavioral aspects of hunger, sex, exploration, play, fear, anger and the like. Bindra argues that it is not possible to make a distinction between "emotional behavior" and "motivated behavior", and he further declares that many of his descriptive and explanatory concepts could be used in dealing with perceptual and learning phenomena as well.

Bindra describes "motivated behavior" as *"goal-directed activities"* and offers a very thorough analysis of this concept (which we shall deal with later).

The problem of the *development* of motivated or goal-directed behavior is explained mainly by *reinforcement* (although constitutional determinants are not ruled out).

Among the factors that affect the *occurrence* of motivated activities Bindra stresses "habit strength", "sensory cues", "arousal level" and the state of the "blood chemistry", which together are assumed to determine completely the occurrence of motivated activity.

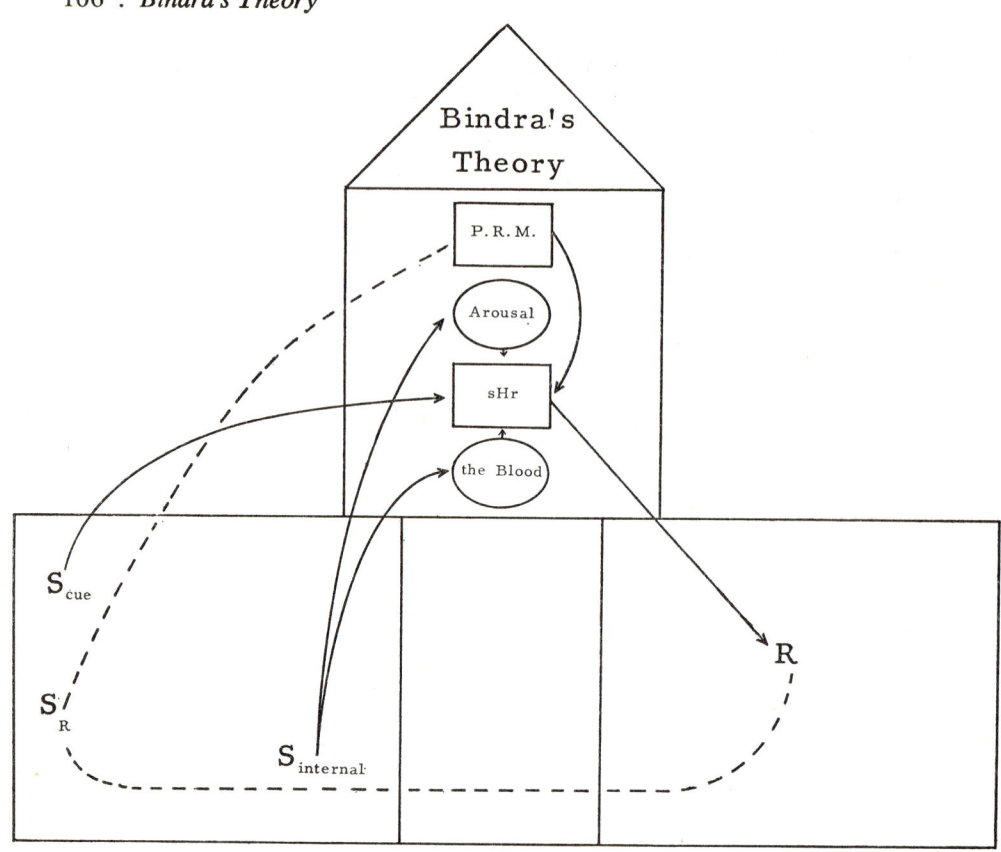

Fig. 5.1. Diagram illustrating Bindra's theory. Behavior (R) is directly determined by "Habit strength" (sHr), which is influenced by "Arousal" in the Reticular Arousal System, and by "Blood", i.e., the chemistry of the blood, which influences the brain. These H-variables are influenced by two S-variables: "cues" and "internal stimuli". The behavior results in a reinforcing event (S_R), which in turn influences the "Positive Reinforcing Mechanism" (P.R.M.) in the brain. This in turn influences sHr, which is increased in strength.

We can illustrate our summary by means of a diagram representing the main variables and hypotheses in Bindra's theory (Fig. 5.1.)

2.1. *The hypothetical terms (H-terms)*

Among the concepts mentioned in the above summary we can classify *"habit strength", "arousal level"* and *"blood chemistry"* as *explanatory terms* or H-terms, while we can classify *"sensory cues"* and *"reinforcers"* as *descriptive terms* or empirical variables. Besides these concepts Bindra has formulated a "hypothetical mechanism" called "the positive reinforcing mechanism or P.R.M." (p. 139).

2.1.1. *The surplus meaning of the H-terms.* As this P.R.M. is introduced after a very thorough analysis of different hypotheses about reinforcement, especially Old's and Milner's explanation of intra-cranial stimulation, it is obvious that the P.R.M. must be described as an H-term with *neurophysiological* surplus meaning (an H_0-term).

"Blood chemistry", of course, also refers to a *neuro*physiological H-variable.

"Arousal level" is more difficult to classify. Bindra sometimes uses the term "arousal level", like Duffy does "activation", so that it is on the border-line between H-terms and general, empirical terms of the very abstract sort. On the other hand he connects it with the reticular activating system (p. 255):

"Thus, it appears that the activation of the cortex, which is related to the behavioral changes we have subsumed under "arousal" is determined by the activity of the reticular activating system."

So it would seem to be justifiable to describe Bindra's "arousal level" as a *neurophysiological* H-term.

Bindra devotes an entire chapter to the discussion of the term "habit strength", which he has adopted from Hull. He writes about this concept (p. 148):

"Thus the concept of habit strength, like that of goal direction, can be considered as a global concept referring to any one or more of a number of different measures. The use of the common label "habit strength" is justified on the ground that the different measures can all describe one and the same response, and on the presumption that they may be determined by overlapping neural mechanisms."

This quotation shows, that "habit strength", like "arousal level" is a term which lies at the border-line between general, descriptive terms and H-terms of the neurophysiological sort.

"This "border-line" feature of Bindra's theory is consistent with his metatheoretical principles: In trying to combine the approaches of Skinner and Hebb he has to use "mediating" variables, which are mostly highly abstract, general, empirical variables with only very little *neurophysiological* "surplus meaning".

2.1.2. *Dispositional or functional terms?* In accordance with our second classification we must describe "arousal level" and "blood chemistry" as *function* variables, while "habit strength" is more of a *disposition* variable, whose function is determined by the other two H-variables and the independent S-variables.

2.1.3. *Dynamic, directive or vector terms?* In our third classification we must place "arousal level" as a *dynamic* term as it refers to a variable which has a purely activating effect on behavior. "Habit strength" is a *directing* term as it refers to a variable having a purely "steering" effect on behavior. "Blood chemistry" and the "Positive Reinforcing Mechanism" are more difficult to classify. They refer to variables having a mainly activating effect. But it is not a *general* activating effect on behavior, rather a *specific* or selective one. Thus these variables indirectly have a guiding or directive effect also. Therefore, in our classification we place "blood chemistry" and P.R.M. as *vector* terms.

2.2. Classifications of the hypotheses

Turning to the hypotheses of Bindra's theory we shall first consider the:

2.2.1. *Basic classification of hypotheses*. This is the classification into S-H, H-H, and H-R-hypotheses. First, we shall look at the *S-H-hypotheses:* "Habit strength" as an H-variable is, in accordance with Bindra's theory (elaborated in Chapter 16), determined by two S-variables, "sensory cues" and "reinforcements".

The H-variable "arousal level", is in Bindra's theory (in accordance with Chapter 8) determined by environmental changes, reduction in sensory variation, task performance, noxious stimulation and the administration of certain drugs.

"Changes in blood chemistry result from the normal metabolic and anabolic processes that characterize all living organisms. These processes lead to variations in the level of oxygen, carbon dioxide, water, sugar, various salts, hormones, and other humoral factors" (p. 258 – introduction to Chapter 9: "The Role of Blood Chemistry")".

These were summaries of the most important S-H-hypotheses in Bindra's theory.

The most important *H-H-hypotheses* are summarized by Bindra in "Some tentative conclusions" (pp. 291–294):

"The habit strength of a response is related to the effects that alterations in arousal level will have on it. In general the greater the habit strength the wider the range of arousal level within which the response will occur in its usual form." (p. 293).
"Again the exact effect on a response of a humoral change is related to the habit strength of a response. The greater the habit strength the more likely is the response to withstand variations in blood chemistry" (pp. 293–294).

As the above quotations show "habit strength" is the central H-variable in Bindra's theory. The other two H-variables ("arousal level" and "blood chemistry") as well as the S-variables "sensory cues" and "reinforcements" determine behavior via "habit strength".

Among the H-H-hypotheses we must also classify Bindra's neurophysiological interpretations. Besides the *"Positive Reinforcing Mechanisms"*, which he postulates mainly on the basis of Olds' and Milner's experiments with intra-cranial stimulation, he also mentions the *"Reticular Activating System"* as the basis for the "arousal level". And in connection with the "blood chemistry" factor, he formulates the following hypotheses (p. 294):

"Two main classes of mechanisms can account for the effects on behavior of variations in arousal level and blood chemistry. The behavioral effects may be brought about by the sensory feedback (to the brain) from changes in peripheral organs associated with variations in arousal and blood chemistry. Alternatively, or in addition to the feedback mechanism the behavioral effects may result from some direct action of the arousal and humoral changes on certain special areas or centers in the brain."

Among the *H-R-hypotheses* in Bindra's theory we have selected[2]) the following as the most important (p. 246):

"Generalization 1. There is an optimum range of level of arousal within which a given measure of performance will reach its highest (or lowest) value; the greater the deviation in either direction from the optimum arousal level, the greater will be the decrease (or increase) in the performance measure."

This is the well known inverted U-shaped relation between level of arousal and performance, which was originally suggested by Freeman and is also included in Duffy's theory.

The above presentation of Bindra's hypotheses can now be supplemented by our partially symbolic reformulations. We abbreviate "habit strength" with "H_S", "positive reinforcing mechanism" with "H.P.R.M.", "arousal level" with "H_{AL}" and "blood chemistry" with "H_{BC}". Thus we get:

1. hypothesis: $S(cue) \rightarrow H_{AL}$
2. hypothesis: $S(reinforcer) \rightarrow H_{PRM}$
3. hypothesis: $S(external\ stimuli) \rightarrow H_{AL}$
4. hypothesis: $S(task) \rightarrow H_{AL}$
5. hypothesis: $S(noxious\ stimuli) \rightarrow H_{AL}$
6. hypothesis: $S(cue) \rightarrow H_{AL}$
7. hypothesis: $S(metabolic\ processes) \rightarrow H_{BC}$
8. hypothesis: $S(anabolic\ processes) \rightarrow H_{BC}$
9. hypothesis: $H_{AL} \longleftrightarrow H_S$
10. hypothesis: $H_{BC} \longleftrightarrow H_S$
11. hypothesis: $H_{PRM} \rightarrow H_S$
12. hypothesis: $H_S \rightarrow R(learned\ behavior)$
13. hypothesis: $H_{AL}(optimal) \rightarrow R(optimal\ performance)$.

On the basis of this systematic reconstruction we can conclude this section with the basic classification of the hypotheses:

1. *Purely theoretical hypotheses (H-H):*
   Hypotheses No. 9, 10 and 11. In all: 3 hypotheses.
2. *Partly empirical hypotheses:*
   a. S-H hypotheses: No. 1, 2, 3, 4, 5, 6, 7 and 8. In all: 8 hypotheses.
   b. H-R hypotheses. No. 12 and 13. In all 2 hypotheses.

2.2.2. *The complexity of the hypotheses.* The reader has probably observed that there are some interrelated H-variables in Bindra's theory. Therefore it cannot be a "mechanistic" theory. On the other hand we do not find so complicated inter-relationships as in some "field" theories, so it should be correct to classify Bindra's hypotheses as *"dynamic"*.

2.2.3. *The functional relationships in the hypotheses.* Bindra is not explicit about the problem of determinism. But he often uses the term "probability" in connection with variables which determine behavior. So it would seem to be correct to describe his hypotheses, like Skinner's, as *"probability-deterministic"*.

The descriptive stratum

3.1. *The abstract D-level*

We shall start the analysis with the *abstractive descriptive terms.* (3.1.1.), first the *dependent R-variable*. Bindra writes in the introductory chapter (p. 17):

"'It is this purposive' or 'moving-in-the-direction-of-goals' aspect of behavior that is the dominant feature of the phenomena that are termed motivational, . . .".

Bindra thus continues Tolman's work with a definition of motivated behavior as "purposive" or *"goal-directed"*, as he prefers to designate it. The present author thinks that Bindra's analysis of "goal direction" is the most thorough and satisfying to be found. The first reason for this evaluation is that Bindra has stressed the descriptive and operational features of the concept (p. 54):

"A *goa*l is thus *an incentive that is chosen by the investigator as a reference point for describing observed behavior.*
The choice of the reference point – called goal – is completely arbitrary and has reference only to the investigator's mode of analysis, not the animal's intention or any other subjective state."

The second reason for our high evaluation of Bindra's analysis is his conclusion that:

"Goal direction is thus a *multidimensional* concept. Appropriateness, persistence and searching as defined above can be looked upon as some of the dimensions that are involved in judging behavior as *more or less* goal-directed" (p. 59).

From the above quotations it is clear that *"goal direction"* in Bindra's theory is a *multidimensional, quantitatively descriptive concept,* which presupposes "goal" as a convenient "reference point".

Turning to the *independent S-variables*, we find that the most important one is *"reinforcer"*, which has a connection with "goal". As the reader will remember *"goal"* is defined as an *incentive* which is chosen as a reference point. And "incentive" is defined thusly (p. 117):

"*Incentive:* An event that is presumed to be a reinforcer for a given response, but which has not yet been shown to be a reinforcer of the response."

Thus, incentive is a *possible* reinforcer, and "a reinforcer" is defined (p. 116):

"*Reinforcer:* An event the occurrence of which changes the overall habit strength of a given response."
"*Reinforcement:* The procedure of presenting a reinforcer in close temporal contiguity with a given response" (p. 117).

There are thus the following relationships between "goal" and "reinforcer": A "goal" is a selected incentive, and an "incentive" is a possible reinforcer, or:

"incentive" ⊃ "reinforcer" ⊃ "goal".

3.1.2. *The general, descriptive propositions* ("laws"). In this connection it is important to point out that Bindra follows Skinner's *empirical* approach concerning the problem of reinforcement[4]), and therefore there is no circularity in the relationship between the S-variable "reinforcer" and the R-variable "goal direction".

Therefore, Bindra can formulate two *empirical generalizations* (S-R-sentences or "laws"), which he summarized (p. 72):

"Thus, in essence, the two generalizations state that *continued or repeated exposure to and reinforcement by a given goal must produce goal-directed activity and, conversely, goal-directed activity cannot develop without the operation of these two factors.*"

Besides the *"reinforcer"* variable Bindra's theory contains another empirical S-variable, *"sensory cue"*, to which a whole chapter is also devoted. This S-variable is defined (p. 178):

"a *sensory cue* may be looked upon as any characteristic of a stimulus to which an organism can learn to make a differential response."

Bindra also formulated some empirical generalizations (S-R-sentences) about "sensory cues". The most important is summarized (p. 293):

"If sensory cues are varied within their effective range for a given response, the response usually shows minor variation in some of its characteristics (e.g., amplitude, latency)."

3.2. *The concrete D-level*

Moving from the *"high level"*, empirical generalizations and abstract terms to the *"basic level"* of protocol statements and basic terms, we find a number of experimental, behavioral and physiological measures. Thus Bindra, in the chapter about "Arousal and Behavior", refers to the same measuring methods and experimental results as we found in Duffy's theory of activation:

1. GSR (galvanic skin response)
2. EKG (electrocardiogram)
3. BMR (basal metabolic rate)
4. EMG (electromyogram)
5. EEG (electroencephalogram) and others

Bindra also refers to many of the same investigations of individual differences in arousal as Duffy does. But, of course, Bindra's chapter about arousal cannot contain as extensive research results as are found in Duffy's whole book about activation.

3.3. *The descriptive units*

In the classification of theories in accordance with the descriptive units employed we must describe Bindra's theory as being rather *molecular*.

The theory as a whole

4.1. *The formal properties*

We shall first describe and classify the formal properties of the theory.

4.1.1. *The systematic organization* of Bindra's theory can be described as being on the borderline between "explanatory sketches" and "explanatory systems". There are some explicit formulations of hypotheses called "tentative conclusions" and "generalizations". If they all had been formulated in a systematic fashion (e. g., with numbers or letters indicating the logical order), then we should undoubtedly have classified his theory as an explanatory system.

4.1.2. *The preciseness of representation* in Bindra's theory is on the level of a *verbal* theory. Neither symbols nor mathematical formulas are employed.

4.1.3. *The properties of the models* employed in Bindra's theory are expressed in two-dimensional diagrams. His diagram of the Reticular Activating System (Fig. 24, p. 255) is typical for Bindra's book.

4. 2. *The epistemological propositions*

As the reader will remember Bindra's program was to *combine* Skinner's and Hebb's approaches to psychology. Bindra's theory should, in accordance with this, as a whole resemble both Skinner's descriptive S-R-theory and Hebb's S-O-R-theory. And this is certainly the case. His theory is an *explanatory, neurophysiological S-O-R-theory*. But it has a smaller content of H-variables than Hebb's theory, and, although they are of the neurophysiological type, they are on the borderline between H-variables and the very abstract and general descriptive concepts.

4.3. *The theory-empiry ratio*

The general impression a reader receives when reading Bindra's book is that the theory is rather *empirical*. On the basis of the classification of hypotheses

Nebraska Symposium on Motivation, 1969

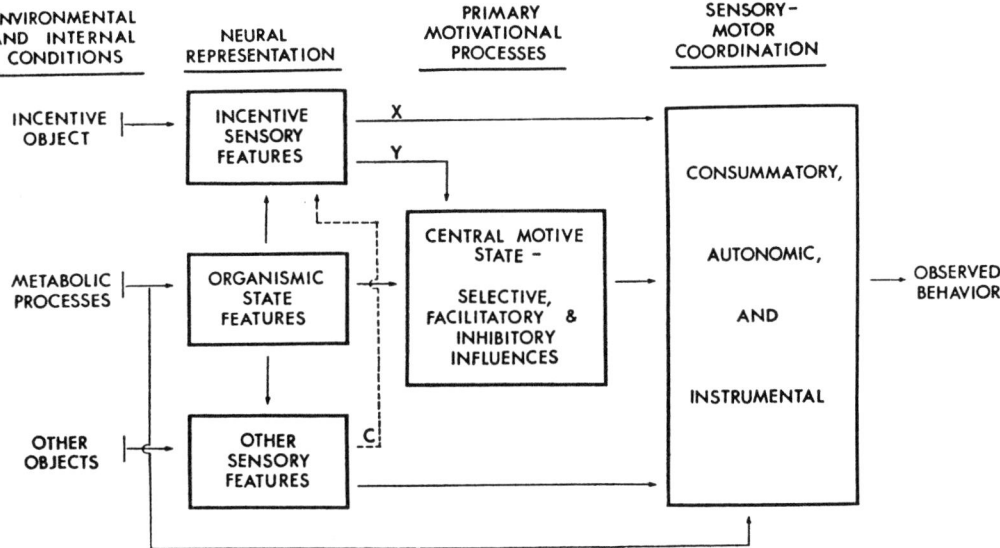

Fig. 5.2. A. Hypothetical Model of Motivation. Showing 1) how the central motive state is generated by an interaction of neural representations of organismic-state features and incentive-stimulation features (Route Y), and 2) how the environmental (incentive and nonincentive) stimuli, together with the central motive state, influence response determination by selective effects (facilitation or inhibition) on sensory-motor coordinations. The stimulation arising from nonincentive environmental stimulation can, through conditioning (Route C) acquire the same properties as Route Y. (From Nebraska Symposium on Motivation, 1969).

made in section 2.2.1. earlier in this chapter, we are able to calculate the Hypotheses Quotient by means of the formula:

$$\text{H. Q.} = \frac{\Sigma(\text{H--H})}{\Sigma[(\text{S--H})+(\text{H--R})]} = \frac{3}{8+2} = \frac{3}{10} = 0.30$$

Later works

Since the above analysis of Bindra's theory was made he has written some papers of great value for motivational theory. Most important from our point of view is his contribution to the *Nebraska Symposium on Motivation*, 1969: "The Interrelated Mechanisms of Reinforcement and Motivation, and the Nature of their Influence on Response".

In this paper Bindra formulates a consistent *incentive motivation theory*.

The main hypothesis is formulated in the summary of his paper in this way (Bindra, 1969), pp. 29–30:

"This paper presents evidence and argument in support of the hypothesis that response reinforcement and response instigation arise form a common set of neuropsychological mechanisms, and that the principle of reinforcement is a special case of the more primary principle of motivation."

The main H-variable is called *"central motive state"*. It is supposed to have selective, facilitatory and inhibitory effects on instrumental and consummatory reactions. As can be seen from Bindra's diagram (Fig. 5, p. 22 in Bindra, 1969), which is presented above (see our Fig. 5.2.) the "central motive state" is determined by the neural representations of "incentive sensory features", "organismic state features" and "other sensory features". These neural representations are in turn determined by the S-variables: "incentive object", "metabolic processes" and "other objects". Among these S-variables the incentive object is the most important both for instigation and reinforcement of behavior.

The supposed relationships between the main variables are clearly represented in the above diagram.

From the hypothesis quoted and the diagram it should be obvious that Bindra still prefers the "neuropsychological" type of theory (or S-O-R-theory as we call it).

Concluding remarks. Bindra's later works reinforce the impression one got from reading his book: He has made a very valuable and original contribution to the integration of some important theories of motivation and reinforcement.

NOTES

1. Italics mine.
2. The reader should be informed, that we have not included all Bindra's hypotheses about the *development* of motivational activities.
3. Italics are the present author's.
4. With the only difference that Bindra postulates a "Positive Reinforcement Mechanism".

6: Berlyne's Theory

Introduction

In this Chapter we shall analyze a theory about curiosity-motivation presented by *D. E. Berlyne* in his book, "Conflict, Arousal and Curiosity" (1960)[1]. Besides this book he has written another one, "Structure and Direction in Thinking" (1965)[2], a number of chapters in reference books and numerous articles[3] Among these the most relevant for this analysis is the Chapter: "Motivational Problems Raised by Exploration and Epistemic Behavior" in *S. Koch* (1963)[4].

Besides this impressive productivity, another outstanding fact about Berlyne is his very broad and many-sided orientation. He is familiar with European psychology, especially the work of *Piaget,* and modern Soviet-Russian as well as North-American psychology, especially the work of *Hull* and *Hebb*. Berlyne has integrated all these inspirations in a very fruitful way into a theory about curiosity.

The metastratum

1.1. *Philosophical propositions*

Berlyne makes no explicit formulations about the psychosomatic problem or about any other philosophical problems. But from the other explicit meta-propositions, we can infer that Berlyne presupposes a *neutral-monistic* theory about the psychosomatic problem and a biological, Darwinian philosophy of Man.

1.2. *Metatheoretical propositions*

Berlyne discusses the value of theory in psychology with the following words in his "1960-book" (p. 163):

"There is a certain amount of controversy in psychological circles about the necessity of theory. . . . But a point of diminishing returns and needlessly inconclusive effort is

---

1. In the following called his "1960-book".
2. Afterwards called his "1965-book".
3. Listed in the bibliography of this book.
4. Called here his "Koch-paper".

soon reached unless specific questions, arising out of attempts at theory, are on hand to take over the helm."

Berlyne is thus moderately favorable to theory construction in psychology. About his attitude to older theories he writes explicitly (in his "Koch-paper" (1963, p. 353):

"The lines of research we have reviewed show how it is possible to recognize serious deficiencies in existing theories and yet to overcome these deficiencies by renovating theoretical fabrics that have given good wear."

Berlyne's "theoretical strategy" may thus be described as an *"integrative* approach".

His most extensive metatheoretical formulations are presented in his "1965-book". In Chapter 1 he describes his approach as "a neo-associationist approach" or *"integrative neo-associationism"*. He presents the positive characteristics in this way (pp. 14–19):

"1. *Primacy of S-R-associations.* The S-R psychologist keeps the elucidation of input-output relations or S-R associations constantly in view as his primary aim. He may make copious use of intervening variables and refer to hypothetical processes within the organism, but he regards these as devices for handling networks of output-input relations that would otherwise be intraceable." . . .
Few are preponderantly concerned with analyzing consciousness, like the introspective, experimental psychologists of fifty years ago . . . Despite this, many psychologists, including some who specialize in thinking, fail to make clear to what extent they are endeavouring to explain behavior and how far they are endeavouring to explain conscious experience. Both of these may be legitimate pursuits, but it is important not to confuse the two."

We have included this extensive citation because it is one of the most clear metatheoretical formulations about modern psychology, we have found. This citation contains an *epistemological* principle about the preference for a *behavioral* data language (instead of a phenomenological one); and Berlyne makes it clear that it is a choice. Besides this the citation contains a *metatheoretical* principle about a "neo-associationistic" way of constructing theories (which was first made by Tolman).

Besides the above-quoted characterization of the neo-associationistic approach Berlyne mentions these (pp. 14–19):

"2. *Insistence on genetic explanations"* . . . It means tracing the course of development from which present behavior sprang, both phylogenetically and ontogenetically. . . .
"3. *Relation of complex to simple.* S-R behavior theory was characterized from the start by a dual ambition, most clearly expressed in the work of Hull. The aim was to construct theories generating predictions that would be (a) maximally precise and (b) applicable to as wide a range of behavior as possible. However, if we examine the record of this current, and especially if we consider the life work of Hull, a certain degree of incompatibility between these two aspirations is revealed, at least of the present stage in the history of psychology.
So later theoreticians of behavior (see Berlyne, 1954) have been faced with a choice.

Some of them, for example, those who have devoted themselves to mathematical models or computer-simulation programs, have pursued precision above all. ... Others, including those who have been most closely in touch with developments in neurophysiology and those who have been most concerned with motivational problems, have given precedence to seeking principles and concepts that will have the widest possible range of applicability and thus be capable of revealing the interrelations of the most diverse psychological phenomena.
The later order of priority will characterize this book, whose approach can thus be described as an integrative neoassociationism".

Again we have presented an extensive quotation, because it is the most precise and informative formulation we have found about this meta-theoretical problem. Berlyne presents his reasons for choosing an approach in motivational theory, which started with *Hebb*'s book (1949).

Thus Berlyne in his approach to psychological theory has borrowed heavily from Tolman (using "intervening variables" or "H-variables") and from Hebb (using "neurophysiological H-variables"). But in his theory about thinking he deviates from these two psychologists by presenting a fourth characteristic of the neo-associationist approach (p. 17):

"4. *Recognition of internal stimuli and responses.* The neoassociationist has the idiosyncrasy of referring to the changes that constitute these inferred mediating processes as "response" and as "stimuli". This is perhaps the most distinctive peculiarity of S-R-psychology."

Berlyne also presents a very clear discussion of this feature of his approach. But it is not his theory of thinking, but of motivation, which concerns us here, and, therefore, we will not go deeper into this.

1.3. *Methodological propositions*

In the quotations above about metatheoretical problems there are also some indications of Berlyne's methodological principles. It is clear that he prefers a *behavioral data language*, and it is also obvious that he prefers an *experimental* approach. Actually his own work is based upon experiments, both with animals and men.

The hypothetical stratum

2.0. *Summary of the hypotheses*

We shall presently turn to the *contents* of Berlyne's explanatory system. But before we go into a deeper analysis, we present here a very short summary of the contents of the theory as a whole. It is very easy to do, because Berlyne has given us an excellent summary of the whole book in his title: "Conflict,

Arousal and Curiosity". In other words: *curiosity-behavior* (which will be described further and classified later) is caused by various *conflicts* (which also will be described under the analyses of the descriptive level). The causal link, the mediating or intervening variable between conflict and curiosity is *"arousal"*. This is the most important explanatory term or *H-variable* in Berlyne's theory. It is a very well-defined variable, which is introduced after a very thorough analysis of the concept of *"drive"* in general. As this analysis is one of the most rewarding the present author has found, we will consider it at some length in the next paragraph. But before leaving this summary of the theory, we shall present a summarizing diagram representing the hypotheses in Berlyne's theory (Fig. 6.1.).

2.1. *The hypothetical terms (H-terms)*

Berlyne (1960) confesses in the preface (p. VIII), that:

"The book has two features that would have surprised me when I first set out to plan it. One is that it ends up sketching a highly modified form of drive-reduction theory. . . . The second surprising feature is the prominience of neurophysiology."

Later in the more theoretical part of the book (Chapters 7 to 11) Berlyne makes a very thorough analysis of the concept of drive. He thus writes (pp. 165–167):

"The concept of drive, which dominates contemporary discussions of motivation, resolves itself into three logically distinct concepts. We may distinguish them as $drive_1$, $drive_2$ and $drive_3$."

"$Drive_1$. There is first the notion of drive as a condition that affects the *level of activity*. It is customary to speak of the "energizing effect of drive" in this connection." . . . "The close resemblance between the manifestations of $drive_1$ and those of arousal will hardly have escaped the reader." . . . "So it will require no great temerity to regard $drive_1$, and arousal as intimately related. Nor will it require great originality, as several writers have been drawn towards the same step (e. g., Hebb, 1955, Lindsley, 1957, Morgan, 1957, Malmo, 1958)." . . .

"$Drive_2$. The second notion represents drive as an *internal condition that makes certain overt responses more likely than others*. It differs from $drive_1$ in its selectivity." . . .

"$Drive_3$. The third notion identifies drive as *a condition whose termination or alleviation is rewarding*, i.e., promotes the learning of an instrumental response."

After this thorough analysis of the drive-concept Berlyne continues (p. 168):

"One of the working assumptions of S-R reinforcement theory as developed especially by Hull (1943, 1952) and his associates, has been that $drive_1$, $drive_2$ and $drive_3$ can be identified."

The rest of the two most theoretically significant chapters (7 and 8) contain an extensive argumentation for *identifying* "$drives_{1,2,3}$" with "*arousal*", which is a function of the *"reticular arousal system"* (RAS). But with this argumentation we move on to the next part of our analysis (the hypotheses), and before doing

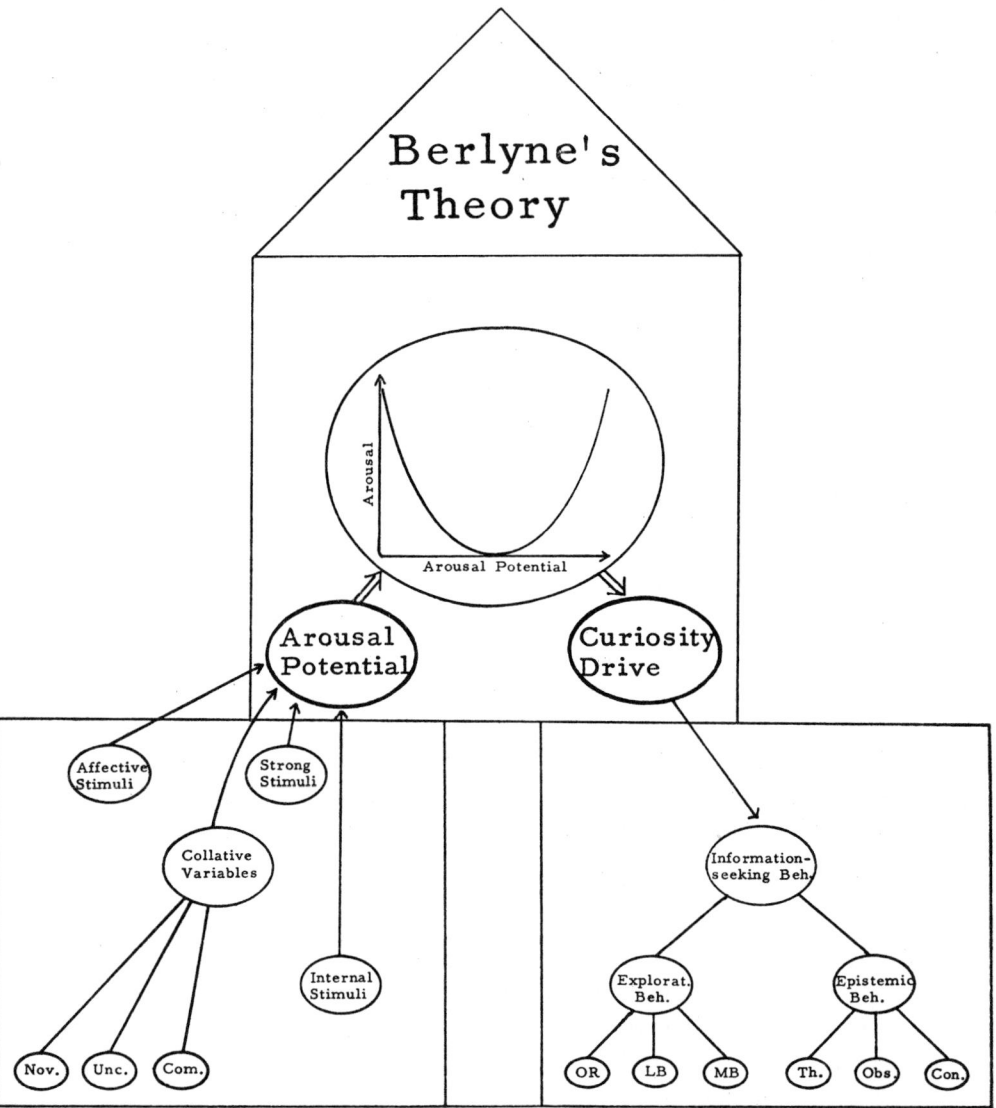

Fig. 6.1. The D-level and H-level of a Psychological Theory – D. E. Berlyne's Theory of Curiosity.

that, we shall conclude this part by classifying Berlyne's important variable, "arousal".

2.1.1. *The surplus meaning of the H-terms.* In accordance with our first classification into neutral-formal, neurophysiological and phenomenological variables it is easy to describe Berlyne's "arousal" as a *neuro-physiological* variable. Berlyne's book is replete with modern American and Russian psychophysiological research-data. And we have already seen that Berlyne in the preface has declared his preference for a neuro-psychological approach.

2.1.2. Dispositional or functional terms? In accordance with our second classification into disposition variables and function variables we can describe "arousal" as a *function variable*. The corresponding disposition variable must be the Reticular Arousal System, as it is the structure which is activated to function.

2.1.3. Dynamic, directive or vector terms? From Berlyne's discussion of the concept of "drive" it is clear that "drive$_1$" and "arousal" are *dynamic* terms, while "drive$_2$" and "drive$_3$" are *vector* terms.

2.2. *Classifications of the hypotheses*

We are now naturally lead to the next part of our analysis: the *hypotheses* in Berlyne's explanatory system.

We will first look at some *S-H-hypotheses*, which formulate the causal or functional relationships between arousal and its antecedents.

Berlyne (1960) discusses the independent variables, which are "Determinants of arousal" (especially, pp. 170–179). They are: 1) intensive variables, 2) affective variables and 3) "collative variables" (the special curiosity-motivating variables, which will be dealt with later). He presents considerable experimental evidence for every class, and then coins a new term (p. 179):

"We shall henceforth refer to all these properties of incoming stimuli with power to affect arousal as *arousal potential*."

This "arousal potential" is perhaps not an H-variable, but rather a very *general* descriptive term standing for abstract properties processed by independent variables of stimuli. It is one of those variables, which makes it extremely difficult to draw a sharp boundary between D-level and H-level, between the descriptive and explanatory contents of a theory.

But we have come to the conclusion that "arousal potential" should be regarded as an "intervening variable" in the narrow sense, i. e., "arousal potential" is an H-term without any surplus meaning. As discussed in Chapter 2 of this book "intervening variables" can be conceived of as belonging to the "lowest" or least abstract part of the H-level.

Berlyne discusses two possible hypotheses about the relationship between "arousal potential" and "arousal".

One hypothesis is set forth by *Hebb* and other psychologists. It postulates:

"that the condition that make for boredom will produce exceptionally low arousa, and that low arousal, as well as high arousal, must therefore be aversive." (pp. 188–89 in Berlyne, 1960).

The other hypothesis is set forth by Berlyne himself. He writes (p. 193):

"When arousal potential is inordinately low, arousal may mount."
Berlyne prefers this hypothesis to the first one, because "a state of low arousal is a state of drowsiness characterized by high-amplitude, low frequency EEG waves" (p. 189).

But he is in agreement with Hebb and others that low arousal potential "boredom", as well as high arousal potential is aversive, and that the optimal arousal potential is preferred or strived for (p. 194):

"Our hypotheses imply, therefore, that for an individual organism at a particular time, there will be an *optimal influx of arousal potential.* Arousal potential that deviates in either an upward or a downward direction from this optimum will be drive inducing or aversive. The organism will thus strive to keep arousal potential near its optimum." ...

This apparently paradoxical part agreement and part disagreement between Berlyne and Hebb is a consequence of Berlyne's special hypotheses (best elaborated in his "Koch-paper"). While Hebb and others presuppose a *linear,* increasing relationship between arousal potential and arousal, Berlyne presupposes a U-shaped relation between arousal potential and arousal. In other words, Berlyne presupposes that only a *medium* strength of arousal potential causes a *low* arousal. But it is a *low* arousal which is preferred, not a medium (which Hebb postulates).

This makes clear that Berlyne and Hebb are in agreement about the fact that *medium* arousal *potential* is *optimally attractive.*

All these confusing agreements and disagreements are perhaps cleared up by Berlyne's own diagram from his "Koch-paper":

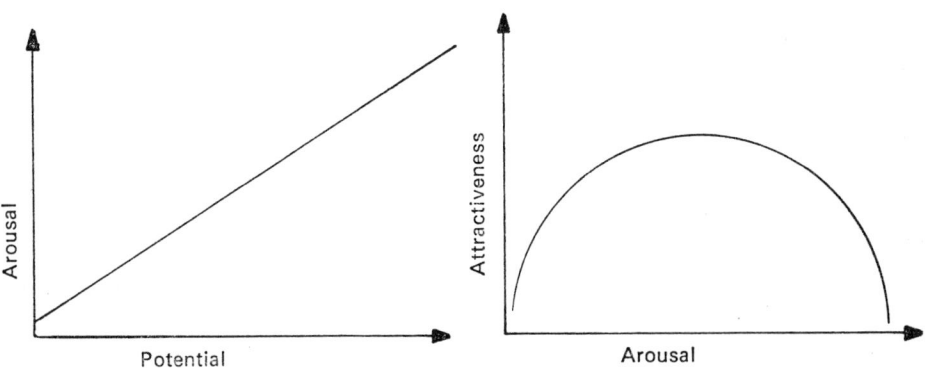

Fig. 6.2. Hebb's hypotheses.

The agreement between Hebb's and Berlyne's hypotheses can here be noted.

While *Hebb*'s hypotheses are the most *simple,* I think that *Berlyne*'s are the most *empirically adequate.* We have already mentioned that his hypotheses can

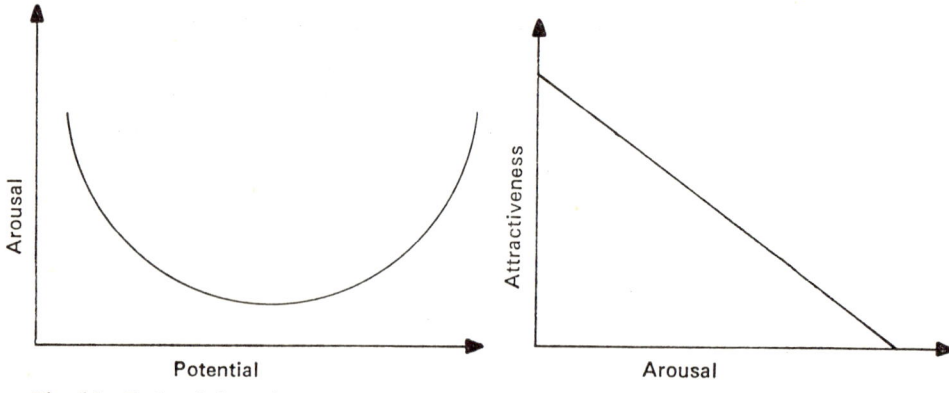

Fig. 6.3. Berlyne's hypotheses.

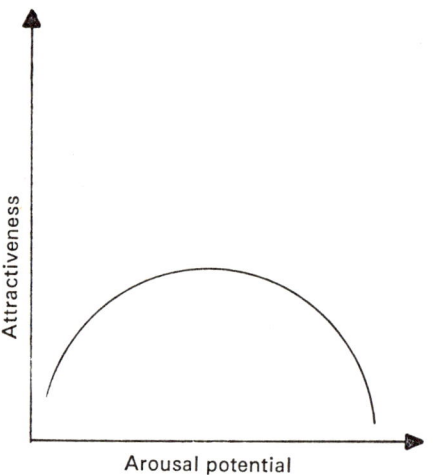

Fig. 6.4 Arousal potential.

explain the paradoxical similarities and differences between *"sleepiness"* (low arousal), which is *preferred*, and *"boredom"* (high arousal, but low arousal potential), which is *avoided*. Berlyne's hypotheses also explain how high arousal caused by high arousal potential is avoided. This "high-high-condition" exists in *all* drives (except boredom). And *"curiosity"* is thus a drive which is caused by *conflicting* stimuli-conditions (called "collative variables", which we will deal with later).

Thus Berlyne could formulate a very general *H-R-hypothesis:* all high-arousal conditions or "drives" determine arousal- or drive-reducing behavior. This drive-reducing behavior must be different in "boredom" and other "drives" (including curiosity). In *"boredom"* (high arousal, but low potential) the behavior of the organism consists of a seeking for *increased stimulation* (increasing potential, but reducing arousal). In *"curiosity"* (and other drives with high potential and high arousal) the *behavior* of the organism consists of a striving for *reducing stimulation* (and potential, which reduces arousal). Berlyne assumes that the reducing of arousal, or drive-reduction, is always rewarding or *"reinforcing"*. He thus *accepts the "drive$_3$"-concept as valid for curiosity-drive* (without necessarily accepting a general reinforcement theory of learning)[5]).

Berlyne also accepts the *"drive$_2$"-concept as valid for* curiosity-drive[6]), as he supposes, that curiosity-drive has a selective effect upon several other processes. These hypotheses may be classified as *H-H-hypotheses*. He elaborates on them in Chapter 3 of his "1960-book" under the title "Attention". He concludes the Chapter with the following summary (p. 77):

"the evidence we have to go on tends to favor the view that the determinants of attention in performance, attention in learning, and attention in remembering are similar. They seem to include many of the factors that affect response strength in general. Moreover the collative variables that are a special concern of ours seem to play a part in all three."

What Berlyne here calls "attention" is a selective function of the reticular system (RAS). He – especially in his "Koch-paper" – mentions several investigations which present evidence for a *specific* activating function in the thalamic part of the RAS. Even the brain-stem part of the RAS has not only a *general* but also a *specific* activating function according to some experiments by the Soviet psychophysiologist *P. K. Anokhin*.

"He has shown that different chemical substances will block the normal reticular reaction to some kinds of stimuli while leaving the potency of other stimuli unaffected." "Anokhin concludes from these and other facts . . . qualitatively different biological reactions (orienting reaction, defensive reaction and alimentary reaction) excite in the reticular formation different complexes of neural elements which are specific to them. These neural elements, in their turn, exert a specific activating influence on the cerebral cortex mobilizing in it intracortical connections adequate to the given reaction." (p. 309 in the "Koch-paper").

As "learning" and "remembering" may be classified as H-variables, it is correct to describe the hypotheses about the relationship between "attention" (-specific activating arousal) on the one side and "learning" and "remembering" on the other side as *H-H-hypotheses*. As "performance" must be classified as a dependent, empirical variable ("R-variable"), we must describe the hypothesis

---

5. In later works (Berlyne, 1967 and 1969) Berlyne modifies his hypothesis about reinforcement. According to the new version of his reinforcement hypothesis reinforcement or reward is the result of either *reduction* of high arousal or *increase* in low arousal. See D. E. Berlyne: "Arousal and Reinforcement" (in D. Levine (Ed.) *Nebraska Symposium on Motivation"*, Lincoln: University of Nebraska Press, 1967) as well as D. E. Berlyne: "The justifiability of the concept of curiosity" (Paper delivered at the XIX International Congress of Psychology, London, 1969).
6. The reader may be reminded, that Berlyne logically accepts the "drive$_1$"-concept too, because "drive$_1$" is *identical* with "activation" or "arousal".

about the relationship between "attention" (RAS) and "performance" as an H-R-hypothesis[7]).

2.2.1. Basic classification of hypotheses. After having presented the most important of Berlyne's hypotheses, we now turn to the basic classification into S-H, H-H and H-R hypotheses. Before doing that we shall make our systematic reconstruction of the hypotheses and reformulate them in partially symbolic formulas.

In this reconstruction we have finally decided to regard arousal potential" (= "A.P.") as an H-term representing the variable which determines "arousal" (= "A"). Thus we have the following hypotheses:

1. hypothesis: S(intensive, external stimuli)→$H_{A.P.}$
2. hypothesis: S(affective stimuli)→$H_{A.P.}$
3. hypothesis: S(collative variables)→$H_{A.P.}$
4. hypothesis: S(internal stimuli from needs)→$H_{A.P.}$
5a. hypothesis: $H_{A.P.}$, low→$H_{A.}$, high("boredom")
5b. hypothesis: $H_{A.P.}$, high→$H_{A.}$, high("curiosity")
5c. hypothesis: $H_{A.P.}$, high→$H_{A.}$, high("other drives")
6. hypothesis: H("boredom")→R(stimulus seeking)
7. hypothesis: H("other drives")→R(stimulus reduction)
8. hypothesis: H("curiosity")→R(explorative, epistemic)
9. hypothesis: $H_{A.}$(specific, "attention")→H(acquisition, learning)
10. hypothesis: $H_{A.}$(specific, "attention")→H(remembering)
11. hypothesis: $H_{A.}$(specific, "attention")→R(performance)

After having made this partially symbolic reformulation of the hypotheses we conclude this section with our basic classification:

1. *Purely theoretical hypotheses (H-H):*
   Hypotheses No. 5, 9 and 10. In all: 3 hypotheses.
2. *Partly empirical hypotheses:*
   a. S-H-hypotheses: No. 1, 2, 3 and 4. In all: 4 hypotheses.
   b. H-R-hypotheses: No. 6, 7, 8 and 11. In all: 4 hypotheses.

2.2.2. The complexity of the hypotheses. It remains to classify the hypotheses in accordance with their degree of complexity. They all seem to be very simple with only two variables, so they can be described as *"mechanistic" hypotheses*. We must remember that Berlyne has constructed some very general abstract and comprehensive variables (e. g., "arousal potential" and "arousal"), and therefore his hypotheses can be simple ("mechanistic"), while the theory as a whole is comprehensive and has the widest possible range of applicability (which is in accordance with Berlyne's metaprinciples).

---

[7]. Berlyne has dealt with the problems of *attention* in later works, see especially D. E. Berlyne: "Attention as a Problem in Behavior Theory" (in D. Mostofsky (Ed.): *Attention.* N. Y.: Appleton, 1968).

2.2.3. *The functional relationships in the hypotheses.* Berlyne is not explicit about the problem of determinism, but it seems to be correct to describe his hypotheses as *"causal-deterministic"*.

We have finished the analysis of Berlyne's hypothetical stratum and turn to the next level of his theory, the descriptive level.

The descriptive stratum

3.1. *The abstract D-level*

We are now going to analyze the independent variables and later on the dependent variables in Berlyne's theory.

Berlyne deals with the *independent empirical* variables in Chapter 2 of his "1960-book". These variables are:

1. *"Novelty"* is a basic characteristic of many stimuli. This stimulus-variable can be classified in several ways. Thus stimuli can be *"completely* novel", when they have never been preceived before. They can have a *"short-term-novelty"*, when they have been perceived recently, and a *"long-term-novelty", when they* have been perceived a long time ago (without being completely novel).

The stimulus *pattern* can be classified as *"absolutely* novel" or *"relatively* novel". In the latter case there are some elements in the pattern which are familiar.

Related to novelty are "change", "surprisingness" and "incongruity". All these characteristics – like novelty itself – are of course *relative* to an organism.

2. *"Uncertainty"* is another basic characteristic of stimuli. Berlyne defines this stimulus-variable in accordance with "information theory", but it would take too long to present it here.

3. *"Complexity"* is a third basic characteristic of stimulus patterns. These stimulus-variables depend on the *number* of elements in the stimulus-pattern, and upon the *dissimilarity* of the elements, and further upon the degree of *"cohesion"* of the pattern.

Some of these stimulus-variables can be defined in terms of information theory, with *uncertainty* as the basic variable (called "entropy" in information theory). Then "complexity" is "content of information" and "surprisingness" is "amount of information".

From a psychological point of view these variables can all be described as having elements of *conflict*. But to distinguish this conflict between *stimuli* from conflict between *responses,* Berlyne calls them *"perceptual conflicts"*. Besides these Berlyne later notes another sort of conflict between *symbolic* stimuli, which he designates *"conceptual* conflict"[8]).

---

8. It is possible to regard "conflict" – just like "arousal potential" – as an *intervening variable* (without surplus meaning), rather than a descriptive, independent variable.

For all these independent empirical variables Berlyne coins the common term: *"collative variables"*.

These collative variables contribute to the "arousal potential", which is also determined by "affective stimuli" (associated with reward and punishment), all intensive external stimuli, and internal stimuli arising from needs. We thus have the following hierarchical system of more or less generalized independent empirical variables in Berlyne's theory.

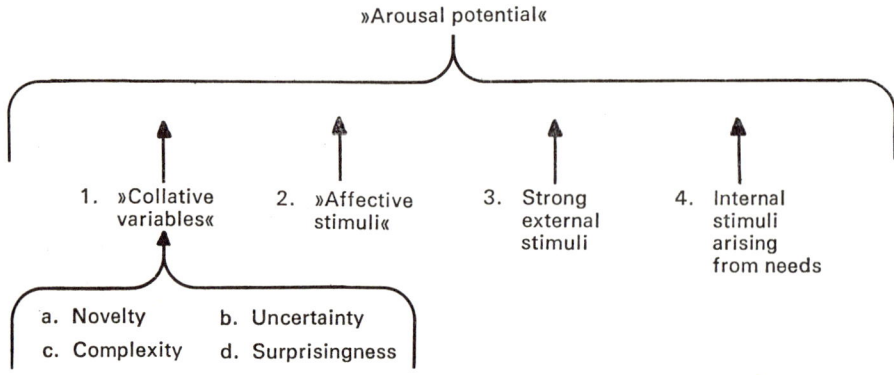

Fig. 6.5. Schematic representation of the *independent* empirical variables in Berlyne's theory. ("Arousal potential" can be regarded as an "intervening variable").

We now turn to the *dependent* empirical variables in Berlyne's theory. He has himself made a very systematic classification of these behavior- or R-variables in his "1960-book" and elaborated it further in his "Koch-paper".

One of his main classifications is into *"exploratory behavior"* and *"epistemic behavior"*.

He gives us a short definition in the "Koch-paper" (pp. 286–87):

"Exploratory responses have the function of altering the stimulus field."

"Exploratory behavior" can be classified in three ways (pp. 288–90):

1. Classification in accordance with *the form* it takes.

    a. "receptor – adjusting responses" (to these belongs the "orienting reflex")
    b. "locomotor exploration"
    c. "investigatory responses" (mostly manipulative).

    These three classes are dealt with in Chapters 4–6 in Berlyne's "1960-book".

2. Classification in accordance with its *motivation:*
    a. "intrinsic exploration" (motivated by curiosity).
    b. "extrinsic exploration" (other motives than curiosity).

3. Classification in accordance with the *object*.
    a. "Specific exploration", which has the function of providing stimulation from a specific source (often motivated by curiosity).
    b. "diversive exploration", which has the function of providing stimulation in general and named "recreation", "entertainment", etc. (often motivated by "boredom").

"*Epistemic behavior*" is defined in this way in the "Koch-paper" (p. 322):

"The term *epistemic behavior* refers to behavior whose function – – – is to equip the organism with *knowledge*, by which we mean structures of symbolic responses."

Epistemic behavior is classified into:

1. *epistemic observation* – which includes the experimental and other observational techniques of science.
2. epistemic *thinking* – which is a sort of *directed* and productive thinking.
3. *consultation* – which includes asking other people questions or consulting reference books.

As we already know Berlyne has made the empirical generalization (S-R-sentence or "law"), that *exploratory and epistemic behavior are determined by perceptual and conceptual conflicts*. It was in order to *explain* this "law" that he elaborated the hypotheses about *arousal*, with which we are now familiar.

3.2. *The concrete D-level*

It goes without saying that Berlyne employs numerous *protocol-sentences* as the basis for his empirical generalizations and hypotheses. The protocol-sencentes are used in all the experiments about curiosity which Berlyne presents in his book and papers. Many of these experiments were made by Berlyne and his co-workers. Others were made by diverse American, European and Soviet psychologists, but it would lead us too far afield to review them in this book. It is sufficient to state that in the present author's opinion Berlyne's theory is based upon "firm empirical ground".

The protocol-sentences themselves are, of course, not quoted in reviews of the experiments, which are – as is usual in a book of this sort – presented in a generalized form.

3.3. *The descriptive units*

We can end this part about the descriptive content of Berlyne's theory with a classification of the protocol-sentences in accordance with the employed descriptive units. It is not easy because it is a matter of degree, but the present author would describe them as rather *molecular descriptions*.

128 . *Berlyne's Theory*

The theory as a whole

4.1. *The formal properties*

(4.1.1.) Turning to our description of Berlyne's theory as a whole, he shall first look at *the systematic organization of the theory*. We think that it is correct to place his theory on the borderline between "explanatory sketches" and "explanatory systems". There are no explicitly formulated hypotheses, but the text is clearly divided into three strata (the M, H, and D).

(4.1.2.) As the reader undoubtedly remembers, Berlyne prefers maximal applicability to maximal preciseness. It is also consistent with his metaproposition that *the preciseness of his representation* must be classified as being on the level of a *verbal theory*. But there are some symbolic and mathematical formulations – especially in the chapter about "information theory" and its application to the definition of "novelty" and other collative variables.

(4.1.3.) *The properties of the model* are developed in such a way that it must be classified as a *two-dimensional model,* because it consists of diagrams presenting the functional relationships between "arousal potential", "arousal" and "attractiveness".

4.2. *The epistemological properties*

The epistemological properties of Berlyne's theory place it safely among the *S-O-R-theories,* because it is an explanatory theory employing hypothetical terms with physiological surplus meaning (H_O-terms) referring to "brain models" (not exclusively to physiological data).

4.3. *The theory-empiry ratio*

On the basis of the general impression Berlyne's theory makes one should undoubtedly classify it as being rather *empirical*. This is confirmed by calculating the Hypotheses Quotient by means of the formula:

$$H.Q. = \frac{\Sigma (H - H)}{\Sigma [(S \div H) + (H \div R)]} = \frac{3}{4+4} = \frac{3}{8} = 0.38$$

Concluding remarks. Although Berlyne's theory is not formally developed to the same extent as Hull's and is more akin to Hebb's, we think that his theory will be highly influential in the future, because he has made a very original integration of many valuable trends in modern psychology. Therefore, we think that his theory will influence both motivational theory and its application to problems of education, the arts and other fields.

7. Konorsky's Theory

Introduction

The Polish neurophysiologist *Jerzy Konorski* is well known both in the East and the West for his work on conditioned reflexes. Besides several experimental reports he has written a book on conditioning: *"Conditioned Reflexes and Neuron Organization"* (1948). And nearly 20 years later he wrote another book: *"Integrative Activity of the Brain"* (1967). This later work includes a very broad and general psychological theory about learning (conditioning), perception and *motivation*. This theory is not only broad in *scope* – a general behavior theory – but is also very broad in *coverage:* the work of both American and European as well as Soviet psychologists is known to Konorski and utilized in his theory. Therefore, we have decided to analyze Konorski's theory and include it in this book.

The metastratum

1.1. *Philosophical propositions*

Konorski's latest book (1967) contains some explicit metapropositions, most of which are collected in the "Introduction", but some of which are spread throughout the book. As usual we systematize the analysis of the metapropositions by following our general systematological plan.

In common with most modern psychological theories, there are very few explicitly formulated epistemological or other *philosophical* propositions in Konorski's book. But we found a few intermingled with methodological propositions.

From these more or less implicit philosophical propositions we can reconstruct Konorski's general philosophical principles in this way:

Konorski presupposes that there is continuity without principal differences between animals and men. This *Darwinian or biological conception of Man* is explicitly expressed in connection with a discussion (p. 4) based on the assumption "that the animal experiences perception of the object in much the same way" [as Man does]. And he continues (pp. 4–5):

"To deny such an assumption would mean to draw a sharp border between the brain function in man and in the higher vertebrates, which would be inadmissible from the biological point of view."

Closely related to his conception of Man are his presuppositions about the *psychophysiological* problem, but it is not easy to reconstruct Konorski's thesis about this matter. Some propositions seem to indicate a thesis of the kind held by Pavlov and called *epiphenomenalism* – that version of dualism which is close to materialistic monism. Thus Konorski writes (p. 3):

"None of us doubts that our mental experiences, which we know from our own introspection, do depend on our cerebral activity – that if this activity is blocked or abolished, the mental processes disappear. Moreover, we believe that different mental experiences depend on different cerebral processes – that is, that exactly the same process cannot give rise to two different psychic phenomena. But if this is true, then why not infer the occurrence of particular nervous processes from our mental experiences in exactly the same way as we infer them from behavioral acts?"

While this indicates a dualism the next passage seems to come closer to epiphenomenalism (p. 4):

"Furthermore, we should clearly realize that the occurrence of a certain subjective experience, similar to the occurrence of a certain objectively observed behavioral act, is not the explanation itself but, on the contrary, a phenomenon which *requires* explanation in terms of physiological processes."

But in other connections we found expressions which seemingly presuppose a *neutral monistic* thesis. Thus Konorski writes about the interpretation of some experiments (p. 330):

"As a matter of fact, this psychological speculation is nothing but the translation of the physiological events deduced from experimental observations into psychological language."

Such a "double-language" thesis is often connected with a version of neutral monism as set forth by the modern analytical philosophers. As already mentioned Konorski does not explicitly express agreement with this neutral monistic thesis, but his principles for theory construction – to which we now turn – apparently presuppose such a thesis.

1.2. Metatheoretical propositions

Konorski's book contains more explicit propositions about theory construction than the above.

Although Konorski favors a *physiologically* based theory he is at the same time aware of the fact that such a theory today has to be a *"constructive" theory with a "brain-model"* – not an old-fashioned "reductive" theory. The present author thinks that Konorski is one of those who earliest and most clearly has expressed such presuppositions about theory construction[1]). We also

---

1. Among earlier expositions we can mention Konorski's evening lecture at the 17th International Congress of Psychology in Washington in 1963. Unfortunately, some of Konorski's most brilliant, didactial remarks about his diagrams are *not* in the printed paper (see J. Konorski. "On the Mechanism of Instrumental Conditioning". Proceedings of the 17th International Congress of Psychology, Washington, 1963).

found in his book (1967) many clear propositions about this attitude toward theory construction. One of the clearest and most extensive metatheoretical propositions is found in the "Introduction" (pp. 5–6):

"A few comments are needed about our attitude to the anatomical controversies concerning the localization of various functionally defined "centers" or regions. Here we follow the prudent thesis of von Holst that at the present stage of the development of brain physiology the questions "how" and "why" are more important than that of "where". In order to be consistent, when dealing with the problems of functional organization of particular systems, we shall make use of block models devoid of too precise anatomical specifications. If anyone should say that in this work we are dealing with the "conceptual" nervous system, we shall readily accept this definition without considering it a reproof. In fact, as long as our concepts on the functioning of the nervous system do not contain essential errors, this way of dealing with it seems to be more profitable for our purpose than dealing with all the intricacies of actual anatomical relations."

What Konorski here refers to as "block models" are in reality diagrams. Later in the book (p. 216) he defends *"diagram-making"* against the kind of criticism made of earlier diagram-making which was based upon inadequate information and claims. Konorski maintains that "this does not mean that diagram-making as such should be rejected, but only that improved diagrams should be used."

Later in this chapter we shall look at some of Konorski's diagrams, but we wish to conclude this section by repeating that the above quotations demonstrate that Konorski conceives of theory-construction as the *construction* of *models of "brain-mechanisms"* – the conceptual nervous system – and that these models are best symbolized or represented by *"block-diagrams"*. This is a kind of theory-construction which is close to that of *"computer-diagrams"*, but the interesting thing is that in Konorski's theory this is integrated with a *physiological* approach to psychology.

1.3. Methodological propositions

Konorski is – just like most modern psychologists – most explicit about *empirical* methods.

The most striking thing in his methodological principles is his acceptance of *all possible methods:* electrophysiological methods, studies of brain defects, behavioral experiments and introspection. Thus he writes in the "Introduction" (p. 5):

"To sum up, the task posed in this work is to present the general architecture of the brain activity of higher animals on the basis of *all* available evidence which can be utilized for this purpose. According to whether the stress is placed on the information provided by the experimental work on animals or on information derived from the observation of subjective experiences and behavior of human beings, the book is composed of two parts."

The two parts mentioned in this quotation are the part about innate activities (drives) and conditioned reflexes, which is mainly based upon animal behavioral and physiological data, and that about perception and memory, based mainly upon human neuropathological and introspective data.

Konorski presents special arguments for adopting introspective data, and after defending this position he presents a new argument (p. 4):

"The utilization of the subjective phenomena as the source of information about the cerebral processes becomes even more important in our time when we are able to correlate more and more these phenomena with the electrical signs of brain function."

But he – of course – does not accept introspective data uncritically. Thus he writes (p. 177):

"As seen fron our previous discussion, the introspective method is most informative in studying the properties of unitary images (and, consequently, of the gnostic units representing them), and it can provide much important and precise material which may be verified and corroborated by other methods. This method cannot, however, be considered fully satisfactory, because it fails to give us complete information about all the associations which are formed in us or in other persons."

For the study of associations Konorski employs several behavioral-experimental methods to supplement the introspective method, which is insufficient in this case, but it would take us too far afield to go into detail about these methods.

In close relationship to arguments favoring the introspective method stand some arguments (pp. 213–14) for supplementing "artificial", experimental methods with a *"naturalistic" observation* of animal and human behavior under natural conditions existing outside the laboratories.

Thus the use of *all* empirical methods are recommended by Konorski: behavioral experiments and natural observations, as well as electrophysiological statements, neuropathological observations and introspection. This illustrates his eclecticism.

The hypothetical stratum

2.0. *Summary of the hypotheses*

Konorski's book comprises more than 500 pages, in which we find many concentrated descriptions of experiments as well as theoretical discussions and hypotheses. Therefore, it is not easy to present a *short* summary, but Konorski has offered valuable help here by writing rather extensive summaries after each chapter and, in addition, a whole chapter summarizing the main content of the book. Therefore, the best we can do is to present a summary of this summarizing chapter. In order to render a fair view of his theory we shall quote rather extensively from the implicit hypotheses of which the present author has found nearly fifty.

We shall begin with a very rough overview of the whole theory (p. 507):

"The gross correlative anatomy of the brain teaches us that this organ is composed of three kinds of functional systems: (1) the *afferent systems* (analyzers) built according to the hierarchical convergence-divergence principle; (2) *associative systems* linking particular afferent systems and their parts; and (3) *efferent systems* controlling the executive organs. In each of these systems two types of intercentral connections may be discerned: in one type the synaptic contacts between nerve cells are fully transmissible because of the ontogenetic development of the nervous system; in the other type the ontogenetically determined transmissibility of the synaptic contacts is only potential, and their actualization depends on the animal's individual experiences accomplished by learning processes."

The main hypotheses of the *afferent* system are about perceptual learning. Konorski's contributions to perceptual theory are his hypotheses about *"gnostic units"*, which are defined and summarized in his way (p. 508):

"We call the units representing functionally meaningful patterns of events perceptive or gnostic units, and the transmission of messages from the receptive surface to these units unitary perceptions. The cortical areas in which gnostic units (potential or actual) are situated are called gnostic (associative) areas." - - - - - -

"We assume that gnostic units are formed by transformation of potential synaptic contacts, linking the units of lower levels of the given afferent system with the units of the appropriate gnostic area, into actual synaptic contacts. New gnostic units representing new stimulus-patterns are formed from potential gnostic units - - -"

The *associative* system consists of an inborn and an acquired part: The inborn associative system consists of *unconditioned* reflexes, which are divided into two categories: *preparatory* and *consummatory*. It is in connection with the preparatory reflexes that motivation occurs. Thus Konorski writes (p. 509):

"The central mechanisms controlling the preparatory reflexes are denoted as drives or emotions. Accordingly the preparatory reflexes are called drive reflexes."

The distinction between "drive" and "emotion" is defined in this way (p. 41):

"The proposed meaning of the term "drive" is in full harmony with its general usage, except that we tend to regard it (as many contemporary authors do) as a strictly physiological term. The subjective experiences corresponding to particular drives, familiar to us from introspection and supposed to be analogous in the higher animals, will be called *emotions*."

The effects (or functions) of drives are summarized in this passage (p. 509):

"- - - in higher animals they [the drives] have mainly facilitatory character in respect to both afferent and efferent systems - - -"

Konorski's hypothesis about drive is supplemented by some hypotheses about what he calls "antidrive", which is his special term for "satisfaction". The shortest explicit formulations about this are found in the "summary and conclusions" to Chapter 1 (pp. 57–58):

"The organization of the drive-controlling systems is somewhat different in preservative and protective drives. In the hunger-satiation system, being the representative of the preservative drive systems, the satiation center is controlled by humoral stimuli, its activation producing the suppression of the hunger center and its inactivation producing the release of that center. Therefore, the satiation center regulates the *excitability of the* hunger center, or rather its particular groups of units corresponding to particular nutritive substances. The hunger center is assumed to be composed of on-hunger units of particular kinds, and reciprocally related with them, off-hunger units. The off-hunger units are activated by particular taste stimuli, whereas the on-hunger units are activated by the taste of elements thrown into operation when the taste stimuli is discontinued.

This dual character probably does not exist in the protective drive systems, where the drive producing stimuli, which are partially identical with the protective consummatory stimuli directly elicit the appropriate drive."

These hypotheses are also presented in two of Konorski's "block models", the diagram in Fig. I–3 (p. 28) and Fig. I–4 (p. 34), which we reproduce here (as our Fig. 7.1.) also with the purpose of demonstrating Konorski's model building.

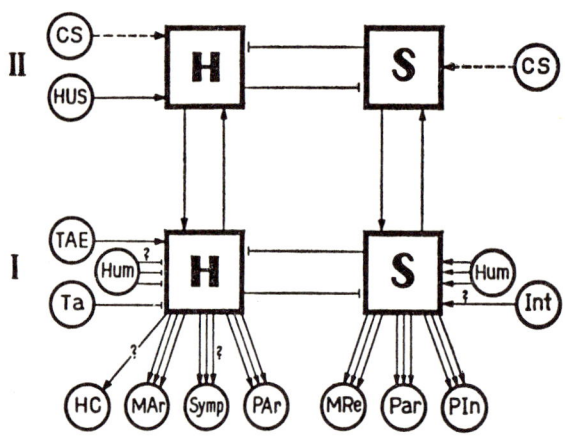

Fig. 7.1.a. Block Model of the Hunger-Satiation System (Simplified)

I, lower level of the system; II, higher level of the system. H, hunger centers; S, satiation centers. → excitatory connections; --|, inhibitory connections; – →, conditioned connections. Ta, effect of taste (see Section 10); TAE, taste aftereffect; Int, interoceptive stimuli; Hum, humoral stimuli; CS, conditioned stimulus; HUS, hunger unconditioned stimulus; HC, hunger contractions; MAr, motor arousal; Symp, sympathetic outflow; PAr, perceptual arousal; MRe, motor relaxation; Par, parasympathetic outflow; PIn, perceptual indifference.

Since it was reported that hunger contractions are present after lateral hypothalamic lesions (J. Mayer and S. Sudsaneh, Mechanism of hypothalamic control of gastric contractions in rat, *Amer. J. Physiol.*, 197 [1959]: 274–85), they may depend also on a lower (vagal) reflex-arc probably thrown into action by irritation of the stomach by the balloon.

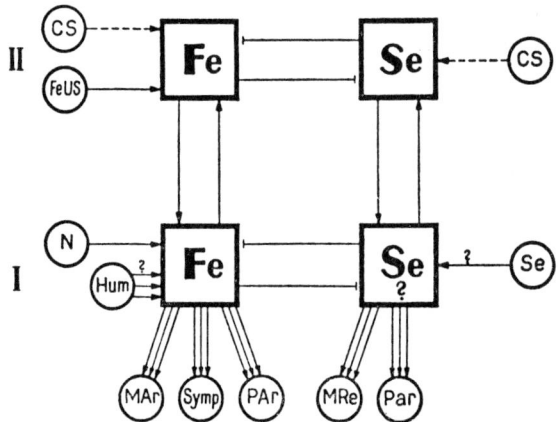

Fig. 7.1.b. Block Model of the Fear-Relief System)
Fe, fear centers; Se, relief centers and security stimulus; N, noxious stimulus; FeUS, unconditioned fear stimulus of non-noxious character. Other denotations as in Figure I-3.
Note that non-noxious fear stimuli are thought to act on the higher level of the fear system. Note also that the lower level of the relief system is considered uncertain.

The concept of "drive" is further elaborated for the hunger drive, where the hunger center is differentiated into "on-drive-units" and "off-drive units". The complicated interaction between the drive units and the antidrive or satiation center, and the taste receptors is hypothesized in another block model presented as Fig. I–6, which we also reproduce here (as our Fig. 7.2.).

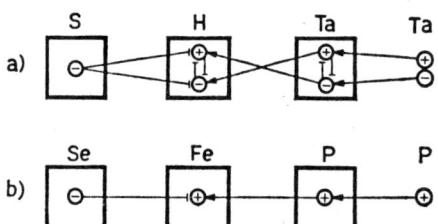

Fig. 7.2. Relations between drive and antidrive units in hunger and fear
a) Hunger-satiation system. S, satiation center; H, hunger center with ondrive units (+) and off-drive units (—); Ta, taste receptors and taste lower center with on (+) and off (—) units. →, excitatory connections; —|, inhibitory connections.
On-food-taste units activate off-hunger units, whereas off-taste units activate on-hunger units. Satiation units both on-hunger units and off-hunger units. Only protopathic pathways of taste are drawn, and the hunger mechanism for one nutritive substance is indicated.
b) Fear-relief system. Se, relief center; Fe, fear center with only on-fear units; P, pain receptors and pain lower center.
The fear center is homogeneous, reacting directly to the protopathic aspect of pain stimuli.

We conclude this summary of Konorski's motivational hypotheses by quoting his hypothesis concerning the localization of drive mechanisms, which is found among other places on p. 57:

"Drives are controlled by the part of the brain which we call the "emotive system" (in contradistinction to the cognitive system). Its centers are situated on two levels: in the hypothalamus, and in the limbic system; the latter is thought to be involved in conditioning of drives."

After these extensive quotations of the inborn associative system we continue with a briefer summary of the *acquired* associative system. About the nature of the learning process and the role of motivation in this process we find the following hypotheses (p. 511):

"Associative learning occurs when two units (one of them being a transmittent unit, the other one a recipient unit) linked by potential connection are synchronously activated and consists in increasing the transmissibility of their synaptic contacts."

Konorski deals with three types of learning: 1) *perceptual learning* (the establishment of gnostic units), 2) *classical conditioning*, and, 3) *instrumental conditioning*.

Classical conditioning is defined in this way (p. 512):

"By classical (or type I) conditioned reflex we denote association (or rather its utilization) between two sets of units of which the recipient set gives rise to an unconditioned reflex."

Drive reflexes as well as consummatory reflexes may be conditioned in the classical way.

The instrumental (or type II) conditioned reflexes are defined in the following way (p. 513):

"Another type of associations is in operation in instrumental conditioned reflexes — those reflexes in which the animal, being under the action of a particular drive, learns to perform a certain motor act when this act leads to the corresponding antidrive. The mechanism of the formation of instrumental CRs is conceived in the following way.

According to our earlier discussion, one of the major effects of drive reflexes is hypermotility produced by arousal of the motor behavioral system. If in this condition, a given movement is followed by immediate satisfaction of drive, connections are established between the units representing that drive and kinesthetic units representing that movement."

The special hypotheses of learning included in the above quotation are described by Konorski himself by means of the following metapropositions (pp. 513–14):

"The proposed concept, being a version of the drive reduction theory, fulfills at the same time the requirements of the hedonistic view claiming that the instrumental movement is learned and performed because the subject anticipates the pleasure of the "reward" or of the cessation of anxiety. In fact, since, according to our concept, a stimulus is pleasant only if it leads to satisfaction of drive, the two formulations are more or less equivalent."

We shall now summarize Konorski's hypotheses about the *efferent* systems. He proposes that the *kinesthetic* analyzer has a certain "programming" function. This is expressed among other places in the following quotations (pp. 516–17):

> "It is assumed that the more or less chaotic movements produced by lower levels of the motor behavioral system after birth become integrated in the gnostic fields of the kinesthetic analyzer into definite patterns, a process analogous to the formation of unitary perceptions in the exteroceptive analyzers.
> - - - - - -
> The kinesthetic analyzer also differs from exteroceptive ones in that it is directly connected with the motor efferent system represented in the cortex by pyramidal and extrapyramidal neurons. - - - And so the kinesthetic gnostic units may be considered as a programming device for skillful movements which the subject has learned to perform."

Finally, we shall cite his hypothesis about the role of motivation in performance (p. 517):

> "- - - the programming of the skilled movement and its execution are possible only when the given drive urges a subject to perform it – that is when the subject is appropriately motivated."

We hope that the reader now has a clear conception of Konorski's broad, precise and well-integrated theory about perception, learning and motivation (see also Fig. 7.3.). These extensive quotations will be used in the following analysis of the hypothetical stratum, where we concentrate on the motivational variables and hypotheses.

2.1. *The hypothetical terms (H-terms)*

In the summarizing quotations we have already presented the most important motivational terms: "drives", "antidrives" and "emotions".

Before going into a detailed systematological analysis of these terms, we shall supplement them with a presentation of Konorski's differentiation of "drives" into categories of drives.

Konorski's main classification of drives – and the related preparatory reflexes – is divided into two categories:

1. *"Preservative drives"* – and unconditioned preservative reflexes which comprise the following groups (p. 9):

> "(1) reflexes concerned with assimilation of necessary materials (inspiratory and ingestive reflexes); (2) reflexes concerned with excretion of waste or unused materials (expiration, urination, defecation); (3) reflexes concerned with recuperation (sleep); (4) reflexes concerned with preservation of species (copulation, bearing progeny, and nurture of progeny)."

2. *"Protective drives"* – and the unconditioned protective reflexes, which include (pp. 9–10):

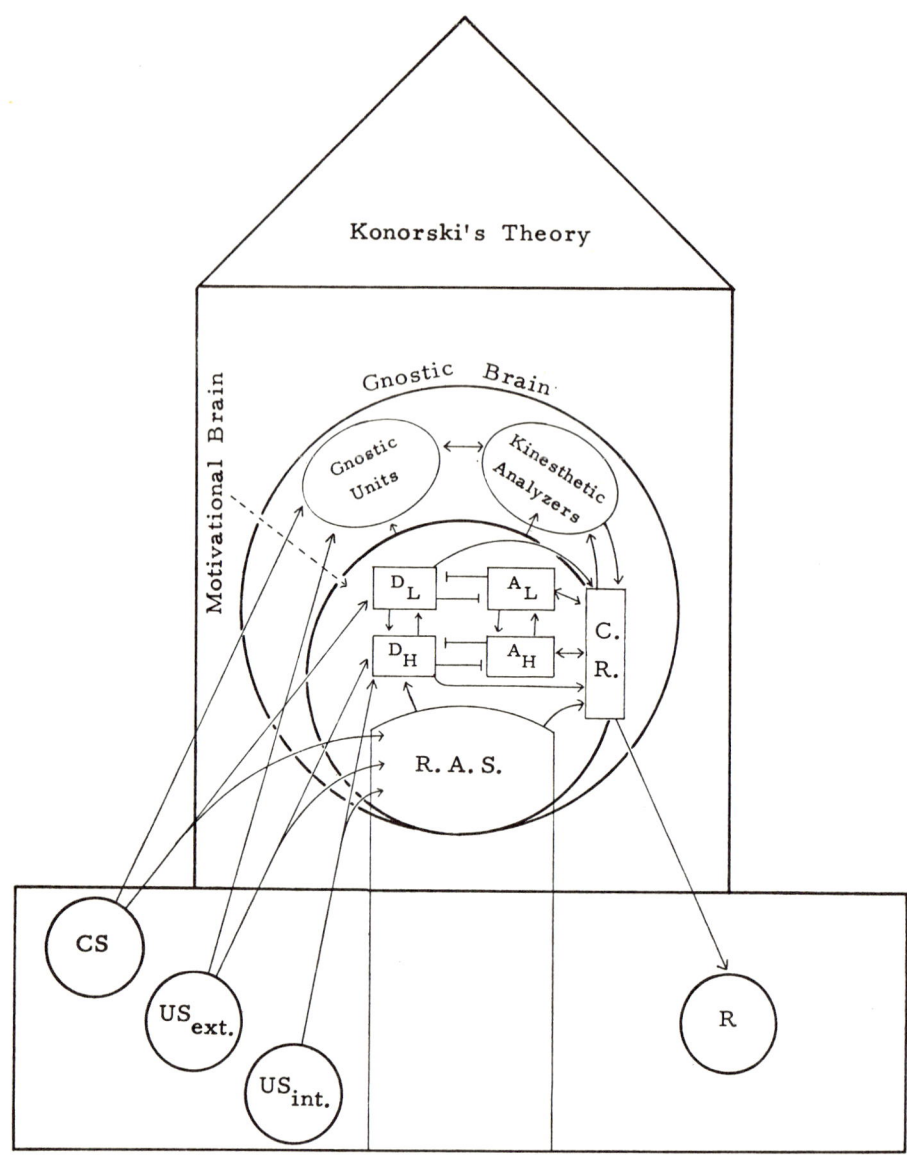

Fig. 7.3. Diagram of Konorski's theory. This diagram represents our summary of Konorski's theory. Behavior (R) is directly determined by the center for *consummatory reflexes* (C. R.). This center is influenced by processes in the *gnostic brain,* which includes both the gnostic units and the kinesthetic analyzers. The C. R. are also influenced by the *motivational brain,* comprising the Reticular System (RAS), the hypothalamus and the limbic system. This motivational brain contains the *drive centers* as well as the *anti-drive centers*. These two categories of drive centers are located on two levels: the *hypothalamic* (D_H and A_H in the figure) and the *limbic* (D_L and A_L). The hypothalamic level is influenced by the unconditioned stimuli, both internal ($US_{int.}$) while the limbic level is influenced by the conditioned stimuli (CS). All the external stimuli influence the gnostic units. There is considerable feedback and interaction between the different centers, but everything cannot be represented in this rough model.

"(1) reflexes concerned with the withdrawal of the whole body or any part from the operation of a noxious or endangering stimulus (retractive or retreat reflexes); (2) reflexes concerned with the rejection of harmful agents from the surface of, or inside, the body (rejective reflexes); (3) reflexes concerned with annihilating or disarming harmful agents (offensive reflexes)."

As was already obvious from the summary section Konorski concentrates his exposition on two drives: the *hunger* drive as representive of the preservative drives, and the *fear* drive as representative of the protective drives. As we have reproduced his instructive "block models" of the hunger drive and the fear drive, we shall not go into further detail concerning them.

We have decided to select another drive, the exploratory drive (or curiosity), for a more detailed presentation.

Konorski distinguishes between the *preparatory, searching behavior* and the *consummatory, targeting reflexes*. As drives generally are defined as "the controlling mechanisms of the *preparatory* activities" (p. 57), the drive corresponding to the preparatory, searching behavior is called *curiosity* or the "exploratory drive". It may be interesting for the reader to compare his hypothesis about curiosity with Berlyne's theory. Therefore, we quote from Konorski (p. 37):

"A prolonged absence of any variegated stimuli acting upon the respective surfaces is known to be hardly endurable for the organism; thus these stimuli are almost as necessary for its well-being as is food or water. If this is true, we may assign exploratory behavior to the category of preservative activities; and in consequence look for some internal (humoral) factors which would regulate it. It may be tentatively postulated that neurons of all afferent systems are, in the normal condition in an active state because they are "nourished" by the external stimuli impinging upon them. If these stimuli are lacking – that is, when there is a "hunger" for external stimulation – a hypothetical "exploration system" in the brain is thrown into action which tends to increase exploratory behavior and thus to restore a *sui generis* homeostasis of the sensory systems."

He also has some hypotheses about the central localization of the exploratory drive mechanism. Thus he writes (p. 38):

"Finally, the problem of the central mechanism governing the curiosity reflexes is still poorly understood. We do not know whether the controlling mechanism for curiosity is represented on the hypothalamic level, but we have good evidence of its existence on the cortical level. In fact, one of the striking effects of frontal lobotomy in man is precisely the decrease, or even loss, of curiosity with total preservation of targetting reflexes."

A summary of his hypothesis about curiosity is presented in connection with a block diagram, Fig. II–18, which we present here (as our Fig. 7.4.).

After this more detailed presentation of Konorski's motivational concepts we are ready for the systematological analysis proper.

2.1.1. *The surplus meaning of the H-terms*. It is obvious that most of Konorski's H-terms have a *physiological* surplus meaning, so obvious, that it is perhaps very important to underline that these terms are *hypothetical* terms, and not descriptive terms borrowed from psychology.

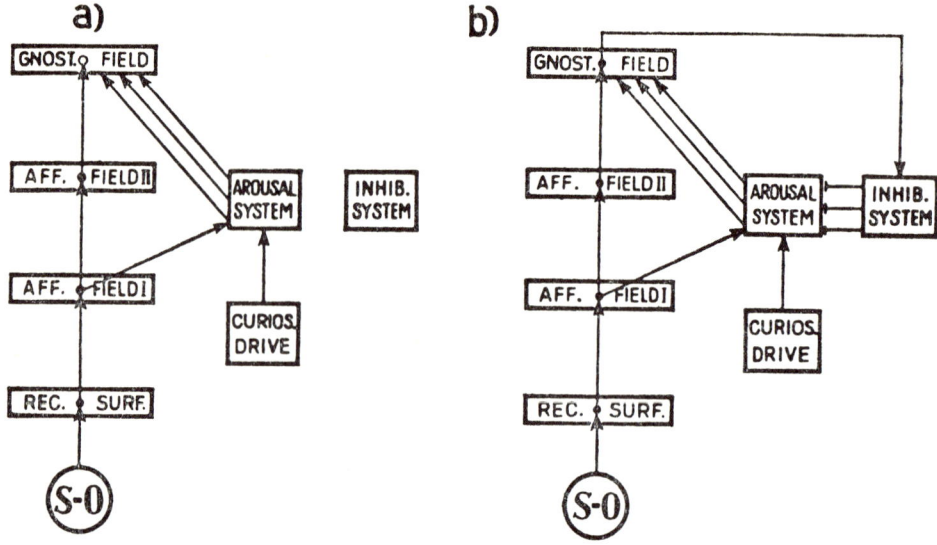

Fig. 7.4. The hypothetical mechanism of habituation

a) The operation of a *new* stimulus-object. The stimulus activates successively: particular elements of the receptive surface, particular units of the first order receptive field, particular units of the second order receptive field and hence the messages converge on some potential gnostic units of the gnostic field. Units of the first order receptive field (or of another central structure) fire to the unspecific arousal system which increases the excitability of the gnostic field. The joint action of the specific and unspecific impulses upon this field enables the formation of appropriate gnostic units.

b) The operation of the *known* stimulus-object. The original course of events is the same as in (a). The messages from the specific and unspecific systems rearch the appropriate gnostic units and produce the perception of the stimulus-object. These gnostic units send impulses to the unspecific inhibitory system (or rather one of its parts), which suppresses the corresponding part of the arousal system, and in this way the perception of the stimulus-object is momentarily stopped. In consequence, the flow of impulses from the gnostic units to the inhibitory system ceases and another perception instigated by the curiosity drive can take place.

But not all his terms have a physiological surplus meaning. "Emotion" is different from the other motivational terms. This is most clearly expressed in the following passage (p. 57):

"The controlling mechanisms of the preparatory activities are called *drives*, and their psychological counterparts are called *emotions.*"

We think it is correct to interpret this in such a way that "emotion" is an H-term with a *phenomenological* surplus meaning. This is a consequence of Konorski's application of the introspective data.

2.1.2. *Dispositional or functional terms?* It is a little more difficult to classify Konorski's terms (and variables) according to the duration of the existence of the variable. Is "drive" a disposition *or* a function? We think that the right answer is that his "drive" represents both a disposition *and* a function.

Thus in a passage previously quoted (p. 57) we found that "the controlling mechanisms of the preparatory activities are called *drives*." And this can be interpreted in such a way that "drive" denotes a *disposition* (a structure or "mechanism"). But at the first point where the term "drive" is introduced we find this (p. 41):

"The nervous *processes* controlling the basic preparatory activities - - - - - - will be called *drives*" (italics added).

We believe that in this case it is just as correct to interpret "drive" as a *function* ("process").

Our conclusion, therefore, must be that *Konorski uses the term "drive" in a double meaning*, sometimes referring to the "drive *mechanism*" (a disposition variable), and sometimes to the "drive *process*" (a function variable).

The same is true for the parallel term "antidrive". But we think that the word "emotion" is exclusively a *function* term.

2.1.3. *Dynamic, directive or vector terms?* This systematological classification is easier to apply to Konorski's H-terms than the above.

Thus in one of the quotations presented earlier it was explicitly stated that drives "have mainly facilitatory character in respect to both afferent and efferent systems" (p. 509). We interpret the word "facilitatory" as being equal to "general activating" or "dynamic". This conception is supported by another clear and concentrated formulation found in the "summary and conclusion" (p. 57):

"The effects of almost all drives are: motor hyperactivity (which we call arousal of the motor behavioral system); increased motor efficiency; arousal of particular afferent systems, probably mediated by the unspecific thalamic nuclei; and increased tonus of the sympathetic system."

As the reader has undoubtedly noticed the word "arousal" is used twice in this quotation – as well as many times in other places – and this term is usually employed in modern psychology to designate a general activating or *dynamic* effect on behavior. Therefore, we think that it is correct to classify "drive" as well as "antidrive" and "emotion" as *dynamic terms* (and variables).

For the sake of completeness we should like to supplement this classification by pointing to the other variables having a *directive* function on behavior according to Konorski's theory.

"Perception" and the corresponding "gnostic units" have a purely *directive* function. The same is true of the *consummatory* reflexes, which we have not yet dealt with in detail. But in this connection let us look at this passage (from p. 56), which defines their function:

"Innate consummatory activities, both preservative and protective, are generally referred to as unconditioned reflexes (URs). They are in operation when the stimulus eliciting the given activity is present and the organism reacts to it in the appropriate way."

Thus the *consummatory* activities are preceded by the preparatory activities, which contain the necessary "arousal", also for the consummatory reflexes.

The *preparatory* reflex systems, on the other hand, contain *both* functions (effects). Thus the *dynamic* effect is determined by the *central* controlling processes and mechanisms referred to as "drives", and the *directive* effect is determined by the *afferent* and *efferent* parts of the total reflex system. We consequently believe that it is correct to classify the whole preparatory reflex system as a vector variable (while the "drive" component of this variable is a dynamic variable).

Before going to the next section concerning "hypotheses" let us summarize our classification of the H-terms (and corresponding variables) in Konorsky's theory by means of a combined classificatory scheme (Table 1).

Effect / Existence	Dynamic terms	Vector terms	Directive terms
Disposition terms	»Drive-mechanisms«	»Preparatory reflex centers«	»Gnostic units« »Consummatory reflex centers«
Function terms	»Drive-processes« Emotions	»Preparatory Activities«	»Perception« »Consummatory activities«

Table 7.0. Classification of the main H-terms and their corresponding variables in Konorsky's theory.

2.2. Classifications of the hypotheses

In the previous sections we have analyzed the single H-terms and variables in Konorsky's theory. We shall therefore concentrate now on the *hypotheses* formulating the *relationships* between the variables. The most explicit formulations of hypotheses are found in the "summary and conclusions" ending every chapter and in the final summarizing chapter, where we find nearly fifty implicit formulations of hypotheses.

In this section we shall concentrate on the motivational hypotheses. First, we shall present the hypotheses and later analyze them.

The main hypotheses about the *interaction between drives* are summarized in the following manner (p. 58).

"The interrelations between various drives and between drives and antidrives obey, in principle, the following rules:
(1) There is a mutual antagonism between each drive and a corresponding antidrive.
(2) Different drives, whether preservative or protective are in mutual antagonistic relation – that is, when a particular drive is in operation, it tends to inhibit all other drives if none of them is stronger than the active one.
(3) If a given drive is satisfied and the antidrive comes into operation, it may facilitate the operation of other drives if the relevant stimuli eliciting them are present."

The relationships between *drives and their antecedent conditions* are perhaps best summarized in the following quotation (pp. 42–43):

"On the other hand, the receptive side of the emotive system is quite different. First, as indicated earlier, the intracentral chemoreceptive surface in the hypothalamus plays a most important role in eliciting preservative drive reflexes and possibly an auxiliary role in protective drive reflexes. Second, in those instances when exteroceptive stimuli serve to elicit drive reflexes, this is accomplished by their "protophalhic" (emotionally tinted) aspect, different anatomically and functionally from their "epicritic" aspect in cognitive reflexes."

Finally, we present the main hypotheses about *drives and their consequences* – especially their relationships with *consummatory activities* (as we have already dealt with the more general "arousal" effect of drives). The most explicit formulations about these relationships are found on pp. 48–49:

"To sum up our considerations, we offer the following statements.
(1) Every drive reflex, connected with either preservative or protective activity, produces a facilitation of the corresponding consummatory reflex.
(2) Whereas the preservative consummatory reflex during its action exerts an inhibitory effect upon the drive reflex, the defensive consummatory reflex does not.
(3) After the consummatory UR is terminated, the appropriate drive UR is in operation. In preservative reflexes it is released by the aftereffect of the consummatory US, but in the defensive reflexes it outlasts the operation of this US."

We believe that these passages from Konorski's book represent the most explicitly formulated hypotheses in his theory, and so we now turn to the systematological analyses proper.

2.2.1. Basic classification of the hypotheses. Before we can make the basic classification of hypotheses, we must make our partially *symbolic reformulations.* We shall concentrate on the motivational hypotheses and a few other main hypotheses which were quoted in the above sections. Thus we get the following reformulated hypotheses.

1. hypothesis: S(humorals) → H(drive)
2. hypothesis: S(protopathic) → H(drive)
3. hypothesis: S(conditioned stimuli) → H(drive)

4. hypothesis: S(humorals) → H(anti-drive)
5. hypothesis: S(unconditioned) → H(anti-drive)
6. hypothesis: S(conditioned) → H(anti-drive)
7. hypothesis: S(epicritic) → H(perception)
8. hypothesis: S(UCS + CS) → H(classical conditioning)
9. hypothesis: S(reinforcing) → H(instrumental conditioning)
10. hypothesis: S(kinesthetic) → H(motor programming)
11. hypothesis: H(increased drives) → H(decreased other drives)
12. hypothesis: H(increased drive$_1$) → H(decreased anti-drive$_1$)
13. hypothesis: H(decreased drive$_1$) → H(increased anti-drive$_1$) → H(increased other drives)
14. hypothesis: H(drive) → H(motor arousal)
15. hypothesis: H(drive) → H(perceptual arousal)
16. hypothesis: H(anti-drive) → H(motor relaxation)
17. hypothesis: H(anti-drive) → H(perceptual indifference)
18. hypothesis: H(drive) → R(consummatory)
19. hypothesis: H(drive) → R(autonomic)
20. hypothesis: H(perception × motor programming × drive) → R(performance)

On the basis of this *systematic reconstruction* we can make the basic classification of hypotheses:

1. *Purely theoretical hypotheses (H-H):*
   Hypotheses No. 11 to 17 incl.
   In all: 7 hypotheses.
2. *Partly empirical hypotheses:*
   a. S-H hypotheses: No. 1 to 10 incl.
      In all: 10 hypotheses.
   b. H-R-hypotheses: No. 18 to 20 incl.
      In all: 3 hypotheses.

In conclusion we wish to emphasize that many of Konorski's H-H-hypotheses are in fact very strongly confirmed by neurophysiological data. Perhaps so strongly founded empirically that many people would classify them as purely empirical hypotheses. But we still think that from a psychological systematological point-of-view they are most correctly classified as H-H-hypotheses.

2.2.2. *The complexity of the hypotheses*. It is not so easy to classify Konorski's hypotheses as being *one-dimensioned or multidimensional*. After a first inspection of the formulations quoted above one perhaps would classify the hypotheses as *one-dimentional*. But after studying his "block models" (or diagrams) it would seem logical to classify them as *multidimensional*.

We think that it is most fair to Konorski and most in accordance with our systematological taxonomy to judge his theory from the block models, which are far more formally developed than the largely implicit hypotheses. Thus our conclusion is that his theory is a *multidimensional theory*.

2.2.3. *The functional relationships in the hypotheses.* Finally, we should classify Konorski's hypotheses according to the presupposed conception of the functional relationship between the variables.

We have not found any explicit formulation about this problem, but we think that all the (implicit) hypotheses, as well as the block models, indirectly presuppose *deterministic, functional relationships* between the variables. This is also in accordance with "classical" natural science metatheory implicitly accepted by Pavlov as well as modern neuropsychologists.

We have finished our analysis of the hypothetical stratum of Konorski's theory and now turn to the descriptive stratum.

The descriptive stratum

3.0. *Introduction*

The D-level of Konorski's text is by far the most extensively and explicitly formulated. But we must remember that we only analyze a small part of the theory in detail, that dealing with drives. There is just as much about perception as motivation and much more about conditioning and learning in general. And this is especially true about the D-level.

We can roughly divide the D-level into two sub-levels, the *abstract* and the *concrete*.

3.1. *The abstract D-level*

This is the part of the D-level containing "empirical laws" and abstract descriptive terms.

3.1.1. *The general descriptive propositions.* The "empirical laws" or rather the description of general, functional relationships between S- and R-variables are especially to be found in the part of the book dealing with conditioning. We shall only select a few to give a representative impression of Konorski's theory.

Thus we found some empirical laws about *"classical* conditioning", or "type I CR", summarized in this way (pp. 290–91):

"Extensive experience with salivary CRs has led to the establishment of the following rules determining the relation between the character of the CS and the magnitude of the conditioned response.
 (a) Other things being equal, the greater the physical strength of the CS (measured in decibels, candles, pressure, and the like), the larger the conditioned response to it.

(b) "Rough" CSs (that is, of irregularly changing intensity) produce a larger CR effect than monotonous CSs, and intermittent CSs produce a larger effect than continuous CSs. The higher the frequency of the intermittent stimulus, the stronger is the effect.

(c) Auditory stimuli (tones, buzzers, and so on) usually produce stronger CR effects than visual stimuli (lamps) and tactile stimuli (rhythmic touch of the body).

(d) Very strong auditory stimuli produce a lower effect than strong ones, at least in alimentary CSs.

(e) According to my own experience, CRs closely related in space with the US produce a larger effect than more remote CSs (contiguity principle)."

Konorski has experimented very much with the *"transformation" of CRs* and revised Pavlov's theory of "inhibition", which he substitutes with a theory about *"formation of new connections"*. In connection with this he formulates the following empirical laws (p. 344):

"It follows from these assumptions that the so-called extinction of a CR is nothing but the substitution of a new reinforcement for the old one (in that case no-US for US) and thus follows the general rules of "transformations" of CRs. These rules are as follows.

(1) Each "transformation" of a CR into the antagonistic one, whether alimentary-defensive CR transformation or positive-negative CR transformation, encounters a certain resistance owing to the fact that the formation of new connections leading from the CS units to the new US units and the new drive units is handicapped by strong excitation of the old US units and the old drive units elicited by that CS.

(2) On the contrary, the restoration of the previous CR is a much easier process, because the old connections on which this CR is built are already there and the reverse training consists only in establishing their relative dominance over the connections with the antagonistic units."

Konorski is one of the first psychologists in the East or West who has experimented with "instrumental conditioning", or *"type II CR"*, as it is also called. On the basis of his own and others' experiments he summarized the following empirical laws (p. 389):

"By type II CRs we have called those CRs in which the movement is performed in response to a given stimulus, because by its performance the animal procures an attractive US such as food (US$^+$) or avoids an aversive US such as the introduction of acid into the mouth or an air puff into the ear (US$^-$).

We have specified four varieties of experimental procedure by which type II CRs are obtained. They are as follows.

(1) If an external stimulus S_E accompanied by a movement M is reinforced by US$^+$ whereas S_E alone is not, then the animal learns to perform this movement in the presence of the external stimulus ($S_E \to M$).

(2) If an external stimulus S_E accompanied by a movement M is reinforced by US$^-$ whereas S_E alone is not, then the animal learns to resist the provocation of this movement by performing the antagonistic movement ($S_E \to \sim M$).

(3) If an external stimulus S_E is reinforced by US$^+$ whereas S_E is accompanied by movement M is not, then the animal learns to resist the provocation of this movement by performing the antagonistic movement ($S_E \to \sim M$).

(4) If an external stimulus S_E is reinforced by US$^-$ whereas S_E accompanied by M is not, then the animal learns to perform this movement in the presence of the external stimulus ($S_E \to M$).

3.1.2. *The abstract descriptive terms.* In connection with all the empirical laws presented here there are implicit definitions and classifications of *abstract descriptive terms* – such as "type I CR" and "type II CR".

In the field of "drives" there are no empirical laws other than "theoretical laws" (or rather hypotheses), which we have already analyzed. But there are some *definitions and classifications* of abstract, descriptive terms, which we must present in order to complete our exposition of Konorski's theory.

These are the "Categories of basic activities of the nervous system" (p. 8), or rather the classification of *observable behavior* related to the "unconditioned reflexes".

Before presenting this it is necessary to introduce explicit distinctions between terms – distinctions which we heretofore have used implicitly. The term "reflexes" in his theory is used as a common term for:

1. *the hypothetical, central "reflex-centers" and the processes going on in these centers,* and
2. *the observable reflex-activity (or behavior).*

The following classification is primarily concerned with the reflex-activities, which may be classified according to *two principles:*

Reflex-activities can be divided according to *biological role* into *preservative* and *protective reflexes*. We have previously presented examples of these reflexes.

Reflex-activities can also be divided according to *sequence* into *preparatory* reflexes and *consummatory* reflexes, which we have also dealt with in detail previously.

These two classifications of reflex-activities can be combined into one classification scheme, which Konorski has done in his Table I–1 (p. 10), which we present here:

Classification of basic activities of organisms

preservative preparatory	preservative consummatory
protective preparatory	protective consummatory

Table 7.1.

After having presented the most important empirical laws and classifications of abstract, descriptive terms, we turn to the next sub-level of the descriptive stratum.

3.2. *The concrete D-level*

This sub-level contains descriptions of singular events, the so-called "protocol sentences".

Konorski's book contains many detailed descriptions of his experiments – besides summaries of others' experiments. The most extensive descriptions of experiments are found in the chapters about "instrumental conditioned reflexes (type II)". Thus in Chapter 8 twenty-five experiments are described. It is, of course, impossible to repeat these descriptions here. The main results are summarized in the previously quoted empirical laws and in the hypotheses.

It only remains to state that Konorski in these experiments for the most part uses *behavioral data* from animal experiments, while in other chapters he also makes use of *physiological* and *introspective data*. This is all consistent with his metapropositions which we analyzed in the first part of the chapter.

3.3. *The descriptive units*

There remains but one systematological classification of the D-level: Which descriptive units has Konorski employed? Although his theory integrates a wealth of data from many sources – as we have just seen – it seems fair to classify the preferred descriptive units as being rather *molecular*. Thus we find that Konorski's theory is one of the most molecular theories we have in this collection..

The theory as a whole

We conclude our analysis of Konorski's theory by classifying it as a whole.

4.1. *The formal properties*

4.1.1. *The systematic organization*. As the reader may have observed, Konorski's theory is not a deductive theory. On the other hand it is not an explanatory "sketch", because there are many explicit and systematically organized propositions – especially in the "summary and conclusion" sections of every chapter. Although there are not any explicit hypotheses with numbers, etc., we think that it is most correct to classify Konorski's theory as an *explanatory system*.

4.1.2. *The preciseness of representation*. The immediate impression one receives on Konorski's theory is that it is very precise. But after closer inspection and a little reflection it is obvious that this theory is not a mathematical theory and no other (non-mathematical) symbols are used. Therefore it is a *purely verbal theory*. The impression of preciseness is undoubtedly created by the extensive use of diagrams, which we shall deal with in the next section.

4.1.3. *The properties of the models.*
As mentioned above Konorski makes extensive use of many elaborate diagrams, which he calls "block-models". Thus they are *two-dimensional models*, and they are the most precise and systematic two-dimensional models we have found among the psychological theories we have investigated.

4.2. *The epistemological properties of the theory*
It is very easy to classify Konorski's theory as to category or type as a *physiological, explanatory or S-O-R theory*. Thanks to the very sophisticated use of highly developed "block-models" it is clear that he himself also conceives of his theory as a physiological explanatory theory using *constructs* rather than a "reductive" or somewhat physiological, descriptive theory. As mentioned in connection with the analysis of the metastratum, the present author has not found a clearer exposition of a theory of this type than Konorski's.

4.3. *The theory-empiry ratio*
The general impression one receives from Konorski's theory would lead one to classify it as a rather *empiristic* theory. On the basis of our systematic reconstruction made in section 2.2.1. we have calculated the Hypotheses Quotient by means of the formula:

$$\text{H.Q.} = \frac{\Sigma(H-H)}{\Sigma[(S-H)+(H-R)]} = \frac{7}{10+3} = \frac{7}{13} = 0.54$$

This is a higher H.Q. than we would have expected from our general impression of Konorski's book. But perhaps we have classified some variables as hypothetical which are really empirical.

Conclusion. The present author has not tried to hide his highly positive evaluation of Konorski's theory. But in spite of this we hope that our neutral systematological taxonomy has made it possible to treat his theory in a satisfactory scientific manner, and besides create an interest for this theory, which is an integration of the best from the East and the West.

8 : Pribram's Theory

Introduction

The work of the American neuropsychologist, *Karl H. Pribram* (born 1919) is of special interest for the metascientist. Pribram has made many experiments in the border area between psychology and the neuro-sciences. It was in the latter area he had his original education and experience. Furthermore, he has integrated his experimental results from neuropsychology with ideas borrowed from another interdisciplinary field, that of information theory and cybernetics. (See especially: Miller, Galanter and Pribram, 1960). Finally Pribram has been interested in the philosophy of science more than is usual for experimental workers in the natural sciences.

The results of Pribram's highly integrative work have until recently been scattered in numerous papers and chapters in handbooks. But now it is easier to study his work as he has collected many of his papers and chapters – together with those of other authors – in a four volume "readings" under the title: *"Brain and Behaviour"* (1969).

Furthermore, Pribram has now presented his whole general psychological theory in one book, *"Languages of the Brain"* (1971), which has been the main source for this metascientific study, although we have also found many interesting formulations – especially about the metastratum – in other sources (which are listed at the end of this chapter)[1]).

The metastratum

1.1. *Philosophical propositions*

As already indicated Pribram has shown great interest in the philosophical presuppositions of neuropsychology and has formulated the results of his investigations very clearly and explicitly.

Pribram has made an explicit statement regarding his *epistemological* theory – most specifically in a chapter called: "Proposals for a Structural Pragmatism" (Pribram, 1965 – here quoted from Pribram, 1969).

---

1. At the moment of writing this chapter Pribram's book had not yet been published. The present study was made on the basis of a pre-publication stencilled copy which Pribram was kind enough to send me. The book appeared in September 1971. We have made some supplementary comments in the last section of this Chapter.

Pragmatic philosophy is selected as the guiding philosophy of science based on the following arguments (from Pribram, 1969, Vol. I, p. 13):

"[Pragmatism is] first, a method; and second, a genetic theory of what is meant by truth (James, 1931, p. 65). Seen as a compromise between the tough-minded empiricist and the tender minded rationalist, pragmatism has maintained the tough spirit in its methods and the tender heart in its aims".

Pribram conceives of pragmatism as a kind of "radical empirism". But pragmatism – contrary to operational logical positivism – contains a genetic theory of truth which regards theories as *instruments*, and therefore Pribram prefers pragmatism. He adds the label "structural" to his version of pragmatism because the concept of "structure" has been so important in the modern natural sciences. After quoting Eddington for support in this matter he continues (Vol. I, p. 17, 1969):

"That is why a *structural* pragmatism. The issue of structure is, of course, implicit in the examination of the mind-brain problem viewed as the relation between psychological and neurological science."

Thus it is obvious that there is an intimate relationship between Pribram's epistemology and his *theory of the psychophysiological problem*. This theory is expounded in several places. Thus Pribram writes (in 1969, Vol. IV, p. 494):

"Once levels of discourse are recognized as such, and the potentialities and limitations of communication between them are accepted, the only recourse is to a truly monistic seemingly pluralistic, multilevel *structural* mindbrain."

In defending this theory Pribram makes a hard attack on the *dualistic* theories, about which he says (Pribram 1962, p. 152):

"Nor is the classical dualistic frame more than a giving-up. For aside from the paucity of empirically precise data soundly systematized, the most important deterrent to fruitful inquiring into the relation between psychology and neurology has been philosophic dualism."

But Pribram also attacks the *"identity theory"* – the analytical philosopher's version of neutral monism – about which he writes (Pribram, 1971, Chapter 20, pp. 377–78):[2])

"The dilemma of the identity theorist is therefore that he can never reach that which is assumed identical without construction which entails an additional language, an additional aspect which though it may subsume others can never become itself identical with them. The identity theorist thus ends up as a pluralist, identity remaining an unachieved goal."

Although Pribram is very explicit in his criticism of the alternative theories it should be clear – also from these quotations – that his own theory can be

---

2. The page numbers refer to the printed edition of "Languages of the Brain" (1971). As there were only a few changes in wording between the original stencilled version and the printed book we have retained the former.

described as a kind of *"pluralistic, multi-level structuralism"*. This description underlines his tendency to emphasize the fact that there are *several levels of discourses* in psychology (the phenomenological and the behavioral) and in the neurosciences (the brain, the neurons and the molecules), but these different discourses can refer to the same *structure* of events. Thus Pribram's pluralistic theory is basicly *neutral monistic*. And this monistic theory concerning the psychophysical problem is logically related to his metatheory.

1.2. Metatheoretical propositions

Pribram is also very thorough and explicit in his discussion of metatheoretical problems (in the narrow sense). Thus in Pribram (1962) he writes about neuropsychology:

"By definition, neuropsychology is a reductive discipline" (p. 121).

But by this statement he is not referring to the old-fashioned "reductive" theory – rather to the role of neuropsychology as an *integrative discipline between* psychology and neurophysiology. Pribram's whole output makes it obvious that he conceives of neuropsychology as an integrative discipline which can only achieve its goals by making *constructive* theories which use *models* in order to explain the collected and systematized data from the two neighboring fields. Thus he writes (in Pribram, 1962) on p. 148:

"Models are practically always used (implicitly or explicitly) to subsume any fairly extensive body of data; at different stages of the science, different levels of precision in models are possible and useful in generating testable hypotheses".

The important role played by models in science is further stressed by Pribram in a paper in which he points out the similarities between his own neuropsychological theory and the pragmatic theory of knowledge created by C. S. Peirce. He has touched on this in an unpublished paper presented at the Second Banff Conference on Theoretical Psychology, 1969.

"To modify Peirce's theory of meaning to this extent is to give primacy to his abductive form of reasoning; hypothesis formation by analogy as against reasoning by deduction or induction. In science abduction takes the form of modeling."

As it will be clear for the reader after the presentation of the hypotheses of Pribram's theory later in this chapter, there is an unusually beautiful and logical consistency in his epistemology, his metatheory and the hypotheses of his own psychological theory.

1.3. Methodological propositions

Pribram has summarized his basic attitude to methodological problems by adopting the label *"subjective behaviorism"*, which was a name born as the result of the team-vork involved in the production of *"Plans and the Structure of Be-*

havior" (see Miller, Galanter and Pribram, 1960). Thus he writes (in Pribram, 1962, p. 153):

"This approach, dubbed psychological or subjective behaviorism, reaffirms that a recently neglected subject matter for a scientific and experimental psychology is after all appropriate – the study of man by man."

The meaning of "subjective behaviorism" is further elaborated in the following quotation (Pribram, 1962, p. 123):

"This approach to the relation between psychology and neurology places emphasis on a laboratory analysis of problems that are often initially posed introspectively."

Thus introspection may be the starting point for a neuropsychological experiment, but it can also be conceived of as the final check-point, as indicated in the following quotation (Pribram, 1971, Chapter 5, p. 100):

"My own procedure is to classify by non-behavioral means separate categories of organismic and environmental circumstances as independent variables. I then consider the interactions between these classes as expressed in behavior. From this constellation I *infer* psychological processes and examine their similarities and dissimilarities to subjective processes. When the fit appears right I use mental language."

This quotation illustrates that Pribram uses behavioral, physiological and phenomenological (introspective) *data*. On the basis of these data he *constructs* his hypotheses regarding psychological processes designated by mentalistic language. In our systematological taxonomy this means that he should use hypothetical terms with *mentalistic* surplus meaning (H_M-variables). We shall later return to the hypothetical terms actually used by Pribram and see if they really are H_M-terms.

Before leaving this section we should like to emphasize that Pribram makes use of a broad range of methods. He not only uses introspection, behavioral methods and physiological methods, but advocates all kinds of neurophysiological methods: electrophysiological as well as neurosurgical. He was educated as a neurosurgeon and makes operations on both human and animal subjects. Most of his experiments are made with monkeys, but they are often initiated by observation of human patients (including these subjects' introspective rapport).

The hypothetical stratum

2.0. *Summary of the hypotheses*

According to Pribram's theory there are three main types of hypothetical variables, which he calls *"images"*:

1. "Images of Events" (approximately equal to "perception").
2. "Monitor Images" (approximately equal to "feeling"), and
3. "Images of Achievement" (approximately equal to "plans" or "intentions").

Images of Events are the prime results of the brain's "coding of information". Thus Pribram formulates his basic hypothesis in this way (Pribram, 1971, Preface):

"The systems approach has shown the brain to be an organ superbly fitted to organize and reorganize its own activity, i.e., to make codes. It codes experience, transforms this coded representation into another form and in turn, re-recodes whatever becomes available in terms of new experiences. The function of the brain is to process and reprocess information just as it is the function of the liver to process and reprocess metabolites. The brain is thus a prime i nstrument for the production of languages, even a language to describe itself." 2a.

The basic neural mechanism for this coding activity is the interaction of excitatory and inhibitory states in neurons (analogous to the off- and on-states of the electronic components of a computer). Patterns of such excitatory and inhibitory states are examples of the brain's coding of information, and the result is the "image" of the events in the outer world. This image is "projected" on the association cortex which functions like a receiving "screen". This screen is not a passive receptor but rather an active modifier of the received information in accordance with previously stored information. Pribram has developed a model of the image, a so-called "hologram", to which we shall return at a later time.

Monitor Images are the neural representations of the state of the organism. They have their origin in neural receptors in the hypothalamus in the same way that the Images of Events have their origin in external sense receptors. These Monitor Images denote the feelings of states like hunger and emotion. Therefore, these images – together with the third form – have an intimate relationship to "motivation", as this concept is conceived of in most theories. We shall therefore return to a more detailed analysis of this later.

Images of Achievement is the third form of images. These images are reural representations on the motor cortex of "learned anticipations of the force and change in force required to perform a task" (Chapter 13, p. 250, Pribram, 1971).

These three categories of hypothetical variables determine behavior: Image of Achievement has the directing and organizing function (much like "Plans" in Miller, Galanter and Pribram, 1960). This directing function is assisted by the Image of Events which processes the necessary information to adapt the plans and behavior to the environment. The dynamic or activating function is mainly carried out by the Monitor Image which provides the "values" which are important for the goal-setting of behavior.

To this interplay of images the complete theory also includes hypotheses about memory, learning and reinforcement as well as about language.

We have made a diagram representing a rough summary of Pribram's theory (Fig. 8.1.).

2a. This passage was *not* retained in the printed edition, but we have kept it here, because it expresses a very basic assumption in Pribram's theory.

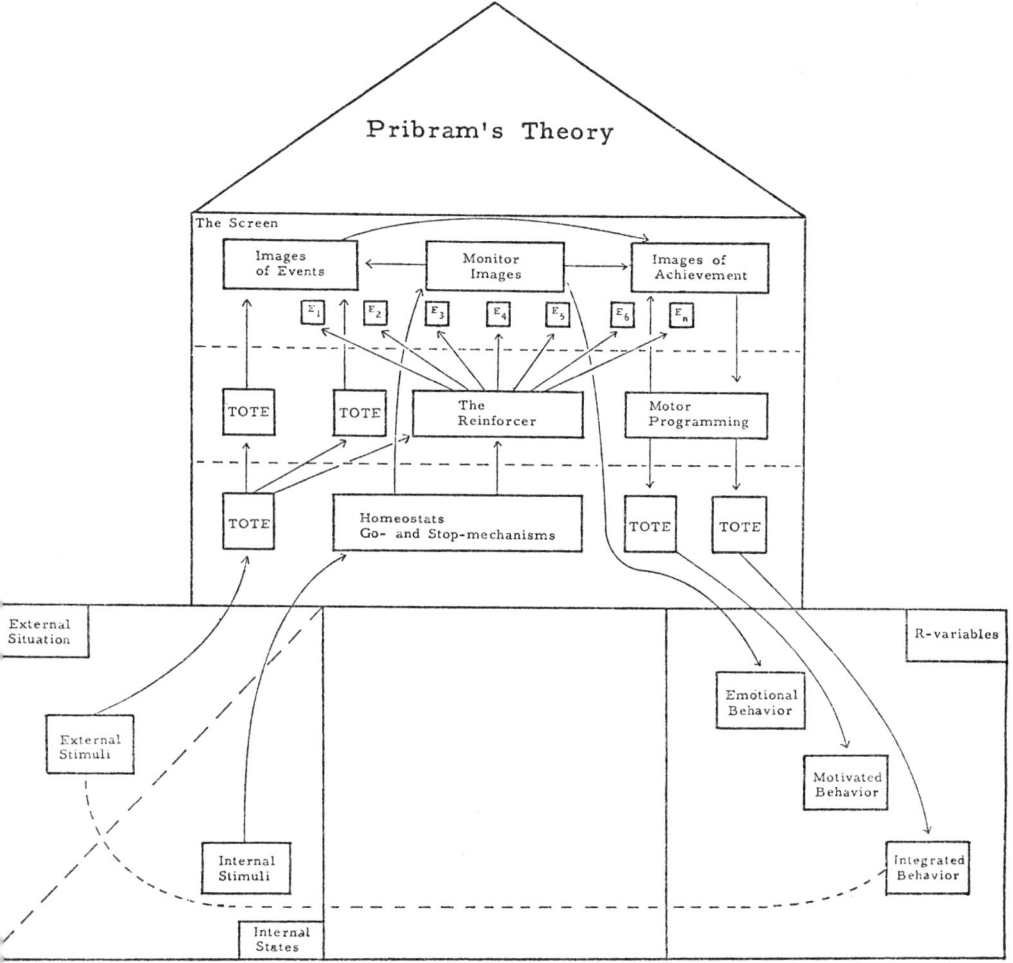

Fig. 8.1. A Diagram representing a rough summary of Pribram's theory.

2.1. *The hypothetical terms*

We now turn to the more detailed analysis of the H-terms in Pribram's theory.

Before making the systematological analyses of the main H-terms, we ought to define them.

The basic mechanism of the *Image of Events* (or "I.E.") is the "TOTE", a construct borrowed from Miller, Galanter and Pribram (1960). This construct is analogous to a servomechanism with feedback in a computer. This hypothetical mechanism is a "Test-Operate-Test-Exit mechanism", which functions in this way: an *input* from a receptor cell (or other neural component) is *tested* (i. e., compared with a pre-established standard). If the test results in *incongruence* between input and standard then an *operation* (a behavioral act or other activity) is performed, and the new input is fed back and *tested*. If *congruence* has been achieved then the process "exits" out of the mechanism. We can represent the whole construct by the following diagrams (Fig. 8.2. and Fig. 8.3.):

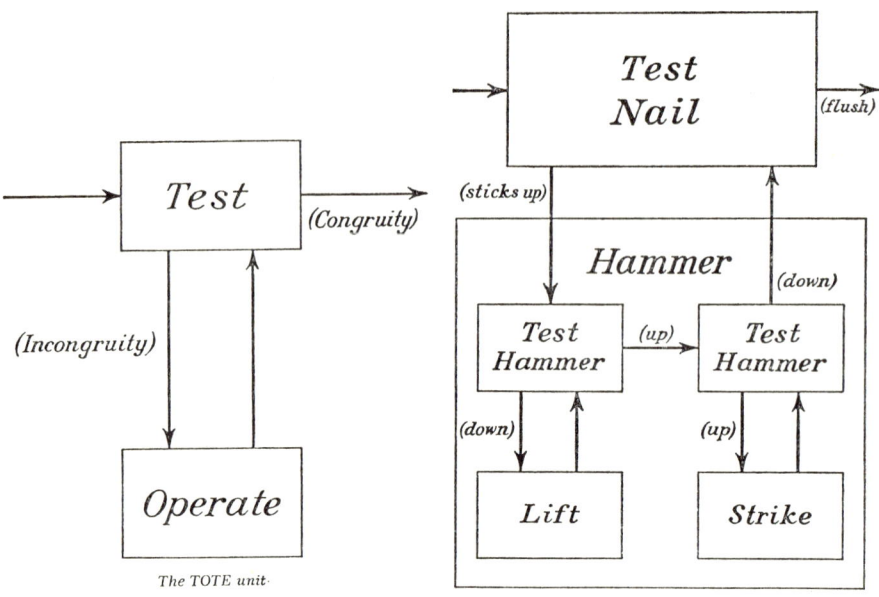

Fig. 8.2. Plans and the Structure of Behavior.

Fig. 8.3. The hierarchical Plan for hammering nails.

Pribram writes in a summarizing section about the TOTE (Chapter 5, p. 95, Pribram 1971):

Part I has been concerned with bringing together a wealth of disparate facts about the brain and its control of behavior into some simplified scheme that can serve as an anchor for further thought and exploration. The scheme adopted is the TOTE, a logic element made up of two reciprocally related processes: (1) a change of state initiated by sensory input or by (2) an operator of nerve impulses generated in the central nervous system. This two process logic element is, of cource, an oversimplified abstraction from the data. But I want to emphasize the usefulness of the TOTE fiction for our time and research purposes just as Sherrington emphasized the usefulness of the reflex arc for his [3]).

The next step in the construction of the I.E. is the interaction of several "neural aggregates" of TOTE units. This interaction is thought to be analogous to a so-called *"hologram"*, which is introduced in the following passage (Chapter 7, p. 13):

3. More about the TOTE concept in a later section.
"The proposal is made that interactions among the patterns of excitation which fall on

receptor surfaces become, after transmission over pathways organized in a parallel fashion, encoded in the slow potential activities of neuronal aggregates to form spatial representations. These representations are not geometric (or iconic) however. Rather, they are, most likely, composed by a special class of more or less linear transformations which have lately been labelled "holographic" because of their resemblance to a photographic process that makes use of interference patterns.

Holograms have many fascinating properties in image making and the storing of information, as will be discussed below. These properties, were they present in the nervous system, would go a long way toward resolving the problem of the paradox posed by the anatomically constraint and functional equivalence of neural input organization. There is good evidence for the existence of just such properties[4]).

The final step in the construction of the I.E. is the *"screen"* upon which the "hologram" or I.E. is presented. Pribram and his colleague, Spinelli, have constructed a model of this screen. This screen model is interpreted as being a model of the function of the association areas of the cortex. It is presented by Pribram in this way (Chapter 8, p. 4):

"We now have good evidence that the so called association areas of the cerebral cortex exert control over the input systems which is in many respects similar to that exercized when a zoom lens is extended and retracted." (from the stencilled version).

As it is seen in the above quotation the function of the screen is co-determined by the individual's past history. Therefore, it is important for Pribram's theory to contain some hypotheses about *memory*. This is dealt with at length in Chapter 2 of Pribram's latest book (1971). He proposes an *"induction model" of memory*. Memory traces or engrams are conceived of as induced changes in the molecular structure of the membrane between nerve cells and the glia cells, and as more permanent changes in growth. Thus he writes (Chapter 2, pp. 42–43):

'Evidence of the importance of RNA in memory storage can at present be best explained by recourse to a model based on this embryogenetic process of induction. The model states that excitation of nerves is accompanied by RNA production. This neural RNA induces changes in the surrounding oligodendroglial cell commencing a chemical conversation indicated by the reciprocal nature of the variations in concentration of RNA and other metabolites between neuron and glia. Induced as a change in the functional interaction of the glial-neural couplet. These changes may in the first instance produce alterations in the conformations of lipids, proteins and lipoproteins all large molecules which make up the membranes which interface neuron with glia. These configurational changes are reversible and can fade or be superceded. When maintained by repetition of the same pattern, however, the alterations in molecular conformation will endure long enough to produce an effective change in membrane permeability which in turn allows more RNA and other metabolites originating in the excited neuron to affect its glial surround to the point where glial cell division is actually induced. Once divested of its encapsulating

---

4. We have kept this quotation from the stencilled version, but a similar passage can be found in the printed version, chapter 8, pp. 152–53.

glia, the growth cone of the neuron is free to plunge between the newly formed glial daughter cells and to make new contacts with the neurons beyond."

Pribram also needs a hypothesis of *reinforcement*. He deals with this problem at length in Chapters 14 and 15 in his 1971 book. We find there a critical discussion of two of the well known hypotheses of learning (contiguity and drive reduction), which are rejected on the basis of neurophysiological data. He prefers a more "cognitive" hypothesis à la Tolman. But he substitutes Tolman's "expectancy" concept with a concept of *"competence"*. About this he writes (Chapter 14, p. 252, 1971):

"There is by now ample evidence for the occurrence of the self adapting mechanism we have come to know in this book as a "screen" through which and against which incoming signals are matched (Chapter 8). The screen is gradually built up; it may be conceived as a coded representation of prior signals generated by organism-environment interaction; it is subject to alteration by signals of mismatch (i.e., a partial match); it leads to "expectancies" of the environment by the organism. The neural composition of the mechanism has been detailed in these chapters and Bruner (1957) has spelled out its implications for psychology in a paper on perceptual readiness. Here I will pursue the theme in terms of the construction of "competences" in the brain of the organism." And continues (p. 264):

"Organisms do not respond to just *any* occurrences that happen simultaneously, contiguously. Their behavior is guided by *the competence of the brain to organize stimuli*, including those consequent to behavior. Stimuli are context-determined events, "sampled" on the basis of a central competence (a neural "set") determined by *prior* experience and by other central events."

Pribram conceives of the reinforcement process as a kind of *"induction"* of changes in electrical potential in the brain. These changes in electrical potential are induced by *"relevant"* stimuli, i. e., stimuli which are relevant to the states of "appetites" and "satiety" in the so-called "homeostates" (to which we shall return later). Pribram furthermore presents neuropsychological evidence for the hypothesis that *amygdala* in the limbic system play an important role in this reinforcement process. Thus he proposes the following hypothesis (Chapter 15, p. 285):

"This result *suggests* that the amygdala is intimately involved in the temporal extension of a process set into operation in reponse to repetition of events – a process of registration of relevant events in memory. It is as if some sort of "internal rehearsal" were taking place in the normal organism, without which registration does not occur."

After presenting the principal variables which determine the "Image of Events on the cortical "screen", we go on to the other main image, the *"Monitor Image"* ("M.I.") (or "feeling" as it is also called).

The similarity between "feelings" and "perceptions" can be found in the fact that they are both "images" produced as holograms in the brain. The difference between feelings and perceptions can be found in the fact that perceptions are "Images of Events" in the world outside and produced by inputs on external sensory receptor cells, while feelings are images of the world within or "Monitor Images" and are produced by inputs on "monitor" receptors in the brain stem. Pribram has the following to say about these receptors (Chapter 9, p. 175):

"These receptors function as "state" sensitive elements of a variety of servomechanisms, christened "homeostats" by Cannon, concerned with the regulation of appetitive-consummatory functions."

These brain stem receptors can according to their functions, be divided into *"go mechanisms"* or *"stop mechanisms"* (e. g., respectively the "hunger" and the "satiation centers", also mentioned by Konorski in his theory).

Pribram connects the terms "emotion" and "motivation" to these centers, as is seen from the following quotation (Chapter 10, p. 195):

"The paradox is once more resolved if the "stop" mechanisms (medial hypothalamic) are more generally seen to regulate affects or feelings of e-motion, processes ordinarily involved in taking the organism "out of motion" and reserving the term "motivation" for those "go" processes (converging in the lateral hypothalamic region) which ordinarily result in behavior which carries forward an action."

The theory of motivation and emotion will be dealt with in more detail when we take up the section about hypotheses (2.2.). But first we must deal with the third main H-term in Pribram's theory, *"Images of Achievement"* (or "I.A."). These images are products of inputs from receptors intimately connected with the motor units represented on the motor cortex, which functions like the sensory cortex. Thus Pribram writes (Chapter 13, p. 250):

"Finally, our conception of the functions of the cerebral motor cortex of the precentral gyrus has become radically revised. This part of the brain cortex has been shown by the experiments detailed in this chapter, to be the sensory cortex for action. An image-of-achievement becomes constructed through a neural holographic process much as is the image-of-events. The image-of-achievement is, however, composed of learned anticipations of the force and changes in force required to perform a task. These force fields become parameters on the servomechanism and are directly (via the thalamus) and indirectly (via the basal ganglia and cerebellum) relayed to the motor cortex where they are correlated with a fast time cerebellar computation roughly predicting the outcome of the action."

In order to complete this presentation of Pribram's main H-terms we must look at his definitions of the terms *"sign"* and *"symbol"* which are summarized in the following passage (Chapter 19, pp. 365–66):

"Let me review briefly the distinction between sign and symbol as set forth in the earlier chapters. Signs are coded representations that refer to the world of the senses. The signs are produced through action on that world, classifying, categorizing and even naming its existences. Signs are constructed in the spatial domain. Symbols are coded representations that refer to the world within the organism. The symbols are produced, just as are signs, through action, but it is the remembrance of the effect of the action on the world within – the reinforcing effect – that produces the symbol. Symbols are constructions that organize the temporal domain.

Signs and symbols are thus acts, environmental effects produced by the organism."

These two terms represent the main elements of *language* and *thought*, which are dealt with in the last four chapters of Pribram's book. He writes the following about these subjects (Chapter 19, pp. 369–70):

"I believe language is used by man as a tool to accomplish whatever purpose he is about."

"Whenever language is used in this internal fashion it becomes thought. Thinking is not, however, a solely linguistic enterprise. Thinking derives from prolongations of states of active uncertainty which can be resolved only when the images involved become reconciled."

"The hypothesis I am proposing is that *all* thinking has, in addition to sign and symbol manipulation, a holographic component. Holographic representations are excellent associative mechanisms as we have seen and they powerfully and instantaneously perform cross correlation. These are the very properties that have been attributed to the thought process – the problem has been to make explicit how they are achieved."

"According to this view, thought is a search through the distributed holographic memory until uncertainty is resolved, i.e., unil the relevant information is obtained."

With these quotations we have tried to give the reader a detailed and relatively representative presentation of the main H-terms in Pribram's theory. But before passing on to the systematological analyses it might be useful to *summarize* this section by formulating a series of *explicit definitions of the main H-terms:*

1. Definition: *"Images of Events"* ("I.E.") are variables (states or processes) produced on the cortical *"screen"* by a *holographic process* in the neural *"TOTE units"*, which are activated by inputs on the external receptor cells.

    1.1. The *TOTE units* are neural structures functioning as servomechanisms.
    1.2. The *holographic process* is a complicated interference between inhibitions and excitations of neural units.
    1.3. The *"screen"* is a complicated neural structure (corresponding to the sensory and associative areas of the cortex) which is composed of memory traces or *"engrams"*.
    1.4. *"Engrams"* are permanent formations of the molecular structure of neural cells and glia, which are determined by – and later influence – the electrochemical processes in the cells.

2. Definition: *"Monitor Images"* ("M.I.") are variables (states or processes) produced in the brain by a holographic process in *homeostats* ("go" and "stop mechanisms") in the brain stem.

    2.1. *"Emotion"* is a Monitor Image produced by a strong activation of homeostats which cannot be appropriately channelled into action.
    2.2. *"Motivation"* is a Monitor Image produced by an activation of the homeostats, which can be channelled into action by an Image of Achievement.

3. *Definition:* *"Images of Achievement"* *("I.A.")* are variables (states or processes) that determine behavior in co-operation with I.E. and M.I. I.A. are produced on the motor cortex by a holographic process determined by a feedback from the sensoric registrations of movements.

2.1.1. *The surplus meaning of the H-terms.* The many quotations presented here were selected as being the most explicit definitions of H-terms we could find in Pribram's book. There is no doubt that they are *hypothetical* terms. But it is more difficult to decide what surplus meaning these H-terms really possess. The reason is that the main H-terms in Pribram's theory have *different* kinds of surplus meaning. It is our opinion that the main H-terms, the *"Images* of Events", "Monitor *Images"* and "Images of Achievement" all contain *mentalistic* surplus meaning. Without being able to demonstrate it by reference to more explicit definitions than the passages already quoted we believe that the "Images" should be classified as H_M-terms.

The term "TOTE" and other terms used in the explanation of images, such as *"hologram"* and *"screen"* are a bit more difficult. The explanations are based upon a large amount of neurophysiological data, but in spite of this we don't think it is correct to classify them as H_O-terms. They have rather a *neutral* surplus meaning as do terms representing real constructs inspired by cybernetics and information theory. This is clear in the case of the "TOTE" and we think that it is also correct to classify "hologram", "screen", "go-mechanism" and "stop mechanism" as hypothetical terms with *neutral* surplus meaning or as H_N-terms. This is *not* to imply that Pribram's theory doesn't contain physiological terms. We can find a considerable number of such terms in explanations, but they normally represent *data*. The real, explanatory, hypothetical terms represent neutral hypothetical *constructs* and thus are H_N-terms.

2.1.2. *Dispositional or functional terms?* It is rather easy to classify the terms in Pribram's theory according to the *existence* of the variables they represent.

Thus the main terms, I.E., M.I. and I.A. refer to *function* variables (processes or states). The same is true for the terms "hologram", "emotion" and "motivation", which are also function terms.

But the "TOTE", "screen", "go mechanism" and "stop-mechanism" are *disposition-terms* as they represent inborn or acquired dispositions (or structures) in the organism.

2.1.3. *Dynamic, directive or vectorial terms?* It is a little more difficult to classify Pribram's terms according to the *effects* of the variables to which they refer. In accordance with the application of cybernetics and information theory he conceives of *all* neurophysiological processes as *information transformation processes,* i. e., processes for the coding and decoding of information. This implies that problems of *energy transformation* are disregarded in such a model. In ac-

11 Modern Theories

cordance with this theoretical orientation *all* variables could be classified as *directive*. But we think this would be too crude and undifferentiated, and, therefore, try to disregard the cybernetical model and classify the variables in accordance with their effect on behavior. Then it should be rather easy to regard *"Images of Events"* as referring to purely *directive* variables, while *"Monitor Images"* refer to purely *dynamic* variables, and *"Images of Achievement"* to *vector variables*. The same is true for all the constituent variables. Thus "TOTE", "hologram" and "screen" refer to *directive* variables, while "emotion", "motivation" and "homeostats" refer to *dynamic* variables.

2.2. Classifications of the hypotheses

We have already (in section 2.0) presented a survey of the content of the hypotheses in Pribram's theory. Therefore, in this section we shall mainly concentrate on the hypotheses concerning motivation.

We shall take our starting point in a section of Chapter 15 where Pribram defines the well known term "drive" in relation to his theory (Chapter 15, p. 272):

"A drive stimulus, just as a sensory stimulus, results from the operation of a biased servomechanism, a homeostat."

"Homeostat" is the common term for all "go-" and "stop-mechanisms". This is clear from the following passage, in which the motivational hypotheses are further elaborated (Chapter 15, p. 272):

"Taking hunger as a model we found that the core brain homeostats with their central and peripheral sensitivities were constituted of two reciprocally active components. One component signals depletion and starts the regulatory process; the other component signals satiety and stops the process. We also aw that the "go" phase of the process is characterized by appetite and that the "stop" phase generates affect. Appetite and affect therefore turn out to be the motivational (as contrasted with sensory) stimuli, the drives sought by the behaviorist. In the language of this book appetites and affects are monitor images, indicators of processes that track brain states and influence the temporal organization of behavior accordingly."

These were the basic hypotheses of motivation. Closely related to these is "emotion", which Pribram deals with very thoroughly, especially in Chapter 11, where he writes (p. 208):

"But action is not the only way in which an organism can achieve variety in control. The possibility exists that he may exert self control, i.e., that he may make internal adjustments with his neurological system, adjustments that will lead to re-equilibration without recourse to action. My thesis will be that it is these internal adjustments that are felt as emotions."

The above quotations contain – together with the quotations in section 2.1.0. – the most important implicit and explicit hypotheses in Pribram's theory. But we think it might be useful to reformulate the hypotheses, as Pribram himself doesn't present any summaries or other explicit formulations. Thus we present the following *explicit formulations of his hypotheses:*[5])

1. *Basic hypothesis:* The function of the brain is to process and reprocess information.
2. *Hypothesis:* The processing of information results in the production of *"images"* of the external environment ("I.E."), the internal state of the organism (M.I.") and the organism's achievement ("I.A.").
3. *Hypothesis:* "Images of Events" ("I.E.") are determined by inputs on external sensory receptors which determine a *"holographic"* process in the neural servomechanisms – the "TOTE-units" – which in turn results in the production of *"Images of Events"* ("I.E.") on the cortical *"Screen"*.
4. *Hypothesis:* The *"Screen"'s* components, the *engrams* or memory traces, are determined by an enhancing process in the *amygdala*, which in turn is determined by the registration of *relevant* inputs, i. e., inputs related to the contemporary states of the homeostats.
5. *Hypothesis:* The *"TOTE-unit"* is activated by inputs, which are *tested* (i. e., compared with an inbuilt standard). If the test results in *incongruence* between the standard and the input, the TOTE-unit *operates* on the environment in order to change the inputs until they are *congruent* with the standard. Then the process *exits* from the unit to other neural units.
6. *Hypothesis:* *"Monitor Images"* ("M.I.") are determined by states of appetite or satiation in *homeostats* (i. e., "go mechanisms" and "stop mechanism") which are in turn influenced by the internal receptor cells and humorals.
7. *Hypothesis:* *"Emotions"* are "M.I." which are determined by strong activations of homeostats, which cannot be channelled into action, and therefore determine emotional reactions.
8. *Hypothesis:* *"Motivations"* are "M.I." which are determined by the activation of homeostats, which can be channelled into action by Images of Achievement.
9. *Hypothesis:* *"Images of Achievement"* ("I.A.") are determined by feedback from sensoric registrations of movements.
10. *Hypothesis:* Integrated behavior is determined by an interaction of Images of Events, Monitor Images and Images of Achievement.

After presenting this reformulation of the hypotheses and a summarizing diagram of all the hypotheses (see Fig. 8.1.), we are ready for the systematological classifications of hypotheses.

---

5. The reader can compare these hypotheses and the definitions already presented with the quotations in order to evaluate how representative the reconstructions are.

164 . Pribram's Theory

2.2.1. *The basic classification of hypotheses.* The above formulated hypotheses must now be classified as *theoretical* (H-H-hypotheses) or partly *empirical* (S-H- and H-R-hypotheses).

The *first* hypothesis cannot easily be classified. It is not a formulation of the relationship between two or more variables. It is rather a proposition defining the fundamental conception of the brain. Therefore, it could be conceived of as a *metatheoretical proposition* defining the kind of information theoretical model which is selected as a basis for the explanations.

The *second* hypothesis is a theoretical hypothesis concerning the relationship between information processing ("H_{in}") and images of different kinds ("H_{im}") and can be symbolized in this way:

(2.) $\qquad H_{in} \to H_{im}$

The *third* hypothesis is partly *empirical* as it represents the relationship between the (external) S-variable, "input", and the H-variables, "holographic processes" and "Images of Events". It can be symbolized in this way:

(3.) $\qquad S_{ext.} \to H_{holog.} \to H_{I.E.}$

The *fourth* hypothesis is also partly *empirical* as it represents the relationship between the (external) S-variable, "relevant stimuli", and the H-variables, "enhancing process in amygdala" and "engrams". It can be symbolized in this way:

)4.) $\qquad S_{ext.} \to H_{enh.} \to H_{eng.}$

The *fifth* hypothesis can be conceived of as partly *empirical* as it is concerned with the relationship between the S-variable, "input", and the processes in the TOTE, all of which can be regard as H-variables. Even "operate" can be regarded as an H-variable, because it influences the environment via the motor-cortex, motor-impulses and overt reactions. The only possible R-variable is "exit". Thus we have:

(5.a.) $\qquad S_{input} \to H_{Test} \to H_{Operate} \to H_{Test} \to R_{Exit}$

But the *fifth* hypothesis can also be interpreted as a *theoretical* hypothesis as both "input" and "exit" can be H-variables in those cases where the TOTE units are parts of a larger hierarchy of TOTE units (see Fig. 8.3.). This interpretation of the fifth hypothesis can be symbolized in this way:

(5.b.) $\qquad H_{inp.} \to H_T \to H_O \to H_T \to H_E$

The *sixth* hypothesis is partly *empirical* as it represents the relationship between the (internal) S-variables – humorals and other influences on internal receptor cells – and H-variables – states in homeostats and M.I. This can be symbolized as follows:

(6.) $\qquad S_{int.} \to H_{homeo.} \to H_{M.I.}$

The *seventh* hypothesis is also partly *empirical* as it represents the relationship between the H-variables – activation of homeostats and M.I. and the R-variable – emotional behavior. We can symbolize this relationship thusly:

(7.) $\qquad H_{homeo.} \to H_{M.I.} \to R_{emot.}$

The *eight* hypothesis is partly *empirical* as it represents the relationship between the H-variables – activation of homeostats, M.I. and I.A. as well as the R-variable – motivated behavior. This can be symbolized:

(8.) $\qquad H_{homeo.} \to H_{M.I.} \to H_{I.A.} \to R_{mot.}$

The *ninth* hypothesis is partly *empirical* as it represents the relationship between the (internal) S-variable, proprioceptive feedback and the H-variable, I.A. Thus we get:

(9.) $\qquad S_{int.} \to H_{I.A.}$

The *tenth* hypothesis is partly *empirical* as it represents the relationship between the three H-variables – I.E., M.I. and I.A. – and the R-variable – integrated behavior. We thus get the following formula:

(10.) $\qquad (H_{I.E.} \times H_{M.I.} \times H_{I.A.}) \to R_{integr.}$

We can now summarize our classification of the nine hypotheses. We shall disregard the first "basic hypothesis" which is a metaproposition, and hypothesis (5.a.) which is a less likely interpretation than (5.b.).

1. *S → H-hypotheses:*
    (3.) $S_{ext.} \to H_{hologr.} \to H_{I.E.}$
    (4.) $S_{ext.} \to H_{enh.} \to H_{engr.}$
    (6.) $S_{int.} \to H_{homeo.} \to H_{M.I.}$
    (9.) $S_{int.} \to H_{I.A.}$

2. *H → H-hypotheses:*
    (2.) $H_{inf.} \to H_{ima.}$
    (5.b.) $H_{inp.} \to H_T \to H_O \to H_T \to H_E$

3. *H → R-hypotheses:*
    (7.) $H_{homeo.} \to H_{M.I.} \to R_{emot.}$
    (8.) $H_{homeo.} \to H_{M.I.} \to H_{I.A.} \to R_{mot.}$
    (10.) $(H_{I.E.} \times H_{M.I.} \times H_{I.A.}) \to R_{integr.}$

Thus we can conclude that Pribram's theory contains 2 *theoretical* hypotheses and 7 partly *empirical* hypotheses.

2.2.2. *The complexity of the hypotheses.* From this reconstruction of Pribram's hypotheses it is obvious that they are rather complex. There are only two hypotheses (the 2nd and 9th) which make reference to only two variables, but there is only one hypothesis (the 10th) in our reconstruction which refers to an *interaction* between variables. The rest of the hypotheses define a "linear" relationship between 3 or more variables. Thus we can conclude that Pribram's theory is *rather complex*.

2.2.3. *The functional relationships in the hypotheses.* Pribram is not explicit when discussing the problem of determinism. But the hypotheses are all formulated with reference to *causal-deterministic* functional relationships. Thus it may be correct to conclude that his theory is (implicitly) causal-deterministic.

We have now finished the analysis of the H-level and proceed to the next level of abstraction.

The descriptive stratum

3.0. *Introduction*

In his book Pribram does not separate the descriptive content from the hypothetical and the metatheoretical. It is not formulated in terms of explicit empirical laws, but it is, nevertheless, possible to extract the most important abstract and concrete descriptive content.

3.1. *The abstract D-level*

We shall present some of the most important of the general, descriptive propositions (empirical laws) which are to be found scattered throughout Pribram's book.

The first part of the book deals intensively with the mechanisms of brain function. Among these are the *role of RNA in memory*. Pribram has the following to say about this (Chapter 2, p. 38):

> "There appears to be no question that RNA production is somehow involved when nerves are stimulated physiologically or by performances undertaken by the organism."

Another general description is concerned with *the inhibition process*, which as we know plays an important rôle in Pribram's holographic process. He says the following about the inhibition process (Chapter 4, p. 63):

> "In other words, stimulation of a retinal locus produces *inhibition* surrounding that locus. This process of "surround" or "lateral" inhibition has been directly observed in the eye of the horseshoe crab *Limulus*."
>
> "This process of "surround" og "lateral" inhibition is not restricted to the visual system."
>
> "In short, surround inhibition is one characteristic of neural networks—especially those organized as sheets whose neuronal depth includes several stages of processing."

A third important relationship is the *central control of inputs*, about which Pribram writes (Chapter 5, pp. 85–86):

"These data show that all of the organism's input mechanisms are directly controlled by the central nervous system. Thus output fibers, efferents, regulate the organism's receptor and therefore sensory functions, as well as his movements."

Neurophysiological research on the *brain stem* is summarized in this way (Chapter 9, p. 175):

"In summary, then, the work of a century of neurophysiological experiment indicates that a series of specialized "monitor" receptors are located near the midline ventricular systems of the brain stem. These specialized receptors are the classical centers for the control of respiration, food intake, etc."

And the relationship between the homeostatic mechanisms and the *reticular system* is formulated as follows (Chapter 9, p. 178):

"Within the reticular core is located a set of systems that is especially effective in biasing the homeostatic mechanism."

Later Pribram summarizes data about the hunger and thirst "centers" in this way (Chapter 10, p. 186):

"Further, the location of brain cells sensitive to the chemicals involved in the regulation of hunger and thirst are most likely distributed in a system within the core brain rather than being concentrated in a single "center"—although nodes in the system can be identified."

The present author thinks that the above quotations account for the most important general descriptive propositions contained in Pribram's book. Let us now turn to the next sub-level.

3.2. *The concrete D-level*

The more concrete descriptions of experiments and other observations are also to be found scattered throughout the book in this instance. It is characteristic for Pribram that he has carried out experiments as well as clinical observations. Most of his experiments have been on monkeys. We shall present some concrete descriptions to give the reader a fair impression of his style.

Thus he writes about some experiments with monkeys (Chapter 17, pp. 313–14):

"Specifically, a great number of experiments done with monkeys have shown that discrimination learning and pattern recognition remain unimpaired after removal of large expanses of cortex surrounding the primary projection areas. Yet much more restricted removals made at some distance from the primary cortex produce severe deficiencies in both sign learning and recognition. Simply disconnecting the intracortical pathways which join these areas with the primary has no effect. On the other hand, cutting the pathways which connect the cortex with subcortical structures produces as severe a disturbance as does removal."

A typical description of a clinical case is found (in Chapter 10, p. 192):

"I once had the opportunity to examine some patients in whom the medial part of the temporal pole—including the amydala—had been removed bilaterally. These patients, just as their monkey counterparts described earlier, typically ate considerably more than is normal and had gained up to a hundred pounds in weight. The opportunity to examine these patients was welcome because I thought that at last I could *ask* the subject how it feels to be so hungry. But much to my surprise, no such answer was forthcoming. One patient who had gained more than one hundred pounds was examined at lunch time. Was she hungry? She answered, "No." Would she like a piece of rare, juicy steak? "No." Would she like a piece of chocolate candy? She answered. "Um-humm," but when no candy was offered she did not pursue the matter. A few minutes later, when the examination was completed, the doors to the common room were opened and she saw the other patients already seated at a long table, eating lunch. She rushed to the table, pushed others aside, and began to stuff food into her mouth with both hands. She was immediately recalled to the examining room and the questions about food were repeated. The same negative answers were obtained again, even after they were pointedly contrasted with her recent behavior at the table. Somehow the lesion had impaired the patient's *feelings* of hunger and satiety and this impairment was accompanied by excessive eating!"

We hope that we have given the reader an impression of Pribram's descriptions, both the more abstract, general propositions (empirical laws) and the more concrete descriptions of observations.

3.3. *The descriptive units*

It is not easy to classify Pribram's theory according to the *descriptive units* which he employs, because they are neither very molar nor very molecular. The descriptions of the *independent* variables in his experiments, which are often *internal* S-variables or more *central* intracranial inputs or disturbances, are often stated in rather *molecular* terms. But the description of the *dependent* variables, the behavior of the experimental subjects and the patients, is often made in rather *molar* terms.

As Pribram's theory is a *psychological* theory, i. e., a theory about the behavior and subjective experiences of animals and human beings, we think it is correct to classify it mainly on the basis of the descriptive units applied in the descriptions of behavior. Therefore, we conclude by classifying his theory as being rather molar.

The theory as a whole

4.1. *The formal properties*

We now turn to the description of the theory as a whole and the first main point is a classification of the theory according to its formal properties. Among these we shall look at:

4.1.1. *The systematic organization.* We think that Pribram's theory as far as the systematic organization is concerned is on the borderline between *"sketches"*

and *"explanatory systems"*, as the text is rather clearly divided into three levels: the M-level is mainly represented in the introductory chapters, and the H-level and the D-level side by side in the rest of the book. But there are so few explicit formulations of definitions and hypotheses that the theory cannot clearly be classified as an explanatory *system*.

4.1.2. *The preciseness of the representation.* As far as this aspect is concerned Pribram's theory must be classified as *purely verbal*, as it is formulated in ordinary language with many exact scientific terms, but with *no* symbols or mathematical formulas.

4.1.3. *The properties of the models.* It is the formal properties of the model which are most highly developed in Pribram's theory. Firstly, there are some *two-dimensional* models in the form of diagrams in various places in the book. Besides, he refers to a *three-dimensional* model of the "screen". Furthermore, there is the possibility of making a *computer-simulation model* of parts of the theory – especially the parts about language and thinking (which we have not analyzed in any detail in this chapter).

This application of information theory and cybernetic models, together with neurophysiological data and hypotheses, is the most important, unique and fruitful property of Pribram's theory. But just this property makes it very difficult to place it in the next classification.

4.2. *The epistemological properties*

It is easy to classify Pribram's theory as an *explanatory* theory, but it is difficult to decide which type it is: Is it an S-O-R-theory, an S-H_N-R-theory or an S-M-R-theory? The heavy use of neurophysiological *data* – together with behavioral and some phenomenological data – should indicate a classification as a *physiological*, explanatory (S-O-R) theory. But the *hypothetical terms* used in the explanations don't have any physiological surplus meaning, neither the H_N-terms nor the H_M-terms (cf. 2.1.1.). Thus the theory could be classified either as an S-H_N-R-theory or as an S-M-R-theory. But we believe that the most important and original explanatory terms in Pribram's theory are H_N-terms because they refer to the cybernetical constructs ("TOTE-units", "holographic process", "screen", etc.). Therefore, we conclude that it is most correct to classify his theory as an *S-H_N-R-theory* because the main explanatory terms have neutral surplus meaning.

4.3. *The theory-empiry-ratio*

The last classification of the theory as a whole is a classification into *speculative contra empirical theories*. I think it is correct to classify Pribram's theory as an *empirical* theory in spite of the use of hypothetical constructs.

In this case we have a possibility of supplementing this rough classification with the calculation of the t/e-ratio or the *Hypotheses Quotient* (H.Q.), as we have made explicit reconstruction of the implicit hypotheses in the theory. By using the formula for the H.Q. we get:

$$\text{H.Q.} = \frac{\Sigma (H \to H)}{\Sigma (S \to H) + (H \to R)} = \frac{2}{4+3} = \frac{2}{7} = 0.29$$

This is an H.Q. of approximately the same size as Hull's (Cf. Chapter 2, section 2.4.3.).

Supplement to Chapter 8 of Pribram's Theory:

Later Developments

Introduction. As mentioned in a footnote to the introduction to this chapter, the above analysis of Pribram's theory was made on the basis of a pre-publication stencilled version of his book.

When the book appeared we studied it in order to detect any changes. The most obvious change was the addition of two hundred figures, most of which are neuroanatomical drawings and diagrams representing experiments. In addition, there are some diagrams representing different versions of the TOTE unit, to which we shall return in a following section.

The book had also grown in length from the version I had seen before (to 432 pages). Most of the additions are descriptions of experiments and empirical results which support the theory.

The most important change from a theoretical point of view is a modification of the hypothetical construct, TOTE unit, to which we now turn.

The TOTE unit. In chapter 5 the reflex arc concept is criticized and replaced by the TOTE unit, which we have analysed earlier in this chapter. But we want to supplement that presentation with a new diagram, Fig. 5–6 to be found p. 90 in Pribram's book, because this diagram demonstrates in a very instructive way the difference between the reflex arc concept and the TOTE concept.

But even in the section of the book where the TOTE concept is introduced Pribram started to revise and expand this hypothetical construct. The expansion consists of the addition of a so-called "Bias" component to the former "Test"

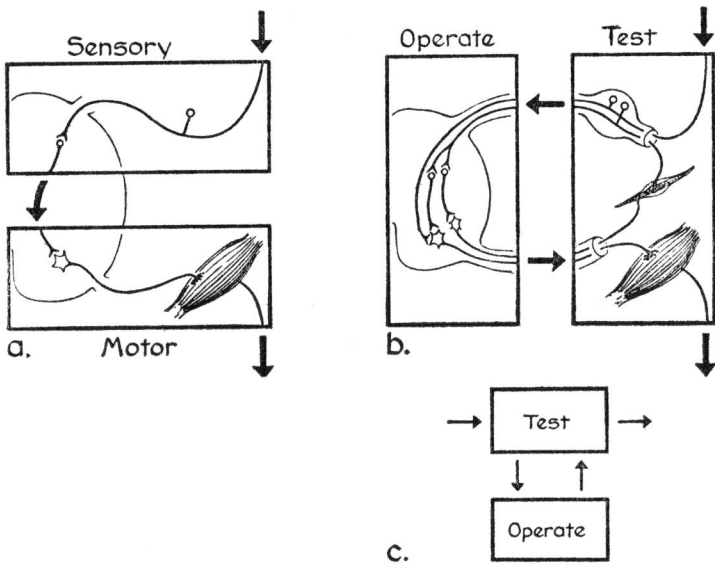

Fig. 8.4. Development of the TOTE from the reflex arc concept. Note that the γ-connectivity of the muscle spindle demands that a "test" be performed.

and "Operate" components. This implies that a "feedforward" process has been added to the important feedback process.

Pribram presents this expanded version in the following passage (pp. 94–95) and in the accompanying diagram.

> The reflex arc was a conception used by Sherrington to explain data he had before him. The success of his explanations made the reflex arc an extremely useful fiction. The TOTE diagram is also a fiction when applied to neurobehavioral analysis. It is a somewhat higher-order fiction than the reflex arc—the reflex arc is the limiting case of a servo in which feedback can be accomplished only via the organism's environment and in which the operation performed is insensitive even to this feedback, i.e., the effect, once initiated, runs itself off to a predetermined state. The usefulness of a higher order fiction must lie in its ability to handle a larger range of facts. The TOTE concept was brought to bear for just this reason: the reflex arc cannot encompass the data that demonstrate the central control of receptor mechanisms. Further, the TOTE concept can handle a variety of other neurobehavioral observations, such as the treatment of adaptation and habituation in Chapter 3. Yet, it is important to bear in mind that the neurobehavioral TOTE just as the reflex arc, is but a fiction and should be supplanted or supplemented whenever it is found restrictive rather than useful. The expanded though still oversimplified TOTE shown in Fig. 5–9, for instance, more clearly diagrams the relationship between feedback and feedforward and the role of coding, memory, and bias in the neurobehavioral process than did our earlier version. As an overall improvement on the reflex arc, however, the TOTE conception is central to any development of a reasonably coherent view of neurobehavioral organization. (See Miller, Galanter, and Pribram, 1960, for one such coherent view.)

172 . *Pribram's Theory*

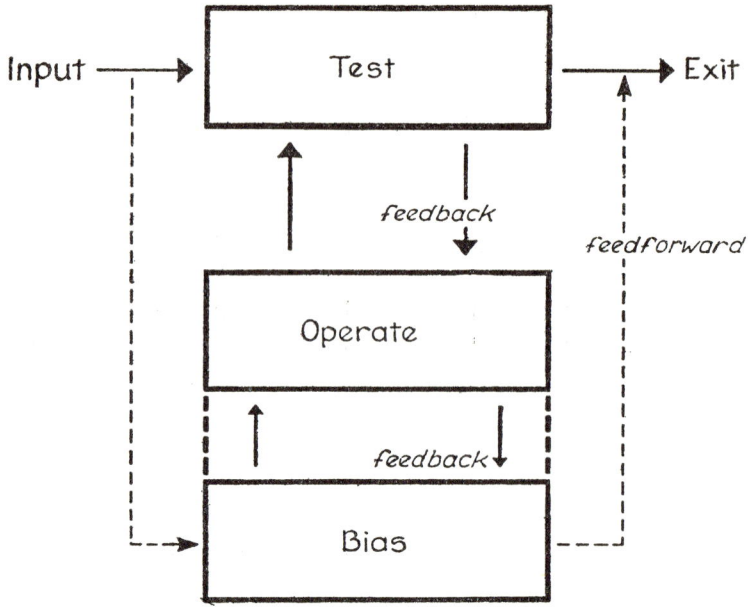

Fig. 8.5. The TOTE servomechanism modified to include feedforward. Note the parallel processing feature of the revised TOTE.

This revised TOTE construct is employed frequently throughout the book. Thus it is applied to represent the different memory processes as shown in Fig. 5–10 p. 96.

Later Pribram applies the TOTE concept – in the simpler, original version – to the "homeostats", the "Go" and "Stop" mechanisms.

These examples do not constitute all the cases in which Pribram has applied the new, expanded TOTE construct in explanation of different problems. But we think that the above examples are enough to demonstrate the utility of the new TOTE construct. The present author thinks that Pribram's expanded TOTE concept in the future will be "the TOTE-TO BE" (as Pribram calls it in the "Epilogue", p. 389).

Other revisions. The only other revision which we regard as being significant for our purpose is a restatement of the author's thesis about the psychosomatic problem.

Pribram calls his solution to this problem: the "Biologist view". The most concentrated formulation of this view is found in the following passage (pp. 383–84):

In the Biologist view, multiple "apects" turn out to become multiple "realizations," multiple embodiments achieved in what is often a long drawn out stepwise process.
   Thus the key to the Biologist view of the mind-brain problem is structure. In a sense

the Biologist view is a form of constructional realism. Biological rather than physicalistic. however, it encompasses a constructional phenomenology–Images have structure; they are made by a complex brain process; they are not the givens of existential awareness. Because the Biologist view is constructional, it shares the rational approach to epistemology and has therefore a neo-Kantian flavor (Pribram, 1970, Pribram 1971). Because of the emphasis on the structure of communicative Acts-language and culture—the Biologist view speaks to the pragmatist with a proposal for a structural pragmatism (Pribram, 1965).

The Biologist view partakes of all of these critical philosophies yet transcends them. Going beyond the analytic preoccupations of philosophy without discarding them, the Biologist view of the mind-body problem simply accepts, it as a biological fact, another manifestation of the biology the scientist encounters at every turn in his explorations. The broad aim of the Biologist position on this vital issue is, therefore, acceptance, and wonder, not critical argument."

As is apparent from this quotation Pribram emphasizes at least three points: First, the Biologist view" is based upon *empirical data* as well as on philosophical analyses. Second, the "Biologist view" is in accordance with much modern – so-called "post-critical-philosophy", among others that of the well known philosopher, *Polanyi* (see Polanyi, 1960). Third, the "Biologist view" is a kind of *realism* – or better, "a multiple realization theory".

Thus once more Pribram has managed to be both up to date and original.

Concluding remarks. After having finished the analysis of Pribram's theory we should like to give explicit expression to our personal evaluation, which has been more or less implicit in the above pages: Pribram's theory is unique in its integration of philosophical sophistication with ingenious model construction and the employment of different experimental methods. And, in addition to this, he integrates psychology and the neurosciences.

Thus we think it is fair to say that Pribram is a truly great integrator.

9: Miller's Theory

Introduction. The American psychologist, *Neal E. Miller*, (born 1909) certainly deserves a chapter in a book about modern theories of motivation. This can be seen by referring to the big German *"Handbuch der Psychologie in 12 Bänden"*. In the volume about "Motivation" (ed. by Hans Thomae) Miller is one of the most frequently referred to among contemporary psychologists. This position was gained through a very large production of high scientific standard. Thus he is one of the co-authors of the well-known *"Frustration and Aggression"* (1939) written by the so-called "Yale group", who were students and co-workers of *C. L. Hull*. In addition, Miller is co-author, with *John Dollard*, of two books which are now among the "classics" in psychology: *"Social Learning and Imitation"*, 1941, and *"Personality and Psychotherapy"*, 1950. Furthermore, Miller is sole author or senior author of a long series of papers in journals and chapters in handbooks. The most important for our purposes are presented in the bibliography at the end of this chapter.

Thus there is not *one* main work which contains Miller's theory, and consequently it is difficult to make the selection of texts for this metascientific study. But we have found it convenient to divide his production into two periods:

The *first* period begins in the 1930s and ends in the early 1950s. The main theme of this period was the development and application of a *"liberal S-R-theory"* inspired by Hull's work, and the most original contribution from this period was Miller's *theory of conflict*, which first appeared in 1944 (see Miller, 1944) and which was later elaborated. (We shall make use of the latest presentation found in Miller, 1959).

The *second* period extends from the early 1950s up to the present. The main theme of this period is physiological-psychological experiments in learning and motivation. Miller has been one of the pioneers in the application of the intracranial stimulation technique. We regard his *theory about the so-called "Go mechanism"* as the main theoretical contribution from this period (see Miller, 1963).

Thus "Miller's theory" in this chapter means his two theories dealing with, firstly, conflict, and, secondly, the "Go mechanism", supplemented with formulations from the other texts.

The metastratum

1.1. *Philosophical propositions*

Miller's philosophy of science is most explicitly and extensively presented in his chapter in Sigmund Koch's metascientific handbook (see Miller, 1959). Miller is least explicit about epistemological and other basic philosophical problems, such as the *psychosomatic* problem. Therefore, we have to draw inferences from the theory as a whole and reconstruct his theory about the psychosomatic problem. We think that his implicit psychosomatic theory is a kind of *neutral monism*.

Intimately related to this problem is the presupposed conception of Man, about which Miller is more explicit. Thus he writes (p. 201 in Miller 1959):

"It is assumed that the basic mechanisms of learning and conflict are similar enough in man and the other mammals so that work on the latter will often generalize to man. More specifically, the assumption is that all the psychological processes found in other mammals are likely also to be present in man. It should be noted that this assumption does not deny the possibility that man may have additional capacities which are much less well developed or absent in the lower mammals. All that is assumed is that what is found in lower mammals will probably be found also in man."

In this quotation we find an expression of the biological or *Darwinian conception of Man*, which is common among most modern psychologists.

1.2. *Metatheoretical propositions*

Miller's theory contains many explicit metatheoretical propositions.

First: He is very clear about the function and nature of scientific theory. Although he is a great experimental psychologist, he is certainly *not* a narrow empiricist. Thus he writes (p. 200 in Miller, 1959):

"Pure empiricism is a delusion. A theorylike process is inevitably involved in drawing boundaries around certain parts of the flux of experience to define observable events and in the selection of the events that are observed. Since multitudinous events could be observed and an enormous number of relationships could be determined among all of these events, gathering all the facts with no bias from theory is utterly impossible. Scientists are forced to make a drastic selection, either unconsciously on the basis of perceptual habits and the folklore and linguistic categories of the culture, or consciously on the basis of explicitly formulated theory.

Scientific theory is only an elaboration and formalization of common-sense processes of perception and communication. Theory is trying to make sense out of observations — to abstract and generalize. The goal of theory construction is to produce a parsimonious system of symbols (in either verbal or other forms) that can be used to make rigorous deductions about some of the consequences of different sets of conditions."

This long quotation demonstrates that Miller's metatheory can in its main principles be equated with *logical empiricism*, which is a common phenomenon among American psychologists. But Miller's version is a very *liberal* one.

Second: Miller has a very *realistic* attitude toward the function of theory, an attitude which is consistent with the history of science, especially as stressed by *Thomas Kuhn* (see Kuhn, 1962). Thus he writes in his paper about the "Go mechanism" (Miller, 1963):

"a theory may be fruitful, leading to valuable research, even though it eventually is proven to be wrong, – – a useful theory is never abandoned because of contradictory evidence, but is overthrown only by a superior one." (p. 66).

The last sentence, especially, reveals strong agreement with one of Kuhn's main theses, which was published at about the same time that Miller wrote this.

Third: Miller strongly emphasizes the *principle of parsimony*. Thus he writes in Dollard and Miller, 1950 (p. 6):

"A theory is more powerful the more generally applicable its principles are. As Einstein has emphasized, the goal is to account for the most facts with the fewest principles."

Another formulation of the same principle is to be found in Miller, 1959 (p. 201):

"The greater the parsimony (e.g., ratio of facts to assumptions), the greater achievement and the more likely the scientist is to conclude intuitively that he is on the track of a fundamental regularity in nature."

The last quoted formulation of the principle of parsimony is nearest to the present author's definition of the Hypotheses Quotient, which is designed to measure what Miller calls "ratio of facts to assumptions".

Intimately related to Miller's support of the principle of parsimony is his argumentation for *the utility of "intervening variables"* (in the broader sense equal to our "hypothetical variables"). As we have already presented his reasoning rather extensively in Chapter 2 of this book (section 3.1.2.) we shall only summarize the main points of the argument: *there is a gain in informational economy by using intervening variables,* when 3 or more S-variables are related to 3 or more R-variables.

The present author thinks that it is of special metascientific interest that this clear and convincing argument for the use of intervening variables is proposed by so great an *experimental* psychologist as Miller.

1.3. *Methodological propositions*

Miller is also very explicit and clear in his propositions about *empirical* methods.

One of his basic methodological principles is *the utility of animal experiments*. We have already touched upon this in connection with his Darwinian conception of Man, but the principle is still more explicit in this formulation (found in Miller, 1959):

"For certain (but not all) problems it may be desirable to work out the laws first in more rigorously controlled experimental situations with animals. Although these laws will have to be checked later at the human level, it will be easier to check them once they have been precisely formulated so that one knows exactly what to look for than it would be to discover them in the complex human situations which are less subject to experimental simplification and control. Furthermore, one's confidence in the conclusions from the less-controlled clinical situation is increased if the same relationship is found in the better-controlled animal experiments."

Another methodological principle is also referred to in this quotation, one which clearly reflects the close co-operation between Miller and his psychoanalytically trained co-worker, John Dollard. This principle, the *utility of clinical observations,* is a supplement to animal experiments, and is further elaborated in Dollard's and Miller's book from 1950, which is dedicated "To Freud and Pavlov and their students", thus indicating an approach to the integration of experimental learning psychology and clinical psychoanalysis. In this book they write:

"The psychotherapeutic situation, however, provides a kind of window to mental life" (p. 3).

And later they continue (p. 6): "Observations made in the situation of psychotherapy are a kind of natural history."

The positive attitude to psychoanalysis is stressed in this formulation (p. 6): "Whatever be the difficulties of data and concept, an attention to Freudian hypotheses can help the experimenter spend his time on important problems and build toward that general systematic account of human personality which is expected of psychologists."

The integrative approach is clearly recommended in this quotation (p. 8): "We believe that giving the solid, systematic basis of learning theory to the data of psychotherapy is a matter of importance."

The present author feels that in this integrative approach Dollard and Miller have been forerunners for the later "behavior therapists", and that their work is much more theoretically sophisticated then that of most of the behavior therapists.

Finally, we should mention an important methodological principle in Miller's theory which he stresses in several places (see Miller 1957, 1965 and 1967). He calls it *"a rationale for using a variety of techniques", a*nd it could be regarded as the "methodological equivalent" to the metatheoretical principle of using intervening variables (in the broad sense). Only by using several methods of experimental manipulation and several methods of measuring results can psychologists hope to get reliable information about intervening hypothetical variables. Thus in his later period Miller applies behavioral as well as several physiological and chemical methods in a very ingenious way.

For the sake of completeness we shall conclude this section about methodological principles by mentioning that Miller prefers and makes use *of behavioral data-language* without presenting much explicit argumentation for this. This is a logical reflection of the liberal S-R-tradition, to which Miller belongs.

The hypothetical stratum

2.0. *Summary of the hypotheses*

As previously mentioned we have decided in our systematological study to lay emphasis on the two theories about *conflicts* and the *"Go-mechanism"*. It is therefore easy to make an outline of Miller's theory – or rather theories – as Miller himself has formulated these theories in sets of hypotheses.

2.0.1. *The conflict theory*. Miller's theory of conflicts is formulated in 6 "postulates" (or "assumptions"), from which 5 "deductions" can be made. We present here the 1959 version of the theory along with the main diagram:

"The Postulates":

(A) The tendency to approach a goal is stronger the nearer the subject is to it.
(B) The tendency to avoid a feared stimulus is stronger the nearer the subject is to it.
(C) The strength of avoidance increases more rapidly with nearness than does that of approach.
(D) The strength of tendencies to approach or avoid varies directly with the strength of the drive upon which they are based.
(E) Below the asymptote of learning, increasing the number of reinforced trials will increase the strength of the response tendency that is reinforced.
(F) When two incompatible responses are in conflict, the stronger one will occur.

"Some deductions":

1. The subject should approach part way and then stop.
2. Increasing the strength of hunger should cause subjects to approach nearer to the goal.
3. Increasing the number of reinforced training trials (below the asymptote) should cause subjects to approach nearer to the goal.
4. Increasing the strength of fear should cause the subjects to remain further away from the goal.
5. Increasing the number of reinforced avoidance trials (below the asymptote) should cause the subjects to remain farther away from the goal.

As mentioned earlier this conflict theory is Miller's most original contribution from the first period. It is applied in his and Dollard's book about "Personality and Psychotherapy" (1950) together with their theory about learning, which is also applied in "Social Learning and Imitation" (1941).

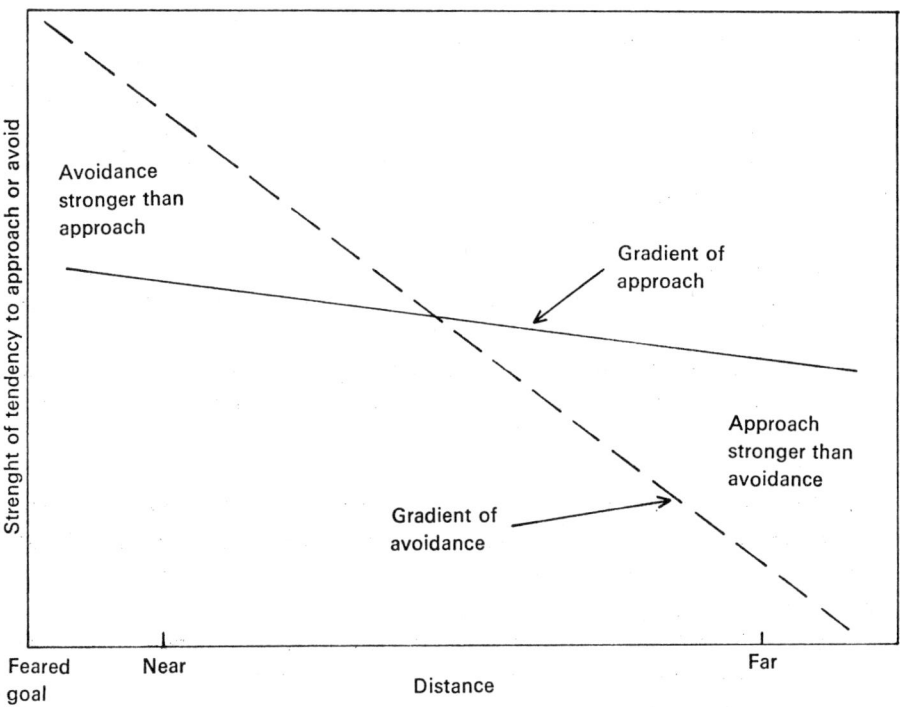

Figure 9.1. Simple graphic representation of an approach-avoidance conflict. The tendency to approach is the stronger of the two tendencies far from the goal, whereas the tendency to avoid is the stronger of the two near to the goal. Therefore, when far from the goal, the subject should tend to approach part way and then stop. In short, he should tend to remain in the region where the two gradients intersect.

It is only for the sake of simplicity that the gradients are represented by straight lines in these diagrams. Similar deductions could be made on the basis of any curves that have a continuous negative slope that is steeper for avoidance than for approach at each point above the abscissa.

Miller's and Dollard's learning theory is a simplified version of Hull's drive-reduction theory. It is a *"drive-cue-response-reinforcement"-theory,* which is summarized in the following passage (from Dollard and Miller, 1950):

"The relationship among the fundamental factors may be grasped in a brief summary. The drive impels responses, which are usually also determined by cues from other stimuli not strong enough to act as drives but more specifically distinctive than the drive. If the first response is not rewarded by an event reducing the drive, this response tends to drop out and others to appear. The extinction of successive nonrewarded responses produces so-called random behavior. If some one response is followed by reward, the connection between the cue and this response is strengthened, so that the next time that the same drive and other cues are present, this response is more likely to occur. This strengthening of the cue-response connection is the essence of learning. The functions of each of the four factors will become clearer as they are described separately in more detail."

The main reason for repeating their learning theory (with slight modifications) in "Personality and Psychotherapy" is that the *neuroses are regarded as results of learning under the conditions of conflict between strong drives*. And psychotherapy is conceived of as the learning of new, more adaptive responses.

The most important of the strong drives contained in the neurosis-producing conflict is *fear*. This drive, according to Miller's theory, is a learned or rather *learnable drive* and it is supposed to be the basis of most learned, human motivation.

We shall later analyze the main terms and hypotheses in the conflict theory and now make a similar analysis of the theory concerning the "Go mechanism".

2.0.2. *The theory concerning the "Go mechanism"*. Throughout his career Miller has been interested in the problem of *reinforcement*. The learning theory which was applied in the two books written in co-operation with Dollard, was a *drive-reduction theory* of reinforcement.

In the 1941 book this theory was presented without reservations, but in the 1950 book they made a slight modification about the *generality* of the drive-reduction theory as can be seen from the following quotation (p. 42 in Dollard and Miller, 1950):

"Although we believe that a consistent, parsimonious drivereduction theory of reinforcement (Miller and Dollard, 1941) is possible and has the advantage of being more likely to stimulate penetrating research on fundamental problems of learning, such a view is not essential to the main line of argument in the present book. All we need to assume here is that a sudden reduction in a strong drive acts as a reinforcement; we do not need to make the more controversial assumption that all reinforcement is produced in that way."

In Miller's second period he has continued to show an interest in the reinforcement-problem. It could even be said that this has proved to be the main problem of the second period, and that the physiological experimental technique was only the common *technique* used for exploring the problem of reinforcement.

Thus the main contribution to psychological *theory* made by Miller in this period – besides his metascientific paper in the Koch volume – is the theory about the "Go mechanism", which he calls his "alternative to drive-reduction theory". This theory is presented in the Nebraska Symposium on Motivation of 1963 (edited by Marshall R. Jones). The theory is systematic, very concentrated and formulated in 7 *"tentative assumptions"*, which we present here:

1. That there are one or more "go" or "activating" mechanisms in the brain which act to intensify ongoing responses to cues and the traces of immediately preceding activities, producing a stronger intensification the more strongly the "go mechanism" is activated.

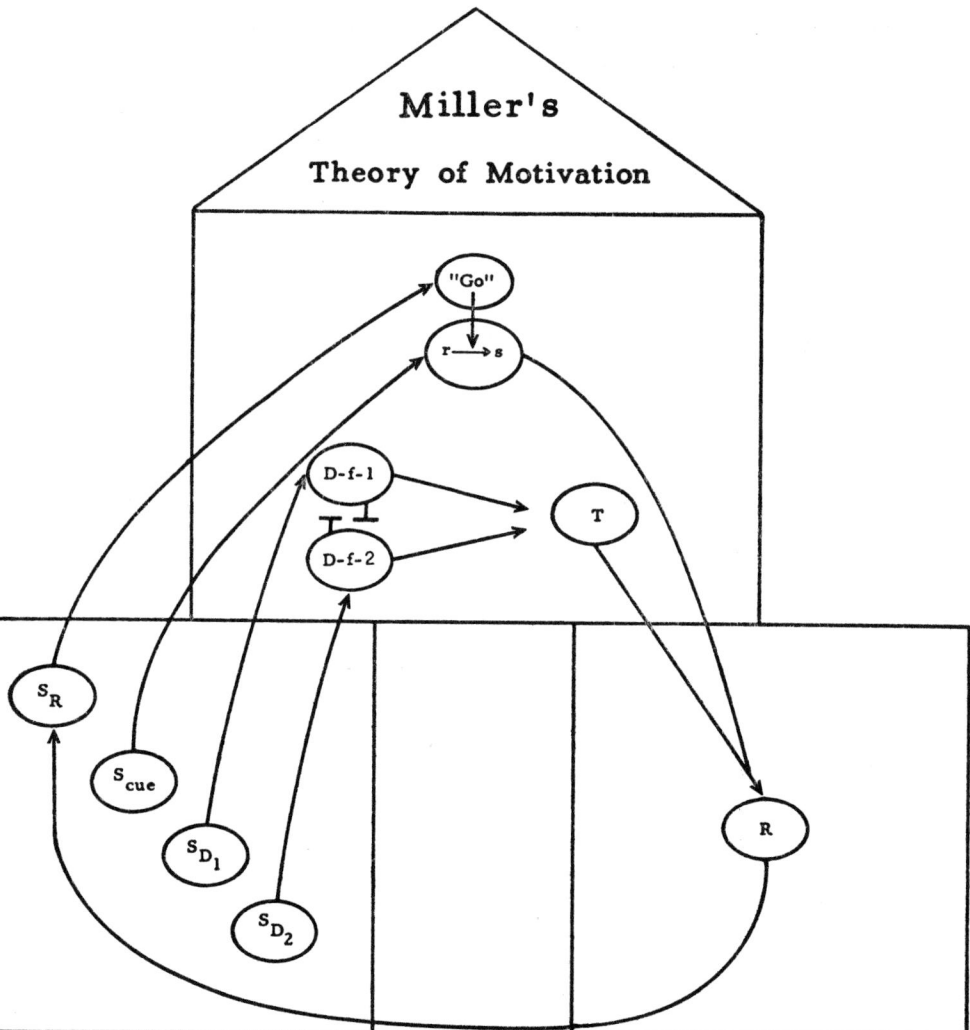

Fig. 9.2 Diagram representing the main hypotheses in Miller's two theories about (1) conflicts and (2) the "Go mechanism". "Go" = the Go mechanism; r s = "cue producing response" or activated "connection"; D-f-1 and D-f-2 = Drive functions 1 and 2; T = tendency to approach or avoid; R = behavior; S_{D1} = Drive stimulus 1 and 2; S_{cue} = cue stimulus; S_R = reward or other reinforcing event.

2. That this "go mechanism" (or "mechanisms" as will be understood but not repeated hereafter) can be activated in a variety of ways, such as by reduction in noxious stimulation, by the taste of food to a hungry animal, possibly by feedback from still more central effects of eating, by the release of a stimulated but inhibited response from blocking, by the removal of a discrepancy between an intention and an achievement, etc.

3. That all responses, including the activation of this "go mechanism" are subject to conditioning with contiguity being sufficient.
4. That the strength of the CR is determined to a great degree by the strength of the UCR (including the intensified trace which automatically serves as a UCR since the activities are similar), but also by the number of pairings.
5. That when a chain of cues leads to a UCS for the "go mechanism", it is most strongly conditioned to those nearer to the UCS, but can be conditioned (perhaps via lingering traces and/or by successive higher-order conditioning) to those farther away with a progressive decline in strength.
6. That every time a CR (including a conditioned "go responce") is repeated without reinforcement from the UCS (or perhaps it should be, a CS is presented without a UCS, or the CR is stronger than the UCR), it is subject to a certain amount of weakening, or in other words, experimental extinction.
7. That there is a certain amount of reciprocal inhibition between the central mechanisms involved in pain, fear, and frustration and the "go" mechanism, or mechanisms.

We shall analyze the terms and hypotheses in the following sections of this chapter. We conclude this summarization of Miller's theory with an illustrative diagram. (Fig. 9.2.)

2.0.3. *Other theories.* Although the conflict theory and the theory of the "Go mechanism" are the most original and formally developed of Miller's theories, we think it important to add a summary of his *theory of learned drives*, because this theory plays an important role in Dollard and Miller: "Personality and Psychotherapy" (1950).

This theory is based upon some "classic" experiments carried out by Miller which demonstrate that fear can be learned (by conditioning), and that such a learned fear can motivate the learning of new instrumental reactions (Miller, 1948). These experiments are also referred to in Dollard and Miller (1950), in which we find the following summaries (pp. 67–69):

"To summarize we say that fear is *learned* because it can be attached to previously neutral cues, such as those in the white compartment; we say that it is a *drive* because it can motivate, and its reduction can reinforce the learning and performance of new responses, such as turning the wheel or pressing the bar. Therefore, we call the fear of a previously neutral cue a *learned drive.* – – –"

"In short, we are assuming (1) that fear obeys the same laws as do external responses; and (2) that it has the same drive and cue properties as strong external stimuli. These hypotheses are purely functional; they say nothing about the anatomical location, central or peripheral, of the inferred process. According to them, fear could be a central state that obeys the same laws as an external response and has the same drive and cue properties as a strong external stimulus.

As a short way of expressing the first hypothesis, fear will be called a response; to express the second one, it will be called stimulus-producing."

In addition to fear Miller and Dollard mention other learned or learnable drives such as anger, nausea and disgust, as well as learnable components in other innate drives. Furthermore, Dollard and Miller put forward *the hypothesis that* many learned human motivations are based upon learned fear (the same hypothesis found in Brown's theory, which is dealt with in this book).

A further elaboration of Miller's and Dollard's theory of learned drives is gained by supplementing it with their concept of *"mediated learned drives"*. These are drives which are aroused by words or sentences. Dollard and Miller have the following to say about this concept (p. 106):

"Since words have no innate tendency to arouse drives, it is apparent that only drives that are learnable (that is, by our definition, response-produced) can be attached to words. After the drive-producing response has been attached to the word as a cue, the response of saying the word will elicit the drive. Since the learned drive is elicited via the word, it is called a *mediated learned drive.*"

These *"mediated learned drives"* combined with the Hullian concept of *"cue-producing responses"* make it possible for Dollard and Miller to deal with the very complicated problems in *human motivation and higher mental processes* as well as the development of neuroses. The reader can gain some impression of this by studying their diagram (Fig. 14, p. 223), which summarizes their whole theory of neuroses (Fig. 9.3.).

Concluding this presentation of Miller's and Dollard's theory of learned drives we should like to mention that Miller has treated the problem in more detail in his well known chapter, "Learnable Drives and Rewards", in Steven's (Ed.): *Handbook of Experimental Psychology* (1951). Later Miller has written another chapter (with *Jay M. Weiss*) for a book about *"Punishment and Aversive Behavior"* (ed. by B. Cambell and R. M. Church, 1969).

2.1. *The hypothetical terms (H-terms)*

In the postulates presented in the *conflict theory* we find the following terms which may be regarded as hypothetical terms: "tendency to approach", "tendency to avoid" and "the drive upon which they are based". These terms are not explicitly defined in the theory, but "drive" is defined in the books written with Dollard. Thus in "Social Learning and Imitation" we find this well-known and frequently quoted definition of "drive" (p. 18):

"A drive is a strong stimulus which impels action. Any stimulus can become a drive if it is made strong enough. The stronger the stimulus, the more drive function it possesses."

In their 1950 book, "Personality and Psychotherapy", Dollard and Miller have modified their definition of "drive" a little. Thus they start with the following sentence (p. 30):

"Strong stimuli which impel action are drives."

The rest of the definition is identical with the old one. But in 1950 the authors added a qualifying footnote, from which we quote (p. 31):

184 . Miller's Theory

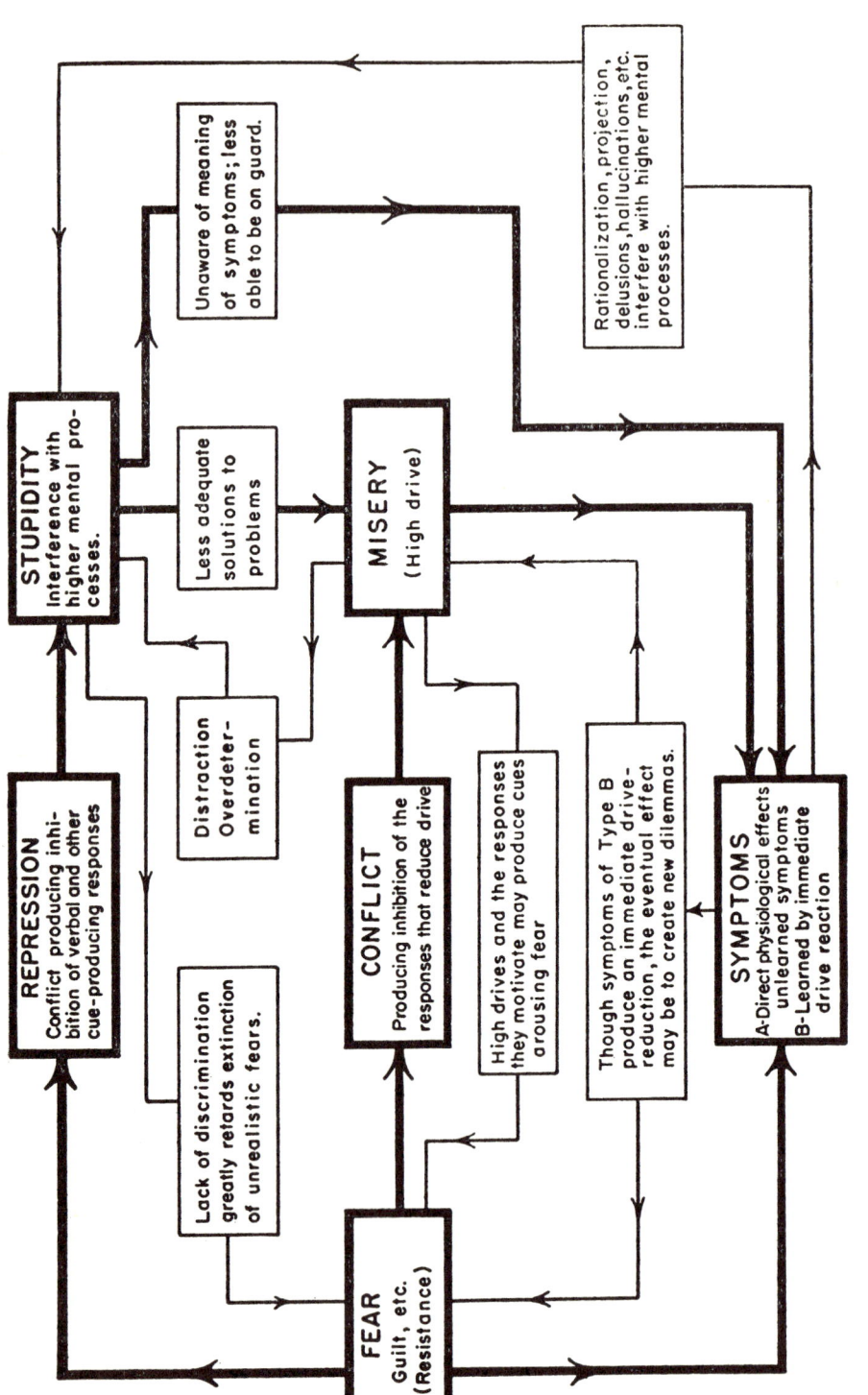

Fig. 9.3 Schematic diagram of some basic factors involved in neuroses. Arrows indicate "produces" or "tends to contribute to." Heavy arrows indicate major causal sequences; lighter arrows, subsidiary ones.

"But we do not care to press this view in the present book. All that needs to be assumed here is (1) that intense enough stimuli serve as drives (but not that all drives are strong stimuli), (2) that the reduction in painfully strong stimuli (or of other states of drive) acts as a reinforcement, and (3) that the presence of a drive increases the tendency for a habit to be performed.

While many needs produce drives, not all of them do."

In the last sentence we find important distinction between "drive" and "need". This distinction is based upon some experiments by Miller and co-workers which demonstrate that both milk fed directly into the stomach via a fistula as well as milk fed through the mouth has a reinforcing effect. The experiments are summarized in Miller, 1957[1]).

Besides drive there is another important term in Dollard's and Miller's learning theory, namely "cue", which is defined and differentiated from drive in the following quotations (from Dollard and Miller, 1950):

"The drive impels a person to respond. Cues determine when he will respond, where he will respond, and which response he will make" (p. 32).

"To summarize" stimuli may vary quantitatively and qualitatively; any stimulus may be thought of having a certain drive value, depending on its strength, and a certain cue value, depending on its distinctiveness" (p. 34)

We shall make a systematological analysis of drive and cue and the important terms in the conflict-theory in the following sections, but first we shall present the main terms from the "Go mechanism" theory.

The most important term in this theory is of course "Go mechanism". This term is not explicitly and formally defined, but implicitly it is very clearly defined in the first of the so-called "tentative assumptions", which we have already quoted.

Except for this new term all those used in the 7 assumptions are common, well-defined terms like "cues", "traces", "central mechanisms", etc.

Thus "Go mechanism" is the only term from this theory which is analyzed in the following sections.

2.1.1. *The surplus meaning of the H-terms.* "Drive" is the most important term in the conflict and learning theories, and it is also the most difficult to classify systematologically. The first definition of drive (1941) seems to suggest that drive is a stimulus, an observable S-variable, and thus *not* an H-variable. But the second version (1950) implies that there are at least *some* drives which are *not* stimuli. Thus some internal drives may be centrally produced excitations. Furthermore, we can see as early as in the 1941 version that drive is *not* identical with the observable stimulus, because *the same stimulus can have both "drive-value" and "cue-value"*.

We thus believe that the most correct systematological interpretation of *Dollard's and Miller's drive is that this term is used loosely as a common designation for S-variables, the external "drive-stimuli" and the internal "need-states"*, as well as for an H-variable, the "drive-value" or "drive-function" as it is sometimes called.

And of course the same is true for the *term "cue"*, which is used as a common designation for *an S-variable, the "cue-stimulus" and an H-variable, the "cue-value"*.

The rationale for using the stimulus terminology for unobservable H-variables is expressed by Dollard and Miller in 1950 (in a footnote, pp. 33–34):

"The functional similarities between the effects of these internal states, such as hunger and thirst, and those of external sources of stimulation, such as illumination and sound, are our justification for tentatively expanding the concept of stimulus to include both of them."

Miller has presented a very extensive, clear and convincing argumentation for the "expanded stimulus conception" in his Koch-chapter (Miller, 1959). This argumentation is in agreement with the tradition which Berlyne has called "Neo-Associationism" (in Berlyne, 1965). According to this tradition unobservable H-variables are treated either as central stimuli or as central responses with the same functional properties as observable peripherical stimuli and responses. The classical prototype of such a liberally expanded S-R-concept is found in Hull's "r_G-s_G-mechanism". In Dollard and Miller it is called a "cue-producing response".

If we accept this systematological classification of drive and cue as being H-terms in the cases where they are equated with drive-value and cue-value – or drive-function and cue-function – we must decide what kind of surplus meaning they have. We think that it is implied in the whole expanded, liberal S-R-terminology that the terms are *H-terms with neutral surplus meaning*. But it is difficult to decide whether they represent *hypothetical constructs* with neutral surplus meaning ("H.C.N.") or *intervening variables* ("I.V.") in the narrow, formal sense. But this uncertainly is not peculiar to Miller's use of H-terms; it is rather a part of the whole distinction between intervening variables and hypothetical constructs. Therefore, we must be content with classifying them as H-variables (including both H.C.N. and I.V.).

After this classification of drive and cue it is rather easy to classify the remaining terms in Miller's conflict theory: "tendency to approach" and "tendency to avoidance". These terms are also H-terms representing *H-variables with neutral surplus meaning*. We think that there is a certain analogy between Miller's (and Dollard's) main terms and those of Hull. Thus Hull's well-known formula:

$$sEr = f(D \times H)$$

could be transcribed to Miller's terminology in this way:

$$\text{tendency} = f(\text{drive-value} \times \text{cue-value}).$$

Leaving the conflict theory and turning to the theory about the "Go-mechanism" the systematological "picture" changes.

While the H-terms in the conflict theory have *neutral* surplus meaning, we find that the "Go-mechanism" is an *H-term with physiological surplus meaning*. This is evident from the whole meaning-context in the 7 assumptions quoted in section 2.1., and is furthermore supported in other places, e. g., in Miller's contribution to the Nebraska Symposium. Thus we find the following (p. 100 in Miller, 1963):

"It seems reasonable to assume that areas in which Olds (1958) secured self-reward are either part of the "Go mechanism" or are directly connected with it."

In this second period the surplus meaning in Miller's drive has also changed from neutral to physiological.

This change in surplus meaning is apparent in Miller's 1957 paper on "Experiments in Motivation" (see Miller, 1957), in which, among other things, he deals with the problem: "Are certain drives heterogeneous clusters?" About this problem he writes (p. 5):

"If a drive really is a single unitary variable – representing the activity of a single substance in the blood, a central state, a center or an integrated system in the brain – it is obvious that all pure measures of the drive should be perfectly correlated."

Miller does not come to a conclusive solution to the problem, because the experimental evidence does not provide the basis for such a conclusion. But it is obvious from the quotation – as from the whole paper – that his drive-concept has developed into a more physiological concept.

This is perhaps even clearer from a later contribution to a "Handbook of Physiology" (Miller, 1967), where Miller uses the terms "thirst" and "osmoreceptors" almost synonymously. Thus he writes (pp. 53–54).

"– – – when we are dealing with the effects of three different types of manipulation on each three measures, describing all the direct relationships becomes quite complicated. It may be simpler to think in terms of an intervening variable, such as thirst, or a mechanism, such as osmoreceptors, – – –."

From these quotations it should be clear that drive now has a *physiological* surplus meaning. But it should also be clear that drive is still a *hypothetical* term referring to a *hypothetical* variable, and not an observable state or mechanism.

We are now ready to turn to other systematological classifications of the terms in Miller's theory.

2.1.2. *Dispositional or functional terms?* From the foregoing quotations it can also be seen that Miller has a tendency to use drive as a term referring both to a *function* (state or process) and to a *disposition* (neural structure or mechanism, etc.). In the first period *drive* was exclusively used as a *function-term*. The same is true of cue, which has always been used as a *functional term*. The related disposition-term referring to the structure, which is activated by the cue-stimulus, is a term which has been mentioned before, namely, *"connection"*. This term is defined in Dollard's and Miller's book from 1941 (p. 25):

"The word 'connection' is used to refer to a causal sequence, the details of which are practically unknown, rather than to specific neural strands."

This definition is repeated later – among other places in Miller, 1963 (in the footnote on p. 96). It is obvious from this definition that connection is an H-term with *neutral* surplus meaning. Perhaps it is not quite so obvious that it is also a *disposition term*. But, as Dollard and Miller write on the same page (p. 25 in the 1941 book): "The connection between cue and response is the new product of learning". We think it is correct to classify connection as a disposition term.

The last term from the conflict-theory, tendency (to avoid or approach), is without doubt a *functional term* referring to a momentary state or process – not a lasting structure.

The main term in the theory about the "Go mechanism" must be classified as a *disposition-term* referring to a hypothetical neural structure or "mechanism". There is no special functional term referring to the state or process of activation of the "Go mechanism". But this is not an unusual case, as we have seen earlier, e. g., in chapters about other theories.

2.1.3. *Dynamic, directive or vector terms?* As Miller and Dollard are very explicit in their formulations about the *effect* of the variables in behavior, it is easy to make the last systematological classification of H-terms. Thus *drive* is very clearly defined as a *dynamic term* referring to an activating variable, while *cue* is just as clearly defined as a *directive term* referring to a directing or "steering" variable. As tendency is defined – implicitly – on the basis of drive, it must be a *vector term* referring to a variable with *both* an activating and a directive effect (guiding behavior to or from a goal object).

Contrary to these clearly defined effects of the three variables mentioned we do not find that the effect of the "Go mechanism" is so easy to classify.

In the first "tentative assumption" we find the "Go mechanism" defined as a mechanism "which acts to intensify ongoing responses". This should indicate that it is a *dynamic* variable. But in the long run the effect of the "Go mechanism" is to indirectly and *selectively reinforce* the traces or "connections" between cues and reactions. Thus the "Go mechanism" has some *directive* effect, too. Therefore, we must conclude that "Go mechanism" is a *vector term* as it refers to a variable with a combined dynamic and directive effect, (although the dynamic effect is the most important or dominant).

We are now able to conclude these systematological classifications of the H-terms in Miller's theory by combining the two last classifications in one classification scheme (Fig. 9.4.):

Effect Duration of Existence	Dynamic variables	Vector variables	Directive variables
Dispositions	Drive-mechanism	Go mechanism	Corrections
Functions	Drive-function	Tendencies to approach and avoidance	Cue-function

Fig. 9.4 Combined classification of the variables in Miller's theory.

2.2. Classifications of the hypotheses:

We have already presented the hypotheses from the conflict-theory and those from the theory about the "Go mechanism". The following systematological classifications deal exclusively with these two theories, because Miller's and Dollard's theory of learning and learned drives is not so formally developed that it is possible to make such classifications – at least not without first making a tine-consuming, systematic reconstruction of the implicit hypotheses.

2.2.1. *The basic classification of the hypotheses.* We shall first analyze the "postulates" in the *conflict-theory*. We make use of a systematic, reconstructive analysis in which we restate the postulates in symbolic form by transforming the main terms into S-, H-, and R-symbols followed by an easily understandable abbreviation. The reader may compare our symbolic version with the postulates quoted in section 2.0.:

Postulate A: $S_{Goal} \rightarrow H_{tendency\ appr.}$
Postulate B: $S_G \rightarrow H_{t.avoid}$
Postulate C: $S_G \rightarrow (H_{t.appr.} \langle H_{t.av})$
Postulate D: $H_{Drive} \rightarrow H_{tendency}$
Postulate E: $S_{Reinf.} \rightarrow H_{tendency}$
Postulate F: a) $(H_{t.av} \rangle H_{t.ap.}) \rightarrow R_{avoid}$
　　　　　　 b) $(H_{t.ap} \rangle H_{t.av}) \rightarrow R_{appr.}$

Thus we find that the 6 postulates can be classified into:

1. *theoretical (or H-H-)hypotheses:* Postulate D
2. *partly empirical hypotheses:*
   a) S-H-hypotheses: Postulates A, B, C and E.
   b) H-R-hypotheses: Postulate F.

The 5 "deductions" are *not* hypotheses (in our terminology), but purely empirical S-R propositions or "laws". This is clearly the case if we substitute such terms as "hunger" (in the 2nd deduction) and "fear" (in the 4th deduction) with the terms for the S-variables determining hunger and fear.

When analyzing the tentative assumptions in the *theory about "Go mechanism"*, we come to the following result:

1. assumption: $H_{go} \rightarrow H_{trace} \rightarrow R$
   or: a) $H_{go} \rightarrow R$, and
   b) $H_{go} \rightarrow H_{trace}$
2. assumption: $S_{Reinf.} \rightarrow H_{go}$
3. assumption: If contiguity, then $CS \rightarrow UCS \rightarrow CRH_{go}$
4. assumption: $\triangle UCRH_{trace} \rightarrow \triangle CRH_{go}$
5. assumption: If $CS_1 \rightarrow CS_2 \rightarrow UCS \rightarrow CRH_{go}$ then $CS_2 \rightarrow CRH_{go} > CS_1 \rightarrow CRH_{go}$
6. assumption: If $CS \rightarrow UCS \rightarrow CRH_{go}$, then $\triangle CRH_{go}$ and if $CS \rightarrow CRH_{go}$, then $-\triangle CRH_{go}$
   (where $\triangle CRH_{go}$ is an *increase* in the strength of a »conditioned go-activity«, and $-\triangle CRH_{go}$ is a *decrease* in the strength of a »conditioned go-activity«)
7. assumption: $H_{go} \rightleftarrows H_{pain}$
   where $\rightleftarrows$ (means inhibition).

Thus we find that the 7 tentative assumptions can be classified into:

1. *theoretical (H-H-)hypotheses:*
   1b., 4th, and 7ht assumptions
2. *partly empirical hypotheses:*
   a. S-H-hypotheses: 2nd, 3rd, 5th, and 6th assumptions
   b. H-R-hypotheses: 1a. assumption.

2.2.2. *The complexity of the hypotheses.* Our reconstructive analyses with the symbolic transformation of the hypotheses in Miller's theories have the advantage that it is also easy to see how complex the hypotheses are.

We can classify the hypotheses in the *conflict theory* in the following way:

1. *One dimensional* hypotheses: Postulates A, B, D and E.
2. *Multi-dimensional* hypotheses: Postulates C and F.

The hypotheses in the theory of the *Go mechanism* can be classified in this way:

1. *One-dimensional* hypotheses: 1a., 1b., 2nd and 4th assumptions.
2. *Multi-dimensional hypotheses:* 3rd, 5th, 6th and 7th assumptions.

We have counted the 7th assumption as multi-dimensional as it contains the *interaction* of two variables.

We can therefore conclude that Miller's two theories contain enough multi-dimensional hypotheses to preclude the use of the label "mechanistic" about the theories as a whole. They are in fact "dynamic" or "field-theoretical" theories.

2.2.3. *The functional relationships in the hypotheses.* Miller is not very explicit about the kind of functional relationship presupposed in his theories. From our analysis of the theories we think that it is correct to describe the hypotheses as *causal-deterministic in principle* although in practice Miller has to accept a kind of probability-determinism.

With this we have finished our analysis of the H-level of Miller's theories and now turn to the D-level.

The descriptive stratum

3.0. *Introduction*

The largest part of Miller's output consists of experimental and other *empirical* reports with suggestions for the *application* of the results to social and clinical problems. Therefore, most of his texts are *descriptive*, although he is certainly not anti-theoretical – as the reader must have understood from our analysis of the M-level and the H-level of his theory. In spite of the fact that the descriptive content forms the largest part of Miller's theory our forthcoming analysis of the D-level will not be as extensive as was the case with the two previous levels of abstraction, which are of primary concern for systematologists.

Looking at the D-level we can find *one general theme* going through both of the periods in Miller's production: *the problem of reinforcement.*

In the *first* period Miller and Dollard were mainly occupied with trying to *apply a reinforcement theory* to problems of social learning, personality and psychotherapy. In the *second* period Miller has been more interested in *physiological- psychological experiments concerning the reinforcement of autonomic responses* and the application of the results to psychosomatic medicine.

We shall now analyze the *description* of the main empirical results.

3.1. *The abstract D-level*

3.1.1. *The abstract descriptive terms.* The most important *abstract, descriptive terms* have already been mentioned in connection with the analyses of the H-terms, because they are so intimately connected with them. We are thinking about the terms drive and cue, which cover some S-variables as well:

1) the *strength* of a stimulus (determining the H-variable "drive-value" or "drive-function", and 2) the *distinctiveness* of a stimulus (determining the H-variable "cue-value" or "cue-function"). For the sake of brevity we can rephrase the terms for these two S-variables as: *drive-stimulus* and *cue-stimulus*.

We also mentioned the S-variable *need* in connection with drive.

We should also mention another S-variable which is important in Miller's and Dollard's theory – although it is only explicitly mentioned in the 1941 book – namely *"reward"*. We conceive of this term as referring to an *S-variable*, which may be an *object* or an *event*, which has the potential property of being a *reinforcer*[2]).

Intimately related to the term "reward" is another term *"incentive"*, which also represents an S-variable. Miller and Dollard write about this in their 1941 book (pp. 30–31):

"The same object may serve as an incentive with acquired drive value in one situation and as a reward in another. Food at a tantalizing distance may serve as an incentive to more vigorous responses, and food in the mouth as a reward strengthening those responses. – – –

– – – The incentive value of the object is based upon the more primary reward function."

In this quotation Miller and Dollard have presented an implicitly formulated "law" about the relationship between reward and incentive, which is important in modern motivational theory.

Before mentioning other laws in Miller's theory we have a few comments about another abstract, *descriptive* term representing an *R-variable:* namely, the term *"response hierarchy"*. This term describes the relationships between several "responses in the order of their probability of occurrence" (p. 36 in Dollard and Miller, 1950). The term is sometimes used with a certain amount of explanatory or hypothetical meaning so it could be conceived of as referring to an intervening variable or hypothetical construct. But it is not necessary to do this, as Miller's and Dollard's theory contains the corresponding *hypothetical* term to response hierarchy, namely "connection". Thus we can regard the term connection as an H-term referring to the H-variable which determines the order of responses described by the *descriptive* term response hierarchy.

3.1.2. *The general, descriptive propositions ("laws")*. Turning from descriptive *terms* to *empirical laws* we shall first deal with the *conflict theory*. We have already found that the so-called deductions in this theory are empirical laws. These laws are applied in "Personality and Psychotherapy" in dealing with the origin and treatment of neuroses. This book is an excellent demonstration of the great explanatory power of Miller's conflict theory.

In the *theory of the Go mechanism* all the "tentative assumptions" are – as we have already demonstrated – *hypotheses* and *not* empirical laws. But the whole set of hypotheses about the Go mechanism is created in order to explain *one* important empirical law: *the law of effect*. We must remember that this law has been accepted throughout the whole period of Miller's production. In order to *explain* it he first applied Hull's *drive reduction theory*, but the increasing difficulties connected with this theory motivated him to construct his "new alternative to drive reduction", the *theory of the Go mechanism*. However, the change in the set of explanatory hypotheses has not altered the *fact* that the empirical law of effect has been a main guiding principle in his whole production.

Thus in the *first* period Miller and Dollard made experiments in order to demonstrate that *a drive reduction reinforcement theory could be applied to:*

1. *social learning:* the tendency to *imitate* is a learned tendency based upon reinforcement through drive reduction of primary drives.
2. *learned drives* – especially *fear* – are learned by reinforcement through the reduction of a strong drive-stimuli (e. g., pain).
3. *neuroses* are *learned* behavior patterns which are learned during *conditions of conflict* between two or more strong drives (one of them often fear). Although the neurotic behavior seems to reflect maladjustment, it is learned on the basis of some reinforcement: the maximum of drive-reduction which the individual can obtain under the difficult conditions of conflict.
4. *psychotherapy* is learning better ways to solve "emotional problems", or, in other words: finding the best way to resolve the conflicts between drives in order to gain more drive-reduction. This learning consists of using insightful problem-solving of the emotional problem by "thinking", i. e., the application of cue-producing responses – especially language – to solve the conflict problem. "Insight learning" is – according to Dollard and Miller – a kind of learning by reinforcement, which only differs in degree from trial-and-error learning.

During the *second* period Miller and his co-workers have conducted two main series of experiments:

1. *physiological-psychological experiments concerning motivation,* which revealed some of the neural and other physiological mechanisms of motivation and reinforcement (see, among others: Miller, 1957),
2. experiments demonstrating that *autonomic responses are learnable through reinforcement*. In these experiments Miller demonstrated that autonomic responses such as: salivation, heart rate, kidney function, gastric functions, peripherical vasomotoric responses, and electrical "brain waves" (measured by EEG) are all modifiable by reinforcement (using intra-cranial stimulation in the Go mechanism). He also points to the possibility – and experimen-

tally demonstrates – that *psychosomatic symptoms* are learnable and can be *treated* by a reinforcement-technique (see Miller, 1969).

One of Miller's motives for the last mentioned series of experiments was to demonstrate that *a reinforcement theory can be applied to both instrumental and autonomical responses*. Thus a so-called "two-factor" theory of learning – like those of Mowrer and Skinner – is neither necessary nor parsimonious. *The empirical law of effect is the basic principle of learning* – according to Miller's very ingenious and convincing experiments.

3.2. The concrete D-level

Leaving the more abstract descriptive terms and empirical laws we now turn to the more concrete descriptive content in Miller's theory. The *protocol sentences* in his experimental reports can be divided into two main categories.

1. *Behavioral data sentences:* these are the protocol sentences describing the results of *observations and measurements of behavior* in experiments with animal and human subjects such as:
a. experiments concerning *imitation* using rats (see Miller and Dollard, 1941).
b. experiments concerning *imitation* using children (see Miller and Dollard, 1941).
c. experiments concerning *conflict behavior* using rats (Miller, 1944, and Dollard and Miller, 1950).
d. experiments concerning *fear* as a learnable drive using rats (Miller, 1948, and Dollard and Miller, 1950).

2. *Physiological data sentences:* these are the protocol sentences describing the results of observations and measurements of *physiological* phenomena such as:
a. experiments using the technique of *intra-cranial stimulation*. Miller and co-workers were among the pioneers in using this method in psychology. (The first results were reported in connection with a film at the American Psychological Association meeting in September, 1953, a year before Olds and Milner reported their experiments).
b. experiments concerning the *chemical stimulation of the brain*. Miller and co-workers have also been pioneers in introducing this technique into psychological experiments (see Miller, 1965).
c. experiments concerning the use of *pharmacological* techniques. Thus Miller has used different *drugs* in his experiments on motivation (Miller, 1957). He has used *curare* in the experiments concerned with the learning of autonomic responses in order to present uncontrollable feed-back from the skeletal muscles (Miller, 1969).

From this short survey the reader has undoubtedly noticed that Miller really uses *a variety of techniques*, as he himself so strongly recommends (especially in Miller, 1967). The present author thinks that Miller is one of those psychologists who has invented the most experimental methods – and without becoming a narrow-minded experimentalist.

3.3. *The descriptive units*

If we use the rough division of descriptive units into *molar* and *molecular* terms, we can make this general, brief description of Miller's theories:

In the *first* period he principally makes use of *molar descriptions of behavioral data*, while in the *second* period he principally makes use of *molecular descriptions of both behavioral and physiological data*.

We have now finished our more detailed analysis of Miller's theory and conclude with a description of the theory as a whole.

The theory as a whole

4.1. *The formal properties*

In this section we again concentrate on the two most formally developed theories, the conflict theory and the theory about the Go mechanism.

4.1.1. *The systematic organization.*

This formal property is found to the highest degree in the *conflict theory*, which is developed as a *deductive system*. The deductions are made in connection with a graphic model, which we shall comment on later.

The theory of the Go mechanism is not quite so formally developed – but it could easily be. This theory can be classified as an *explanatory system* consisting of 7 explicitly formulated hypotheses. If some formal deductions were made as in the conflict theory, the theory of the Go mechanism would also have been a deductive system.

4.1.2. *The preciseness of representation.*

Both of Miller's theories are *purely verbal theories*. They are, however, so precisely formulated that they could easily by *symbolized* as we have demonstrated in our reconstructive analysis. And the present author thinks that it may be possible to transform the conflict theory into a *mathematically* formulated theory, as we possess exact measurements of the tendencies to approach and avoidance. (The rats were strapped into harnesses through which they could pull weights which were the measure of the strength of the tendency to approach or avoidance).

196 . Miller's Theory

4.1.3. *The properties of the models.* It is only in connection with the *conflict theory* that Miller makes use of a model. As the reader will recall from the presentation of the hypotheses (section 2.0) he uses a special *"graphic"* or *"two-dimensional model"* (as we have called it in our systematological taxonomy). And this model is not only used for illustrative and didactical purposes, but also in making *deductions of explanations.* Thus this conflict theory is one of the finest examples of a model explanation we have found. He specifies the advantages (and disadvantages) of this kind of explanation in the following quotation (Miller, 1959, p. 209):

"The advantage of the graphic type of exposition and deduction that we have employed is that it is simple and readily understood. The disadvantage is that one must draw some particular type of curve, thus implying a more specific assumption concerning the exact shape of the function that is necessary for immediate purposes or desirable on the basis of available evidence. Then, this implication has to be denied by a somewhat awkward disclaimer. It would be possible to make a more rigorous and elegant deduction using either the algebra of inequalities or symbolic logic. Such a deduction, however, would consume more space and be harder for the average reader to follow."

The present author finds this a convincing demonstration of the utility of models in scientific theories.

4.2. *The epistemological properties*

There are also differences between Miller's two theories in regard to their epistemological properties. Both theories are *explanatory* theories, but the *conflict theory is a neutral, explanatory theory (an S-H_N-R-theory)* as it contains neutral H-terms (representing intervening variables or hypothetical constructs with neutral surplus meaning), while the *theory of the Go mechanism is a physiological, explanatory theory* (or S-O-R-theory) as it contains H-terms with physiological surplus meaning (cf. the analysis in section 2.1.1.).

4.3. *The theory-empiry-ratio*

The impression one receives from reading Miller's theories is that they are theories with a *low theory-empiry-ratio*, or, in other words: *empirical* theories – not speculative theories.

As the theories are rather highly developed in their formal properties it is possible to calculate the *Hypotheses Quotient.*

Thus we have the following for the *conflict theory:*

$$\text{H. Q.} = \frac{\Sigma(\text{H}-\text{H})}{\Sigma(\text{S}-\text{H})+(\text{H}-\text{R})} = \frac{1}{4+1} = \frac{1}{5} = 0.20.$$

(The reader can check this calculation by comparing it with our classification in section 2.1.1.). This is one of the lowest H.Q.s. Of the 10 H.Q.s calculated in "Theories of Motivation", only 3 are lower, those of Tinbergen, McClelland and Hebb. *If* we had counted the "deductions" of the conflict theory and – as S-R-propositions – placed them in the denominator in the fraction for calculating the H.Q., we would have got an even lower H.Q. (0.10). But we do not feel that this is fair. Anyway, the conflict theory *is* very empirical.

The calculation of the Hypotheses Quotient for the theory of the *Go mechanism* is:

$$H.Q. = \frac{3}{4+1} = \frac{3}{5} = 0.60.$$

(The reader may check this by comparing it with the classification of the 7 assumptions made in section 2.2.1. – and will notice that we have counted the two parts of assumption 1. as two hypotheses). This gives a somewhat higher H.Q., but we think that it is still correct to describe the theory as being *empirical*.

Concluding remarks. We wish to emphasize that our last section indicates that Miller's theory is really one of the psychological theories which is *most formally developed and at the same time experimentally well founded.*

NOTES

1. As far as the present author knows it was Miller's experiments which forced C. L. Hull to make the important distinction between need and drive in his theory.
2. We believe that the terms "reward" and perhaps also "reinforcer" – can be used as *descriptive* terms, independent of the presupposed *hypothesis about reinforcement*, whether this be a drive-reduction or another kind of reinforcement hypothesis (e.g., Miller's later "Go mechanism theory").

10: Brown's Theory

Introduction

In 1961 appeared "The Motivation of Behavior" by *Judson S. Brown*, who was already known as the author of several articles about motivation and learning. Brown's book holds special interest for anyone making a study of motivational theories, because it is the first attempt to build a theory of motivation mainly upon the basis of C. L. Hull's general behavior theory, which Brown views as "The most useful theory of motivation we possess" (p. VIII). As we have analyzed Hull's theory in our former book, it is natural also to select Brown's theory for a metascientific analysis in this chapter.

The metastratum

1.1. *Philosophical propositions*

Brown makes no explicit formulations about philosophical problems. But it would probably not be incorrect to infer from the other metapropositions that he – like most other modern American psychologists – presupposes a *neutral monistic* theory of the psychosomatic problem and a *biological, Darwinian* philosophy of Man.

1.2. *Metatheoretical propositions*

Brown is very thorough in his discussion of problems of theory construction and gives many explicit formulations of metatheoretical principles, which we therefore will deal with a little more extensively.

First he discusses two different approaches to psychology (pp. 21–22):

"Given a well-established empirical law, the psychologist may follow two principal paths toward the enrichment of his understanding of the law. One of these, which involves detailed analyses and descriptions of the bodily mechanisms of behaving organisms is usually described as the "physiological approach". The second often characterized as the "behavioral approach" leads to further study of the range of conditions under which the law holds and to the search for "explanatory" laws in which only behavioral and experimental variables are contained."

Brown does not explicitly state if – or why – he prefers the behavioral approach, but so he does, and it is a consequence of his preference for Hull.

He states that the use of "explanatory concepts" or "intervening variables" is characteristic of the "behavioral approach". He thus writes (p. 23):

"Gaps in the network of explanatory laws are filled, in part, by "guessed-at laws" (Spence, 1948) and by the introduction of "explanatory" concepts – – – The concepts of drive and motivation to which we now turn, are often encountered in the writings of those who subscribe to the behavioral approach, and generally speaking, occupy a position of considerable importance therein."

Brown devotes a whole chapter (Chapter 2) to a very thorough discussion of the problem of intervening variables. About the reason for using these concepts he says (p. 29):

"One rather obvious reason for the use of intervening variables, even when ill defined and loosely connected to a theory, is that the users regard them as having real value as summarizing or interpretive concepts."

But Brown also realizes the dangers of using intervening variables – especially "circular reasoning". He therefore discusses rather thoroughly how these dangers can be avoided and summarizes his opinion in the following manner (p. 35):

"This (avoiding circular reasoning) can be accomplished, in principle, by making certain that one's definition of an intervening variable is completely independent of the specific responses that are assumed to be determined by that variable. This requirement can be met by basing the definition upon (1) the subject's previous experiences, (2) the responses he makes in other test situations, (3) one or another of his organic states, or (4) the stimuli impinging upon him."

1.3. *Methodological propositions*

As a follower of a "neo-behaviorist" it is natural for Brown to prefer a behavioristic protocol language. He thus writes (p. 1):

"The psychologist concentrates his attention primarily upon the *behavior* of living organisms, – – –".

And later he writes (p. 26):

"The attainment of satisfactory explanations of behavior is described as the psychologist's principal aim and the observing and recording of the activities of organisms as his initial task."

This is a clear statement about the data language of psychology.

It is also consistent with a "Hullian approach" to stress the experimental method and especially the measuring procedures. Brown presents in a part of Chapter 2 a very thorough discussion of "the Problem of Drive Quantification". He summarizes the discussion with this moderately optimistic statement (p. 56):

"No procedures have yet been devised by means of which drive may be measured in the *fundamental* sense that length and weight are measured, but the quantification of drive by what is termed *derived* measurement may eventually prove to be feasible."

The hypothetical stratum

2.0. *Summary of the hypotheses*

Before analyzing the contents of variables and hypotheses in Brown's explanatory system, we will present a short *summary* of the content of the theory as a whole.

Behavior is determined by "Habit" (H) and "Drive" (D) in multiplicative interaction:

$$B = f(H \times D).$$

"Drive is a general activating, intervening state or process in the organism, which only activates but does not guide behavior (this guiding or directive functon is performed by H). There are thus not different drives but different specific *sources* of a general drive. These sources of drive can be primary (organic needs and noxious stimuli) or secondary (learned responses). Reaction tendencies may be in conflict and then we have the state of "frustration". Drive influences performance and perception in several ways, which it would be too complicated to elaborate on in this short summary.

But we have presented another kind of summary in the form of a diagram (Fig. 10.1):

2.1. *The hypothetical terms (H-terms)*

The most important motivational variable in Brown's theory is "Drive", which is a *general activating, non-directing H-variable*. He presents one of the most extensive and thorough discussions of the utility or necessity of motivational variables the present author has found, and therefore we will present it here in detail.

Brown first (in Chapter 2) discusses the cases where a special motivational variable may be useful or desirable. The cases are:

1. "The evocation of vigorous responses by weak stimuli." (p. 29).
2. "Variability of responses in the presence of constant stimulation conditions" (p. 30).
3. "Equality or constancy of behavior in the presence of normally effective changes in the external stimulus stiuation" (p. 32).

Perhaps we could further concentrate these summaries by the formulations:

Motivational H-variables may be useful or necessary in cases of irregular *S-R-relationships*.

Brown also includes a discussion of the "criteria for the identification of motivational variables", which he summarizes as follows[1]) (pp. 41–42):

---

1. The reader may compare these criteria with Berlyne's analyses of the three drive concepts.

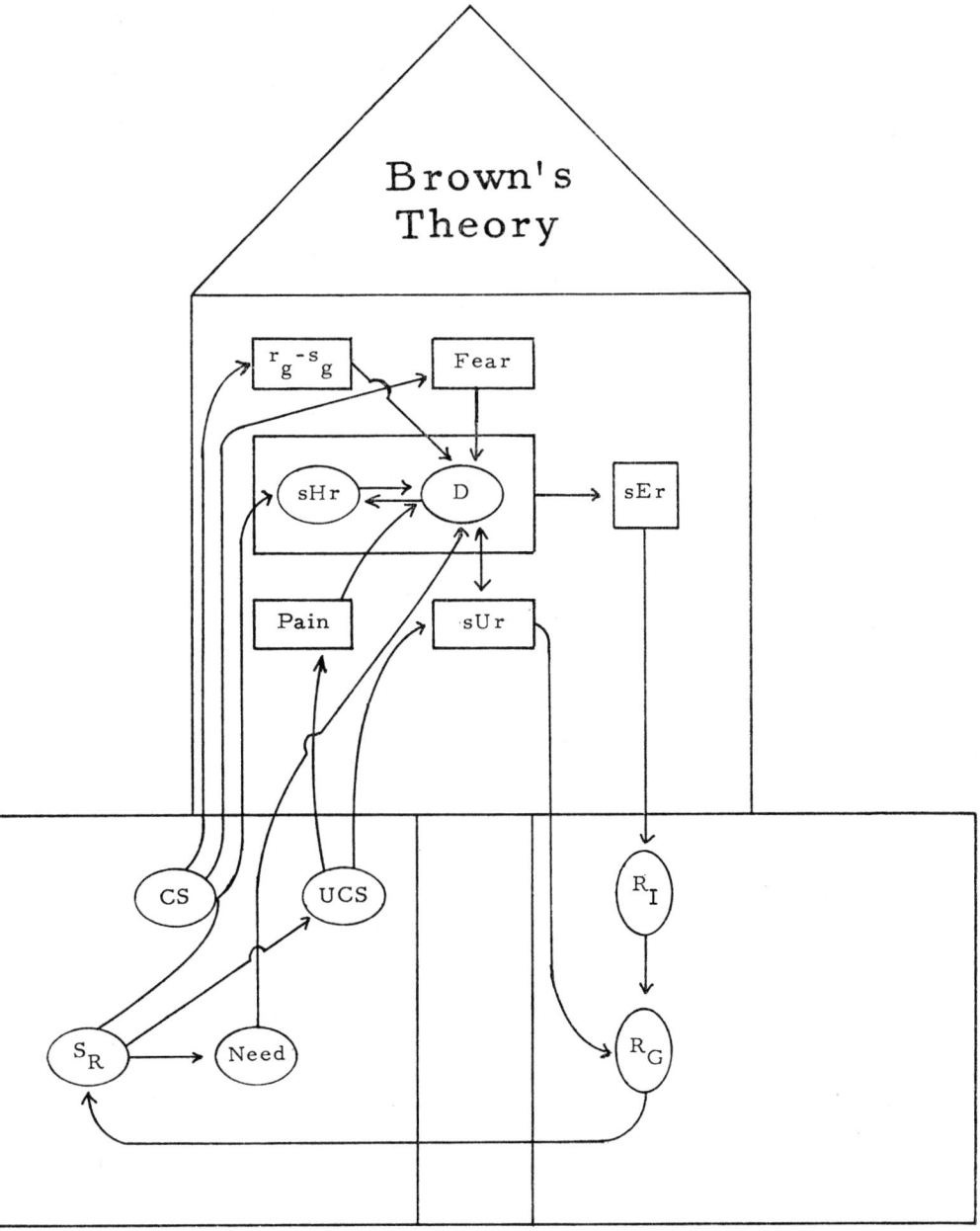

Fig. 10.1 Diagram representing Brown's theory; Behavior – instrumental (R_I) and goal activity (R_G) – is a function of "reaction potential", which in turn is determined by "drive" (D) and "habit" (sHr) in interaction. Drive is determined by "primary sources" – "need" and "unconditioned pain" – as well as by "learned sources of drive", fear and r_g–s_g. The H-variables are all influenced by conditioned stimuli (CS) and reinforcing events (S_R). Unconditioned stimuli (UCS) can determine unlearned connections (sUr). which – in interaction with drive – can determine a goal reaction (R_G).

"1. A variable is often said to be motivational if it facilitates or energizes a wide variety of responses."
"2. A variable is commonly said to be motivating if the learning of new responses seems to depend upon appropriate manipulation of that variable."
"3. A variable is sometimes regarded as motivational if changes in that variable lead to the weakening of certain responses."

As the reader has undoubtedly noted, the only generally accepted criterion is the first one which *identifies motivational variables with energizing or activating variables.*

Besides this, Brown makes (in Chapter 4) a very interesting analysis in which he compares the *"motivational* interpretations" with what he calls non-motivational or *"associative* interpretations". He analyzes several "motivational" interpretations among which Hull's theory is the most important. He also presents some of his own "associative" interpretations, including brief mention of Estes's theory.

He concludes his analyses with the following words (p. 132):

"Although associative conceptualizations appear to possess the virtue of simplicity, it would be premature to conclude that the idea of a general energizing drive must, therefore, be rejected completely."

2.1.1. *The surplus meaning of the H-terms.* From the above quotations it is undoubtedly clear for the reader that Brown's "Drive" is an H-term with *neutral* surplus meaning (an H_N-term).

But later he summarizes certain experimental evidence and writes (p. 135):

"– – it appears from the above summary of experimental evidence that many diverse findings are consistent with the concept of a nonspecific activating drive."
"In Chapter 9 additional evidence is presented from the field of physiological psychology that is consistent with the general-drive conception."

The present author would like to stress the last quoted sentences, because they show that *Brown's (and Hull's) "general activating drive" can be integrated with more physiological concepts like Berlyne's, Bindra's, Duffy's and others.*

But although Brown points to the possibility of interpreting "Drive" as related to the function of the brain stem's reticular arousal system, his "drive concept" must still be described as a neutral H-term.

2.1.2 *Dispositional or functional terms?* While it thus was easy to use our first classification, it is certainly more difficult to use the other classifications into dispositional contra functional terms. Brown is not explicit about this dichotomy, and the present author thinks that he confuses the disposition-function distinction with the motivating-directing distinction.

If we then try to describe his main H-variables in accordance with the disposition-function distinction, we must classify *"Drive" as a function variable*. But *"Habit strength"* is more difficult: it is *both* a *function* variable and a *disposition* variable (which determines some of the individual differences in behavior).

2.1.3. *Dynamic, directive or vectorial terms?* This classification is very easy to apply to Brown's terms, because he is very clear on this point. Thus he writes in Chapter 3 in a paragraph (pp. 57–58) about "Some terminological distinctions":

"With few exceptions, contemporary theorists make a distinction between independent variables that seem to have motivational effects upon behavior and those that direct or guide behavior."

"Moreover, two kinds of intermediary constructs are introduced that correspond with these two groups of variables. Thus drives, motivations, conations, emotions, and libidos function as the activating agents; while cognitive maps, associative tendencies, and habit strength serve, in conjunction with external and internal stimuli, to determine the direction behavior will take.

In some instances, however, difficulties arise in attempting to maintain these distinctions."

Brown then discusses these difficulties – especially in connection with his own two main variables "Drive" and "Habit strength" – and he concludes (p. 59):

"Certain *variables* may thus be seen to have dual consequences, but *drive* is assumed to have only motivational effects and *habit strength* only directive functions."

The present author agrees with Brown's proposals for the use of "Drive" as a purely activating variable; and his distinction[2]) has – in combination with ideas from other theorists (especially K. Lewin) – been one of the foundations of the classification into "dynamogenic, directive and vector variables", which is introduced in Chapter 18 of "Theories of Motivation". But in spite of this, the present author thinks that he confuses the dynamic-directive distinction with the function – disposition distinction – or at least that he neglects this other distinction.

---

2. Which first appeared in his paper from the first Nebraska Symposium on Motivation of 1953. In a recent letter to the author Brown has stated the following: "Following Hull, I assumed in my book, that D multiplied all learned associative tendencies ($_sH_Rs$). Thus D, irrespective of its source, was thought to affect all reactions indiscriminately. More recently, however, I have tentatively adopted the view that D, while indeed multiplying or energizing all reaction tendencies, *affects some more powerfully than it does others*. On this view, termed a *graduated drive theory*, level of hunger, say, affects both approach and avoidance tendencies but multiplies approach more than it does avoidance. This is obviously a position that lies between a purely selective drive notion (hunger affects only food-related responses, etc.) and Hull's extreme version of a nonselective energizer."

2.2. Classification of the hypotheses

We have already presented a rough overview of Brown's hypotheses (in 2.0.0.). A more detailed presentation of them can be made in connection with the first classification of hypotheses.

2.2.1. Basic classification of hypotheses.
We thus turn to the classification of hypotheses according to their constituent terms.

Among the *S-H-hypotheses* we will pay special attention to Brown's hypotheses about *"sources of drive"*. As a logical consequence of his non-specific activating drive concept, he prefers to deal with drive as a unitary concept. There is only one drive, not several different drives. But there are several different "sources of drive". These sources of drive may be primary or secondary.

"Broadly speaking, primary motivational variables are those that produce their effects through the action of inherited bodily mechanisms" (p. 61).

"*The secondary sources of drive* differ from their primary counterparts in that their efficacy as motivators rests largely upon learning" (p. 62).

Brown's terminology is thus very consistent, and his hypotheses about the working of secondary sources of drive are the most thorough and extensive the present author has found concerning this important problem.

He builds his hypotheses upon Mowrer's and Miller's well known experiments dealing with fear as a learned drive – or learned source of drive in his terminology.

He has formulated the hypothesis that fear is the secondary source in most instances of so-called "acquired drives" in human beings.

He thus writes (p. 172):

"At the heart of this interpretation, then, is the basic idea that an *"important motivating component of many of the supposed acquired drives for specific goal objects is actually a learned tendency to be discontented or distressed or anxious in the absence of those goals"* (Brown, 1953).

Brown elaborates this hypothesis in connection with money, and shows that:

"anxiety might serve as a learned motivating agency for money-seeking responses if it is aroused by cues indicating the absence of money" (p. 172).

But he also mentions, that the same relationship could be valid for the goals of power, prestige and the like. He thus writes (p. 175):

"Anxiety-arousing properties could certainly be acquired by stimuli denoting a lack of prestige or affection or power, and could thus provide a motivational mainspring for responses directed toward these goals as well."

Besides these hypotheses Brown also elaborates rather extensively hypotheses about the function of *words* and *language* as acquired sources of drive. He thus formulates the following hypothesis, that (p. 183):

"these verbal commands serve as conditioned stimuli to arouse learned responses that have motivating effects upon other responses."

And Brown goes further and asserts the hypothesis that words "would also be motivating when spoken by an individual to himself" (p. 183). This hypothesis is applied to the problem of "need-achievement" and he arrives at this conclusion (p. 185):

"In short, self-administered "try-hard" instructions such as these may constitute the basic "acquired drive" of the high need-achiever and may be used by him in a wide variety of circumstances."

Brown's theory about the function of secondary sources of drive is a very clear, consistent and parsimonious theory, as he lays by far the most stress on fear as the basis for all acquired sources of drive. But *incentive motivation* (K) is also treated in his book (pp. 176–180[3]).

However, he also analyzes the possibility of other sources. Hunger is experimentally investigated, but he reaches (p. 190) the conclusion that:

"there is no convincing experimental evidence to support the contention that hunger, like fear, can after training, be elicited as a learned response to a conditioned stimulus."

Turning to the *H-H-hypotheses* in Brown's theory, we shall first consider the most important, which he has borrowed from Hull. It is the hypothesis about the multiplicative relation between "Drive" (D) and "Habit strength" (H) which combine to produce "Reaction (or Excitatory) Potential" (E):

$$B = f(E) = f(D \times H).$$

Besides this H-H-hypothesis Brown has elaborated (in Chapter 6) a hypothesis about "Frustration". This H-variable is defined as a state which raises the subject's level of drive. This Frustration is thus an H-variable, which is the result of conflict or competition between several reaction tendencies (Es). One of these reaction tendencies may be an inhibitive tendency (I) determined by "Thwarting" (or response interference)[4]. Brown gives us an excellent overview of his (and Farber's) frustration theory in this diagram Fig. 6.1., p. 203, which is reproduced below as our Fig. 10.2.:

---

3. In a later survey of "Secondary Motivational Systems" (in "Annual Review of Psychology", Vol. 19, 1968) Brown and E. E. Farber added *incentive motivation* to the important secondary motivations. They discuss these phenomena in the light of K. W. Spence's and Hull's theory about "K", which stands for the motivational component of the "r_g-s_g-mechanism", or the fractional antedating goal-response. Brown and Farber seem to favor a *"frustration interpretation"* of K:

"This view implies that it is the lack of an incentive or goal object, in the presence of cues previously associated with that incentive that is motivating." (Brown and Farber, 1968, p. 115).

4. The reader should be informed that "thwarting" is used in the same way as "frustration" is by other psychologists.

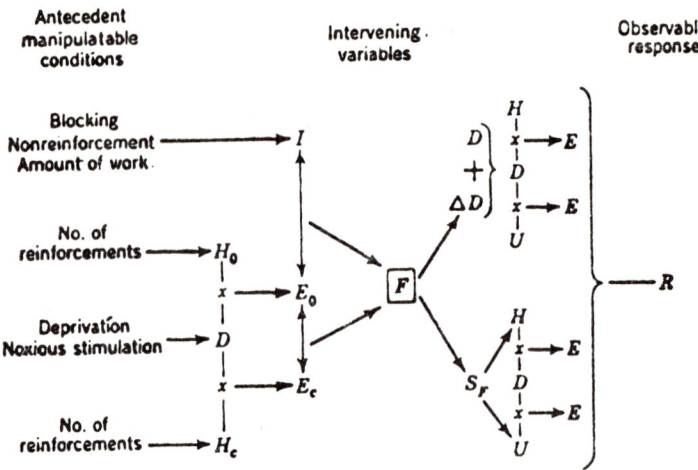

Fig. 10.2 This diagram summarizes the antecedent conditions and hypothetical variables of the frustration theory of Brown and Farber (1951). The state of frustration (F) is assumed to be produced by competition (indicated by double-headed arrows) between an ongoing excitatory tendency (E.) and either an inhibitory tendency (I) or a competitive excitatory tendency (E.). These interacting tendencies are shown to depend upon their respective habit strengths (H. and H.), drive (D), and upon the indicated antecedent conditions. The consequences of frustration are shown as either an increment in general drive (ΔD), or frustration-specific stimuli (S_F), or both. These factors are assumed to have respectively, the same kinds of motivational and associative functions assigned to them in Hull's behavior theory.

The last H-H-hypothesis deals with the interaction between "Drive" and "perception", which enter into theories of behavior in the role of a "scientific construct" (p. 324). Brown reviews the experiments about "motivational variables and perception" in Chapter 8. He summarizes them in the following formulations (p. 325):

Studies of the effects of primary sources of drive upon behavior in perceptual situations have yielded suggestive but inconsistent results."

"A review of representative investigations purporting to show that the judged size of objects is affected by their value leads to the conclusion that the effect at best is slight, especially when the valued objects are physically present."

Brown is also a little sceptical about a motivational interpretation in the areas of research in "perceptual defense" and "perceptual sensitization" and recommends that:

"alternative interpretations couched in terms of individual differences in familiarity with certain classes of stimuli merit careful appraisal" (p. 326).

These views about the influence of Drive upon the responses that define perception are consistent with Brown's non-specific, activation drive concepts.

From this general drive concept are also deduced the *H-R-hypotheses* about "motivational variables and human performance", which are elaborated in Chapter 7. The general H-R-hypothesis is formulated by Brown in the summary (p. 263):

"According to generalized drive theory, hunger should enhance all reactive tendencies, thereby leading to better performance when correct habits are strongest and to poorer performance when incorrect tendencies are dominant."

But Brown regrets that "experiments to evaluate these expectations have seldom been conducted" (p. 263); and the reviewed experiments may be interpreted in accordance with associative principles.

After the above review with quotations from Brown's hypotheses, we make our customary partially symbolic reformulation of the hypotheses. We have changed the usual abbreviations made by Hull's co-workers in this was: "sEr" or "reaction evocation potential" is abbreviated as H_E. "D" or "Drive" as H_D, "sHr" or "habit strength" as H_H. "I_R" or "inhibitory strength" as "H_I", "Frustration" as H_F, "r_g-s_g" or fractional antedating goal response" as $H(r_g$-$s_g)$. With these symbols we have made the following systematic reconstruction:

1. hypothesis: $S(need) \rightarrow H_D$[5])
2. hypothesis: $S(UCS) \rightarrow H(pain)$
3. hypothesis: $S(CS) \rightarrow H(fear)$
4. hypothesis: $S(UCS) \rightarrow H(sUr)$
5. hypothesis: $S(CS) \rightarrow H(r_g$-$s_g)$
6. hypothesis: $S(lack\ of\ affection) \rightarrow H(anxiety)$
7. hypothesis: $S(lack\ of\ power) \rightarrow H(anxiety)$
8. hypothesis: $S(lack\ of\ prestige) \rightarrow H(anxiety)$
9. hypothesis: $S(lack\ of\ money) \rightarrow H(anxiety)$
10. hypothesis: $S(motivation\ words) \rightarrow H(anxiety)$
11. hypothesis: $S(amount\ of\ work) \rightarrow H_I$
12. hypothesis: $S(blocking\ of\ response) \rightarrow H_I$
13. hypothesis: $S(non\text{-}reinforcement) \rightarrow H_I$
14. hypothesis: $S(reinforcement) \rightarrow H_H$
15. hypothesis: $H_{r-s} \rightarrow H_D$
16. hypothesis: $H(fear) \rightarrow H_D$
17. hypothesis: $(H_D \times H_H) \rightarrow H_E$
18. hypothesis: $(H_I \longleftrightarrow H_E) \rightarrow H_F$
19: hypothesis: $(H_{E1} \longleftrightarrow H_{E2}) \rightarrow H_F$
20. hypothesis: $H_F \rightarrow H_D$
21. hypothesis: $H_E \rightarrow R(instrumental\ and\ goal\ reaction)$
22. hypothesis: $H(UCS) \rightarrow R_G$

5. "Need" embraces both "deprivation" and "noxious stimuli".

This systematic reconstruction of Brown's hypotheses forms the basis for this classification into:

1. *Purely theoretical hypotheses (H-H):*
   Hypotheses No. 15, 16, 17, 18, 19 and 20. In all: 6 hypotheses.
2. *Partly empirical hypotheses:*
   a. S-H-hypotheses: Hypotheses No. 1 to 14 incl. In all: 14 hypotheses.
   b. H-R-hypotheses: No. 21 and 22. In all: 2 hypotheses.

2.2.2. The complexity of the hypotheses: There are only a few multi-dimensional hypotheses (No. 17, 18 and 19). The rest are *one-dimensional*. Therefore the degree of complexity of the hypotheses may be described in terms of the "in between category": *dynamic hypotheses*. They are certainly not "mechanistic" as the multiplicative relationships between D and H show, but neither are they so complex as in field theories. The only hypothesis in Brown's theory which is almost field-theoretical in complexity is his hypothesis about "Frustration" (Cf. Fig. 10.2.).

2.2.3. The functional relationships in the hypotheses. There are no explicit formulations about the kind of determinism assumed in Brown's theory. But implicitly the hypotheses indicate *causal determinism*. The more statistical or "probability-deterministic" views in Hull's later works play no role in his theory.

The descriptive stratum

3.1. *The abstract D-level*

Brown presents a very thorough discussion of the problem of defining responses and stimuli independently to avoid circular reasoning. He arrives (p. 26) at:

> "the conclusion that, given precise criteria of observation, responses can be identified and recorded reliably even when observers know nothing of the stimuli that elicit the responses. Similarly, the conclusion is reached that environmental events such as lights, sounds, and odors, can be identified and measured by physical procedures, irrespective of whether these events are correlated with responses."

Besides this analysis of the independent S-variables and the dependent R-variable, Brown also makes a detailed analysis of "varieties of functional relations" or empirical generalizations ("laws"). This is done by using Spence's classification of laws which we also have employed. Besides S-R-relations he also mentions R-R and O-R-relations. In the last case "O" stands for empirical, independent variables in the organism (*not* H-variables with physiological "surplus meaning" as is the case in this book).

Brown also shows that S-R and O-R-laws can be combined by varying both the condition of the organism and the stimulus situations.

"Relations obtained under such conditions might be termed S O–R–laws, since the dependent variable (the response) is a joint function of both an organic variable and an environmental one" (p. 19).

As an example of an O-condition which *can* be treated as an *independent* variable (as well as an intervening variable) he mentions the activity of the reticular system.

As concrete cases of S-R-laws Brown discusses some experimental findings about the relationships concerning "performance as a function of variations in primary sources of drive" (pp. 70–94), but it would lead us too far afield to go into a more detailed analysis of this part of the book.

3.2. *The concrete D-level*

The protocol statements and fundamental terms in Brown's theory deal with classes of responses. He summarizes his reasons for this (p. 26):

"Since no two responses are ever exactly alike, the investigator in gathering his basic data, must deal with classes or groups of responses."

Related to this is the problem of the level or units of description.

3.3. *The descriptive units*

Brown discusses this problem in his book in connection with "the behavioral approach" (contra the "physiological approach"), and he writes (p. 23):

"In following the behavioral approach, therefore, one deals primarily with molar rather than molecular behavior. – – –".

And on the same page (p. 23) he defines the term:

"molar behavior, meaning relatively gross movements or goal-oriented actions of the entire organism."

As his approach is what he calls "behavioral", and as his book mainly deals with "gross movements and goal-oriented actions", it should be correct to classify the theory as a *molar theory*.

The theory as a whole

4.1. *The formal properties*

As usual we conclude by describing Brown's theory as a whole. Following our outline we first look at the formal properties of the theory.

(4.1.1.) *The systematic organization* of Brown's theory is on the level of an *explanatory sketch*. There are some very clear "summaries" of the chapters in his book, but no explicitly formulated hypotheses and definitions, so the theory cannot be classified as an "explanatory system" – and of course not as a "deductive system" like Hull's theory. In fact many of Hull's students – Spence, Brown, Mowrer and others – have *not* followed him in his deductive theorizing.

(4.1.2.) *The preciseness of representation* in Brown's theory is mainly on the *verbal* level although there is *some partial symbolization* because of the employment of some of Hull's symbols (D, sHr, sEr, etc.).

(4.1.3.) *The properties of the models* employed in Brown's theory are on the level of *two-dimensional models*. He includes several diagrams among which we have selected and reproduced (in section 2.2.1.) his diagram representing his and Farber's frustration model.

4.2. The epistemological properties

The epistemological properties of Brown's theory clearly place it in the category of *explanatory* theories and in the sub-type of *neutral* explanatory or $S\text{-}H_N\text{-}R$-theories.

4.3. The theory-empiry ratio

The general impression made by Brown's theory is such that we feel confident in classifying it as a rather *empirical* theory. We can calculate the Hypotheses Quotient on the basis of our systematic reconstruction of the hypotheses (made in Section 2.2.1. of this chapter). We thus get:

$$\text{H. Q.} = \frac{\Sigma(H-H)}{\Sigma[(S-H)+(H-R)]} = \frac{6}{14+2} = \frac{6}{16} = 0.38.$$

Concluding remarks. The H.Q. is almost the same as that of Hull's, which we calculated as being 0.30. (Later calculated by computer as 0.36). This confirms the impression that Brown has been faithful to Hull's traditions. At the same time he has developed the clearest and most elegant theory of secondary motivation we have found.

11 : Woodworth's Theory

Introduction

The American psychologist, *R. S. Woodworth* (1869–1962), certainly needs no introduction. Among psychologists he is very well-known – especially as the author of several textbooks and handbooks, which are based upon an unusually all-round orientation and deep insight into psychology.

As early as 1918 he wrote a book, "Dynamic Psychology", in which he introduced a drive concept which was different from both Freud's and McDougall's. Forty years later, in 1958, Woodworth wrote a new book about the same subject with the title "Dynamics of Behavior". In this book he reconsidered the drive concept, criticized contemporary theories of motivation and formulated a new theory of motivation[1]), which deserves to be analyzed here.

The metastratum

1.1. *Philosophical propositions*

As is usual among modern psychologists Woodworth has no explicit formulations about philosophical problems. But from the explicit metatheoretical and methodological propositions it would seem that he presupposes a *neutral-monistic* theory of the psychosomatic problem, and that he presupposes a biological Darwinian philosophy of Man, as did the other functionalistic American psychologists.

1.2. *The metatheoretical propositions*

It is consistent with Woodworth's broad, functionalistic attitude to psychology that he criticizes a purely descriptive S-R-psychology. He summarizes his criticisms thus (p. 31):

"The objections raised to the S–R-formula mean that it is too limited. It seems to imply that nothing important occurs between the stimulus and the motor response. Or it seems to imply that the sensory stimulus is the only causative factor in the arousal of a response.

---

1. His motivational theory is presented in the first 5 chapters of the book. The remaining 7 chapters deal with perception and learning.

These limitations can be avoided by the addition of another symbol to stand for the organism.

The S–O–R-formula.
The O inserted between S and R makes explicit the obvious role of the living and active organism in the process; O receives the stimulus and makes the response."

Earlier in the book Woodworth identifies his "O-variables" with *Tolman's* "intervening variables". He also discusses *Skinner's* view of substituting "A (antecedent) variables" for intervening variables which he argues against with the words (p. 7):

"Any competent psychologist, we may argue, will be alive to the pitfall pointed out by Skinner and stilll find it more than merely convenient to conceive of intervening variables. It is necessary to bear in mind that antecedent operations have produced effects in the organism which persist in some form and only so can be factors in the present behavior. At the present time they are O-factors and no longer A-factors.

As we shall see later it is these variables that the organism perceives and reports about in the introspective method. Therefore, Woodworth's positive attitude towards the introspective method is consistent with his metatheoretical position expressed in the S-O-R-formula.

Finally, it should be stated explicitly that Woodworth's "O-variables" are not identical with the "O-variables" as used in this book, as they are *not* intervening variables with physiological surplus meaning, but rather hypothetical variables with neutral surplus meaning.

About the possibility of constructing physiological variables and theories Woodworth writes (p. 25):

"It may be a long time before convincing physiological theories of thinking, of learning and retention, and of behaving in general can be achieved. Meanwhile we wish not only to assemble miscellaneous behavioral facts but also to interrelate them dynamically. It can be done at the molar level. And it is probable that molar psychological dynamics will be more serviceable in the understanding, prediction, and control of behavior than even well-developed physiological theories."

What Woodworth here calls "molar psychological dynamics" is what we call H-terms with neutral surplus meaning. He implicitly makes the assumption that "molecular" is always identical with "physiological" (and "molar" with "behavioral" or "psychological"). As we know from the analyses made in "Theories of Motivation", this is often, but not always the case (e. g., Hebb's theory is rather molar and physiological).

1.3. *Methodological propositions*

About his preference for a data language Woodworth writes in the preface (p. 6):

"The point of view is not behavioristic, however, though most of the recent experimental material cited is objective rather than subjective."

Later he writes more explicitly about his view of "behaviorism" (p. 7):

"A student of behavior is not necessarily a behaviorist. A loyal adherent of the behavioristic school is subject to certain restrictions: he must not make use of introspective data; he must not speak of "mental" processes; he must regard animal behavior as better suited for fundamental research than the more complicated human behavior."

It is especially the anti-introspective attitude which Woodworth objects to. He writes for the use of introspection with these words (p. 9):

"There is usually no reason for rejecting this introspective report as untrustworthy. And can we say that he is ascribing his act to a "mental" cause in the sense that is so objectionable to the behaviorists, i.e., a non-physical cause that lies outside the fields of natural cause and effect? On the contrary – – – without perceiving the physiological details, he perceives the familiar bodily state as a whole."

We found the clearest formulation about the use of introspective data on p. 12:

"The difficulty of drawing any sharp line between introspective and non-introspective observation makes it seem rather ridiculous to exclude all introspective data from the study of behavior, as if such exclusion were required by scientific morality. The requirement is, rather, to separate the introspective sheep from the goats, for undoubtedly much goes on in a person's learning, thinking and deciding that he cannot observe accurately. Often the most promising line of attack on a problem is to use introspective results as suggestive of hypotheses which can be put to the test of quantitative objective experiments."

We have quoted Woodworth's view so extensively, because it is so clear why he permits psychologists to use introspection, while he at the same time is aware of its shortcomings.

But in spite of this positive attitude to introspection, we cannot describe his view as showing a preference for a phenomenological data language, because he writes the following about the definition of psychology (p. 20):

"Even before the advent of behaviorism, about 1912, psychologists were beginning to regard the word *behavior* as a good term for the subject matter of their science, a better term for the purpose than *consciousness* or *mind* or even *mental processes*. One reason was the obvious fact that mental processes became of practical or social importance when they gave rise to overt activity, including, of course, spoken or written language. Another reason was the increasing emphasis on objective, rather than introspective methods in psychology, though many psychologists who liked the word *behavior* refused to join Watson in his attempt to eliminate introspection altogether. Probably the main reason was that *behavior* was a more comprehensive term. It could include motor activity, often regarded as different from mental activity, and it could include unconscious processes and factors."

Woodworth has in the above quotation summarized all the good reasons for defining "psychology" as "the science of behavior".

It is obvious from the extensive quotations we have presented that he prefers a *behavioral data language* (rather than a phenomenological one) in spite of the fact that he at the same time doesn't wish to exclude introspection as a useful method. He avoids inconsistencies and combines these metatheoretical principles by considering introspective data as verbal (behavioral) reports. The present author thinks that this is the most fruitful solution to this epistemological problem.

He presents no explicit formulations about methodological principles – other than the already quoted discussions of the introspective method.

The hypothetical stratum

2.0. *Summary of the hypotheses*

Before analyzing the contents of explanatory terms and sentences, we shall present a very short *summary* of the hypotheses.

The function of behavior is "dealing with the environment". This function requires the interaction of "abilities" and motivation. "Abilities" to deal with the environment are the results of perception and learning (which Woodworth deals with in the last 7 chapters of his book). The primary motivation of behavior is this tendency to deal with the environment; the satisfaction of organic needs is only a sort of secondary goal which is the result of certain behavior acts. As he formulates it (p. 124):

"Here we are making the claim that this direction of receptive and motor activity toward the environment is the fundamental tendency of animal and human behavior and that it is the all-pervasive primary motivation of behavior. That is what we mean by a behavior-primacy theory of motivation."

Or perhaps better (p. 127):

"What the present theory says is that the inclusive drive is the tendency to deal with the environment, and that capacities are capacities for dealing with the environment in various ways."

We can present the theory in a diagram (Fig. 11.1.).

2.1. *The hypothetical terms (H-terms)*

As these summarizing quotations show the main *H-variables* in Woodworth's theory are "abilities" and "motivation". And "motivation" – which is our concern – contains two main variables: *"preparatory set"* and *"drive"*.

2.1.1. *The surplus meaning of the H-terms*

The definition of preparatory set or *"pre-set"* is formulated as follows (p. 41):

"For a formal definition we may say that preparatory set is a state of readiness to receive a stimulus that has not yet arrived or a state of readiness to make a movement that cannot be done until a preliminary movement has been made."

About the metascientific classification of his concepts Woodworth writes (p. 41):

"The state of readiness is an O-factor in the ensuing behavior. – – –
  Probably brain readiness more than the muscular tension is responsible for the contributions of this O-factor to efficient behavior."

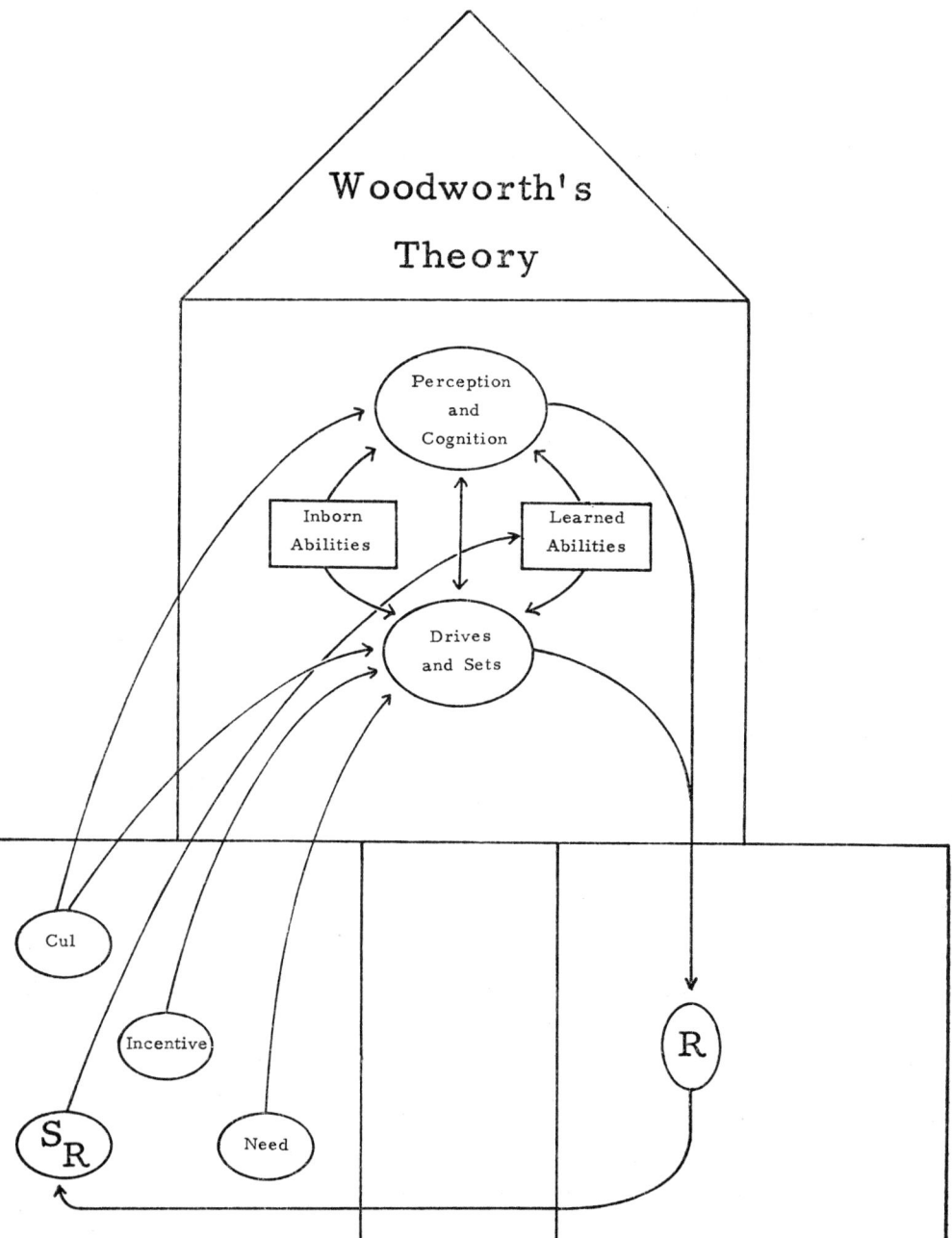

Fig. 11.1 Diagram presenting Woodworth's theory: Behavior (R) is determined by "drives" and "cognitive processes". These are in turn determined by the independent variables "need", "incentive", "cue" and "reinforcing stimuli" (S_R). In addition, "drives" and "cognitive processes" are influenced by inborn and learned "abilities".

This quotation could perhaps give the impression that "preparatory set" is a neurophysiological H-variable. But that is not the case. On the next page (p. 42) he makes it clear that:

"We can treat it as an intervening variable and tie it to observable stimuli and A-factors on the input side and to observable results on the output side."

This quotation demonstrates that "pre-set" *is an H-term with neutral surplus meaning* (despite Woodworth's special use of the symbol "O"). But the next to the last quotation shows, as do many other passages, that he is not far from or completely against a neurophysiological interpretation.

This is also the case with the other main motivational variable, *"drive"*. Concerning this explanatory term he writes (p. 58):

"– – – drive is a "construct" rather than an observable datum in animal behavior. Human beings, however, give introspective evidence of an active drive when they report "wanting" to do something and proced to do that very thing. Human beings thus manifest numerous drives which do not depend on any known physiological needs.

Another term which should be added to our collection is *set* (preparatory set, preset, goal set). Any fundamental difference between set and drive would be hard to find, though "set" suggests limited activities and "drive" broader fields of activities."

It is from this quite obvious that Woodworth's *"drive"-concept is an H-term with neutral surplus meaning.*. But it is clear from some of the following quotations that in this case too, the H-variable is not completely without neurophysiological "surplus meaning".

2.1.2. *Dispositional or functional terms?* Now that we have classified Woodworth's H-terms as being H_N-terms, we turn to our second classification into disposition and function variables. It is easy to describe "set" and "drive" as *function variables*. But Woodworth also has something to say about factors which contribute to individual differences. In connection with an exposition of what he calls "outgoing" motives (including achievement, affiliation, domination and other motives) he writes (p. 96), that "Individuals differ in the relative strength of these motives". As far as the causes for individual differences are concerned he lays special emphasis both on home environment, and different cultures and subcultures. "But the individual's genes should not be disregarded" (p. 95). He does not go deeper into these problems, and he has no names to designate the disposition variables (genes and so on) which influence the motivational function variables.

2.1.3. *Dynamic, directive or vectorial terms?* It is rather easy to classify Woodworth's term "drive" as a *vector* term because he clearly states (p. 60):

"By analogy with a force in physics, a drive has two distinguishable characteristics, *intensity* and *direction*. – – – If we disregard for the moment its direction, we can say that any drive activates the organism."

It is the "intensity- or activation-component" of the "drive concept" that can be neurophysiologically interpreted. About this Woodworth writes (p. 62):

"We are beginning to obtain some data on the physiology of drive, or at least of activation. – – – These levels of cortical activation seem to be controlled by that part of the interbrain called the *hypothalamus* which sends nerve fibers upward to all parts of the cortex and also downward to the autonomic system."

As the reader may observe from this quotation, Woodworth ascribes the activation function solely to the hypothalamus. And he does not mention the Reticular Activation System here in this connection or in other places in the book. It is certainly curious if the RAS should have escaped the attention of the fabulously well-oriented Woodworth. It is especially strange as he was familiar with the experiments of *Olds and Milner* with intracranial stimulation, the results of which he received "with a shock of surprise" (p. 121).

As "pre-set" is regarded by him as a special kind of drive, we can also classify it as a *vector* term.

"Abilities" and "perception" are purely *directive* terms.

Thus there are no purely dynamic terms in Woodworth's theory.

2.2. Classifications of the hypotheses

We have already (in 2.0.0.) summarized the main content of Woodworth's hypotheses. A more detailed understanding of the content of the hypotheses can be gained by studying the next classification.

2.2.1. *Basic classification of hypotheses.* In this classification we shall first present the *S-H-hypotheses*.

One of these hypotheses deals with the relationship between "need" and "drive". Woodworth writes (p. 58):

"Though drive is to be distinguished from need, a physiological need is likely to generate a drive – – – and the intensity of the drive can be increased by prolonging the deprivation period."

Not all drives are determined by needs, as we can see from the following (p. 59):

"The drive to escape from a noxious or obnoxious stimulus – – – is not built up gradually to internal physiological processes, as hunger is, but is aroused by a persistent external stimulus. Here we have an important class of cases where a drive is aroused by an incentive."

Intimately related to the "escape drive" is the "avoidance drive" which "is aroused by a signal or "cue" from the oncoming incentive" (p. 60).

Among Woodworth's most important *H-H-hypotheses* we find one on the first page (p. 1):

"Motives do not operate in a vacuum, and the behavior in which they do operate is affected by the processes of perception, learning and thinking. Not only are these processes motivated, but motives themselves depend on how a situation is perceived and understood and on habits and ways of meeting a situation that have been previously learned."

The same hypothesis is formulated in a slightly different way (p. 48):

"Ability and motivation seem to be two necessary factors in any performance. They are complementary factors; if both are present the performance will occur, but not if either one is lacking."

This formulation looks like Hull's multiplicative "drive × habit" hypothesis, if we identify his "habit" with Woodworth's "ability". But there is the difference that "ability" after all is more important in Woodworth's theory, as "abilities" or "capacities to deal with the environment" are main sources of motivation. This is the main hypothesis in his special *"behavior-primacy theory"* (as distinguished from a "need-primacy theory"). The most concentrated formulation we found was on p. 133:

"The behavior-primacy theory regards the tendency to deal with the environment as a primary drive, and indeed as *the* primary drive in behavior. The various capacities for dealing with the environment afford outlets for the general behavior drive and give it different forms – given the necessary environmental opportunities. So the manifold human interests are predictable from the combination. – – –
Perhaps the behavior-primacy theory, even though no great intellectual achievement, will have practical value in education, where the need-primacy theory certainly appears to be useless."

The present author thinks that Woodworth is right in his evaluation of the importance of his behavior-primacy theory for education; but the same educational utility *can* be achieved by supplementing a need-primacy theory with some sort of primary "activity motives" and a primary curiosity motive (cf. the chapter about Berlyne's theory).

Among the *H-R-hypotheses* in Woodworth's theory we have already touched upon the most fundamental, which perhaps is most clearly formulated on p. 63:

"In general, a drive has direction as well as intensity; it is selective as well as activating."

We have quoted from some of Woodworth's discussions of the *activating* function of drive. Curiously enought he presents little positive evidence for the *directing* function of drive; his evidence is mainly negative and formulated as criticism of "the theory of non-directive drive" (i. e., Hull's and Brown's theories).

The most positive evidence for the directing function of drive is presented by Woodworth in his attempt to explain *"activation"* as in reality a *"sensitization function"*. His empirical evidence for this hypothesis is knowledge about sensitization effects: e. g., the effects from sex hormones, adrenalin and poorly nourished blood on the stimuli that cause behavior.

After this review of quotations from Woodworth's hypotheses it remains to make the partially *symbolic reformulations*. In these we shall use "cognition" as a common term covering perception as well as other cognitive processes, "motives" for "drive" and "set", and "abilities" for inborn abilities, learned skills, knowledge, etc. Thus we get:

1. hypothesis: S(need) → H(drive)
2. hypothesis: S(need) → H(set)
3. hypothesis: S(incentive) → H(drive)
4. hypothesis: S(incentive) → H(set)
5. hypothesis: S(cue) → H(cognition)
6. hypothesis: S(cue) → H(motives)
7. hypothesis: H(abilities) → H(motives)
8. hypothesis: H(abilities) → H(cognition)
9. hypothesis: H(motives) → H(cognition)
10. hypothesis: H(cognition) → H(motives)
11. hypothesis: H(motives × cognition) → R(performance)

This systematic reconstruction results in the following basic classification:

1. *Purely theoretical hypotheses (H-H):*
   Hypotheses No. 7, 8, 9 and 10. In all: 4 hypotheses.
2. *Partly empirical hypotheses:*
   a. S-H-hypotheses: No. 1 to 6 incl. In all 6 hypotheses.
   b. H-R-hypotheses: No. 11. In all: 1 hypothesis.

2.2.2. *The complexity of the hypotheses.* Concerning the *degree of complexity* of the hypotheses we can describe them as *dynamic hypotheses*. The hypotheses about the general interaction between "abilities" and "drives" show most clearly that they are certainly not "mechanistic"; but, on the other hand, they are not so complicated that they deserve to be described as "field *theoretical*".

2.2.3. *The functional relationships in the hypotheses.* Concerning the problem of *determinism* Woodworth takes up the old dichotomy between teleology contra mechanism rather than the more modern dichotomy "deterministic contra statistic laws". About the old problem he writes (p. 54):

"Mechanism and teleology seem both to be involved. The question is whether one of them can be reduced to the other. To attempt a reduction of all organic processes to teleology – – – would seem hopeless and worse than useless. But to discover causal mechanisms for goal-seeking activities, along S-R lines, might be possible and would be practically useful; – – –"

In connection with a discussion of McDougall's teleological viewpoint Woodworth concludes (p. 35):

"Cause and effect of the ordinary, mechanistic sort appear to be sufficient."

So it is correct to describe Woodworth's theory as a *deterministic theory*, but it is "causal determinism", not the modern "probability" determinism.

The descriptive stratum

3.1. *The abstract D-level*

Among the most important abstract descriptive terms in Woodworth's theory are, of course, the independent S-variables and the dependent R-variables.

Concerning the *S-variables* he underlines the distinction between the "stimulus" and the "stimulus object". The object is a source of stimulation, and a stimulus is defined (p. 29) as:

"Any physical energy, to be a stimulus, must arouse some receptor to at least minimal activity."

Among the *R-variables* he stresses the importance of integration of movements. He writes (pp. 37–38):

"In general, integrated sequences of movement seem to be characteristic and even essential in the behavior of organisms, whether high or low in the animal scale."

Woodworth further distinguishes between "two-phase motor units" and "polyphase motor units". In the two-phase motor units "the first phase is preparatory, the second effective or consummatory" (p. 37).

The most important R-variable in his theory is perhaps the concept *"retroflex"*, which he introduces with the words (p. 33):

"To complete the formula for any bit of behavior, we must add a symbol for the retroflex, such as "Rx". We can then write S–O–R–Rx, to be read that a stimulus, acting on the organism, elicits a response and that the response generates new stimuli, which feed back into the organism. The term, *retroflex,* to identify sensory feedback, was introduced by Troland in 1928."

It is about this retroflex that Woodworth formulates an important, well-known *S-R-generalization* or "law" (p. 34):

"Prompt feedback of reward or punishment for a certain response to a situation is likely to have an after-effect when the person meets the same situation again. The success or failure of an attempt has a similiar after-effect. In this connection the retroflex (or at least a favorable one) is called a *reinforcement.*"

3.2. *The concrete D-level*

The basic terms and protocol statements which Woodworth's theory contains come from the descriptions of the experiments, which he presents as empirical evidence for this theory. They are mainly based on other psychologists' experiments with animals and men. There are no special sorts of preferred experiments; even introspective reports are accepted in consistence with his meta-principles.

3.3. *The descriptive units*

Woodworth's preferred descriptive units are *molar units*. About Tolman's distinction he writes (p. 22):

"The distinction is really not between two kinds of behavior, for the same behavior can be taken either way; it is a distinction between two kinds of description, a psychological description being always molar and a physiological description being often though not always molecular. Tolman's main point was that the molar description could bring to light characteristics of behavior that would not be known by a molecular description."

We have earlier in this chapter had the opportunity of commenting on Woodworth's identification of "molar" with "psychological" and "molecular" with "physiological". As the reader can see from the above quotation, the last identification is not satisfactory.

The theory as a whole

4.1. *The formal properties*

Let us now consider Woodworth's theory as a whole. Firstly, the formal properties of the theory.

(4.1.1.) *The systematic organization* of the theory is on the level of an *explanatory sketch*. There are neither explicit formulations of hypotheses nor definitions, so there is no doubt about the validity of this classification.

(4.1.2.) *The preciseness of the representation* is on the level of a purely *verbal* theory, as there is no symbolization and no mathematical formulas are employed. But Woodworth's style of writing is certainly very clear.

(4.1.3.) *The properties of the models* employed are on the level of *verbal analogies*, but there are only a few in Woodworth's theory.

4.2. *The epistemological properties*

The epistemological properties of Woodworth's theory clearly place it in the main category of *explanatory theories*. And despite his special use of the symbol "0" in the formula "S-O-R", we are sure that his theory belongs to the sub-category of *neutral* explanatory theories or $S-H_N-R$-theories.

4.3. *The theory-empiry ratio*

We think that Woodworth's theory belongs to the middle part of the continuum going from the most speculative to the most empirical theories.

We have calculated the Hypotheses Quotient on the basis of the systematic reconstruction presented in section 2.2.1. of this chapter:

The result reads:

$$\text{H. Q.} = \frac{\Sigma(H-H)}{\Sigma[(S-H)+(H-R)]} = \frac{4}{6+1} = \frac{4}{7} = 0.57.$$

Concluding remarks. If the reader has got the impression – in spite of the attempt to make an objective analysis – that the present author admires Woodworth, it is not wrong. I think he and Tolman are the greatest integrators and systematizers in psychology. They have contributed more than others to bring about the integration of the conflicting schools into one unitary science of psychology.

12: Festinger's Theory

Introduction

In 1957 a book appeared by the American psychologist, *Leon Festinger*, entitled "A Theory of Cognitive Dissonance". It presented a "cognitive" theory of motivation which is very original and which has been fruitful in stimulating experimental and other empirical research. Therefore we have selected Festinger's theory for a comparative analysis. In this chapter we shall concentrate on Festinger's main book from 1957, which we feel provides a balanced picture of his theory. In a concluding section we shall comment on other books by Festinger and his co-workers[1]).

The metastratum

1.1. *Philosophical propositions*

There is a very clear stratification of the text in Festinger's book in such a way that it is clear that the chapters belong to the *hypothetical* stratum (called "Theory" by Festinger) or the *descriptive* stratum (called "Data"). But there are no chapters explicitly belonging to the metastratum. However, the first chapter contains (under the title: "An Introduction to the Theory of Dissonance") some metapropositions. We find many historical, some metatheoretical and many methodological propositions, but no philosophical propositions in this chapter. Thus we must go on the assumption that Festinger's theory of the psychosomatic problem and his philosophy of man are not radically different from those of other American psychologists – otherwise he would have indicated it by some explicit propositions. If this guess is correct he presupposes a *neutral monistic theory* of the mind-body problem and a Darwinian, *biological conception of man*.

1.2. *Metatheoretical propositions*

There are very few metatheoretical propositions (in the narrow sense) and most of them are dispersed throughout the book in the form of comment to passages

---

1. Festinger's theory is unique, because it grows out of social psychology and thus does not belong to any of the main traditions in motivational psychology. Therefore we have placed this chapter between those influenced by learning theory and those influenced by personality theory.

with hypothetical or descriptive content. Besides the above there are a few more general metatheoretical propositions. Thus Festinger writes about the general *level of preciseness*, which he intends to work with (p. 9):

> "Most of the remainder of this chapter will deal with a more formal exposition of the theory of dissonance. I will attempt to state the theory in as precise and unambiguous terms as possible. But since the ideas which constitute this theory are by no means yet in a completely precise form, some vagueness is unavoidable."

Festinger also has some metatheoretical propositions concerning the *range of applications* which exist for his theory. Thus he writes at the end of Chapter 1 (p. 31):

> "Although the core of the theory is simple, it has rather wide implications and applications to a variety of situations which on the surface look very different. The remainder of the book will spell out these specific implications of the theory and will examine data relevant to them."

From these quotations we can understand that his "ideal" psychological theory is one possessing *optimal preciseness combined with the widest possible application*. And we believe that he has succeeded in reaching his "ideal".

1.3. Methodological propositions

There are many methodological propositions in Festinger's theory. Most of them are scattered throughout the book as comments to the many investigations he builds his theory upon, but some of them are of a more general character.

Festinger includes many analyses of the relationship between theory and data. One of the best formulations, which is typical of Festinger's methodological approach, is found on p. 243:

> "In order to test a theory and its derivations, one usually appeals to instances which are not obvious so as to rule out alternative explanations. If the theory has any validity, however, it should also be consistent with a large body of data which are obvious. Certainly a theory which elegantly handles some nonobvious aspect of behavior, but is inconsistent with much that we know of an obvious sort, is not a very satisfactory theory."

This is a good formulation of the age-old *"principle of parsimony"*.

In several places he stresses the importance of *preciseness* in theoretical definitions and empirical methods. Thus he writes (p. 15):

> "The conceptual definitions of dissonance and consonance present some serious measurement difficulties. If the theory of dissonance is to have relevance for empirical data, one must be able to identify dissonances and consonances unequivocally."

Festinger *favors experimental investigations* – especially those involving control groups – over other kinds of empirical investigations. Thus he writes in connection with one of his many discussions of investigations (p. 140):

"This kind of ambiguity of interpretation and concomitant lack of cogency with regard to the hypothesis we are considering is typical of data on such matters. Rather than present a large variety of such data concerning the question on hand, we have selected a pair of studies to discuss, one of which, fortunately, contains a control group which makes the interpretation unequivocal."

Festinger also devotes a single passage to a discussion of the *introspective method* and the related *phenomenological data*. He writes (p. 72):

"Before we proceed, it may be well to say a word about the validity and trustworthiness of the kind of data which this study yields. The study used trained subjects (professionnal psychologists or students trained in introspection) and depended almost exclusively on introspective reports for its data. For many years now this type of data has been in disrepute, perhaps justifiably so. One may not want to trust a person's introspections as giving an adequate description of psychological processes, nor may conscious processes be of central importance. But for present purposes one can treat these data just as one would treat data collected from interviews."

We interpret this passage as being an expression of the methodological propositions, which conceive of the *behavioral data language* as the basic one, but at the same time accept the phenomenological *data* as *verbal behavior*. This is the neo-behavioristic principle, which Tolman made so popular among American psychologists.

The hypothetical stratum

2.0. *Summary of the hypotheses*

Festinger's theory is formulated in such a precise and systematic way, that it is easy to present a summary of it. We can do no better than quote his own summary of Chapter 1: "An Introduction to the Theory of Dissonance". In this chapter he presents all his main terms and hypotheses, and he summarizes them in the following fashion (p. 31):

"*Summary*

The core of the theory of dissonance which we have stated is rather simple. It holds that:
1. There may exist disonant or "nonfitting" relations among cognitive elements.
2. The existence of dissonance gives rise to pressures to reduce the dissonance and to avoid increases in dissonance.
3. Manifestations of the operations of these pressures include behavior changes, changes of cognition, and circumspect exposure to new information and new opinions."

From this quotation we get a good picture of the main elements and relationships in Festinger's theory. Perhaps some readers have wondered if this theory really is a *motivational* theory rather than a purely cognitive theory. Festinger explicitly uses the term "motivate" in his first presentation of the basic hypotheses on p. 3:

"The basic hypotheses I wish to state are as follows:
1. The existence of dissonance, being psychologically uncomfortable, will motivate the person to try to reduce the dissonance and achieve consonance.
2. When dissonance is present, in addition to trying to reduce it, the person will actively avoid situations and information which would likely increase the dissonance."

But toward the end of the book we find the following passage (p. 276):

"There are many factors affecting people's behavior, attitudes, and opinions about which the theory of dissonance has nothing to say. For example, we have said little or nothing about motivation throughout the course of this book. Dissonance itself can, of course, be considered as a motivating factor, but there are many other motives which affect human beings and we have skirted the question of any relationship between these other motivations and the pressure to reduce dissonance. There are, however, in some circumstances, clear relationships."
And Festinger continues on p. 277:
"But what I want to stress here is that I have not dealt with problems of motivation, and that these problems would, by and large, be distinct from the problems with which the theory of dissonance does deal."

In spite of his own ambivalent attitude toward motivational theory, we think that his theory really is a motivational theory whose subject is a special cognitive kind of motivation. This is even more clearly stated by he himself in the following passage (p. 3):

"In short, I am proposing that dissonance, that is, the existence of nonfitting relations among cognitions, is a motivating factor in its own right. By the term *cognition,* here and in the remainder of the book, I mean any knowledge, opinion, or belief about the environment, about oneself, or about one's behavior. Cognitive dissonance can be seen as an antecedent condition which leads to activity oriented toward dissonance reduction just as hunger leads to activity oriented toward hunger reduction. It is a very different motivation from what psychologists are used to dealing with but, as we shall see, nonetheless powerful."

Therefore, we think it well-justified to include Festinger's theory in this book.

2.1. *The hypothetical terms (H-terms)*

There are very few H-terms in Festinger's theory, which is another indication of the simple structure of the theory.

The important terms are of course "dissonance", its opposite, "consonance", and the related term, "irrelevance". These terms are defined in the following quotations. But before doing that Festinger had to define the *"elements"* which can be dissonant, consonant or irrelevant to each other. These "elements" are *cognitive* elements or pieces of "knowledge" defined in a broader sense in the following (pp. 9–10):

The terms "dissonance" and "consonance" refer to relations which exist between pairs of "elements". It is consequently necessary, before proceeding to define these relations, to define the elements themselves as well as we can.

These elements refer to what has been called cognition, that is, the things a person knows about himself, about his behavior, and about his surroundings. These elements, then, are "knowledges", if I may coin the plural form of the word. Some of these elements represent knowledge about oneself: what one does, what one feels, what one wants or desires, what one is, and the like. Other elements of knowledge concern the world in which one lives: what is where, what leads to what, what things are satisfying or painful or inconsequential or important, etc.

It is clear that the term "knowledge" has been used to include things to which the word does not ordinarily refer – for example, opinions. A person does not hold an opinion unless he thinks it is correct, and so, psychologically, it is not different from a "knowledge". The same is true of beliefs, values, or attitudes, which function as "knowledges" for our purposes. This is not to imply that there are no important distinctions to be made among these various terms. Indeed, some such distinctions will be made later on. But for the definitions here, these are all "elements of cognition", and relations of consonance and dissonance can hold between pairs of these elements."

The more formal definition of these terms is presented on p. 13:

"It is appropriate now to attempt a more formal conceptual definition.

Let us consider two elements which exist in a person's cognition and which are relevant to one another. The definition of dissonance will disregard the existence of all the other cognitive elements that are relevant to either or both of the two under consideration and simply deal with these two alone. *These two elements are in a dissonant relation, if, considering these two alone, the obverse of one element would follow from the other.* To state it a bit more formally, x and y are dissonant if not-x follows from y."

And finally we have a definition of "irrelevance" (p. 11): "That is under such circumstances where one cognitive element implies nothing at all concerning some other element, these two elements are irrelevant to one another."

2.1.1. The surplus meaning of the H-terms.

In the first quotation of definitions presented above there is possibly a small amount of mentalistic surplus meaning connected to the term "knowledge". But in the second quotation containing the formal definitions this mentalistic surplus meaning has completely disappeared and left terms with *no* surplus meaning ("intervening variables") or with *neutral* surplus meaning, i. e., H_N-terms. As there are no principle differences between the last two categories, we shall not pursue the question further.

2.1.2. Dispositional or functional terms?

It is rather difficult to classify "dissonance" and "knowledge" (cognitive elements) according to the duration of their existence.

A "cognitive element" – a piece of "knowledge" – refers to a variable, which can exist for years, once a person has acquired it. Thus it is a *disposition*. But when a cognitive element is actualized or activated – and perhaps conscious – it is at the same time a function – process or state. In Festinger's terminology there is no difference between the "knowledge as disposition" and the "knowledge as function".

"Dissonance" refers to a state or process which exists for an indefinite period until the person succeeds in reducing it by changing it to "consonance", which may then last years. Thus *"dissonance"* must be regarded as a *function*, while "consonance" is a disposition. Only in people with a very high dissonance tolerance can this variable exist for years and thus be regarded as a disposition.

2.1.3. *Dynamic, directive or vectorial terms?* It is easiest to classify the H-terms according to their effect on behavior.

"Cognitive elements" (or "knowledge") refers to variables which have an exclusively *directive* effect on behavior. This would seem to follow from the definition of the term "cognitive".

"Dissonance" refers to a variable which has a *dynamic* effect on behavior. This should be clear from the definitions quoted above. And in another place Festinger made the following comparison (p. 18):

"In other words, dissonance acts in the same way as a state of drive or need or tension."

Later he has the following to say (p. 260): "– – – there is a drive toward consonance among cognitions."

Although the terms "drive", "need" and "tension" – with which Festinger compares "dissonance" – are not always used as purely dynamic terms, but can also be used as vector terms, we think it correct to classify his "dissonance" as a purely *dynamic* term.

2.2.0. *Classifications of the hypotheses.* Before making the classifications of the hypotheses in Festinger's theory, we ought to present the hypotheses for consideration. Festinger himself has formulated his definitions and hypotheses precisely and systematically in the last chapter, we can do no better than quote his own recapitulation (see also Fig. 12.1.). Therefore, we present pages 260 to 266 incl. from his book:

Festinger's hypotheses

The various definitions, asumptions, and hypotheses which constitute the theory of cognitive dissonance have been stated in the five theoretical chapters of the book. In an effort to provide a brief summary of the theory, I will restate some of these definitions, assumptions, and hypotheses in as organized a manner as seems feasible.

The basic background of the theory consists of the notion that the human organism tries to establish internal harmony, consistency, or congruity among

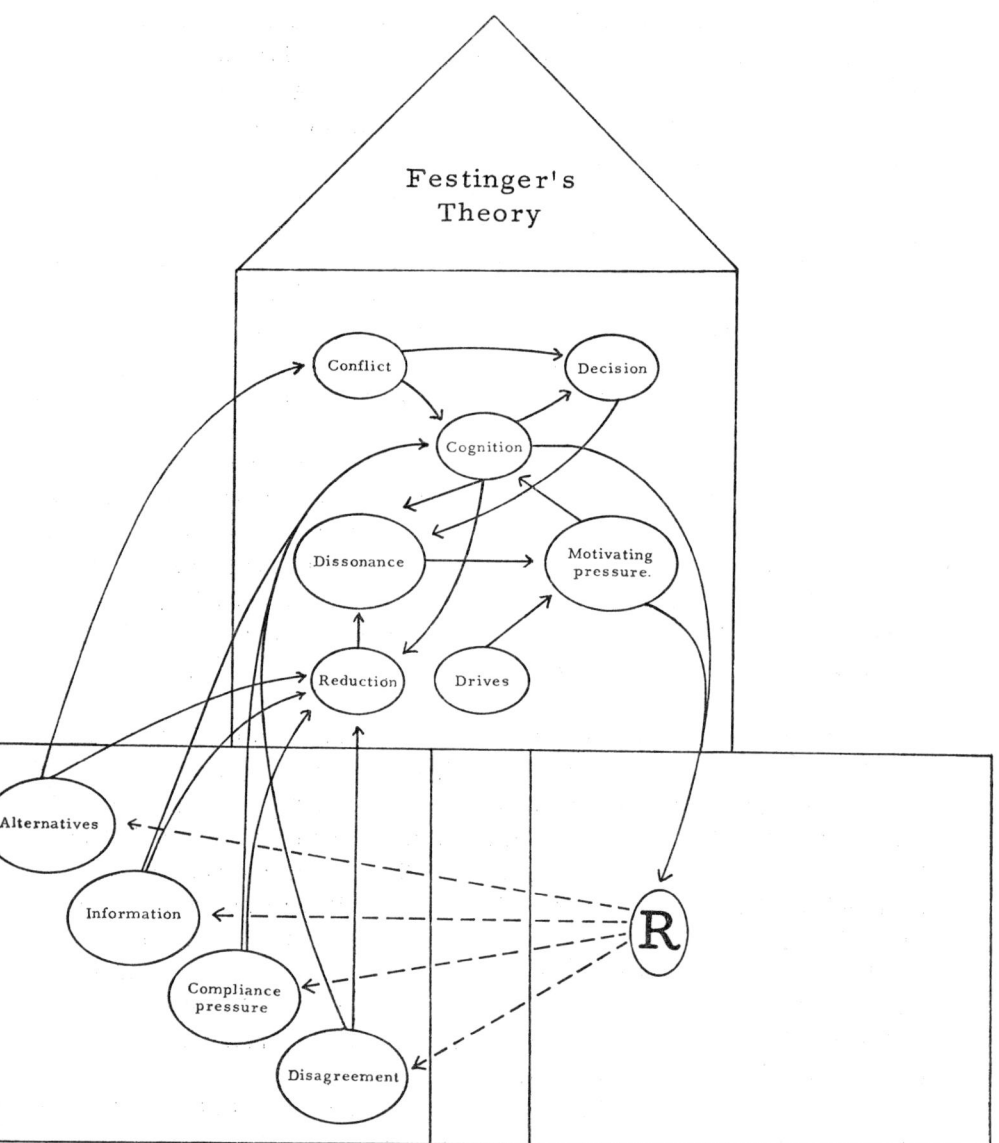

Fig. 12.1 Diagram concering Festinger's theory. "Information", "Compliance pressure" and "Disagreement" determine "Cognition" which in turn produces "Cognitive dissonance". The latter determines "Motivating pressure", which together with other kinds of motivation ("drives") determines behavior, which may result in "Reduction of dissonance". This may also be done through "Cognitive processes" (re-evaluation, etc.). A more complicated process is started by "Alternatives, which produce "conflict", which determines impulsive decision – or, via cognition – more rational decisions. These in turn produce dissonance.

his opinions, attitudes, knowledge, and values. That is, there is a drive toward consonance among cognitions. In order to deal with this notion in a somewhat more precise manner, I have imagined cognition to be decomposable into elements or, at least, clusters of elements. The following theoretical statements have been made about the relations among these cognitive elements:

1. Pairs of elements can exist in irrelevant, consonant, or dissonant relations.

2. Two cognitive elements are in an irrelevant relation if they have nothing to do with one another.

3. Two cognitive elements are in a dissonant relation if, considering these two alone, the obverse of one element follows from the other.

4. Two cognitive elements are in a consonant relation if, considering these two alone, one element follows from the other.

Starting from these definitions, a number of situations have been denoted as implying the existence of cognitive dissonance.

1. Dissonance almost always exists after a decision has been made between two or more alternatives. The cognitive elements corresponding to positive characteristics of the rejected alternatives, and those corresponding to negative characteristics of the chosen alternative, are *dissonant* with the knowledge of the action that has been taken. Those cognitive elements corresponding to positive characteristics of the chosen alternative and negative characteristics of the rejected alternative are *consonant* with the cognitive elements corresponding to the action which has been taken.

2. Dissonance almost always exists after an attempt has been made, by offering rewards or threatening punishment, to elicit overt behavior that is at variance with private opinion. If the overt behavior is successfully elicited, the person's private opinion is dissonant with his knowledge concerning his behavior; his knowledge of the reward obtained or of the punishment avoided is consonant with his knowledge concerning his behavior. If the overt behavior is not successfully elicited, then his private opinion is consonant with his knowledge of what he has done, but the knowledge of the reward not obtained or of the punishment to be suffered is dissonant with his knowledge of what he has done.

3. Forced or accidental exposure to new information may create cognitive elements that are dissonant with existing cognition.

4. The open expression of disagreement in a group leads to the existence of cognitive dissonance in the members. The knowledge that some other person, generally like oneself, holds one opinion is dissonant with holding a contrary opinion.

5. Identical dissonance in a large number of people may be created when an event occurs which is so compelling as to produce a uniform reaction in everyone. For example, an event may occur which unequivocally invalidates some widely held belief.

Thus far, dissonance and consonance have been defined as "all or none" relations – that is, if two elements are relevant to one another, the relation between them is either dissonant or consonant. Two hypotheses have been advanced concerning the magnitude of dissonance or consonance.

1. The magnitude of the dissonance or consonance which exists between two cognitive elements will be a direct function of the importance of these two elements.

2. The total magnitude of dissonance which exists between two clusters of cognitive elements is a function of the weighted proportion of all the relevant relations between the two clusters which are dissonant, each dissonant or consonant relation being weighted according to the importance of the elements involved in that relation.

Starting with these hypotheses about the magnitude of dissonance, a number of operational implications seem clear.

1. The magnitude of postdecision dissonance is an increasing function of the general importance of the decision and of the relative attractiveness of the unchosen alternatives.

2. The magnitude of postdecision dissonance *decreases* as the number of cognitive elements corresponding identically to characteristics of chosen and unchosen alternatives *increases*.

3. The magnitude of the dissonance resulting from an attempt to elicit forced compliance is greatest if the promised reward or threatened punishment is either *just sufficient* to elicit the overt behavior or is *just barely not sufficient* to elicit it.

4. If forced compliance is elicited, the magnitude of the dissonance *decreases* as the magnitude of the reward or punishment *increases*.

5. If forced compliance fails to be elicited, the magnitude of the dissonance *increases* as the magnitude of the reward or punishment *increases*.

6. The magnitude of the dissonance introduced by the expression of disagreement by others *decreases* as the number of existing cognitive elements consonant with the opinion *increases*. These latter elements may correspond either to objective, nonsocial items of information or to the knowledge that some other people hold the same opinion.

7. The magnitude of the dissonance introduced by disagreement from others *increases* with *increase* in the importance of the opinion to the person, in the relevance of the opinion to those voicing disagreement, and in the attractiveness of those voicing disagreement.

8. The greater the difference between the opinion of the person and the opinion of the one voicing disagreement, and, hence, the greater the number of elements which are dissonant between the cognitive clusters corresponding to the two opinions, the greater will be the magnitude of dissonance.

One now comes to the point of stating the central hypotheses of the theory, namely:

1. The presence of dissonance gives rise to pressures to reduce that dissonance.

2. The strength of the pressure to reduce dissonance is a function of the magnitude of the existing dissonance.

These hypotheses lead, naturally, to a consideration of the ways in which dissonance may be reduced. There are three major ways in which this may be done.

1. By changing one or more of the elements involved in dissonant relations.
2. By adding new cognitive elements that are consonant with already existing cognition.
3. By decreasing the importance of the elements involved in the dissonant relations.

Applying these considerations to actual situations leads to the following:

1. Postdecision dissonance may be reduced by increasing the attractiveness of the chosen alternative, decreasing the attractiveness of the unchosen alternatives, or both.
2. Postdecision dissonance may be reduced by perceiving some characteristics of the chosen and unchosen alternatives as identical.
3. Postdecision dissonance may be reduced by decreasing the importance of various aspects of the decision.
4. If forced compliance has been elicited, the dissonance may be reduced by changing private opinion to bring it into line with the overt behavior or by magnifying the amount of reward or punishment involved.
5. If forced compliance fails to be elicited, dissonance may be reduced by intensifying the original private opinion or by minimizing the reward or punishment involved.
6. The presence of dissonance leads to seeking new information which will provide cognition consonant with existing cognitive elements and to avoiding those sources of new information which would be likely to increase the existing dissonance.
7. When some of the cognitive elements involved in a dissonance are cognitions about one's own behavior, the dissonance can be reduced by changing the behavior, thus directly changing the cognitive elements.
8. Forced or accidental exposure to new information which tends to increase dissonance will frequently result in misinterpretation and misperception of the new information by the person thus exposed in an effort to avoid a dissonance increase.
9. Dissonance introduced by disagreement expressed by other persons may be reduced by changing one's own opinion, by influencing the others to change their opinion, and by rejecting those who disagree.
10. The existence of dissonance will lead to seeking out others who already agree with a cognition that one wants to establish or maintain and will also lead to the initiation of communication and influence processes in an effort to obtain more social support.

11. Influence exerted on a person will be more effective in producing opinion change to the extent that the indicated change of opinion reduces dissonance for that person.

12. In situations where many persons who associate with one another all suffer from the identical dissonance, dissonance reduction by obtaining social support is very easy to accomplish.

To conclude this brief summary of the theory, there are a few things to be stated concerning the effectiveness of efforts directed toward dissonance reduction.

1. The effectiveness of efforts to reduce dissonance will depend upon the resistance to change of the cognitive elements involved in the dissonance and on the availability of information which will provide, or of other persons who will supply, new cognitive elements which will be consonant with existing cognition.

2. The major sources of resistance to change for a cognitive element are the responsiveness of such cognitive elements to "reality" and the extent to which an element exists in consonant relations with many other elements.

3. The maximum dissonance which can exist between two elements is equal to the resistance to change of the less resistant of the two elements. If the dissonance exceeds this magnitude, the less resistant cognitive element will be changed, thus reducing the dissonance.

This brief summary can hardly hope to give an adequate picture of the theory, but perhaps it can help the reader to see more clearly the nature of the theory and where it goes. I will not attempt to provide any summary of the empirical evidence which has been presented.

In the course of thinking about the theory, conducting studies designed to test its implications, and searching the literature for data, numerous ideas have suggested themselves which seem promising but about which there is no evidence. The degree of confirmation of the theory of dissonance in those areas where data have been obtained seems sufficient to encourage me to spell out here those implications from, and ideas about, the theory of dissonance for which no evidence is available. The remainder of this chapter consists, then, of an assortment of suggestions which vary all the way from derivations from the theory to hunches about variables which affect the processes of dissonance reduction".

2.2.1. *Basic classification of hypotheses.* On the basis of the above reprinted pages from Festinger's book we can make the first basic classification of his hypotheses. On page 230 in our book he recapitulates his four definitions of the main terms. Then follows (p. 230 in our book) five hypotheses about those *situations* which determine dissonance.

We can reformulate these hypotheses in our partly symbolic version in this way using "H_D" as the abbreviation for the hypothetical term "dissonance":

1. S(alternatives) → H(decision) → H_D
2. a. S(punishment) → H_D
2. b. S(reward) → H_D
3. S(information) → H_D
4. S(disagreement) → H_D
5. S(common events) → $H_{D\ common}$

As may easily be seen from the above reformulations the first five hypotheses are all S-H-hypotheses.

On page 231 Festinger presents two hypotheses about the *magnitude* of dissonance. In our reconstruction they appear as follows:

6. H(importance of elements) → $H_{D\ magnitude}$
7. H(weighted importance) → $H_{D\ total\ magnitude}$

We have classified these as H-H-hypotheses.

On page 231 we find 8 hypotheses which can be regarded as quantitative reformulations of the first 5 hypotheses, and can consequently be regarded as S-H-hypotheses:

8. S(alternatives) → H(importance of decision) → $H_{D\ magnitude}$
9. S(alternatives) → H(decreasing conflict) → $H_{D\ decreasing}$
10. a. S(reward, just sufficient) → $H_{D\ max}$
 b. S(reward, not just sufficient) → $H_{D\ max}$
 c. S(punishment, just sufficient) → $H_{D\ max}$
 d. S(punishment, not just sufficient) → $H_{D\ max}$
11. a. S(reward increases) → $H_{D\ decreases}$ → R(compliance succeeded)
 b. S(punishment increases) → $H_{D\ decreases}$ → R(compliance succeeded)
12. a. S(reward increases) → $H_{D\ increases}$ → R(compliance failed)
 b. S(punishment increases) → $H_{D\ increases}$ → R(compliance failed)
13. S(disagreement decreases) → $H_{D\ decreases}$
14. S(importance of disagreement) → $H_{D\ increases}$
15. S(disagreement) → $H_{D\ magnitude}$

At the middle of page 231 Festinger formulates two "central hypotheses", which we regard as H-H-hypotheses:

16. H_D → H(motivating pressure)
17. $H_{D\ magnitude}$ → H(strength of pressure)

The reader may have noticed the appearance of a new term, "motivating pressure", which is not defined formally in the book. This term can either be interpreted as referring to the dynamic effect of the cognitive dissonance, or to a specific hypothetical variable which is determined by the cognitive dissonance. We have chosen the last interpretation.

At the middle of page 232 Festinger presents three propositions concerning the ways in which dissonance can be reduced. We regard them as hypotheses and restate them in the following way:

18. H(changing elements) → H_D reduction
19. H(new consonant elements) → H_D reduction
20. H(importance of elements decreases) → H_D reduction

As can be seen from this reconstruction we regard these hypotheses as H-H-hypotheses.

These three main hypotheses about the ways of reducing dissonance are followed by 12 more specific propositions concerning dissonance reduction in the four situations which produce dissonance: alternatives (conflict and decision), new information, forced compliance and disagreements. These hypotheses are presented on pages 232 and 233 and we bring our reformulations here:

21.a. H(increase in attractiveness of the chosen alternative) → H_D reduction
   b. H(decrease in attractiveness of unchosen alternative) → H_D reduction
22. H(perceiving elements identical) → H_D reduction
23. H(decreasing importance of alternatives) → H_D reduction
24.a. H(changing opinion) → H_D reduction → R(compliance)
   b. H(increasing value reward → H_D reduction → R(compliance)
   c. H(increasing strength of punishment) → H_D reduction → R(compliance)
25.a. H(increasing strength of opinion) → H_D reduction → R(non-compliance)
   b. H(decreasing reward) → H_D reduction → R(non-compliance)
   c. H(decreasing punishment) → H_D reduction → R(non-compliance)
26.a. H_D → R(seeking consonant information)
   b. H_D → R(avoidance dissonance information)
27. H(changing cognition of behavior) → H_D reduction
28. H(dissonance information) → H(misperception) → H_D reduction
29.a. H(cognition of disagreement) → H(opinion change) → H_D reduction
   b. H(cognition of disagreement) → R(influencing others) → H_D reduction
   c. H(cognition of disagreement) → H(misperception) → H_D reduction
30. H_D → R(seeking social support) → H_D reduction
31. S(compliance) → H(opinion change) → H_D reduction
32. H(identical dissonance) → R(social support) → H_D reduction

These hypotheses belong to the following categories:

1. H-H-hypotheses: No. 21, 22, 23, 27, 28, 29a and 29c.
2. H-R-hypotheses: No. 24, 25, 26, 29b, 30 and 32.
3. S-H-hypotheses: No. 31.

Finally, Festinger formulates three propositions "concerning the effectiveness of efforts directed toward dissonance reduction". We can reconstruct them on the basis of his owe formulations (found on page 233 in our book):

33. a. H(resistance to change of cognitive elements)→ H_D reduction resistance
    b. S(availability of information)→ H_D reduction resistance
34. a. H(cognitive elements ' »reality« contact)→ H_D reduction resistance
    b. H(amount of dissonant element)→ H_D reducton resistance
35. a. H(max.dissonance)→ H(resistance to change of weakest element)
    b. H(increase of max.dissonance)→ H(change of weakest element)

These hypotheses are mainly H-H-hypotheses – except for No. 33.b., which may be classified as an S-H-hypothesis, and No. 35.a., which is actually a definition.

After completing the reconstruction of Festinger's hypotheses we conclude this section with a restatement of the classification of hypotheses:

1. *Purely theoretical (H-H) hypotheses:*
   Hypotheses No.: 6, 7, 16, 17, 18, 19, 20, 21, 22, 23, 27, 28, 29, 33, 34 and 35.
   In all: 16 H-H-hypotheses.

2. *Partly empirical hypotheses:*
   a. *S-H-hypotheses:* Hypotheses No.: 1, 2, 3, 4, 5, 8, 9, 10, 11, 12, 13, 14, 15 and 31.
      In all: 14 S-H-hypotheses.
   b. *H-R-hypotheses*: Hypotheses No.: 24, 25, 26, 30 and 32.
      In all: 5 H-R-hypotheses.

The reader may have noticed that we have disregarded the different versions of the hypotheses, which in our reconstruction were indicated by the letters a, b, c, etc. Only in two cases (No. 29 and 33) do the hypotheses belong to different classes (although they have the same number but with different letters added). But this is only a minor irregularity.

2.2.2. *The complexity of the hypotheses.* If the reader inspects the reformulated hypotheses again he will notice that all Festinger's hypotheses are *one-dimensional*. Most of the hypotheses contain only two "elements" (terms or variables). But none of the hypotheses encompass *interaction* between two or more elements, so they cannot be classified as "multi-dimensional". This would seem to confirm the general impression that Festinger's is a clear and simple theory.

2.2.3. *The functional relationships in the hypotheses.* Festinger does not explicitly state his presuppositions about what kind of functional relationships he assumes in his hypotheses. But there are some implicit statements which indicate the presupposition of *causal determinism*. Thus he writes (p. 154):

"Before presenting the data, however, there are a few points concerning interpretation which should be made. In most instances where one considers the relationship between holding or not holding some opinion and engaging in some behavior relevant to that opinion, the interpretation with respect to direction of causality is bound to be somewhat equivocal. Certainly we will all grant that cognition steers behavior. Consequently, any relationship between behavior and holding or not holding an opinion could result from this direction of causality. The theory of dissonance, however, predicts the same relation with the causality in the opposite direction. In order to identify clearly the direction of causality then, and eliminate any ambiguity of interpretation, it is necessary to be able to say definitely that at some previous time the behavior existed in the absence of the opinion."

From this it is quite clear that Festinger assumes the existence of causal determinism, even in the cases where the direction of causality is opposite to that usually assumed.

The descriptive stratum

3.1. *The abstract D-level*

Festinger's book contains descriptions of many experiments and empirical investigations conducted by him and his co-workers as well as by other psychologists. Some of the experiments were planned in order to test the implications of his theory; other research is reported because it confirms the theory, although it was conducted by other researchers without any connection with or knowledge about his theory. It is the present author's opinion that his theory is empirically very well founded and that it has inspired much fruitful research. This is indicated by the considerable quantity of descriptive content in the book. The eleven chapters include five dealing mainly with empirical research (which is indicated in the titles of the chapters by the word "data"). Four chapters deal with hypotheses concerning different problems (which is indicated in the titles of the chapters by the word "theory"). The first and last chapters present and summarize the theory respectively. Thus approximately half of the book belongs to the D-level.

Although there is considerable descriptive content in the book, very little of it belongs to the *abstract* D-level. There are very few *general, descriptive propositions* (empirical "laws"). The empirical results are summarized in propositions, which are not expressed in *abstract, descriptive terms*, but rather employ the hypothetical terms used in the hypotheses.

In order to give the reader a fair impression of the abstract, descriptive stratum in Festinger's theory we have decided to quote at some length the summary – parts of the chapters about data.

As already indicated by the hypotheses, he deals with four main areas involving cognitive dissonance.

The first field of research is concerned with the consequence of *decisions*. The *data* from this field are presented in Chapter Three, where we hear about an investigation of "advertising readership" and "an experiment on confidence in decisions", as well as "an experiment on change in attractiveness of alternatives" and "the difficulty of reversing decisions". All these research results are summarized at the end of the chapter (p. 83):

"Summary

This chapter has reviewed a number of studies which in one way or another deal with events that occur after a decision has been made. The data show:
1. Following a decision there is active seeking out of information which produces cognition consonant with the action taken.
2. Following a decision there is an increase in the confidence in the decision or an increase in the discrepancy in attractiveness between the alternatives involved in the choice, or both. Each reflects successful reduction of dissonance.
3. The succesful reduction of postdecision dissonance is further shown in the difficulty of reversing a decision once it is made and in the implication which changed cognition has for future relevant action.
4. The effects listed above vary directly with the magnitude of dissonance created by decision."

The second field of research is concerned with "the effects of forced compliance" and the data are reported in Chapter 5. Five such studies are discussed and the results are summarized in this way (p. 122):

"Summary

Data from five studies have been presented, all of which are relevant to the theoretical analysis presented in Chapter Four, namely, that dissonance follows from situations which elicit forced compliance and that this dissonance may be reduced by change of private opinion.
 The data show that:
1. Following public compliance there is frequently a subsequent change of private opinion over and above what the variables in the situation, not including dissonance, would account for.
2. Taking the magnitude of such opinion change as reflecting the magnitude of the pressure to reduce dissonance, the data fit the hypothesized relations with importance of the issue and with amount of reward used to elicit the compliant behavior."

The third field of research deals with "voluntary and involuntary exposure to information", and the data are presented in Chapter 7. This chapter includes reports about 8 investigations and one experiment, and the results are summarized at the end of the chapter (p. 176):

"Summary

This chapter has dealt with data concerning one aspect of the process of dissonance reduction, namely, obtaining new cognition which will be consonant with existing cognition and avoiding new cognition which will be dissonant with existing cognition.
 It has been shown that much of the data concerning selectivity in exposure to propaganda ,information, and mass media can be interpreted along the lines of attempted dissonance reduction. Unfortunately, most such data are causally equivocal and cannot be regarded as providing strong corroboration for the theory of dissonance.

The data concerning reactions of people when involuntarily exposed to new information are, fortunately, more adequate.

When dissonance exists, persons will be able to evade the impact of dissonance-incearsing information, even when forcibly exposed to it, by various means such as misperception, denying its validity, and the like. If persons do not expect a source of information to produce dissonant cognition and, hence, are not alert to avoid the dissonance, the information will have more impact.

The interaction between the amount of dissonance which exists and the expectation concerning some particular source of new information in determining whether or not a person will expose himself to, or avoid, this source of information is made particularly clear by the results of an experiment designed to test these implications of the theory."

The fourth field of research is concerned with "the role of social support". This field is covered by one theoretical chapter and *two* chapters concerning data. Thus in Chapter 9 we find data from a half dozen investigations about the "influence process", and in Chapter 10 data from another half dozen investigations about "mass phenomena". Unfortunately, Festinger does not provide us with any summaries for these two chapters, so we can only tell the reader that the empirical data confirm the hypotheses of dissonance.

However, from the summaries already presented it should be clear that he uses his own hypothetical terms when summarizing empirical results. Nor does he present any operational definitions of the hypothetical terms in connection with the description of the research carried out.

But in spite of this formal deficiency in Festinger's theory, the present author received a strong impression of intimate relationships between the hypothetical stratum and the descriptive stratum of his theory, as well as of a very well verified theory.

3.2. *The concrete D-level*

Much of Festinger's text belongs to this level.

First, there are many very detailed and precise descriptions of the research procedures employed in the various investigations, coupled with thorough discussions and interpretations of the results. These descriptions and discussions of methods are consistent with Festinger's methodological propositions discussed in Section 1.3. of this chapter.

Second, there are many detailed, specific descriptions – "protocol sentences" in his empirical chapters. The present author especially enjoyed the description of the study of "mass proselytizing" which Festinger conducted as a participant observer in a religious movement, which postulated the destruction of the earth on a certain day. This description reads lihe a novel[2]).

---

2. See L. Festinger, H. Riecken and S. Schachter: *When prophecy fails.* (Minneapolis: Univ. of Minnesota Press, 1956).

3.3. *The descriptive units*

Festinger's theory employs rather *molar* descriptive units, which is natural for a theory which is mainly based upon empirical research carried out within the field of social psychology.

The theory as a whole

4.1. *The formal properties*

It is rather easy to classify Festinger's theory according to its formal properties. (4.1.1.) *The systematic organization* of the theory is developed to such a degree that the theory must be classified as an *explanatory system*. There is a very clear stratification of the text into the three levels. The hypotheses are explicitly formulated and coherently presented in the last chapter. But they are not organized into a deductive system.

(4.1.2.) *The preciseness of representation* is on the level of a *purely verbal theory*. There are no symbolic or mathematical formulations of hypotheses. But the verbal formulations are presented in a very clear and precise manner.

(4.1.3.) *The properties of the models* used in connection with Festinger's theory are those which characterize a *two-dimensional model*. A few diagrams are presented which illustrate the relationship between cognitive dissonance and other variables.

4.2. *The epistemological properties*

Festinger's theory is clearly an *explanatory theory* and as H-terms with neutral surplus meaning are employed it must be classified as belonging to the subcategory called "neutral explanatory" or $S-H_N-R$-theories.

4.3. *The theory-empiry ratio*

In this last classification we must define Festinger's theory as being rather *empirical* as there are many experiments and other empirical research connected with it.

After having made a partly symbolic, systematic reconstruction of the hypotheses, we have calculated the Hypotheses Quotient as:

$$H.Q. = \frac{\Sigma(H-H)}{\Sigma[(S-H) + (H-R)]} = \frac{16}{14+5} = 0.84.$$

Later production. We have now finished our systematological analysis of Festinger's "A Theory of Cognitive Dissonance" (1957). But Festinger has been very productive since the above work appeared. Although this book, from a theoretical point-of-view, is still his main work, we shall make a few comments about his later production.

He has co-authored several books, perhaps the most well-known being "Deterrents and Reinforcement – The Psychology of Insufficient Reward" (Stanford University Press, 1962), which was co-authored by *Douglas Lawrence*. But this book is more relevant for those concerned with the psychology of learning.

For our purposes the most significant of the later books by Festinger is his "Conflict, Decision and Dissonance" (Stanford University Press, 1964). This book was written in collaboration with some of his graduate students and assistants. The book contains reports and discussions concerning 10 experiments, all made to further clarify the problems about decision and dissonance which were dealt with in two chapters in "A Theory of Cognitive Dissonance". These experiments have resulted in a more detailed theory about the decision process, and to some extent a revision of the original theory.

We shall first make a summary of Festinger's most recent theory about decision – (based on the last chapter in his 1964 book):

A conflict between alternatives starts the *pre-decision* process, which is largely oriented toward making an objective and impartial evaluation of the merits of the alternatives. This is done by collecting information, evaluating this information and establishing preference order between the alternatives. The subject continues to seek new information and re-evaluate old information until he has reached a sufficient level of confidence in his established order of preference.

Then the person makes a *decision*.

After the decision has been made and the person is committed to a given course of action we have the *post-decision* process, which differs markedly from the predecision. There is now less objectivity and more bias in the evaluation of the alternatives. And we note the appearance of *dissonance*. (But only after the person had committed himself to the decision – contrary to what Festinger said in 1957).

The dissonance is most salient in the first period, just after the decision has been made. The following dissonance reduction occurs by thinking about and re-evaluating the alternatives until sufficient reinterpretation has been made and the reduction of dissonance ended. In the very beginning of the post-decision period there may be signs of regret – and possibly a change of decision. But if commitment to action has begun – and, especially, if support from the environment is given – then the dissonance reduction succeeds, and a change of decision seldom occurs.

We can summarize our review of Festinger's theory of the decision-process in this way:

S(alternatives) → H(conflict) → H(information and evaluation of alternatives) → H(preference order established) → H(decision) → H(dissonance) → H(re-evaluation of alternatives) → H(reduction of dissonance) → H(consonance).

In addition to the revision already mentioned in a parenthesis in the above summary, we have found two other revisions of Festinger's theory:

1. He now maintains that "there does seem to be evidence for selective exposure to new information so as to help in the dissonance-reduction process" (p. 96). In the 1957 theory he maintained that there would be avoidance of expected dissonance-increasing information.
2. A regret is now conceived of as a natural implication of the beginning of the dissonance reduction – and *not* an attempt to change the decision and avoid dissonance (as stated in 1957).

Concluding remarks. The present author has a strong impression of Festinger's theory as a very *research stimulating and ever growing theory*. Although his 1957 book is a highly elaborated and systematically organized work, it is certainly not a "finished" theory, but rather the beginning of a whole new research tradition, which seems to establish a bridge between the psychology of motivation and social psychology.

13: Cattell's Theory

Introduction

The British-American psychologist *Raymond B. Cattell* (born 1905) has gained acknowledgment as a leader in the development of the factor analytical approach to the psychology of personality. He is a student of the founder of factor analysis, C. Spearman, and he has founded a "Laboratory for Personality Assessment and Group Behavior" in the United States which has produced more than 500 tests. In addition, Cattell himself has written many books and papers and edited several big handbooks, so that he is recognized as one of the most productive contemporary psychologists. Cattell's writing has motivated psychologists all over the world to join his team or to organize local teams inspired by him and his ideas.

In the last decennium Cattell has broadened the scope of his theory so that it now covers not only the *structure* of personality but also the *dynamics* of personality (= motivation) as well as *learning*.

Therefore, we have previously presented an analysis of Cattell's theory in the first edition of "Theories of Motivation" (1959), but we think that Cattell's theory has been developed so much since that time that it deserves a new analysis.

As Cattell's production is so great, we must make a selection for this analysis. We have based our chapter upon the following books by Cattell: "Personality: A Systematical, Theoretical and Factual Study" (1950), "Personality and Motivation, Structure and Measurement" (1957), and "The Scientific Analysis of Personality" (1965). The last mentioned can be recommended as the best introduction to Cattell's theory. In addition to the above we have gained much from studying Cattell's own chapters as well as many other chapters in Cattell (Ed.): "Handbook of Modern Personality Theory" (forthcoming). This last mentioned book has been of special value for the first part of this chapter, to which we now turn.

The metastratum

1.1. *Philosophical propositions*

Cattell is least explicit in formulating the general philosophical presuppositions for his work. Thus we have found no explicit propositions about the psychophysiological problem or other philosophical problems related to psychology. The most explicit philosophical propositions deal with the subject matter of psychology and the preferred *data-language* of psychology. Thus he writes in Cattell, 1965, p. 239:

> "Most professional psychologists (except for a few ideosyncratic philosophical psychologists) are behaviourists nowadays. But the form of behaviourism on which learning theory, in particular, has sought to nourish itself is really only one form or model within behaviourism, though it is sometimes mistaken for the whole. For clarity this particular sub-model should be distinguished as *reflexology*.

Thus Cattell presupposes the use of a *behavioral* data-language, so we may be sure that his philosophy is not dualistic. As we later shall demonstrate Cattell makes heavy use of neutral hypothetical constructs (the "factors" of personality). We can thus draw the tentative conclusion that Cattell presupposes a *neutral-monistic philosophy* concerning the psychophysiological problem. In addition, it seems probable that he presupposes a *biological,* or Darwinian philosophy of man, because most modern psychologists do; and Cattell does not seem to depart from this rule.

1.2. Metatheoretical propositions

Cattell is much more explicit about the more specific metatheoretical problems. His metatheory is especially elaborated in his introductory chapter: "The Direction of Personality Theory" (Cattell, forthcoming) in connection with what he calls a "taxonomy of theories". He defines a theory "as an integrated set of explicit definitions and explanations" (p. 2). He stresses the importance of logical consistency, systematic integration of several areas of data and deductions of new hypotheses. There are in all 6 "dimensions for a taxonomy of theories", which Cattell discussed. The dimensions are (Table 1-1, p. 3)[1] :

1. Precise Model – vs – Purely Verbal Formulation.
2. Local "Construct" Properties – vs – Imported Metaphorical Properties.
3. Few Areas Connected – vs – Many Areas Integrated.
4. Low Complexity – vs – High Intricacy of Formulation.
5. Mathematical Starkness – vs – Physical Enrichment of Model.
6. Few Deductions Possible – vs – Many Deductions Possible.

Cattell's metatheory favors a precise model with local "construct" properties, which integrates many areas in formulations possessing high intricacy and mathematical starkness and many possibilities for deductions.

Later in the same chapter Cattell criticizes the generally accepted philosophy

---

1. The present author has taken advantage of Cattell's taxonomy of theories and integrated some of his dimensions in the systematological taxonomy applied in *this* book.

of science – which has its origins in Logical Empiricism – according to which *the* scientific method is "the hypothetico-deductive method". Cattell argues for the proposition that *the* scientific method is "the inductive-hypothetico-deductive (or IHD) method".

The present author thinks that a still better formulation would be the one suggested by *Norwood Russell* (see Hanson, 1958), which could be rephrased as *"the abductive-hypothetico-deductive method"*. The term *"abduction"* is – especially by Charles S. Peirce – used to designate the method or process of proposing hypotheses based upon *combined theoretical-empirical evidence*. The proposed hypotheses are tested by the *deductions* of observable consequences. The present author believes that the sequence: abduction → hypothesis → deduction is a more correct description – or reconstruction – of *the* scientific method according to both historical evidence (see Kuhn 1962, and Hanson, 1958) and cognitive-psychological evidence as presented by *Jean Piaget*.

Besides these more general metatheoretical statements Cattell has additional specific propositions about the type of theory he wants to develop. Thus he writes (in 1965, p. 250):

"A scientific theory must finally be expressed in a 'model', and a model forces us to ask exactly what our assumptions are about mathematical formulae, causal connexions, and so on."

And still more specifically about the factor analytic approach (in 1965, p. 78):

"– – – the factor analytic approach, which presents a mathematical 'model' – that is to say a set of precise rules for handling and combining the measurements involved. Any such model in science is the very heart of a theory. By it the theory is tested quantitatively, and on the 'fit' of the experimental results to the quantities predicted the theory stands or falls. By this test the factor theory of personality does very well – – –".

From these quotations it is obvious that Cattell's theory is of the type which *Tolman* called "constructive" and which we have more precisely designated as the *"neutral-constructive type of theory"*. The present author thinks that it is important to emphasize that Cattell's theory is a *constructive* theory, because so much misunderstanding of the status of the theory has been expressed by opponents of the factor analytic approach. Some critics argue that factor analytic theory is *pseudo*-objective and *pseudo*-exact theory, which under the cover of highpower mathematics conceals arbitrary and subjective theory-building. These critics often refer to the *technique of rotation* of co-ordinates representing the hypothetical factors. This rotation and the succeeding interpretation of the factor-structure *is* dependent on the skill and insight of psychologists, but this is the *constructive* or *creative* element which is found in the construction of *all* scientific theories. In order to be *scientific* this creation has to be checked by empirical methods. And the very exact nature of factor analytical theory construction makes it much easier to test the empirical validity of the theory.

This leads us to the next level of the metastratum.

1.3. Methodological propositions

Cattell is much more explicit about methodological problems than about the other metascientific problems. Thus he presents a very strong and extensive collection of arguments for what he calls the "multivariate experimental method"[2]). This method has been developed by a combination of statistic methods and test methods which were developed by *Francis Galton*. And the factor analysis developed by Galton's student, *C. Spearman*, is the mathematical counterpart of the tests and other measuring devices employed in this method. Cattell was the first to apply this approach to personality theory. He contrasts the multivariate method with the *"univariate method"*, which is the classic experimental method developed in physics and other natural sciences. As is well known this method consists in *isolating* one component of the total field of investigation and manipulating it as a variable while all other components are kept constant. According to Cattell this method does not furnish the possibility of finding the *interaction* between all the components of the whole field. That can only be accomplished by naturalistic of clinical observations and by the multivariate experimental method. This last mentioned method thus combines the comprehensiveness of the clinical and naturalistic methods with the exactness of the classical, "univariate" method. Thus Cattell writes (in 1965, pp. 21-22):

"The univariate, laboratory method, with its isolation of the single process, has worked well in the older sciences, but where total organisms have to be studied, the theoretical possibility must be faced that one can sometimes hope to find a law only if *the total organism* is included in the observations and experiences – not just a bit of its behaviour. In this respect, the emphasis on 'wholeness' in the multivariate method is actually the same as in the clinical method, but it is quantitative and follows explicit calculations of laws and general conclusions."

The multivariate method has another practical advantage which Cattell mentions (in 1965, p. 22):

"The fact that he can study behaviour in its natural setting means that he can deal with emotionally important matters and real personality learning."

In spite of Cattell's strong interest in the multivariate method he is not one-sided, but argues for a combined approach (in 1957, p. 46):

"Scientific method, especially in psychology, is most effective with a "two-handed" strategic application of analytical multivariate and controlled univariate methods, each generating personality hypotheses and each providing checks more effectually than the other at some stages of reseacrh."

---

2. The most comprehensive and profound exposition of this method is presented in R. B. Cattell (Ed.): *Handbook of Multivariate Experimental Psychology* (Chicago: Rand McNally, 1966).

Intimately related to the multivariate experimental approach is Cattell's conception of *"objective tests"*. These tests are described in this way (in 1965, p. 104):

"In these the subject is placed in a miniature situation and simply acts, while his responses are observed and measured. His cooperation is required to the extent that he agrees to be tested, but the objectivity in this type of test may be defined by the criterion that the *subject does not know on what aspect of his behavior he is really being evaluated.*"

In addition to the objective tests Cattell also uses data from *questionnaires* and from *ratings* of behavior in everyday situations. We shall go into further detail about these data when we deal with the descriptive stratum of Cattell's theory, but first we shall analyze the hypothetical stratum.

The hypothetical stratum

2.0. *Summary of the hypotheses*

It is difficult to present an overview of Cattell's theory as the content is both very comprehensive and very detailed.

Cattell's theory may be conceived of as an extremely elaborated version of the formula:

$$R = f(S,O).$$

Thus the "O" is broken down into a long chain of traits, T, which are specific to an individual, i, and stimulated by a situation, j. Thus we have:

$$R_{ji} = s_{j1}T_{1i} + s_{j2}T_{2i} + \ldots + s_{jn}T_{ni}$$

Cattell classifies the traits, T, in several ways.

The main classification related to the content of the theory is the division into:

1. *Ability traits* (A), which are factors that determine how *well* the performance is carried out.
2. *Temperamental traits* (T), which are factors which determine the *style* of behavior.
3. *Dynamic traits*, which are factors that determine the "power" or *activation* of behavior. They can be subdivided into:
    a. *Ergic drives* (E), which are factors hypothesized to be *innate* reactions to consummatory goals.
    b. *Sentiments* (M), which are factors hypothesized to be *learned* reactions to goals and sub-goals.

The dynamic traits are components in a structure called the *"dynamic lattice"*. This hypothetical structure is activated by stimuli from the external si-

248 . *Cattell's Theory*

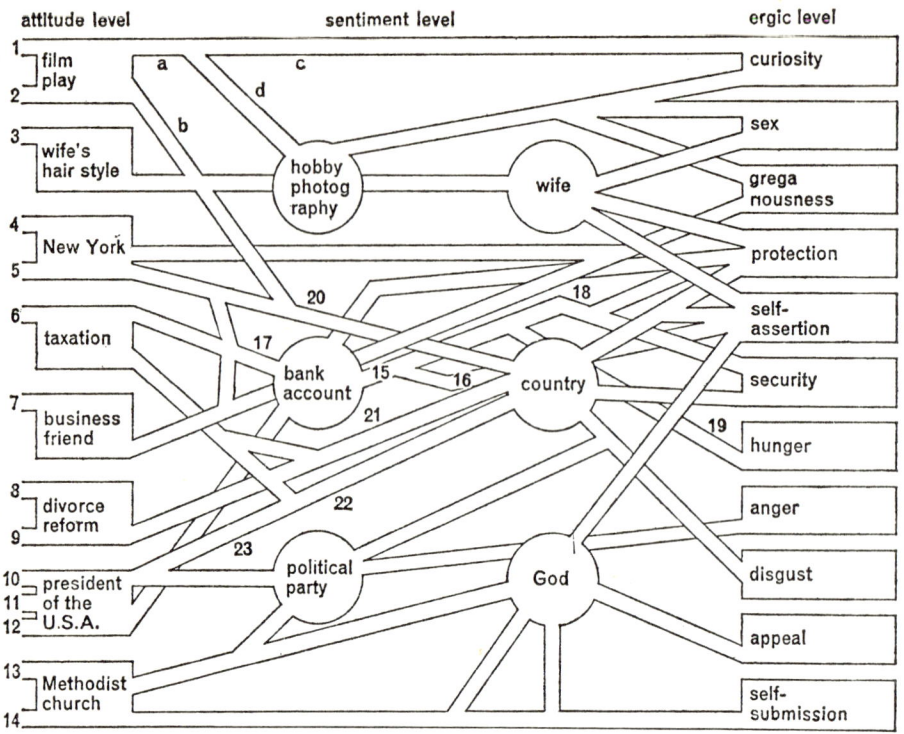

Fig. 13.1 Fragment of a dynamic lattice, showing attitude subsidiation, sentiment structure, and ergic goals (Diagram 21 from Cattell, 1965).

tuation and the internal physiological state. This structure is influenced by the ability traits (A) and the temperamental traits (T), which together with the dynamic lattice (E and M) determine the reaction of the individual. These reactions are classified into categories called *"attitudes"*, which are variously defined as: "the manifest dynamic variable or motivational unit", or: "a response to a stimulus situation", or: "a stimulus-response unit" (in 1957, pp. 442–43).

Before going into further detail with the analysis of Cattell's theory we can represent this overview by means of two diagrams, one borrowed from Cattell (1965), which illustrates the "dynamic lattice" (Fig. 13.1.).

The other is a diagram by means of which the present author has tried to present an overview of the content of Cattell's theory (Fig. 13.2.).

2.1. *The hypothetical terms. (H-terms)*

We have already presented the main hypothetical terms in Cattell's theory. Before going into a systematological analysis and classification of these terms, we should look at the *motivational* terms in more detail.

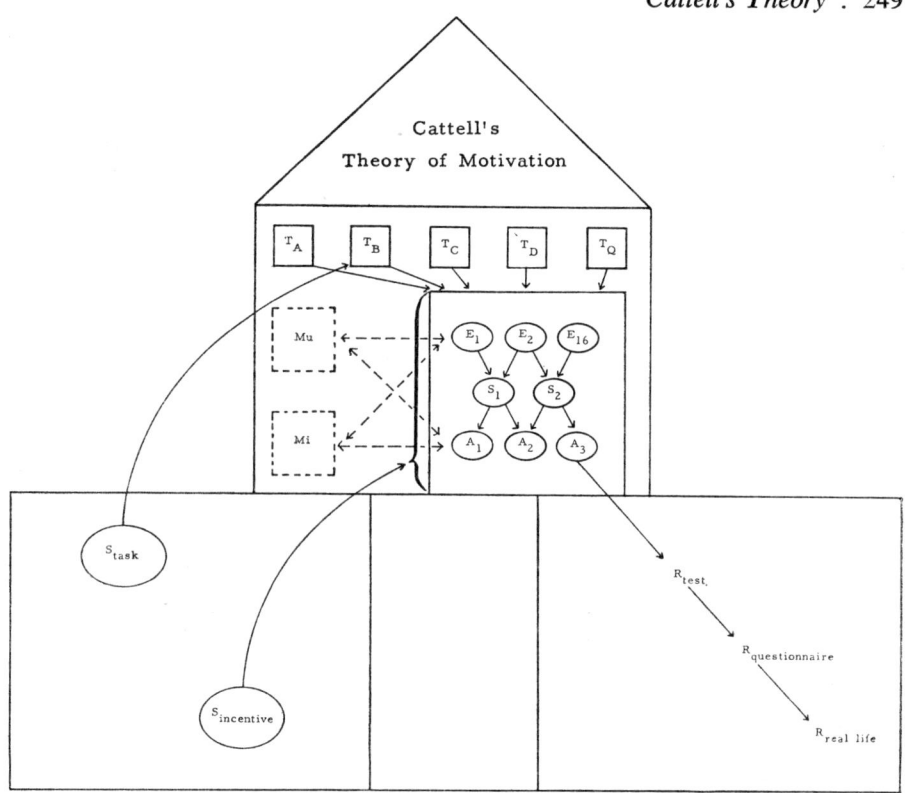

Fig. 13.2 Diagram representing the main hypotheses in Cattell's theory of motivation. T_A to T_Q are the *temperamental* traits. One trait, T_B, is a cognitive trait or *ability*, which is influenced by the complexity of the task-situation. Mu and Mi are the *motivational component factors,* which perhaps have another metascientific status (indicated by broken lines symbolizing that these factors are not causal-determining factors similar to all the factors or hypothetical variables in Cattell's Theory). The box containing E_1 to E_{16} and S_1 to S_2 and A_1 to A_3 is the *"dynamic lattice",* which is influenced by the incentives in the situation. E_1, E_{16} are ergs, S_1 and S_2 are *sentiments,* A_1 to A_3 are attitudes, which are possibly on the border-line between the H-level and the D-level.

The specific motivational variables in Cattell's theory are the so-called "dynamic traits", which include *"Ergs", "Sentiments",* and *"Attitudes",* among others.

1. *Erg.* The main dynamic variable is the *erg.* This term is Cattell's substitute for more traditional terms such as "instinct", "need" or "drive", which are expressions for the concepts used in the older clinical and uni-variate experimental psychology, whose methods, according to Cattell, are unsatisfactory when applied to the dynamic variables. Therefore Cattell has constructed the new concept and term "erg", which he defines in this way (pp. 185–86 in Cattell, 1965):

"It seems that we are so constructed that our final satisfactions have to be instinctive ones, or *ergic* ones. The term *erg,* from the Greek *ergon* for work or energy, is used in the dynamic calculus for a structure which has hitherto been called, at once too vaguely and elaborately, an instinct or drive which is the energy source behind behaviour. As we shall see in a moment, an erg (hard g) can be precisely factor-analytically located and defined, whereas instinct, need, drive, etc., have become all things to all men and can no longer be used with scientific precision. An erg, and ergic (pronounced as in allergic) tension, an ergically determined attitude, etc., can, on the other hand, be demonstrated by analysis and measured by objective tests."

In another place (Cattell, 1957) we find a more formal definition (p. 543):

"Our concluding definition of an erg, anticipating certain confirmations by researches along these lines is as follows (109): "An innate psychological structure which permits the organism to acquire reactivity (attention, response) to certain classes of objects more readily than others, to experience a specific emotion common to each class, and to start various courses of action (equivalents) which cease more completely at a certain common, definite, consummatory goal activity than at any other. This common goal character is demonstrable by, among other methods, a factor-analytic proof of functional unity in attitude action courses that can be perceived (or demonstrated) by the psychologist to lead to a common goal"."

This last definition has some similarity to McDougall's often quoted definition of "instinct", which Cattell himself has pointed out (in Cattell, 1950). Also the number of ergs approximates the number of "instincts"[3] contained in McDougall's list, which can be seen in the following table (Table 13-2 in Cattell, 1957, p. 541):

TABLE 13.3. Hypothesized List of Human Ergs

	Goal title	Emotion	Status of evidence
1	Mating	Sex	Replicated factor; measurement battery exists
2	Gregariousness	Loneliness	Replicated factor; measurement battery exists
3	Parental protectiveness	Pity	Replicated factor; measurement battery exists
4	Exploration	Curiosity	Replicated factor; measurement battery exists
5	Escape to security	Fear	Replicated factor; measurement battery exists
6	Self-assertion	Pride	Replicated factor; measurement battery exists
7	Narcistic sex	Sensuousness	
8	Appeal	Despair	Factor, but of uncertain independence
9	Rest-seeking	Sleepiness	Factor, but of uncertain independence
10	Constructiveness	Creativity	Factor, but of uncertain independence
11	Self-abasement	Humility	Factor, but of uncertain independence
12	Food-seeking	Hunger	Factor absent through absence of variance
13	Pugnacity	Anger	Factor absent through causes unknown
14	Acquisitiveness	Greed	Factor absent for lack of markers
15	Disgust	Disgust	Factor absent for lack of markers
16	Laughter	Amusement	Factor absent for lack of markers

3. McDougall's list of "instincts" – or as he later called them: "propensities" – increased from 12 in 1908 to 18 in 1932. The reader is referred to the chapter about McDougall's theory in "Theories of Motivation" (4th ed., 1968).

Besides defining and classifying ergs Cattell has made a more detailed analysis of ergs as being constituted of various components according to the following formula:

$$E = (S + k) [C + H + (P - aG) - bG].$$

The symbols in this formula are:

E = the *ergic tension* level (as measured at a certain moment).
$S + k$ = the *stimulus* situation (k is a constant added with the purpose of preventing the whole E equalling zero when the S equals zero).
C = the constant *constitutional*, individual difference component.
H = the *historical* component, which is an effect of the individual's personal experience with the erg in question.
P = the *physiological* state component.
G = the *gratification* level (thus –G represents absence of gratification, usually called "deprivation").
a, b = personal constants added to the gratification level, respectively to the physiological (a) and to the more general ergic gratification level (b).

Thus Cattell's concept of "erg" is much more specific and differentiated than the more common motivational concepts – "needs" and "drives". Cattell himself sometimes makes reference to these concepts by stating that $C+H+P$ is equal to "drive strength", while $[C+H+(P-aG)-bG]$ is equal to "need strength". Thus erg is a broader concept than drive and need as it also includes the situational component $(S+k)$.

It remains to emphasize that all ergs are conceived of as being *primary*. The *secondary* or acquired dynamic variable is "sentiments", to which we now turn.

2. *Sentiments*. The other kind of variable in the dynamic lattice is "sentiments". The term is defined in the "Glossary" to Cattell, 1957, p. 900:

"Sentiment. A factor among attitudes corresponding to an acquired pattern from a social institution."

The relation between ergs and sentiments is expressed in this quotation from Cattell, 1965, p. 192:

"The sentiment brings together attitudes, in fact, with several *different* ergic roots, but only *one* source of learning – the repeated experiences of rewarded behaviour simultaneously affecting a wide set of attitudes."

From this it is obvious that sentiments are the products of *learning*. Therefore, Cattell also uses the term *"engrams"* (and the symbol M, standing for "memory") as an equivalent term to "sentiments"[4]. The specific role of learning in

---

4. To be more specific: "engrams" is a broader term including both "sentiments" and "complexes", which are psychopathological forms of engrams.

Cattell's theory is dealt with later in this chapter. The "social institution" mentioned in the definition of sentiment refers to such things as religion, profession, sport, nation, etc. Through tests and factor-analytic methods sentiments have been identified which correspond to these institutions as well as to some other goal-objects (wife, children, etc.). Also the person's own "self" is the object of a sentiment (the so-called "self-sentiment").

3. *Attitude*. The third kind of variable in the dynamic lattice is "attitude". Cattell gives the term attitude a broader meaning than is usual in social psychology and sociology, "where one speaks of an attitude as being only *for or against* an object" (p. 176, Cattell, 1965). In variance with this Cattell defines attitudes in this way (in Cattell, 1965):

"An attitude may, therefore, be defined as *an interest in a course of action, in a given situation*" (p. 175).

At other places Cattell calls attitude "the 'brick' in the dynamic structure". It is obvious from these quotations that attitude is a variable belonging to a level of abstraction which is different from that to which erg and sentiment belong. We shall return to this problem later, after we have presented some other motivational variables.

4. *Other variables*. Besides the three sub-categories of "dynamic traits", which constitute the "dynamic lattice", Cattell's theory contains another set of variables called the *"motivational component factors"*.

Both the "motivational component factors" *and* the "dynamic traits" (ergs and sentiments) are based on *measurements of attitudes*. The *difference* between the two sets of factors is determined by the *purpose* of the measurement. If measurement of the *strength or intensity* of attitudes is the main purpose, some *"motivational component factors"* can be established by factor analysis. On the other hand, if the main purpose of the measurement is the *structure and direction* of the attitudes, then the previously mentioned dynamic traits can be established by factor analysis (ergs and sentiments).

The difference between the two sets of factors could possibly also be expressed in this way: the *dynamic traits* are mainly determined by the structure of the *personality* tested, while the *motivational component factors* are mainly determined by *measuring devices* used in testing.

This last way of expressing the difference between the two sets of factors is in consistence with Cattell's formal definition (in Cattell, 1957, p. 896):

"Motivation Component Factors. Components, found in measurement *devices,* which may enter into *any* dynamic structure factor."

If the present author's interpretation of Cattell's motivational component factors is correct, it is a little confusing – at least for me that Cattell has named these factors with terms borrowed from the psychoanalytic theory about the *structure* of personality. Thus the five motivation component factors best established by him at the moment are:

        A = conscious *id*
        B = realized *ego*
        Γ = ideal self or *superego*
        Δ = unconscious, sympathetic nervous system
        E = repressed *complexes.*

By making a further factor analysis Cattell has found two *second-order factors* in addition to the five mentioned above: "*Integrated* (self-sentiment) interests" and "*unintegrated* (unconscious) interests". This is illustrated by the following diagram (from Cattell, 1965, p. 182):

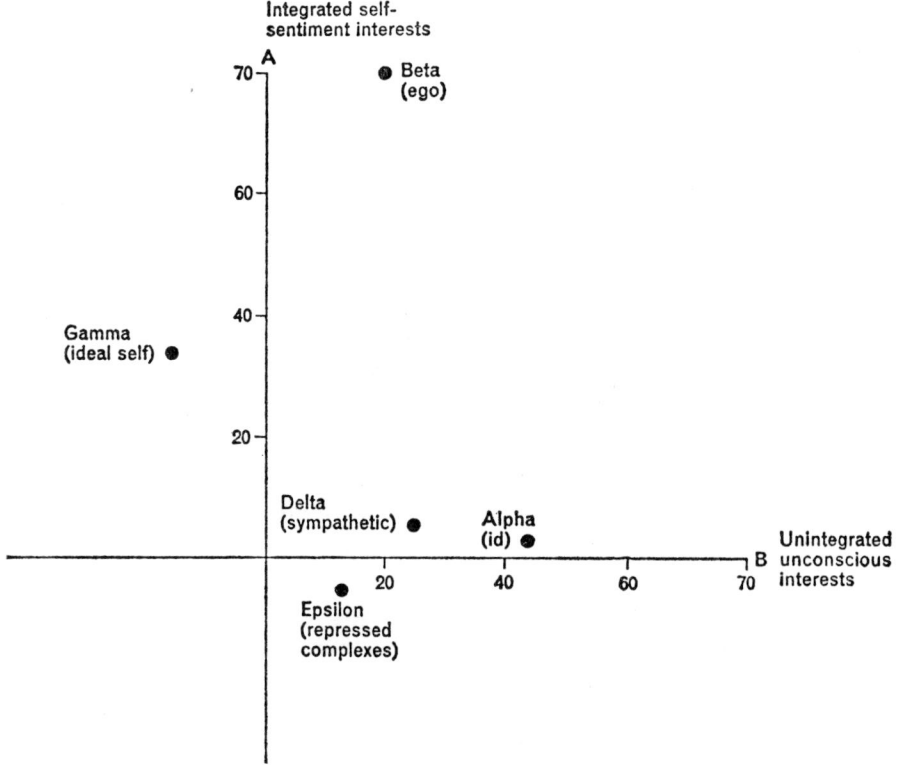

Fig. 13.3 Relation of second-order to primary motivation factors (Diagram 20 from Cattell, 1965).

The two *second-order* motivation component factors are analogous to the two *dynamic (source) traits*, which determine every *attitude*, which can be conceived of as a *vector* defined in terms of:

1. *ergic strength* (analogous to the *unintegrated* interests), and:
2. *engrams* (sentiments which are analogous to the *integrated* interests).

This analogizing is based upon some passages in Cattell's 1957 book, such as the following (p. 584):

"Factors found in dynamic variables (i.e., dynamic trait structures), are either ergs or engrams (sentiments, complexes). A given attitude response (or any response) is therefore expressible as a vector in two adjoining spaces. One defines ergic strength and quality, i.e., "orectic direction", and is representable by E coordinates; the other defines the learning experience, i.e., the "sociological direction" or institutional-personal history, and is representable by M coordinates. The first is in units of ergic tension; the second is in units of reward-frequency (reinforcement) plus ergic tensions. Resemblances and differences of this formulation and that independently reached by reflexological learning theory can be noted.

In addition to the M measurement a sentiment factor can be given an *ergic investment* score from vector addition of the ergic dimensions of the attitudes which intersect in the sentiment (preferably in the Alpha motivation component measures). This yields a single vector resultant for a sentiment object which should equal, experimentally, the total interest in having the object continue (or be destroyed). This is the defensible, logical, definable basis for measuring 'for or against' an object; but it refers to a sentiment, not an attitude."

This interpretation of the motivational component factors forms the basis for the following systematological classification, to which we now turn.

2.1.1. *The surplus meaning of the H-terms*. After the above detailed representation of the terms (and variables) in Cattell's theory it should be rather easy to make the different systematological classifications of the terms.

All the *traits* – cognitive, temperamental and dynamic are *H-variables*. Furthermore, all the traits – with the possible exception of "attitudes" – can be classified as *hypothetical constructs* with *neutral* surplus meaning (without "imported metaphorical properties", to use Cattell's own terminology).

"*Attitude*" deviates from other dynamic traits in that it belongs to another level of abstraction. Cattell has indicated this in a diagram (p. 538 in Cattell, 1957), where attitudes are located on the so-called "manifestation level", while the other "dynamic traits" are located on the so-called "abstraction level". If we interpret these two levels as being analogous to our D-level and H-level respectively, then it means that *attitude is a descriptive term*. But then it must be a highly abstract descriptive term, which summarizes all the test-results measuring dynamic traits. This interpretation is also supported by the fact that attitudes in Cattell's formula are always represented by an "R" (or some other symbol) standing for "reaction", "performance" or some other *observable* behavior-pattern.

There is an alternative possibility, that of classifying attitude as an intervening variable (in the narrow sense) belonging to the border zone between the D-level and the H-level[5]).

It is more difficult to classify the *"motivation component factors"*; but *if* our earlier expressed conception is correct, then motivation component factors is a term representing a truly *intervening variable* (in the formal and narrow sense). This means that these factors are *abstractive concepts* based upon some aspects of the measurements of attitudes, while the dynamic traits are *constructive concepts* representing factors or variables which mediate between independent S-variables and dependent R-variables. In other words: *all traits are causal determiners of behavior*. Cattell has in several places stressed "the position that factors are not categories, but causes" (among other places in a personal letter to the present author). A more elaborated formulation is found in Cattell, 1966, from which we quote the following (pp. 237–39):

"It behoves us, at this point, to define more closely the status and meaning of the term factor. The epistemological status of a simple structure factor is that of an empirical *construct*, but it commonly has degrees of 'surplus meaning' borrowed from beyond the immediate system, which can turn it into a theoretical concept (see also Henrysson). However, for such uniquely determined common factors in general, our view is that their only surplus meaning, beyond what is given by the properties of a *mathematical factor*, is that they are *influences*. Operationally, this additional meaning is derived from simple structure and confactor rotation operations."

The present author agrees in general with Cattell's conception of factors, because he and his co-workers have presented strong evidence – among other things from their nature-nurture studies – that supports this view of factors. But I believe that the motivation component factors are exceptions, as they are *abstractions* from the measurement of the strength or intensity of attitudes which do *not* correspond to any other set of causal determining factors parallel to the dynamic traits. *If* the motivational component factors are regarded as another set of *cuasal* determining factors, then Cattell's theory would be less parsimonious and there would be a problem regarding the functional relationship between the two sets of H-variables (or factors), the dynamic traits and the motivation component factors.

We therefore conclude this section with the classification of motivation component factors as intervening variables (in the formal, narrow sense), while cognitive, temperamental and dynamic traits are hypothetical constructs (with

---

5. The reader should be warned that this classification is different from the classification of attitude presented in my chapter in Cattell's *Handbook of Modern Personality Theory* (in press). The present author has made some changes in his conception of Cattell's theory in the time between writing the two chapters.

neutral surplus meaning – except attitudes, which are abstract, descriptive R-variables[6]).

2.1.2. *Dispositional and functional terms.* We now turn to the second systematological classification of terms and variables into "dispositions" and "functions" according to the *duration* of their existence. You may well have a suspicion that all traits of factors are dispositions, as the purpose of personality theory is to establish a stable set of personality factors in order to explain ever-changing behavior. This is also the case with Cattell's theory – at least for the majority of traits. Thus *all cognitive and temperamental traits are dispositions, and so are some components of the dynamic traits: the M-factors (engrams in sentiments) and the C and H components of ergs* (i. e., the constitutional and the historical components), as well as the personal constants (k, a, b) in the formula for ergic tension level.

The remaining two components of the erg, *the physiological state, P, and the gratification level, G, are in reality functions.*

In the case of Cattell's theory it is possible to make *a further differentiation of functions into "processes", "states" and "changes"* as this theory is very explicit and precise on this point, too. Thus we have the following classification:

1. *"Processes":* variables of very short duration (seconds to hours): the momentary stimuli, the physiological component of an erg (P), and the "reverberatory level of engrams" (a concept which belongs to Cattell's learning theory, which we shall examine later).
2. *"States":* variables with somewhat longer duration (from hours to days): the gratification level of ergs, G, and *perhaps* the physiological state, P, as well as certain "state levels" such as "arousal", "anxiety", "depression" and "fatigue", which are dealt with in Cattell's complete personality theory (but not in this chapter).
3. *"Changes":* variables which change over periods from seconds to years: endogenous change, C_e, capacity change, C_c, and learning change, C_l, as well as the decline rate of the reverberatory processes in engrams (equal to "forgetting").

And for the sake of completeness we add here:

4. *"Dispositions":* variables with the longest duration of existence (from years to a lifetime): cognitive and temperamental traits as well as the M, C and H components of the dynamic traits.

---

6. In the following two systematological classifications motivational component factors are *not* included, as these classifications presuppose that the variables are causal determiners or functional mediating variables.

This classification can be combined with the next systematological classification:

2.1.3. *Dynamic, directive and vectorial variables.* It would seem to be easy to classify the three categories of traits according to their effects on behavior into *dynamic* variables (including "dynamic traits"), *directive* variables (including "cognitive traits") and *vectorial* variables (including "temperamental traits"). But a further analysis of Cattell's text reveals that the so-called dynamic traits are not purely dynamic variables. Thus it is clear that "attitude" is defined as a *vectorial* term, and, furthermore, we find a cognitive or *directive* component in *sentiments*, the engram factor (M), which thereby defines "sentiments" (as a whole) as *vectorial* variables (as they are constituted of ergs and the M-factors).

Even "erg" is not a purely dynamic term as its definition includes reference to consummatory goals specific for each of the 16 ergs. This brings an element of *directive effect* into ergs. But this directive effect is not very strong or dominant as is the case with sentiments (and temperamental traits). Therefore, we have chosen *not* to classify ergs as vectorial variables but to keep them as dynamic *variables*[7]).

Thus we can conclude the classification of variables according to *effect on behavior* with this summary:

1. *Dynamic variables:* Ergs.
2. *Directive variables:* Cognitive traits, the engram component (M) of sentiments.
3. *Vectorial variables:* Temperamental traits, attitudes and sentiments (as wholes).

The two last systematological classifications can be combined in one classification scheme (Fig. 13.4.).

2.2. *Classification of the hypotheses*

We have already, in our overview of Cattell's theory (cf. paragraph 2.0.), outlined the content of the hypotheses in Cattell's theory. A more detailed pres-

---

7. If we want to make a distinction between such clear dynamic terms as Hull's "drive", Lewin's "tension", and Hebb's and others' "arousal" on the one side and Cattell's "erg" on the other side, we could introduce a new classification with the sub-categories *general* dynamic variable (like "drive", "tension", "arousal", etc.) and *specific* dynamic variables (like "erg"). The last sub-category is placed between the general dynamic and the vectorial variables (such as Lewin's "force" and Hull's "sEr"). This new classification is presented in my chapter in Wolman's *Handbook of General Psychology* (1973).

Effect \ Duration	Dynamic Variables:	Vectorial variables:	Directive variables:
Processes:	Physiological conditions?		Reverbatory processes ($r_{h,t}$)
States:	Physiological conditions? Arousal Anxiety Depression Gratification level Es. and Ed.		M_s (sentiment sensitivity index)
Changes:		C_l: learning C_c: capacity change C_e: endogenous change	Declinerate of reverbatory processes (d_r)
Dispositions:	Dynamic traits: E_T, C, H	Temperamental traits Attitudes	Ability traits M_T (sentiment-engram)

Fig. 13.4. A short inspection of this classification-sheme shows that Cattell's thery has very few process-terms. But it can be explained by the fact that it was orginally a personality theory, which has been expanded to include motivation and learning.

entation of his hypotheses is not easy, because they are scattered through his voluminous production without many summaries or explicit formulations. The most explicit and broadest set of hypotheses is found in his "Personality" (1950), where the last chapter contains 17 explicit "laws" (which are not empirical laws but *hypotheses* according to our terminology). It would, however, be of little use to quote all these laws or hypotheses here, because Cattell's theory – and his terminology – has been developed so much since 1950.

The latest explicit and systematic formulation of the hypotheses in Cattell's theory is to be found in Chapter 19 in his "Handbook of Modern Personality Theory" (in press). In this chapter a "comprehensive learning theory" is presented in 22 formulas. Although this is really a very concise, exact and systematic theory, it would take us too far afield to present and comment on all the 22 formulas. Instead, we have chosen to present the main content of Cattell's "comprehensive learning theory" in the following few sentences:

Learning is a function of the following "factors" (or variables) at the *beginning* of the learning sequence:

E = ergic tension level, which in this case is subdivided into a constant, E_T, and a variable, E_S (called the "ergic sentivity index").
M = engram action level (including sentiments and complexes), subdivided into the constant, M_T, and the variable, M_S, or "sentiment sensitivity index".
S = state level (arousal, anxiety, etc.).

In addition to this, learning is influenced by the following "factors" at the *end* of a learning sequence:

E_d = drop in ergic level, which is a function of:
G = consummatory gratification or reward magnitude.
r_{ht} = reverberatory level of the cognitive process from situation "h" at time "t".
d_r = decline rate of the cognitive reverberatory process.
f = frequency of repetition after the first sequence.

All these factors or variables are functionally related as indicated by one of the most important among the 22 formulas:

$$a_{hj_{(ft_1)}} = \text{Log } f\,[r_{hxt_1} - d_r(t_1 - t_2)]\,[E_{si}\,(S_{h_x}es - S_g)]$$

Concerning this formula Cattell states (Chapter 19, p. 32):

"Thus frequency, reward, and 'goal distance' consolidation are brought into a single theory."

We have found this comprehensive learning theory worth comparing with the classical learning theory of Hull and present it in an appendix to this chapter[8]).

2.2.1. *The basic classification of the hypotheses.* From the former analyses it should be obvious to the reader that Cattell's theory contains many explicitly and precisely formulated hypotheses. They are also organized into explanatory systems in some of his books (*"Personality"*, 1950, and *Handbook of Modern Personality Theory,* forthcoming). But for our purpose we need a more comprehensive system of hypotheses covering most of Cattell's production. Therefore, we shall make a *systematic reconstruction* of his theory – or rather theories – as presented in his main books. Although his hypotheses are certainly formulated in precise symbolic versions it has been necessary to reformulate them in accordance with our S-H-R-symbolism. We take our starting point from our diagram (Fig. 1.), and use the following abbreviations:

S_C = constitutional determinants,
which in principle are independent (or S-variables).

---

8. This appendix is taken from my Chapter 34 in Cattell's "Handbook of Modern Personality Theory" forthcoming).

S_H = life history determinants,
which also in principle are independent (or S-variables).
S_T = task requirements, instructions
and other stimuli for problem solving.
S_I = incentives.
S_D = deprivations.
S_S = organic states other than deprivations
(fatigue, illness, arousal, etc.).
H_{AT} = ability traits.
H_{TT} = temperamental traits.
H_E = ergs.
H_M = sentiments (and other memory factors).
H_S = hypothetical personality states.
$H_{att.}$ = attitudes (which are on the border-line
between the H-level and the D-level).

Through the employment of these symbols we can make the following systematic reconstruction of Cattell's main hypotheses:

1. hypothesis: $S_{C+H} \to H_{AT}$
2. hypothesis: $S_{C+H} \to H_{TT}$
3. hypothesis: $S_{C+H} \to H_E$
4. hypothesis: $S_H \to H_M$[9])
5. hypothesis: $S_T \to H_{AT}$
6. hypothesis: $S_I \to H_{E+M}$
7. hypothesis: $S_D \to H_E$
8. hypothesis: $S_S \to H_S$
9. hypothesis: $(H_{AT} + H_{TT} + H_E + H_M + H_S) \to H_{att.}$
10. hypothesis: $H_{att.} \to R(\text{Test})$
11. hypothesis: $H_{att.} \to R(\text{Questionnaire})$
12. hypothesis: $H_{att.} \to R(\text{Life data})$

These 12 hypotheses represent a *very* concentrated reconstruction of Cattell's main hypotheses. Perhaps it is too concentrated to furnish a fair picture of his theory. But for our purposes it is useful, among other things, as the basis for the following classification of hypotheses:

1. *Purely theoretical hypotheses (H-H):*

Only one hypothesis: No. 9.

---

9. This formula could be replaced by a more sophisticated reformulation of Cattell's main formula from his comprehensive learning theory: $Ha = S(\text{Reward, magnitude and frequency}) \, H \, [(E + M + S) t_1 - (E + M + S) t_2 \to H_{M_{t_3}}]$.

2. *Partly empirical hypotheses:*

   a. S-H-hypotheses: Hypotheses No. 1 to 8 incl.
      In all: 8 hypotheses.

   b. H-R-hypotheses: Hypotheses No. 10, 11 and 12.
      In all: 3 hypotheses.

2.2.2. *The complexity of the hypotheses.* In our systematic reconstruction of Cattell's hypotheses there has only been one (No. 9) which is *multi-dimensional*, all the others being *one-dimensional*. But the reader should bear in mind that this is *our* reconstruction. By reading Cattell's own books you will find *many* complicated multi-dimensional hypotheses. Consequently, his theory must be classified as a rather complicated ("dynamic") theory.

2.2.3. *The functional relationships in the hypotheses.* From the presentation of the theory and the above notation it should be clear that Cattell's theory is a *causal-deterministic theory in principle*. In practice it is, of course, not possible to make predictions with 100 % probability regarding Cattell's or any other psychological theory.

We have now finished the analysis of the H-level in his theory and turn now to the next level.

The descriptive stratum

3.1. *The abstract D-level*

This stratum of Cattell's theory, the border-zone to the H-level, is very rich in new, precise terms. We have already commented upon the most important abstract, descriptive term, "attitude", which could possibly be conceived of and classified as a term referring to an intervening variable.

3.1.1. *The abstract, descriptive terms.* Cattell's theory contains many other abstract, descriptive terms referring to *both S-variables and R-variables*. But it is difficult to present a short and meaningful summary of these terms, because they are strongly connected with his and his co-workers' many tests and the specific terminology they have developed.

This is consistent with a methodological principle in his theory according to which the hypothetical personality factors or traits should always be operationally defined by referring to a battery of tests. Cattell has expressed the principle in this way (in Cattell, 1965, p. 136):

"One must recognize that the so-to-speak Newtonian phase of psychology has given way to an Einsteinian Relativity in which we are more cautious about assuming that our measures are absolutes. Every psychological measurement made in the rating and the questionnaire media contains both the movement of the observer and of the observed. The effect of the perception of the observer must be scientifically allowed for, and, as Digman and others have shown, with sufficient nicety of calculation, something which we may call the real traits of the person can be extricated from its contamination with instrument factors – provided the latter are understood."

3.1.2. *The general, descriptive propositions.* In the D-level of Cattell's theory there are also many abstract, *general descriptive propositions* ("laws"), both S-R- and R-R-propositions. Most of these are correlations between test results (which are the bases of the construction of the hypothetical personality factors). Besides, there are some more general propositions ("hypotheses" or "laws" – depending on how one regards them) dealing with the *interaction between heredity and environment* on the one side and the formation of personality factors (hypotheses) or the determination of test performances (laws) on the other. Thus in Cattell, 1965 we find 5 laws about the interaction between heredity and environment, which could be summarized in this way (quoted and rephrased from pp. 48–52):

1. *Law of "imprinting":* "The environment is far more powerful in the early stages of life."

2. *Law of "aids":* "The interaction with environment often goes by fits and starts. – – – It is of such stuff that the 20 per cent environmental contribution to individual differences in intelligence may be made."

3. *The law of coercion to the bio-social mean.* The development of personality factors and intelligence in a population is in the long run coerced toward the bio-social mean.

4. *Law:* "The effects of *environment* often determine the *area* in which a trait is displayed, whereas *heredity* more often governs its *amount.*"

5. *Law: Heredity* by and large determines the level of the broad *general traits* (e. g., the sex erg), while *environment* by and large determines the *particular attachment* to objects, etc. (e. g., sex partner).

Besides these laws (and hypotheses) about the interaction between heredity and environment we think that another set of general, descriptive propositions should be mentioned as typical for Cattell's theory: the "laws" about the development of personality summarized in the so-called *"adjustment process analysis chart"*, which represents the so-called *"dynamic cross-roads"* (Diagram 38 in Cattell, 1965, p. 275):

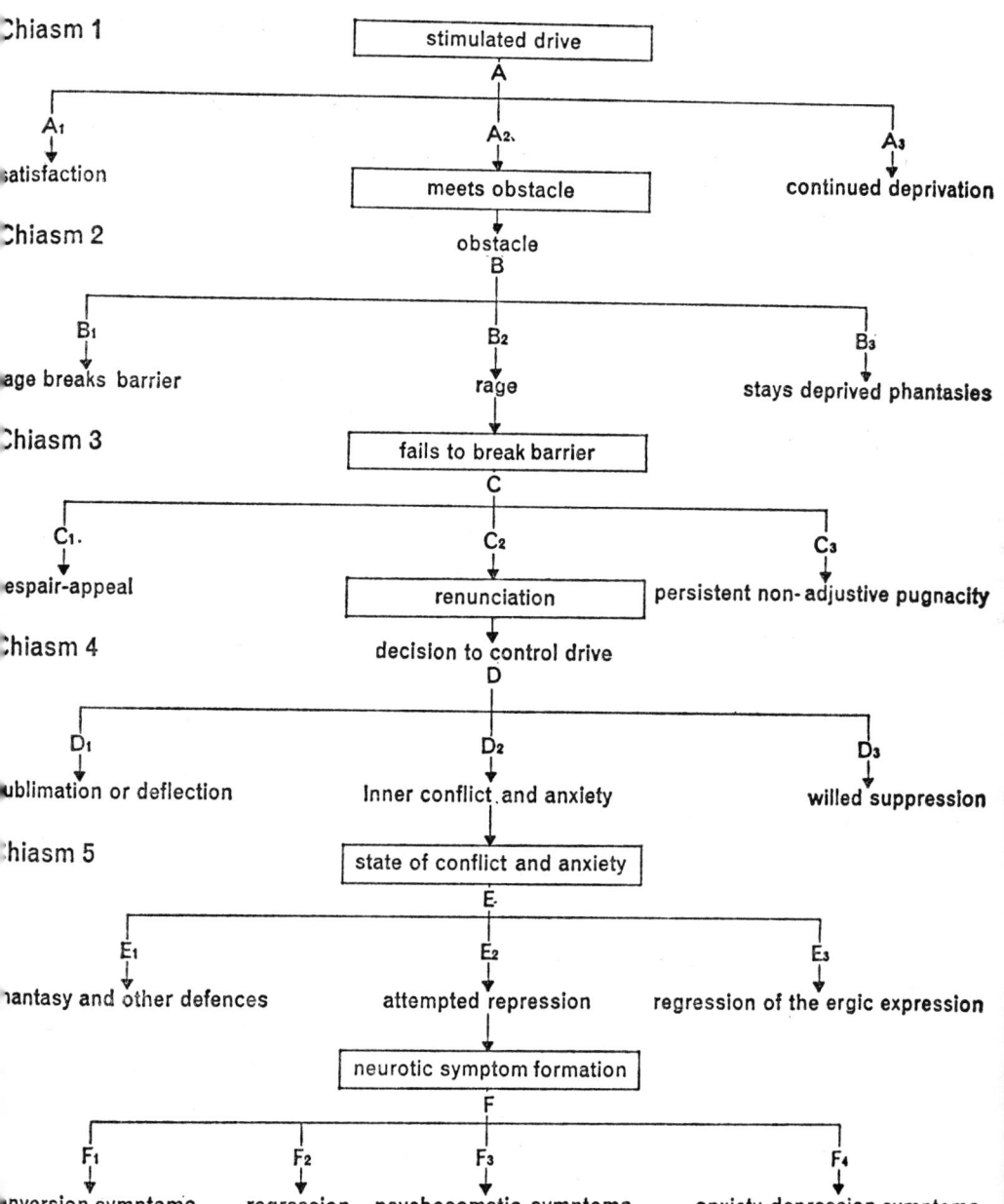

Fig. 13.5. "The dynamic cross-roads" or the adjustment process analysis cart (after Cattell (1965) diagram 38).

We could use Cattell's own words (p. 274) as an explanatory text for the diagram:

"In connexion with the dynamic calculus, and particularly its use in studying integration and adjustment, the clinician's experience of human conflicts has been schematized into a potentially quantifiable system called *adjustment process analysis*. This considers all the possible alternatives in trial-and-error 'emotional learning', providing a scheme of successive 'dynamic crossroads' whereby any individual's particular learning position can be codified."

3.2. *The concrete D-level*

The protocol sentences in Cattell's theory are descriptions of three sets of data:

1. *"L-data" or "Life record data":* ratings made by observers on the frequency and intensity with which specific kinds of behavior occur in the people they observe in actual, everyday-life situations.
2. *"Q-data" or Questionnaire data":* answers to questionnaires based upon the observed person's own self-observation and introspection.
3. *"T-data" or "Objective test data"* "miniature situations set up for a person to react to in which he does not really know on what aspect of his behavior he is being scored (hence "objective")." (p. 61).

It is clear from these descriptions that Cattell's theory is based upon both *behavioral and phenomenological* (introspective) data. Cattell himself regards objective tests as the most reliable observation medium, and prefers questionnaires to ratings. It should be emphasized that Cattell restricts the term "objective" to tests in which the person cannot fake. Thus questionnaires are not objective although they may have high inter-observer correlations. And they are still regarded by him as useful tools.

Without being an expert in psychological testing the present author thinks it is safe to evaluate Cattell's and co-workers' test-battery (including more than 500 tests) as the most comprehensive, detailed, precise and systematic to be found in the field of personality.

Among these tests are two which are especially dseigned for measuring motivation: the Motivation Analysis Test and the School Motivation Analysis Test.

3.3. *The descriptive units*

It is not easy to classify Cattell's theory-as-a-whole as being molar *or* molecular, because he uses all kinds of descriptive units from the most molecular (e. g., GSR measurements) to the most molar (e. g., description of the whole person by means of personality profile). Therefore, it can be said that Cattell's theory contains many molecular descriptions of the reactions of people, but at the same time is able to describe the individual person as a whole.

The theory as a whole

4.1. The formal properties of the theory.

4.1.1. The systematic organization of the theory.
According to this formal property Cattell's theory must be classified as an *explanatory system* which could easily be developed into a *deductive* theory. This is intimately related to the next property.

4.1.2. The preciseness of representation.
According to this property Cattell's theory must be classified as a *partly symbolized theory* on the way to becoming a mathematical theory.

4.1.3 The properties of the model.
The models used in Cattell's theory are *two-dimensional diagrams* (except for the mathematical "model": factor-analysis).

4.2. The epistemological properties of the theory

According to these properties Cattell's theory must be classified as a *neutral explanatory theory* (an S-H_N-R-theory).

4.3. The theory-empiry ratio

The general impression one gets when reading Cattell's production is that his theory is very well-founded on a great deal of empirical research. In addition, the many operational definitions of H-terms gives the impression of an *empirical theory*. On the basis of our reconstruction of his hypotheses we have calculated the Hypotheses Quotient by means of the formula:

$$\mathrm{H.Q.} = \frac{\Sigma(\text{H–H})}{\Sigma[(\text{S–H}) + (\text{H–R})]} = \frac{1}{8+3} = \frac{1}{11} = 0.09$$

This a very low H.Q. – in fact the lowest we have calculated, either in "Theories of Motivation" or in this book. There is always the possibility of error that we have, e. g., made the reconstructed theory too simple. We are confident, however, that a more objective and exact calculation (e. g., by a computer program) would give a similar result.

Concluding this chapter we hope that we have presented an objective metascientific analysis of Cattell's theory in spite of the fact that we are "biased" in favor of his theory.

Appendix

A Comparison Between the Theories of Cattell and Hull

Systematological classifications make a general comparison between theories possible. But besides what has already been presented in this chapter the present author would like to compare Cattell's "comprehensive learning theory" with one of the most comprehensive and precise theories among the "classic" learning theories, that of *Hull*. For the sake of this comparison we may present the essentials of Hull's theory by means of his "Postulate VIII, the Constitution of Reaction Potential (sEr)", which is summarized in this formula (Hull, 1952, p. 7):

$$sEr = D \times V \times K \times sHr.$$

We can compare the terms in Hull's formula with the terms in Cattell's theory. If we do so we find that some terms are *"systematologically equivalent"*, i. e., they have analogous functions in the two theories without being identical in every aspect. A lesser degree of correspondence is indicated by the term "parallel". Direct comparisons are made on the following points:

1. sEr = "reaction evocation potential", which is equivalent to Cattell's "a_{hij}".
2. D = "drive", which parallels, but is not equivalent to Cattell's "Erg", the latter being much more differentiated (among other things including both a personality factor, E_T, and a more motivational factor, E_S). Besides, "E" is made up of many components: constitutional (C), "historical" (H), physiological (P) as well as a special term for "gratification level" (G).
3. V = "stimulus intensity dynamism", which is parallel to the many "S_s" in Cattell's formulas.
4. K = "incentive motivation", which is not directly equivalent or parallel to any term in Cattell's theory. But the "gratification level" (G) and perhaps also the "ergic sensitivity index" (E_S) have analogous functions in his theory.
5. sHr = "Habit strength" is parallel to Cattell's "engram action level" (M), which is broader, as it includes not only instrumental skills or habits (like sHr) but also more cognitive or conceptual variables, as well as the personality organizing variables, "sentiments" and "complexes". But it is perhaps a lack of differentiation in Cattell's terminology that there are no special terms for all these subcategories.

6. Besides the variables quoted in the formula Hull has one more important variable, *"inhibition"*, which is subdivided into "reactive inhibition" (I_R) and "conditioned inhibition" (sIr). But these are not thought to be necessary in the "comprehensive learning theory" according to Cattell (cf. Chapter 19, p. 37, Cattell, forthcoming).

We may therefore *conclude* this comparison by stating that there are *some systematological equivalencies and parallels between Cattell's and Hull's theories.* But Hull has one main term ("Inhibition") which Cattell thinks is unnecessary, and Cattell has several terms (especially for personality and motivational variables) which have no equivalent or parallel in Hull's theory. *Cattell's theory may therefore be described as a more comprehensive and differentiated theory than Hull's,* to which it is equal in formal development.

14. Atkinson's and Birch's Theory

Introduction

The American psychologist *John W. Atkinson* was McClelland's closest Coworker while he was engaged in writing "The Achievement Motive", which appeared in 1953[1]).

Since the publication of this book McClelland and Atkinson have not worked together very much. McClelland has mainly been working with the continuation of the empirical study of motivation and the application of his motivational theory to history and economics[2]).

Atkinson, on the other hand, has mainly been occupied with the theoretical elaboration of the original theory. This he has done to such an extent that I think it is now correct to speak about "Atkinson's theory". This theory deserves an analysis of its own, because he integrates valuable theoretical trends from McClelland, Lewin, Tolman and decision theory.

This theory is presented in its most elaborated form in the last two chapters of his textbook: "An Introduction to Motivation" (1964), which will be the object of the following analysis.

Later Atkinson wrote a book with *Norman T. Feather: "A Theory of Achievement Motivation"* (1966). This book contains a series of empirical studies in support of his theory. This book is analyzed later in this chapter in the section about "The Descriptive Stratum".

More recently he co-authored a book with *David Birch:* "The Dynamics of Action" (1970). The latter contains a new highly formalized theory which we have decided to analyze in a later section of this chapter.

The metastratum

1.1. *Philosophical propositions*

There are no explicit formulations of philosophical propositions in Atkinson's book. But we can infer from the text – especially from his many explicit meta-

---

1. This book was analyzed in K. B. Madsen: "Theories of Motivation" (1st ed., 1959, 4th ed., 1968).
2. Results of these studies are presented in "The Achieving Society" (1961) and "Motivating Economic Achievement" (1969).

theoretical propositions – that he presupposes a *neutral-monistic theory* of the psychosomatic problem. He probably also presupposes a biological Darwinian conception of man as most modern psychologists do, but this cannot be clearly inferred from the text.

1.2. Metatheoretical propositions

Atkinson is much more explicit about metatheoretical problems, which he deals with at several points in the book.

He characterizes his own theory as "ahistorical" and "aphysiological", but in connection with a later mentioned discussion of "the several languages of motivation" he writes (p. 10):

"The several levels of discourse which may be found in the contemporary psychological literature are deliberately referred to as several "languages" in the present discussion in order to suggest the possibility of translation from one to the other."

Later he writes about the possibility of the integration of the two most popular approaches to present psychology (p. 203):

"The two orientations *mathematical* and *neurophysiological,* are viewed as alternative foundations for the theoretical development of psychology. At present, the mathematical orientation provides a more useful approach to systematic analysis of the problem of *human* motivation and integrative discussion of studies of molar behavior in animals and humans than does the neurophysiological orientation. The two will one day be fused, but that day still seems a long way off."

The present author thinks that this "integrative attitude" to the different approaches, which is characteristic of Atkinson's theory, is badly needed and fruitful.

Another remarkable feature of Atkinson's theory is his use of analogies from physics, which he has borrowed from Lewin. About this he writes (p. 305):

"It is worth noting the extent to which certain concepts and theoretical issues which have arisen in the psychology of motivation are in some respects analogous to those which arose much earlier in the attempt to explain the motions of physical objects. For it may be that Lewin's belief that physics provides a useful guide for conceptual analysis of the problem of motivation will in the end turn out to be more correct than the alternative belief that psychology should look to physiology for its guiding concepts."

But there is a difference between Lewin's and Atkinson's ways of using physical concepts. Lewin used physical (or perhaps "quasi-physical") concepts like "force" as *integrated elements* of his theory. Therefore he was especially criticized for his "misuse", as *I. D. London* called it[3]), of physical (and mathematical) concepts. Atkinson's way of using physical concepts cannot be challenged by such criticism, because he does not use physical concepts directly as elements

---

3. Cf. Chapter 9 in "Theories of Motivation", which deals with Lewin's theory.

of his theory, but rather uses physical conceptual analysis as *a guiding analogy or an heuristic model* for theory construction and his conceptual analysis is very fruitful.

1.3. Methodological propositions

Atkinson does not write very much about methodological problems. The most explicit formulations are found in the introductory chapter, where he, among other things, writes about "the several languages of motivation" (pp. 9–10): 1) the "experiential" language, 2) the "neurophysiological" language, 3) the "behavioral" language and 4) the "mathematical" language.

These different languages are not all on the same level. The present author thinks, that only the experiential and the behavioral languages belong to the basic, descriptive level and can be chosen as a "protocol" or "data language". The other two languages belong to a higher descriptive level or perhaps an explanatory level. But this problem need not to be discussed further as Atkinson gives the behavioral language priority.

He also writes a little about more specific methodological problems. In accordance with his preference for the behavioral language he writes in connection with a discussion about Freud (p. 270):

"This notion of unconscious motivation means in simplest terms, that an individual cannot employ the method of introspection and hope to identify fully the determinants of his own behavior."

Besides this Atkinson is especially interested in combining experimental methods and tests in the study of human motivation. He criticizes very thoroughly research with "ad hoc tests", which are not guided by any theory or conceptual system:

"Many studies of this sort are neither fish nor fowl. They produce isolated facts which, after taxing the memory of students for a short time, are soon forgotten because they lack any relatedness to the central task of the science" (p. 272).

Atkinson's own research and theory provide a very promising example of bridge-building between general psychology with its experimental methods and differential psychology with its tests and clinical methods.

The hypothetical stratum of Atkinson's original theory

2.0. *Summary of the hypotheses*

Before we analyze the contents of hypotheses and variables in Atkinson's original theory (from 1964), we shall try to present a *summary of the contents:*

Atkinson's theory is a specific theory about "achievement motivation" but it is thought to be applicable to all sorts of human motivation. The theory is an *"Expectancy × Value"* theory, which is founded on the work of Lewin and Tolman. This theory is distinct from a *"Drive × Habit"* theory, which has its origin in Hull's work. Atkinson has made several elaborations of his "Expectancy × Value" theory. First, he (sometimes) substitutes for "expectancy" the term "Probability" or P; next he breaks down "value" into "Motive" (M) and "Incentive" (I), which are determined by dispositions in the individual and qualities of the goal object respectively. He further adopts the term "Tendency" (T) for the actual state of motivation. The main hypothesis in Atkinson's theory then can be stated thusly:

$$T_{R,g} = M_G \times P_{R,g} \times I_g.$$

When the tendency refers to "achievement motivation", the symbols in the hypothesis are supplemented with an "S" standing for "Success" (or "succeed").

$$T_s = M_s \times P_s \times I_s.$$

Just like McClelland, who early distinguished a "need of achievement" (nAch) from a "fear of failure" (f Fail.), Atkinson distinguishes a "tendency to achieve success" (Ts) from a "tendency to avoid failure" (T_{-f}) which is determined in the same way:

$$T_{-f} = M_{AF} \times P_f \times I_f.$$

These two tendencies then interact with some "external tendencies" ($T_{ext.}$), which produce the resultant tendency to achieve ($T_{res.}$) according to the following formula:

$$T_{res.} = (T_s + T_{-f}) + T_{ext.}$$

In Chapter 10 Atkinson has expanded and generalized this hypothesis into the following:

R_A occurs when

$$T_A > T_B + T_{Gi}.$$

where T_A and T_B are the tendencies to perform the acts R_A and R_B respectively. T_{Gi} is "the inertial tendency", the persistent unsatisfied tendency to perform the act R_B. This can be applied to the general problem: *change* of behavior from one goal, e. g., achieving success (R_s) to another goal, e. g., achieving affiliative contact with other people (R_{Aff}). This is explained by the hypothesis:

R_s occurs when

$$T_s = f(M_s \times E_s \times I_s) + T_{si} > T_{Aff} = (M_{Aff} \times E_{Aff} \times I_{Aff}) + T_{Aff}.$$

2.1. *The hypothetical terms (H-terms)*

Before conducting our systematological analysis and making classifications of the H-terms, it would seem to be worthwhile to have a look at Atkinson's own definitions of the terms. He opens the first chapter of his book with a discussion of the meaning of "Motivation" (p. 1):

"The study of motivation has to do with analysis of the various factors which incite and direct an individual's actions."

Later Atkinson introduces some refinements of these motivational terms (pp. 263–64):

"The reader is reminded that in studies of Achievement the term *motivation* is often used in reference to the aroused state of a person to strive for some goal. It refers to the strength of the tendency to act in a certain way in order to get on the goal. The term *motive* is used in reference to a relatively general and stable personality disposition which is assumed to be one of the determinants of *motivation*, the tendency to strive for the goal. We may avoid confusion by substituting the term tendency for motivation – – –".

After presenting Atkinson's definitions of "motivation" and "tendency", let us turn to his definition of the other variables in the formula: $T_s = M_s \times P_s \times I_s$ (p. 242):

"The first variable, M_s, is a relatively general and stable characteristic of the person which is present in any behaviour situation. But the values of the other two variables, P_s and I_s, depend upon the individual's past experience in specific situations that are similar to the one he now confronts. These variables change as the individual moves about from one life situation to another and so are treated as characteristics of particular situations or particular tasks."

We are now ready for the classifications.

2.1.1. *The surplus meaning of the H-terms.* Atkinson has very explicit formulations concerning this problem, and his theory is very consistent on this point.
He several times mentions the following two possibilities:

1. explanations using *neutral* H-terms, and
2. explanations using *physiological* H-terms[4]).

He writes among other places (p. 277):

"Thus we see a clear-cut separation of fundamental interests within the S–R-tradition: one directed towards further development of a physiological psychology, which, with the aid of new techniques of investigation, is making rapid strides in filling the gaps in empirical knowledge concerning the relation of brain functions to behavior; the other now directed towards elaboration of a systematic and mathematically stated theory of behavior

---

4. A third possibility – explanations using mentalistic H-terms – is mentioned by Atkinson in his historical introducton.

in terms of relations between antecedents, which may be observed without use of special instruments which get under the skin of the organism being studied, and observable characteristics of molar behavior."

He also presents clear arguments for his selection of the neutral H-terms. Thus he writes (p. 276):

"One striking characteristic of several programs of research which have produced Expectancy x Value conceptions of motivation of behavior is the extent to which the task of explaining purposive characteristics of molar behavior is divorced from the *"physiological language"* of motivation. – – – In each case, the task of explanation is conceived as one calling for conceptualization of the process which intervenes between observable stimulus situation and observable behavior in terms of variables, whose functional properties are defined in a mathematical principle which states how they combine to influence the strength of a tendency to act in a certain way."

In accordance with these explicit formulations Atkinson's H-terms can all be counted as H_N-terms.

Some readers perhaps think that the term "expectancy" has some *mentalistic* surplus meaning, but substituting it with "probability" (P) demonstrates that the term *is* a neutral, operationally defined H-term.

2.1.2. *Dispositional or functional terms?* In this case also it is easy to classify Atkinson's H-terms, because he defines them so precisely. In the quotations already presented in section 2.1.0. of this chapter, we have seen, that "Motive" is defined as "a relatively general and stable personality disposition". Thus it is clearly a *dispositional* term. The other terms are said to refer to variables which "change as the individual moves about from one life situation to another". Thus they should be classified as *functional* terms. But there remains some doubt about this, because these variables are also said to "depend upon the individual's past experience", which indicates that they have some dispositional components. There are two solutions to this problem: *either* there are assumed but not explicitly defined variables in the theory, i. e., some dispositions connected with "expectancy" (E) and "incentive value" (I), *or* the dispositional components are completely covered by the dispositional term "motive" (M), and the remaining terms – T, E, and I – are functional.

2.1.3. *Dynamic, directive or vector terms?* It is not so easy to classify Atkinson's H-terms in accordance with the corresponding variables' effect on behavior, because he makes very few explicit formulations about the problem. But we think that it is most correct to classify "motive" and "incentive value" as purely *dynamic* terms (although they *might* be regarded as vector terms). But the main effect of these variables is after all to *activate* behavior.

"Expectancy" is a directive term, as it refers to a cognitive variable which selects the specific act and guides it to the goal. The combined variable, "tendency", is a well-defined vector variable.

It is interesting to compare the main formula in Atkinson's theory with that in Hull's, because both theories are so precise and systematic. If we look at the two formulas:

$$\text{Hull: sEr} = f(\text{sHr} \times D \times K), \text{ and}$$

$$\text{Atkinson: } T_{R,g} = f(M_G \times E_{R,g} \times I_g),$$

we find the following similarities: sEr and $T_{R,g}$ are both functional vector terms while K and I_g are both functional dynamic terms. But here the similarities end and the differences begin: M_G and sHr are both dispositions but M_G dynamic and sHr directive. $E_{R,g}$ and D are both functions, but $E_{R,g}$ is directive and D dynamic. We think that the most important difference is that Atkinson's theory does not include any variable similar to Hull's "drive", D. According to Atkinson's theory, behavior is *not* determined by biological needs and drives, but by external incentives, expectancy of outcome as well as a personal disposition, the motive. This is the main difference between the "Expectancy × Value" theory and the "Drive × Habit" theory.

2.2. Classification of the hypotheses

In this section we shall analyze the hypotheses in Atkinson's theory. We shall concentrate here on the hypotheses about achievement motivation and take up the more generalized ones in a later section.

As the reader undoubtedly remembers the main hypotheses are:

$$T_s = f(M_s \times E_s \times I_s)$$

$$T_{-f} = f(M_{AF} \times E_f \times I_f).$$

All the terms in these hypotheses are H-terms. The variables they refer to are determined by certain S-variables, but the functional relationships are not presented in formulas as are the two main formulas. Consequently we have supplemented Atkinson's theory with an explicit formulation of these implicit hypotheses:

First: the motives, M_s and M_{AF}, are supposed to be dispositions. Nothing is explicitly stated about their origin, but we know from the research carried out by McClelland, Atkinson and co-workers that these dispositions are acquired as a result of upbringing. We could formulate it in this way:

Childhood conditions S(C.C.) determine motives (M_s and M_{AF}), or, in symbolic formulation:

1.a. $S(C.C_s) \rightarrow H(M_s)$
1.b. $S(C.C_f) \rightarrow H(M_f)$.

Second: the expectancies, E_s and E_f, are determined by stimuli from the task situation, S_T. The important feature is the degree of difficulty of the task, or, in other words: the relative probability of success or failure. This probability is of course also dependent on the person's earlier experience with similar situations. Therefore we think that it should be explicitly stated in our reformulation of Atkinson's theory that earlier frequency of success, $S_{E.S.}$, produces a memory trace of these experiences, H(Mem.). And this memory trace, together with the perception, H(P), of the present situation, S_P, determines the expectancies of success, E_s, and failure, E_f. For these we have two parallel sets of formulations:

2.a. $S(E.S_s) \rightarrow H(Mem. s)$
2.b. $S(E.S_f) \rightarrow H(Mem.f)$
3.a. $S(P_s) \rightarrow H(P_s)$
3.b. $S(P_f) \rightarrow H(P_f)$
4.a. $[H(P_s) \times H(Mem.s)] \rightarrow H(E_s)$
4.b. $[H(P_f) \times H(Mem.f)] \rightarrow H(E_f)$

Third: the incentive value, I_s, of achieving success is dependent upon the probability of success, P_s (or E_s), according to the formula:

$$I_s = 1 - P_s$$

or, symbolically:

5.a. $[1 - H(P_s)] \rightarrow H(I_s)$.

The parallel formulation for tendency to avoid failure is:

$$I_f = -P_s$$

or symbolically:

5.b. $[-H(P_s)] \rightarrow H(I_f)$.

Having formulated all the relationships between S-variables and H-variables, we can now reformulate Atkinson's main hypotheses symbolically:

6.a. $[H(M_s) \times H(E_s) \times H(I_s)] \rightarrow H(T_s)$
6.b. $[H(M_{AF}) \times H(E_f) \times H(I_f)] \rightarrow H(T_{-f})$
7. $[H(T_s) + H(T_{-f})] \rightarrow R(\text{achievement-oriented})$.

We are now able to make the basic classification of the hypotheses.

2.2.1. *Basic classification of hypotheses.* For the reader's convenience we recapitulate here our *systematic reconstruction* of Atkinson's hypotheses:

1.a. $S(C.C_s) \rightarrow H(M_s)$
1.b. $S(C.C_f) \rightarrow H(M_f)$
2.a. $S(E.S_s) \rightarrow H(MT_s)$
2.b. $S(E.S_f) \rightarrow H(MT_f)$
3.a. $S(P_s) \rightarrow H(P_s)$
3.b. $S(P_f) \rightarrow H(P_f)$
4.a. $[H(P_s) \times H(MT_s)] \rightarrow H(E_s)$
4.b. $[H(P_f) \times H(MT_f)] \rightarrow H(E_f)$
5.a. $[1 - H(P_s)] \rightarrow H(I_s)$
5.b. $[- H(P_s)] \rightarrow H(I_f)$
6.a. $[H(M_s) \times H(E_s) \times H(I_s)] \rightarrow H(T_s)$
6.b. $[H(M_{AF}) \times H(E_f) \times H(I_f)] \rightarrow H(T_{-f})$
7. $[H(T_s) + H(T_{-f})] \rightarrow R(\text{achievement-oriented})$

On the basis of this we can make the following classification:

1. *Purely theoretical hypotheses (H-H):*
   Hypotheses No. 4a, 4b, 5a, 5b, 6a and 6b. In all: 6 hypotheses.
2. *Partly empirical hypotheses:*
   a. S-H-hypotheses: No. 1a, 1b, 2a, 2b, 3a and 3b. In all: 6 hypotheses.
   b. H-R-hypotheses: No. 7. In all: 1 hypothesis.

2.2.2. *The complexity of the hypotheses.* On the basis of our systematic reconstruction we can also classify the hypotheses according to the degree of complexity into:

1. *one-dimensional hypotheses:*
   Hypotheses No. 1a, to 3b plus 5a and 5b. In all: 8 hypotheses.
2. *Multidimensional hypotheses:*
   Hypotheses No. 4a, 4b, 6a, 6b and 7. In all: 5 hypotheses.

Thus the theory contains a considerable number of *complex* hypotheses and can therefore be characterized as a rather *dynamic (or even a field) theory.*

2.2.3. *The functional relationships in the hypotheses.* It is more difficult to classify Atkinson's theory in accordance with the presupposed type of functional relationship. Atkinson has no explicitly formulated metapropositions about this problem, but he presents the following quotation at the beginning of Chapter 9 in: "A Theory of Achievement Motivation" (p. 240):

"Causes certainly are connected with effects; but that is because our theories connect them, not because the world is held together by cosmic glue" (N. R. Hanson, 1958, p. 64).

If we assume that this quotation expresses Atkinson's own point of view about determinism, we may describe it as a very "modern" interpretation of *"causal determinism"*. It is in fact so "radical", that it is very close to what we can describe as "probability determinism". Many of the empirical generalizations cited in his book are also formulated statistically. On the other hand, he – as a true follower of K. Lewin – formulates all his hypotheses as causal deterministic relationships (in principle). So perhaps the most correct description of his theory is that it is a *"causal deterministic theory in principle"*, which *in practice* acknowledges the necessity of formulating psychological hypotheses *statistically*.

The hypothetical stratum of the Atkinson and Birch theory

2.0. *Summary of the hypotheses*

In this section we shall analyze the hypotheses presented in *John W. Atkinson's and David Birch's: "The Dynamics of Action"* (1970) in which they have presented the most formalized and mathematically elaborated theory found in motivational psychology.

We shall begin with a summary of the hypotheses, which can also serve as a systematic reformulation of the hypotheses.

The fundamental presupposition of this theory is that *the living organism is always active*. Consequently, the main problem of motivational psychology is *not* to explain why the organism is active, but to explain *change of activity*. This problem is basic to the traditional problems of motivational psychology: 1) initiation, 2) persistence, 3) vigor and 4) preference (or choice) of activity, which are all related to the basic motivational problem: change of activity.

In accordance with these presuppositions the *first* hypothesis in our reconstruction states that *behavior is determined by action tendencies (T), which persist in their present state unless acted upon by certain forces*.

The forces that determine the change in persisting action tendencies and ongoing activity are *instigation, consummation* and *resistance*.

The *second* hypothesis states that *stimuli determine instigating forces (F) which produce changes – an increase – in the strength of action tendencies*. Thus it should be clear that stimuli do not cause or elicit the action tendencies, but only produce *changes* in them.

A *third* hypothesis states that *behavior determines consummatory forces (C), which produce changes – a decrease – in the strength of action tendencies*. According to this theory all behavior has a "consummatory value", and only a difference in degree between the kinds of activities traditionally called "instrumental" and "consummatory (or goal)" behavior is assumed.

The combination of instigating and consummatory forces is expressed in a *fourth* hypothesis, which is stated in this way in Atkinson-Birch (p. 12):

"The Principle of Change in Strength of Tendency is stated: *the rate of change in the strength of a tendency at any moment in time is equal to the instigating force minus the consummatory force.* This is most conveniently written as a differential equation:

$$\frac{dT}{dt} = F - C.$$

Both instigating forces and consummatory forces can spread their influence from one action tendency to others in the same "family of tendencies". This spread of effect is called *"displacement"* (= spreading the effect of instigating forces), and *"substitution"* (= spreading the effect of consummatory forces). We must leave out the hypotheses about displacement and substitution in our summarizing reformulation, because it would bring us too far afield. We include, however, the concepts: "negaction tendency", "inhibitory force" and "resistance".

"Negaction tendency" (N) is the tendency *not* to engage in an activity. It determines behavior together with the action tendencies. Thus we can reformulate the *fifth* hypothesis in this way: *Behavior is determined by a "resultant action tendency" (T), which is the algebraic sum of the strengths of action and negaction tendencies for that particular activity.*

And close to this is the concept of "inhibitory force" (I), which can be introduced as the *sixth* reformulated hypothesis in this way: *Stimuli determine inhibitory forces (I), which increase the strength of negaction tendencies.*

Parallel to the concept of the "consummatory force" of an action tendency is the "force of resistance" (R) of a negaction tendency. This is introduced in the *seventh* hypothesis, which is formulated by Atkinson and Birch in this way: (p. 208):

"*A change in the strength of a negaction tendency depends on the magnitude of the inhibitory force, the magnitude of the force of resistance and the duration of the exposure to these forces. The differential equation that describes the change in the strength of a tendency not to undertake a particular activity is*

$$\frac{dN}{dt} = I - R.$$

All these basic hypotheses – and the related mathematical formulas – are combined into one integrating hypothesis, called "the programmatic Principle of Change of Activity", which is expressed in the following formula (9.4):

$$^tB/A = \frac{(T_{AF} - N_{AF}) - (T_{BI} - N_{BF})}{\hat{F}_B}$$

which reads as follows: the time it takes for the change from activity A. to activity B. is a function of a ratio between, on the one hand, the difference between the differences between the action tendencies (T_{AF} and T_{BI}) and negaction tendencies (N_{AF} and N_{BI}) in their final and in their initial strengths, and, on the other hand, the instigating force (F_B) for the activity *not* occuring (B).

We think that our seven reformulated hypotheses and formula 9.4 represent the main hypotheses in the Atkinson-Birch theory.

We do not have space to take up Atkinson's and Birch's applications of these hypotheses to such psychological problems as choice, learning, etc. We shall only mention that the instigating forces and the inhibitory forces of stimuli are supposed to be either inborn (unconditioned) or learned (conditioned).

Atkinson's and Birch's theory presupposes a *recency principle* of learning combined with a "drive-induction", or, rather an *incentive motivation principle* of reinforcement. They are combined in the following manner (p. 147):

"*A Principle of Learning.* We propose the following partial and preliminary statement of a Principle of Learning: *A stimulus acquires for its next occurrence a magnitude of instigating force for an activity that is a positive function of the strength of the action tendency expressed in the activity.*"

Atkinson and Birch give a very interesting account of the relation between *covert activity* ("thought") and *overt activity* ("action").

They think that three possible relationships exist:

A. "thought" and "action" are instigated by the same stimuli and are parallel and *correlated*.
B. "thought" is partly *correlated* to action and partly mediates between stimulus and overt action. "Thought" may have an amplifying effect on overt action,
C. "thought" is a *mediating* variable between stimulus and overt action.

The three possible relationships are presented graphically in Fig. 10.1. on p. 336 in Atkinson and Birch, which we reproduce here (as our Fig. 14.1).

Atkinson and Birch prefer the first possibility, because it is very practical as a basis for using TAT and other projective tests as diagnostic devices for measuring motivational variables.

In this connection A and B also discuss "affect" and "emotion" in the light of their theory. They believe that the affective states are determined by the relationships between instigating forces (F) and consummatory value (c) in the following manner (p. 338):

"It would appear that whenever one or the other of these factors (F or c) is increasing in magnitude faster than the other, and there is a change in the F/c ratio, there is also positive affect."

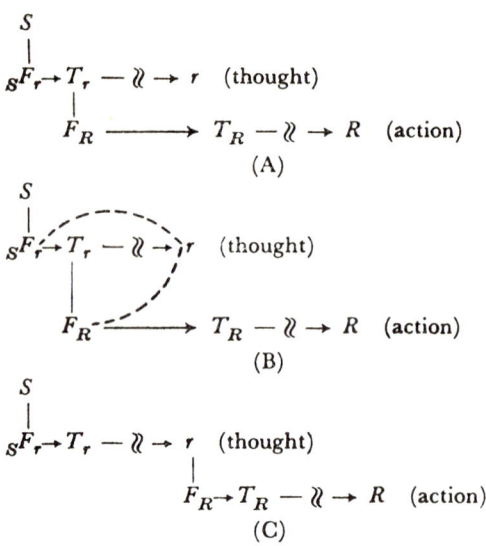

Figure 14.1. The graphic representation of three possible relationships between conscious thought (r) and action (R), treated as covert and overt activity in the text. In (A) instigation to action is mediated by the perceptual-imaginal tendency (T_r) which, when dominant, is expressed in thought. The content of thought and action are correlated and so the content analysis of thought is diagnostic of action. In (B) conscious thought is considered an additional source of instigating force for both covert and overt activity. It, thus, functions to amplify trends that are already implicit in the unconscious proces. In (C) all instigation and resistance to over action is mediated by consvious thought. The unconscious perceptual-imaginal tendency (T_r) does not mediate instigation or'resistance to overt action. (From Atkinson and Birch, 1970, Figure 10.1).

And furthermore (p. 339):

"On the other hand negative affect occurs whenever one or another of the two factors (F or c) is decreasing more rapidly than the other."

The four possible affective states are presented in a table (Table 10.1. on p. 338), which we present here (as our table 14.1).

We shall conclude this summary with a comparison between Atkinson's original theory and that of Atkinson and Birch.

The main terms in Atkinson's theory are:

$$T = f(M \times E \times I).$$

Among these, T, or "tendency", is equated with "action tendency" in the A. and B. theory. M, or "motive, is regarded by A. and B. as being mainly a product of learning, about which they write (A. and B. p. 185):

STATE AFFECTIVE	CRITICAL DETERMINANTS		STRENGTH OF ACTION TENDENCY
	F	*c*	
Hope (+)	Increase in magnitude	Relatively constant	Increase
Satisfaction (+)	Relatively constant	Increase in magnitude	Decrease
Disappointment (−)	Decrease in magnitude	Realitively constant	Decrease
Frustration (−)	Relatively constant	Decreare in magnitude	Increase

From Atkinson and Birch, 1970.

Table 14.1. Positive and Negative Affective States Are Associated with the Nature of Changes in the Magnitude of Instigating Force of the Stimulus Situation Relative to the Consummatory Value of the Activity in Progress.

"Thus, to say that an individual is either strong or weak in motive to achieve is to say an equivalent thing for him about the potential strength of a whole family of instigating forces to achieve. And, in so doing, we define the functional significance, that is, the behavioral implications, of this partial description of his personality."

The last two terms, E, expectation, and I, incentive value, are regarded as belonging to the covert activity, which is correlated to the overt activity. Thus they write (A. and B., p. 198):

"We have taken the position that the concepts of expectancy (or subjective probability) and valence (or utility) in theory about human decision making are descriptive dimensions of the covert activity that normally antedates or accompanies overt behavioral preference." From Atkinson and Birch, 1970.

We conclude this summarizing reformulation of the Atkinson-Birch theory with a graphic model or diagram representing the main variables and their relationships (Fig. 14.2).

2.1. *The hypothetical terms*

The main H-terms in the A. and B. theory are: T. action tendency; F, instigating force; C, consummatory force; N, negaction tendency; I, inhibitory force and R, force of resistance.

2.1.1. *The surplus meaning of the H-terms.*
As all the terms in the Atkinson and Birch theory appear in mathematical formulas representing psychological variables, they must be classified as H-terms with *neutral* surplus meaning.

2.1.2. *Dispositional or functional terms?*
We think that all the terms in the A. and B. theory are *functional* terms, although some of them, e. g., T and N, refer

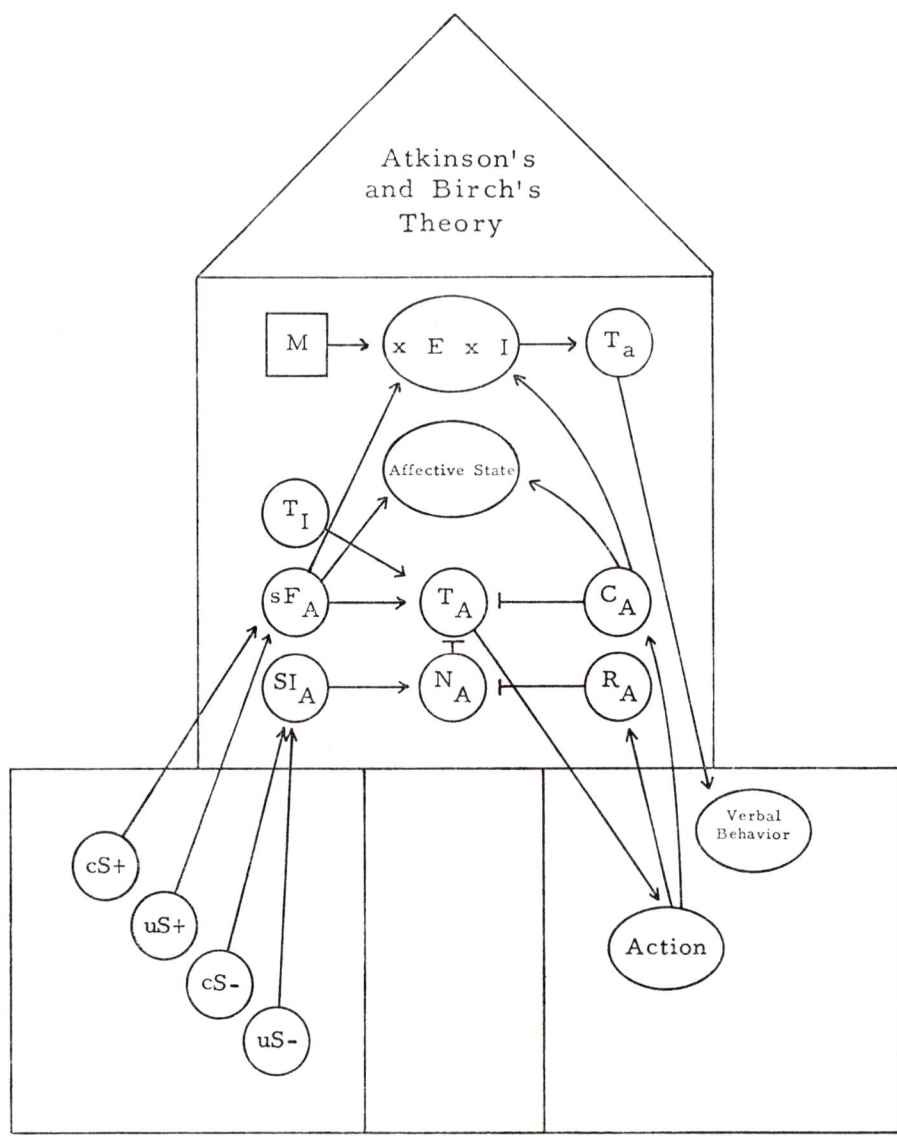

Fig. 14.2. Diagram representing the main hypothesis in the Atkinson and Birch theory: Action is determined by an action tendency (T_A), which is increased by inertial action tendency (T_I) as well as instigating force (sF_A) and *drecreased* by consummatory force (C_A) and the negaction tendency (N_A). This negative action tendency is determined in the same way by inhibitory force (sI_A) and force of resistance (R_A). The instigating and inhibitory forces are influenced by positive (reward) and negative (punishment) stimuli, conditioned and unconditioned. The consummatory force and the force of resistance are influenced by feedback from the behavior. The instigating force and the consummatory force determine the affective state as well as expectation (E) and incentive value (I), which, together with motive (M) determine a tendency (T_a) for "thought" (covert action) expressed in verbal behavior.

to states which can last for some time. The only typical dispositional term is M, motive, which does not belong to this theory, but to Atkinson's original theory.

2.1.3. Dynamic, directive or vector terms?
All the H-terms mentioned are *vector terms* as they have a combined dynamic and directive effect upon behavior. This is a typical trait of the A. and B. theory.

The authors discuss the possibility of introducing a dynamic – or "nonspecific" – variable into the theory. Their conclusion is (p. 328):

"In summary, a nonspecific excitant, acting on both action tendencies and instigating forces or on instigating forces alone, can be expected to produce a greater intensity of performance and/or degree of involvement of the individual in the ongoing activity, but no such general statement about effects on latency can be made."

2.2. Classification of the hypotheses

We have already presented our summarizing reconstruction of the hypotheses in the A. and B. theory. In order to make our basic classification of the hypotheses in the next section we must reformulate them symbolically. In this case it is easy to do because the theory is already highly symbolized. We employed some symbols from the A. and B. theory, but have put them in parentheses after the letter H, indicating their status as H-terms. This produces the following reformulations of the main hypotheses:

1. hypothesis: $H(T_{AI}) \to R_A$
2. hypothesis: $S_A \to H(F_A) \to H(T_A)$
3. hypothesis: $R_A \to H(C_A) \to H(T_A)$
4. hypothesis: $[H(F_A) - H(C_A)] \to H(\frac{dT_A}{dt})$
5. hypothesis: $[H(T_A) - H(N_A)] \to H(T_A) \to R_A$
6. hyposhesis: $S_A \to H(I_A) \to H(N_A)$
7. hyposhesis: $[H(I_A) - H(R_A)] \to H(\frac{dN}{dt})$
8. hypothesis: $H[\frac{(T_{AF} - N_{AF}) - (T_{BI} - N_{BF})}{\hat{F}_B}] \to R(t_{A/B})$

2.2.1. Basic classification of the hypotheses.
The above reformulation serves as a starting point for our classification of the hypotheses into purely theoretical and partly empirical hypotheses:

1. *Purely theoretical (H-H) hypotheses:*
   Hypotheses No. 4 and No. 7. In all: 2 hypotheses.

2. *Partly empirical hypotheses:*
   a. S-H-hypotheses: No. 2 and No. 6. In all: 2 hypotheses.
   b. H-R-hypotheses: No. 1, No. 3, No. 5 and No. 8. In all: 4 hypotheses.

2.2.2. *The complexity of the hypotheses.* Our systematic reconstruction of the theory is also the basis for the classification of the hypotheses according to the degree of complexity. We have obtained the following results:

1. *One-dimensional hypotheses:*
   Hypotheses No. 1, No. 2, No. 3, No. 5 and No. 6.

2. *Multidimensional hypotheses:*
   Hypotheses No. 4, No. 7 and No. 8.

2.2.3. *The functional relationship in the hypotheses.* Atkinson and Birch make the following statement about this problem in the Preface (p. VIII):

"Fairly early we decided on a theory that is continuous in nature rather than discrete, deterministic rather than probabilistic. We made tentative beginnings in the other directions but turned away from them because of a preference for a deterministic theory and the convenience of a theory that is based on continuous functions."

Thus it is clear that the presupposed functional relationships are *deterministic*.

The descriptive stratum

3.0. *Introduction*

In this section we shall analyze *"A Theory of Achievement Motivation"*, edited by John W. Atkinson and Norman T. Feather (1966). This book contains the results from a series of empirical studies of achievement motivation conducted by Atkinson, Feather and their co-workers: Nathan Brody, Harry J. Crockett, Matina S. Horner, Lawrence W. Littig, George H. Litwin, Charles H. Mahone, James N. Morgan, Robert W. Moulton, Patricia O'Connor and Charles P. Smith.

These empirical studies are based upon the methods originally tried out by McClelland, Atkinson, Clark and Lowell in *"The Achievement Motive"* (1953), and upon the more detailed methodological studies presented in John W. Atkinson (Ed.): *"Motives in Fantasy, Action, and Society"* (1958), which we have not included in this analysis.

Atkinson's, Feather's and co-workers' empirical studies were based on the theory about achievement motivation which Atkinson formulated in 1964, and which has already been analyzed in the first two sections of this chapter.

3.1. *The abstract D-level*

3.1.1. *The abstract descriptive terms.* It is obvious from the above analysis of the H-level of the A. and B. theory, that the *main R-variable is "time to change from one activity to another."* As mentioned in several places this R-variable can be conceived of as including *other R-variables*, namely: 1) *persistence* of the ongoing activity, 2) *latency* of the alternative that is initiated and 3) *choice* or preference of activities. All these R-variables can be regarded as determined by the H-variable "Tendency" (T), which through these measurements of time, is measured *indirectly* with some degree of exactness.

Among the *S-variables* which the original Atkinson theory had to take into account and make measureable are those determining the H-variables: "Expectation" (E) and "Incentive value" (I). Atkinson and co-workers have been especially interested in P_s, *probability of success*, as a determinant of "expectation", which is sometimes defined as the "subjective probability of success".

Atkinson and co-workers have been less interested in the S-variable determining the incentive value, because the theory for achievement motivation assumes the following relationship between I_s and E_s (or rather P_s):

$$I_s = 1 - P_s.$$

Therefore, it is enough to know and measure the probability of success, P_s, when one is mainly interested in achievement motivation.

The final H-variable in the determination of tendency and behavior is "Motive" (M). This H-variable can be *indirectly* measured by *tests*. For the "motive to achieve" (M_s) Atkinson and co-worker have decided to continue to use McClelland and co-workers' version of the TAT, but for the "motive to avoid failure" (M_{AF}) they have adopted the Test Anxiety Questionnaire (TAQ) constructed by *Mandler* and *Sarason*.

3.1.2. *The general, descriptive propositions ("laws")*. Atkinson and co-workers have found some general relationships between the achievement motives (M_s and M_{AF}) – or, rather, the test scores on the TAT and the TAQ – on the one hand and other S- and R-variables on the other. These general relationships may be regarded as "laws" about achievement motivation. We shall now look at some of these "laws" as they are reported in Atkinson and Feather (1966):

1. *Aspiration:* Persons with $M_s > M_{AF}$ are found to:
   a. prefer tasks of intermediate difficulty,
   b. show greater persistence in working at an achievement-related task and
   c. show more efficiency in performance.
2. *Persistence:* Persons with $M_s > M_{AF}$ are found to:
   a. persist longer at an initial achievement task than persons with $M_{AF} > M_s$, when the initial P_s is high (e. g., $P_s > 0.50$), and
   b. persist for a shorter time at an initial achievement task than persons with $M_{AF} > M_s$, when the initial P_s is low (e. g., $P_s < 0.50$).
   c. persist longer at insoluble tasks than persons with $M_{AF} > M_s$ – even when they have the possibility of choosing another task with intermediate P_s.

3. *Success and Failure:*
   a. Persons with $M_s > M_{AF}$ are found to *increase* their level of aspiration after *success* and *decrease* it after *failure*.
   b. Persons with $M_{AF} > M_s$ are found to *increase* their level of aspiration after *failure* and *decrease* it after *success*.
4. *Vocational preference:*
   a. Persons with $M_{AF} < M_s$ have *unrealistic* vocational aspirations (either too high or too low compared to their abilities), while persons with $M_s > M_{AF}$ have *realistic* vocational aspirations.
   b. Persons with $M_s > M_{AF}$ exhibit *upward* vocational mobility.
5. *School performance:*
   It was found that ability grouping in schools increases performance and interest in school work among students with $M_s > M_{AF}$.

We believe that the above "laws" formulated by Atkinson and co-workers are those possessing the greatest general interest.

3.2. *The concrete D-level*

The concrete D-level of Atkinson and co-workers' theory contains descriptions of data from the various empirical studies, they have made. The most important part of these data are the test-data – from which we have already mentioned the *Test Anxiety Questionnaire (TAQ)* and the *Thematic Apperception Test (TAT)*.

Test data must in principle be classified as *behavioral data*, as they are results of the subject's *verbal behavior* – oral or written. However, we should like to draw the reader's attention to McClelland's conception of the data from projective tests – especially the TAT. McClelland regards *TAT data as data intermediate between behavioral and phenomenological data*. They combine the subjective richness found in the phenomenological data with the objective exactness found on the behavioral data. The present author thinks that this is especially true after the development of a computer program which is able to make content analyses of TAT-stories: *"The General Inquirer"*, A Computer Approach to Content Analysis" by P. J. Stone, D. C. Dunphy, M. S. Smith and D. M. Ogilvie (1966)[5].

3.3. *The descriptive units*

The descriptive unit employed in Atkinson and co-workers' theory is rather *molar*. This is also consistent with Atkinson's metatheoretical propositions. Thus he wrote (in his 1964 book, p. 305):

5. It is also "The General Inquirer" which has inspired our work with the development of computer programs for the purpose of theory analyses.

"The present conception handles the matters of initiation of an acitivity, and interruption of an activity all in a single breath. It does this by: (a) acknowledging that from the viewpoint of a psychologist, the behavioral life of an organism must be considered a succession of molar activities, and (b) by viewing change of activity as the most fundamental problem."

The theory as a whole

4.1. *The formal properties*

We think that it is correct to regard the three books by Atkinson (1964), Atkinson and Birch (1970) and Atkinson and Feather (1966) as *one* theory. In this section we shall deal with them as one whole theory.

(4.1.1.) *The systematic organization* of the theory as a whole is such that it is placed on the borderline between explanatory systems and deductive theories. The theory is not axiomatized, but there are many examples of *deductions* from the formulas – especially in the "mathematical notes" attached to each chapter in Atkinson and Birch. Therefore we decided to classify the theory as a *deductive* theory.

(4.1.2.) *The preciseness of representation* is very high. In the Atkinson and Birch book the theory reached such a degree of preciseness that it is one of the most *mathematized* theories found in the fields of motivation, learning and personality. Of the 356 page text in this book there are approximately 50 pages of "mathematical notes". In addition, the rest of the text contains many mathematical formulas. We think that Atkinson and co-workers' theory can be favorably compared with the theories of Lewin, Hull and Cattell, which are the most mathematized theories the present author has analyzed.

(4.1.3.) *The properties of the model* approximate those of a *"mathematical model"*. Atkinson and Birch have the following to say about this in their book, p. VIII:

"These [dynamic] processes are dealt with mathematically, but the dynamics of action is not intended to be a mathematical model of motivation. We did not take an abstract mathematical system and use it as a representation of motivation. Therefore, no mathematical structure specifically dictated relationships within the theory. Instead, we have taken our ideas about motivational processes, phrased them in the language of mathematics, and used mathematical operations to derive consequences."

The present author thinks that it is fair to say that although Atkinson and Birch have *not used* a mathematical model, they *have*, in fact, *developed* a mathematical model for motivational psychology.

In addition to this their book is full of two-dimensional or *graphic models*.

4.2. *The epistemological properties*

In full consistency with Atkinson's metatheoretical principles the theory is developed as a *neutral explanatory or S-H_N-R-theory*, using hypothetical terms with neutral surplus meaning. Even though the terms are represented by mathematical symbols, we think that they actually represent *hypothetical constructs* rather than "purely" intervening variables without surplus meaning.

4.3. *The theory-empiry-ratio*

The immediate impression one receives from reading Atkinson's 1964 book and Atkinson and Birch's book (1970) is that the theory is rather speculative – though not without relationship to empirical research. In fact most of the Atkinson and Feather book is empirical in nature.

In this instance it is not necessary to rely solely upon impression and judgement, but we can supplement these with the calculation of the Hypotheses Quotients. We have done this for Atkinson (1964) and for Atkinson and Birch (1970) and reached the following results by using the formula:

$$H.Q. = \frac{\Sigma(H-H)}{\Sigma[(S-H)+(H-R)]}$$

Atkinson (1964): $H.Q. = \frac{6}{6+1} = 0.86$

Atkinson and Birch (1970): $H.Q. = \frac{2}{2+4} = 0.33$

These results confirm the above mentioned impression in the first case, but not in the second. The A. + B. theory must be classified as rather empirical. The difference between the two theories is found among other things in the fact that many more of the hypothetical terms are operationally defined or related to descriptive S- and R-terms.

Concluding remarks. Although Atkinson started as one of McClelland's co-workers, it is our opinion that he and his co-workers have developed a theory of their own – inspired not only by McClelland, but also by more classic theories like those of Freud, Lewin and Tolman. And this theory has placed Atkinson and co-workers in a leading position in *motivational* psychology proper, which could be compared to Cattell's in the more general field of personality theory, and to Hebb in the *physiological tradition* represented in this book by such important theories as those of Berlyne, Bindra, Duffy, Konorski, Miller and Pribram.

15. Maslow's Theory

Introduction

The American psychologist *Abraham H. Maslow* (1908–1970) was the organizer and first President of the "Association of Humanistic Psychology". This new school of psychology regarded itself as a "third force in psychology", in many ways in opposition to the behavioristic and the psychoanalytic schools.

The humanistic psychologists have been inspired by existential philosophy, which in Europe has influenced among others, many psychiatrists. Some of the European pioneers in existentialism are themselves psychiatrists (e. g., Binswanger, Heidegger, Frankl and others).

This existential philosophy came to the United States after the Second World War and was received very positively by many psychologists and psychiatrists. *Gordon W. Allport, Charlotte Bühler, Rollo May, Carl Rogers* and others worked in co-operation with Maslow to establish the Association of Humanistic Psychology as well as a Journal for Humanistic Psychology.

In this chapter we shall concentrate on Abraham Maslow[1], because he has created a very original and influential theory of motivation. This theory is presented in its most complete version in his book *"Motivation and Personality"* (1st ed., 1954; 2nd ed., 1970). The following analysis deals mainly with this book. In addition we shall analyze Maslow's philosophy of science as presented in his book *"Psychology of Science"* (1966). We have surveyed a large part of his very considerable production and found that the two books selected are most convenient for our purposes[2].

The metastratum

1.1. *Philosophical propositions*

Maslow has formulated his philosophical propositions very explicitly and in a very detailed manner.

---

1. Gordon Allport's theory is analyzed in my book "Theories of Motivation" (4th ed., 1968). The theory of Charlotte Bühler is analyzed in a later chapter (16) of this book.
2. I am very much in debt to Abraham Maslow, because he took time just prior to his death to correspond with me about my project which was a great help to me. I am sorry that I didn't finish this chapter before his death, but the chapter has been carefully checked and approaved by *Charlotte Bühler*.

First of all he emphasizes that philosophy and psychology are intimately connected, and that psychologists should be more interested in philosophy than they have been in the past. In the period between the two World Wars it was mainly the philosophy of science which was studied by psychologists, but Maslow proposes that the *philosophy of values* should also be of interest to psychologists. In addition he claims that psychology is of great importance for the philosophy of values. He suggests the possibility of establishing an *empirical* value theory on a psychological basis. This is based on *free choice:* What people choose *are* values, and a list of preferences establishes the *value hierarchy*. Thus to establish a value theory we have to study the free choices of people. But not all people are of equal interest in this connection, because he conceives only of the choices of *healthy* people when determining the generally valid values and norms.

There is a close connection between his philosophy of values and his theory of motivation (which we shall take up later) as well as with his *philosophy of man*.

He argued strongly for the position that psychologists should make an explicit formulation of their philosophy of man, *before* they started their psychological research and theorizing.

The present author was previously of the opinion that a philosophy of man could be a *result* of psychological research, and should not be formulated without empirical data as the basis. But a discussion with Maslow – and Allport – convinced him that it is true that *psychologists always have a conception of man* before they start their research and theorizing. And this conception of man influences their way of theorizing – e. g., their choice of hypothetical constructs, empirical research and methods. Therefore, it is important to make a critical analysis of this conception of man. Otherwise it cannot be revised and developed. It is very important that the psychologists presupposed philosophy of man is formulated as explicitly and clearly as possible.

Maslow's own philosophy of man is *humanistic* and opposed to the prevalent biological or Darwinian conception of man. This implies that he conceives of man as *different in principle* from other species. Thus he writes (in "M. and P.", p. 7):

"The laws of human psychology and of nonhuman nature are in some respects the same, but are in some respects utterly different."

This point of view is also manifested in his theory of motivation – especially his conception of "growth motivation" or "metamotivation", which we shall take up at a later point.

But in spite of this anti-Darwinian conception of man Maslow regards the *"core of human nature" to be biologically determined, inborn possibilities*. This implies that man is born with the possibility of developing certain personality traits, abilities, etc., which are qualitatively different from traits and abilities found in other species. Among these specific human possibilities is the *need for self-actualization.*

According to Maslow the *qualities* of "human nature" are determined biologically. This means that *society and culture only influence* the development of human personality *quantitatively*. Thus cultural and social conditions can facilitate or inhibit the development of human possibilities, but they cannot change the inborn possibilities *qualitatively*.

Maslow's philosophy of man is imbedded in his whole *world view*, which he calls a *"holistic-dynamic view"* and describes in these words ("M. and P.", p. 299):

"The general point of view that is being propounded here is holistic rather than atomistic, functional rather than taxonomic, dynamic rather than static, dynamic rather than causal, purposive rather than simple-mechanical. In spite of the fact that these opposing factors are ordinarily looked upon as a series of separable dichotomies they are not so considered by the writer. For him they tend strongly to coalesce into two unitary but contrasting world views. This seems to be true for other writers as well, for those who think dynamically find it easier and more natural to think also holistically rather than atomistically, purposively rather than mechanically, and so on. This point of view we shall call the holistic-dynamic point of view. It could also be called organismic in Goldstein's sense."

Although Maslow has presented his philosophy of man and his world view very explicitly, it is nevertheless, confusing – at least to the present author – that he has not formulated his conception of the *psychosomatic problem*. From his "holistic" or "organismic" conception of the universe it should logically follow that "body" and "mind" are conceived of as constituting a whole, integrated organism or person. Thus his theory of the psychosomatic problem can be regarded as a version of *neutral monism*. But we shall later see that he makes considerable use of H-terms with *mentalistic* surplus meaning, and this should indicate a *dualistic* theory of the psychosomatic problem. Unfortunately, Maslow's lack of clarity makes the solution of this problem very difficult.

1.2. Metatheoretical propositions

Maslow is even more explicit in his formulations of metatheoretical propositions. In addition to certain chapters in "Motivation and Personality" (especially Chapters 1 and 2) he has written a whole book, "The Psychology of Science" ("P. of S."), which is mainly devoted to his philosophy of science. The latter work covers his more basic *epistemological* propositions as well as his *metatheoretical* propositions (in the narrow sense). As they are so intimately related we shall deal with them in this section.

The *first* and most important of his metatheoretical propositions states that *science is created by human beings*. Thus in the opening statement of Chapter 1 in "M. and P." (p. 1) we find:

"A psychological interpretation of science begins with the acute realization that science is a human creation, rather than an autonomous, nonhuman, or *per se* "thing" with intrinsic rules of its own. Its origins are in human motives, its goals are human goals, and it is created, renewed, and maintained by human beings. Its laws, organization, and articulations rest not only on the nature of the reality that it discovers, but also on the nature of the human nature that does the discovering."

This "psychological interpretation" of science implies that it is important to study *the motives and the abilities of scientists*. Maslow has a *"pluralistic" view* of these matters. He emphasizes that scientists have *many motives* for studying science. Some of them – e. g., the so-called "need for knowledge" and "need for understanding" facilitate the growth of science, while other motives – especially the "need for security" – inhibit the development of science. Maslow also emphasizes that scientific work involves *many different abilities*, because it consists of several different functions. These different abilities are not present in the same degree in all scientists, so team-work is an essential thing in science. He writes the following about this ("M. and P.", p. 9):

"If the ideal scientist combines within himself the creative hypothesizer, the careful checker-experimenter, the philosopical system builder, the historical scholar, the technologist, the organizer, the educator-writer-publicist, the applier, and the appreciator, then we can easily conceive that the ideal team might be composed of at least nine individual specialists in these different functions, *no one of whom need himself be a scientist in the rounded sense*."

One of the important consequences of Maslow's psychological and pluralistic approach to science is the importance of *tolerance*. Thus he writes ("M. and P.", p. 5):

"We all complement and need each other in science."
 "Science *needs* all kinds of people."
 "Clearly we need the same kind of tolerance and acceptance of individual differences among scientists as we do in other human realms."

This conception and attitude toward science is very encouraging and reinforcing – especially for people who – like the present author – have been educated in terms of the more rigid, narrow and formalistic conception of science created by the logical empiricists.

In addition to his main metatheoretical proposition about the pluralistic-psychological conception of science he has formulated a series of related metatheoretical propositions – most thoroughly elaborated in "P. of S.", where most of them have been given a whole chapter each.

In the first of these propositions Maslow states that *problem centering facilitates the growth of science*, while means centering inhibits it. He elaborates this in a whole chapter (2) in "M. and P.". He states that means centering facilitates over-evaluation of technical and formal perfection at the cost of significance and meaningfulness. Means centering facilitates quantification as a goal in itself instead of as a means. Means centering also facilitates "departmentalizing" and hierarchy among the sciences as well as scientific orthodoxy and security-seeking.

Maslow's second metatheoretical proposition proposes that *psychology should be a humanistic and personal science* rather than mechanistic and impersonal as it has been until now. About this he writes ("P. of S.", p. 2):

"while it was necessary and helpful to dehumanize planets, rocks and animals, we are realizing more and more strongly that it is *not* necessary to dehumanize the human being and to deny him human purposes."

A *third* metatheoretical proposition states that *fear creates defensive scientists,* who, of course, do not become creative problems-solvers. Thus he writes ("P. of S.", pp. 22–23):

"In other words, the scientist can be seen as relatively defensive, deficiency-motivated, and safety-need-motivated, moved largely by anxiety and behaving in such a way as to allay it. Or he can be seen as having mastered his anxieties, as coping positively with problems in order to be victorious over them, a growth motivated toward personal fulfillment and fullest humanness, and therefore as freed to turn outward an intrinsically fascinating reality, in wholehearted absorption with it rather than its relevance to his personal emotional difficulties, i.e., he can be problem-centered rather than ego-centered."

On the basis of fear some so-called *"pathologies of cognition"* may develop such as "the compulsive need for certainty", "the premature generalization", "the denial of ignorance", "the denial of doubt", "intolerance of ambiguity", "the need to conform" and many others.

A fourth metatheoretical proposition introduces a distinction between *experimental knowledge"* and *"spectator knowledge",* which resembles Freud's "primary processes" and "secondary processes". About this distinction Maslow writes ("P. of S.", pp. 46–47):

"My thesis is that experiential knowledge is prior to verbal-conceptual knowledge but that they are hierarchically-integrated and need each other."

He relates this distinction to the philosophy of science created by the logical empiricists and adopted by the behaviorists with the following words ("P. of S.", p. 47):

"Nor need these affirmations in any way contradict a "minimal" behaviorism, that is, a doctrine of levels in the reliability of knowledge in which public knowledge is granted to be more trustworthy and more constant for many purposes than private and subjective knowledge."

Thus it is obvious that he regards humanistic psychology as a *supplement* to a kind of pure behaviorism – not as an alternative in opposition.

A *fifth* metatheoretical proposition expresses preference for an *empiristic* philosophy versus a purely rationalistic one. Thus he writes ("P. of S.", p. 79):

> "A scientist's first duty, then, is to describe the facts. If these conflict with the demand for a "good system", then out with the system. Systematizing and theorizing come after the facts. Or, to avoid ruminating over what a fact is, let us say that the first task of the scientist is to experience truly that which exists. It is amazing how often this truism gets lost."

This leads directly to the *sixth* metatheoretical proposition in which Maslow introduces a distinction between *two kinds of meaning:* the *concrete*, so-called "suchness" meaning and the *abstract* meaning. These two kinds of meaning are related to *two kinds of cognitive processes:* "understanding" (related to concrete meaning) and *"explanation"* (related to abstract meaning). He elaborates this in a whole chapter in "M. and P." – Chapter 13: "Cognition of the Individual and the Generic". In this chapter he warms against what he calls "pathological abstracting" or "rubricizing".

A *seventh* metatheoretical proposition introduces a distinction between *"Taoistic versus controlling science"*. Classical, experimental science – including experimental psychology – is "controlling science" as it presupposes interference and active influence on the phenomena under investigation. Clinical psychology is "Taoistic science" as it presupposes the passive non-interfering attitude toward nature, which prevails among Eastern philosophers. Thus Maslow writes ("P. of S.", p. 97):

> "Eastern writers have stressed more the concept of the observer's harmony with the nature that he studies. Here the stress is a little different, for it is implied that the observer is himself part of the nature he observes. – – – Mastery of nature is not the only possible relation to it for a scientist."

This distinction between two kinds of science resembles – though no reference is made to it – Jürgen Habermass's distinctions between *the natural, dialectical and hermeneutic sciences.* (The last two categories include the social sciences and the humanistic sciences respectively. See Habermass, 1967, and Radnitzky 1970).

The eighth metatheoretical proposition claims that *science is not value-free.* Science cannot be value-free, because it presupposes that scientists make several *choices* – and choices are the realization of values according to Maslow. First, the scientist chooses to find "truth", which is a basic value, and, second, he chooses an area of research, methods, etc. He summarizes it in the following quotation ("P. of S.", p. 123):

> "But beyond this insistence that choosing necessarily implies principles of choice, i.e., values, there is the even more obvious point that the whole enterprise of science is concerned with "Truth". That's what science is all about. Truth is considered intrinsically desirable, valuable, beautiful. And of course truth has always been counted among the ultimate values. That is to say, science is in the service of a value, and so are all scientists"

Science is not only value-free because it presupposes choices, but it – at least psychology – can also *study* values by studying the choices and preferences of people. About this Maslow writes (p. 124):

"Any studies of choice or preference or selection may be considered to be, in a particular and useful sense, the study of values, either instrumental or final.
    The crucial question to be asked is: can science discover the values by which men should live? I think it can, and I have advanced this thesis in various places, supporting it with whatever data I could muster."

The *ninth* metatheoretical proposition – and the last one we shall deal with in this book – states that *there are stages, levels and degrees of knowledge*. By means of this "fundamental truth" Maslow tries to emphasize that different sciences – like physics and psychology – may be regarded as being at different stages or levels of development. In addition, he also attempts to emphasize that there are many degrees of knowledge between the absolutely true and the absolutely false.

We have devoted considerable space to Maslow's philosophy of science. We feel this justified for two reasons: 1) It is an original, *psychological* approach to the philosophy of science, and 2) it is in harmony with various trends in *the evolution of a new conception of "science"* which have emerged from many different areas[3]).

Our main criticism is of a purely formal nature: we think that Maslow's exposition of his philosophy of science could have gained considerably by being more *systematic* and without so much superfluous and redundant overlapping. But the same thing could be said about his theory of motivation, which we shall take up later, after having dealt with his methodological propositions.

1.3. *Methodological propositions*

Maslow deals with methodology both in "P. of S." and in "M. and P." – in Chapter 15 and Appendix B respectively.

He favored the *clinical method*. About this he writes ("M. and P.", p. 241):

"It is amazing that experimental psychologists have not turned to the study of psychotherapy as to an unworked gold mine. It is the best technique we have ever had for laying bare men's deepest nature as contrasted with their surface personalities."

We think that Maslow here does a little injustice to experimental psychologists. He could at least have mentioned *Dollard and Miller's* "Personality and Psychotherapy" (1950) as being an exception to his statement[4]).

He elaborates his opinion about the clinical method in "P. of S." (p. 12):

---

3. See in the bibliography the books of: J. Habermass, Norwood Russel Hanson, Thomas Kuhn, Karl Popper, Gerard Radnitzky and Håkan Törnebohm.
4. The reader is referred to the chapter about Miller's theory.

"By far the best way we have to learn what people are like is to get them, one way or another, to tell us, whether directly by question and answer or by free association, to which we simply listen, or indirectly by covert communications, paintings, dreams, stories, gestures, etc. – which we can interpret."

He has no explicitly formulated propositions concerning a preference of *data language*, which is perhaps related to his lack of an explicit formulation of a proposition about the psychosomatic problem. The nearest he comes to an explicit formulation is contained in the following quotation ("P. of S.", p. 47):

"This is why I can think that (1) most psychological problems do and should begin with phenomenology rather than with objective, experimental, behavioral laboratory techniques, and also (2) that we must usually press on from phenomenological beginnings *toward* objective, experimental, behavioral laboratory methods."

We interpret this statement – in connection with many others – to mean that Maslow does *not* propose a phenomenological data language as an alternative to a behavioral data language. He seems rather to favor *a kind of integration of these two data languages*, just as in many other ways he regards his own theory as a supplement to behavioristic and psychoanalytic theories. Of course his theory is more akin to psychoanalysis and the Gestalt tradition – especially to *Kurt Goldstein*'s version – than to behaviorism.

Maslow's close relationship to psychoanalysis will be more obvious when we analyze his theory of motivation.

The hypothetical stratum

2.0. Introduction

Before we present our customary overview of the hypotheses let us look at some principles for the construction of a theory of motivation. These principles are not "hypotheses" in the sense of explanatory propositions about the functional relationship between variables. They are rather metapropositions: propositions dealing with the driving forces within human beings as well as propositions about the construction of motivational theories. Some of the propositions are perhaps vaguely formulated hypotheses. Thus they are on the borderline between the hypothetical stratum and the metastratum. Consequently we present them in the following special section before the usual overview of the H-level.

2.0.1. *Principles for construction of a motivational theory.* Maslow elaborates these principles, especially in Chapter 3 of "M. and P.", which has the title: "Preface to Motivation Theory". We shall present the most important of his principles in a systematic reconstruction.

Maslow's *first* principle for the construction of a motivation theory is the *"humanistic" or "anthroprocentic" principle,* which he describes in this way (p. 27, "M. and P."):

"– – – motivation theory must be anthroprocentric rather than animalcentric."

A corollary to this principle is that hunger is an atypical drive in human beings because: "Most drives are not isolable, nor can they be localized somatically" ("M. and P.", p. 20). Therefore hunger should *not* be used as a paradigm in a humanistic motivation theory. Perhaps it is also wrong to use it as a paradigm in a theory about animal motivation.

Maslow's *second* principle is the *"eupsychian principle"*, which states that:

"Any theory of motivation that is worthy of attention must deal with the highest capacities of the healthy and strong man as well as with the defensive manoeuvres of crippled spirits" (p. 33).

Maslow's *third* principle is a *classification principle*. It is formulated in this way (p. 26):

"The weight of evidence now available seems to me to indicate that the only sound and fundamental basis on which any classification of motivational life may be constructed is that of the fundamental goals or needs, rather than on any listing of drives in the ordinary sense of instigation (the "pulls" rather than the "pushes"). It is only the fundamental goals that remain constant through all the flux that a dynamic approach forces upon psychological theorizing."

A corollary to this principle states (p. 25) that:

"We should give up the attempt once and for all to make atomistic lists of drives or needs. For several different reasons such lists are theoretically unsound."

Maslow continues later on the same page (pp. 25–26):

"Too many of the listings that we now have available have combined indiscriminately needs at various levels of magnification. With such a confusion it is understandable that some lists should contain three or four needs and others contain hundreds of needs. If we wished, we could have such a list of drives contain anywhere from one to one million drives, depending entirely on the specificity of analysis."

In spite of these argumentations against classifications of drives or needs he employs one himself. His "hierarchy principle" – which we shall examine later – presupposes at least a rough classification of drives or needs in terms of physiological needs, safety needs, etc.

Maslow's *fourth* principle deals with *the importance of unconscious motivation*. Concerning this he writes (p. 22):

"We may thus assert that sound motivation theory cannot possibly afford to neglect the unconscious life."

The reasons for this principle are among others that *conscious* motives or desires refer to *means* rather than to *ends*. The ends are always the basic needs.

They are called "basic" because they are ends in themselves, and are common to all human beings in all cultures.

We regard the above principles as the most important metatheoretical propositions to be found in Maslow's "Preface to Motivation Theory". Some of those not mentioned here in this systematic reconstruction have been omitted because it is very difficult to classify them either as philosophical propositions about the "nature of man" or as rather vaguely formulated motivational hypotheses. That is especially the case with the first principle, which he elaborates in this chapter (p. 19):

"Our first proposition states that the individual is an integrated, organized whole. – – – In motivation theory this proposition means many specific things. For instance, it means the whole individual is motivated rather than just a part of him."

Thus we think that the first part of the above quotation is a philosophical presupposition, while the last part comes nearer to being a hypothesis about motivation.

We shall present a summary of the most important hypotheses in the following section.

2.0. Summary of the hypotheses

The most important hypothesis in Maslow's motivation theory is his *"hierarchy hypothesis"*, which states that *human beings are motivated by an hierarchical system of basic, "instinctoid" needs*. The hierarchy of needs includes: the physiological, the safety, the affiliative, the esteem and the self-actualization needs (the latter including the needs for creativity, for knowledge and understanding, and the aesthetic needs). The hierarchical organization of the needs implies that unsatisfied "lower" needs will dominate over and conquer in a conflict with unsatisfied "higher" needs. Thus self-actualization requires the satisfaction of all other needs. Therefore, self-actualizing people must generally be satisfied and mentally healthy. Only unsatisfied needs are motivating forces. When a need is satisfied – or "gratified" as Maslow prefers to put it – a higher need can dominate and determine the individual's behavior. Gratification of needs also changes the individual's cognitive processes and his attitudes and evaluations.

Frequent gratification or frustration of needs in childhood determines permanent personality traits in the individual.

The higher needs appear at a later time in both the phylogenetic and the ontogenetic development. Thus the motivational life of an individual may be described as a "climbing up" through the different levels of the "pyramid of needs". Infants are dominated by the physiological needs of hunger and thirst as well as the safety needs. Young children are dominated by the safety needs and the affiliative needs, while older children are dominated by the affiliative needs and the esteem needs. At the start of adolescence we first encounter the needs for self-actualization, but it is not until we reach the adult level that we find people completely dominated by the self-actualization needs.

If basic needs are permantly frustrated there is bound to be evidence of psychopathology in the individual.

Only *instrumental* behavior – or "coping acts" – is motivated, while purely *expressive* behavior is unmotivated (later Maslow calls it "metamotivated", i. e., motivated by self-actualization needs).

Before turning to the more detailed analyses of the H-terms and the hypotheses in his theory we present the main lines of this summary in two diagrams of his theory (Fig. 15.1. and 15.2.).

2.1. *The hypothetical terms (H-terms)*

It is very difficult to say how many and which terms in Maslow's theory are *hypothetical* terms, because he only presents a few *explicit* definitions of terms. Most terms are defined implicitly by using them in the context. Therefore it can prove difficult to place them in our systematological tables. Even the most basic classification into meta-, hypothetical or descriptive terms is difficult.

We have therefore decided to include the most important terms, which we think are H-terms.

"*Need*" is the most important term in Maslow's theory of motivation. It is sometimes used as a synonym for "drive" – or rather a class of needs – the physiological needs – which are sometimes called "drives". The word "desire" and "motive" are also used in this connection. The nearest we come to an explicit definition of "need" is in the following passage ("M. and P.", p. 22):

"It is characteristic of this deeper analysis that it will always lead ultimately to certain goals or needs behind which we cannot go; that is to certain need-satisfactions that seem to be ends in themselves and seem not to need any further justification or demonstration. These needs have the particular quality in the average person of not being seen directly very often but of being more often a kind of conceptual derivation from the multiplicity of specific conscious desires. In other words then, the study of motivation must be in part the study of the ultimate human goals or desires or needs."

We think that it is rather obvious from the passage above that "need" is a *hypothetical* term ("a kind of conceptual derivation").

The role of need in motivation is expressed in this way ("M. and P.", p. 57): "a satisfied need is not a motivator."

Needs are classified into several categories which we mention briefly (cf. "M. and P.", pp. 35–47):

1. *Physiological needs:* hunger, thirst, sex, etc. Many of these needs – but not all of them – are *homeostatic*.

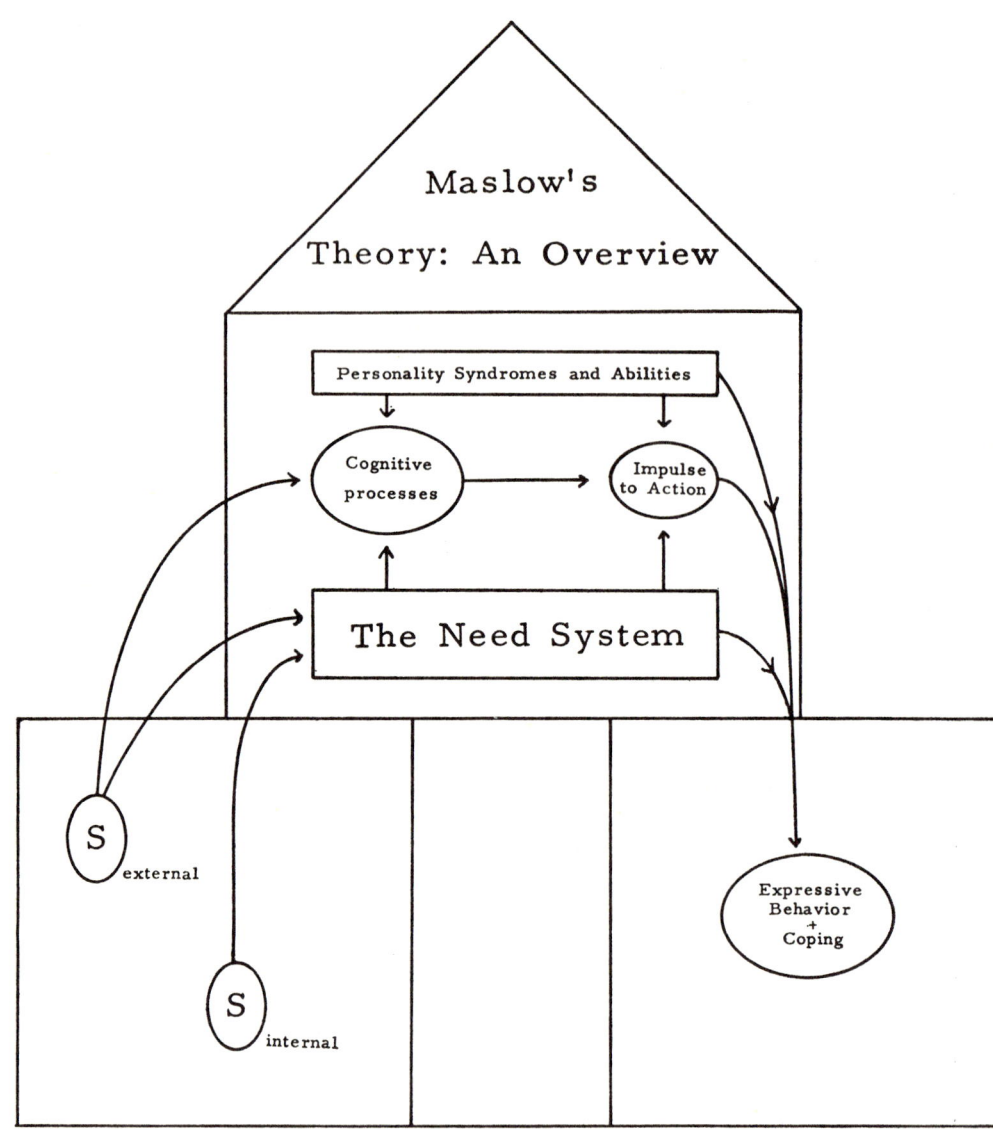

Fig. 15.1 An Overview of Maslow's Theory. Behavior consists of an expressive and a coping component. It is determined by "impulses to action", which are in turn determined by "the need system", "cognitive processes" and "personality syndromes and abilities" in combination. The cognitive processes are determined by external stimuli, while the need system is activated by both external and internal stimuli. The function of the need system is illustrated in more detail in Fig. 15.2.

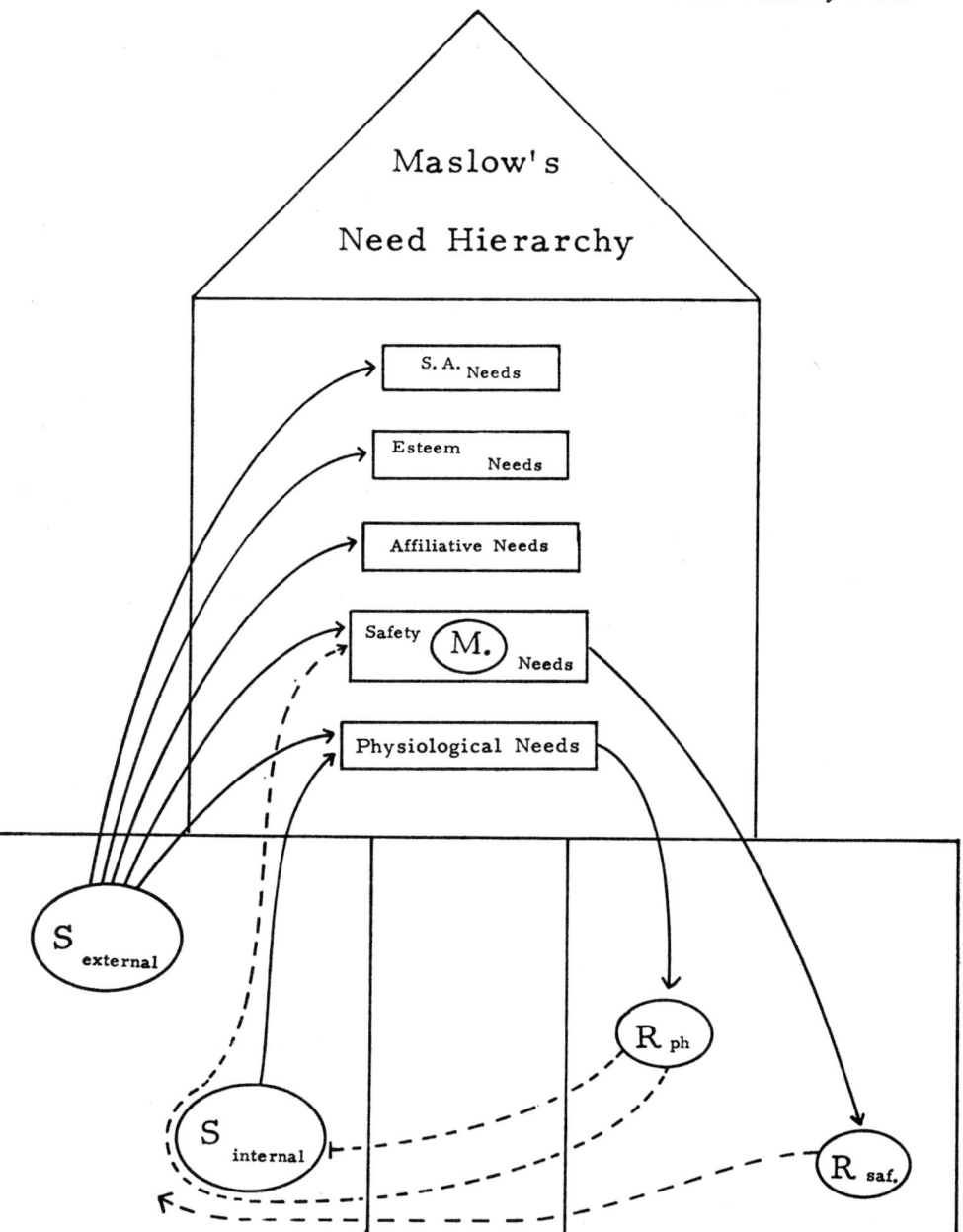

Fig. 15.2 A model of Maslow's motivation theory. The need system is activated by external and internal stimuli, but only the most prepotent need in the hierarchy determines behavior for the moment. The prepotency is determined by: 1) the pre-established hierarchy with the physiological needs as the most prepotent; and the self-actualization needs as the least prepotent; 2) the state of gratification after which a less prepotent need may for the moment be dominant and motivate behavior, if the more prepotent needs are gratified. In our diagram the safety needs for the moment act as "motivators". Their gratification is the condition for the next level of need being motivators and so on.

2. *Safety needs:* security; stability; dependency; protection; freedom from fear; from anxiety and chaos; need for structure, order, law, limits; strength in the protector; and so on.
3. *Affiliative needs:* the needs for love, affection and belongingness[5]).
4. *Esteem needs:* the needs for achievement and prestige.
5. *Self-actualization needs:* This important class of needs is defined in this way ("M. and P.", p. 46):

"It refers to man's desire for self-fulfillment, namely, to the tendency for him to become actualized in what he is potentially."

Included in the latter class of needs or closely connected with it – Maslow is not clear on this point – we find the *needs for knowledge and understanding* and the *aesthetic needs*.

In some connections he uses the term *"growth needs"* about the self-actualization needs in order to distinguish them from all the others, which are designated by the collective term *"deficiency needs"*. The terms "meta-motivation" and "metaneeds" are used in such a way that they are nearly equivalent to "self-actualization needs". Thus he writes (p. 134):

"I have suggested the word "metaneeds" to describe the motivations of self-actualizing people."

In addition to the above mentioned classifications of needs Maslow makes a distinction between *"lower" and "higher" needs*. This distinction is a *relative* one: one class of needs – e. g., safety needs – is lower in the need hierarchy than, e. g., the affiliative needs – but higher than others, e. g., the physiological needs.

If we combine all his classifications of needs we get the following result:

Classification Scheme

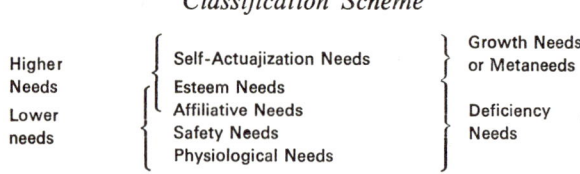

We have tried to indicate the relativity of the distinction between lower and higher needs by making use of two overlapping braces.

Finally, we ought to mention that all the needs in the hierarchy – also the "highest" (self-actualization) needs – are *"basic* needs" in Maslow's terminology. This means that they are what he calls *"instinctoid"*. He devotes a whole chapter (6) to the older instinct theories and analyzes his basic needs in the light of these theories. He concludes his analysis with these words (p. 88):

5. Maslow does not use the term "affiliative" – this is our term.

"All the foregoing considerations encourage us to the hypothesis that basic needs are in some sense, and to some appreciable degree, constitutional or hereditary in their determination."

While *"need"* is the main concept in his motivational theory, *"personality syndrome"* is the main concept in his personality theory (both of which are included in the book "Motivation and Personality").

Maslow introduces this concept in Appendix B with the following definition (p. 303):

"Our preliminary definition of a personality syndrome is that it is a structured, organized complex of apparently diverse specifities (behaviors, thoughts, impulses to action, perceptions, etc.) which, however, when studied carefully and validly are found to have a common unity that may be phrased variously as a similar dynamic meaning, expression, "flavor", function, or purpose."

This definition is unclear concerning the systematological status of the syndrome concept. The reader has probably noticed that Maslow defines a personality syndrome as a complex of apparently diverse specificities (behaviors, thoughts, impulses to action, perceptions, etc.) – and among these specificities we find both *descriptive* terms like "behavior" and *hypothetical* terms like "thoughts", "impulses to action" and "perception". Some of these H-terms may be interpreted as descriptive terms if a phenomenological data languge is presupposed. As Maslow is not clear on this point, however, we shall return to the problem later, and provisionally regard the "personality syndrome" as an H-term. This H-term refers to a set of H-variables ("thoughts", "impulses to action", "perception", etc.), which *determine* the overt behavior. This relationship between "behavior" and the other terms mentioned in the above quotations is much more clearly stated in the following formulation (p. 321):

"In a broad fashion, preliminary to more specific analysis, we can say that the relations between the syndromes and overt behavior are about as follows. Each act *tends* to be an expression of the whole integrated personality. This means, more specifically, that each act tends to be determined by each and all of the personality syndromes (in addition to other determinants to be spoken of below)."

In addition to these two important concepts Maslow mentions other H-terms such as "cognitive processes", "cognitive capacities", "talents", etc., but as they are not an integral part of his theory we shall limit the following systematological classifications to the two most important terms.

2.1.1. *The surplus meaning of the H-terms*. It is difficult to classify Maslow's H-terms systematologically, because there are so few explicit definitions. But we think it correct to classify the two main H-terms – "need" and "personality syndrome" – as H-terms with *mentalistic* surplus meaning. We base this on the fact that he sometimes uses the term "desire" synonymously with "need" (and "desire" is certainly an H_M-term). In addition, he uses such terms as "thoughts", "perception" and "impulses to action" in the definition of "personality syndrome", and of these terms "thoughts" at least has mentalistic surplus meaning.

But the evidence is not conclusive, and one *could* argue that Maslow's H-terms have *neutral* surplus meaning.

2.1.2. Dispositional or functional terms? This classification as well presents difficulties – at least concerning the term "need". This term is used in such a way that it sometimes refers to a variable with a long duration of existence, a *disposition* – a latent need in the need hierarchy – and sometimes to a variable with shorter duration of existence, a *function* – the unsatisfied need which is a "motivator". Thus "need" in Maslow's theory – similar to in Murray's – is *both a dispositional and a functional term*.

"Personality syndrome" is, however, used only as a *dispositional term* referring to a disposition pattern or structure, which manifests itself in various "thoughts", "impulses to action" and different kinds of behavior.

2.1.3. Dynamic, directive or vectorial terms? Maslow uses "need" – as does Murray – as a *vector term:* in both theories needs are variables having *both* dynamic and directive effects on behavior. There is, however, the difference that Murray explicitly and thoroughly defines "need", while Maslow uses it without an explicit definition. But Murray's and Maslow's use of "need" has been incorporated into the traditional terminology of personality theory, which unfortunately is very unlike that of learning theory, where "need" is used in quite another sense (see Madsen, 1968).

We must classify "personality syndrome" as a *vector* term because there are not explicit definitions defining it as a dynamic or a directive term.

2.2. Classifications of the hypotheses

We have – in section 2.0.2. – presented a summary of the content of the hypotheses in Maslow's theory. As there are no – or at least very few – explicit formulations of the important motivational hypotheses, we shall quote some of the most important passages and then make a systematic reconstruction of the hypotheses before making the systematological classifications.

The most important hypotheses of the *hierarchical organization* of the need-system are implicitly included in the following passages from "M. and P.":

"If all the needs are unsatisfied, and the organism is then dominated by the physiological needs, all other needs may become simply nonexistent or be pushed into the background" (p. 37) ..

The most implicit formulation of the hierarchy hypothesis is found in the following (p. 38):

"*At once other (and higher) needs emerge* and these, rather that physiological hungers, dominate the organism. And when these in turn are satisfied, again new (and still higher) needs emerge, and so on. This is what we mean by saying that the basic human needs are organized into a hierarchy of relative prepotency."

The important hypotheses about *self-actualization* are contained in the following (p. 46):

"Even if all these needs are satisfied, we may still often (if not always) expect that a new discontent and restlessness will soon develop, unless the individual is doing what *he*, individually, is fitted for. A musician must make music, an artist must paint, a poet must write, if he is to be ultimately at peace with himself. What a man *can* be, he *must* be. He must be true to his own nature. This need we may call self-actualization."

A third important hypothesis about *multi-determination* is found in the following quotations (all from p. 55):

"− − − most behavior is overdetermined or multimotivated." − − − " "Not all behavior is determined by the basic needs. We might even say that not all behavior is motivated. There are many determinants of behavior other than motives." − − −

"Some behavior is highly motivated, other behavior is only weakly motivated. Some is not motivated at all (but all behavior is determined)."

An important hypothesis about *gratification* is found in the following quotation (p. 60):

"The most basic consequence of satiation of any need is that this need is submerged and a new and higher need emerges. Other consequences are epiphenomena of this fundamental fact."

The epiphenomena to which Maslow refers in the above quotation are: changes in values, changes in interests and changes in cognitive capacities and learning.

An important hypothesis about *functional autonomy* – first formulated by Woodworth, modified by Allport – is restated by him in the following quotation (p. 72):

"Although it is generally true that we move to higher need levels after gratification of the lower needs, it yet remains an observable phenomeon that once having attained these higher need levels and the values and tastes that go with them they may become autonomous, no longer depending on lower need gratifications."

A hypothesis about the *origin of needs* is formulated by Maslow in this way (pp. 80–81):

"Our main hypothesis is that human *urges* or *basic needs* alone may be innately given to at least some appreciable degree. The pertinent behavior or ability, cognition or affection need not also be innate, but may be (by our hypothesis) learned, canalized, or expressive. – This is to say that the hereditary component of basic needs may be seen as simple conative lack, tied to no intrinsic goal-achieving behavior, as blind, directionless demands like Freud's id impulses."

306 . *Maslow's Theory*

The last quotation creates some doubts about the classification of "need" as a vector term. In this quotation it is defined as referring to a *dynamic* "directionless" variable.

Maslow has a whole chapter dealing with the distinction between higher and lower needs. The main content is concentrated in 16 propositions, which can be regarded as hypotheses about or hypothetical definitions of higher needs. We shall quote these propositions here as they represent some of the most explicit formulations in his book ("M. and P.", pp. 98–100):

" 1. The higher need is a later phyletic or evolutionary development."
" 2. Higher needs are later ontogenetic developments."
" 3. The higher the need the less imperative is it for sheer survival, the longer gratification can be postponed, and the easier it is for the need to disappear permanently."
" 4. Living at the higher need level means greater biological efficiency, greater longevity, less disease, better sleep, appetite, etc."
" 5. Higher needs are less urgent subjectively."
" 6. Higher need gratifications produce more desirable subjective results, i.e., more profound happiness, serenity, and richness of the inner life."
" 7. Pursuit and gratification of higher needs represent a general healthward trend, a trend away from psychopathology."
" 8. The higher need has more preconditions."
" 9. Higher needs require better outside conditions to make them possible."
"10. A greater value is usually placed upon the higher need than upon the lower by those who have been gratified in both."
"11. The higher the need level, the wider is the circle of love identification, i.e., the greater is the number of people love-identified with, and the greater is the average degree of love identification."
"12. The pursuit and the gratification of the higher needs have desirable civic and social consequences."
"13. Satisfaction of higher needs is closer to self-actualization than is lower need-satisfaction."
"14. The pursuit and gratification of the higher needs leads to greater, stronger, and truer individualism."
"15. The higher the need level the easier and more effective psychotherapy can be: at the lowest need levels it is of hardly any avail."
"16. The lower needs are far more localized, more tangible, and more limited than are the higher needs."

With these quotations we think we have presented the most important hypotheses about motivation in Maslow's theory. There *are* other hypotheses in his book, but they are more concerned with frustration, neuroses, psychotherapy and other matters, and belong more to his clinical personality theory than to his motivation theory.

Therefore we conclude this section with a summary containing a *systematic reconstruction of the hypotheses of motivation found in Maslow's theory:*

1. *The multi-determination hypothesis:* Behavior is determined by many interacting hypothetical variables: the need system, the personality syn-

dromes, the abilities, the cognitive processes and the impulses to action (cf. our overview diagram, Fig. 15.1).
2. *The activation hypothesis:* The activation of behavior is determined by one or more unsatisfied needs.
3. *The need system hypothesis:* The unsatisfied needs are determined by external and internal stimuli as well as by interaction with other unsatisfied needs in the need system.
4. *The hierarchy hypotheses:*

4a. The interaction of unsatisfied needs is determined by the inborn need system, which is organized as a hierarchy or prepotency with the physiological needs as the most prepotent, followed by the safety, the affiliative, the esteem, and the self-actualization needs.

4b. When an unsatisfied need has been satisfied (gratified) for a period it no longer determines behavior, which is instead determined by a higher (less prepotent) unsatisfied need and so on, until the individual's behavior is completely determined by the self-actualization needs.

4c. *The self-actualization hypothesis:* When all lower deficiency needs are satisfied, then the individual's behavior will be completely determined by the highest growth or metaneeds for self-actualization.

4.d *The functional autonomy hypothesis:* A higher need may acquire a functional autonomy or independence of the lower needs and so counteract the system of prepotency.

5. *The gratification hypothesis:* The satisfaction or gratification of a need results in a restructuring of the cognitive processes (perception, attention, thinking, evaluation, etc.).

6. *The origin hypothesis:* The system of "basic needs" (including the self-actualization needs) is determined by heredity and maturation and is thus unlearned.

2.2.1. *The basic classification of hypotheses.* Before making our basic classification of hypotheses into purely *theoretical* and partly *empirical* hypotheses, we must reformulate them as symbolic formulas. The result reads:

1. hypothesis: $(H_{need} \leftrightarrow H_{pers.\ syndr.} \leftrightarrow H_{cog.\ proc.} \leftrightarrow H_{imp.}) \rightarrow R$
2. hypothesis: $H_{uns.\ need} \rightarrow R_{dynamic}$
3. hypothesis: $(S_{int.} + S_{ext.}) \rightarrow (H_{uns.\ need_1} \leftrightarrow H_{uns.\ need_2})$
4a. hypothesis: $(H_{ph-} \dashv H_{s-} \dashv H_{af-} \dashv H_{es-} \dashv H_{S.A.}) \rightarrow R_{ph}$.
4b. hypothesis: $(H_{ph+} \rightarrow H_s \dashv H_{af-} \dashv H_{es} \dashv H_{S.A.}) \rightarrow R_s$.
4c. hypothesis: $(H_{ph+} \rightarrow H_{s+} \rightarrow H_{af} \rightarrow H_{es+} \dashv H_{S.A.-}) \rightarrow R_{S.A.}$
4d. hypothesis: $(H_{es-} \dashv H_{ph-} \dashv H_{s-} \dashv H_{af-} \dashv H_{S.A.-}) \rightarrow R_{es}$.
5. hypothesis: $H_{gratification} \rightarrow H_{cog.\ proc.}$
6. hypothesis: $S_{heredity} \rightarrow H_{need\ system}$

The abbreviations employed in the above symbolic formulations should be easy to understand. Arrows indicate facilitatory influences, double arrows interaction, and a ⊣ indicates inhibitory influences. Plus and minus signs are used for satisfied and unsatisfied needs respectively.

On the basis of our symbolic reformulation of Maslow's motivation hypotheses we can finally make the classification of hypotheses into:

1. *Purely theoretical (H-H-hypotheses):*
   1. hypothesis: No. 5.

2. *Partly empirical hypotheses:*
   a. S-H-hypotheses: 2 hypotheses: No. 3 and 6.
   b. H-R-hypotheses: 6 hypotheses: No. 1, 2, 4a, 4b, 4c and 4d.

The reader should bear one important thing in mind: the above classification is based upon *our* reformulation of Maslow's theory, or, more exactly, of his *motivational* hypotheses. And in this case we have had to work harder in making the reformulation than usual in order to transform the text into a systematic and precise theory. Therefore, there are more possibilities of making errors. This will have special implications for our later calculation of the Hypotheses Quotient (in section 4.3.0).

2.2.2. *The complexity of the hypotheses.* From the above symbolic reformulations of Maslow's hypotheses it is easy to see that many of them are rather complex. If we make a classification according to complexity, we get:

1. *One-dimensional hypotheses:* 3 hypotheses: No. 2, 5 and 6.
2. *Multi-dimensional hypotheses:* 6 hypotheses: No. 1, 3, 4a, 4b, 4c and 4d.

Thus we must admit that Maslow *has* realized an holistic program by constructing a rather field-theoretical motivation theory.

2.2.3. *The functional relationships in the hypotheses.* If we examine the implicit and explicit formulations of hypotheses in Maslow's book, "Motivation and Personality", we rather frequently find the word "determined". From the whole context it is rather clear that he presupposes the existence of *causal determinism*. There is no statement in "M. and P." which can be interpreted as presupposing any form of indeterminism.

This is important to bear in mind as he later in "Toward a Psychology of Being" (1st ed., 1962) made explicit statements in favor of indeterminism. But this philosophical doctrine, which is an important part of existential philosophy, had not influenced him at the time the first edition of "M. and P." was written (1954).

Nor do we find any indeterministic propositions in the second edition (1970), not even in the preface to this book, which is probably the last thing he wrote for publication before he died in the summer of 1970.

The descriptive stratum

3.0. Introduction

The data in Maslow's book are mainly presented in Chapters 11 and 12, which deal with his investigations of the so-called "Self-Actualizing People": But in the rest of the book he frequently refers to this search as well as to his general experience with psychotherapy. Before we take up the results of this investigation let us look at some abstract descriptive terms.

3.1. The abstract D-level

(3.1.1.) The most important content of the arstract D-level in Maslow's theory consists of the *abstract descriptive terms*. Among these we shall emphasize the distinction between *"expressive" and "coping" behavior*. Inspired by Gordon W. Allport he presents this distinction in Chapter 10, where we find the following (implicit) definitions ("M. and P.", p. 132):

"1. Coping is by definition purposive and motivated; expression if often unmotivated.
2. Coping is more determined by external environmental and cultural variables; expression is largely determined by the state of his organism.
3. Coping is most often learned; expression is most often unlearned or released or disinhibited.
4. Coping is more easily controlled; expression is more often uncontrolled and sometimes even uncontrollable.
5. Coping is usually designed to cause changes in the environment and often does; expression is not designed to do anything.
6. Coping is characteristically means behavior, the end being need gratification or threat reduction. Expression is often an end it itself."

To these implicit definitions he adds a warning (in a footnote on p. 131):

"We must be careful here to avoid sharp, either-or dichotomizing. Most acts of behavior have both an expressive and a coping component, – – –."

(3.1.2.) In addition to the empirical laws included in the above implicit definitions we find some other "empirical laws" or *general, descriptive propositions about self-actualizing people*. These "laws" are presented as section headings in Chapter 11: "Self-actualizing People: A Study of Psychological Health".

We shall look at these "laws" in more detail below, but to get a full understanding of them as implicitly formulated laws, we must presuppose the following formulation as an implicit, introductory part of each "law":

Self-actualizing people have in a higher degree than normal people the following personality traits:

1. "More efficient perception of reality and more comfortable relations with it."
2. "Acceptance (self, others, nature)."
3. "Spontaneity; simplicity; naturalness.
4. "Problem centering."
5. "The quality of detachment; the need for privacy."
6. "Autonomy; independence of culture and environment: will; active agents."
7. "Continued freshness of appreciation."
8. "The mystic experience; the peak experience."
9. "Gemeinschaftsgefühl."
10. "Interpersonal relations."
11. "The democratic character structure."
12. "Discriminations between means and ends, between good and evil."
13. "Philosophical, unhostile sense of humor."
14. "Creativeness."
15. "Resistance to enculturation; transcendence of any particular culture."
16. "The imperfections of self-actualizing people."
17. "Values and self-actualization."
18. "The resolution of dichotomies in self-actualization."

We must admit that we have had our doubt about classifying these propositions as "empirical laws". They could just as well be classified as hypotheses as they contain hypothetical terms. But we have interpreted them as laws, because Maslow uses *both a phenomenological and a behavioral data language,* so we must classify these sentences as being general, *descriptive* propositions ("laws") and not explanatory propositions (hypotheses). If we accept this interpretation we can classify the above propositions as the most important "laws" found by Maslow in his investigation of self-actualizing people.

3.2. The concrete D-level

Maslow describes the subjects and methods in Chapter 11, pp. 150–153 in "M. and P." The subjects were selected according to the following criterion (p. 150):

"This criterion implies also gratification, past or present, of the basic needs for safety, belongingness, love, respect, and self-respect, and of the cognitive needs for knowledge and for understanding, or in a few cases, conquest of these needs. This is to say that all subjects felt safe and unanxious, accepted, loved and loving, respect-worthy and respected, and that they had worked out their philosophical, religious, or axiological bearings. It is still an open question as to whether this basic gratification is a sufficient or only a prerequisite condition of self-actualization."

After the application of the criterion the following subjects were finally selected (p. 152):

"The subjects have been divided into the following categories

Cases:	7 fairly and highly probable contemporaries (interviewed) 2 fairly sure historical figures (Lincoln in his last years and Thomas Jefferson) 7 highly probable public and historical figures (Einstein, Eleanor Roosevelt, Jane Addams, William James, Schweitzer, Aldous Huxley and Spinoza)
Partial Cases:	5 contemporaries who fairly certainly fall short somewhat but who can yet be used for study
Potential or Possible Cases: Cases suggested or studied by others:	G. W. Carver, Eugene V. Debs, Thomas Eakins, Fritz Kreisler, Goethe, Pablo Casals, Martin Buber, Danilo Dolci, Arthur E. Morgan, John Keats, David Hilbert, Arthur Waley, D. T. Suzuki, Adlai Stevenson, Sholom Aleichem, Robert Browning, Ralph Waldo Emerson, Frederick Douglass, Joseph Schumpeter, Bob Benchley, Ida Tarbell, Harriet Tubman, George Washington, Karl Muenzinger, Joseph Haydn, Camille Pissarro, Edward Bibring, George William Russell (A. E.), Pierre Renoir, Henry Wadsworth Longfellow, Peter Kropotkin, John Altgeld, Thomas More, Edward Bellamy, Benjamin Franklin, John Muir, Walt Whitman."

While the *subjects* thus are described rather thoroughly the *methods* are only briefly touched on. It appears that the main method employed with living subjects was the interview, although certain tests (e. g., the Rorschach) seem to have been employed in the selection of subjects.

There is no detailed description of data in the form of protocol sentences.

3.3. *The descriptive units*

It is rather easy to classify Maslow's theory as a *molar* theory, because he employs molar descriptive units such as "the coping act", "the personality syndrome" and "the whole personality". Even the "smallest" of these descriptive units, "the coping act", is a rather molar descriptive unit.

The theory as a whole

4.1. *The formal properties*

When we turn to the final classifications of Maslow's theory and deal with it as whole, we must first classify it according to its formal properties.

(4.1.1.) *The systematic organization* of this theory is such that it must be classified as a loosely organized text or "sketch". There is no clear stratification of the text. The first two chapters and the last two belong mainly to the M-level,

Chapters 11 and 12 mainly to the D-level, and the rest of the chapters mainly to the H-level. But there are many breaks in this systematic order, and it can even be difficult to determine to which level a given proposition belongs. We have already mentioned that there are practically no explicit formulations of definitions and hypotheses.

(4.1.2.) *The preciseness of representation* in Maslow's theory corresponds to that of a *purely verbal theory*. There are no symbolizations and of course no mathematization.

(4.1.3.) *The properties of the models* used in Maslow's theory are equivalent to *verbal analogies*. There are, however, very few verbal analogies in his explanatory text.

4.2. The epistemological properties

We think it is most correct to classify Maslow's theory as *an explanatory theory*. Among the sub-categories of explanatory theories his belongs to the S-M-R, as he uses H-terms with *mentalistic* surplus meaning.

We have thought about the possibility of classifying Maslow's theory as an *M-theory*, an interpretative or intuitive "Verstehen" theory. If he had not included his investigation of self-actualizing people, we should have regarded his theory as based solely on intuitive "Verstehen" which is in turn based upon clinical experience. Although Maslow's theory is near to – the nearest we have found – an M-theory, we think that his presentation of data in Chapters 11 and 12 transforms his theory into an explanatory theory.

4.3. The theory-empiry ratio

On the basis of our immediate impression after having read Maslow's books we might well feel justified in calling his theory *rather speculative*. But after calculating the Hypotheses Quotient we began to have our doubts. The result was:

$$\text{H.Q.} = \frac{\Sigma(\text{H–H})}{\Sigma[(\text{S–H}) + (\text{H–R})]} = \frac{1}{2+6} = \frac{1}{8} = 0.13$$

This is a surprisingly *low* H.Q. – among the lowest we have found. Thus there is a discrepancy between our first rough impression and classification of Maslow's theory as *speculative*, and the calculation revealing a very low H.Q., thus indicating an extremely *empiristic* theory. After some deliberation we have come to the conclusion that the reasons for the discrepancy are that the H.Q. is based upon *our* reconstruction of his *motivation* theory. Our reconstruction has improved upon the preciseness of presentation and systematic organization of his theory, which is one of the most undeveloped as far as these formal properties are concerned. And we have concentrated on Maslow's motivational theory which perhaps is that part of his whole theory which is the least undeveloped in formal respects. Thus the discrepancy arises from the differences between our systematic reconstruction of a part of his theory and our rough impression of his unformalized theory as a whole.

We hope this is enough to "explain away" this discrepancy between our rough judgement of a theory as being *speculative* and the result of the exact calculation of the H.Q. which reveals it to be an *empirical* theory. But we must confess that the above has left a doubt in the mind of the present author about what the correct *interpretation* of the H.Q. is. We shall take up this problem in more detail in the last of the comparative chapters.

Concluding remarks. In spite of our reservations concerning the formal properties of Maslow's theory, we must conclude with an evaluation of the theory as one of the most original and broadest of those appearing after the Second World War.

In both its originality and its informal development his theory reminds us of Freud's. It will be for future historians of psychology to judge if Maslow's theory will have the same wide and profound influence on psychology as that of Freud.

16. Other Important Theories

Introduction

In contemporary, motivational psychology there are of course many more than the 12 theories which we have analyzed in Chapters 4–15. Many of these other theories also deserve a whole chapter. But unfortunately, time limitations and the space available to the author in this book have made it impossible to do justice to all these other theories.

In order to "solve" this problem we have decided to present brief analyses of 10 more theories and some very brief remarks about a few additional ones. We hope that in a possible later edition of this book – or perhaps in another book – we can treat some of these theories more thoroughly. The present author has received valuable assistance from some of his graduate students, who have made preliminary unpublished analyses of several theories. Five of the following systematological analyses have been made on the basis of the work of graduate students, who are identified in the respective sections.

Bolles's Theory

Introduction

The American psychologist *Robert C. Bolles* has, in addition to an impressive number of articles, written the book *"Theory of Motivation"* (1967). In this book he makes a very extensive analysis of the historical development of motivational psychology. Of special interest is the very thorough critical analysis of the "drive" concept contained in Hull's (and co-workers') theory. And in the last third of the book he presents a theory of motivation which is very similar to *Skinner's*.

1. *The Metastratum*

(1.1). Bolles presents his *philosophical presuppositions* in the first chapter of the book. He seems to believe that psychologists have three principal philosophical doctrines to choose between:

1. *Traditional Rationalism:*
   This is a kind of rationalistic epistemology often connected with a *dualistic* – or "mentalistic" – theory of the psychosomatic problem. Bolles regards this as an unsound basis for scientific psychology.
2. *Mechanism or Physicalism:*
   This also denotes a kind of *rationalistic* epistemology, but connected with a *materialistic* theory of the psychosomatic problem. Bolles regards the *neurophysiological* approaches to psychology as modern versions of the mechanistic approach.
3. *Empirical Determinism:*
   This is a type of *empiristic* epistemology often connected with a *neutral monistic* theory of the psychosomatic problem. Bolles believes that this is the soundest foundation for scientific psychology, as it has been for other natural sciences.

(1.2). The *metatheoretical propositions* are also explicitly and precisely presented in the first chapter of Bolles's book.

First, it should be emphasized that Bolles is more positive in his attitude toward theory construction than Skinner is. Bolles regards *theory as necessary* if we want to systematize and explain in psychology. But he formulates certain requirements which theories must meet if they are to pass as *scientific* theories.

The first requirement is that all "constructs" must be precisely defined. The next requirement is that the hypothetical – or *theoretical* constructs (as Bolles prefers calling them) must be both *syntactically* related to each other, and *semantically* related to the *"empirical* constructs" (our abstract descriptive terms). Third: these empirical constructs must be firmly related to "the thing language, the language of common perceptual experience, through operational definitions" (p. 14)[1]).

Bolles also discusses the different kinds of "theoretical constructs", each with its particular kind of surplus meaning. He abandons the "mentalistic" or "animistic" constructs (the H_M-terms in our terminology) as well as the "neurological" constructs (the H_o-terms in our terminology). He prefers working with the so-called "intervening constructs", which are called H_N-terms (without surplus meaning – or with some neutral surplus meaning) in our terminology.

But he does not go as far as the radical empiricists (like Skinner) who reject all theoretical constructs (H-terms). Thus he writes (p. 19):

"It is certainly possible to have a theory of behavior involving terms with no surplus meaning, terms which do not commit the theorist to a particular variety of explanation, or betray his personal belief in one.

1. Bolles uses the term "data language" in this way: "The empirical constructs, taken together, constitute what we will call the data language" (p. 13). This is different from our use of "data language", which refers to what he calls "thing language" or "reduction language".

Radical empiricism is too big a price to pay. All that it buys can be purchased more cheaply by demanding that constructs be validated solely by being tied syntactically and semantically to the data language.

From the above quotation we can conclude that although Bolles agrees with Skinner's approach in general his metatheoretical orientation is more like that of N. E. Miller (first period).

(1.3.). We have not found any explicit formulations of *methodological propositions* in Bolles's book. But it is obvious from the book that he favors *experiments with animals*. The book contains 70 pages of references, mainly to animal experiments.

Therefore the data language (according to our definition of the term) is clearly *behavioral*.

2. The Hypothetical Stratum

(2.0.) As already mentioned in the introduction, the main part of Bolles's book is devoted to an historical and critical analysis of various motivational theories. The most thorough analysis is made of *Hull's drive theory*. We have decided to summarize this critical analysis as it is necessary background for making a *summary* of Bolles's own theory. We believe that we can best do this by quoting the page on which he summarizes his more than 200 page long discussion of the drive concept (p. 329):

"A Final Word on the Drive Concept.

The same troubles have plagued us in the area of acquired drives that bothered us in the area of the primary drives. The attempt to find supporting evidence has led us to an understanding of behavior which cannot be improved by talking about drives (or D). Wherever we investigate motivated behavior, its associative determinants, i. e., the stimuli and reinforcements that give it structure loom ever more important, while the role played by drive becomes ever less clear.

The first chapters of our survey of the data on drive indicate that what Hull proposed for drive in general had only been demonstrated for hunger. There is a further limitation, however, in that not all of what Hull proposed for drive is valid even for hunger. Indeed, about all we can say with assurance is that the rat's hunger-produced weight loss is directly related to the strength of its eating behavior and of the instrumental behavior upon which eating is contingent. As soon as the contingencies between behavior and reinforcement are removed, the evidence for any kind of motivational effects begins to collapse. It is true that the hungry rat explores and runs in activity wheels more than nonhungry rats, but this seems more parsimoniously explained in terms of specific connections between hunger and these kinds of behavior. In other areas, we have failed to find that D and H are independent, that the stimulus concomitants of drive have any real existence, that drive reduction constitutes reinforcement, that different sources of drive are motivationally equivalent, or that there are consistent individual differences in drive strength. The different sources of drive seem to be marked more by their different effects than by their common properties, and even in the case of hunger, which conforms best with the theoretical requirements, its effects suggest that it is more like a source of incentive than a source of drive. However, the worst failure of the drive concept continues to be that it does not help us to explain behavior.

We can find some semblance of acquired aversive drives, but again, having found them, we discover that we cannot explain behavior very well with them.

The drive concept is like an old man that has had a long active, and yet, even useful life. It has produced a notable amount of cenceptual and empirical work; it has, perhaps indirectly, made a great contribution to our understanding of behavior. But the fruitful days are nearly gone. The time has come when younger, more vigorous, more capable concepts must take over. So, as sentimental as we may feel about our friend, we should not despair at his passing."

Bolles continues in the following chapter with "incentive theories of motivation", and concludes his analysis with this remark (p. 367):

"Thus, incentives can explain anything drives can explain, and they can explain a vast number of transient and short-term effects that drives cannot explain."

Although this evaluation of the incentive concept seems very positive, Bolles continues his critical analysis and ends with discounting it. In the last chapter he discusses "Reinforcement Theories of Motivation". This chapter opens with the following statement (pp. 434–35):

"Here in the final chapter it is perhaps appropriate to consider the possibility that the explanation of behavior can proceed better without any motivational concepts, without involving needs or drives or wants or anything of the sort, either in our data language and among our theoretical concepts. Specifically, we will consider the possibility that what we have called motivated behavior is neither more nor less than learned behavior, and that all of the phenomena that have been called motivational can be translated without loss, into phenomena af reinforcement."

Thus Bolles's extensive, thorough and thought-provoking critical analysis of motivational theories concludes with *reinforcement taking the place of motivation.* This is so much more impressive, because he starts his book with a moderately positive attitude toward theories employing explanatory, hypothetical constructs. Yet, in spite of this, his own theory contains – as far as we can see – *no* hypothetical terms and therefore no hypotheses.

We can thus go on to the next stratum of the theory.

3. The Descriptive Stratum

(3.1.). The main part of the *abstract D-level* in Bolles's theory is concerned with the *empirical "law of effect"* – or the empirical "law of reinforcement", as he also calls it. His evaluation of this law is concentrated in the following lines (p. 445):

"If we are to analyze behavior in search of its lawfullness, then we should surely welcome the empirical law of reinforcement; it is one of the best we have found so far."

(3.2.). The *concrete D-level* of Bolles's theory consists of the numerous experimental results recorded in connection with the discussion of the motivational theories. The experiments were, for the most part, carried out on animals. The data language (in our sense of the term) is *behavioral*.

(3.3.). The *descriptive units* are rather *molecular*.

4. The Theory as a Whole

(4.1.). The *formal properties* of the theory are rather *systematically organized* (although Bolles does *not* formulate a system of hypotheses). It is a very *precise*, but purely verbal presentation. No explanatory models are used.

(4.2.). The *epistemological properties* of Bolles's theory are – like Skinner's – those of a *behavioral descriptive theory, an S-R-theory* (although in principle Bolles is not against an explanatory theory).

(4.3.). The *theory-empiry* ratio is very low. The theory must consequently be classified as being *very empirical*. If the Hypotheses Quotient had been calculated, it would probably have approximated zero.

Concluding Remarks. We think that Bolles has made a major contribution by making a critical analysis of motivational theories from a Skinnerian point of view. The main criticism which could be raised against Bolles's book is its nearly total limitation to animal experiments. He has *not* demonstrated that *motivational constructs are superfluous in the explanation of complicated human behavior*[2]).

Bühler's Theory

Introduction

The German-American psychologist, *Charlotte Bühler*, has had a long career as a psychologist, during which she has made important contributions to several fields of psychology. It is well known that Charlotte Bühler was among the pioneers in the establishment of child psychology in the 1920's. The best known work from this period is *Kindheit und Jugend* (1928). As a real developmental psychologist she continued with studies of the whole course of life, which were presented in *Der menschliche Lebenslauf als psychologisches Problem*. (1933). This is – as far as we know – the first book dealing with this problem, which was later studied by Allport, Erikson, Maslow, Murray and other personality psychologists. Charlotte Bühler continued her work in the United States, where she worked as a professor in clinical psychology. With this triple background in

---

[2]. It should be added that Bolles has changed his theory in some respects since the appearance of his 1967 book. See, among other things: C. R. Bolles: "Species-Specific Defense Reactions and Avoidance Learning" *(Psychological Review, 1970, Vol. 77, pp. 32–48).*

developmental psychology, personality theory and clinical psychology she became one of the leaders in the new school of "humanistic psychology". Thus she led the first international conference in humanistic psychology in Amsterdam in August, 1970, and has gained the position of the "grand old lady" of humanistic psychology. She gained this position, among other ways, through her authorship of numerous books and papers about humanistically oriented personality theory.

Charlotte Bühler has formulated a motivational theory as a part of her theory of the course of human life, which we have systematically analyzed below. The following analysis is based upon two of her latest books: the textbook, *Psychology for Contemporary Living* (which has been published in 10 languages – the American edition in 1968) and a book co-edited with *Fred Massarik: The Course of Human Life: A Study of Goals in the Humanistic Perspective* (1968), which is a continuation of her above-mentioned main work, which appeared in 1933.

1. The Metastratum

There is a clear connection between Charlotte Bühler's personality theory and *existentialist philosophy*. It should also be mentioned that her personality theory, both historically and epistemologically, was formulated *prior* to the emergence of existentialist philosophy. She is convinced that human beings – at least from about middle age – are consciously occupied with *life goals*, and that they need an *integrating belief* (philosophy of life, religion, etc.). She believes that existentialism is an expression of ideas to be found in humanistic personality theory.

(1.1.). We think that it is correct to describe Charlotte Bühler's *philosophical presuppositions as belonging to empiristic epistemology,* althoug she does not make any explicit statements about this matter.

Nor does she explicitly formulate her philosophy of the psychosomatic problem. The author believes, however, that there is evidence that she embraces a dualistic point of view regarding this problem. Thus in the textbook she makes the following definition: "Psychology is the science of the mind; it deals with mental, or psychic, life" (p. XIV).

But later in the same book she states that "everything that happens is psychophysical" (p. 17). In addition, she explicitly presents two different theories in this section (p. 17):

"There are, in the main, two theories that attempt to explain the psychophysical occurrence. One of them credits *interaction* between psychophysical processes, and the other sees the psychophysical happening as a *total happening.*" And she concludes the same section with the following passage (p. 17):

"The one fact to be kept in mind is that everything which happens inside us has a psychic and a physical side."

We think that the phrase "a total happening" is an expression of the *neutral monistic* philosophy of the psychosomatic problem, which is also called the "double aspect theory". The latter term came to our mind when we read the last quotation (p. 17). If we could conclude that this passage was a declaration of preference on the part of Charlotte Bühler, then we should describe her philosophy as *neutral monistic* rather than *dualistic*. But we must leave the problem for the present. We shall return to it later in Section 2.1.

Charlotte Bühler is much more explicit in her statements about the presupposed "philosophy of man". She frequently refers to *a humanistic philosophy of man*. The sub-title of "The Course of Human Life" *(A Study of Goals in the Humanistic Perspective)* also reveals this concern with the humanistic.

(1.2.). There are only a few explicit formulations of the *methatheoretical propositions*. We feel, nevertheless, that it is correct to state that Charlotte Bühler conceives of her works as mainly *descriptions of empirical studies*. But she admits at several places that it is necessary to have some *hypothetical constructs* or "theoretical concepts" as organizing principles for both the guidance of the empirical studies and the systematic presentation of the results. Thus after a discussion of the theories of *Kurt Goldstein* and *Heinz Hartman*, she writes (p. 6):

"But neither these nor other occasional differences of opinion seemed serious enough to endanger our collaboration. On the contrary, it appeared to us that the hypothetical nature of the theoretical concepts would serve us well in a collaborative venture and that our differences could add a new dimension of interest to the study, particularly since the theoretical bias that determined the selection of the material will be explained."

And after discussing methodological problems she adds (p. 10):

"Theoretical considerations, of course, play an essential role in this book; they appear in all sections and culminate in Part V."

Thus it is obvious that Charlotte Bühler and her co-workers conceive of their work as containing a set of hypothetical constructs and hypotheses (which we shall analyze further in a following section). As they contain no other explicit formulations of metatheoretical propositions we can turn to the methodological problems.

(1.3.). Charlotte Bühler and her co-workers are much more explicit in their formulations of *methodological propositions,* which is the case with most other modern psychologists. Thus she writes (p. 9):

"A study of life goals encounters several methodological problems. The first is the sheer mass of material involved in the examination of a complete life history. The second results from the multitude of factors that codetermine the process of goal setting. To consider these methodological problems properly requires not only a study of several different scientific resources but also an integration of different kinds of data obtained by varying methods. What complicates the process is the necessity for dealing with statistical observations and interview data on the one hand, and long-range views and detailed studies conducted over a short period of time, on the other.

I would suggest, therefore, that we use two separate approaches: the macroscopic and the microscopic. The macroscopic approach will be applied when we consider the course of life as a whole, and view primarily its major outlines and aspects. The microscopic approach will be used to examine in detail individual behavior at specific moments in certain phases of development."

It is obvious from this passage that Charlotte Bühler is very broad-minded in her attitude toward psychological methods. She accepts and employs classical *experimental* methods and *tests* as well as the more unconventional – at least for psychology – *historical-biographical* methods. The latter are called "macroscopic", while the first two are called "microscopic". These terms are equivalent to Tolman's well known terms "molar" and "molecular".

No preference is stated regarding a *data language,* but Charlotte Bühler and her co-workers for the most part use *behavioral* data language; they describe the behavior – especially *verbal* – of their subjects.

Thus we can summarize our analysis of Charlotte Bühler's metapropositions by observing that she presupposes the same principal philosophical, metatheoretical and methodological presuppositions that others in the field of scientific psychology do, although she deals with a much more complicated problem than usual, namely, the whole course of human life.

2. *Hypothetical Stratum*

(2.0.). A very short *summary* of the hypotheses in Charlotte Bühler's theory is presented in the preface to Bühler and Massarik (p. V):

"The theory that all goal setting must be understood as it relates to the course of life as a whole is presented as a basic hypothesis. - - -"
"Concern with the person's goal setting as a procedure contributing to his eventual fulfillment (based largely on self-realization) or failure represents the book's humanistic orientation."

Thus "goals" are important components of the course of human life. This important concept is defined in this way (p. 4):

"As we are going to deal with the goal aspects of life, a word should be said obout the difference between goals and needs. Both are motivational concepts, but each represents a different aspect of motivation.
The common denominator of most definitions of need is the belief that it results from deficiencies in the organism. These deficiencies cause tensions, which, in turn, initiate processes. The inherent aim of these processes is to relieve the pressures of the need and/or to satisfy it. This inherent aim may or may not also be the goal. It becomes the goal if by his action the individual strives for the satisfaction of the need as an end, that is, if, besides the urge, he also has the intent."

According to the above, "goals" are determined by "needs", but not all needs result in "goals." A "goal" requires that the termination of need satisfaction becomes an "intent" for the individual. Charlotte Bühler's exposition continues logically (p. 4):

> "This leaves the question of how these intents occur. There is no doubt that in purposeful actions the anticipated end appears in an image based on a previous perceptual experience. There are, however, stages of action, specifically in creative work, where the urge seems to contain an aim directed toward an end which is not yet clearly defined. This is true particularly in the early stages of creative development. A young person, for instance, may feel an urge to write or the desire to help others without knowing specifically how or why. The initial urge is part of a process that, once achieved, will then be identified as having been the inherent goal."

This can be summarized in this way: *"Goals" are endstates of need satisfaction, which can be – but are not always – consciously anticipated by an "intent"*.

After these basic definitions Charlotte Bühler introduces the following basic hypothesis (p. 12):

> "This book starts with the assumption that the individual's course of life has a definite basic structure and that this structure is evident in his biological life cycle as well as in his psychophysical development. By structure we mean an organized system with certain consistent properties and potentialities. It is also a basic assumption that the life-cycle structure codetermines the goals the human being sets for himself."

The "basic structure of life" comprises certain basic needs or "tendencies" as Charlotte Bühler calls them. They are defined in this way (pp. 17–18):

> "I furthermore hypothesized that there are four basic tendencies that work toward what I call the fulfillment of life: need satisfaction, self-limiting adaptation, creative expansion, and upholding of internal order. Need satisfaction and upholding of order involve principles of stability, while self-limiting adaption and creative expansion involve principles of change. Human beings go through life changing and creating change, satisfying needs, adapting themselves to given circumstances, and upholding internal order. The different tendencies determine, with changing predominance, the utilization of a person's inner and outer potentials, and the availability as well as management of these determine the attainable fulfillment. These tendencies, it is assumed, are present at birth, since from the very beginning an infant has to adapt himself in order to satisfy his needs and to extend himself and coordinate his behavior, if only to a small degree. And obviously, the newborn's drive is directed primarily toward need satisfaction.
>
> Thus, normatively speaking, we find fluctuating degrees of predominance in the various stages. The growing child develops his self-imiting adaptation during the learning process, the adolescent and adult move into a widened world during a period of predominant creative expansion, the adult begins to assess his past and himself in the climacteric age, probably because he wants to restore his inner order, and the old person either regresses to need-satisfying tendencies or continues to follow his previous adaptive or creative drives. One aspect of fulfillment is believed to be the experience of having used these basic tendencies toward the most complete realization of one's own potential."

Thus it is clear from the part of the theory we have quoted that these four basic tendencies occur in a different pattern of dominance in the different phases of life. Roughly *need satisfactions* dominate in the first phase (childhood), *self-limiting adaptation* in the second phase (adolescence), *creative expansion* in the middle phase of life (25–50 years old), and *upholding of internal order* in the fourth phase (50–65 years old), while the last phase (65 years old and older) *can* be dominated by a regression to need satisfaction though in some people there can be a continued dominance of "creative expansion"[3]).

This leads us directly to the next theme: the existence of individual differences in the goal pattern. Charlotte Bühler and her co-workers have constructed a questionnaire called the "Goal Inventory". A factor analysis resulted in 11 factors, which could be organized in terms of the four basic tendencies. This is shown in the following list (p. 100):

"I. *Need satisfactions*
  A. Satisfactions in life
  B. Love and family
  C. Sex and self-gratification

II. *Self-limiting adaptation*
  D. Self-limitation caution
  E. Adaptiveness and submissiveness
  F. Avoidance of hardships

III. *Creative expansion*
  G. Self-development
  H. Power, fame

IV. *Upholding of internal order*
  J. Moral values
  K. Political and/or religious commitments
  L. Success"

We shall later return to the results of the studies made with the help of the Goal Inventory.

There remains to be mentioned one more main concept in Charlotte Bühler's theory, the "integrating self". This term is implicitly defined in this way (p. 349):

"As indicated in the Introduction and in the first chapter, we believe that integration is being accomplished by the self, which we assume to be the core system of the personality. We consider the ego, to which modern ego psychologists ascribe the role of integrator, as primarily a conscious, organizing agency within the realm of reality.

The self, however, appears to us to be a subconscious system which stores the individual's potentialities and their imminent directives. It represents and develops his intentionality toward ultimate fulfillment, a stage he is expected to reach by realizing his potential, modified as it may be by external influences."

3. According to recent correspondence Dr. Bühler has further developed her theory about the four basic tendencies in her contribution to "Essays in Honor of Maslow" (in press).

Finally, we shall *summarize* the above representations of terms and hypotheses in Charlotte Bühler's theory:

The individual is born with an inherited *"Life-cycle structure"*, which co-determines the *goals* of life in conjunction with environmental factors.

The life-cycle structure includes four *basic tendencies*, which determine different goal patterns in different phases of the life-cycle and in different individuals. The four basic tendencies are:

1) the tendency to *need satisfaction,* 2) the tendency to *self-limiting adaptation,* 3) the tendency to *creative expansion* and 4) the tendency to upholding of *internal order*. These four basic tendencies normally dominate four successive phases of the life-cycle.

In addition to these four basic tendencies there is a fifth goal-determining factor, the *"integrating self"*, which is the unconscious "core system of personality".

The *"goals"* determined by all these goal-determining factors are *end states of the basic tendencies* – including the basic needs of hunger, thirst, sex, etc. If a goal is conscious it is called an *"intent"*.

(2.1.). *The main H-terms* in Charlotte Bühler's theory are: "goal", "need", "intent", "tendencies", "self" and "life-cycle structure". They are all defined – explicitly or implicitly – in the quotations above.

We have found it difficult to classify these H-terms according to their *surplus meaning*. Nevertheless, we have come to the conclusion that most of Charlotte Bühler's H-terms are H_N-*terms* referring to hypothetical variables with a *neutral* surplus meaning.

It is possible that intent is an exception and can be classified as an H_M-term, as it refers to a hypothetical variable with mentalistic surplus meaning ("an image based on a previous perceptual experience", p. 4).

"Self" and "life-cycle structure" are *dispositional* terms, as they refer to certain hypothetical structures which have a lifelong existence; "intent" is a *functional* term. But "tendency", "need" and "goal" are terms with *double-meaning:* they refer both to certain *dispositional* variables (lasting structures) and to the *functional* variables – the corresponding variables in an *activated* state. This is similar to the use of the term "need" found in the theories of Maslow, Murray and Rogers.

(2.2.). *The hypotheses* in Charlotte Bühler's theory are not formulated – or reformulated in such a way that it is possible to make the classification into *theoretical* and partly *empirical* hypotheses. Nevertheless, we think that it is possible to classify the hypotheses as being rather *complex*.

Although we have found no explicit statements about the kind of *functional relationships* presupposed, we believe that it is correct to classify the functional relationships as being *causal deterministic*. We have *not* in any case found any formulations of *indeterministic* presuppositions, which occasionally are found in humanistic theories and especially in existentialist philosophy.

3. The Descriptive Stratum

3.1. The *abstract* D-level contains Charlotte Bühler's "laws" of the life-cycle consisting of five life phases. A very concise description of this is presented by her on p. 44, which we reproduce here as Fig. 16.1.

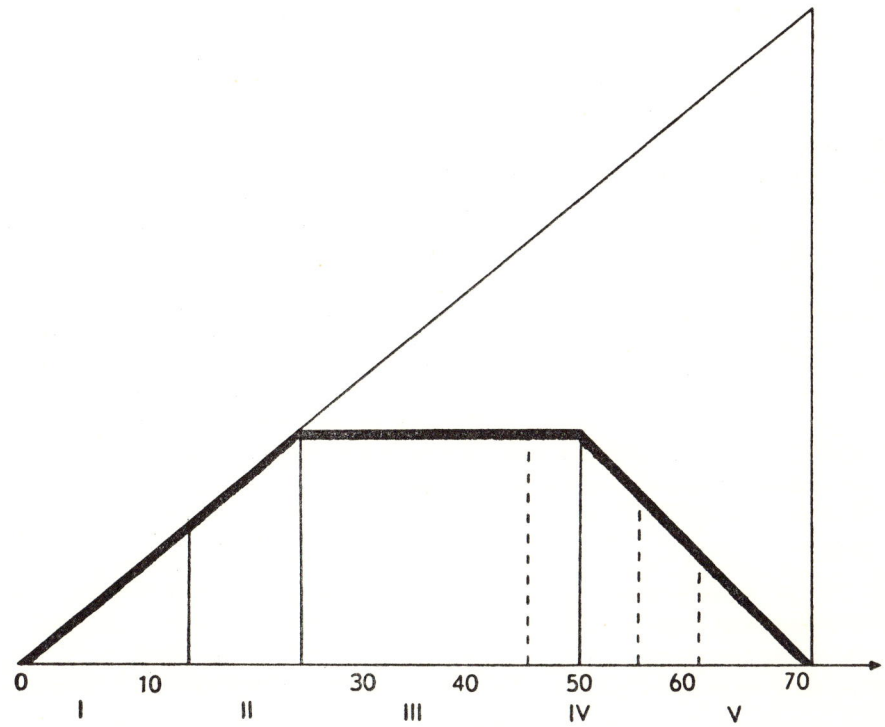

Fig. 16.1. Schematical Model Showing the Underlying Biological Process of Growth, Reproduction and Decline.

The straight line represents the years from 0 to 70 +, with subdivisions of decades. The heavy line represents the curve of accelerated growth from birth to a maximum of about 25 years, of relative stability between about 25 to about 50 years of age, of decline from approximately 50 years to the end. These phases are still essentially applicable, even though modern medicine has increased longevity.

The diagonal line represents schematically the onset and continuous growth of reproductive products.

The vertical full and dotted lines represent at 15 the mean age of beginning of reproductivity, which may occur any time between 10 and 20 years of age; at 25 the latest end of accelerated growth; at 45 to 55 to 60 the end of reproductivity, varying between individuals and both sexes; at 50 to 60 the beginning of decline.

The Roman figures I to V represent schematically conceived five phases of life: I: Period of accelerated growth before reproductivity sets in; II: Period of continuing of accelerated growth with beginning ability to reproduce; III: Period of relative stability between accelerated growth and decline, period of reproductivity; IV: Period of loss of reproductivity, at least for the female sex, and beginning decline; V: Period after reproductivity and of decline.

326 . *Bühler's Theory*

Another part of Charlotte Bühler's theory contains a rather general, abstract description of empirical relationships found in connection with the research carried out on the Goal Inventory. We quote from Bühler's and Massarik's book in order to give the reader an impression of the research results (pp. 100–101):

"A comparison of ten relatively well-adjusted and well-functioning nonpatients was made with 30 patients who were classified in three groups of ten, according to the severity of their neuroses. It allows the following tentative statements:

Theoretically speaking, we can distinguish between favorable and unfavorable goal patterns. Favorable patterns are patterns of factorial percentiles which, in a clinical evaluation, would indicate a personally and socially constructive attitude toward life. People who set their goals according to these patterns may be expected to have love in their life, to care for other people's welfare, and also to believe in their own self-realization. Furthermore, they seem to be aware of reality and able to accept reasonable degrees of limitations and/or hardships.

Unfavorable patterns are patterns of factorial percentiles which indicate a personally and socially unconstructive attitude toward life. These include patterns revealing lack of love, lack of concern for others, or also an overemphasis on the rights of others, disbelief in one's own self-realization or unrealistic expectations, disregard of reality, an inability to accept limitations and hardships, an unreasonably selfrestrictive or submissive attitude and/or an exaggerated willingness to take burdens on to oneself. The goal patterns of the well-functioning person on the whole were more in agreement with a factor distribution that could be called "favorable" to a fulfilling way of life. Their profiles show high factors B, G, and F, with the exception of older pepole's G being regressed. They also appear to have adequate degrees of A, C, D and L, while the distributions of E, F, H, J and K vary with each individual. In addition, these profiles tend to distribute themselves over medium and high percentiles. "Unfavorable" profiles tend to show great variations of percentiles and excessively high and low scores. Depressed persons tend to score in the low to medium percentiles, while very demanding persons have excessively high scores."

3.2. The *concrete D-level* of Charlotte Bühler's theory consists of the many descriptions of life histories which she and her co-workers have studied. In addition, there are descriptions of material from therapeutical interviews.

3.3. The *descriptive units* employed by Charlotte Bühler (and co-workers) are both *molar* ("macroscopic") and *molecular* ("microscopic"). But the molar unit – the course of life – is the most characteristic for her.

4. *The theory as a Whole*

(4.1.). The formal properties of Charlotte Bühler's theory place it in the class of *explanatory sketches*. The presentation is purely *verbal*, but very clear and precise. No models are used in the *explanations;* the above reproduced "schematical model" of the life-cycle is a *descriptive* model.

(4.2.). The *epistemological properties* of Charlotte Bühler's theory are those of an $S\text{-}H_N\text{-}R\text{-}theory$, i. e., a neutral explanatory theory (as most of the H-terms employed are H_N-terms).

4.3. We have not been able to calculate the Hypotheses Quotient, but we should judge the *theory-empiry ratio* to be in the middle range: i. e., a rather *empiristic theory*.

Concluding Remarks. We hope that our analysis of Charlotte Bühler's theory has demonstrated the original combination of *developmental and humanistically oriented personality theory*, through which she has integrated some of the best qualities from classic experimental, developmental studies with a broad humanistic and existentialist orientation. Through this contribution she has gained a position as *one of the great integrators in psychology*.

Eysenck's Theory

Introduction

The British psychologist *H. J. Eysenck* is one of the well known contemporary psychologists, because of his work within the field of personality theory. Since the Second World War he has written a dozen books, edited or co-authored another dozen and written numerous papers in journals. He is the only European personality theorist who can be compared to the (British-)American personality theorist, *R. B. Cattell*, both in his approach to personality (factor analysis) and in his productivity.

The only reason for not devoting a whole chapter to Eysenck – as we did to Cattell – is that Eysenck first included motivational concepts and hypotheses in his theory at a much later point than did Cattell.

Eysenck's production until now is divided into three periods: In the first period he constructed a purely *descriptive system* of personality based upon factor analysis and presented in his first book: *Dimensions of Personality* (1947).

In the second period he related his descriptive system to *explanatory theories in experimental psychology* – especially the theories of *Pavlov* and *Hull*. The main works from this period are: Eysenck (Ed.): *Dynamics of Anxiety and Hysteria* (1957), *Experiments in Personality* (1960), Eysenck (Ed.): *Experiments in Behavior Therapy* (1964) and Eysenck (Ed.): *Experiments in Motivation* (1964)[4]. As can be seen from the titles of these books, he became interested in the *application* of his experimental personality theory during this period.

In the third period he has concentrated on the *biological* – especially the neurophysiological – basis of personality factors. The chief work from this period is *The Biological Basis of Personality* (1967).

---

4. This book was reviewed in the 4th edition of my "Theories of Motivation" (1968).

328 . *Eysenck's Theory*

As this book contains a general theory of personality – including some motivational constructs – we have decided to make a systematological analysis of it.

1. *The Metastratum*

(1.1.). Eysenck makes no explicit formulations of his *philosophical presuppositions*. But we can infer from the context as a whole that he – like most other modern psychologists – has adopted *logical empiristic epistemology* and the related *neutral monistic* theory of the psychosomatic problem. We can also infer a presupposed *biological* conception of man.

(1.2.). The *metatheoretical propositions* are rather explicitly stated. Thus Eysenck writes in the *Epilogue*, p. 340:

"What has been presented is a *model* of certain aspects of personality and a *theory* to explain the working of that model."

Thus it is obvious that he regards his type of explanation as a *"model explanation"*.

Eysenck also expresses his view of the *functions* of theories in the *Epilogue*, p. 340:

"Any theory in this perplexing field is almost by definition a "weak" theory (Eysenck, 1960); its purpose is to guide research along promising and fruitful lines rather than to fulfill the function of a "strong" theory, which is to provide universally accepted laws from which rigourous deductions can with safety be made. All "strong" theories started out as "weak" theories; the heliocentric view of the universe as advocated by Aristarchus or even by Copernicus, was weak in this sense and was rejected by such men as Archimedes for what at the time were excellent reasons (e.g., the failure to observe stellar parallax). The theory here put forward will have to earn its bread and butter rather by giving rise to interesting and important experiments than by being "right" in some absolute sense; it may in due course grow into a strong theory - - -."

From this quotation the reader can understand that Eysenck has an *instrumentalistic*, metatheoretical point of view, which – in our opinion – is in no way in contradiction with his latest interest in "reduction" to physiological theory. We have found precisely the same metatheoretical position in the theories of *Berlyne, Konorski, Pribram, Sokolov* and others analyzed in this book. Eysenck's own evaluation is clearly set forth in the preface (p. XII):

"To me its seems that the causal links postulated between personality variables on the one hand, and neurological and physiological discoveries on the other, make the whole model more realistic and take it out of the field of solipsistic speculation in which the shool of the "empty organism" thrives."

From this quotation it seems to be correct to infer that Eysenck regards his latest theory as a true "reductive" theory – or at least as an approach in that direction. We shall return to this later.

(1.3.). He is still more explicit in the formulations of his *methodological pro-*

positions. Thus he devotes almost the whole of Chapter 1 ("The Two Faces of Psychology") to the presentation of his methodological propositions. The "two faces" alluded to in the title of the chapter are the two main methodological divisions of psychology: *general, experimental psychology and differential, personality psychology*. He presents – in connection with reports concerning many concrete empirical studies – a very convincing argumentation for the *methodological position that these two parts of psychology must be integrated* if psychology is to develop along the same lines as the older natural sciences.

Eysenck discusses the various ways in which such an integration between the two disciplines could be achieved. He concludes the chapter in this way (p. 33):

"We would suggest therefore that the most useful approach to the problem of reuniting the two large areas of psychology which are at present so sadly disjointed would be the one which made use first of the descriptive approach to isolate the main dimensions of personality and then of the hypothetico-deductive approach. In the latter, the main dimensions were tentatively identified with concepts in experimental and general psychology, deductions were made from this identification, and experiments were carried out to test the value of these deductions. In this way we might hope to end up with a unified psychology presenting a single face to the world rather that the present somewhat schizophrenic, Janus-like apparition."

With this integrative methodology Eysenck is in company with such psychologists as Cattell, McClelland and Atkinson. The last two have, however, started their synthesis from the other side, the experimental psychology of motivation. It is very encouraging when psychologists approach the same goal from different angles. Perhaps we shall get some results in the near future.

2. *The Hypothetical Stratum*

(2.0.). We can *summarize* the content of Eysenck's theory in this way:

On the basis of *specific responses* in concrete situations the psychologist can infer the existence of certain *habits* which are found to be correlated. On the basis of these correlations and with the help of factor analysis Eysenck has constructed a number of *traits*. The correlations between these traits form the basis for the construction of some *personality factors of a higher order*. He calls them *"types"* or *"dimensions"* and postulates the existence of two independent "types" or "dimensions" of personality: *"Emotional stability vs. Neuroticism"* ("N") and *"Extraversion vs. Introversion"* ("E")[5].

Eysenck has constructed these two personality types which are rather similar to Cattell's and other psychologists' second-order factors. Later – in his second period – he has related these personality factors to some of the *hypothetical variables* dealt with in experimental psychology.

---

5. The reader may remember, that Cattell also found the same two higher-order factors, but Cattell prefers to work with the less abstract *traits*.

"Emotional Stability vs. Neuroticism" (N) is related to the hypothetical variable *"anxiety"* (or "general, emotional *drive"*) found in the theories of Hull and Spence. Eysenck summarizes the relationships in this way (p. 52):

"We may perhaps summarize our evaluation of the general theory of emotionality as a personality trait and its influence on learning and other psychological variables by making the following points: (a) In a very broad sense there is much evidence to support the suggestion that emotion acts as a drive. (b) Emotionality, neurotism, or anxiety, conceived of as personality variables, are descriptive concepts which refer to a greater emotional arousability of certain people, as compared with others. (c) Emotionality as so conceived is productive of stronger than average drive in emotion-producing situations. (d) Such emotions acting as drives may lead to facilitation of performance or to deterioration of performance depending on complex interactions between amount of drive present, task difficulty, stress experience, and the various other independent variables discussed in this chapter. (e) Proper quantification of all these variables is essential before confident predictions can be made in the individual case. (f) Without such quantification the theory may still be useful in predicting performance at extreme ends of the scale (where there can be little doubt about the precise predictions to be made) and in mediating an understanding of certain everyday life phenomena which otherwise might be difficult to comprehend."

The next step in Eysenck's theorizing is the presentation of evidence for the *neurophysiological basis* of the two main variables. The two personality dimensions, "Extraversion vs. Introversion" ("E") and "Emotional stability vs. Neuroticism" ("N") are related to two different parts of the brain; E to the ascending reticular activating system (the ARAS) and N to the so-called "visceral brain" (the "VB") including the limbic system and the hypothalamus. He summarizes this on p. 230:

"The position which will be argued in this chapter accepts as a fundamental reality the existence of two major, independent dimensions of personality, E and N. It identifies differences in behaviour related to the former with differential thresholds in the various parts of the ascending reticular activating system, and differences in behavior related to the latter with differential thresholds of arousal in the visceral brain (MacLean, 1958, 1960), i.e., the hippocampus, amygdala, cingulum, septum, and hypothalamus. It does not postulate complete independence of these structures but only relative and partial independence; as Gellhorn and Loofbourrow (1963) have pointed out, "it is obvious, since ascending and descending pathways connect the reticular formation with the hypothalamus, that under experimental conditions similar effects may be produced by stimulation of either structure, but this fact should not obscure the fundamental functional difference between the two structures." Similarly, we may say that, depending upon external stimulation, similar or different effects may be produced by these two structures."

Eysenck criticizes *Elisabeth Duffy* and others for not discriminating between these two systems in their theories of activation (cf. Chapter 4 of this book). He suggests the following terminology (p. 233):

"For ease of discussion we will use the terms "activation" and "arousal" in this specialized sense, as referring to autonomic and reticular activity respectively; to use them as synonyms, as is the custom, seems to invite confusion between two clearly distinct types of excitation."

The more exact relationship between the "Extraversion vs. Introversion" dimension and the RAS is formulated very precisely in the following summarizing passage (p. 241):

"Our general statement of the theory relating extraversion-introversion and the reticular formation arousal system postulated a higher level of arousal in introverts and a higher level of inhibition in extraverts."

Eysenck makes reference to Sokolov's theory which we have also analyzed in this chapter. He seems to agree with Sokolov to a considerable extent concerning the rôle of the RAS. Finally, he concludes his evaluation of the status of his own theory with the following words (p. 255):

"A similar statement may perhaps be made in summary of all the theoretical discussions offered in this chapter. The psychological data quoted in Chapters II and III demand certain neurophysiological structures as explanatory concepts; neurophysiologists have discovered structures of the requisite type which fit surprisingly well the requirements of the psychologists. One might almost say that if the hypothalamus and the reticular formation had not been discovered, psychologists would have had to invent them – and up to a point, as Hebb forcefully pointed out in his allusion to the "conceptual nervous system", that is precisely what they did. The fact that the needs of psychological data and the findings of the neurophysiologists agree so well is not of course proof of the propositions advanced in this chapter; it is conceivable, although perhaps not altogether very likely, that different and as yet unknown structures might exist in the brain stem and the midbrain which served the function of mediating the personality features associated with neuroticism and extraversion. Until methods of obtaining direct evidence of the postulated association are worked out, one can only acknowledge the weaknesses of the theory presented, while pointing out at the same time that even in its existing state it has enabled many investigators to make testable predictions and to verify these predictions experimentally; this of course is one of the main functions of a good theory. Similarly, the theory has enabled us to give a unified account of the experimental facts as they are known to date; this is the other main function of a good theory. Only future work will tell whether much or any of the theory will survive further testing, particularly the direct kind of neurophysiological study which so needs to be done."

It is obvious from this passage that Eysenck's theory has developed in the direction of a physiological explanatory theory.

(2.1.). After this summary of his theory we shall turn to the systematological classification of *the H-terms*. The main H-terms from the first descriptive theory are the *personality factors* E and N. In the second theory they are identified with – or at least related to – the following hypothetical variables: The E factor is related to *excitation and inhibition* and the N factor to *"emotional drive"*.

In the third theory these variables are related to the *arousal of the RAS* and the *activation of the visceral brain* (VB) respectively.

(2.1.1.). The *surplus meaning* of these H-terms is *neutral* for the first two theories and *physiological* for the last one. In other words the personality factors E and N and the hypothetical variables "excitation", "inhibition" and "emotional drives" are H_N-*terms*, while the "arousal of RAS" and the "activation of VB" are H_o-terms.

(2.1.2.). The H-terms can be classified according to the *duration of the existence* of the corresponding variables in this way: The *personality factors* are *dispositional* terms. (Eysenck devotes a whole chapter to the presentation of evidence for the inheritance of the personality factors E and N). The *hypothetical variables* "Excitation", "inhibition" and "emotional drive" are all *functional* terms. But the terms "activation of the VB" and "arousal of the RAS" refer to both a set of *functions* ("activation" and "arousal") and a set of *dispositions* (the RAS and the Visceral Brain).

(2.1.3.). Because of the *effect* of the corresponding variables all H-terms can be classified as *dynamic* terms. Eysenck's theory presupposes that the addition of some *cognitive* variables will have a directive effect.

(2.2.). *The hypotheses* in Eysenck's theory can be classified on the basis of a systematic reconstruction of his own explicit formulations on pp. 52 and 79, which have already been quoted. They may be stated as follows:

1. hypothesis: *Behavior*(R) is determined by a complicated interaction between *excitation and inhibition* (E/I) of cognitive (cortical) processes as well as of *motivational processes*, i. e., emotions and drive states (D_e). As a formula: $[H(E/I) \times H(D)] \to R$.

2. hypothesis: The *excitation-inhibition* (E/I) of the cortex is determined by *arousal of the RAS* ("RAS-arousal"). As a formula:
   H(RAS-arousal) → H(E/I).

3. hypothesis: *Arousal* of the RAS is determined by internal and external *stimuli* ($S_i + S_e$). As a formula:

   $S_i + S_e$ → H(RAS-arousal).

4. hypothesis: The *motivational processes* (D_e) are determined by *activation of the "Visceral Brain"* (VB-activation"). As a formula:

   H(VB-activation) → H(D).

5. hypothesis: The *VB-activation* is determined by internal and external stimuli ($S_i + S_e$). As a formula:

   $S_i + S_e$ → H(VB-activation).

6. hypothesis: Optimal *performance* ($R_{performance}$) is determined by an optimal balance setween *motivation* (D_e) and *task difficulties* (S_T). As a formula:

$S_T \rightarrow H(D_e) \rightarrow R_{performance}$.

7. hypothesis: The courses of the *cognitive* processes (E/I) and the *motivational* processes (D) are influenced by a hierarchy of *inherited personality factors* (H(E) and H(N)). As a formula:

$[H(E) + H(N)] \rightarrow [H(E/I) \times H(D)]$.

8. hypothesis: The *personality factor* "E" (extraversion-introversion) via the *cognitive* processes (E/I) determines individual differences in behavior. These individual differences in behavior vary from *hysterical-psychopathic disorders* via *extraverted* and *introverted behavior patterns* to *dysthymic disorders*. As a formula:

$H(E) \rightarrow H(E/I) \rightarrow R(extra/intro)$.

9. hypothesis: The *personality factor* "N" (emotional stability vs. neuroticism) determines individual differences in behavior via the *motivational* processes (D_e). These individual differences vary from *normal emotional stability* to the *neurotic, emotional instability* found in dysthymics and psychopaths. As a formula:

$H(N) \rightarrow H(D_e) \rightarrow R(emotional)$.

We have reconstructed the above hypotheses placing emphasis on the more general and on the motivational aspects.

We have summarized these reformulated hypotheses in a diagram (Fig. 16.2.).

(2.2.1.). On the basis of these symbolic reformulations of Eysenck's hypotheses we can make the following classification into S-H, H-H and H-R-hypotheses:

1. *Purely theoretical (H-H) hypotheses:*
   Hypotheses No. 2, 4 and 7. In all: 3 hypotheses.

2. *Partly empirical hypotheses:*
   a. S-H-hypotheses: No. 3, 5 and the first part of No. 6. In all: 3 hypotheses.
   b. H-R-hypotheses: No. 1, the second part of No. 6, No. 8 and 9. In all: 4 hypotheses.

   (2.2.2.). The *complexity* of the hypotheses:

---

6. This is a restatement of the so-called Yerkes-Dodson Law.

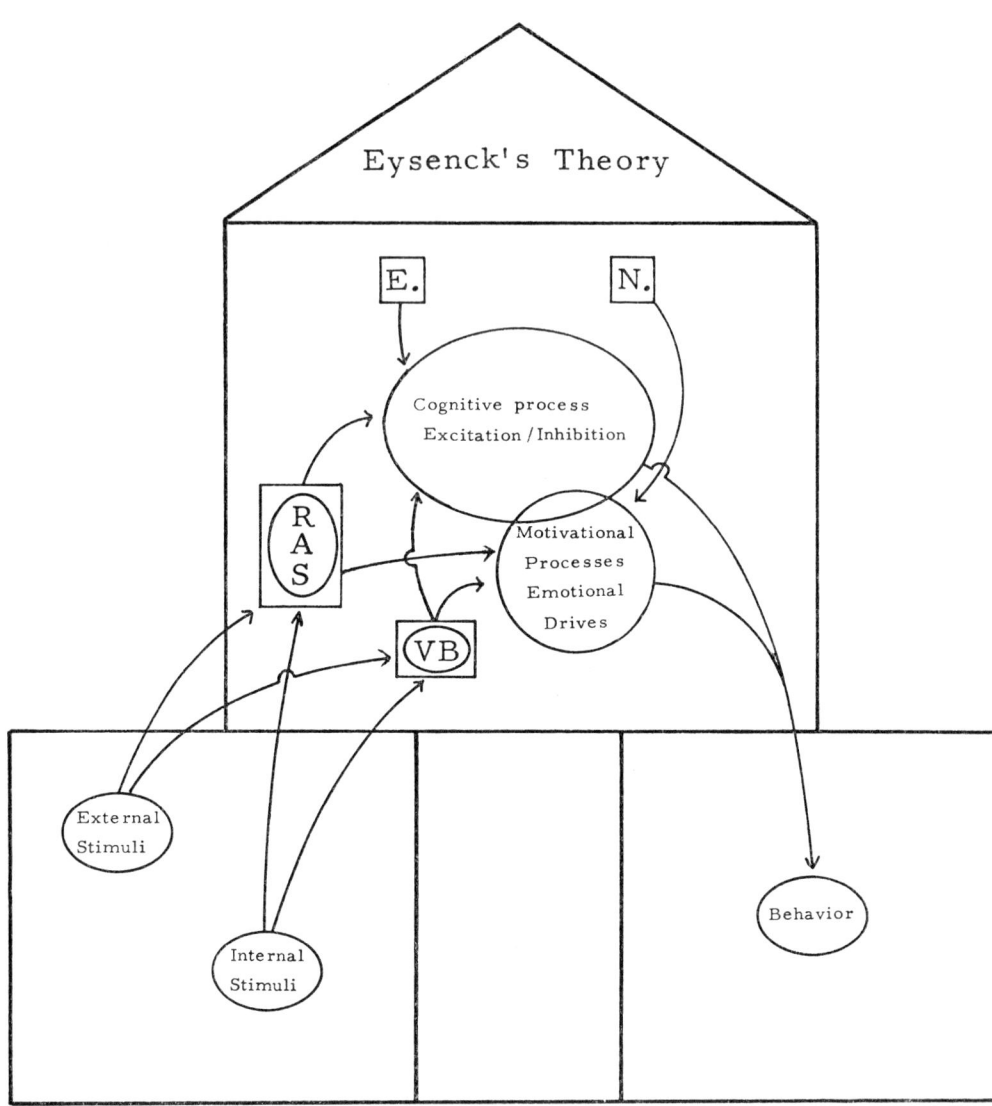

Fig. 16.2 Diagram representing the main hypotheses of Eysenck's theory: Behavior is determined by an interaction of cognitive and motivational processes. Cognitive processes are developed by an excitation-inhibition reaction produced by an arousal of the RAS. The motivational processes are produced by activation of the "Visceral Brain" (limbic system and hypothalamus). These brain structures are aroused or activated by internal and external stimuli. The processes are influenced by the inherited personality factors E (Extraversion-introversion) and N (emotionality or neuroticism) which produce individual differences in behavior.

1. *Multidimensional hypotheses:*
   Hypotheses No. 1 and 7.

2. *One-dimensional hypotheses:*
   The remaining hypotheses.

(2.2.3.). The *functional relationships* can be described as *causal deterministic*. We feel that this is obvious from some of our quotations from Eysenck's book.

3. *The Descriptive Stratum.* Eysenck's theory contains descriptions of a great quantity of empirical data.

(3.1.). The *abstract D-level* contains among other things many abstract *descriptive terms*. The most important D-terms are related to Eysenck's descriptive personality system. It is, however, somewhat difficult to draw a sharp boundary between the H-terms and the D-terms in his hierarchical descriptive system.

The personality factors E and N from the *"type level"* are certainly *hypothetical* as we have already indicated in the above section. But we are in doubt about the classification of *"traits"*. They could be classified as belonging to the H-level. Thus the *extraversive traits:* "sociability" "impulsiveness", "activity", "liveliness" and "excitability" could all be regarded as H-terms. And the same is the case for the *emotional stability traits:* "emotionality", "neuroticism", "ego-strength" and "anxiety". However, the position that the *"traits" are all highly abstract D-terms* could also be defended, as they are terms for correlations between test results.

If the last classification is the most correct, then it follows that all the terms for different kinds of *"disorders":* "psychopaths", "hysterics", "dysthymics", "psychosomatics", "psychotics", neurotics, etc., are all *descriptive terms*.

However, we are not in doubt about the classification of the so-called "habits" in Eysenck's hierarchical system: *"Habits" are D-terms.*

The abstract D-level also comprises all the *general abstract descriptions* of empirical results, the *empirical "laws"*. In the case of Eysenck's theory as well as other empirical personality theories (e. g., Cattell's), the empirical "laws" are not all *S-R-relationships* but also contain *R-R-relationships* (i. e., correlations between test data). It would require much more space, than we have at our disposal to present even the most important of the empirical laws found by Eysenck and his co-workers. Even in the one book we have dealt with – *"The Biological Basis of Personality"* – there are innumerable general empirical (S-R and R-R) relationships. We can only indicate some of the empirical results found by combining experimental methods with test methods. Thus Eysenck has found how the various personality "types" react to: 1) involuntary rest pauses and blocking, 2) sensory thresholds, 3) formation of conditioned responses, 4) learning, 5) perceptual phenomena, 6) motor movements, 7) achievement and aspiration and 8) autonomic reactions.

(3.2.). From these brief indications of the general, empirical results it is obvious that the *concrete D-level* of Eysenck's theory contains empirical data drawn from a variety of sources. The most original data are those collected through his so-called *Maudsley Personality Inventory* (which has recently been revised and is now called the "Eysenck Personality Inventory"). This test battery resembles Cattell's – especially the many "objective tests" in both sets, which are very similar.

In addition to these test data Eysenck also builds upon *experimental data* such as those drawn from experiments with conditioning, learning and performance. Furthermore, he includes considerable *physiological data* (EEG, GSR, etc.) as well as some *pharmacological data* obtained from experiments with drugs.

We think that it is fair to say that *Eysenck's theory is one of the personality theories founded on the broadest empirical basis.*

(3.3.). Finally, we should point out that the *descriptive units* employed by Eysenck are of different kinds, but more *molecular* than molar in sum.

4. The Theory as a Whole

(4.1.). The *formal properties* of Eysenck's theory are the basis for classifying his theory as a *hypotheses system* (as there are only a few explicitly formulated hypotheses or "postulates"), which is very *precisely formulated in partly symbolic form*. Many *graphic models* are employed (most of these being descriptions by means of coordinate systems).

(4.2.). The *epistemological properties* of Eysenck's theory have changed from those of a *neutral* explanatory theory – an $S\text{-}H_N\text{-}R$-theory – in the first two periods of his production to those of a *physiological* explanatory theory – an S-O-R-theory – in the most recent period of his production. This is from a metascientific point of view a very interesting development.

(4.3.). The *theory-empiry ratio* of the theory is very low. We received the impression from reading Eysenck's book that it is a *very empirical theory*. We have calculated the Hypotheses Quotient on the basis of our reconstruction of the theory and reached the following result:

$$\text{H.Q.} = \frac{\Sigma(\text{H--H})}{\Sigma[(\text{S--H}) + (\text{H--R})]} = \frac{3}{3+4} = \frac{3}{7} = 0.43.$$

This result is perhaps not consistent with the above description of Eysenck's theory as being very empirical, but the reader must remember that the H.Q. is calculated solely on the basis of *our reconstruction* of Eysenck's *physiological* explanations and with emphasis placed on the more general and motivational hypotheses. If we had been able to include more of his *differential* personality hypotheses the H.Q. certainly would have been lower.

Concluding Remarks. The present author has until recently regarded Eysenck's theory as a *differential personality theory* with a large number of empirical results and many *practical applications*. But the latest period in his production has forced us to change this "image" of his theory. We feel that it is on the way to becoming a very fruitful *synthesis* of differential personality theory with general experimental psychology. And this synthesis is attained through a *neuropsychological* approach.

Irwin's Theory

Introduction

The American psychologist *Francis W. Irwin* has presented a very original theory of motivation in his book: *Intentional Behavior and Motivation – A Cognitive Theory* (1971). Unfortunately, this book appeared too late to receive the thorough and extensive treatment it deserves, so we are only able to present a short systematological analysis.

1. *The Metastratum*

(1.1.). Irwin's book is – compared to the usual American standards – a rather small book (201 pages), but it is very condensed. The relatively small size may account for the absence of any explicit formulations of the *philosophical presuppositions*. Thus the only grounds we have for inferring the presupposition about the *psychosomatic* problem is a statement (p. 105) that the theory does *not* presuppose a reduction to physics and physiology. It is also stressed, however, that the "theory at no point supposes that behavior violates physical or biological laws; it is not 'vitalistic'." (p. 105). From this we may conclude that Irwin presupposes a kind of *neutral monistic* philosophy.

(1.2.). He devotes a whole chapter (Chapter 8) to his *metatheoretical propositions*. Thus he discusses whether or not the first part of his book actually contains "a theory" and concludes (p. 104):

"It may be concluded, then, that Part I contains elements of a psychological system together with some theory explicitly stated and a good deal more informally assumed in the illustrations. The words "system" and "theory" will be used freely in the remaining chapters as each seems appropriate to the context.

The present author feels that Irwin is fully justified in characterizing his work as "a theory". It is in fact one of the clearest and most consistent psychological theories we have analyzed. But it is not easy to place his theory in one of our systematological categories, because it is so original. We feel quite safe, however, in describing it as a *"constructive theory"* which presupposes an "instrumental" metatheory. We have already quoted a statement against reduction to physics and physiology. Irwin furthermore declares his debt to Tolman, the leader of the "constructionist" (or "instrumentalist") conception of psychological theories.

(1.3.). There are no explicit formulations of *methodological propositions*. But Irwin analyzes several *experiments* both on animals and people, and describes some of his own experiments as well. He shows a preference for the *discrimination-preference experiments*.

A *behavioral* data language is used despite the absence of any explicit argumentation. There is, however, a *very* interesting discussion about the utility of the concept of "consciousness", which may be regarded as an indirect statement about data language. Thus he writes (pp. 107–108):

"As the reader has seen, it has not been necessary to introduce the notion of "consciousness" in defining intentional acts, intended outcomes, and the psychological states prior to these in the present system. The notion itself is extraordinarily vague; and Miller (1942) claims to have found as many as sixteen distinct meanings of its opposite, "unconsciousness."

To say that an organism is conscious of something becomes meaningful in an SAO system if appropriate behavioral criteria can be found to assess the factual correctness of such a statement. The problem hardly arises seriously as long as we are dealing with organisms that display differential responses and biases but not discriminations and act-outcome expectancies, of which the blowfly (Dethier, 1964, 1966) is probably an example. When the latter states appear, some might wish to claim that the organism was conscious of the discriminanda and outcomes that are the objects of these states, which we have already loosely described above as cognitive. The demand would no doubt be still stronger if the organism were able to meet criteria of "perception" of objects; such criteria have not been offered here, but would presumably be stronger than those of discrimination. If, finally, the organism were able to perceive its own psychological states, as human beings can no doubt sometimes do, then, if ever, it would surely be said to be "conscious" of them.

A reader who follows this line of thought with any degree of sympathy may be led, like the writer, to wonder whether the concept of consciousness has any nonredundant meaning at all. If it does, it would seem to have the same criteria as those of perception but to be more general, in that it would refer to cognitions of all kinds of objects whatsoever, including psychological states themselves, rather than being restricted, as perception often is, to cognitions of objects that are non-psychological.

At any rate, SAO theory supposes that to perceive something and to be conscious that one perceives it, or to desire something and to be conscious that one desires it, are two different things, and that the former member of each of these pairs by no means implies the latter. In the writer's view, consciousness in this sense is much less prevalent and accurate than it is often taken to be. Freud has perhaps done psychology a disservice, not by insisting upon the significance of unconscious processes (in his special meaning of this term), but by unintentionally giving more significance that it deserves to the difference between states of which the person is conscious and those of which he is not."

The present author thinks that it should be clear from this long analysis of the concept of "consciousness" that Irwin does *not* favor a phenomenological data language.

2. The Hypothetical Stratum

(2.0.). As Irwin's theory is very clear and precise in its presentation, we can find the best *summary of the hypotheses* by referring to his own summaries found at the end of each chapter. The summary after Chapter 1 thus presents an overview of the whole theory. We present here a diagram (Fig. 16.3A.) which is a model of the theory.

(2.1.). After this summary of the main concepts in his theory we turn to the systematological classification of these concepts.

Provisionally, we have decided to classify the terms "situation", "act" and "outcome" as *descriptive terms* (to which we shall return in a later section) and the rest of the terms in his Fig. 16.3A. as *H-terms*.

We have used the word "provisionally", because it is much more difficult than usual to classify the main terms in Irwin's theory. We should have unhesitatingly classified them as H-terms if Irwin himself had not written the following passage (pp. 106–107):

"Preferences and expectations are dispositional states of the organism, and changes in such states, such as "learning," are processes. Psychology attempts to relate such states and processes to prior and concomitant variables, on the one hand, and to acts, on the other. In a logical sense, then, they are intervening variables. The view taken here is, however, that they are observable objects, and no more hypothetical than the inflammability of a dry match or the noninflammability of a wet match. Furthermore, such states and processes are not only observable, but have been observed. As observed facts, their significance for psychology can be debated but their existence cannot be doubted without questioning the numerous experiments whose results can be put into the standard forms described in Chapters 3 and 5."

From this passage it is obvious that Irwin does *not* regard the main terms "preferences" and "expectancies" as hypothetical terms but rather as "observational" or *descriptive* terms (in our terminology). But in the passage subsequent to that just quoted we find the following statements (p. 107):

"The existence of preferences, expectancies, and other states and processes is known by way of behavior; – – – –"

This statement indicates that "preferences", "expectancies" and other states are observed *indirectly* via behavior, and this means that these terms are *hypothetical terms* according to our systematological taxonomy (i. e., explanatory terms referring to not directly observable entities intervening between situation and behavior).

(2.1.1.). If we then classify Irwin's H-terms, according to *surplus meaning* we must admit that the first impression is that the main terms – "expectancy" and "preference" – are H_M-terms, terms with *mentalistic* surplus meaning. But after some reconsideration we think it is correct to classify his H-terms with *neutral* surplus meaning as H_N-*terms*, because they are defined in a systematic context on the basis of behavior – *not* of phenomenological data.

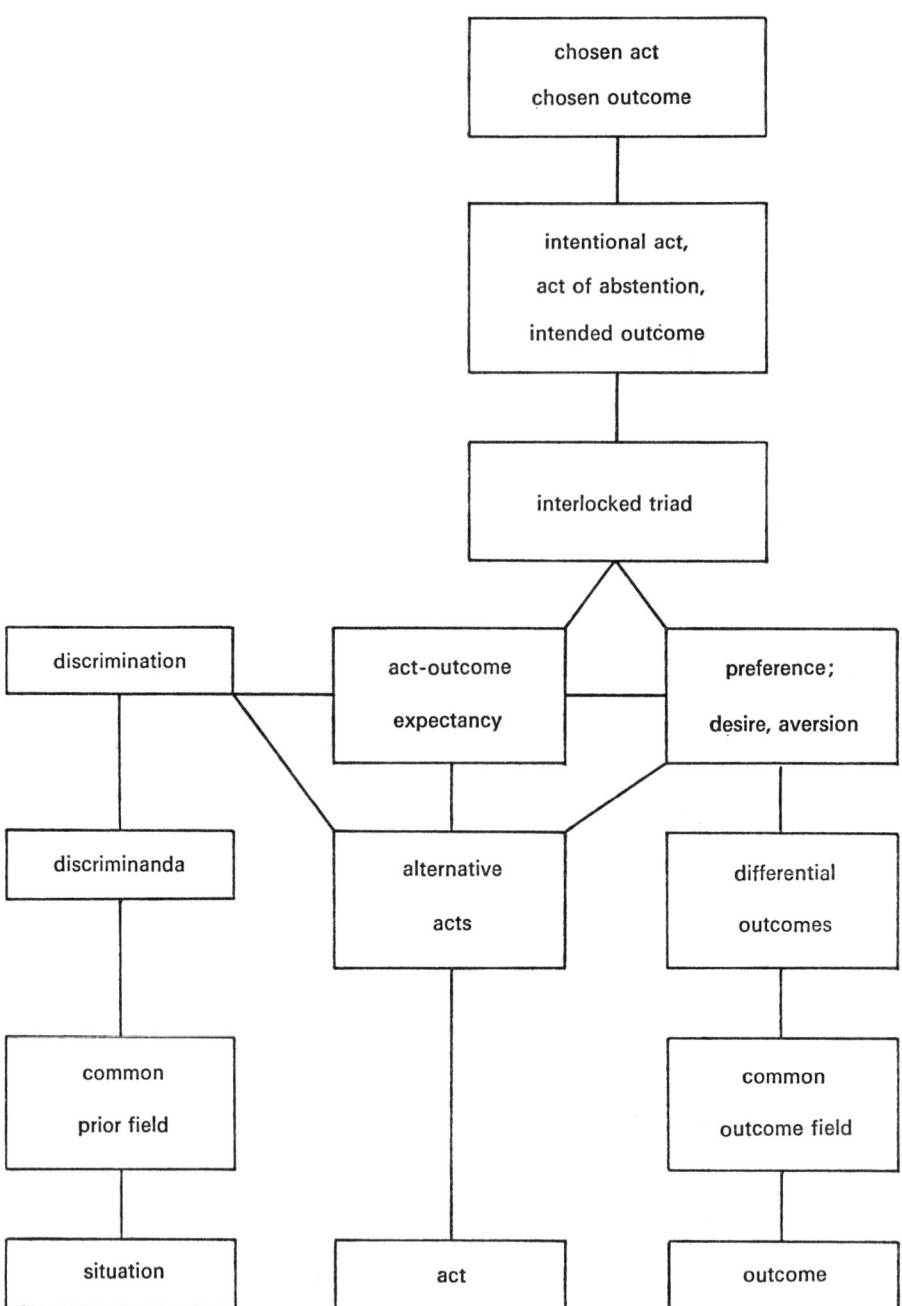

16.3A. Principal concepts introduced in chapter 1 (from F. Irwin: "Intentional Behavior and Motivation", 1971).

(2.1.2.). Classification of the variables according to their *existence* as being either dispositions or functions is also difficult. At one place in the book (p. 68) Irwin writes about the "logical properties of act-outcome expectancies":

"The relation *aa'Eo* is a state of an organism and like preferences, discimdinations, and other psychological states, is not a permanent property of the organism but changes during the course of time under the influence of variables the discovery of which is a principal task of psychology."

This passage shows that he regards the variables as *functional variables* (which in our terminology includes both states and processes). But in another passage already quoted (p. 106) he calls them "dispositional states", which could indicate that they exist for such a long time that they are more like dispositions. But we do not think that he uses the word "disposition" in this sense. Perhaps it is more akin to what the logical empiricists mean when they talk about "dispositions" as *inferred* properties. So we conclude that "expectancies", "preferences" and the other H-terms are actually *functional terms*[6]).

(2.1.3.). Classification of the variables according to their *effect* on behavior is less difficult. Irwin explicitly discusses the relationship of the main terms to the more common terms "motivation" and "cognition" and writes (p. 139):

"The words "motive" and "motivation" are not technical terms in the system and therefore will not be defined. They may be used to refer loosely to matters concerned with preferences, just as "cognition" may be used to refer loosely to matters concerned with discrimination, expectancy, and other aspects of the acquisition and use of knowledge, when precision is either not possible or not aspired to. Thus, the preference in an interlocked triad may be thought of as the motivational element, and the complementary act-outcome expectancies as the cognitive elements, in the definition of an intentional act."

From this quotation it is clear that "expectancy" is a cognitive concept, or, as it is called in our systematological taxonomy: *a directive term*. Irwin refers to "preference" as a "motivational" concept, which in our taxonomy includes both "dynamic" and "vector" terms. We feel, nevertheless, that it is most correct to classify *"preference" as a vector term*, because it refers to a variable having a *combined* dynamic and directive effect on behavior.

Before leaving the classification of the H-terms in Irwin's theory, we should mention that he also discusses the more traditional motivational terms like "drive" and "emotion". Thus he touches on the drive concept and discards it with the following words (pp. 136–137):

"From an SAO point of view, the word "drive", if retained at all, should be understood to mean "any aversive emotional state." The present chapter has set forth the criteria of aversiveness of psychological states; the criteria of "emotionality" will be discussed in Chapter 12. The "energizing," but also the depressing," characteristics of drive are

---

6. Irwin has in Note 4 on pp. 84–85 introduced a distinction between "latent" vs. "active" states, which is similar to our distinction between "dispositions" and "functions". Thus his terms have double meaning – as often seen in psychological theories.

its emotional properties, while the organism's tendency to avoid situations that arouse drive and to seek situations that reduce or eliminate it would reflect its aversiveness. The one-sidedness of this view would be compensated for by the conception of *desired* states, which may also be emotional and thus energizing or depressing, but whose arousal the organism will seek and whose reduction or elimination the organism will resist. Where intentional behavior is concerned, the learning that is required for seeking and avoidance is here presumed to be th acquisition and modification of act-outcome expectancies."

Irwin is a little more positive in his evaluation of the term "emotion", which is discussed in the last chapter of his book. This discussion is summarized in the following conclusion (p. 171):

"The writer's opinion is that the word "emotion," as was said above about "motivation," is useful when precision is either not desired or not attainable; again, like "motivation," it is not a technical term in an SAO system and will not be formally defined. It has been implicit in the discussion of emotional states that they are biasing dispositions, and that they may be desired or aversive or may be associated with, or responsible for, the desiredness or aversiveness of other outcomes; and it should be noted that the concepts of bias desiredness, and aversiveness *are* technical terms and *are defined* in the present system. It is not clear that an attempt to distinguish sharply between emotional and non-emotional biases, desires, and aversions is worth the effort and would, even if successful, reflect a genuine psychological distinction rather than an arbitrary set of criteria drawn from such disparate considerations as those of neural and endocrine physiology, genetics, the topography of behavior, the psychology of learning, and mere convenience. The notion of a biasing disposition is always in the neighborhood when emotions are discussed; what seems to be important is not whether such a disposition is emotional but whether the behavior that one is trying to understand is subject to such and such a disposition and, if so, what concretely the relations happen to be."

From this quotation it is obvious that "emotions" is included in Irwin's theory as a kind of "bias" or "biasing disposition", which influences the preference of outcome[7]).

(2.2.). Turning from the classification of H-terms to the hypotheses we must first determine if there are any explicitly formulated hypotheses in Irwin's theory. We believe that the so-called "diagnostic rules" are hypotheses, and we also interpret Irwin's own metatheoretical statement about these rules as being in accordance with our conception. Thus he summarizes the rules and comments upon them in this way (p. 89):

7. Irwin has made the following comment about our text: "I feel that your statement that emotions "influence the preference of outcome" is a bit vague and not quite what I was trying to say. My view is that (1) emotional states may themselves *be* objects of preference, and that in fact they often *are* markedly desired or aversive; and that (2) like other desired or aversive objects, they may induce desiredness or aversiveness in other objects that bring them about or reduce or eliminate them. These views are expressed on pp. 166–170. This means also that I do not think that, in your Fig. 16.3A, the box containing the word "bias" and the arrow leading to "preference" are appropriate to my conceptions."

"These diagnostic rules can be condensed into the following statements: if *an act is intentional and depends upon two members of an interlocked triad, then it also depends upon the third member of the triad. If, in addition, one of these rules holds and the act occurs (i.e., is chosen), then the third member of the triad exists.*

Rules I, II, and III are taken to be basic principles of a cognitive psychology. That they do not follow from the definition of intentional acts was asserted above and is demonstrated in Note 1 of this chapter. Nor can they be regarded as induced from experimental results; the required experiments do not exist. Rather, their formal status is that of empirical postulates, the credibility of which depends upon the fruifulness of their application and the absence of persuasive counterexamples."

We regard Irwin's formulation about these rules in the above quotation – "empirical postulates" – as equivalent to our term "hypotheses", i. e., explanatory propositions containing H-terms. Thus the condensed statement of the rules could be reformulated in this way:

The basic hypothesis: An intentional act is determined by an "interlocked triad", i. e., a preference and a pair of act-outcome expectancies.

The basic "diagnostic rule": It can be inferred from the knowledge of the existence of two elements in an "interlocked triad" plus the observation of the occurrence of an intentional act, that the third element in the interlocked triad also exists.

We regard this diagnostic rule as a *metaproposition* (or more specifically: a methodological proposition). The above "basic hypothesis" is implicitly contained in Irwin's formulations of the diagnostic rules.

In order to make our reconstruction of Irwin's theory complete we also bring the following explicit formulations of the other implicit hypotheses:

1. Hypothesis: An act-outcome *expectancy* is determined by a *discrimination* of the discriminanda in the *situation*.

2. Hypothesis: A preference – a desire or an aversion – is determined by *expectancies* of act-outcomes influenced by *biasing dispositions* (including "emotional states").

3. Hypothesis: The simultaneous occurrence of *expectancies* and *preference* determines the *act*. If the expectancies and the preference constitute an "interlocked triad", then the act is an intentional act. (This is our reformulation of the above formulated "basic hypothesis" included in the diagnostic rules).

We can reformulate the above three hypotheses in our usual half-symbolic fashion:

1. hypothesis: S(discriminanda) → H(discrimination) → H(expectancy).

2. hypothesis: H[expectancy, bias] → H(preference).

3. *hypothesis:*
   3a. H[preference, expectancies] → R(act).
   3b. H[(preference), (expectancy a + expectancy b)] → R (intentional act).

After this reconstruction of Irwin's theory we are ready for the systematological classification of the hypotheses.

(2.2.1.). *First,* the classification into *theoretical and partly empirical hypotheses.* From the above symbolic reformulation it is obvious, that hypotheses No. 1 is an S-H-hypothesis, hypothesis No. 2 an H-H-hypothesis and hypothesis No. 3 an H-R-hypothesis.

(2.2.2.). The classification according to *complexity* of the hypotheses shows that hypothesis No. 1 is a *one-dimensional* hypothesis, while hypotheses No. 2 and 3 are *multidimensional*. We have not in our reformulations specified the kind of interactions between the hypothetical variables (except in 3b). We do not know if there should be a multiplicative or an additive interaction, so we have only used a comma between the H-terms.

(2.2.3.). The classification of hypotheses according to presupposed *functional relationship* is quite difficult. But we think that Irwin presupposes *causal deterministic* relationships.

Before turning to the descriptive stratum we shall summarize our reconstruction of his theory by presenting it in the form of a model (Fig. 16.3A.).

3. *The Descriptive Stratum*

As already stated it is more difficult than usual to distinguish between the H-level and the D-level in the case of Irwin's theory.

(3.1.). As indicated in our diagram we have classified all the "basic terms": *Situation, Act,* and *Outcome* as belonging to the *abstract D-level*. It is not without hesitation that we have made this classification, because these terms are *not* defined as independent and dependent variables as is usually the case with S-R-terms.

"*Situation*" is defined as including "the physical and social environment of the organism and its own psychological and physiological properties and states prior to an act" (p. 12). Thus Irwin seems to include some *hypothetical* variables in the situation – what he in the above quotation calls "psychological properties". But shortly after he says (p. 12) that "a situation must be describable", and on the next page (p. 13) he describes the properties of the organism in this way:

"To interpret an act, one may need to know the species of the subjects, their age, their sex, their intelligence, their state of nutrition, their emotional state, their states of expectancy or preference, etc."

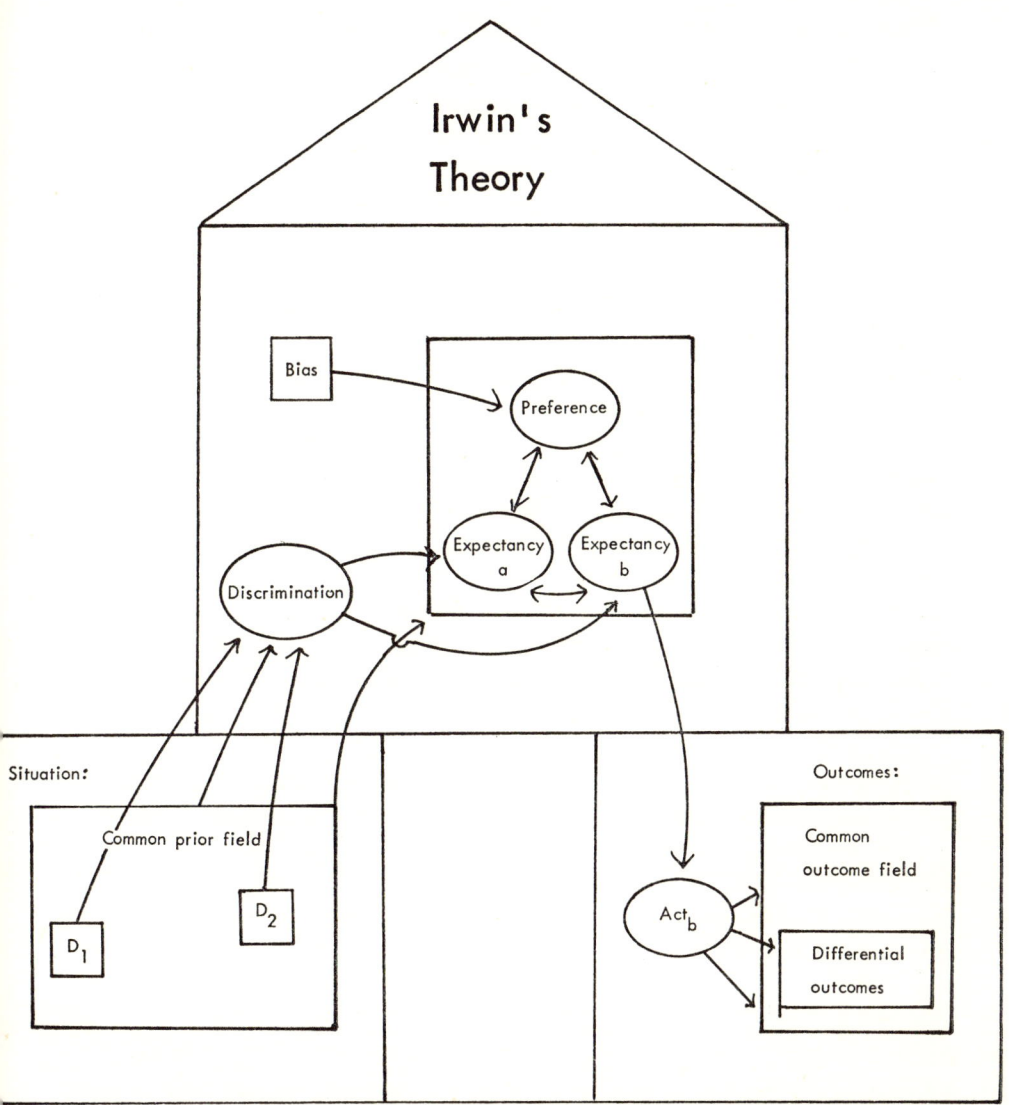

Fig. 16.3A Diagram representing the main hypotheses in Irwin's theory. The *Act* results in *Outcomes* including the "common outcome field" and the "differential outcomes". The Act is determined by the interlocked triad": "preference," "expectancy, a" and "expectancy, b" (related to act, b and its alternative, act, a). The preference is influenced by "bias" (including "emotional states"), and expectancies are influenced by the *Situation*, including the "common prior field" and the "discriminanda" (D_1 and D_2).

Most of these properties would also be classified as independent (S-)variables in other psychological theories. Thus the resemblance to Tolman's "HATE" (heredity, age, training and endocrines) is obvious. Therefore, although all the variables mentioned are not external stimuli, we think it safe to say that they are independent variables which in principle are *descriptive*.

We think that the same is true about the two other basic terms.

"*Act*" is defined as "anything that an organism can be said to do" (p. 17).

"*Outcome*" is defined as "the circumstances of the organism's environment, states, and properties at some time after an act" (p. 20). Thus this is very similar to "situations", which are the circumstances at the time of the act or before it.

If we accept the classification of "situation", "act" and "outcome" as abstract *descriptive terms,* we must also accept "common prior field" ("c.p.f."), "discriminanda", "common outcome field" and "differential outcomes" as *descriptive terms*, (as indicated in our diagram above). To be consistent we must classify "*intentional act*" and "*chosen act*" as descriptive terms. We are in complete agreement with Irwin when he points to the similarity between "intentional act" and Tolman's "purposive behavior". We also think that "intentional act" is similar to Bindra's "goal-directed behavior", although the last mentioned theory does not presuppose such complicated cognitive processes as we find in Irwin and Tolman.

(3.2.). The *concrete D-level* in Irwin's theory consists of the descriptions of experiments – mainly experiments about *discrimination and preference*. Many of these experiments are repetitions of "classic" experiments earlier performed by other psychologists, but some are original contributions to the field by he and his co-workers.

(3.3.). The *descriptive units* of Irwin's theory are mainly *molar,* although he himself quite explicitly states (p. 19) that:

"– – – – it seems wise to refrain from setting boundaries for fundamental concepts and to relegate to the development of the science whatever sharpening is to be done. Acts as minute as action potentials from single nerve cells may be admitted together with acts as extensive as Beethoven's composition of his C-sharp minor Quartet."

4. *The Theory as a Whole*

(4.1.). *The formal properties* of Irwin's theory are those of a very systematically organized system. Even though there are very few explicitly formulated hypotheses, we think that his theory can be classified as a *hypotheses system* which comes close to being a deductive system. The presentation is very precise with many *symbolic formulations*, although they are all of the qualitative kind.

A *graphic model* is used which we presented above.

(4.2.). The *epistemological properties* are those of a *neutral explanatory theory*, an $S-H_N-R$-theory.

(4.3.). The *theory-empiry ratio* is estimated to lie in the middle range. We are able to calculate the Hypotheses Quotient on the basis of our systematic reformulation:

$$H.Q. = \frac{\Sigma(H-H)}{\Sigma[(S-H)+(H-R)]} = \frac{1}{1+1} = \frac{1}{2} = 0.50$$

The H.Q. is also in the middle range, but we wish to point to a source of possible error created by the very small number of explicitly (re-)formulated hypotheses.

Concluding Remarks. Irwin's theory is one of the most original theories we have analyzed. It is more "cognitive" than any other motivational theory we have seen. It is more systematic and precise than most of the phenomenological and humanistic theories of motivation, while at the same time it is able to cope with the most complicated kinds of human motivation. Thus his theory integrates the best things from the behavioristic and the humanistic approaches to psychology.

Irwin's theory really deserved a whole chapter, but its late appearance just before this book was to be finished is the explanation for this relatively brief treatment.

Fowler's Theory

Introduction

The American psychologist *Harry Fowler* has elaborated a theory of curiosity which is presented among other places in his book *"Curiosity and Exploratory Behavior"* (1965) and as a chapter entitled "Satiation and Curiosity" (in K. W. Spence and J. T. Spence (Eds.): *"Psychology of Learning and Motivation"*, Vol. I, 1967). The present analysis is based upon an unpublished analysis made by one of my graduate students, *Anne Vibeke Fleischer*.

1. *The Metastratum*

(1.1.). Fowler presents no explicit formulations of his *philosophical presuppositions*. But we maye feel safe in taking for granted that he – as an American psychologist who belongs to the Hull-Spence tradition – presupposes a *neutral monistic* philosophy of the Mind-Body problem and a *biological* conception of man.

(1.2.). Fowler does make some explicit formulations about *metatheoretical* problems. Thus he states that the contemporary theories of motivation are inadequate in their treatment of curiosity and exploratory behavior. But he found it

348 . *Fowler's Theory*

possible to elaborate one of the existing theories, namely that of Hull and Spence. Thus he has a metatheoretical orientation similar to that of Berlyne, although the two theories' explorations of curiosity are rather different.

Fowler explicitly formulates a metatheoretical conception of hypothetical variables, which is near to that of Miller. Thus he states that the main function of hypothetical variables is to *integrate* the empirically determined relationships between behavior and its determinants. But he stresses that hypothetical terms have to be *operationally defined* and *predictive* if they are to be fruitful.

(1.3.). He also makes some explicit formulations about *methodological* problems. Thus he prefers to study publicly observable phenomena, i.e., behavior, concentrating on measureable aspects. Therefore, he experiments on animals and describes the results in *behavioral data language*.

2. *The Hypothetical Stratum*

(2.0.). Fowler's theory can be summarized in this way: Constant and homogeneous stimulation determines a state of "boredom", which becomes a "source of drive" – in the sense of Brown's theory. The increased drive determines exploratory behavior, which in turn results in a change of stimulation. This reduces boredom and drive, and this drive reduction reinforces the exploratory behavior. The main H-variable, drive, is related to other H-variables in accordance with Spence's version of Hull's main postulate, thus:

R(diversive exploratory) = $f(E) = f[H \times (D + K) - I]$.

In this well known formula "E" is "excitatory potential (or reaction-evocation potential). "H" is "habit strength" (which is determined by the number of trials), "D" is drive (which in this case is largely determined by the constancy of the stimulus situation), "K" is "incentive motivation" (which in this case is determined by the change in stimulation contingent upon the response – cf. Berlyne's "collative variables") and "I" is "inhibition" (which in this case is determined by, among other things, the number of non-reinforced or no-change trials).

From this short summary we can see that Fowler has differentiated "curiosity" motivation into two variables: a "boredom drive" and a kind of "change-incentive motivation".

(2.1.). The H-terms can be classified as H_N-terms with *neutral* surplus meaning. They are all *functional* terms referring to processes or states – except "H" (habit strength), which is a disposition term. D, K and I are *dynamic* terms referring to variables, which have an exclusively activating effect on behavior (although K – or rather the related r_g-s_g – has some directive effects). H is a *directive* term because "habit strength" is a variable with an exclusively directing or steering effect on behavior. E is a *vector* term.

(2.2.). *The hypotheses* are by and large partly *empirical* hypotheses with rather few purely theoretical hypotheses. The main hypothesis – Spence's version of Hull's postulate – is a *complex*, multidimensional hypothesis. There are no explicit formulations about the supposed functional relationships, but we venture the guess that it is a kind of causal *determinism*.

3. The Descriptive Stratum

Through his experiments with rats Fowler has formulated certain "laws" which can be stated in this way:
1. The animal responds to and for *change* in the stimulus situation by specific and diversive *exploratory* behavior.
2. The *intensity* of the exploratory behavior is proportional to the *magnitude* of change in the stimulus situation (up to a certain limit, when change in the stimulus situation results in *avoidance* behavior).

The descriptive unit of Fowler's theory is *molar*.

4. The Theory as a Whole

(4.1.). *The formal properties* of Fowler's theory are such that they must be classified as a *hypotheses system*, which is rather precisely formulated in *partly symbolic* statements. Some *graphic models* are employed.

(4.2.). *The epistemological properties* of Fowler's theory are of such a nature that it must be classified as a *neutral explanatory theory* – an S-H_N-R-theory.

(4.3.). *The theory-empiry ratio* is low. On the basis of a detailed reconstruction of Fowler's theory formulated into 15 hypotheses, Miss Anne Vibeke Fleischer has calculated the following:

$$H.Q. = \frac{3}{6+6} = 0.25.$$

Conclusion. The present author thinks that Fowler has demonstrated the fruitfulness of elaborating the Hull-Spence theory into a theory of curiosity, which is a valuable alternative to Berlyne's neuropsychological theory.

Luria's Theory

Introduction

The Soviet psychologist, *A. R. Luria*, is one of the most well known, contemporary Soviet psychologists in the Western World. He has been working in the field of neuropsychology since the 1920's and several of his books have been translated into English. We have selected one of his latest books which is available in English translation as: *"Human Brain and Psychological Processes"* (1966). Although this book does not contain a motivational theory as such we find so much of a general psychological theory that it can prove useful to compare it with other neuropsychological theories analyzed in this book, e. g., those of Berlyne, Konorski, Pribram, etc. The following systematological analysis is based upon a preliminary, unpublished study made by Miss *Jutta Gravsholt,* one of my graduate students.

1. The Metastratum

(1.1.). Although Luria has not explicitly formulated his *philosophical presuppositions* about the Mind-Body problem, we can infer from the text that he has a *materialistic* point of view regarding this problem. It is, however, a very sophisticated kind of "materialism", which comes close to neutral monistic philosophy, so common among Western philosophers and psychologists.

His "philosophy of Man" is expressed very clearly in the following passage (Luria, 1966, pp. 21-22):

"In one respect, however, human mental activity differs radically from the reflex activity of the animal. This refers to its *social-historical origin and its structural organization."*

Among the more important achievements of Soviet psychology, as may be found in the writings of many authors (Vygotsky, 1956, 1960; Leont'ev, 1959, 1961) are the introduction of the historical method into psychology and the confirmation of Marx's statement that the human mind is the result of the social form of life and that the formation of the five external senses is the work of basic processes of world history (K. Marx and F. Engels, *Early Works,* Moscow, 1956, pp. 593-594). This fundamental principle has received concrete application in the work of Soviet psychologists and of a number of Western scholars (Wallon, 1942, etc.), and it has provided a completely new approach to human psychological processes which is completely different from that advocated by contemporary positivism.

The behavior of an animal, however complex, is the result of two factors: inborn tendencies, on the one hand, and direct, individual experience, formed in the course of conditioned-reflex activity, on the other. In contrast to this, the conditions in which human behavior is formed include yet a third factor, beginning to play a decisive role in the development of human faculties: the assimilation of the experience of mankind in general, which is incorporated in objective activity, in language, in the products of work, and in the forms of social life of human beings.

This social experience not only forms the methods of human work and operations with objects in the external environment but it also creates complex and plastic methods of controlling the individual's own behavior and the wide range of generalized images and ideas composing human consciousness."

This long quotation is presented, because the present author thinks that the Soviet psychologists' conception of Man as expressed by Luria is a very fruitful, "dialectical", synthesis of the purely biological, Darwinian conception of Man, which is shared by most Western psychologists and the old humanistic conception of Man, which at present is having a renaissance in the West due to the so-called "humanistic psychologists". According to the Soviet conception *Man is both a biological and a social historical product*.

(1.2.). Luria does not formulate any *metatheoretical propositions*. It looks as though he conceives of his work mainly as *descriptions* of the results of his empirical studies. But a closer look shows that he also works with some *explanatory* principles containing *hypothetical constructs*. These hypothetical constructs can be conceived of as constituting a brain model, although he does not present it as a graphic model as does Konorski.

(1.3.).Luria is much more explicit in his formulations of *methodological propositions*. Thus he discusses the *factor analytical* method of Spearman and Thurstone, which he criticizes as being too formal and statistical. Notwithstanding he retains some of the most valuable features of factor analysis in his own method, the so-called *"syndrome analysis"*, which he described in this way (Luria, 1966, p. 52):

"In such cases the investigator analyzing the relationship between the mental processes in any one individual usually has a sufficiently accurate idea of the character of the disturbance arising as a direct result of a lesion of the cortical end of one of the analyzers. By observing the secondary disturbances of the systemic consequences of these primary defects and by analyzing them quantitatively and comparing them with a careful description of the mental processes remaining intact in these cases, the investigator can study in its concrete form the mutual relationship between individual forms of mental activity and can deduce from this relationship the factor on which it is based. This method of investigation of patients with local brain lesions has many advantages and, despite the large number of complicating conditions, it may be used as an additional method of factor analysis."

The *methods* employed are *clinical tests* combined with *neurological investigations* of brain lesions in the patients. Sometimes these methods were supplemented by *experiments* in classical conditioning.

The results are presented for the most part in the *behavioral data language*.

2. *The Hypothetical Stratum*

(2.0.). An excellent *summary* of the hypotheses in Luria's theory is presented in the Preface (Luria, 1966, p. XVII):

"According to this ideal human mental processes are to be understood as complex functional systems, having a social-historical origin and exhibiting in their structure different levels of organization. These processes take place as a result of the combined activity of several cortical zones, each of which plays its own specific role in these functional systems and supplies an essential factor for the normal working of the functional system as a whole. A local brain lesion, directly causing the loss of one of the factors concerned in the construction of mental processes, thus leads to a secondary disturbance of the functional system as a whole; however, every disturbance has its own individual character depending on which link of the functional system is affected by each particular local brain lesion. For this reason the analysis of changes in mental processes in patients with local brain lesions may serve not only as an important means of topical diagnosis of brain lesions, but also as a method of study of the structure of mental processes themselves, and may be of fundamental importance for the subsequent development of scientific psychology."

One important concept is his *"complex functional system"*. He refers in this way to "a complex adaptive activity of a whole system" (p. 17). This must be differentiated from another meaning of "function", in which the term denotes a particular property of a tissue. In the latter case "function" always refers to a particular tissue or a particular organ, while in the previously mentioned sense it always refers to an entire functional system consisting of several tissues or organs.

The "complex functional systems" involved in psychological processes such as perception, memory and thinking are constituted of *cortical zones* and *subcortical systems*.

The *cortical zones* are classified into:

1. *primary zones:* the projective areas of the cortex.
2. *secondary zones:* the associative areas of the cortex.
3. *tertiary zones:* these are the so-called "overlapping zones", which consist of an overlapping of the cortical nuclei of the individual analyzers.

The *subcortical systems* are:

1. the Reticular Arousal System.
2. the limbic system.

The cortical zones are involved in the complex functional systems whose functions are *analysis* and *synthesis*. The last mentioned function can be further divided into 1) *simultaneous synthesis* (including perception and conception of relational systems) and 2) *successive synthesis* (including perception of sequences and performance of skilled movements).

The *RAS* is involved in "the maintenance of the general tone of the cerebral hemispheres necessary for preservation of a state of wakefulness" (p. 32).

This system is closely co-ordinated with parts of the cerebral cortex and with *the limbic system*. It is involved in emotional behavior and "there is considerable evidence that it may be regarded os the apparatus for comparing the desired and actual effects, which P. K. Anokhin calls the "action acceptor" – –" (p. 34).

The only place where we have found an explicit statement about motives is in the following passage (Luria, 1966, p. 34):

"The limbic region, which may be regarded as an intermediate formation, belonging partly to the archipallium (Filimonov, 1940, 1944, 1951 and others), plays an essential role in the regulation of animal behavior. In man this region has lost much of its importance. Because of the incomparably greater role of the highly organized motives, social in origin and formulated by means of speech, the function of the formation of intentions and comparison of the results of an action with the motor plan must inevitably be transferred to higher cortical structures. These structures forming part of the cortical end of the motor analyzer, integrate impulses arriving both from other (extero- and proprioceptive) regions of the cortex, and also from lower formations, with impulses in the motor analyzer itself."

As this quotation demonstrates, Luria conceives of "motives" – or at least "the highly organized motives" – as being "social in origin and formulated by means of speech".

This is a conception which is very similar to that of many Western psychologists – especially those belonging to the Hull tradition (Cf. especially the chapters in this book about N. E. Miller's and Brown's theories).

Thus we find that Luria's theory places *language* in an important rôle both in *cognitive* processes and in *motivation*.

(2.1.). The main *H-termini* in this theory are – from our point of view: "functional systems", "syntheses" (successive and simultaneous), "action acceptor", "motor plan", "motives" and "state of wakefulness", "general tone" and "natural drives"[8]).

All these H-termini are H_o-termini with *physiological* surplus meaning.

"Functional systems" and "action acceptors" are *dispositional* terms, while "syntheses", "motor plan", "motive" and "drive" are *functional* terms.

Drive" is a purely *dynamic* term, while "motive", "motor plan", "action acceptor" and "functional system" are *vector* terms. "Syntheses" is a purely *directive* term.

(2.2.). *The hypotheses* are not explicitly stated, but from a systematic reconstruction made by Miss Jutta Gravsholt it appears that there are both purely *theoretical* (H-H) hypotheses as well as partly *empirical* (S-H and H-R) hypotheses. All the hypotheses are rather *complex* or "multidimensional", and they presuppose *causal-deterministic* functional relationships.

3. *The Descriptive Stratum*

The main part of Luria's book consist of descriptions of the results of neurological investigations, clinical tests and experiments with patients suffering from brain lesions. In these descriptions several *abstract*, descriptive terms are used, uch as "analyzer", "signal reflexes", "kinetic melodies", "goal-directed behavior", "voluntary behavior", etc. In addition, there are many anatomical descriptions in connection with individual cases of lesions.

There are no formulations of S-R-laws of the traditional kind, but the *syndromes* may be conceived of as general, empirical relationships between various "symptoms" (which are R-variables). Thus they are *R-R-* rather than S-R-*laws*.

The *descriptive units* employed are rather *molecular*.

---

8. The last mentioned term is used in Luria's letter to Professor Douglas Bowden (1971), which is published in the Danish Journal, *Skolepsykologi* (1971, 8, pp. 407–408).

4. The Theory as a Whole

(4.1.). *The formal properties* of Luria's theory correspond to those of an *explanatory sketch*. It contains a very precise, but purely *verbal* discourse.

(4.2.). *The epistemological properties* of the theory are those of a *physiological explanatory, or S-O-R-theory*, and comes very close to being a *descriptive, physiological* theory (a "reductive" theory in the narrow sense).

(4.3.). From the above analysis we should expect *the theory-empiry ratio* to be rather low. But the preliminary reconstruction made by Miss Jutta Gravsholt resulted in the calculation of an H.Q. = 0.75. She thinks, however, that a more thorough and broader analysis – including more of Luria's many books – would result in a lower H.Q.

Concluding Remarks. The above analysis has – we hope – made it clear for the reader, why Luria is so well known – also among Western psychologists. It is a very original and fruitful theory and very broad in its orientation (more than half of the references are to Western psychologists). Therefore, this theory can be an important bridge between Soviet and Western psychology.

Nuttin's Theory

Introduction

The Belgian psychologist, *Joseph (R.) Nuttin*, has worked in the field of motivation for several years and published several papers and books about learning, motivation and personality. We have selected the book *"Reward and Punishment in Human Learning"* (1968) for the purposes of this analysis. It can be regarded as a summary of Nuttin's theoretical and experimental work up to 1968[9]).

The following brief analysis is based upon a preliminary, unpublished analysis made by Gorm Uhrenholdt, one of my graduate students.

1. The Metastratum

(1.1.). Nuttin is not explicit about his *philosophical presuppositions,* including the psychosomatic problem. He is, however, explicit about his philosophy of man. Thus he writes (p. 9):

"The most striking aspect of human behavior is its constructive character – its modifiability in response to new situations and through formulation of new goals. It seems quite

---

9. The book is translated by *Anthony G. Greenwald,* who also has written an appendix to the American edition, which contains Greenwald's own experiments.

inappropriate to seek to understand this constructive property of behavior by studying the habit formation process."

From this passage it is obvious that his conception of man is *humanistic*, close to that of the so-called "humanistic psychologists". But it should be pointed out that he developed his humanistic philosophy before the school itself was organized (c. 1960).

(1.2.). Nuttin's *methatheoretical propositions* are not extensively formulated because he regards his book as an experimental work. He is not, however, negative in his attitude toward theories. He regards his own theory as a general guide to experimental work. Thus he writes (p. 144):

"These theoretical views are intended as a general framework in which more concrete hypotheses about human behavior can and should be developed."

(1.3.). Nuttin is more explicit in his *methodological propositions*, where he presents arguments for carrying out experiments with *human* subjects – rather than animals.

2. Hypothetical Stratum

(2.0.). We can summarize Nuttin's theory in this way:

The human organism (personality) and the environment (world) constitute together one functional unit. The general *types of interaction* which are "required" for the well-functioning of the organism (or personality) are inborn *needs*. These needs are conceived, on the behavioral level, as demands for some patterns of behavioral relations with the physical and social environment *(relational theory of needs)*. Due to the cognitive functions, these needs develop into dynamic means-end structures (plan, projects or tasks) which initiate and direct coordinated series of behavioral acts. Learning occurs either automatically through the very fact that needs find an outlet (reward) via concrete behavioral dealing with objects and are, thus channeled into these behavioral pathways *(canalization* learning), or through a more *cognitive* process by which some behavioral responses are *recognized* (e. g., on the basis of their outcome or reward) as interesting and useful for further accomplishment of the behavioral plan or task. Thus, the rewarded response arouses the attention or activity level of the organism and i s *incorporated* in the dynamic task tension. This incorporation of rewarded or selected responses in a dynamic task tension system (plan, interest, etc.), or the arousal itself of the activity level (attention) of the organism by the reward or any other relevant signal, constitute the process by which better learning of these responses occurs.

Nuttin has the following to say about "learning and motivation" in general (p. 128):

"In our view, the psychological processes that facilitate acquisition and retention of either cognitive expectations or behavioral skills are essentially motivational in nature. The subject's motivational orientation is responsible not only for the fact that certain $S_1R_1S_2$ sequences are selectively preceived and acquired, but also for superior preservation of those expectations and skills that play a role in the projects and tasks at which the subject is performing."

With regard to learning by canalization he continues (p. 131):

"In terms of the present theory of learning, stimulus-response units can be preserved or retained by their being integrated in a dynamic system by the canalization process. Canalization is a quite primitive mechanism by which a specific behavior pattern becomes integrated with a motivational state of the organism; the behavioral response is conceived as the channel through which a vague need for interaction with an environmental object finds outlet. It is, in fact, impossible to speak of a specific need until some canalization has occurred – i.e., until the organism has established a behavior pattern for extracting a specific object from its environment, or, in other words, until the need tension has established a channel into a specific response. Nonrewarding responses, on the other hand, are those which are not able to serve as channels for the required type of environmental contact. Because these successful responses provide no outlet for the need tension, they are not integrated in the dynamic system of the need and, theefore, tend not to be preserved among the behavioral capabilities of the organism.

It should be clear from the foregoing that the canalization process is simultaneously a process of development of needs into concrete motives and development of behavioral reaction patterns (or learning)."

(2.1.). The most important *H-terms* in Nuttin's theory are "need", "task tension" and behavioral "plans" or "projects".

Need is defined pp. 129–130:

"Needs may be defined as those organism-environment interactions that demonstrate the characteristic of requiredness, which manifests itself (a) by the existence of a coordinated hierarchy of activities within the organism's behavioral repertoire serving to maintain the required interaction, and (b) by the fact that the organism deteriorates physically or mentally if the relationships cannot be established or maintained. Needs are conceived here not merely as states of deficiency in the organism; the fundamental structure of a need includes the required interactions with the environment. Since a wide variety of the organism's activities function to ensure that the state of deficiency is never, or, at best, rarely experienced, it seems appropriate to regard the deficiency state as only a phase in the total structure that constitutes the need."

Thus "need" is more than a state of deficiency, which is the usual conception. According to Nuttin it is a state of interaction between organism and environment in as far as it is found to be "required" for the well-functioning of the personality as a whole.

"Tensions" occur not only as parts of needs but also in the special form called *"task tensions"*. This is the state of tension in which a specific response is incorporated by the occurrence of a reward. Task tension is a centrally located reinforcing agent acting upon those connections which are the permanent results of learning. Task tension is defined implicitly in this hypothesis (p. 82):

"Our hypothesis is as follows. When a task remains to be performed, there exists for the performer a cognitive state that may be called "task tension". Each component of the task participates in this state of tension as long as the subject perceives it as a part of the to-be-performed task. In the case of a learning task, the fact that a response is successful, or rewarded, results in the perceptual inclusion of the response in the to-be-performed task. The unsuccessful response is correspondingly excluded. Thus, correct responses may be considered as becoming incorporated in a task-tension system from which incorrect responses are excluded. The experiments of the present chapter will be oriented around this hypothesis, that incorporation in a task-tension system is the essence of the connection-strengthening property of rewards."

The main difference between "task tension" and "need tension" is that task tension is a cognitive elaboration of a need tension.

All the H-termini mentioned are H_N-termini, hypothetical termini with *neutral* surplus meaning.

They are all *functional* terms – except "connections", which are *dispositional*.

"Need" and "task tension" are *dynamic* terms, while "cognitive processes" and "cognized objects" are *directive* terms. It is possible that "connection" is a vector term.

The only explicitly stated hypothesis is *complex* (multidimensional). The presumed functional relationship would seem to belong to the category of *"probability-determinism"*.

3. *The Descriptive Stratum*

The largest part of the book belongs to the D-level as 6 out of 8 chapters contain descriptions of the results of experiments.

They can be reformulated into descriptions of empirical relationships or "laws" as follows:

1. *"Canalization"* is a kind of reinforcement learning, i. e., the formation of connections determined by reward and punishment according to the law of effect.

2. *"Incorporation"* belongs to the category of *cognitive* learning, i. e., the strengthening connections resulting in new, complex behavior patterns determined by cognitive processes, including information covering the results of past behavior and an evaluation of the future significance of a behavior pattern. This kind of learning is more likely to occur the more mature the person is. It is faster than canalization.

(3.3.). The *descriptive units* employed in Nuttin's theory are *molar*. He emphasizes that it is necessary to describe *human* behavior and personality in *molar* terms.

4. The Theory as a Whole

(4.1.). The *formal properties* of Nuttin's theory are such that it must be classified as an *explanatory sketch* presented in purely *verbal* form without any use of models.

(4.2.). The *epistemological properties* are such that the theory must be classified as an S-H_N-R-*theory* i. e., a neutral, explanatory theory.

(4.3.). The *theory-empiry ration* is low and the theory must be classified as rather *empirical*. The main deductions from the theory have been experimentally tested.

Concluding Remarks. It is our opinion that Nuttin's theory is an original *"cognitive"* theory of learning and motivation which in some respects resembles the "humanistic theories". With his more than 100 experiments, he has made a very original and lasting contribution to the age old debate about the law of effect. We think that his work deserves to be much better known in the United States than it seems to be.

Reventlow's Theory

Introduction

The Danish psychologist *Iven Reventlow* has made an original contribution to psychology which is of interest for several reasons:

First, Reventlow has from the beginning had as his aim the integration of ethology and humand psychology – especially the application of ethological methods to the study of psychoanalytical problems. *Second*, this integration is accomplished by the introduction of a *mathematical* model as the main instrument of integration. *Third*, in his argumentation for this integration Reventlow has presented many original and systematically interrelated *metapropositions* which are of relevance for our purposes. *Fourth*, Reventlow's theory can be regarded as *a theory of motivation* – the motivation of nest-behavior in the three-spined stickleback.

His main work is the book: *Studier af komplicerede psykobiologiske fænomener* (Studies of complex psychobiological phenomena)[10]. In this book he presents the main results of his experimental studies of the nest-behavior of the three-spined stickleback (Gasterosteus aculeatus). The results are summarized in the mathematical model and presented in a highly elaborated metatheoretical framework.

The following systematological analysis is based upon an unpublished study made by one of my graduate students, *Jørn Thaning Christiansen*.

---

10. Copenhagen: Munksgaard, 1970. Only available in Danish (English summary).

1. *The Metastratum*

(1.1.). As already indicated Reventlow makes use of a very elaborated argumentation of *philosophical presuppositions* as well as of other metapropositions. He has formulated his epistemological presuppositions very explicitly. He presupposes an *empiristic* epistemology, but it is not a question of simple and straightforward empiricism, but of psychologically elaborated empiricism as can be seen from the following passage (p. 28):[1]

> "The method of ethology consists – – – – mainly in the observation of animals in their normal biological milieu – or at least, under circumstances which are as close to this as possible. Therefore, ethologists have to work with such complex stimulus situations and such complicated conditions of motivation that it is impossible to present descriptions which are as exhaustive as those normally found in presentations of experiments in the laboratories, where stimulus situation can be simplified and the animal's behavior can be determined by one dominant kind of motivation. In addition to this the many possibilities of action outside the laboratory preclude making as objective a registration of behavior as in the laboratory. The results of ethological experiments thus build to a greater degree than laboratory experiments upon the observer's immediate conception of the external stimuli facing the animal, why it has reacted, and how it has done this."

Reventlow has presented his epistemological presuppositions in a diagram, which includes both the experimental subjects' behavior as well as the cognitive processes used by the experimenter. We have reproduced the following diagram from Reventlow's book (p. 32):

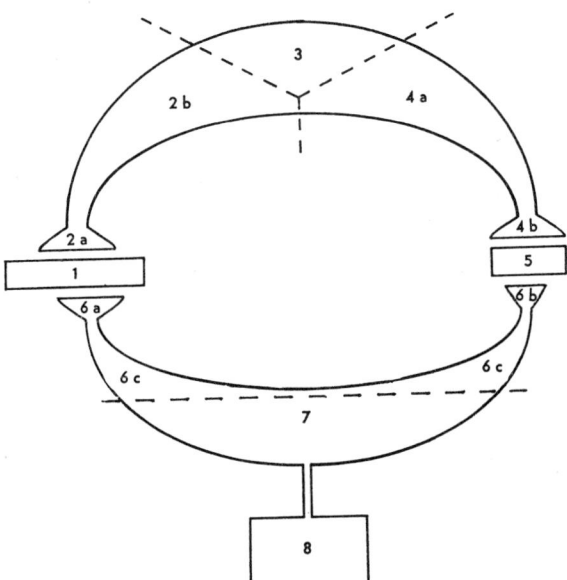

Fig. 16.4

---

1. The English translation is our own.

This diagram illustrates the relationship between the experimental subject's reactions to stimuli and the observer's perception and cognition of this behavior "1" represents the external world, which stimulates the experimental subject as well as the experimenter. "2a" denotes the sense organs of the experimental subject. "2b" illustrates the perceptual area of the central nervous system. "3" is the co-ordinating and motivating part of the CNS. "4a" is the motor area of the CNS and "4b" represents muscular movements. "5" denotes external behavior as a whole. Numbers 2, 3 and 4 together represent the so-called Innate Releasing Mechanisms (IRM). No. 1 covers a larger area than 2a to underline the fact that the animal's sense organs are not complete physical registration instruments. "6a" and "6b" represent the observer's sense organs. "6c" is the perceptual part of his nervous system, which determines the observer's phenomenal experience of the observed behavior ("7" in the Figure). "8" indicates the observer's description, which comprises the scientific data and is the basis for the scientific elaboration. "6a" is not symmetrical to "2a" in the diagram, which symbolizes that animals react to stimuli which we do not know about and, on the other hand, we know – through measuring instruments – aspects of the physical world which the animals's sense organs cannot register.

Similarly "6b" is not equal to "4b" and "5", which illustrates that the experimenter is not able to perceive the whole of the animals' reaction.

We can now summarize Reventlow's epistemological theory in this way: A selection of information occurs based on the total amount of information. This selection is determined by the observer's current state (motivation, etc.) and his more stable personality factors, including his experience and metascientific presuppositions. The information is elaborated cognitively into a phenomenal experience depicting the animal's reaction, the stimuli, etc. A feed-back goes to the information-selecting variables, which influence later experiments and their results.

Reventlow makes no explicit formulations about the psychophysical problem, but it would seem that he presupposes *a neutral-monistic* philosophy. He is more explicit in the formulations of his conception of man. He states that there are so many similarities between the behavior of animals and man that it is possible to enrich human psychology through the study of animal experiments. His whole integrative approach presupposes a *biological* philosophy of man.

(1.2.) *The metatheoretical propositions* are also formulated very explicitly and elaborated in Reventlow's book. Thus he supports a *naturalistic conception of science*, according to which it is the purpose of science to make explanations and predictions.

In accordance with his epistemological presuppositions he employs a constructionist or *instrumentalist conception* of the function and status of theories. Thus he does *not* support reductionistic realism, which is so common among ethologists. Rather, he conceives of a theory as a construction which has the purpose of integrating data from ethology and psychology.

It is consistent with this instrumentalist conception of theory to favor explanations by *analogies and model construction* rather than by formalized deductive systems.

Reventlow uses two different models.

The first is an *explanatory* model borrowed from the well known and widely accepted theory of *Niko Tinbergen*, to which we shall return in the main section about the H-level.

The second model is a *descriptive* mathematical model. It is called "descriptive" because it has the function of making calculations of quantitative estimates of measurable aspects of observations. The argumentation for application of a mathematical model is presented thusly (p. 55):

"One can conceive of mathematical expressions as statements in a special language. It can, among other things, be easier to carry through reasoning in mathematical language than in the language of daily life, and, in addition, the mathematical language can be more fitted to summarize many confused details in a single clear expression."

Reventlow distinguishes between complex and relatively simple mathematical models. The complex models are – according to Reventlow – constructed "on the basis of theoretical reflections about the phenomena under investigation, their structure and those factors which possibly have an influence on them" (p. 55). Reventlow is not enthusiastic about such models, because it is very difficult to translate the theoretical constructs into mathematical concepts and to establish operational definitions of these concepts.

Furthermore, it is difficult to estimate the effect of the single variables which are introduced in the experiment.

Therefore, Reventlow recommends the use of simple mathematical models, which can be elaborated while the complexity of the phenomena under investigation is increased. Such a simple model does not require other hypotheses than those under direct investigation. He expresses his reflections about models in this way (p. 57):

"By working successively with a priori presuppositions, model construction, statistical check, revision of presuppositions, new model construction, etc. it is possible to construct a model which is empirically sounder than the more complex models, which may be based on more detailed theoretical presuppositions, but which are less controllable."

As Reventlow himself presents a very profound discussion of the problem of *determinism*, we shall review it here in connection with the other metatheoretical problems. He started his work with a *probability* model, because it was most *convenient*, not because he believes in indeterminism. After the end of his experimental work he again discusses the problem of why deterministic predictions seem to be impossible in psychology. He mentions three possibilities:

1. The existence of some effective factors which have been overlooked.
2. Psychological phenomena are fundamentally indeterministic.

3. Psychological phenomena are dependent upon so many factors of equal strength that it is impossible in practice to register all of them in one experiment.

The first possibility presupposes the existence of *causal determinism,* while the second presupposes the existence of *indeterminism.* The third possibility does not allow the making of a choice between these two fundamental philosophical theses, but requires the use of a *probability model* as in the second case.

Reventlow does not conclude with a final acceptance of one of the two fundamental theses, but decides to recommend the use of probability models for the sake of convenience. This is consistent with his *instrumentalist* metatheory.

(1.3.) *Methodological propositions* about the data language are also discussed very explicitly. Reventlow regards himself as a "behavioristic phenomenologist". This label indicates that he combines behavioral and phenomenological data. But we think that it is more correct to call the position "phenomenological behaviorism", because he uses a *behavioral* data language. The adjective "phenomenological" signifies that every behavioral *fact* has to perceived by a human observer and registered – perhaps even classified – before they can be accepted as *data.* Thus it follows that all behavioral data should be expressed in this phenomenological way: "the experimenter observed that the subject reacted in this or that way."

The majority of Reventlow's metapropositions deal with discussions of *methods.* About this he writes (p. 73):

"Some may have the opinion that we have used too much space to discuss our choice of method, but we think that the choice of method – as far as we can see – determines the results which are achieved."

Reventlow believes that the provisional working hypothesis about the phenomena under investigation ought to determine the choice of method. He writes (p. 14):

"In biology, and especially in psychology, variables can be linked together in such a way that one cannot exclude them from an experiment in the same way as in physics – – – – The "wholes", which we in all probability meet in daily life, are hierarchically structured functional phenomena, which are produced by means of a complicated and many-sided interaction between the components, which again may be hierarchical wholes – – – –."

Therefore, the *univariate* method which is usually used in the physical sciences, is not applicable in the biological and behavioral sciences.

Reventlow recommends the *multivariate* method, because it neither *controls* nor excludes variables, but rather *registers them.* The complicated mathematical and statistical work this method entails can now be done by computers.

This is an argumentation similar to Cattell's who also argued for the multivariate method. But among the different sub-types of the multivariate method Reventlow chooses the *ethological* method, because it encompasses the following qualities (p. 25 and following):

1. "As ethology observes the animal's complete way of life, it does not have the "mosaic-psychological" character which in reality characterizes such a large part of comparative psychology."
2. "In ethology the experimental animals are presented with problems which are biologically relevant for them, while the problems in other types of animal experiments resemble 'human problems'."
3. It is possible for the ethologists to experiment with many kinds of animals, not only those which are specially fitted for or even developed exclusively for life in the laboratory. This makes it possible to gain insight into many different types of behavior; and to find fundamental similarities in the behavior of different kinds of animals."
4. "Ethologists work with many more kinds of motivation or rather with a more biologically relevant distribution of them."
5. "In ethological experiments the experimenter cannot avoid getting to know about the animal's general behavior and this places, moreover, a demand on him if he wishes to apply the method in a responsible way. Such knowledge is of great importance for the interpretation of the results."

The sources of error which are connected with the ethological method, namely, the observer's interference with the observation, can be mitigated to some extent in the following ways:

1. The observer should be aware of his own possible rôle as a source of error. But it is not enough to avoid anthropomorphism. More basic research into this methological problem is required.
2. To employ technical methods in connection with the registration of behavior – if these methods do not inhibit the experimental situation. Thus the use of film makes it possible to have several observers, who can make a more detailed study of the behavior, e. g., by slow exposition of the film, which furthermore has the advantage that the unreflected experience of causality and goal directedness in behavior is destroyed.
3. To select experimental animals which do not invite anthropomorphic interpretations.
4. To a greater extent to formalize and summarize the description of behavior in short mathematical expressions.
5. To include the observer's personal characteristics in the model used for description and explanation of behavior (as already demonstrated in Figure 16.4.).

2. The Hypothetical Stratum

Reventlow adopts *N. Tinbergen*'s theory and hierarchical model of the instincts. This theory is analyzed in detail in *"Theories of Motivation"* (Madsen, 1968).

364 . *Reventlow's Theory*

Therefore, in this chapter we shall hold ourselves to an examination of the most important aspects of Reventlow's version of Tinbergen's theory.

The main variables are presented in a diagram (Fig. 16.5.) made by *Jørn T. Christiansen* on the basis of Reventlow's exposition.

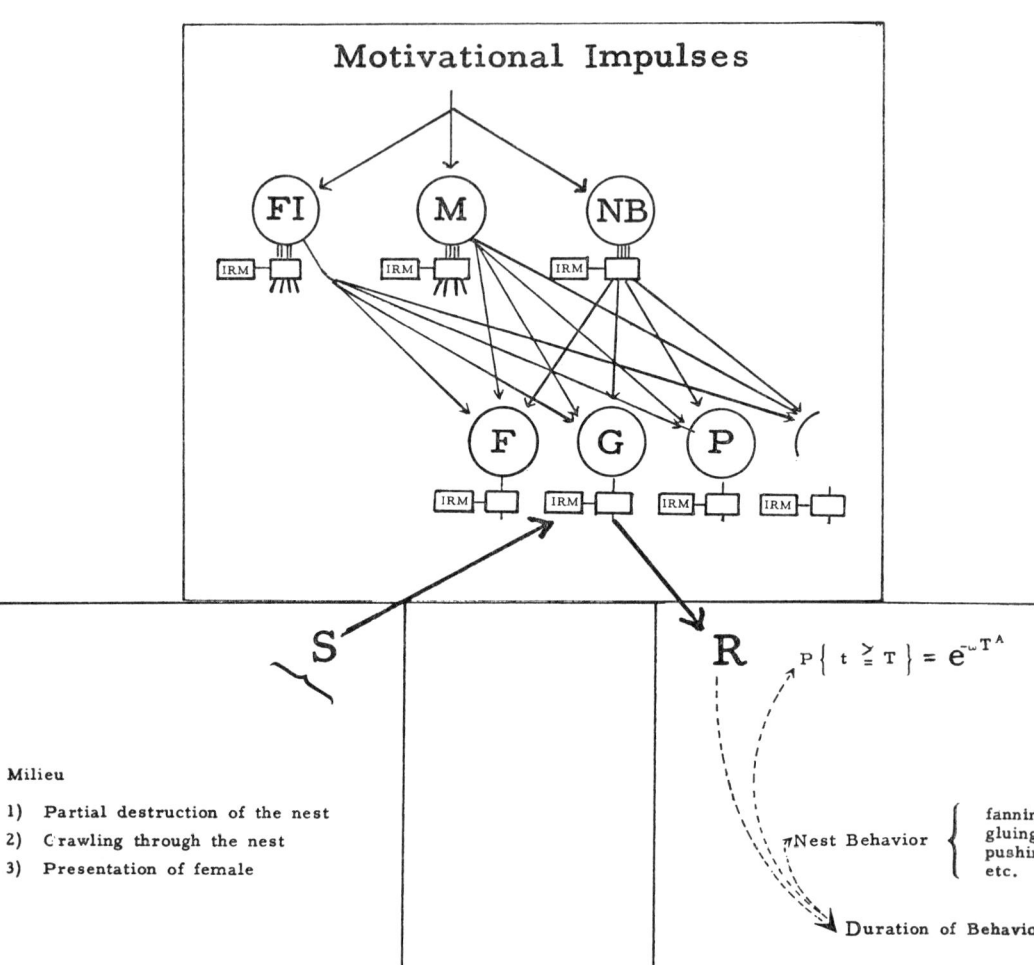

Fig. 16.5 A section of the ethological model as used by Reventlow. The figure comprises two levels of the hierarchical structure of centers on the H-level. Fi = fight, M = mate, NB = nest-behavior, F = fanning, G = gluing and P = pushing. The upper shown in *this* figure are "loaded" with motivational impulses from centers above (which are *not* on this diagram). The NB Center has been released by its IRM by means of which all the centers for molecular behavior have become "loaded". The balance between Fi and M is supposed – together with the S-variable – to determine the specific molecular behavior. The D-level in the diagram depicts the S- and R-variables in Reventlow's theory.

One of the differences between Tinbergen's and Reventlow's theories is that Tinbergen uses H termini with physiological surplus meaning while Reventlow uses H-termini *without* any surplus meaning. They refer to pure "intervening variables" in the narrow sense.

Another difference is that Tinbergen assumes reciprocal inhibition between the centers on the same level, while Reventlow assumes facilitating interactions (see Fig. 16.5.). Reventlow formulates the following hypotheses (p. 124):

"It is the balance between the two latently active centers plus the stimulus situation that determines the kind of molecular behavior which occurs during the steering of the third center." (see Fig. 16.5).

This hypothesis is – as are Tinbergen's – multidimensional. It is also a *probability-deterministic* hypothesis which is in accordance with his metatheoretical propositions.

In addition to this explicitly formulated hypothesis, Reventlow presents some discussion of a loosely formulated verbal analogy to the explanation of some empirical constants found in the experiments and expressed in the descriptive model to which we now turn.

3. *The Descriptive Stratum*

The D-level in Reventlow's theory contains descriptions of four experimental series carried out with male sticklebacks. He was interested in the period between the completion of the nestbuilding and the presentation of a sexually aroused female.

(3.1.). The *abstract D-level* contains both *S- and R-variables* (3.1.1.). There are 4 different S-variables in the four different experimental series: 1) the whole environment, 2) partial destruction of the nest, 3) moving through the nest and 4) presentation of a female.

The main R-variable is the rather abstract *nest-behavior*. This molar behavior is divided into the following categories of molecular behavior: fanning, gluing, pushing, removing material from the nest, building, vertical boring, nest digging. The most important measurable aspect of the R-variable is the *duration* of nest-behavior and the *duration* of no nest-behavior.

All these R-variables are treated in a mathematical equation, which is a probability model:

$$p\{t \geq T\} = e^{-\omega T^A}$$

This formula is not an explanatory but a *descriptive* model. It is a summarizing, formalized description of behavior through the use of statistical methods. The important *parameter* ω in the formula, is *not* a hypothetical term, but a highly abstract *descriptive R-term*. It is determined by an interaction between all the S- and H-variables.

The formula presented here is the third in a series of successive revisions on the basis of several experiments.

The presuppositions of the model can be stated in this way:

1. The quantity of behavior can be described in terms of *duration*.
2. The probability of an interruption of behavior is constant – independent of how long the behavior lasts. (This presupposition has later been rejected).
3. The observed behavior acts are presumed to be stochastically independent.

The final version of the formula:

$$p\{t_f \geq T\} = e^{-\omega T^A}$$

should be read in this way (p. 199):

"This formula merely expresses that the probability that the stickleback is at its nest for a period (t) which is equal to, or longer than, one or other arbitrarily chosen periods (T), is determined by the quantity to the right of the sign of equation. In this formula e is a mathematical constant without psychological interest, and T the arbitrarily chosen period, which is of no interest either. A is a constant equal to 1.513 and common to all sticklebacks in situations identical to those in which they were observed. The quantity of psychological interest hereby becomes ω, the value of which varies from individual to individual and from one situation to another."

In addition to the descriptive model we can reproduce the following *empirical laws* (3.1.2.):

1. "The probability of the fish leaving (or going to) its nest grows exponentially according to a constant factor (of 1.513) as the fish has been longer and longer at the nest" (p. 69).

This law shows that the second of Reventlow's presuppositions concerning the descriptive model cannot be retained.

2a. "Certain behavior must be described by the frequency of its initiation, as well as by its duration, and there seems to be no relation between these two data" (p. 95).
2b. "The state of the nest has no influence on the duration of the nest behavior" (p. 104).
3. "The state of the nest has decisive influence on what kind of specific molecular nest-behavior occurs" (p. 108).
4. "After having moved through the nest the fish leaves it much more quickly than before, and stays away from it a long time" (p. 112).
5. "The nest-behavior increases greatly after the sight of the female, as there is less probability of the male leaving the nest when they are there, and greater probability of going to the nest when they are away from it" (p. 121).

(3.2.) The *concrete D-level* of Reventlow's book includes many tables with quantitative results from experiments.

The *descriptive unit* is rather *molecular*.

4. The theory as a whole

(4.1.). The formal development of the theory is that of a *hypotheses system* combined with a *concrete model*.

(4.2). The *epistemological* category to which the theory belongs – the "type of theory" – is that of an *S-H-R-theory*, a constructive, explanatory theory.

We have not calculated the H.Q., but we estimate the *theory-empiry ratio* to be very low, as there are few hypothetical variables and many empirical variables.

Conclusion. The present author thinks that Reventlow's theory is so original that it deserves comparison with well known American theories. It is particularly interesting to compare his methods to *Cattell*'s multivariate approach, and his descriptive model may be compared with *Atkinson and Birch*'s latest theory with a mathematical model in which the time of changing behavior also plays an important role. In addition, his theory is original in its approach to the integration of ethology and human psychology.

Schultz's Theory

Introduction

The American psychologist *Duane P. Schultz* has in his book *Sensory Restriction: Effects on Behavior* (1965) surveyed a great number of experiments connected with the problems of sensory restriction. The enormous quantity of data is systematized and integrated by means of a theory of "sensoristasis", i. e., a drive for sensory variation.

During the last few years this subject has gained in importance in motivational psychology. We have seen related hypotheses in the theories of Duffy, Bindra, Berlyne, Konorski and Sokolov. Therefore we have decided to include Schultz's theory in our systematological studies also.

1. The Metastratum

1.1. Schultz's book is largely devoted to the recording of experimental results. Only 35–40 of the 200 pages are theoretical. Therefore, we cannot expect an extensive treatment of metatheoretical problems. We have not found any – explicit or implicit formulations of *philosophical pressuppositions*.

(1.2.). But there are some explicitly stated *metatheoretical propositions*. Thus Schultz – indirectly through a quotation from another author – takes the metatheoretical position that the *function of the theories* is to stimulate new ideas and investigations. He shows a preference for *neurophysiological*, explanatory theories.

(1.3.). He is, quite naturally most explicit in his *methodological propositions*. Thus, in the preface he expresses his preference for a *behavioral* data language and *experimental* methods (p. V):

> "Thus, more emphasis is placed on data obtained from objective test results or physiological measures than on strictly subjective reports with no objective referents."

And this principle is followed throughout the book.

2. The Hypothetical Stratum

(2.0.). Schultz *summarizes* his own theory in the preface by advancing the "proposition that man needs varying sensory stimulation in order to function adaptively" (p. V).

After having surveyed and analyzed the data and hypotheses about the Reticular Arousal System and its interaction with other parts of the brain, Schultz formulates his theory, which contains a definition of the main variable and a number of hypotheses. The formulations are so precise and concise that we can do no better than quote them.

First, the definition of the main H-term, *sensoristasis*, which is designed as an integration of various terms found in contemporary theories, such as the "curiosity", "exploratory", "manipulatory" and "activity" drives. The definition appears on p. 30:

> "Sensoristasis can be defined as a drive state of cortical arousal which impels the organism (in a waking state) to strive to maintain an optimal level of sensory variation. There is, in other words, a drive to maintain a constant range of varied sensory input in order to maintain cortical arousal at an optimal level. Conceptually, this sensory variation-based formulation is akin to homeostasis in that the organism strives to maintain an internal balance, but it is a balance in stimulus variation to the cortex as mediated by the ARAS. The word, *sensoristasis,* is used in the same manner in which Cannon (1932) spoke of homeostasis."

After this definition of the variable Schultz presents the following formulations of the theory (p. 31):

> "The essential corollaries of the sensoristatic model are seen as the following:
> (1) The drive mechanism invoked in the concept of sensoristasis is synonymous with arousal as facilitated or mediated by RAS.
> (2) An optimal range or level of external stimulation exists which functions to influence the level of cortical arousal. - - -
> (3) The organism will behave so as to maintain this optimal arousal level. Those behaviors which increase or decrese sensory variation to the optimal level will be reinforced while those which increase stimulation above the optimal level will not be reinforced. - - -
> (4) The optimal range of sensory variation is capable of shifting as a function of several variables such as the task to be performed, present state of the organism, and level of preceding stimulation. More important the range is subject to both inter- and intra-organism differences. - - -"

These are the main hypotheses in Schultz's "sensoristatic model". In addition to these he makes some deductions based on the hypotheses. They are conceived of as predictions, which are studied in the rest of the book. We quote these seven predictions from p. 32:

"(1) Conditions of reduced sensory input will result in measurable changes in activation level.

(2) The sensoristatic drive state is induced by conditions of restricted sensory variation input and becomes increasingly intense as a function of time and amount of deprivation or restriction.

(3) When conditions of sensory restriction disturb the sensoristatic balance, the organism will exhibit gross disturbances of functioning; e.g., perception, cognition, learning.

(4) When stimulus variation is restricted, central regulation of threshold sensitivities will function to lower sensory threshold. Thus, the organism becomes increasingly sensitized to stimulation in an attempt to restore the balance.

(5) Organisms will exhibit evidence of learning in situations where the only apparent reinforcement is a change in sensory variation. Thus, under conditions of sensory restriction, increases in stimulus variability will have reinforcing properties.

(6) There exist individual differences in the need for sensory variation. These individual differences may be partially due to the early postnatal levels of stimulation as discussed above.

(7) Reduction of the patterning of stimulus input will result in greater behavioral effects than simply reduction of the level of stimulation. Deprivation of variation in stimulation rather than level of stimulation, *per se,* induces a more intense sensoristatic drive state. Hence, behavioral disturbances should be greater under perceptual deprivation conditions than under sensory deprivation conditions, as these where defined in Chapter I.

The validity of these predictions is considered in the following chapters."

After this presentation of Schultz's theory in summary form we turn to our systematological analysis.

(2.1.). The *H-term* in the theory is "sensoristasis". It is actually an H_o-term as it refers to an hypothetical variable with *physiological* surplus meaning.

It is a *functional* term as it refers to a "drive" state. The corresponding dispositional term is "drive mechanism" which in this case refers to the RAS.

"Sensoristasis" is a *dynamic* term as it refers to an exclusively *activating* or "energizing" effect on behavior.

(2.2.). *The hypotheses* contained in Schultz's theory can be classified in this way:

1. *Purely theoretical (H-H)hypotheses:*
   No. 1 and No. 2 of the so-called "corollaries" of the sensoristatic model" (cf. the above quotation).

2. *Partly empirical hypotheses:*
   S-H-hypotheses: No. 4 of the corollaries and predictions No. 1 to No. 5 (cf. the above quotation).
   H-R-hypotheses: No. 3 of the corollaries.

We are in doubt about the classification of "predictions" No. 6 and No. 7. It is possible that they are not hypotheses (according to our definition) but empirical laws. "Prediction" No. 1 could also be regarded as an empirical S-R-law, if "activation level" is regarded as an operationally defined descriptive term standing for "arousal" of the RAS.

The hypotheses are mostly of the *one-dimensional* type.

Although we have found no explicit formulations about the problem, we think that the presupposed functional relationship is *causal deterministic*.

3. The Descriptive Stratum

The main part of Schultz's book – Chapters 3 to 8 – belongs to the D-level, as it contains a survey and analysis of the experimental results.

(3.1.). The *abstract D-level* contains a definition of the most important descriptive term – included in the title of the book – namely: "sensory restriction". This term is used synonymously[11]) with "sensory deprivation", which is defined in this way (p. 6):

"Sensory deprivation experiments involve attempts to reduce sensory stimulation to an absolute minimum."

Another important D-term is "perceptual deprivation", which is defined in this way (p. 7):

"Perceptual deprivation involves an attempt to reduce the patterning and meaningful organization of sensory input while maintaining a somewhat normal level of input."

In addition to these abstract descriptive terms, the abstract D-level contains *empirical "laws"*. We regard the *summaries* in Chapter 9 as empirical "laws", as they are *general, abstract descriptions*. We have included the most important of Schultz's summaries (from pp. 169–172):

"Chapter III noted a variety of physiological effects as a consequence of sensory restriction. A progressive slowing of the frequencies of brain waves in the alpha band was demonstrated which seemed to persist for some time after release from isolation. This disturbance of electrical activity of the brain was greater under perceptual deprivation than sensory deprivation.

A somewhat consistent decrease in the electrical resistance of the skin as measured by GSR was demonstrated. Rather consistent increases appeared in cutaneous and pain sensitivities with some suggestion of an increase in visual and auditory sensitivities.

Dealing with cognitive functions, evidence introduced in Chapter IV revealed that most subjects in sensory and perceptual deprivation conditions reported difficulties in directed thinking, concentration, *etc.*, to a rather high degree.

---

11. Schultz might have distinguished between "sensory deprivation" and "sensory restriction" in this way: "sensory restriction" is the reduction to a minimum in the stimulation of an adult individual, while "sensory deprivation" is the long term reduction in stimulation of a young individual.

Of great interest for further research was the suggestion that some cognitive abilities might show an improvement under sensory restriction. The evidence was, however, contradictory. The proposition that a subject may be rendered more persuasible under sensory restriction received some degree of support and the implications of this for a brainwashing technique were noted.

Most subjects undergoing sensory restriction reported a rather wide range of perceptual disturbances during isolation which persisted, in some cases, for as much as one day after isolation. Objective tests of perceptual functioning, however have not revealed such a wide range of perceptual deterioration.

Chapter VI revealed evidence indicating varying degrees of emotional impairment in subjects undergoing sensory restriction, which effects often, but not always, increased in severity as a function of time in isolation.

Chapter VII dealt with a variety of techniques attempting to predict a person's tolerance for sensory restriction. In general, most of the attempts at prediction, using paper – and pencil and projective tests, provided very discouraging and inconsistent results.

In general it seems that individual social isolation produced the most severe effects as compared to isolation with a small group. However, even confinement with a group of other people seemed to produce emotional and cognitive impairments when the period of confinement was as long as several months."

(3.2.). The *concrete D-level* of Schultz's theory consists of many detailed descriptions of single experiments in which he used *physiological* (EEG, GSR, etc.) and *behavioral* data, as well as a number of "subjective reports" (which *can* be regarded as verbal behavior).

The *descriptive units* (3.3.) employed are rather *molecular*.

4. The Theory as a Whole

(4.1.). The *formal properties* of Schultz's theory are developed to the level of a *system of hypotheses*, which is almost equivalent to a deductive system. The presentation is purely *verbal*, but very precise. There are some diagrams of the brain which may be regarded as *graphical models*.

(4.2.). The *epistemological properties* of the theory are those of a *physiological* explanatory or *S-O-R-theory*.

(4.3.). The *theory-empiry ratio* is low. We have calculated the Hypotheses Quotient on the basis of our classification in Section 2.2.:

$$H.Q. = \frac{\Sigma(H-H)}{\Sigma[(S-H) + (H-R)]} = \frac{2}{6+1} = \frac{2}{7} = 0.29$$

If the two doubtful "predictions" (No. 6 and No. 7) were classified as partly empirical, the H.Q. would have been still lower (0.22).

Concluding Remarks. We regard Schultz's book as a very interesting example of a primarily empirical monograph containing a very systematic and concise theory, which can be favorably compared to the other neuropsychological theories which we have analyzed in this book.

Sokolov's Theory

Introduction. Another Soviet psychologist who is highly regarded in the Western world is *Ye. N. Sokolov*.

From among his papers and books we have selected his book *"Perception and the Conditioned Reflex"*, which appeared in English translation in 1963.

The reason for selecting this book is that it contains a theory of the orientation reaction – or exploratory behavior – which can be compared to those of Berlyne, Fowler and Konorski.

The present analysis is based upon a preliminary, unpublished analysis made by one of my graduate students, Miss *Jutta Gravsholt*.

1. The Metastratum

(1.1.). There are no explicit formulations of *philosophic presuppositions*. But Sokolov regards himself as a follower of Pavlov. Therefore, we can assume that he also presupposes a *materialistic* – or perhaps an *epi-phenomenalistic* – philosophy of the psychosomatic problem as well as a biological Darwinian conception of Man.

(1.2.). Nor does Sokolov make very many statements concerning *methatheoretical* problems. It is quite likely that he – like Luria, Pavlov and other Soviet psychologists – conceives of his book as a *description* of empirical facts. In the Appendix, however, he presents "A Neuronal Model of the Stimulus and the Orienting Reflex". This is clearly a "constructive", explanatory theory although the "model" is neural. Thus in this respect Sokolov's theory comes close to Berlyne's, Konorski's and Pribram's, although the metapropositions are more explicitly formulated in the last three.

(1.3.). Sokolov is – in accordance with Soviet tradition – much more explicit in his formulations of *methodological propositions*. Thus a whole chapter – Part I, Chapter 2 – is devoted to the "Measurement of the Functional State of Analysers". In this chapter he presents a strong argument for "poly-effector reaction recording", also called the "electropolygraphic technique". This method involves a quantitative, simultaneous registration of several motor and autonomic reactions.

Thus Sokolov's data are physiological and behavioral, and the methods experimental.

2. The Hypothetical Stratum

(2.0.). We can summarize Sokolov's hypotheses in this way; *Perception* is the function of a *"complex functional system"* (in the same sense that Luria uses the term). This system consists of several conditioned and unconditioned *reflex activities* occuring in *analysers* which are conceived of as *self-regulating systems*.

The reflex activities are classified into 1) *adaptive,* 2) *defensive* and 3) *orientation reflexes.* Among these are the orientation reflexes of greatest interest for motivational psychology. Therefore, we shall focus on Sokolov's model of the orientation reflex. The clearest and most concentrated conception of his model is presented in Fig. 16[12]).

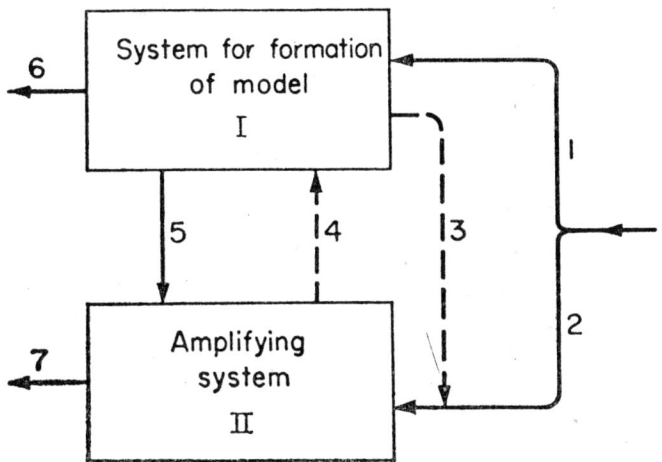

Fig. 16.6 Sokolov's model for the orientation reaction. I: modelling system. II: amplifying system. 1: specific pathway from sense organs to cortical level of modelling system. 2: collateral to reticular formation (represented here as amplifying device). 3: negative feedback from modelling system to synaptic connections between collaterals from specific pathway and reticular formation (RF) to block input in the case of habituated stimuli. 4: ascending activating influences from the RF to the modelling system (cortex). 5: pathway from modelling system to amplifying system (this is the pathway through which the impulses signifying non-concordance between input and existing neuronal models are transmitted from cortex to RF. 6: to specific responses caused by coincidence between the external stimulus and the neuronal model (habitual responses). 7: to the vegetative and somatic components arising from the stimulation of the RF. (From Sokolov, 1960.)

The reader may have noticed that *there are models in the model:* According to Sokolov's model of the brain, "the nervous system produces exact models of the properties of external objects acting on the sense organs". (Sokolov 1963, p. 286). These "neural models" of stimuli are produced by "the system for formation of models", which can be equated with the cortex. If a stimulus acting upon the cortex is not already "modelled", then the "amplifying system" (which can be equated with the RAS) will react with an orientation reflex, and this

---

12. This figure is found in Ye. N. Sokolov: "Neural Models and the Orienting Reflex" (in M. A. Brazier (Ed.): *"The Central Nervous System and Behavior",* New York: Macy, 1960). We have borrowed the figure and the text from R. Lynn: *"Attention, Arousal and the Orientation Reaction"* (Oxford: Pergamon Press, 1966).

will later result in the production of a neural model of the stimulus (learning). If there already is a neural model in the cortex, then there will be no orientation reflex, but only a conditioned reflex.

(2.1.). Some of the most important *H-terms* in Sokolov's theory are: "neural model", "System I" (cortex), "System II" (RAS), "connections" and "reflex systems". They are all H_o-terms with *physiological* surplus meaning. They are *dispositional* terms which are also used as functional terms. In other words, Sokolov's theory lacks special terms referring to the *activated* dispositions. It is difficult to classify the terms and variables according to their effect on behavior, but we think that "System II" (RAS) is a *dynamic* variable, while "System I" (cortex) and the "neural models" are directive – or perhaps vector-variables.

(2.2.). The hypotheses are not explicitly formulated, but on the basis of a systematic reformulation made by Miss Jutta Gravsholt we can conclude that there are more (partly) *empirical* hypotheses than *theoretical* hypotheses. There are also many *complex* (multidimensional) hypotheses. Sokolov makes no explicit formulations about the functional relationships assumed, but it is probably not incorrect to conclude that he assumes a kind of *causal determinism*.

3. The Descriptive Stratum

(3.1.). The abstract D-level in Sokolov's theory contains the classification of the *R-variables*, i. e., reflex activities, into orienting, adaptive and defensive reflexes. (The corresponding reflex *systems* are conceived of as hypothetical variables (dispositions) although there is very little "hypothetical" – in the other meaning of the word – in the existence of these systems).

The orienting reflex *activity* is operationally defined by measurable aspects of electroencephalographic autonomic, motorial and sensorial responses.

Sokolov is not so explicit in his statements about *S-variables*, but he stresses that even the simplest stimulus is in fact a *stimulus complex*. He underlines that the stimulus determining the orienting reflex consists of every change in stimulation (Cf. Berlyne's "collative variables").

For our purposes this is a most important empirical relationship – "law" – which can be reformulated in this way: "Every *change* in stimulation determines an *orienting* reflex activity."

(3.2.). *The concrete D-level* in Sokolov's theory contains many descriptions of the measurement of *behavior* and *physiological* processes. There are also some *verbal* reports, but in principle they are treated as behavior. Thus the *data language is behavioral* (+ physiological).

(3.3.). The *descriptive unit* employed in Sokolov's theory is *molecular*. He explicitly states, in fact, that his theory differs from that of Hull, which is a molar theory.

4. The Theory as a Whole

(4.1.) *The formal properties* of Sokolov's theory are such that it must be classified as an *explanatory sketch* with a purely *verbal presentation*. The *model* is also presented verbally, but we have taken the *graphic model* presented here as Fig. 16.6. from another book of Sokolov.

(4.2.) *The epistemological properties* of Sokolov's theory are such that it must be classified as an *S-O-R-theory*, a *physiological*, explanatory theory.

The theory-empiry ratio makes it necessary to classify his theory as being rather *empirical*. Miss Jutta Gravsholt has calculated the Hypotheses Quotient on the basis of her systematic reconstruction of the theory and found the H.Q. to be *0.38*.

Concluding Remarks. We hope that even this brief analysis of Sokolov's theory has demonstrated that the theory integrates the best from the Pavlovian tradition – the neuropsychological approach – with something found in modern Western psychology, constructive "model-building".

Reviews of Other Theories

Introduction

In the foregoing parts of this chapter we have presented brief analyses of 10 theories, so we have thus far covered 22 theories in this book. If these are added to the 20 theories from the period 1930–1957, which we analyzed in "Theories of Motivation", we have analyzed a total of 42 theories of motivation. But, of course, this does not cover *all* theories of motivation. In the first book because of space limitations we had to exclude Freuds's theory and the production of motivational theories has been growing markedly in the period covered by this book. And, of course, there are theories of motivation which we have never heard about. But even those known to the present author have not all been included. Lack of time and space has made it impossible for us to touch on all the additional theories we should like to examine, but we have selected a few for very brief mention.

1. Berkowitz's theory

The American psychologist *Leonard Berkowitz* has written a book entitled *Aggression: A Social Psychological Analysis* (1962), which in our opinion is one of the best surveys and integrations of research and theory about aggression to have appeared.

He adopts the so-called *"Frustration-Aggression hypothesis"* advanced in 1939 by the "Yale group" (Dollard, Doob, Miller, Mowrer and Sears), because he regards it as being "still the best theoretical framework for the analysis of social aggression" (p. XI). He presents a very concise and precise summary of his version of the theory in the introduction (pp. XI and XII).

"Many of the concepts employed here are defined more or less as they were by Dollard and his colleagues. These definitions can be summarized briefly. Generally speaking, a *frustration* is said to be any interference with some on-going goal-directed activity. Such thwartings usually (if not always) produce an emotional reaction, *anger*, the intensity of this emotional state being a function of certain aspects of the frustration. Anger, in turn, is regarded as an internal condition making aggressive responses relatively likely to occur. Anger, we can say, heightens the probability of hostile behavior. However, the anger "drive state" generally produces aggressive responses only in the presence of relevant cues, stimuli having some association with the anger instigator. The strength of the aggressive reaction to a frustration is in direct ratio to the intensity of the resulting anger and the degree of association between the instigator and the releasing cue. The aggressive reaction may not, of course, be displayed in overt behavior; other responses elicited in the situation can inhibit the hostile actions. *Aggression* and *hostility* are synonymous terms in this book and denote behavior aimed at the injury of some object.

The use of the Dollard et al. approach to aggression does not mean this book is committed to employ only those theoretical concepts favored by the Yale group. In actuality, the present work is conceptually eclectic. The terms used will be the ones that seem most appropriate for the given problem being discussed. Thus, the language of S–R learning theory will be utilized in analyzing hostility generalization, interpretations, belief systems, and the like. There is no real incompatibility between these theoretical constructs; all can contribute to our understanding of aggression."

Berkowitz analyzes the "Instinct Conceptions of Aggression" in Chapter 1 and comes to the conclusion that both the Freudian version and McDougall's version are unacceptable.

In Chapter 2 "The Frustration-Aggression Hypothesis" is analyzed. As already mentioned Berkowitz adopted this hypothesis with some revisions which have served to neutralize some of the criticism of the frustration-aggression hypothesis.

In Chapter 3 he deals with "Situational Determinants of the Strength of the Instigation to Aggression", and modifies some of the principles in the frustration-aggression theory. The most important of the propositions in the theory is, however, retained in its original form, because it was found to be as valid today as when it was originally formulated. This is the proposition that the instigation to aggression aroused by frustration is in direct proportion to the degree of thwarting.

Chapter 4 is concerned with "The Inhibition of Aggressive Acts". The main sources of the inhibition of aggression are anticipation of punishment and conflict with the moral standards accepted by the individual himself.

Chapter 5 deals with "The Nature and Target of the Aggressive Response". In this chapter Berkowitz examines Neal Miller's theory of "displacement" which he equates with a *generalization* of stimuli and responses. From this basic hypothesis he deduces several hypotheses about displacement of aggression and evaluates their validity on the basis of recent experimental research.

This displacement-generalization theory is applied to "Intergroup Hostility" in Chapters 6 and 7. Among other things the so-called "scapegoat" theory is discussed as well as the conditions of conflicts between groups and individuals in a group.

The problem of "Catharsis" is investigated in Chapter 8, and the results point to the conclusion that "catharsis" in the form of discharge of pent-up energy is not so likely to occur as when in the form of a completion tendency of an aggressive act.

Berkowitz summarizes the research about "Violence in the Mass Media" in Chapter 9 and comes to the conclusion that "there is no evidence, however, that their (peoples') hostile predispositions are weakened by viewing fantasy aggression" (p. 254).

Chapter 10 presents a theory of "Aggressive Personalities", which is summarized in this way:

"The present book regards the highly aggressive person as an individual who has a latent disposition to make hostile responses to relevant, aggression – evoking cues rather than someone who is chronically angry" (pp. 298–299).

In the 11th and final chapter Berkowitz turns to "Aggression in Crime, Homicides and Suicides". In this chapter a distinction is made between "unsocialized" or "individual" criminals and "socialized" criminals. The first type of criminal has often been frustrated by extreme parental rejection, while the second type has been less frustrated during childhood, but they have on the other hand been strongly influenced by a criminal subculture (in which both parents and peers can be members).

In conclusion, we wish to emphasize that Berkowitz's book has made a very valuable contribution to psychology by adopting and critically revising the frustration-aggression hypothesis and by integrating so much new data not available at the first appearance of the "Yale group's" theory in 1939[13]).

2. *Cofer and Appley's theory*

C. N. Cofer and M. H. Appley have in their book *Motivation: Theory and Research* (1964) presented a theory which integrates most motivational theory.

---

13. It should be added that since 1962 Berkowitz has developed his theory and changed it to some extent. Thus he now regards *frustration as an aversive experience,* and pain are not – as in 1962 – regarded as a kind of frustration, but rather frustration is regarded as a particular kind of painful experience. See especially L. Berkowitz: "The Frustration-Aggression Hypothesis Revisited" (in L. Berkowitz (Ed.): "Roots of Aggression" (N. Y.: Atherton Press. 1969).

This excellent and very comprehensive (958 pages) book covers a vast amount of the literature dealing with motivation (c. 100 pages of references). After a discussion of "The Concept of Motivation" and a very instructive presentation of "Motivation in Historical Perspective" there are chapters about instinct, bodily conditions, activity and exploration, homeostatic and hedonistic theories, frustration and conflict, motivation in learning and performance, psychoanalytic theory, self-actualization, human motivation and social motivation.

They cover – in accordance with the sub-title of their book – both experimental research (e. g., "bodily conditions") and theoretical discussions (e. g., "psychoanalytic motivation theory").

The most interesting chapter from our point of view was the last one: "Toward a Unified Theory of Motivation". It is in this chapter that Cofer and Appley propose their theory of motivation on the basis of their analysis and integration of the concepts and theories they have surveyed.

The main concept in their theory is "invigoration" (i. e., "arousal") which takes the place of "drive", the main concept in most theories of motivation. They believe that modern neuropsychological research has presented satisfactory evidence for the function of "arousal" as the main variable in motivational processes and behavior. But they prefer the *neutral* H-term, "invigoration" to "arousal", which has a physiological surplus meaning.

Cofer and Appley postulate the existence of two hypothetical "mechanisms" of motivation, which they propose as explanation for all motivational phenomena:

1. *"The sensitization-invigoration mechanism"* (SIM), which is a hypothetical variable or "mechanism". This mechanism is influenced by external stimuli and the internal state of the organism (e. g., the hormonal state). The results of these influences on the mechanism are arousal or "invigoration" of the whole organism. The SIM is conceived of as being *inborn*.

2. *"The anticipation-invigoration mechanism"* (AIM), which is a hypothetical variable – or "mechanism". This mechanism is *acquired* or learned, but its function is similar to the SIM. Thus AIM is also influenced by external stimuli and by the internal (e. g., hormonal) state of the organism. The result of these influences on the AIM is invigoration.

The present author believes that these two hypothetical constructs actually make it possible to integrate two traditions in motivational psychology, the "Habit × Drive"-theories and the "Expectation × Value" theories (Cf. Atkinson's classification in our chapter 10). And, furthermore, they claim that their "mechanisms" integrate the neuropsychological concept "arousal" with the traditional concepts "drive" and "expectation". This is really a great contribution to the synthesis of different motivational theories.

3. Heckhausen's Theory

The German psychologist, *Heinz Heckhausen* has gained the position of one of the most well known motivational psychologists in Western Europa. He has been inspired by McClelland's and Atkinson's theories and research and has contributed many papers and books about *achievement motivation*. We regard the following as his main works: *Hoffnung und Furcht in der Leistungsmotivation* (1963) and *The Anatomy of Achievement Motivation* (1967) as well as the paper *Achievement Motive Research* (in Nebraska Symposium on Motivation, 1968), and another one *The Emergence of a Cognitive Psychology of Motivation* (1972). (H. Heckhausen & B. Weiner, in P. C. Dodwell (Ed.), *New Horizons in Psychology*[2]. Harmondsworth: Penguin, 1972. Pp. 126–147)[14].

Heckhausen's contribution to motivational psychology consists in his further development of the thematic apperceptive instrument. He has constructed two separate scoring keys for the measurement of the two independent tendencies of the achievement motive, i. e., "hope of success" and "fear of failure". The construct validity of both measures has been corroborated in many studies up to now with regard to data on level of aspiration, risk-taking, performance, time perspective, experience of time, neurophysiological measures, incentive, causal attribution of success and failure, self-reinforcement, demographic survey, teacher-student interaction, child-rearing patterns etc. In addition, he has contributed *theoretically* with supplements to the theories of achievement motivation developed by McClelland and Atkinson. From our point of view these theoretical contributions are very significant and therefore we shall summarize them in this section.

First: Heckhausen emphasizes that *"motive arousal is an interactive product of motive and various conditions,* circumstances, and/or constraints of a presently given situation or setting (Heckhausen, 1968 p. 104). Heckhausen and his co-workers have therefore broadened the range of variables included in traditional motivational research. We wish to underline that he has paid more attention to the *incentive* component in motivation than have McClelland or Atkinson.

Second: Heckhausen stresses that a motive is *"a complex cognitive system"*. By doing this he has anticipated the development of motivational theory along the lines followed at a later date by McClelland in a book co-authored by D. G. Winter: *Motivating Economic Achievement* (1969).

---

14. Heckhausen is the first non-American psychologist to have been invited to this symposium, which has developed into an important institution in the field of motivational psychology.

Third: Heckhausen has developed a much more complex set of hypotheses about the origin and *development* of achievement motivation, than did McClelland and Winther. We can reformulate his hypotheses in this way:

1. *The development of the achievement motive is dependent on the development of certain cognitive and motor functions.*

A necessary precondition, e. g., is the child's ability of tracing back the outcome of his own activities to himself as the originator of that outcome. This requires causal attribution of activity effects to internal factors like one's own ability, an accomplishment which emerges at the mental age of three. Till the age of four to five individual differences in the achievement motive become gradually apparent.

2. *The development of the achievement motive is dependent on other motives ("precursor motives").* The "independence motive" is a particularly important precursor motive in its relationship to the achievement motive.

3. *The development of the achievement motive is dependent on reinforcement learning.* Parental rewards and punishment are very important in the shaping of the achievement motive.

4. *The development of the achievement motive is dependent on observational learning.*

5. *The development of the achievement motive is dependent on experienced incongruities.* Thus "the possibility of presenting or self-administrating paced levels of difficulty in the home or in the school appears to have an important influence on motive development" (Heckhausen, 1968, p. 137).

Heckhausen conceives motives as self-reinforcing systems with standards for self-evaluation. He stresses the role of intervening cognitions like anticipated immediate and delayed consequences of action outcome (incentives), the waging of probabilities of outcome, causal attribution of outcome, comparison of achieved outcome with standard norms and, dependent on the result of this comparison, contingent self-reward of self-punishment (H. Heckhausen, 1973)[15].

We have found the above aspects of Heckhausen's work of great importance in the advancement of a general theory of motivation.

---

15. (H. Heckhausen, Intervening Cognitions in Motivation. In D. E. Berlyne & K. B. Madsen (Eds.), *Pleasure, Reward, and Preference.* New York: Academic Press, 1973).

4. Logan's theory

Frank A. Logan has among other things written a book: *Incentive* (1960). It may be of more interest to theory of learning than to theory of motivation, but the book will be mentioned here because Logan is a student of Hull and Spence.

It contains a temporary account about experimental results of "incentives", and also a so-called "micromolar theory" as an explanation to the results.

The experimental results can be summed up, as follows (p. 258):

"rats adjust to the various conditions of reinforcement in terms of the principles of maximization of reward and minimization of effort."

The main thing about a "micromolar" theory is that "responses that differ quantitatively are considered to be different responses", and therefore "a micromolar theory must make predictions in terms of probability of response" (p. 100). These bases bring back Skinner's theory to our mind: the constructs and the postulates of the theory, however, lean heavily on the Hull-Spence approach. The most important hypothetical constructs are: "habit" (sHr), "incentive" (sJNr), "drive" (D), "effort" (sFr), and "temporary inhibition" (sTjr). The three first constructs have been directly borrowed from Hull's theory, only little changes have taken place in the definitions. The two last ones are partially new (although similar variables can be found in Tolman's and Hull's theories respectively). The three first mentioned work positively together for the increase of a reaction tendency ("excitatory potential" sEr), while the two last mentioned work negatively for a decrease of the potential. Logan writes about "primary motivation" (p. 104):

"There are five states of affairs which produce (D), namely: "hunger", "thirst", "sex", "pain" and "fear". The different constructs are defined nearly as in Hull's theory. Logan's theory is likewise formulated in 17 postulates, and an example of deduction is given on the postulates. The very quantitative formulation of the theory has been influenced by statistics-in conformity with Skinner's and other late theories of learning. It ought to be added that Logan has developed his theory further in the years since 1960. His conceptualizations have changed in the interior, although the fundamental constructs remain the same. Later versions of Logan's theory appear in his book with *Wagner:* "Reward and Punishment" (1965) and his latest book: "Fundamentals of Learning and Motivation" (1970)."

5. Mowrer's theory

The American psychologist, *O. Hobart Mowrer* was a member of the so-called "Yale group", which was inspired by C. L. Hull and had among its other well known members N. E. Miller, John Dollard, L. W. Doob and Robert R. Sears. Mowrer co-authored with those mentioned above the well known and influential *Frustration and Aggression* (1939). Later he carried out experimental research and theoretical analysis concerning the role of *anxiety* as a learned drive. This application of experimentally based learning theory to the field of personality has been continued in his later works. Many of his earliest papers were collected in the book *Learning Theory and Personality Dynamics* (1950)[16].

Mowrer elaborated his theory of learning during the 1950s. On the basis of the original Hullian reinforcement theory of learning he developed a so-called "two-factor theory of learning". This theory was propounded in papers in different journals, and after some revisions he included the final version of the theory in his two volume work: *Learning Theory and Behavior* and *Learning Theory and the Symbolic Processes* (both 1960). As the title of the last mentioned book shows, he has expanded his theory to cover the thinking process and language. And in the 1960's he applied his theory to clinical psychology and psychotherapy.

Although Mowrer has not constructed a specific theory of motivation, we think that his *two-factor theory of learning* is of interest for motivational psychology and therefore we review it in the following:

The theory was called a "two-factor" theory of learning, because Mowrer – like Skinner, Konorski and others – postulated *two types of learning:* 1) classical conditioning or *sign learning*, and 2) instrumental conditioning or *solution learning*. These two types of learning were supposed to follow the two principles of *contiguity* and *reinforcement* respectively.

After some intermediate revision he presented his "final version" of the two-factor theory of learning in 1960. According to this version there is only *one type of learning:* classical conditioning or "sign learning". "Solution learning" and all other possible kinds of learning are regarded as derivative forms of classical conditioning.

But Mowrer's theory postulates *two kinds of reinforcement:* 1) *"incremental"* reinforcement (= drive *induction*), which is determined by *punishment* and results in *"fear-learning"*, and 2) *"decremental"* reinforcement (= drive *reduction*), which is determined by *reward* and results in *"hope-learning"*. *Fear* and *hope* can be conceived of as two basic *hypothetical motivational variables*. Fear and hope are involved in *response facilitation* ("habit" learning) and *response inhibition* respectively, as well as in *place approach behavior* and *place avoidance behavior* in the same manner.

As we can see Mowrer's theory includes a motivational hypothesis which comes close to Atkinson's and especially Heckhausen's theories of "hope for success" and "fear of failure".

---

16. This book was briefly commented upon in the first edition of my *Theories of Motivation* (1959).

6. Murray's theory

The American psychologist *Edward Murray* has contributed to motivational psychology through his experimental research and a small, popular textbook. But his main work is the book *Sleep, Dreams and Arousal* (1965). In this book he reviews the growing field of sleep research and formulates a theory of sleep motivation which is of great interest from the point of view of general motivational theory. Therefore, we have decided to review the book here.

In the first chapter of his book Edward Murray writes about "The Motivational Context". He analyzes the current concepts and main theories of motivation and of sleep and concludes with his conception of the sleep motive.

He emphasizes the utility of intervening variables (or hypothetical constructs) such as "motive". Thus he writes (p. 15):

"The theoretical analysis of the sleep motive will begin with the assumption that sleep shares the basic characteristics of other primary, physiological motives. It serves a biological function, it operates through physiological mechanisms, and its deprivation motivates learning and performance. Its deprivation also poses a biological, behavioral, and personality adjustment problem. Through the influence of cultural and social learning, the sleep motive is shaped and developed and may become involved in psychopathology.

While the emphasis will be on showing that sleep has the essential features of a motive, the reader should be alert for important differences between this motive and others. After all, one reason for writing this book is to broaden the base of motivational phenomena on which our general conceptions rest. Thus the peculiarities of sleep may be of importance in assessing the adequacy of current concepts of motivation."

Thus Murray emphasizes that the sleep motive in principle is similar to other physiological motives, although there are some differences.

His definition of the sleep motive deserves to be quoted (pp. 15–16):

"The terms *sleep motive* or *the motive to sleep* are used throughout in a general sense to refer to the entire gamut of phenomena in this area. It really should be read as "the disposition to sleep, serving a biological need, controlled by physiological mechanisms, with a specific goal response, and with specified relationships to deprivation and other motivating conditions." This is the general sense of the word as used by several theorists."

The *goal* response mentioned in this definition is the "act of sleeping" or the "sleeping state". This is the *consummatory* response to which all other kinds of behavior (e. g., finding and paying for a hotel room, preparing to go to bed, etc.) are related as *instrumental* behavior.

In the second chapter Murray discusses at length the biological need for sleep, which was mentioned in the above definition. He concludes his summary of this chapter with the following concentrated conclusion (p. 60):

"In conclusion, while the evidence is incomplete, the sleep motive appears to be comparable to the other homeostatic motives. A reasonable working hypothesis is that sleep permits: the conservation of energy; the diversion of energy for growth, repair, and resistance; and the restoration of energy reserves for muscular, neural, and all other bodily processes in advance of their actual exhaustion. The exact functions of the synchronized and dream phases of sleep are not known."

The third chapter is devoted to "dreams and sleep". Murray adopts *Calvin S. Hall*'s theory that dreams involve a simpler level of cognitive functioning than waking life, and he believes that Freud's hypotheses about complex dreaming processes are superfluous. The summarizing section is aptly concluded in this way (p. 93):

"In conclusion, regardless of the exact function of dreams, they occur in a unique stage of sleep. This stage is characterized by cortical and autonomic arousal, loss of muscle tonus and possibly heightened thresholds, rapid eye movements, and primitive thought processes."

In the fourth chapter Murray deals with certain "physiological mechanisms", which were also referred to in the above quoted definition of the sleep motive. The sleep motive is different from all other physiological motives, all of which are corollated with the reticular activating system (RAS) which is the most important brain mechanism. The sleep motive is corollated with a whole system of brain mechanisms, which are antagonistic to the RAS. Thus he writes (p. 134):

"There is a sleep system in the brain but it seems to be more complex than the activating system. There are at least three major components of the sleep system-a sleep inducing mechanism in the lower brain stem, a descending limbic hypnogenic circuit, and the neocortex. All of these influences affect a thalamic moderating system and the reticular arousal system. The complex sleep system appears to be antagonistic to the reticular arousal system important in wakefulness and most motivational states."

In addition to these three sleep mechanisms in the lower brain stem, the limbic system and the neocortex, there is an additional sleep center in the hypothalamus. Thus the sleep motive has a much more complicated physiological basis than any of the other physiological motives which it otherwise resembles.

The relationship of the sleep motive to learning and performance is covered in the fifth chapter. Although the sleep motive apparently seems to *decrease* learning and performance, Murray finds that under special conditions, e. g., where sleep is a relevant reward for the learning or performance of a response, the sleep motive *increases* learning and performance. Of course, sleepiness and fatigue interfere with most cognitive activities. Other motives can also interfere with learning and performance when there is a conflict between the sleep motive and other relevant motives. Thus the sleep motive is similar to the other physiological motives in this aspect as well.

Murray also deals with the relationships between the sleep motive and arousal, aggression, anxiety and defensive adaptations. In all these relationships the sleep motive also resembles the other physiological motives.

The pathology of sleep and the socialization of sleep also demonstrate that sleep is a physiological motive similar in many fundamental aspects to other physiological motives.

In conclusion, we wish to emphasize that Murray with this book has made a very valuable contribution to motivational theory by collecting such a large number of experimental results about sleep, which he convincingly demonstrates can be integrated by means of the hypothetical construct of the sleep motive.

7. Schachter's theory

Stanley Schachter has written a small book *The Psychology of Affiliation* (1959) which contains the results of an exceptionally interesting and fruitful research concerning social motivation. On the basis of several theoretical considerations the author makes up his mind to investigate the relation between anxiety and the affiliative tendency. The experimental subjects (college students) are placed in an anxiety-producing situation (by "threats" of electrical shock), and are allowed to choose between loneliness and company while they are waiting for the anxiety-producing stimulus. Most people choose to be together with other people – even if verbal communication is prohibited. They prefer, however, to be together with persons (though unknown) who are subject to the same situation, rather than outsiders, which indicates that company has anxiety-reducing effects. Great individual differences are characteristic features of the reactions, which prove to be dependent on the position among the siblings. An only child and the child first born will be more anxious, and will react more socially in the same anxiety-producing situation than later children. These facts are due to differences of child-rearing practices, which have been proved by several investigations.

The experimental principal results concerning the relation between position among the siblings, anxiety and affiliative tendency are supplemented with other experiments (about the influence of hunger), and are supported by references to other psychologists' experiments dealing with factual situations of life (e. g., fighter pilots' reactions during the Korean war).

8. Thomae's Metatheory

In *Hans Thomae* (Herausg.): *Allgemeine Psychologie II. Motivation* (1965) is presented a metatheoretical study of motivational theories. This impressive handbook of close to one thousand pages forms the second volume of "Handbuch der Psychologie in 12 Bänden", which at this writing is not completed. The book is the result of a considerable amount of team-work between many authors: R. Bergius, O. M. Ewert, H. Feger, W. D. Fröhlich, C. F. Graumann, H. Heckhausen, U. Lehr, P. Leyhausen, F. Merz, A. Mischerlich, E. Mittenecker, H. Schmidtke, H. Thomae, H. Vogel and F. Weinert. All these contributors are German psychologists, but the book deals not only with German and continental psychology but with Anglo-American psychology as well. I think that the "Handbuch" is a sign of an over-all up-to-dating in present day German psychology. In addition the "Handbuch" shows the special German interest in systematic classifications and theory construction. Thus the book is divided in the following way:

"I Teil: Allgemeine Motiviationslehre", "II Teil: Differentielle Motivationslehre", "III Teil: Specielle Motivationslehre" and "IV Teil: Ansätze zu einer Theorie der Motivation".

The present author has not seen any book with such a systematic and thorough treatment of the problems of motivation. This book may come to be regarded as a standard when making "motivational classifications". The present author finds that this "Handbuch" contains a fruitful combination of both empirical and theoretical (and metatheoretical) analysis.

In this last respect it is comparable to the big American standard work initiated by the American Psychological Association and edited by *S. Koch*.

PART III
COMPARATIVE
STUDY

In this part of the book we present the results of our *comparative*, systematological studies of modern theories of motivation. For practical purposes we decided to follow our systematological questionnaire or taxonomy, which we used in our *analytical*, systematological studies of the single theories as a kind of outline.

Therefore, in this part of the book we have: First, a chapter about "the metastrata of the theories"; second, one about "the hypothetical strata"; third, one about "the descriptive strata"; and fourth, one about "the theories as wholes".

17. The Metastrata of the Theories

Introduction

In this chapter we bring the results of our comparative, systematological study of the metastrata of those modern theories of motivation which we have analyzed in this book[1]).

In this and the following chapters we include as well our comparative study of the earlier theories of motivation which we presented in "Theories of Motivation". The earlier theories are those of: McDougal (McD), Tolman (To), Young (Y), Lewin (L), Allport (A), Murray (Mu), Hull (Hu), Hebb (He), Tinbergen (Ti) and McClelland (McC), each covered by a chapter in the above work. In addition, the following ten theories were studied in one common chapter: Frenkel-Brunswik (FB), Masserman (Mas), Freeman (Frm), Moore (Mo), Maier (Mai), Cattell (Ca), French (Frh), Stagner and Karworski (S+K), Skinner (S) and Holt-Hansen (H-H)[2]).

As we are following the same outline as in the analytical studies of the single theories, we shall in this chapter deal with the *philosophical*, the *metatheoretical* and the *methodological* propositions of the theories.

The Philosophical Propositions of the Theories

Epistemological propositions

The most important philosophical problems related to the different sciences are the *epistemological* and the *ontological*.

The psychological theories we have studied have not very often had explicitly formulated presuppositions about epistemological problems, such as the nature, conditions and critical evaluation of knowledge (including scientific information).

1. Unfortunately we have only been able to include in our comparative study the theories having their own chapters, and we have *not* included the 10 theories from Chapter 16.
2. We did not include Freud in our "Theories of Motivation", because that would require a whole book, which unfortunately, we have not written as yet! For the following comparative studies we have selected 12 in all: the ten taken up in separate chapters plus Skinner and Moore.

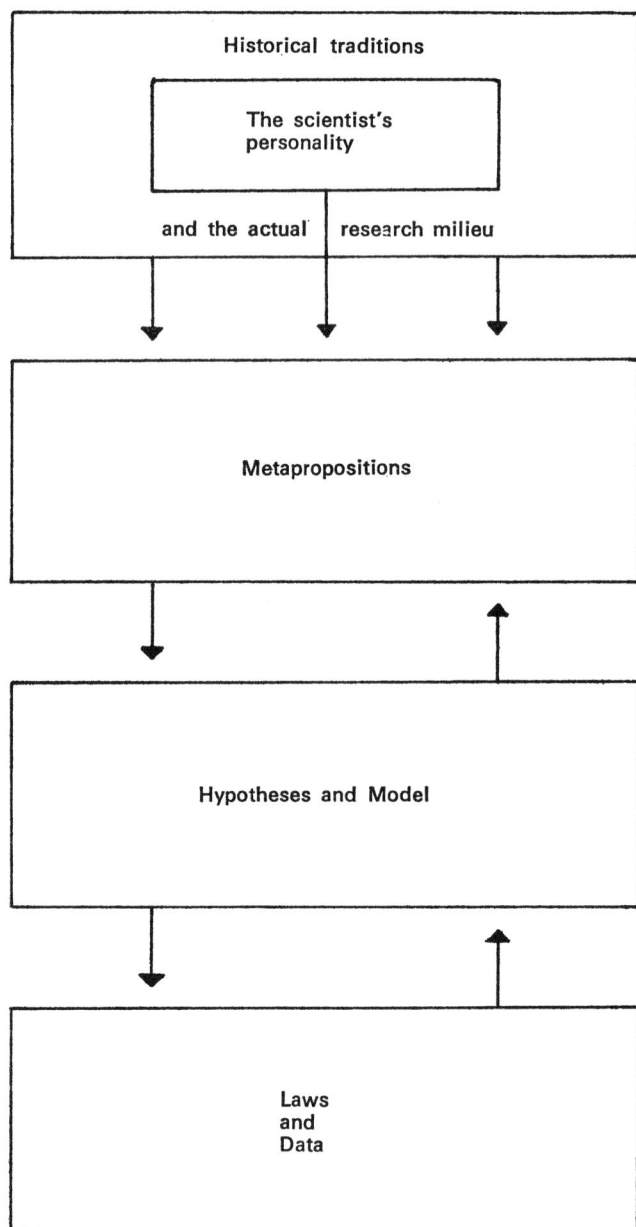

Fig. 17.1. A model of the general metascientific theory: The personal, social and historical factors determine the M-, H- and D-levels of the theory. We presuppose critical feedback between the three levels of the theory, but not feedback to the determining factors.

It is thus often necessary to infer from the whole context what position a psychologist has taken to the epistemological problems.

We have found it useful to employ *Joseph Royce's psycho-epistemological theory*, which classifies the different epistemological positions into three main theories of knowledge: the two "classic" theories, *empiricism* and *rationalism*, as well as a new one, *metaphorism* ("intuitionism"). The main reason for choosing Royce's theory is that he combines epistemological classification with a psychological theory (cf. our introduction in Chapter 2). Royce's *psycho-epistemological* theory states that the scientist's personality determines the kind of epistemological theory he prefers.

We think that Royce's psycho-epistemological theory can be expanded into a *general metascientific theory:* The scientist's personality determines – together with social and historical factors – the *metapropositions* he prefers, and as a consequence of this what kind of *theory* he constructs, and what kind of *data* he collects. We can illustrate this metascientific theory by means of a graphic model (Fig. 17.1.), which should be compared with our diagram (Fig. 1.2.) in Chapter 1.

After this generalization of Royce's theory into a more general metascientific theory, we return to our comparative study of the theories. For this purpose we find it convenient to differentiate between two categories of empiristic positions: "Radical empiricism" (or "positivism"), and "rational empiricism" (or "logical empiricism").

We can now apply this classification of epistemological positions to the modern and earlier theories of motivation which we have studied. This is presented in the following classification (Fig. 17.2.).

Theories of Knowledge	Radical Empiricism	Rational Empiricism	Rationalism	Metaphorism
Modern Theories	Duffy? Bindra?	Berlyne Konorski Pribram Miller Brown Woodworth Festinger Cattell Atkinson		Maslow?
Earlier Theories	Skinner Young? McClelland?	McDougall Tolman Lewin Murray Hull Hebb Tinbergen		Allport? Moore

Fig. 17.2. Classification of the modern and earlier theories of motivation according to their presupposed theories of knowledge. Of the earlier theories we have selected 12 of the 20 studied.

Psychosomatic Theories	Materialism	Neutral Monism	Dualism
Modern Theories	Duffy? Bindra? Konorski?	Pribram Miller Brown Woodworth Festinger Cattell Atkinson Berlyne?	Maslow?
Earlier Theories	Hebb Tinbergen Skinner	McDougall Murray Lewin Young Tolman Hull McClelland	Allport Moore

Fig. 17.3. Classification of the theories according to their presupposed psychosomatic theses. The question mark after some of the names indicates doubt about the classification. The three modern theories classified as materialistic could also be classified as neutral monistic. It is their application of H_O-terms which is the basis for the present classification. We have selected 12 of the earlier theories, which were classified as "behavioristic", "neutral formal", and "mentalistic", which we regard as similar to the present classification.

The mind-body problem

The most important *ontological* problem for psychologists is the *psychosomatic* or "mind-body" problem. Psychologists are a little more explicit in their theories about this problem than when dealing with the epistemological problem. Of the different theories about the mind-body problem presented in Chapter 2, we have only found the following three included in the theories we have studied: *materialism, neutral monism* and *dualism*. The last one is not formulated so explicitly that we can decide whether it represents parallelism or epiphenomenalism. But we think that the third possible version of dualism, the interactionistic theory, can be excluded, as it is very difficult to defend on the basis of modern scientific knowledge.

It has been difficult to classify all the theories we have studied concerning their presupposed propositions about the psychosomatic problem. We decided to classify all the *doubtful* cases as *neutral monistic* theories. Thus – while writing the single chapters – we interpreted indifference or lack of explicit formulations as an implicit statement favoring neutral monism.

But there is another possibility, namely to classify the theories according to the kind of surplus meaning connected with the H-terms. Thus one might conclude that theories with H_O-*terms* (possessing physiological surplus meaning) presuppose a *materialistic* theory of the "mind-body" problem, and similarly, theories with H_N-*terms* (with neutral surplus meaning) are believed to presuppose a *neutral monistic* theory, and, finally, theories with H_M-*terms* (with mentalistic surplus meaning) presuppose a *dualistic* theory. This interpretation is the basis for the above classification scheme, in which the doubtful cases are indicated by a question mark.

The reader may have noticed that we have placed *Pribram*'s theory among the neutral monistic theories, even though Pribram himself has explicitly formulated a *pluralistic* theory of the "mind-body" problem. But it is our opinion that this very original theory comes much closer to the neutral monistic theories, because he assumes that plural levels of discourses reveal a common structure.

After these discussions it is time to present our classification of the modern and earlier theories of motivation in the above classification scheme (Fig. 17.3.).

The philosophy of man

Thanks to Maslow and the other humanistic psychologists we have included the presupposed *conception of man* in the different theories.

Maslow has formulated a humanistic conception of man which he sets up against the generally accepted biological conception which has – often implicitly

Conception of Man	Biological Conception	Humanistic Conception
Modern Theories	11 Modern Theories	Maslow
Earlier Theories	18 Earlier Theories	Allport Moore

Fig. 17.4. The modern and earlier theories classified according to their presupposed conception of man.

– been presupposed by psychologists since its inception as an independent, experimental science. All the other psychologists explicitly formulate – or seem to presuppose implicitly – a biological conception of man.

Among earlier theorists Allport and Moore explicitly presupposed a humanistic conception of man, while the others presupposed a biological conception. Thus we have the above classification scheme (Fig. 17.4.).

The Metatheoretical Propositions of the Theories

Introduction

This part of the metastratum is often formulated much more explicitly and in a more detailed fashion in modern psychological theories than the philosophical propositions. We have discussed several metatheoretical problems in the introductory chapters, and we shall use this conceptual frame-of-reference as the basis for the following comparative studies. In the first section, however, we shall deal with a metatheoretical problem which we have not mentioned earlier in this book. It concerns the different *conceptions ("images", "ideals") of science* which exist in different cultural traditions. We have not introduced this subject earlier because it first came to our knowledge after work on this book was begun. Our interest in the problem was excited by a book by the Swedish metascientist *Gerard Radnitzky:* "Contemporary Schools of Metascience", which first appeared in 1968.

Conceptions of science

In his book Radnitzky introduces three schools of metascience, each possessing its own conception of "science".

First is the Anglo-Saxon School (or schools) of metascience. The chief representative of this school is *logical empiricism*, which equates "science" with the *natural* sciences. If psychology, the social and the humanistic sciences are to be regarded as "real" sciences, they have to develop according to the "naturalistic ideal of science". According to this conception the tasks of science are 1) *objective observation,* 2) *description* of the observations, 3) *explanation and prediction* of the observed "facts", and 4) *application* of this knowledge to technology.

It is obvious from this summary that most modern psychologists seem to have a naturalistic conception of science. But, nevertheless, there are psychologists who have another conception of science.

The second school of metascience is the so-called "hermeneutic-humanistic". This school has a long tradition among the humanistic sciences, especially in history and the text-interpreting philological sciences. A leading figure in the contemporary hermeneutic schools is the German philosopher, *Karl-Otto Apel*[3]). According to Radnitzky the tasks of *humanistic* science are: 1) *description*, 2) *interpretation*, and 3) *understanding* (i. e., "Verstehen").

We find this conception of science quite similar to *Gordon W. Allport's* conception of an *idiographic* personality theory (as opposed to a "nomothetic" psychology). We also think that this conception of science is similar to Maslow's and the humanistic psychologists' conception of "humanistic psychology". The aim of these psychologists is also "understanding". But it is our opinion that the European hermeneutic school of metascience has developed a much more elaborate, systematic and precise metatheory of hermeneutics than their American counterparts with their implicit conceptions of humanistic psychology.

The third school of metascience is the so-called "Frankfurter Schule" with its conception of the *dialectical, critical social sciences*. The most well known leaders of this school are *T. Adorno, J. Habermas* and *H. Marcuse*. According to this school the task of *social* science is *criticism* of social institutions, organizations and the implicit *ideologies* behind societies. As the reader may know this dialectical-critical social metatheory has been the inspiration for the recent "revolutions" in various European universities.

We think that this school's conception of science as being neither "value free" nor "value neutral" comes near to Maslow's and other humanistic psychologists' claim that psychologists ought to explicitly present their philosophy of man and their value system.

These three conceptions of science are not necessarily in contradiction. Only one of them has been proclaimed as *the* ideal, toward which all science must inevitably develop. This was the case with the logical empiricists with their naturalistic conception of science. All three conceptions can be regarded as having their own individual domains and thus supplementing each other. Furthermore, there is a possibility of making a *synthesis* of these three conceptions of science. Radnitzky has – in co-operation with the Swedish-Finnish psychoanalyst, *Carl Lesche*, and inspired by the ideas from *K.-O. Apel* – demonstrated how *psychoanalysis* can be regarded as a science which is both *naturalistic* and *hermeneutic*. We have attempted below to summarize this conception of psychoanalysis.

The psychoanalytic treatment starts as a *dialogue* between the patient and the psychoanalyst, who *possibly understands* at once what the patient tells him. If he does *not* understand he tries to *interpret* what the patient says – among other things his descriptions of dreams. If he succeeds in this interpretation the dialogue will continue to produce understanding, but if he does *not* succeed he

---

3. An introduction to Apel's considerable production can be found in: K.-O. Apel: Analytic philosophy of language and the "Geisteswissenschaften". (In: *Foundations of Language.* Suppl. Series, Vol. 5. Dodrecht: Reidel, 1967).

must *explain* the patient's behavior by turning to the psychoanalytic theories. If this explanation succeeds it is perhaps "translated" for the patient in the form of an interpretation, and the dialogue may continue with mutual understanding until a new explanation is necessary and so on. Thus the psychoanalysis can be regarded as "dialectical reversal" between two levels: the hermeneutic interpretation and the naturalistic explanation, which we can illustrate by means of a diagram (Fig. 17.5.).

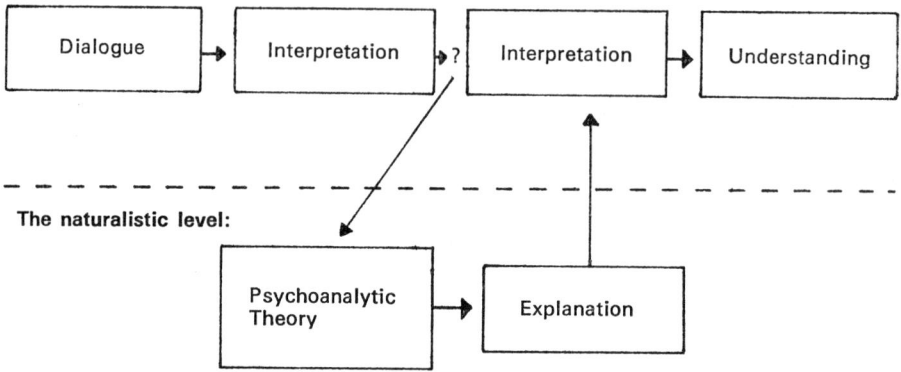

Fig. 17.5. Diagram illustrating the synthesis between the hermeneutic and naturalistic conceptions of science, integrated in the psychoanalytic process (according to Radnitzky).

We can conclude this section with a classification scheme (Fig. 17.6.).

Conception of Science	Tasks of Science:	Examples from Modern Theories:	Examples from Earlier Theories:
The Naturalistic Conception	Explanation, Prediction	11 Modern Theories	18 Earlier Theories
The Hermeneutric Conception	Interpretation, Understanding	Maslow	Allport Moore?
The Dialectical Conception	Criticism, Emancipation	None	None

Fig. 17.6. Classification of the theories according to their presupposed conception of science. There are none which seem to presuppose a dialectical conception. The only psychological theory known to the present author which perhaps can be regarded as dialectical-critical is that of *Eric Fromm*.

The cognitive status of theories

In his well known work about "The Structure of Science" (1961), *Ernst Nagel* has a chapter with the same title as we have used for this section. In this chapter he deals with a very important problem, which has also been discussed among theoretical psychologists, namely: what relation do theories have to "reality"? Nagel maintains that there are three different positions, which he describes as the "descriptive", the "realist" and the "instrumental views" of theories.

The descriptive view can be equated with the metatheoretical position which conceives of theories as systems of *abstract descriptions of observations*. In psychology we find this view among those who – like Skinner – limit the task of science to descriptions of single events or of regular relationships between events ("laws"). This view is also shared by those psychologists who accept *intervening variables* without any surplus meaning.

The realist view can be equated with the metatheoretical position, which conceives of theories as representing certain *unobserved, hypothetical, but "real"* entities behind the observed phenomena. In psychology this view is shared by two different groups.

There are those psychologists who have as their final goal the "reduction" of psychology to physiology. If this goal were realized the result would be a physiological, *descriptive* theory which would belong to the first view. But nobody believes that this goal has been reached, and therefore conceive of their theories as hypotheses referring to the *neuro-physiological structrues and processes behind behavior* – the "conceptual nervous system" as Skinner ironically called it. This view is shared by those – like Hebb and Konorski – who employ hypothetical terms with physiological surplus meaning (S-O-R-theories). *Merle B. Turner* has produced a very detailed and thorough argumentation for the reductionist view (Turner, 1967).

The other group sharing the realist view is composed of psychologists who conceive of theories as referring to *the mental structures and processes behind behavior and conscious experiences*. This view is held by those who use hypothetical terms with mentalistic surplus meaning (S-M-R-theories).

The difference between the two sub-groups of psychologists sharing the realist view is to be found in their presupposed theory of the psychosomatic problem. *The mentalistic realists* have a dualistic theory of the "mind-body" problem, while the *reductive realists* have a materialistic or a neutral monistic theory of this problem.

The instrumentalist view is the metatheoretical position that conceives of theories as *"instruments" or "tools" for making explanations and predictions*. This view has also been called "conventionalism", which was the name given to it by the famous mathematician and physicist, *Henri Poincaré*. In psychology the instrumentalist view is represented by well known psychologists such as *Freud, Lewin* and *Tolman*. Tolman made it popular among American psychologists under the label *"constructive" theories* (in opposition to "reductive" theories). In the past few years the instrumentalist view has gained many adherents, because mathematical and cybernetic models have demonstrated their utility in psychology. The instrumentalist view is shared by all those psychologists who use hypothetical terms with neutral surplus meaning ($S-H_N-R$-theories).

We can summarize this section by making a classification scheme encompassing the modern and earlier theories of motivation which we have studied (Fig. 17.7.).

Type of explanation

In this section we shall deal with a problem related to the above. In Chapter 2 we discussed the two different types of explanations: *deductions* and *models*. A psychologist may use both kinds of explanation in the same theory. But there are some logical relationships between the metatheoretical positions – descriptive, realistic or instrumentalistic – and the preferred type of explanation. Thus we think that an instrumentalist would logically prefer model explanations, while a descriptivist would prefer deductive explanations. Realists could logically be indifferent and use both kinds of explanation.

Metatheoretical positions	Descriptive view	Realist view: Reductionism	Realist view: Mentalism	Instrumentalist view
Modern Theories	Duffy?	Bindra Konorski Pribram Miller (II)	Maslow	Miller (I) Brown Woodworth Festinger Cattell Atkinson Berlyne
Earlier Theories	Skinner	Tinbergen Hebb Young	Allport Moore	McClelland McDougall Murray Hull Lewin Tolman

Fig. 17.7. Classification scheme of modern and earlier theories of motivation according to their view of the metatheoretical status of the theories. Miller is presented in two places, because his first theory is instrumentalistic, and his second reductionistic.

Preferred Type of Explanation	Deductive Explanations	Mixed Type of Explanations	Model Explanations
Modern Theories	Duffy Brown Woodworth Festinger Maslow	Bindra Miller Cattell Atkinson	Berlyne Konoski Pribram
Earlier Theories	Murray McClelland Skinner	McDougall Allport Hull Hebb Moore Young	Tolman Lewin Tinbergen

Fig. 17.8. Classification scheme of the theories studied according to their preferred type of explanation. The mixed type refers to theories including both types of explanation.

We shall classify the theories studied according to the preferred type of explanation. When inspecting the classification scheme the reader should bear in mind that "deductive explanations" include all kinds of verbal or formal explanations, from loose sketches via explanatory systems to deductive systems in the narrow sense, just as "model explanations" include all kinds of models from verbal analogies via two- and three dimensional, concrete models to computer simulation programs and mathematical models.

With these in mind we present our classification scheme (Fig. 17.8).

The Methodological Propositions of the Theories

Introduction

We have found two categories of methodological propositions in the theories we have studied. The first kind we shall deal with contains the arguments for the preferred type of *method*, and the other the arguments for the preferred type of *data language*.

The type of methods

We have found three main types of methods used in the theories we have studied: *Experimental, test* and *clinical*. The same theory may combine

Preferred methods	Experimental methods		Test methods	Clinical methods
Modern Theories	Duffy Berlyne Bindra Konorski Pribram Brown Woodworth	Festinger Atkinson Miller	Cattell Atkinson Festinger	Maslow Konorski Pribram Miller
Earlier Theories	McDougall Tolman Young Lewin Murray Hull Hebb	Tinbergen McClelland Skinner	Allport Murray McClelland Moore	McDougall Allport Murray Moore

Fig. 17.9. Classification scheme with the modern and earlier theories classified according to the preferred methods. Some theories are placed in more than one category, because they use more than one method.

two or three methods. Nevertheless, we can classify the modern and the earlier theories of motivation according to the most preferred method used (Fig. 17.9).

The data language

In Chapter 2 we presented a discussion of the problems about data language. Most modern psychologists have used the *behavioral* data language, but a few have used the *phenomenological*. Many psychologists have used a mixed data language, but often with the behavioral as the basic one. There has not, however, been much discussion of this problem in the last decade. Most psychologists seem to have found the behavioral data language to be most convenient, without committing themselves to a classic behavioristic metatheory and methodology. The reason for this is that the phenomenological data is presupposed to be translatable to the behavioral data language. Even the humanistic psychologists seem to have accepted a behavioral data language, although they criticize the biological philosophy of man as well as the naturalistic philosophy of science, which is a common trait among American psychologists.

The most serious attack upon the dominance of behavioral data language has come from a number of modern philosophers. The *hermeneutic* school of metascience has claimed that there is a basic, qualitative difference between *behavior* and *acts*. Behavior – even *verbal* behavior – can be *described, explained and predicted* in accordance with the *naturalistic* concept of science. *Human acts*

– to which *language* belongs – can neither be explained nor predicted, but the intention (or "meaning") of the act and the linguistic message may be *interpreted* and *understood* in accordance with the *hermeneutic* conception of science.

This philosophically important distinction between *behavior* and human *acts and language* has not only been set forth by the *hermeneutic* philosophers (Cf. Radnitzky, 1970), but also by *analytic philosophers* belonging to the so-called "Oxford school of philosophy". Thus the Danish philosopher, *Justus Hartnack*, has presented a very thorough analysis of this problem (Cf. Hartnack, 1971).

But, unfortunately, these European philosophers' analyses of the problems of behavior and language have not yet come to the attention of any American psychologists. On the other hand most European philosophers seem to be unfamiliar with *Tolman*'s original distinction between *molecular behavior and molar behavior acts*. (Cf. Tolman, 1932). This distinction is similar to the philosophers' distinction between behavior and acts (including language). But Tolman thought it was possible to deal with molar behavior acts in the S-R-paradigm, if supplemented with the intervening hypothetical variables and thus expanded into an S-H-R-paradigm.

We must leave this philosophical discussion until Chapter 19 and return to our systematological classifications. In our next classification scheme (Fig. 17.10) we bring the classification of the modern and earlier theories according to their preferred data language.

Preferred Data language	Behavioral data language	Mixed or combined data language	Phenomenological data language
Modern Theories	Duffy Berlyne Bindra Brown	Konorski Pribram Miller Woodworth Festinger Maslow? Cattell Atkinson	Maslow?
Earlier Theories	Hebb Tinbergen Hull Skinner	Allport McDougall Murray McClelland Lewin Young Tolman Moore?	Moore?

Fig. 17.10 Classification of the modern and earlier theories according to their preferred data language. Two theories – Maslow's and Moore's – were a little difficult to place.

402 . *The Metastrata of the Theories*

Epistemo-logical Theories	Radical Empiricism		Empiristic	Pure	Metaphorism
			Rationalism		
Psycho-somatic Theories	Materialism		Neutral Monism		Dualism
Meta-theories	Descrip-tionism	Reductive Realism	Instrumentalism		Mentalistic Realism
Preferred H-terms	H_O-terms		H_N-terms		H_M-terms
Preferred Data languages	Behavioral		Mixed or combined datalanguages		Phenomenological

Fig. 17.11 A classification scheme presenting the different metascientific views which psychologists may have on different problems. The scheme is made so that it is easy to conceive of three metascientific patterns of preference or "paradigms":
1) The Empiricist paradigm: The empiristic-materialist-descriptionist (or reductionist)- H_O-terms – behaviorist pattern.
2) The Intuitionist paradigm: The metaphorist – dualist – mentalist – H_M- terms – phenomenologist pattern.
3) The Rationalist paradigm: The rationalist – neutral monist – instrumentalist – H_N-terms – integrationist pattern.

Concluding remarks

The reader may have noticed that in this chapter we have mentioned the possibility of relationships between the different positions concerning the philosophy of science. These remarks are expressions of our general metascientific hypotheses. If the personality of the scientist determines his preference for some of the major philosophical propositions – such as the epistemological and the psychosomatic – then it is logical to assume that these first preferences or choices[4]) may well imply some of the later preferences of metapropositions. In

---

4. We think that the term "preference" is more adequate than the term "choice", because it is rarely a matter of consciously choosing a particular metascientific "strategy", but rather a matter of unconscious personal preferences.

turn this should imply some consequences for theory construction and the collection of data. In other words, we expect some relationships between the preferences or some patterns in the metatheoretical positions adopted by a particular psychologist. E. g., we expect a radical empiricist to be a materialist rather than a dualist, a Darwinian rather than a humanist, a descriptivist rather than a realist or instrumentalist, a behaviorist rather than a phenomenalist and so on.

Such a metatheoretical pattern should influence the H-level and the D-level of the same theory.

We shall illustrate our theory by means of a diagram (Fig. 17.11) and in a later chapter[5]) we can see how "correct" the evidence for the theory is in terms of our material.

---

5. Cf. Appendix A attached to Chapter 20.

18. The Hypothetical Strata of the Theories

Introduction

In this chapter we shall present the results of our comparative study of the hypothetical strata of the theories. As we are following the systematological taxonomy as an outline, we have divided this chapter into two main parts: one dealing with the *hypothetical terms*, and another with the *hypotheses* of the theories studied.

The Hypothetical Terms of the Theories

Introduction

In our systematological taxonomy we have made three classifications of hypothetical terms, namely: 1) Classification of the terms according to their *surplus meaning*, 2) classification of the terms into *dispositional* and *functional* terms and 3) classification of the terms into *dynamic, directive* and *vectorial* terms. To these we have added two sections about: 4) the *definitions* of motivational terms and 5) *classifications* of motivational variables.

The surplus meaning of the H-terms

In Chapter 2 we introduced and discussed the classification of hypothetical terms according to their metascientific status as expressed by their surplus meaning. And in our analytical study of the individual theories we used a simplified version of this systematological classification including:

1. H_O-terms, i. e., hypothetical terms referring to *organic*, especially neurophysiological process and structures. H_o-terms thus have *physiological* surplus meaning.
2. H_M-terms, i.e., hypothetical terms referring to *mental* processe and structures. H_M-terms thus have *mentalistic* surplus meaning.
3. H_N-terms, i. e., hypothetical terms referring to genuine hypothetical *constructs* perhaps inpired by other scientific fields (e. g., cybernetics). In this class we also included the *intervening variables* without any surplus meaning. H_N-terms are thus terms with *neutral* (or no) surplus meaning.

We have classified the terms in the chapters about single theories, and we can now compare these theories by presenting this classification in a classification scheme (Fig. 18.1.).

Name of tye Psychologist	H_O-terms	H_N-terms	H_M-terms
Duffy	Activation Responsiveness		
Bindra	Arousal Blood Chemistry Positive Reinforcing Mechanism	sHr	
Berlyne	Arousal Arousal Potential Drive		
Konorski	Drive Anti-drive Gnostic Units Kinesthetic Analyzers		
Pribram	Homeostats	TOTE-unit Holographic process Screen	Images of Events Monitor Images Images of Achievement
Miller	Go-mechanism Drive	Drive value Cue value Tendencies	
Brown		Drive Frustration Habit sEr	
Woodworth		Drive Set Ability Cognition	
Festinger		Cognitive elements Consonance Dissonance	
Cattell		Ability traits Temperamental traits Dynamic traits: Erg, Sentiment Motivational Components	
Atkinson		Tendency Motive Expectation Incentive	
Maslow			Need system Personality syndrome Mental processes

Fig. 18.1. Classification scheme representing the classification of the H-terms in modern theories of motivation according to the surplus meaning attached to the H-terms. H_O-terms are terms with physiological surplus meaning (referring to hypothetical processes and structures in the organism). H_N-terms are terms with neutral surplus meaning (referring to genuine constructs or to intervening variables without any surplus meaning). H_M-terms are terms with mentalistic surplus meaning (referring to hypothetical mental processes and structures).

406 . *The Hypothetical Strata of the Theories*

Name of the Psychologist:	H_O-terms	H_N-terms	H_M terms
McDougall		Instinct Propensity Tendency	
Tolman		Demand (1932) Need (1951) Drive (1959)	
Young	Drive	Set Attitude	Desire
Allport		Motivational Trait Instrumental Trait	
Lewin		Force Valence Tension	
Murray		Need Beta press Cathexes Thematic Dispositions	
Hull		sEr, sHr Drive Incentive Motivation	
Hebb	Phase sequence Cell assemblies Cue function, Arousal		
Tinbergen	Instinct, Motivation		
McClelland	Affective Arousal	Motive	
Skinner		Response strengh	
Moore			Temperament, Character Reception, Construction Conservation Representative and Active Reactions

Fig. 18.2 Classification scheme representing a classification of the H-terms from the earlier theories of motivation according to their *"surplus meaning."*

We have made a similar classification of the H-terms used in the earlier theories and present the results concerning 12 selected theories in another classification scheme (Fig. 18.2.).

Dispositional and functional terms

In Chapter 2 we introduced the classification of H-terms into *dispositional* and *functional* terms as a classification according to the duration of the existence of the variables. Later, in the chapter about Cattell's theory, we broke down the functional terms which resulted in the following classification:

1. *Dispositional terms*, i. e., H-terms referring to hypothetical variables with a relatively long duration of existence (from years to a lifetime). This includes the hereditary dispositions as well as (mental or neural) "structures" and "factors" based on the results of personality and intelligence tests. These dispositions have a rather *indirect* influence on behavior via the functional variables.

2. *Functional terms*, i. e., H-terms referring to hypothetical variables with a relatively shorter duration of existence:
   a. *"processes":* variables with a very short duration (seconds to hours).
   b. *"states":* variables with a somewhat longer duration (from hours to days).
   c. *"changes":* variables (such as learning and growth processes) which change over periods from seconds to years. Changes may produce new dispositions (structures, etc.).

Unfortunately, we have not found any other theories besides Cattell's containing such precisely defined variables that it is possible to apply to them the more detailed classification. Therefore we present the results of our study of the modern and the earlier theories in the following classification schemes (Fig. 18.3. and 18.4.).

Dynamic, directive and vectorial terms

In Chapter 2 we introduced a third classification of H-terms which we developed in connection with our study of the earlier theories of motivation on the basis of ideas found in the writings of Lewin, Duffy and other theorists. It is a classification of terms according to the *effect* of the variables in behavior. Thus we get:

1. *Dynamic terms*, i. e., terms referring to variables having an exclusively activating, energizing effect on behavior.
2. *Directive terms*, i. e., terms referring to variables having an exclusively directing, steering or regulating effect on behavior.
3. *Vector terms*, i. e., terms referring to variables having a combined dynamic and directive effect on behavior. Vaguely defined terms are also classified as vector terms.

Name of the Psychologist:	Disposition Terms	Function Terms
McDougall	Instinct Propensity Sentiment	Tendency
Tolman	Capacities and Temperamental Traits Means-End-Readiness Belief-Value-Matrix	Expectations Demands (1932) Needs (1951) Drives (1959)
Young	Attitude	Drive, Need, Set, Desire
Allport	Motivational and Instrumental Traits	Motivational and Instrumental Traits
Lewin	Structures of Personality and Environment	Tension, Valence, Force
Murray	Need (1938) Thematic Dispositions, Cathexes (1959)	Need (1938) Press and Cathexes (1938)
Hull	Habit strength (sHr)	Drive (D) Reaction potential (sEr) Incentive motivation (K)
Hebb	Cell assemblies	Phase Sequences (1969) Cue functions and Arousal (1955)
Tinbergen	Instinct mechanisms Innate Releasing Mechanisms	Motivation Motivational Factors
McClelland	Adaptation level	Motive Affective Arousal
Skinner	Reaction probability or Response-strength	Deprivation Reinforcing Aversive stimulation
Moore	Temperament Character Habits	Reception Construction Conservation Actions of circumstances

Fig. 18.3 Classification scheme representing a classification of the H-terms in modern theories of motivation according to the *duration of their existence* into disposition terms and function terms.

Name of the Psychologist:	Disposition Terms	Function Terms
Duffy	Responsiveness	Activation
Bindra	sHr; PRM	Arousal Blood Chemistry
Berlyne	RAS	Arousal
Konorski	Drive mechanism	Drive process Emotion
Pribram	TOTE Screen Homeostats	Image of Event Monitor Image Image of Achievement
Miller	Connection Go-mechanism	Drive value Cue value Tendency
Brown	Habit	Drive sEr
Woodworth	Ability	Drive Set Cognition
Festinger	Cognitive element	Knowledge Dissonance
Cattell	Ability Traits Temperamental Traits M, C and H.	Ergic Tension Physiological State Gratification level
Atkinson	Motive	Tendency Expectation Incentive
Maslow	Need system Personality syndrome	Motivator Mental processes

Fig. 18.4 Classification scheme representing the classification of the terms in the earlier theories of motivation according to the duration of existence into *disposition* terms and *function* terms.

Name of the Psychologist:	Dynamic Terms		Vector Terms	Directive Terms
	General	Specific		
Duffy	Activation			
Bindra	Arousal-level	Blood Chemistry	PRM	sHr
Berlyne	Arousal (D_1)	Drive $_2$ Collative Variables		Cognitive Processes
Konorski		Drive Emotion	Preparatory Reflexes and Activities	Gnostic Units Consummatory Reflexes and Activities
Pribram		Monitor Image	Images of Achievement	Images of Event
Miller	Drive		Tendency Go-mechanism	Cue. Connections
Brown	Drive	Sources of Drive	sEr	sHr
Woodworth		Drive. Set		Ability. Cognition
Festinger		Dissonance		Cognitive elements
Cattell		Dynamic Traits Ergs	Temperamental Traits. Attitudes	Ability Traits. Sentiment
Atkinson		Incentive. Motive	Tendency	Expectation
Maslow				

Fig. 18.5 Classification of the H-terms in the modern theories of motivation according to the corresponding variables' *effect* on behavior.

We have frequently felt the need for another intermediate category between dynamic and vectorial terms. We therefore think it worthwhile to introduce a distinction between *general* and *specific* dynamic terms. The last category includes terms referring to variables which activate a *special* class of behavior. Thus specific dynamic variables differ from general dynamic variables by not

Name of the Psychologist:	Dynamic Terms		Vector Terms	Directive Terms
	General	Specific		
McDougall		Propensity Tendency	Instinct Sentiment	
Tolman		Drive (1951) Demand Need (1951)	Drive (1932) Belief-Value Matrix	Expectation Belief
Young		Drive Need	Desire Motive	Set Attitude
Allport		Drive Motivational trait		Instrumental trait
Lewin		Tension Valence	Force	Structure of Environment
Murray		Press Cathexes	Need Thematic Dispositions	
Hull	Drive	$C_K D$	sEr	sHr
Hebb	Arousal (1955)		Phase sequence (49) Cell assemblies (49)	Cue function (1955)
Tinbergen		Motivational factors Motivation		Instinct
McClelland		Affective arousal	Motive	Cues
Skinner		Deprivation	Aversive Stimuli Reinforcer Response Strength	
Moore		Impulse Desire	Temperament Character Instinct	Reception Construction Conservation Habits

Fig. 18.6 Classification of the H-terms in the earlier theories of motivation according to the corresponding variables' *effect* on behavior.

activating all behavior – only a specific class – and they differ from vector variables by not having a directive or steering function.

We have utilized this classification in a classification scheme including the main terms (and variables) in the modern theories of motivation (Fig. 18.5.) and the earlier theories of motivation (Fig. 18.6.).

Classification According to Effect: / Existence Classification:	Dynamic Terms	Vector Terms	Directive Terms
Dispositions Terms	Dynamic traits (Cattell) Motive (Atkinson)	Need (Murray) Instinct (McDougall) Temperamental traits (Cattell)	Instinct (Tinbergen) Ability traits (Cattell) Sentiment engram (Cattell) sHr (Hull)
Function Terms	Drive (Hull) Incentive (Atkinson) Tension, Valence (Lewin) Ergic tension (Cattell)	sEr (Hull) Tendency (Atkinson) Force (Lewin) Need (Murray)	Expectation (Atkinson)

Fig. 18.7 Combined classification scheme with some selected terms from earlier and modern theories of motivation.

The last two classifications can be combined into one classification scheme (Fig. 18.7.). This combined classification scheme has the advantage of making it easier to see how confusing the motivational terminology is in both modern and earlier theories of motivation. The same term – e. g., "drive" – is used with different meanings, and different terms are used about the same class of variables – e. g., "sEr", "force", "tendency" are all used about a single functional vector variable.

If we had included other classifications, too – e. g., the classification according to surplus meaning – then the picture would have been even more confusing.

For the purpose of demonstrating the utility of this combined classification, we have made a combined classification scheme and included a few representative examples.

Proposals for definitions of motivational terms

Our classifications of terms from the many different theories of motivation reveal two major deficiencies in the present stage of motivational psychology.

The first deficiency concerns the many theories of motivation which are not sufficiently precise in their motivational terminology: They lack different terms for different variables. One particularly striking deficiency is that theories lack different terms for the corresponding functions and dispositions. More precisely it can be stated that the theories having their origin in experimental *learning* psychology lack terms for the *disposition* variables, while theories having their origin in *personality* psychology lack terms for the *function* variables. We hope that our systematological studies in conjunction with the increasing interest in

The Terms proposed	Definitions in Systematological terminilogy	Possible neural bases	Equivalent terms in some theories			
			Hull	Cattell	Lewin	Atkinson
1. "Motivation"	Generic term including all dynamic and vector variables					
2. "Central Motive State" x)	Vector functions, H variables consisting of 2a, 2b and 2c	Sub-cortical brain processes or states	sEr	"E" Ergic tension level	Force	Tendency
2a. "Central sensitization processes" or "Sensitization" xxx)	Specific dynamic xx) functions, H-variables	Activation of hypothalamic and limbic centers	S_D	P Physiological component		
2b. "Central incentive processes" or "Incentive-motive"	Specific dynamic functions H variable	Activation of acquired cortico-sub-cortical structures	K		Valence	Incentive value
2c. "Central activating processes" or "Arousal"	General dynamic xx) functions, H variables	Arousal of Reticular Formation	D		Tension	
3. "Motivational Dispositions"	Dynamic and Vector dispositions, H variables	Individual differences in neural centers or acquired neural structures		Constitution and History	Structural differences in "P" and "E"	Motive
4. "Motivational Stimuli"	Dynamic functions, S variables	Stimuli with inborn releasing effect or with acquired dynamic effect	S+K			
5. "Motivational Impulses"	Dynamic functions, S variables	Neural impulses and humoral influences on sub-cortical centers	C_D (Need)	G Gratification	Need	
6. "Informational processes" or "Cognition"	Directive functions, S and H variables	Sensoric and cortical processes	sHr r_g $-s_g$			Expectation

*) The Term "Central Motive State" was originally proposed by *Clifford T. Morgan*, who has developed a very consistent "physiological theory" of motivation (Morgan, 1957, 1959).

**) We have introduced a distinction between *"specific* dynamic" and *general* dynamic functions, referring to specific, selective activation and unspecific, general activation respectively.

***) The sub-division of "Motive state into "incentive", "sensitization" and "arousal" was inspired by *Cofer and Appley* (1964).

metascientific problems may contribute to improvement of this condition in motivational psychology.

The second deficiency in motivational psychology is concerned with the lack of a common terminology for common variables. It is an obvious hindrance for communication and co-operation between psychologists that they do not have a common language. In order to contribute to an improvement of this situation, we venture to present a series of proposals for common definitions of motivational terms. These proposals are based upon our systematological study of more than fourty theories of motivation. We have added to our proposed definitions an overview of the definitions of similar variables in four of the theories which have been most precise in their definitions of terms.

We present our proposals in a classification scheme (Fig. 18.8.) which is adopted from Madsen (1973)[1].

Classifications of motivational variables

In this part of the chapter we shall deal with the problem of defining the *number* and *main classes* of motivational variables. These are really two interrelated problems. We shall deal with the question of defining the *number* first.

The number of motivational variables. There would be no problem about defining the number of motivational variables if they were all *empirical*. But the historical fact that motivational variables were introduced into psychology for the purpose of *explanation* of (goal-directed) behavoir created the following problem: How many different *hypothetical,* motivational variables must we postulate to explain behavior?

This problem is really a part or version of a more general problem in the philosophy of science: the problem of the fruitfulness, validity or "explanatory power" of hypothetical constructs.

The question can be conceived of as a question of avoiding two dangerous extremes:

One extreme is the explanatory approach which involves the construction of so many hypothetical variables that we have one for every fact we wish to explain. This is the *"pseudo-explanatory approach"*. Thus in this case we have just as many motivational variables as there are goal-directed behavior acts to be explained. It is easy to see that this approach leads to a pseudo-explanation with a superfluous duplicity of all terms: a set of *descriptive* terms and a parallel set of *hypothetical* terms. This was the chief failure of the old "instinct" theories, that they deprived their hypothetical constructs of any "explanatory power" or predictive validity by creating too many constructs.

The other extreme explanatory approach is the one which tries to explain everything by one or very few hypothetical constructs. This is the *"speculative philosophical approach"*. The most well-known case in the history of psychology is Freud's "life instinct" vs. "death instinct".

Perhaps it is not so easy to see the shortcomings in this speculative philosophical approach, because the purpose of theories is always to *reduce the number of data by organizing or systematizing them into fewer categories*. And further the number of *abstract descriptive categories* may be organized into a coherent

---

1. The principles for the proposals of definitions of terms are elaborated in Chapter 18 of my "Theories of Motivation" (1st ed., 1959, 4th ed., 1968).

system by introducing a few *hypothetical constructs*. So it seems to be a consequence of this general scientific approach that we try to reduce as often as possible by introducing the fewest possible hypothetical variables – perhaps only one. But the danger of this approach is that it may be very difficult – even impossible – to connect such an abstract hypothetical variable to empirical variables with *operational* definitions.

Thus the solution of the problem is to construct *the optimal number of hypothetical variables:* enough variables to avoid speculative philosophical vagueness by making operational definitions possible, and not so many variables that they become pseudo-explanatory.

N. E. *Miller* has demonstrated very clearly (in Miller, 1959) that the introduction of an intervening or hypothetical variable is justified by the old epistemological *"principle of economy"* if – and only if – *the hypothetical variable is connected with at least three S-variables on one side and three R-variables on the other*. This may be conceived of as a rule for avoiding the pseudo-explanatory fallacy. Unfortunately we do not know a similar simple rule for avoiding the speculative philosophical fallacy. Psychologists have, in this case, to make use of their scientific self-control.

Fortunately most modern theories of motivation demonstrate that most psychologists of to-day have avoided the two extreme explanatory approaches and instead have used what we could call *"a moderate parsimonious reduction"* or perhaps better: an *"optimal explanatory conceptual system"*.

These terms were selected because the history of science demonstrates – as strongly emphasized by the provocative theory of *Thomas Kuhn* (1962) – that scientists prefer the most *parsimonious* theories with the most *explanatory "power"* and avoid the oversimplified "philosophical" approach as well as the pseudo-explanatory "theories".

Fortunately, we may characterize the majority of modern theories of motivation as belonging to the group of optimally parsimonious systems. Thus in most modern theories of motivation parsimonious reduction is obtained by assuming the existence of an optimal system of basic motivational variables or *"primary motives"*. These primary motives – also called "biogenic", "viscerogenic", "organical", "instinctive", "inborn" or "unlearned" motivational variables – are often estimated to number about 10–15. In addition to this most – but not all – theories presuppose the existence of an indeterminate number of *"secondary motives"* – also called "psychogenic", "learned" or "acquired" motivational variables. Furthermore, many theories of motivation presuppose the existence of certain principles for *combinations* of motivational variables into *"motivational systems"* (such as "sentiments", etc.). By this addition the explanatory power of the theories is increased without sacrificing the parsimonious number of basic, explanatory concepts.

But this *categorizing* into *"primary" and "secondary"* motives" has raised at least two problems:

1. What criteria should be used in defining a system of "primary motives"?
2. How is the development of "secondary motives" explained?

We shall deal with these two problems in the following two sections of this chapter.

Criteria for the definition of "primary motives"

In a comparative study of 20 theories of motivation the present author found (Madsen, 1968) that three different criteria for defining "primary motives" are used.

The most commonly used criterion may be called the *"physiological criterion"*. According to this rule the definition of "primary motives" is accomplished by selecting those motivational variables which are known to be functionally related to observable physiological states or processes (outside the central nervous system). Thus *"primary motives" are organically determined motivational variables.*

At the present time psychologists using this physiological criterion can agree about the existence of a dozen "primary motives" – such as hunger, thirst, sex, etc. They are known to be mainly determined – but not necessarily exclusively – by organic states or processes outside the CNS. In most instances it is possible to determine – by the use of electrophysiological or other methods – the location of "motivational centers" in the hypothalamus or other parts of the brain.

The physiological criterion has many advantages: it results in maximum agreement among psychologists and it facilitates co-operation between psychologists and physiologists.

Another widely used criterion for defining "primary motives" may be called the *comparative-psychological criterion* (or by *H. Thomae*, the "universal behavior repertoire" ("universellen Verhatlensinventar"), (Thomae, 1965). According to this principle "primary motives" are selected from among the motivational variables that are supposed to determine universal classes of behavior – or at least species-specific behavior. In other words: *"primary motives" are motivational variables which determine universal behavior acts.* If we apply this criterion we arrive at almost the same set of "primary motives" as that established by the physiological criterion. But the comparative-psychological criterion has the disadvantage that only a few species-specific or common human behavior acts exist. Most human behavior is learned and consequently varies very much among individuals. Only in a rather homogeneous group with a common cultural background do we find any common behavior acts.

A *third* criterion for the definition of "primary motives" Thomae calls *"the cue criterion"* ("Schlüsselreiz-"criterion, *Thomae*, 1965). According to this criterion "primary motives" are selected from among motivational variables which are known to be determined by a species-specific releasing stimulus which presupposes the existence of IRM ("Innate Releasing Mechanisms", as defined by *Tinbergen*, 1951). In other words: *"Primary motives" are motivational variables determined by innate "cues"*.

The cue criterion has the same disadvantage as the criterion of universal behavior: we know about very few innate cues in Man.

With these three criteria we have exhausted all the possibilities for *directly operational definitions:* the *hypothetical motivational variables* called "primary motives" are defined either by their *causes* (organic processes *or* innate cues) or by their *consequences* (species-specific or universal behavior).

We shall only discuss one more criterion which McDougall, among others, applied. It may be called the *psychopathological* criterion" as it defines "primary motives" as motivational variables which the organism must have "satisfied" or reduced in order to retain health and life (therefore, it may also be called the "survival criterion"). If we apply this criterion, we arrive at approximately the same – perhaps a smaller – number of "primary motives".

In concluding this discussion of criteria for the definition of "primary motives" we may propose: that *maximum agreement about definitions or "primary motives" may be accomplished by using all the criteria in combination* and only selecting those as "primary motives" which are so-defined by all the criteria. The one criterion which alone is the most useful is – as mentioned earlier – the *physiological criterion*. By using this criterion we arrive at the following list of "primary motives" (see Fig. 18.9.). Alongside we have placed those established by Cattell, McDougal, Murray and Young.

Secondary Motivation

This important problem has been studied intensively during the past few decades. A very extensive and penetrating review of research and theories has been made by *J. S. Brown* and *L. F. Farber* (Brown and Farber, 1968). In addition, Brown has proposed one of the clearest and most consistent theories concerning secondary motivation (in Brown, 1961). Therefore, in the following pages we shall draw considerably on these sources.

The earlier theories of motivation – such as Tolman's and Murray's – introduced the notion of "acquired drives" or "psychogenic needs", but they did not possess any explanatory hypotheses with experimental support concerning the origins of secondary motivation.

The first experimental investigation of the origins of secondary motivation was carried out by *O. H. Mowrer* (1939). This was supplemented by N. E. Miller (1941 and 1948), who later made extensive use of the concept of secondary motivation in his and Dollard's book about "Social Learning" (1941). In these early experiments and theories *fear* (or anxiety) was regarded as the basis for secondary motivation. In their classic experiments they first demon-

Fig. 18.9. Primary motivational variables in some theories

McDougall's "Propensities" 1932	Young's "Primary Drives" 1936	Murray's "Viscerogenic Needs" 1938	Cattell's "Ergs" 1950	Madsen's "Primary Motives" 1959
1. Food seeking p	1. Hunger	1. n Inspiration	1. Escape	1. Hunger Motive
2. Disgust p	2. Nausea	2. n Water	2. Appeal	2. Thirst Motive
3. Sex p	3. Thirst	3. n Food	3. Acquisitiveness	3. Sex Motive
4. Fear p	4. Sex	4. n Sentience	4. Laughter	4. Nursing Motive
5. Curiosity p	5. Nursing	5. n Sex	5. Pugnacity	5. Temperature Motives
6. Protective and parental p	6. Urinating	6. n Lactation	6. Self-assertion	6. Pain-avoidance Motive
7. Gregarious p	7. Defecating	7. n Expiration	7. Sleep	7. Excretory Motives
8. Self-assertive p	8. Avoiding heat	8. n Urination	8. Play	8. Oxygen Motive
9. Submissive p	9. Avoiding cold	9. n Defecation	9. Self-abasement	9. Rest and Sleep Motive
10. Anger p	10. Avoiding pain	10. n Noxavoidance	10. Mating	10. Activity Motives
11. Appeal p	11. Air hunger	11. n Heatavoidance	11. Gregariousness	11. Security Motive (or fear)
12. Constructive p	12. Fear and Anger	12. n Coldavoidance	12. Parental drive	12. Aggression Motive
13. Acquisitive p	13. Fatigue	13. n Harmavoidance	13. Curiosity	
14. Laughter p	14. Sleep		14. Construction	
15. Comfort p	15. Curiosity		15. Disgust	
16. Rest or sleep p	16. Social instinct		16. Hunger	
17. Migratory p	17. Tickle			
18. Coughing, sneezing, breathing, evacuation, etc.				

strated that fear as an unconditioned reaction to noxious stimuli could be conditioned to a previously neutral stimulus. Next, they demonstrated that this conditioned fear could motivate the learning of a new instrumental reaction. This first experimental establishment of fear as an acquirable drive was followed up by many experiments. Many of these have been conducted to *disprove* the original notions of Mowrer and Miller, but in spite of this, Brown and Farber conclude their critical survey with these words:

"– – it is worth noting that the concept of conditioned fear as a secondary motivational system has proved unusually robust" (in Brown and Farber, 1968, p. 110).

The present author consequently believes that Brown's own theory (Brown, 1961) is based on convincing experimental evidence. In his theory he proposes the hypothesis that fear is the basis for (almost) all secondary motivation.

In their review Brown and Farber further emphasize the possibility that Hull's and Spence's *incentive motivation* (K) may be another important source of secondary motivation. Brown and Farber survey the numerous experimental investigations and theoretical discussions concerning this concept. They seem to be inclined to accept a sort of *"frustration interpretation"* of the motivating function of "K" (or "$r_g - s_g$") with these words:

"This view implies that it is the lack of an incentive or goal object, in the presence of cues previously associated with that incentive that is motivating. Anticipatory motivation is thus transformed into deficit motivation with aversive properties and the conditions leading to this sequence of events are indistinguishable from those that produce frustration" (p. 115 in Brown and Farber, 1968).

Thus Brown and Farber have reduced all (secondary) motivation to the same formula: "deficit or aversive motivation".

They further discuss – and seem to accept – the possibility of an *"incentive motivation interpretation"* of *sensory* reinforcements from novel stimuli, etc. This interpretation seems to be close to that proposed by *Harry Fowler* (1967) but contrary to *D. E. Berlyne*'s drive interpretation of curiosity (Berlyne, 1960).

Brown and Farber conclude that other *primary* need states like hunger and thirst do not seem to be conditionable.

We can thus *conclude* this discussion of *secondary motivation* in this way: Secondary motivation seems to be based on – or perhaps is identical with – *conditioned fear* and *incentive motivation*. Both sources of secondary motivation may be interpreted as *types of aversive or deficit motivation*. We can thus see a clear similarity to *primary motivation* as conceived by *Hull* and his followers.

But there are, of course, other explanations of primary (and secondary) motivation, and, therefore, we shall analyze and compare the basic hypotheses of motivation in the next section of this chapter.

The Hypotheses of the Theories

Introduction

In accordance with our systematological taxonomy we begin with a comparison of the summaries of the theories we have studied. It is presented in the form of a *new classification* of motivational theories according to their *basic hypotheses*, axioms, postulates or *"models of motivation"*.

In the following sections we continue with the classifications of hypotheses according to their *complexity* and later according to their presupposed *functional relationships*[2]).

Basic hypotheses of motivation

We have found it convenient to classify the basic hypotheses – axioms or postulates – of motivation into four categories. We call them "models of motivation" because they are often *systems of interrelated hypothetical variables, which can be represented by a "model"*. These models may be concrete, diagramtic models, but in many cases they are only verbal analogies. In some cases they are mathematical models. However, in this section we are not interested in the formal development of the models, which we shall return to in Chapter 20, but instead concentrate on the content of the models of motivation.

According to the main content of the basic hypotheses in the models, we can classify them into four categories: 1) The "homeostatic" model, 2) the "incentive" model, 3) the "cognitive" model and 4) the "humanistic" model.

1. *The homeostatic model*. This is the oldest model in the history of motivational psychology. The concept of "homeostasis" was formulated by the famous American psychologist *Walter B. Cannon* in 1915 (see Cannon, 1915). He was inspired by the French physiologist *Claude Bernard*'s conception of the "internal milieu". Besides, a similar conception was formulated by *Freud* at the same times as Cannon (see Freud, 1915).

The special feature of the homeostatic model is that *all biological processes – including behavior – are determined* by a disturbance of "homeostasis", i. e., the optimal conditions of equilibrium in the organism. And the biological processes – including behavior – go on until homeostasis is restored (or the organism is dead). Formulated in more familar psychological terms the homeostatic model indicates that: A disturbance of homeostasis constitutes a *need* which in turn determines a central *drive*. Together with cognitive processes this drive determines *behavior*, which reduces – or "satisfies" – the need, and thus reestablishes homeostasis (Cf. Fig. 18.10.).

2. The classification of hypotheses in S-H, H-H and H-R-hypotheses is dealt with in connection with the Hypotheses Quotient in our last chapter.

The Hypothetical Strata of the Theories . 421

Fig. 18.10. Models of Motivation

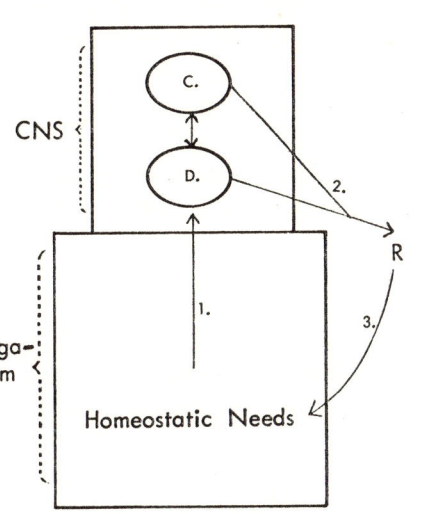

Homeostatic Hypotheses

R. = f (Dynamic, Cognitive)
Dyn. proc. = f (Needs)

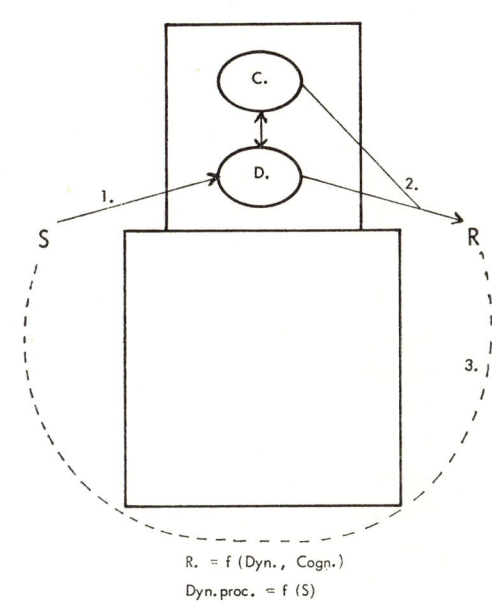

Incentive Hypotheses

R. = f (Dyn., Cogn.)
Dyn. proc. = f (S)

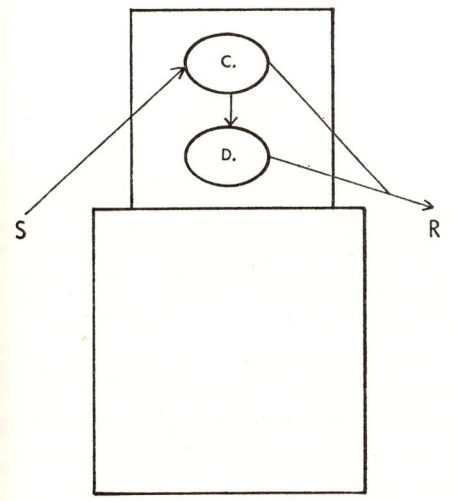

Cognitive Hypotheses

R = f (Dynamic, Cognitive)
Dyn. proc. = f (Cogn.)
Cogn. proc. = f (S)

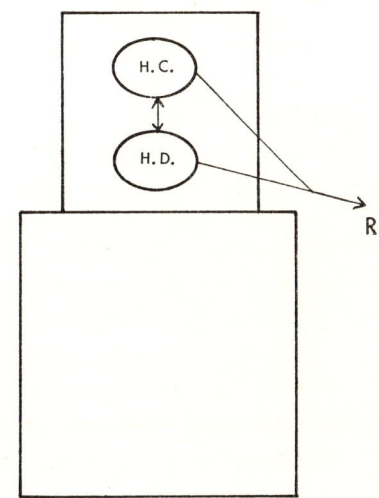

Humanistic Hypotheses

R = f (Human Dyn., Human Cogn.)
Hum. Dyn. proc. = f (?) } Indeterministic
Hum. Cogn. proc. = f (?)

This homeostatic model is found in such influential theories as those of Freud and Hull. And many other psychologists have adopted this model, because it has several advantages. The most important of these are: 1) it is a *simple* model, which is always an important quality for scientists and 2) it is a *biological* model, which was important for psychologists in the post-Darwinian period.

The popularity of the model led psychologists to misuse it and to ignore for a long time facts, which did not fit into the model. Finally, the homeostatic model was so severely criticized that it could not retain its position as the only valid motivational model. Other models were created as alternatives to the homeostatic model.

2. The incentive model

The "homeostatic period" lasted from about 1915 (the year of Cannon's first formulation) until about 1953 (the year of the first Nebraska Symposium on Motivation). Thus *H. F. Harlow* criticized the homeostatic model as being too narrow at the first Nebraska Symposium. He pointed out that there were other biological primary motivations besides homeostatic drive. He was especially concerned with the existence of a visual exploratory drive (see Harlow, 1953).

Later it was demonstrated by many experiments that even the so-called "homeostatic drives" (especially hunger, thirst and sex) cannot be completely explained by the use of a homeostatic model. The earliest and strongest experimentally based attack on the narrow homeostatic model was made by *P. T. Young*. As early as the beginning of the 1940's he presented experimental evidence regarding food preferences in animals which were *not* based on homeostasis (see Young 1941 and 1961. Also the chapter about Young in Madsen, 1968).

The main propositions contained in the incentive model are summarized below.

Certain external stimuli have a *dynamic* effect, i. e., they determine a state of activation or energy mobilization in the organism. This dynamic state determines – together with cognitive processes – the behavior of the organism. This behavior often results in a reduction of the external, dynamic stimuli (Cf. Fig. 18.10b). These stimuli have their origin in stimulus objects called "incentives", i. e., motivating (dynamic, activating, energy mobilizing) stimulus objects. In some theories incentives include "reinforcers" and "goal objects".

There are two kinds of incentives: *primary and secondary.*

The *primary incentives* are S-variables which have an *innate* dynamic effect. These primary incentives play an important role in the so-called *"hedonistic" theories*, among which P. T. Young's is the most elaborate we have studied. He claims that external stimulation has *affective* as well as sensory consequences, and that the affective "arousal" orients the organism towards or against the stimulus object, and thus influences choice and preference.

Among other well known hedonistic theories we have studied we can mention *Hebb's* earliest theory (1949), *McClelland's* theory and Tinbergen's theory.

We should mention that the hedonistic theory is very old – even older than the homeostatic theory. It goes back to the ancient philosophers such as Epicurus and the so-called "Utilitarians" (e. g., J. Bentham) in the 1700's. The hedonic conception is also inherent in *Thorndike*'s "law of effect" and Freud's "pleasure principle".

The *secondary incentives* are S-variables which have an acquired dynamic effect. Therefore such incentives play an important role in modern learning theory. Thanks to the fact that *K. W. Spence's* incentive motivation was included in Hull's theory (denoted by the symbol "K" in honor of *K. W. Spence*).This "incentive motivation, K", together with "drive, D" and "habit strength, sHr" determines the "reaction potential, sEr" and the subsequent behavior. K is thus a *hypothetical* variable which is determined by the S-variable: magnitude and quality of the reward (e. g., fodd) used in the learning experiments to which the theory refers.

Spence developed the conception of incentive motivation on the basis of Hull's earlier concept of the "r_g-s_g mechanism" or the so-called "fractional antedating goal response". In Hull's theory this "r_g-s_g mechanism" has only a *directive* effect, but Spence pointed to the possibility that the *frustration* of R_G – the *complete* goal response – has an *activating* effect similar to drive. This activating or *dynamic* effect of r_g-s_g was separated from the *directive* effect by the label "K".

In Spence's later version of his own theory (see Spence, 1960), K was more important than D as a determiner of behavior. They were here supposed to interact in an additive way, so that Spence's version of Hull's well known formula reads:

$$sEr = f[sHr \times (D+K)].$$

K is thought to be acquired by *reinforcement*, defined as *drive reduction*, while sHr is acquired according to Spence, by *contiguity*.

Among the modern theories of motivation we have dealt with we find *Atkinson*'s to be the most elaborate one based upon an incentive model. Among the earlier theories we should especially like to mention *K. Lewin*'s because it contained the "valence" concept. Freud's concept of "cathexis" is also similar to the modern incentive concept.

After this survey of different incentive theories we now turn to the third model of motivation.

3. The cognitive model

This model of motivation was implicitly included in many earlier theories of perception and cognitive processes, but without being elaborated as a theory of motivation.

Thus there was – according to *Fritz Heider* (see Heider, 1960) – a motivational hypothesis contained in the classic Gestalt theory. The "tendency to closure" or "to create the good figure" was treated by the classic Gestalt psychologists as a dynamic variable, a "force". This conception was never elaborated into an explicit motivational hypothesis and the "tendency to closure" was perhaps only intended to explain the motivation of cognitive processes. But the Gestalt psychologists inspired K. Lewin, who elaborated a general theory of motivation and personality, which was – as already mentioned – an incentive rather than a cognitive theory.

The Gestalt psychologists also inspired – via K. Lewin – *E. C. Tolman*. His original theory (see Tolman, 1932) included both cognitive and motivational variables in order to explain purposive behavior in animals and man. And some of the variables – especially Tolman's "Sign-Gestalt-Readiness" – were mixed cognitive motivational variables. Later Tolman (Tolman, 1951) elaborated these mixed variables into his "Belief-Value Matrix", which, together with his "Need System" and "Behavior Space" determined behavior. He has himself called his theory "A Cognition Motivation Model" (see Tolman, 1952).

Modern theories of motivation contain two slightly different versions of a cognitive model.

According to one version *cognitive processes determine dynamic processes,* and thus cognitive processes have both a *directive* and – indirectly – a *dynamic* effect (see Figure 18.10c). As a good example of a clear and consistent theory of this type we can point to *Festinger* (see Chapter 12).

Another version of the cognitive model of motivation presupposes that *cognitive processes have their own "intrinsic motivation"*.

The best illustration of this we have found is *Woodworth*'s theory (see Chapter 11). This theory contains a *generalization of the idea of "intrinsic motivation" into a "behavior primacy theory"*, which claims that the most basic kind of motivation consists of dealing actively with the environment. This theory does not exclude the fact that "extrinsic" motivation – needs and incentives – also may sometimes co-determine behavior. But the main idea is that even without these "extrinsic" sources of motivation the organism would be active.

In a very thorough and thought-provoking paper *J. Mc. V. Hunt* (see Hunt, 1965) presents a modern "information theory version" of earlier cognitive models of motivation. In the same paper he claims that *Jean Piaget*'s theory contains an implicit hypothesis of intrinsic cognitive motivation. Hunt also claims that *Karl H. Pribram*'s theory belongs to the same category. The present author believes, however, that the latest version of Pribram's theory, which we have analyzed in Chapter 8, is a broader and more comprehensive theory, although it comes nearer to the cognitive model than to any of the other models of motivation.

As the more complex cognitive processes are exclusively concerned with *human beings*, the cognitive model comes nearer to the following model of motivation.

4. *The humanistic model*

This model of motivation is not so clearly defined as the three others. But we think that there is a group of motivational theories which has so much in common that they can be differentiated from the other theories and classified together in one class. They have two important features in common: 1) A humanistic conception of psychology, 2) the hypothesis that a special class of human motivation exists. This class of motivation – or human behavior as a whole – is conceived of as being *un*determined (Cf. Fig. 18.10d).

We have studied two theories which typify the above class.

G. W. Allport presented his theory in his well known book, *"Personality"* (1937, rev. ed. 1961). In this book he made a distinction between *idiographic* and *nomothetic* science, which comes near to the two conceptions of "natural science" and "hermeneutic science" which we referred to in Chapter 17. He also introduced the conception of the *"functional autonomy" of motivation*, which was inspired by an idea presented in Woodworth's first book (1918). According to this conception there is evidence for a class of motivation in adult, mature and mentally healthy people which is functionally independent of the basic, primacy motivation found in animals and infants. Allport claims that the motivational theories contained in learning theories are too narrowly based on animal experiments and that the motivation theory contained in psychoanalysis is too narrowly based on studies of neurotic people, who are more infantile in their motivation than healthy mature adults. (Cf. our Chapter about Allport's theory in Madsen, 1959, 4th ed., 1968).

Abraham Maslow's theory, which we have studied and presented in Chapter 15 of this book, is inspired by Allport as well as others. He has been the leader of the "humanistic psychologists" and has exposed the necessity of another humanistic conception of science in opposition to the naturalistic, which dominated American psychology until recently. In connection with this he has also defended a special humanistic conception of man in opposition to the prevailing biological one. Included in Maslow's conception of man is his hypothesis about a special humanistic adult kind of motivation, the so-called "growth need" or *"metamotivation"*.

A less welll snown example of a humanistic theory is that of *Thomas V. Moore* (see Moore, 1948), which we have studied as one of our earlier theories (see Madsen, 1959). This theory is very much influenced by scholastic, Thomistic

Names of Psychologists	Basic Hypotheses	Homeostatic Hypotheses	Incentive Hypotheses	Cognitive Hypotheses	Humanistic Hypotheses
		Hull	Lewin	Tolman	Allport
		Murray (1938)	Young	Woodworth	Maslow
			Tinbergen	Festinger	Moore
		Duffy	Hebb	Pribram	
			Murray (1959)		
			McClelland		
			Atkinson		
			Miller		
			Konorski		
			Brown		
			Cattell		
			Berlyne		
			Skinner		
			Bindra		
			McDougall		

Fig. 18.11

philosophy. It presupposes a humanistic conception of science and an indeterministic "free-will" theory about human motivation.

We can conclude this section about models of motivation by presenting the results of our study in a classification scheme (Fig. 18.11.). In this scheme we have presented the modern and earlier theories of motivation according to the *dominant* hypothesis of motivation. But the reader must bear in mind that many of the theories studied are so comprehensive that they include two or three kinds of motivation.

A combined model

The present author has considered the possibility of making a synthesis of the different models of motivation. We have at the moment integrated the first three models, but have not succeeded in including the last one, the humanistic model.

Our synthesis is based upon a metatheoretical presupposition and a hypothesis. *The metaproposition states that all three models are "partly true" as they correspond to different categories of motivation.* Or, in other words: The models of motivation are all true, but have limited applicability. Thus each model is supposed to be valid for a special category of motivation.

Our hypothesis states that each category of motiation involves a specific structure in the brain (in addition to the Reticular Arousal System which is involved in *all* kinds of motivation). Thus we have the following categories of motivation:

1. *The hypothalamic motives:*[3]) This is the category of motivation which is assumed to involve *hypothalamic centers* – as well as the RAS. This is the category of motivation for which the *homeostatic* model is most valid. But even in this instance we cannot regard the homeostatic model as completely true, as the homeostatic motives include, for example, the sex motive, which is not a completely homeostatic motive. Incentives may also determine this kind of motive as well as other organic motives: hunger, thirst pain avoidance, cold avoidance, heat avoidance, etc. Thus we could also call this category of motivation "organic motives", "homeostatic motives" or "hypothalamic motives".
2. *The limbic motives:* This is the category of motivation which is assumed to involve *the limbic system* as well as the R.A.S. We have adopted Konorski's hypotheses that "emotional motives" involve limbic "drive centers" and that "social motives" are *conditioned* to the emotional motives. We find that the *incentive* model is especially applicable to these motives. Thus the "emotional" and "social" motives could also be called "limbic" or "incentive".
3. *The cortical motives.* The category of motivation which is supposed to involve the *cerebral cortex* – as well as the RAS. These are the motives which function in accordance with the first mentioned version of the *cognitive* model: cognitive processes determine their own motivation.
   Consequently the category of motives could be called "cognitive" or "cortical".
4. *The RAS motives.* This is the category of motivation which is assumed to involve only the *Reticular Arousal System*. These motives are those for which the *intrinsic model* – e. g., Woodworth's behavior primacy theory – is supposed to apply. Therefore, these could be called "intrinsic" or "activation" motives.

---

3. The reader may have noticed that we equate the term "motive" with the longer phrase "category of motivation".

428 . *The Hypothetical Strata of the Theories*

»Motive« or Category of Motivation	Brain Structures Involved	Model of Motivation Applicable	Examples of Motives
Hypothalamic (»organic« or »homeostatic«) Motives	Hypothalamus and the RAS	Homeostatic Model	1. Hunger 2. Thirst 3. Sex Motive 4. Maternal Motive 5. Excretion Motives 6. Sleep Motive 7. Breathing Motive 8. Acquired »hungers« for tobacco, narcotics, etc.
Limbic (»incentive«) Motives	Limbic System and the RAS	Incentive Model	Emotional motives: 9. Fear 10. Aggression Social Motives: 11. Affiliation Motive 12. Achievement Motive 13. Power Motive
Cortical (»cognitive«) Motives	Cerebral Cortex and the RAS	Cognitive Model (first version)	14. Curiosity 15. Dissonance Reduction
The RAS Motives (intrinsic activation motives)	Only the RAS	The Intrinsic Version of the Cognitive Model	16. Motives for Motoric Activities Sensoric Activities Brain Activities Autonomic Activities

Fig. 18.12 Classification scheme representing our integration of the different models of motivation into one classification of motives according to the brain structures involved.

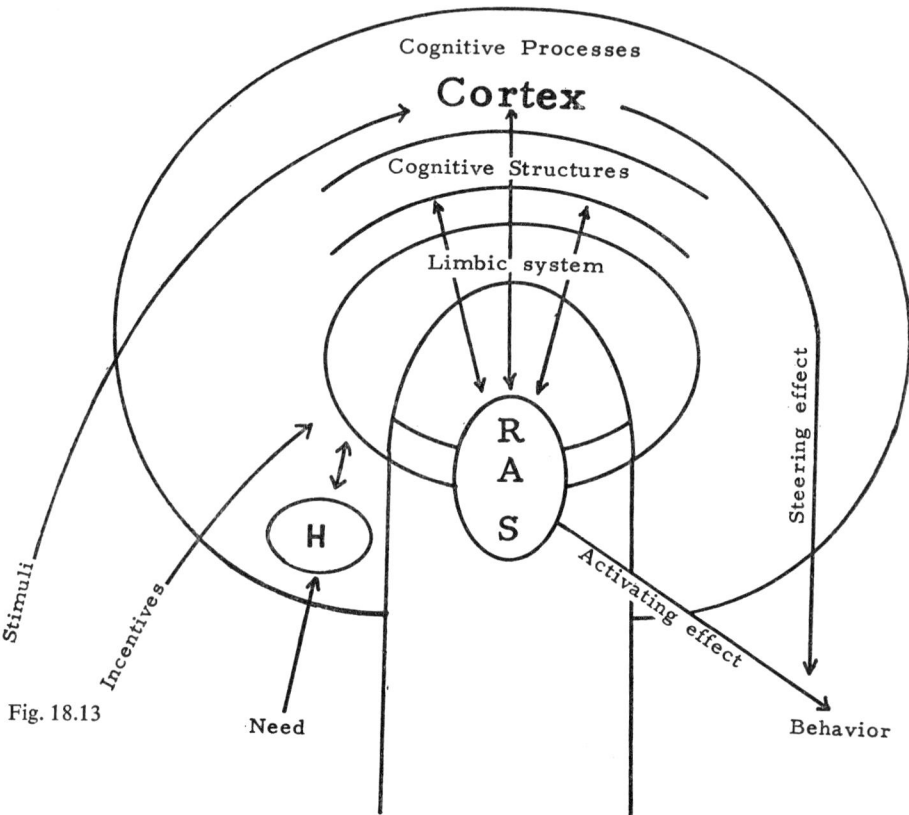

Fig. 18.13

We can summarize this combination of the models in the form of a classification scheme (Fig. 18.12) and a brain model illustrating our integrated model of motivation (Fig. 18.13).

The complexity of hypotheses

This classification is one of those which we have adapted from traditional theoretical psychology, where it has been discussed under such labels as *"mechanistic"*, *"dynamic"* and *"field-theoretical"* hypotheses. We do not believe that the problem has the same interest as it had when we started our systematological studies 20 years ago. But we have retained the classification and redefined it on the basis of *R. B. Cattell*'s conception of *"one-dimensional"* and *multi-dimensional* hypotheses. We have classified the hypotheses in the theories on the basis of this classification. And now we can classify all the theories according to the complexity of their hypotheses and present the results in our next classification scheme (Fig. 18.14.). It is possible – though we have not done so – to calculate a ratio for each theory similar to the Hypotheses Quotients.

The functional relationships of the hypotheses

This is also a problem which has not been discussed very much in the last decade. Most psychologists seem to take the position that it is a matter of convenience to presuppose either causal *determinism* or *probabilism* (stochastic or statistic relationships). The "new" perspective in this discussion is that the

Complexity of Hypotheses	Mainly one-dimensional hypotheses	Both one-dimensional and multidimensional hypotheses	Mainly multidimensional hypotheses
Modern Theories of Motivation	Duffy Berlyne	Bindra Konorski Pribram Miller Brown Woodworth Festinger, Maslow	Cattell Atkinson
Earlier Theories of Motivation	Hebb Tinbergen Allport Skinner Moore	Hull McDougall Young McClelland	Tolman Lewin

Fig. 18.14 Classification scheme representing the classification of the modern and earlier theories of motivation according to the complexity of their hypotheses.

430 . The Hypothetical Strata of the Theories

Functional Relationship	Causal Determinism	Probabilism (Statistic assumption)	Indeterminism (»Free will«)
Modern Theories of Motivation	Duffy Berlyne Konorski Pribram Brown Woodworth	Bindra Miller (?) Cattell (?) Atkinson (?) Festinger (?)	Maslow (?)
Earlier Theories of Motivation	Allport (?), McDougall Tolman, McClelland Lewin, Murray Hebb, Hull Tinbergen, Young	Skinner Hull (?)	Moore Allport (?)

Fig. 18.15 Classification scheme representing the classification of the modern and the earlier theories of motivation according to the presumed kind of functional relationships.

humanistic psychologists have given the old *"free will"-indeterminism* a renaissance. Therefore, we present a classification scheme with the modern and earlier theories classified according to the presupposed functational relationships. (Fig. 18.15):

19. The Descriptive Strata of the Theories

Introduction

According to our systematological taxonomy there are three main units concerning the descriptive stratum of a theory: 1) the *abstract* D-level, 2) the *concrete* D-level, and 3) the *descriptive units*.

It seems most logical to *compare* the theories in relation to these three units, so this chapter has the same three divisions.

The Abstract D-levels of the Theories

The abstract descriptive terms

These terms are important in the construction of theories because they are abstract "summaries" of the more concrete descriptions, and at the same time are empirical "anchor points" for the H-terms. If the hypothetical stratum with its hypotheses and models is to serve its function as an instrument for explanations and predictions, the *H-terms must be "operationally defined", i. e., related by definitions to abstract descriptive terms*. At least *some* of the H-terms must be operationally defined, and the *rest* must be related to them. To require that *all* H-terms be operationally defined would be equal to requiring intervening variables without surplus meaning, and equal to the adoption of a strictly empiristic epistemology and a "descriptive" metatheory. And this is not something most modern psychologists do. But even a more rationalistic epistemology, – at least an "empiristic rationalism" – would require that *all* H-terms be directly or *indirectly* related to abstract descriptive terms. If there are any H-terms which are in *no* way connected with the D-level, then it is doubtful if they can be of any utility as explanatory or predictive instruments. Perhaps they should instead be conceived of as belonging to the M-level, i. e., be regarded as part of the philosophy of man.

One of my graduate students, *Svend Jørgensen*, is working on the development of a computer program which can analyze and simulate the logical structure of a psychological theory, and thus detect how consistently the H-terms are connected to each other and to the abstract descriptive terms. Because of the significance of these terms we now turn to their classification.

Most of the theories have employed *behavioral* data language or a *mixed* data language, the latter frequently placing behavioral data language in the most favorable position, as all introspective and phenomenological data are "translated" into behavioral data language. Therefore we may assume that the abstract descriptive terms can be classified as S- and R-terms.

We have made a classification scheme presenting the descriptive terms contained in the *modern* theories (Fig. 19.1.) and a similar classification scheme for the descriptive terms found in the *earlier* theories (Fig. 19.2.).

The "laws" contained in the theories

There are not many general S-R-relationships formulated as general, descriptive propositions ("laws"). Those laws which have been formulated in motivational psychology are not suited for a comparative study, because the theories concentrate on several "areas" of motivation.

As examples we can point out that *Berlyne*'s theory contains a "law" stating that *collative variables determine explorative and/or epistemic behavior.* And this "law" – which is explained by means of Berlyne's theory about "arousal" – is applied to various fields (e. g., education).

We can regard *Miller*'s theory as being based on the well known *"law of effect"*. He has concentrated on the explanation of this law and its application to the field of learning and therapy.

A third theory which contains one or more empirical "laws" is *Atkinson's*. Together with McClelland and their co-workers they have found many "laws" concerning relationships between *high achievement scores* and other measurements of performance. These are *"R-R-laws"*, as they are between R-variable high achievement score and other R-variables, such as academic achievement and economic achievement, choice of profession, etc. But McClelland and co-workers have also found some *"S-R-laws"*, such as the relationship between educational influences – in childhood and as adults and a high achievement score on a TAT.

A fourth very productive theory is that of *Cattell*, which contains many *"R-R-laws"* about relationships between numerous test scores.

Many other theories have revealed empirical relationships described in general propositions or "laws", but the examples we have mentioned may be enough to demonstrate that the theories deal with such divergent areas of motivation that they are not easy to compare at the D-level.

The Concrete D-levels of the Theories

The concrete descriptions (the data) of the theories

The same difficulties for making a comparative study are present when we study the concrete descriptive strata of the theories. They all contain different *concrete descriptions* (data), and they vary from theory to theory.

The Descriptive Strata of the Theories . 433

Name of Psychologist	S-variable	R-variable
Duffy	Stimuli: External and Internal	Intensity Direction
Bindra	Incentive Reinforcer Goal; Cue	Goal-directed Behavior
Berlyne	Collative Variables	Exploratory and Epistemic Behavior
Konorski	UCS; CS Interoceptive Stimuli Humoral Stimuli	Preparatory and Consummatory Reflex-behavior
Pribram	Internal and External Stimuli	Behavior
Miller	Drive Stimulus Cue Stimulus Reinforcer	Approach and Avoidance Behavior
Brown	Stimuli Primary Sources of Drive	Molar Behavior
Woodworth	Needs Incentives Stimuli	Two-phase and Poly-phase Motor Units. – Retroflex
Festinger	Alternatives Information Compliance pressure Disagreement	Behavior
Cattell	Task Incentive Physiological State	T-data Q-data L-data
Atkinson	Stimuli Probability of Success	TAT-responses Behavior
Maslow	External and Internal Stimuli	Expressive and Coping Behavior

Fig. 19.1 Classification scheme presenting the S-variables and the R-variables in modern theories of motivation.

434 . *The Descriptive Strata of the Theories*

Name of Psychologist	S-variable	R-variable
McDougall	External Stimuli	Purposive Behavior
Tolman	Physiological State Drive; Stimuli	Purposive Behavior
Young	Needs Stimuli	Behavior
Allport	Drives Stimuli	Expressive Behavior Instrumental Behavior
Lewin	Needs Stimuli Goal-objects	Behavior
Murray	Alpha-press Sources of Needs	Actones: 1. Verbones 2. Motones
Hull	C_D or Need External Stimuli	$R \left\{ \begin{array}{l} str \\ n \\ P \\ A \end{array} \right.$
Hebb	External and Internal Stimuli	Organized Behavior
Tinbergen	Releasing Stimuli Motivational Factors	Appetitive Behavior Consummatory Acts
McClelland	Cues Adaption Level	TAT-responses and Other Behavior
Skinner	Deprivation Reinforcers Aversive Stimuli	Respondent and Operant Behavior
Moore	Not Specifically Defined	Not Specifically Defined

Duffy's and *Bindra*'s theories contain a considerable amount of *physiological* data from measurements in addition to purely *behavioral* data. This also applies to *Berlyne*'s, *Konorski*'s, *Pribram*'s and *Miller*'s theories. The three last mentioned theories contain other concrete descriptions as well. Thus Konorski's and Pribram's theories contain data from *pathological* studies of brain-injured people. Both these theories also contain introspective or phenomenological data.

Miller's theory contains in addition to the physiological data, data from *learning experiments* with animals. This is also the case with *Brown*'s and *Woodworth*'s theories.

Atkinson's and *Cattell*'s theories both contain data from psychological *tests*, but from different tests. Both theories also contain experimental data.

Festinger's theory is the only one which contains data from *social psychological* research.

Maslow's theory contains a peculiar set of data – or rather he refers to, but fails to thoroughly describe his data from interviews, questionnaires and tests of the so-called "self-actualizing" people. In addition he – like Miller (and Dollard) – makes some reference to data from *psychotherapy*.

Thus it is difficult to see what all these theories have in common.

Goal directed behavior

If all motivational theories have anything in common it must be to *describe, explain and predict "motivated" behavior, i. e., "purposive" or "goal-directed" behavior*. We must remember that motivational psychology developed in American psychology *after the "behavioristic revolution"*. Neither "classic", introspective experimental psychology nor Gestalt psychology developed any motivational theory. Only psychoanalysis had developed a motivational theory before the behavioristic revolution, which later inspired more behaviorist-oriented circles in psychology.

But the "classic" behaviorist, *Watson*, and his followers, as well as their great contemporary follower, *Skinner*, did not develop a motivational psychology. The reason is that these theories deal for the most part with rather simple kinds of behavior or aspects of behavior.

It was *Tolman and the other neo-behaviorists who first developed an elaborate motivational theory* – of course inspired by *Woodworth, Lewin* and other psychoanalytically inspired personality theorists. *The reason for this was Tolman's explicit concentration on "molar behavior" (or "behavior acts")* which is much more complicated than "molecular behavior", which the classic bevahiorists – and Skinner – have selected as the object for their psychological

---

Fig. 19.2. Classification scheme presenting the S-variables and R-variables in earlier theories of motivation.

studies. It is important to bear this historical fact in mind as it has been overlooked by many critics of modern American psychology. *There is a great difference between molecular behavior and molar behavior – between movements and actions.* It is *molar behavior* (or *actions*) which is similar – or perhaps identical – to the human activities which interest people in their daily lives. It is because of this that studies of molar behavior are more directly applicable to the problems of everyday life. This does not imply that studies of molecular behavior are without practical utility. But the utility comes more indirectly via the information they produce about *aspects* of molar behavior.

But it is just because molar behavior is identical with the actions of everyday life that Tolman and the neobehaviorists had to develop motivational theories.

Tolman's great contribution to psychology was his development of the conceptual system, which made it possible to *describe* molar or "purposive behavior" in man as well as in animals. Inspired by McDougall he found some aspects of behavior which could be *described intersubjectively* ("objectively"), and which defined behavior as "purposive" or "molar". We shall later return to the descriptive aspects of molar behavior. But first we should like to underline the historical fact that *it was in connection with the description of "purposive" behavior that Tolman developed his explanatory concepts, the so-called "intervening variables"*. In order to explain the *dynamic* aspects of purposive behavior, Tolman had to introduce *motivational*, intervening variables such as "drive", "demand" and later "need system". And it was in order to explain the *directive* aspect of purposive behavior that he had to introduce *cognitive*, intervening variables such as "expectation", "cognitive maps" and, later the "belief-value matrix". It is important to remember that he described and explained purposive behavior in both men and animals with the same theory. We shall later return to the criticism of this historical fact, but first we must continue with the description of purposive behavior.

Tolman's description of "purposive" behavior has been revised by *Dalbir Bindra*. As the reader may remember from reading our Chapter 5 about Bindra's theory, he preferred the term *"goal-directed"* to "purposive". "Goal-directed" *behavior* is defined by Bindra as having the following aspects: *"appropriateness"*, *"persistence"* and *"searching"*. It is important that these aspects or "dimensions" – as Bindra prefers to call them – can be described intersubjectively as occurring in *degrees*. Thus it is not an all-or-none matter if behavior is "goal-directed", but *all* behavior can be goal-directed to some degree, greater or lesser. In addition, it is very important to notice that he defines "goal-directedness" in relation to "goal" in this way:

"A *goal* is thus *an incentive that is chosen by the investigator as a reference point for describing observed behavior.*

The choice of the reference point – called goal – is completely arbitrary and has reference only to the investigator's mode of analysis, not the animal's intention or any other subjective state" (p. 54 in Bindra, 1959).

In the above quotation he refers explicitly to animal behavior, but *man's behavior can just as well be described and explained by motivational theories.*

Consequently, motivational psychology competes with a classic manner of dealing with human beings, that is found in the humanistic disciplines and reborn in humanistic psychology.

We have already discussed the differences between the naturalistic and the humanistic conceptions of science (Cf. Chapter 17), as well as the *Apel-Lesche-Radnitzky* synthesis (Cf. Fig. 17.5.). Therefore, we shall conclude this section by presenting our conception of the relationship between the *naturalistic* (neo-behavioristic and psychoanalytic) *theory* of goal-directed behavior and the *humanistic* study of man's actions.

The *naturalistic* theory describes molar behavior as goal-directed and *explains* it with the aid of hypothetical variables – motivational and cognitive.

The *humanistic* approach *aims at understanding and interpreting human actions.*

Thus the two approaches have separate function tasks: explanation and interpretation. But do they study the same thing? We think that they only do this to a *limited* extent: the naturalistic approach studies *behavior* – both *molecular* and *molar*. We think that *molecular* behavior is more intimately related to the subject of *physiology*, i.e., *organic processes*, while *molar* behavior (including "verbal behavior") is more related to the *humanistic study*, i.e., *man's actions*, which include his language. The Danish philosopher *Justus Hartnack* (see Hartnack, 1971) even defines *"action" as something presupposing language.* An "action" is identifiable by a description of its "intentions". The "intention" is not the same as the "motive". The difference – according to Hartnack – is that the "motive" for an action is an answer to the question "why", while the "intention" of an action is an answer to the question "what". According to Hartnack an "intention" is more like a "decision" than a "motive".

From a psychological point of view a *decision* is determined by a *conflict between motives*. Thus we perhaps can conclude that *"intention" can be equated with "decision"*. The only difference between the two concepts is that they belong to different conceptual frames of reference – the humanistic and the naturalistic. *All these conceptual frames-of-reference belong to different "logical categories" or levels of discourse".*

We can summarize our discussion of the concepts "goal-directed, molar behavior" and "human action" by means of a diagram (Fig. 19.3.), which was inspired by *Karl Pribram*'s "pluralistic structuralistic pragmatism".

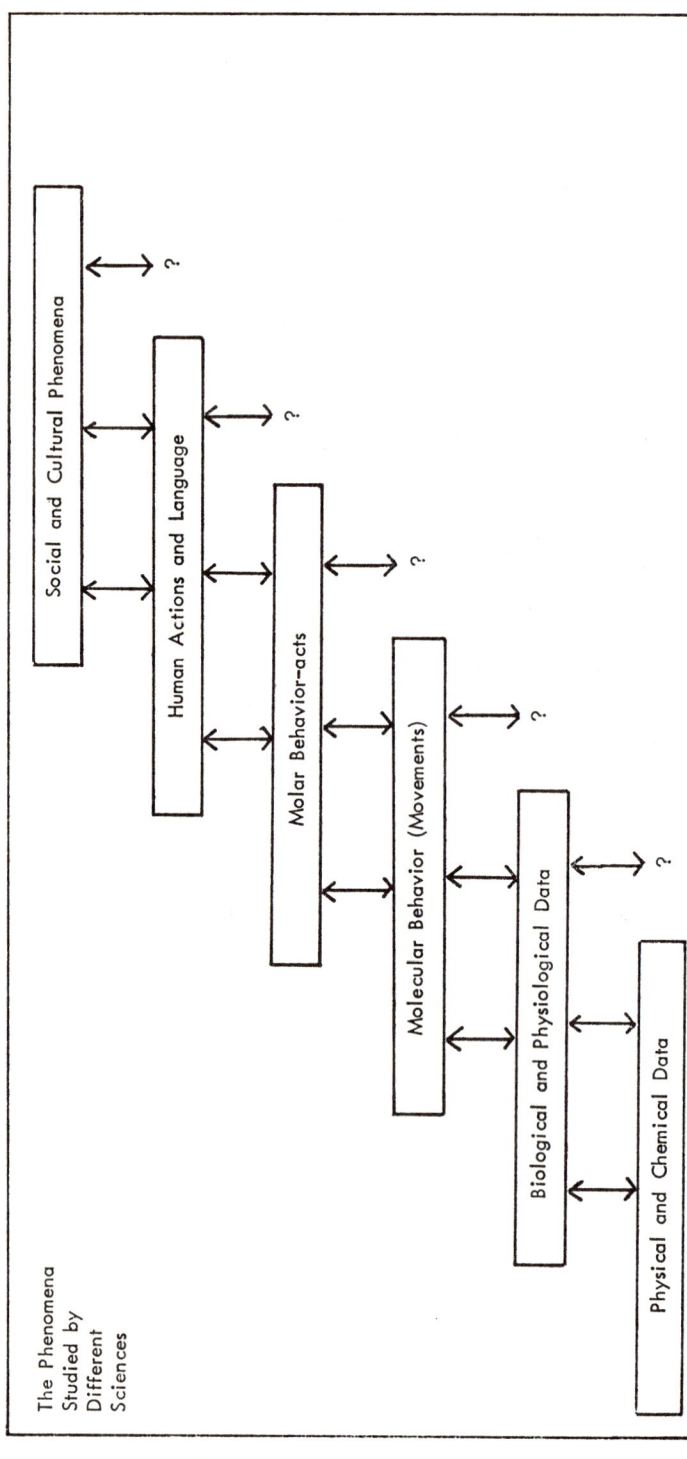

Fig. 19.3. Diagram representing our multi-level conception of scientific discourses. The different sciences are conceived of as being studies of the same universe, different points-of-view resulting in different "slices" of the world. Determined by the different epistemological metatheoretical and methodological points-of-view the different sciences generate different data. This data may be "translated" from one level of discourse to another. But each level contains some "new" data, which cannot be translated "back" to the more "basic" level of discourse.

Descriptive Units:	Molecular Units:	Intermediate Units:	Molar Units:
Modern Theories	Duffy Bindra Berlyne Konorski	Pribram Miller (II) Cattell Festinger?	Miller (I) Brown Woodworth Atkinson Maslow
Earlier Theories	Tinbergen	Young, Lewin Hull, Hebb McClelland McDougall Skinner	Tolman Allport Murray Moore

Fig. 19.4 Classification scheme denoting the classification of the modern and the earlier theories of motivation according to the descriptive units employed.

The Descriptive Units of the Theories

In our last section about the D-level we, according to our outline, usually deal with the descriptive units of the theory being analyzed. Therefore, in this comparative study we shall classify the modern and the earlier theories according to the descriptive units they normally employ.

Although we have already emphasized the great difference between "molar" and "molecular" behavior, we must admit that it is very difficult to draw a sharp boundary line between these two descriptive units. *The difference between "molar" and "molecular" behavior is a difference of degree, but that in no way contradicts our statement that the difference is of great importance.*

We therefore present a classification scheme containing the modern theories and the earlier theories of motivation according to the descriptive units they most often employ (Fig. 19.4.).

20. The Theories as Wholes

Introduction

As we are still following our systematological outline this chapter contains three sections: 1) the formal properties of the theories, 2) the epistemological properties of the theories and 3) the theory-empiry ratios.

Both the earlier and the modern theories of motivation are included in this comparative study.

The Formal Properties of the Theories

The systematic organization

One of the formal properties of the theories we have studied is their systematic organization. We have worked out a classification of the theories into three categories according to their systematic organization:

1. *Explanatory sketches*, i.e., loosely organized texts with very little systematic organization.
2. *Explanatory systems,* i.e., more systematically organized texts. As a minimum requirement the texts must be clearly divided into the three strata: the M-, H-, and D-levels. The "typical" explanatory system also contains explicit formulations of hypotheses, definitions, etc. If the hypotheses are relatively well organized then the explanatory system comes close to the next category.
3. *Deductive theories*, i.e., scientific texts in which the propositions are organized into a deductive system. This last category is the most well defined, so the problems of classification are concentrated on the differences between the first two categories.

We present below the classification of the modern and the earlier theories of motivation in one classification scheme (Fig. 20.1.).

As can be seen from this classification scheme most of the modern and earlier theories are explanatory systems. There seem to be very few differences between the earlier and the modern theories – only a reduction in the number of explanatory sketches in the latter, but not a similar increase in the number of deductive theories. So we cannot see any evidence of a significant development in the systematic organization of the theories.

Systematic Organization	Explanatory Sketches	Explanatory Systems	Deductive Theories
Modern Theories	Maslow Woodworth	Berlyne, Cattell Duffy, Miller(II) Bindra, Festinger Brown Konorski Pribram	Atkinson Miller (I)
Earlier Theories	McDougall Hebb Allport Moore	Young McClelland Murray Tinbergen Tolman Skinner	Hull Lewin

Fig. 20.1 Classification scheme representing modern and earlier theories according to their systematic organization.

Preciseness of Formulation	Purely Verbal Theories	Partly Symbolized Theories	Mathematized Theories
Modern Theories	Maslow Berlyne Duffy, Festinger Bindra, Brown Konorski, Woodworth Pribram, Miller	Cattell	Atkinson
Earlier Theories	McDougall, Skinner Hebb, Murray Allport, Tinbergen Young, Tolman McClelland, Moore		Hull Lewin

Fig. 20.2 Classification scheme representing the modern and the earlier theories of motivation according to the preciseness of representation.

The preciseness of representation

This classification is of course intimately related to the first one, but inspired by our co-opration with R. B. Cattell (See Cattell, 1973) we made a distinction between these two classifications. This classification includes three categories:

1. *Purely verbal theories,* i. e., scientific texts formulated in ordinary language which may possibly contain some scientific terms.

2. *Partly symbolized theories*, i. e., scientific texts partly formulated with mathematical, logical or other special symbols.
3. *Mathematized theories*, i. e., scientific texts containing a complete system of mathematical formulas – a so-called "calculus" – which supplements the verbal formulation.

The last classification is the most well defined, so again the problems of classification are concentrated around the differences between the first two categories.

The results of our classification of the modern and the earlier theories of motivation are presented in the accompanying classification scheme (Fig. 10.2.).

As can be seen from this classification scheme most of both the modern and the earlier theories are purely verbal. There is no significant difference between the earlier and the modern theories, and thus no development in the preciseness of the theories.

The properties of the models

This classification is more independent than the two previous ones. We have worked with a classification of the theories according to the kind of models employed. We have constructed the following categories:

1. *Verbal analogies*, i. e., verbal formulations using metaphors or analogies in the explanatory hypotheses.
2. *Two-dimensional models,* i. e., diagrams, maps or other graphic representations of the explanatory hypotheses. With the development of the mathematical graph theory, this kind of model could be formally developed to a very high degree.
3. *Three-dimensional models*, i. e., three-dimensional structures or mechanisms which represent the explanatory hypotheses. This kind of model cannot of course be represented in the text, but there can be a verbal description, picture or drawing in the text which refers to the model built by the author.
4. *Computer simulation programs*, i. e., programs for computers which simulate the logical structure and sequence of the phenomena to be explained. This is a new and very promising kind of model for psychologists. But it is so new that it has not yet been widely applied.
5. *Mathematical models*, i. e., systems of mathematical formulas representing the hypotheses used in the explanations.

Thus a "mathematical model" is equal to "a calculus" as mentioned in the second classification. We did not include the mathematical model in the presentation of the classification in Chapter 2, but have decided to include it now because it is a very common conception in scientific discussions.

We present below the results of our classification of modern and earlier theories of motivation by means of a classification scheme (Fig. 20.3.).

Types of Models	Verbal Analogies	Two-dimensional Models	Three-dimensional Models	Computer-simulation	Mathematical Models
Modern Theories	Duffy Maslow Woodworth Festinger	Bindra Berlyne Konorski Miller Brown Cattell	Pribram		Atkinson Cattell
Earlier Theories	McDougall Murray Moore Skinner	Tolman Young Allport Lewin Hull, McClelland Hebb, Tinbergen			Hull Lewin

Fig. 20.3 Classification scheme presenting the results of our classification of modern and earlier theories of motivation according to the kind of *models* applied.

As can be seen from the classification scheme most theories make use of verbal analogies and two-dimensional models. There are no computer simulation models and few mathematical models. Again there seems to be no difference between earlier and modern theories of motivation and thus no sign of development.

The Epistemological Properties

The types of theories

We have worked with a classification of theories according to some important epistemological properties. In principle there are seven "types of theories":

1. *S-R-theories*, i. e., purely *descriptive* theories employing a *behavioral* data language.
2. *Phenomenological theories*, i. e., purely *descriptive* theories employing a *phenomenological* data language.
3. *Physiological-descriptive theories*, i. e., purely *descriptive* theories employing *physiological data* as intervening variables between S- and R-data. (This represents "reductive" theories in the narrow sense).
4. *S-O-R-theories*, i. e., *explanatory* theories using H_O-terms (H-terms with physiological surplus meaning).
5. *S-H_N-R-theories*, i. e., *explanatory* theories using H_N-terms (H-terms with neutral surplus meaning).
6. *S-M-R-theories*, i. e., *explanatory* theories using H_M-terms (H-terms with mentalistic surplus meaning).
7. *M-theories*, i. e., *interpreting* theories presenting an intuitive "Verstehen" of others' "minds".

444 . *The Theories as Wholes*

Epistemological Types of Theories	S-R- theories	S-O-R- theories	S-H$_N$-R- theories	S-M-R- theories
Earlier Theories	Skinner	Hebb Tinbergen	McDougall McClelland Murray, Lewin Young, Tolman Hull	Allport Moore
Modern Theories		Duffy Bindra Berlyne Konorski Pribram Miller(II)	Miller(I) Woodworth Brown Cattell Atkinson Festinger	Maslow

Fig. 20.4. Classification scheme presenting the classification of earlier and modern theories of motivation according to the epistemological types of theories.

We have not found any examples of purely *phenomenological*, descriptive theories, and we think that they are not likely to occur in psychology. Some philosophers – e. g., *Husserl* and the Danish philosopher, *Herbert Iversen* – have developed such theories, but in psychology they may possibly be replaced by S-M-R-theories if they are to be applicable to other people (and not be a solipsistic description of the theorist's own consciousness).

Nor have we found any purely *physiological*-descriptive theories. We think that the development of neurophysiology for many years in the future will be behind the need for explanatory help in psychology. Therefore, the physiologically interested psychologists must use *hypothetical* terms (with physiological surplus meaning) and so the planned physiological-descriptive theories become S-O-R-theories.

We have only found one theory which could possibly have been classified as an M-theory, namely Maslow's. But as Maslow makes some reference to data from this research with self-actualizing people, we think it is most correct to classify his theory as an S-M-R-theory.

Thus three of our seven categories are "empty", and we only have to use the four remaining ones in our classification scheme (Fig. 20.4.), namely: The S-R-, the S-O-R-, the S-H$_N$-R- and the S-M-R-theories.

As can be seen from the classification scheme most of the theories are S-O-R- and S-H$_N$-R-theories. In this case there seems to be a difference between earlier and modern theories which indicates a development in the direction of more S-O-R-theories.

The Theory-Empiry Ratios of the Theories

The Hypotheses Quotients

We have made a classification of the theories according to the ratio between the purely *theoretical* (H-H) hypotheses and the partly *empirical* (S-H and H-R) hypotheses. These ratios were calculated according to our formula for the *Hypotheses Quotient*:

$$H.Q. = \frac{\Sigma(H-H)}{\Sigma[(S-H)+(H-R)]}$$

The results of these calculations for both the modern and the earlier theories of motivation are:

Modern Theories:	H.Q.:	Earlier Theories:	H.Q.:
Cattell	0.09	Tinbergen	0.11
Maslow	0.13?	Hebb	0.13
Duffy	0.14	McClelland	0.14
Miller (I)	0.20	Hull	0.36
Pribram	0.29	McDougall	0.43
Bindra	0.30	Lewin	0.50
Atkinson and Birch	0.33	Murray	0.71
Berlyne	0.38	Young	0.82
Brown	0.38	Allport	1.00
Konorski	0.54	Tolman	1.43
Woodworth	0.57		
Miller (II)	0.60		
Festinger	0.84		
Atkinson	0.86		

As the reader undoubtedly knows, we had to make precise *systematic reformulations ("reconstructions")* of the hypotheses before we could make the necessary classification into S-H- H-H, and H-R-hypotheses. *These reformulations introduce a source of error in the calculation of the H.Q.* It is not equally easy to reformulate all the theories. The most systematic and precise theories – like Hull's – are easiest to reformulate without changing the original content of purely theoretical and partly empirical hypotheses. And the least systematic and precise of the theories – like Maslow's – are very difficult to reformulate without changing the original theory-empiry-ratio[1]).

In order to avoid the source of error embedded in the reformulations of the hypotheses, we decided to construct a computer program which would be able to make the calculation of the H.Q. This program was developed by one of our

---

1. That is one of the reasons for putting a question mark behind the H.Q. of Maslow's theory in the above list. Another reason is that the result turned out to be much lower than expected from the general impression we have gained from studying Maslow's theory.

graduate students, *Svend Jørgensen*, but it is a preliminary program, which has only been able to calculate the H.Q. of Hull's theory until now. And even in this case it was necessary to make a slight editorial reformulation of the text before making the calculation of the H.Q. (The result was 0.36 – as indicated in the above list).

Interpretation of the H.Q.

Since we first formulated the Hypotheses Quotient in 1959, we have thought a great deal about the *interpretation* of the H.Q.

Originally, we conceived of the H.Q. as an estimation of the "explanatory power" of the theory – or what N. E. Miller has called "the ratio of facts to assumptions" (Miller, 1959). At that time we thought that we could just as well have included *purely empirical formulations* ("S-R-laws") in the calculation of the H.Q. (The S-R-laws in that case should be added to the S-H and the H-R-hypotheses). But we did *not* include the S-R-laws, because only a few of the theories analyzed had any explicit formulations of S-R-laws. In order to make the theories more comparable we therefore decided to exclude the S-R-laws from all the H.Q.s[2]).

Later we came to doubt if it were correct – or rather if it served any purpose to include S-R-laws in the calculations of the H.Q.'s. The reason for this was that in the case of living psychologists – as most of our subjects are – there could still be an increment in the number of S-R-laws which could be predicted – or found empirically and explained from the set of hypotheses in their theories. And even for no longer living psychologists, there could be an increase in the number of S-R-laws produced by followers, who used the theory in predictions and explanations.

If we do not include S-R-laws in the calculations of the H.Q., then we must re-interpret the Hypotheses Quotient. In such a case it is not an estimation of the "explanatory power" of a theory, but of the *potential* explanatory power. In other words: the H.Q. is an estimation of how broadly the hypothetical terms are anchored to the descriptive terms by means of the postulated functional relationships.

This new interpretation of the H.Q. together with the source of error of the reformulations of the hypotheses, have motivated the construction of a new ratio.

---

2. If we had included the S-R-laws from Hull's theory – his 133 theorems – the H.Q. would have been:

$$H.Q. = \frac{\Sigma(H-H)}{\Sigma[(S-H) + (H-R) + (S-R)]} = \frac{3}{7 + 3 + 133} = 0.02.$$

The M-H-D-ratio

This new ratio should be defined as an estimation of the ratio between the amount of words contained in the Metalevel, the Hypothetical level and the Descriptive level of the text. In order to calculate this ratio we simply counted the number of pages which were classified as belonging to the M-, H- and D-levels respectively[3]). If a theory is not so systematically organized that the three levels are clearly separated, we count a page as belonging to a certain level if most of the content on the page belongs to that level.

In order to make the M-H-D-ratios comparable we have transformed the number of pages belonging to each level into percentages. Thus the formula for the M-H-D-ratio became:

$$M/H/D = \frac{M}{M+H+D} \times 100 \quad \frac{H}{M+H+D} \times 100 \quad \frac{D}{M+H+D} \times 100$$

If we compare the calculated figures presented in Fig. 20.5. we find some interesting things. The 3 highest percentages for the M-level are those of Maslow, Woodworth and Cattell, while the 3 lowest figures are those of Duffy, Berlyne and Bindra. It is not surprising that Maslow has devoted so many pages to the exposition of his metalevel, but it is perhaps more surprising that Cattell has the third highest figure for the M-level. The reader must remember, however, that there is a great difference between the metastrata of Maslow's and Cattell's theories. Maslow deals very thoroughly with philosophical problems but to a lesser degree with metatheoretical and methodological problems, while Cattell deals very thoroughly with methodological problems but to a lesser degree with metatheoretical and philosophical problems. This could, of course, have been demonstrated by counting the figures for the philosophical, the metatheoretical and the methodological sub-levels of the metalevel.

The most interesting thing about the figures for the H-and the D-levels is the ratios between them. Therefore, we have calculated the H/D ratio for the theories. These ratios are directly comparable to the H.Q.s for the theories. The calculation of the H/D ratio has the advantage, compared to the calculation of the H.Q., that it is not necessary to make a systematic reformulation of the hypotheses in the theory before making the calculation. The H/D ratio is simply calculated on the basis of counting the pages classified as belonging to the H- and D-levels respectively. It is therefore interesting to note that the highest H/D ratio is that of Maslow's theory. We think that in this case, at least, the H/D ratio is a more reliable and valid measurement of the theory's theory-empiry ratio than is the H.Q. The next highest H/D ratio is that of Woodworth's theory, but in this case the reader should take into account that we have based

---

3. The M-H-D-ratio could, of course, be calculated more exactly by a computer, which could be programmed to count all the words in the different levels.

Name of Psychologist	Total of M+H+D in percentages	H/D ratio
Duffy	4.2.+24.8+71.0	0.35
Bindra	8.7+42.7+48.6	0.88
Berlyne	6.3+52.5+41.2	1.29
Konorski	7.7+53.9+38.3	1.42
Pribram	20+44.7+34.3	1.32
Brown	18.8+43.1+37.9	1.13
Woodworth	33.8+40.6+25.6	1.95
Festinger	11.7+43.3+45.4	0.96
Cattell	29.7+38.9+31.3	1.29
Atkinson	10.7+48.0+41.5	1.14
Maslow	45.7+36.6+17.7	2.06
Average		1.25

Fig.20.5 This table presents the M-H-D ratio in percentages and the H/D ratio. These figures are calculated from the number of pages in the books dealt with and classified as belonging to the M, H, or D-levels respectively. In the M-H-D ratio the numbers are transformed into percentages in order to make them comparable.

The H/D ratio is calculated on the basis of the percentage figures for the H and D-levels of the theories. The H/D ratio is comparable to the H.Q.

The above figures are calculated on the basis of counting the pages in the main books analyzed. In the case of Atkinson we have used Atkinson and Birch (1960) and Atkinson and Feather (1965). In the case of Cattell we have used Cattell (1965). We have not calculated the figures for Miller's theory because his work is distributed in several papers and in several co-authored books.

our calculation solely on those chapters dealing exclusively with motivation. And that only represents a third of the book.

In order to investigate the correlation between the H.Q. and the H/D ratio we have placed both of them in the same co-ordinate system, with the H/D ratio on the y-axis and the H.Q. on the x-axis. (See Fig. 20.6.).

As can be seen from the figure there is a positive correlation between the H.Q.s and the H/D ratios of the 11 theories. Although we think the number of theories is too small to make an actual calculation of the correlation coefficient between the H.Q.'s and the H/D ratios, the graphic demonstration would seem to recommend the use of the H/D ratio in estimating the potential explanatory power. And as already mentioned the H/D ratio has the advantage of being easier to calculate – so easy that it could be done by a computer.

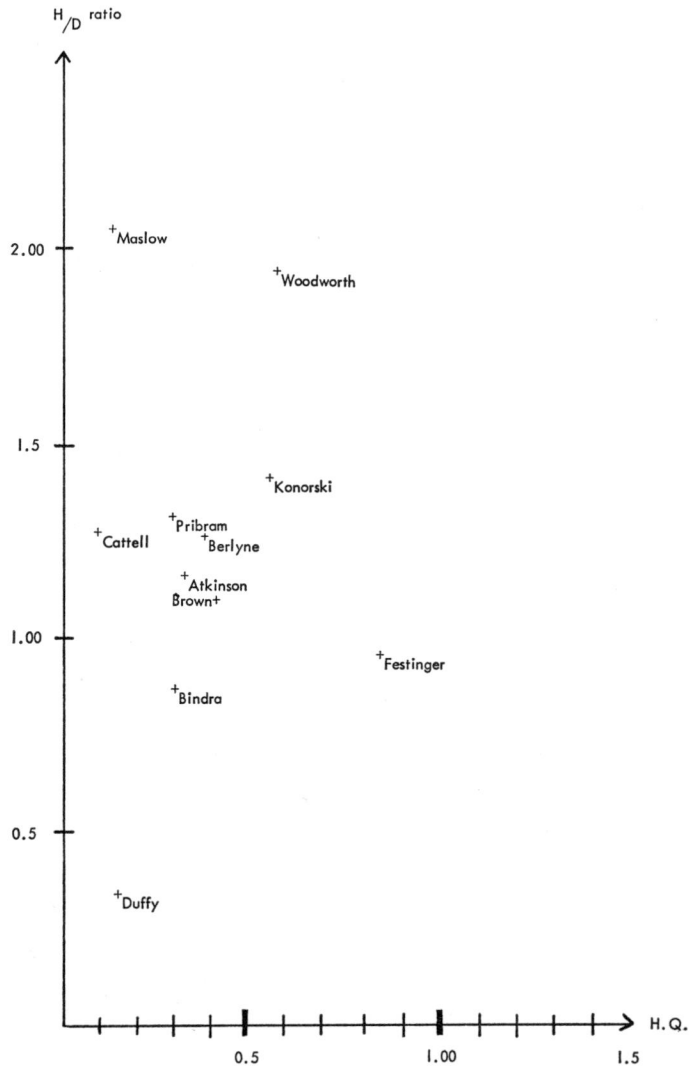

Fig. 20.6 Correlation between the H.Q. and the H/D ratio.

Concluding Remarks

We have now finished our comparative study of the modern theories of motivation selected.

We hope that the reader has acquired a broad impression of modern theories of motivation and deeper *insight* into psychological theorizing in general.

If this is the case we have demonstrated the *utility* of the comparative metascientific study of theories, *systematology*. And in the last chapter we showed that *systematology can be based upon exact methods*. Although these results are only a beginning, we look forward to developing these exact methods with the help of computers. They can *calculate* the H.Q. and other ratios as well as *simulate* the logical structure of theories. And *exact scientific methods have been regarded as the ideal* – at least in the *natural sciences*. The present author still accepts this ideal – although he knows now that it is not the *only* possible ideal of science.

Appendix A:
Patterns of Preferences

In Chapter 17 we introduced the concept "patterns of preferences" of points-of-view about metascientific problems. We postulated the existence of 3 main patterns of preferences or "paradigms":

1. *The Empiricist Paradigm:*
   Radical Empiricism, Materialism and Descriptionism (or Reductionism) with H_O-terms and Behavioral Data Language.

2. *The Intuitionist Paradigm:*
   Intuitionism (or Metaphorism), Dualism, Mentalism with H_M-terms and Phenomenological Data Language.

3. *The Rationalist Paradigm:*
   Rationalism, Neutral Monism, Instrumentalism with H_N-terms and Combined Data Language.

We now have a possibility of confirming our postulate, as we have the results of all the classifications of modern and earlier theories of motivation. We present them here in one combined classification scheme (see Fig. 20.A).

As can be seen from the scheme, there are 3 theories which almost exclusively belong to the Intuitionist paradigm. Those of: Maslow, Moore and Allport. (The last mentioned belongs to the Intuitionist paradigm in 4 out of the 5 possible classifications).

And there are also 3 theories which belong exclusively to the Empiricist paradigm. Those of: Duffy, Bindra and Skinner.

Furthermore there are 9 theories which belong exclusively to the Rationalist paradigm, those of: Miller, Woodworth, Festinger, Cattell, Atkinson, McDougall, Tolman, Lewin and Murray.

The rest of the theories belong more or less consistently to the Rationalist paradigm *or* to the Empiricist paradigm.

In order to get more precise information about the consistency of the paradigms (and the confirmation of our postulate) we have counted the number of theories which consistently follow a pattern of preference or paradigm in all five classifications. There are 14 theories which are "100 % consistent". *This gives us a 58 % ratio of 100 % consistency.* If we also add the 7 theories which – like Allport's – are "inside" the paradigm in 4 out of the 5 possible classifications (i. e., theories which are "80 % consisten", *we get an 88 % ratio of 80–100 % consistency.*

The remaining three theories follow the pattern of preference in 3 out of the 5 possible classifications.

Metascientific paradigms	Empiricist paradigm	Rationalist paradigm	Intuitionist paradigm
Epistemological theories	Duffy Bindra Skinner McClelland Young	Miller; Woodworth Brown; Festinger Cattell; Atkinson McDougall; Tolman Tinbergen; Lewin Murray; Pribram Hull; Berlyne; Hebb Konorski	Maslow Moore Allport
Psychosomatic theories	Duffy; Tinbergen Bindra Skinner Hebb Konorski	Miller; Woodworth Brown; Festinger Cattell; Atkinson McDougall; Tolman Lewin; Murray; Young Hull; McClelland Pribram Berlyne	Maslow Moore Allport
Metatheories	Duffy; Konorski Bindra; Young Skinner; Tinbergen Hebb Pribram	Miller; Woodworth Brown; Festinger Cattell; Atkinson McDougall; Tolman Lewin; Murray Hull; McClelland Berlyne	Maslow Moore Allport
Preferred h-therms	Duffy; Young Bindra; Tinbergen Skinner Berlyne Hebb Konorski	Miller; Woodworth Brown; Festinger Cattell; Atkinson McDougall; Tolman Lewin; Murray Hull; McClelland Pribram	Maslow Moore Allport
Preferred data languages	Duffy; Hebb Binra; Tinbergen Skinner Brown Hull Berlyne	Miller; Woodworth Allport Festinger; Cattell Atkinson; McDougall Tolman; Lewin; Murray Young; McClelland Pribram; Konorski	Maslow? Moore

Fig. 20.A Metascientific paradigms. A classification of the earlier and modern theories of motivation according to the metascientific patterns of preferences or paradigms.

On the basis of these calculations *we regard our meta-scientific postulate about the patterns of preferences as fairly well confirmed.*

Thanks to the explicit calculations the reader may judge for himself.

Supplementary Comments. The above results about "patterns of preferences" were presented by the author at an international conference about "Pleasure, Reward and Preference" in Korsør, Denmark (June 5–9, 1972). One of the participants who also read a paper, was the English psychologist *H. J. Eysenck*, who proposed a very interesting hypothesis: The above 3 paradigms constitute a "dimension" if they are arranged in this way:

Rationalism	Empiricism	Intuitionism

And this dimension is – according to Eysenck – correlated with the personality dimension: Introversion-Extraversion. He has found the same correlation between this personality dimension and the selection of courses, as Royce found between his "psycho-epistemological profile" and the selection of studies. Thus mathematicians and physicists are introverts and rationalists, while chemists and biologists are ambiverts and empiricists and humanists and artists are extraverts and intuitionists.

If this hypothesis proposed by Eysenck is confirmed, we have made a step toward the integration of systematology and the psychology of scientists.

Appendix B.
Computer-Assisted Theory Analysis

Introduction

Since the publication of "Theories of Motivation" (1959) we have worked with the possibility of using computers for the calculation of the Hypotheses Quotient. The idea was rejected by computer experts in this country until the publication of the book "The General Inquirer" by *Philip J. Stone* et al. in 1966. In this book there is a description of the development of a computer program designed for *content analysis*[1]). As theory analysis can be regarded as a special kind of content analysis, it was natural to think that this program could also be developed for use in systematology. One of my graduate students, *Svend Jørgensen*, became interested in the project, and with the assistance of a

---

1. Among the various kinds of texts which the "General Inquirer" has been used to analyze are TAT stories. The program has been applied to McClelland's content analysis system.

computer expert, Licentiate in technology *Thomas Skousen*, he developed first a program for the calculation of the H.Q. and then went on with a program for the analysis of the logical structure of a theory.

In the following pages we present a very brief description of the project.

Calculation of the H. Q . . .

Introduction

The "General Inquirer" was designed for the identification and calculation of the number of certain words, e. g., those relevant for the motivational analysis of TAT stories. Therefore, it seemed natural to postulate that a program could be developed which identified certain theoretical terms and calculated the numbers and ratios between them.

In order to calculate the H.Q. the program should be able to:

1. classify sentences as being S-H, H-H, or H-R-hypotheses according to the content of S-, H-, and R-terms in the sentence,
2. count the number of sentences in the three categories, and
3. calculate the H.Q. according to the formula:

$$H.Q. = \frac{\Sigma(H \to H)}{\Sigma[(S \to H) + (H \to R)]}$$

For the purpose of trying out such a program Svend Jørgensen selected Hull's theory, because it is one of the most exact in psychology. A program has successfully been developed for the calculation of the H.Q. in Hull's theory, but it can in principle be expanded to calculate the H.Q. of any psychological theory which is formulated – or reformulated – systematically and precisely enough. The program comprises a "dictionary" and a "reading program".

The Dictionary

This part of the program consists of a list of words. It contains all the important S-, H-, and R-terms in Hull's theory. In addition, it includes all words – or phrases – which represent functional relationships, e. g., words like "determine", "is a function of", etc. The dictionary is stored in the computer's memory file.

The Reading Program

This part of the program instructs the computer to *identify* those words in a particular text which are to be fed into the computer. The identified words are then *checked* with the dictionary and *classified* according to the above mentioned system. On the basis of this classification of words, the program can identify *sentences* as hypotheses and place them in one of the three categories: S-H, H-H or H-R-. Then the program makes the calculation of the H.Q.

Editorial Work

Before the text can be fed into the computer, it has to be "edited". This means that all the sentences have to be single sentences ending with a / instead of a period. All reference words have to be substituted by the word they refer to. It was easy to carry out this editorial work with Hull's postulates without changing the content.

The Result

On the basis of a slightly "edited" version of Hull's postulate system (Cf. "A Behavior System", 1952) the computer calculated the H.Q. of Hull's theory as being 0.36. Our earlier (1959) calculation of his H.Q. gave a result of 0.30. The difference between these two results can be explained by the fact that the earlier calculation made "by hand" was based upon a reformulation, in which the motivational hypotheses of the theory were especially selected. Thus there is no doubt that a computer program can be developed, which can calculate the H.Q. – and other ratios of interest – if the theories are as precisely formulated as Hull's.

Analysis of the Logical Structure

Svend Jørgensen has continued his work with the development of computer programs for theory analysis. The next program, which is about to be finished, is designed for the *analysis of the logical structure of a theory*. It constitutes an analysis of all the *relationships* between the *terms* (variables, concepts), which appear in a particular theory. The word "relationship" includes in this case both the *functional* relationships, which can be formulated as *hypotheses*, and *constitutional* relationships, which can be formulated as definitions of terms. The quantitative relationships, which can be formulated in the theory analyzed, have been disregarded. The result of the logical analysis of a theory is a "catalogue" of the *terms and relationships* in the theory. In the case of each term it is indicated how many other terms the given term is related to and what kind of relationship it is. This catalogue of terms and relationships is presented by the computer as a *matrix* or as a *graphic model* of the theory. The graphic model of the theory makes it possible to obtain a quick and clear overview of the structure of the theory. It also makes it possible to see if the relationships between H-, S- and R-terms are direct or indirect. If there is an H-term, which has no relationships to any S or R-terms it can easily be detected[2]).

---

2. This program is general and can be applied to any systematic and precise theory as here to Hull's.

Positive Features of Computer Analysis

The positive features of such a computer analysis of the logical structure of a theory are manifest.

First: the development of a computer program certainly *increases the amount of systematological knowledge considerably*. The "dialogue" with the computer forces the metascientist to think and communicate much more clearly than he might otherwise do. Thus clarification and better problem formulation in systematology are the first and most direct results.

Second: computer analysis can be the basis for a *critical development of the theory*, which can be formally improved in the direction of a more consistent logical structure.

Third: computer analysis – especially in the form of making a graphic model of the theory – can be used as the basis for the detection of new functional relationships, which can be empirically investigated. Thus the computer program also facilitates *the empirical development of the theory*.

Finally: the computer program can become the basis for *the development of a computer assisted instruction program*. Such a program would be a valuable tool in the teaching of psychology in colleges and universities. The student would be aided in gaining a better overview of the various psychological theories and a deeper insight into metascientific problems.

To summarize we can state *that the development of computer-assisted theory analysis may have metascientific, psychological and educational value.*

Bibliography

ALLPORT, G. W. (1937): Personality: A Psychological Interpretation (N.Y.: Holt, Rinehart and Winston).
- (1961): Pattern and Growth in Personality (N.Y.: Holt, Rineholt and Winston).
AMONS, R. B. and C. H. AMONS (1962): Psychology of the Scientist: I. Introduction. Perceptual and Motor Skills, 1962, 15 (3), 748–50).
ANDREWS, P. M. (1963): Creativity and the Scientist. (Dissertation Abstracts, 1963, 23 (9)).
APEL, K.-O. (1967): Analytic Philosophy of Language and the Gesteswissenschaften (Foundations of Language. Suppl. Series Vol. 5. Dordrect: Reidel).
ATKINSON, J. W. (1958): Motives in Fantasy, Action and Society (Princeton, N. J.: Van Nostrand).
- (1964): An Introduction to Motivation (Princeton, N.Y.: Van Nostrand).
- and David Birch (1970): The Dynamic of Action (N.Y.: Wiley).
- N. T. Feather (Eds.) (1966): A Theory of Achievement Motivation (N.Y.: Van Nostrand).
AYER, A. J. (1959): Logical Positivism (Free Press Illinois).

BECK, L. W. (1950): Constructions and Inferred Entities (Philosophy of Science, 17, 1950).
BENTON, M. (1961): Creativity in Research and Invention in the Physical Sciences. An Annotated bibliography (USN Res. Lab. Rep. 1961).
BERGMAN, G. (1953): Theoretical Psychology (Annuar Review of Psychology, 1953, 4, 435–58).
- (1957): Philosophy of Science (Univ. Wisconsin Press).
BERKOWITZ, L. (1962): Aggression: A Social Physiological Analysis (N.Y.: McGraw-Hill).
- (1969): The Frustration-Aggression-Hypothesis Revisited (Berkowitz, L. (Ed.) Roots of Aggression (N.Y.: Atheoton Press).
BERLYNE, D. E. (1960): Conflict, Arousal and Curiosity (N.Y.: McGraw-Hill).
- (1963): Motivation Problems Raised by Exploratory and Epistemic Behavior (S. Koch (Ed.): Psychology – A Study of a Science. Vol. V. N.Y.: McGraw-Hill).
- (1965): Structure and Direction in Thinking (N.Y.: Wiley).
- (1967): Reinforcement and Arousal (David Levine (Ed.): Nebraska Symposium on Motivation. Lincoln: Nebr. Univ. Press).
- (1968): Attention as a Problem in Behavior Theory (D. Mostofsky (Ed.): Attention. N.Y.: Appleton).
- (1969): The Justifiability of the Concept of Curiosity (Paper delivered at the XIX International Congress of London).
- and K. B. Madsen (1973): Pleasure, Preference and Reward (N.Y.: Academic Press).
BINDRA, D. (1959): Motivation: A Systematic Reinterpretation (N.Y.: Ronald Press).
- (1969): The Interrelated Mechanism of Reinforeement and Motivation, and the Nature of their Influence on Response (David Levine (Ed.): Nebraska Symposium on Motivation. Lincoln: Nebr. Univ. Press).
BJØRKMAN, M. (1962): Psykologisk Forskning (Stockholm: Almquist).
BLOOMFIELD, L. (1939): Linguistic Aspects of Science (International Encyclopedia Unified Science, 1939, I, (4)).
BOHR, N. (1929): Atomteori og Naturbeskrivelse (Univ. Festskrift. Copenhagen).

BOLLES, R. C. (1967): Theory of Motivation (N.Y. and London: Harper).
- (1970): Species-Specific Defense Reactions and Avoidance Learning (Psychological Review 1970), 77, 32–48).
BORING, E. G. (1950): A History of Experimental Psychology (N.Y.: Appleton, 2nd. ed.).
- (1961): Psychological Factors in the Scientific Process (E. G. Boring: Psychologist at Large. N.Y.: Basic Books).
- (1963): History, Psychology and Science: Selected Papers (N.Y. and London: Wiley).
- Bridgman, Feigl, Israel, Skinner and Pratt (1945): Symposium on Operationism (Psychological Review 1945, Vol. 52, 5).
BRAITHWAITE, R. B. (1953): Scientific Explanations (London: Cambridge Univ.).
BROWN, J. S. (1961): The Motivation of Behavior (N.Y.: McGraw-Hill).
- and E. E. Farber (1968): Secondary Motivational Systems (P. R. Farnsworth (Ed.): Annual Review of Psychology. Palo Alto: Cal. Ann. Rev. Inc. Vol. 19).
- and E. E. Ghiselli (1955): Scientific Method in Psychology (N.Y.: McGraw-Hill).
BRUNSWIK, E. (1952): The Conceptual Framework of Psychology (Int. Encycl. Univ. Sc. Vol. II, 1952 (5)).
BUNGE, M. (1967): Scientific Research (N.Y.: Springer).
- (1969): Models in Theoretical Science (Wien: Verlag Herder (Akten des XIV Internationalen Kongresses für Philosophie, Wien, 1968).
BÜHLER, Charlotte (1933): Der Menschliche Lebenslauf als Psychologisches Problem (Göttingen: Verlag für Psychologie, 2. Aufl. 1959).
- (1928): Kindheit und Jugend (Leipzig: S. Hirzel.; 3. Aufl.).
- (1951): Maturation and motivation (Dialectica, 1951, 5, pp. 312–361).
- (1968): Psychology for Contemporary Living (N.Y.: Hawthorne).
- and Fred Massarik (1968): The Course of Human Life: A Study of Goals in the Humanistic Perspective. (N.Y.: Springer).

CAMPEL, N. R. (1920): Foundations of Science. (N.Y.: Dover).
CAMPELL, D. P. (1965): The Vocational Interests of American Psychological Association Presidents (American Psychologist 1965, 20, 636–44).
CANON, W. B. (1915): Bodily Changes in Pain, Hunger, Fear and Rage (N.Y.: Appleton-Century-Crofts).
CARLSSON, D. (1949): Dimensions of Behavior (Lund: Gleerp).
CARNAP, R. (1936–37): Testability and Meaning (Phil. Science).
- (1934): Formal and Factual Science (Erkenntnis).
- (1953): The Interpretation of Physics (H. Feigl and N. Brodbeck: Readings in the Philosophy of Science N.Y.: Appleton, pp. 309–18).
- (1953): The Two Concepts of Probability (Feigl and N. Brodbeck: Readings in the Philosophy of Science N.Y.: Appleton, pp. 435–55).
CATTELL, R. B. (1946): Description and Measurement of Personality (N.Y.: Harcourt).
- (1950): Personality: A Systematic Theoretical and Factual Study (N.Y. MacGraw-Hill).
- (1957): Personality and Motivation Structure and Measurement (N.Y.: World Book Co.).
- (1965): The Scientific Analysis of Personality (Penguin Books).
- (Ed.) (1974): Handbook of Modern Personality Theory (Englewood-Cliffs: Prentice-Hall).
CHAMBERS, J. A. (1964): Relating Personality and Biographical Factors to Scientific Creativity (Psychol. Monographs, General and Applied 1964, 78 (7), Whole No. 584, 20 pp.).
CLARK, K. E. (1957): America's Psychologists: A Survey of a Growing Profession (Washington D.C. American Psychological Association).
COFER, C. N. and M. H. Appley (1964): Motivation: Theory and Research (N.Y.: Wiley).
COLBY, K. M. (1955): Energy and Structure in Psychoanalysis (N.Y.: Ronald Press).
COOLEY, W. W. (1964): Research Frontier: Current Research on the Career Development of Scientists (Journal of Counseling Psychology, 1964, 11 (1), 88–93).

DATTA, LOIS-ELLIN (1963): Test Instructions and the Identification of Creative Scientific Talent (Psychological Reports, 1963, 12 (2), 495–500).
DEUTSCH, J. A. (1960): The Structural Basis of Behavior (Chicago: Univ. of Chicago Press).
DIEL, P. (1948): Psychologie de la Motivation (Paris: Presses Universitaires de France).
DOLLARD, J. and N. E. Miller (1950): Personality and Psychotherapy (N.Y.: MacGraw-Hill).
DUFFY, ELISABETH (1962): Activation and Behavior (N.Y.: Wiley).

EINSTEIN, A. (1953): Geometry and Experience (H. Feigl and M. Brodbeck: Readings in the Philosophy of Science N.Y.: Appleton, pp. 189–94).
- (1953): The Fundamentals of Theoretical Physics (H. Feigl and M. Brodbeck: Readings in the Philosophy of Science. N.Y.: Appleton, pp. 263–71).
- (1953): The Laws of Science and the Laws of Ethics (H. Feigl and M. Brodbeck: Readings in the Philosophy of Science. N.Y.: Appleton, pp. 779–80).
EPSTEIN, S. (1962): The measurement of drive an conflict in humans (in M. R. Jones (Ed.): Nebraska Symposium on Motivation (Lincoln: Nebr. Univ. Press)).
ESPER, E. A. (1965): A History of Psychology as a Biological Science. (Philadelphia: Saunders).
ESTES, W. K. (1958): Stimulus-response theory of drive (in M. R. Jones (Ed.): Nebraska Symposium on Motivation (Lincoln: Nebr. Univ. Press)).
- et al. (1954): Modern Learning Theory (N.Y.: Appleton-Century-Crofts).
EYSENCK, H. J. (Ed.) (1964): Experiments in Motivation (Oxford: Pergamon Press).
- (1967): The Biological Basis of Personality (Springfield: C. C. Thomas).

FEIGL, H. (1951): Principles and Problems of Theory Construction in Psychology (W. Dennis et al.: Current Trends in Psychological Theory. N.Y.: Prentice-Hall).
- (1953): Notes in Causality (H. Feigl and M. Brodbeck: Readings in the Philosophy of Science. N.Y.: Appleton, pp. 408–18).
- and M. Brodbeck (1953): Readings in the Philosophy of Science (N.Y.: Appleton).
FESTINGER, L. (1957): A Theory of Cognitive Dissonance (Evanstone, Illinois: Row, Peterson).
- (1962): The Psychology of Insufficient Reward (Stanford: Stanford Univ. Press).
- (1964): Conflict, Decision and Dissonance (Stanford: Stanford Univ. Press).
- H. Riedam and S. Schachter (1956): When Profecy Fails (Minneapolis: Univ. of Minnesota Press).
FOWLER, H. (1965): Curiosity and Exploratory Behavior (N.Y. and London: McMillan).
- (1967): Satiation and Curiosity (in K. W. Spence and Janet Taylor Spence (Eds.): The Psychology of Learning and Motivation. Vol. I. N.Y. and London: Academic Press).
FREEMANN, G. L. (1948): The Energetics of Human Behavior (N.Y.: Cornell Univ. Press).
FREUD, S. (1915): Instincts and Their Vicissitudes (The Collected Papers of S. Freud. Paberback edition publ. by Collier Books. N.Y.).

GARRETT, H. E. (1941): Great Experiments in Psychology (N.Y.: Appleton).
GARWOOD, D. S. (1964): Personality Factors Related to Creativity in Young Scientists (Journal of Abnormal and Social Psychol. 1964, 68 (4), pp. 413–19).
GOLANN, STUART E. (1963): Psychological Study of Creativity (Psychol. Bull. 1963, 60 (6), pp. 548–565).
GRIFFITH, C. R. (1943): Principles of Systematic Psychology (Illinois: Illinois Univ. Press).

HABERMAS, J. (1967): Zur Logik der Sozialwissenschaften (Tübingen: J. C. B. Mohr).
HANSON, NORWOOD S. (1958): Patterns of Discovery. Reprinted. (Cambridge: Univ. Press).
HARLOW, H. F. (1953): Motivations as a Factor in the Acquisition of Responses (in M. R. Jones (Ed.): Nebraska Symposium on Motivation. Lincoln: Nebr. Univ. Press).
HARRE, R. (1961): Theories and Things (London).

HARTNACK, J. (1971): Mennesket og Sproget (København: Berlingske Forlag).
HAYS, R. (1962): Psychology of the Scientist: III. Introduction to Passages from the 'Idea Books' of C. L. Hull (Percep. & Motor Skills, 1962, 15 (3), pp. 803–806).
HEBB, D. O. (1949): Organization of Behavior (N.Y.: Wiley).
- (1952): The Role of Neurological Ideas in Psychology (in D. Krech and G. S. Klein (Eds.:) Theoretical Models and Personality Theory (Durham: Duke Univ. Press).
- (1955): Drives and the CNS (Conceptual Nervous System). (Psychol. Rev. 1955, 62, pp. 243–54).
HECKHAUSEN, H. (1963): Hoffnung und Furcht in der Leistungsmotivation (Mesenheim: Glan).
- (1967): The Anatomy of Achievement Motivation (N.Y.: Academic Press).
- (1968): Achievement Motive Research (in David Levine (Ed.): Nebraska Symposium on Motivation. Lincoln: Nebr. Univ. Press).
HEIDER, F. (1960): The Gestalt Theory of Motivation (in Marshall R. Jones (Ed.): Nebraska Symposium on Motivation. Lincoln: Nebr. Univ. Press).
HEMPEL, C. G. (1935): Analyse Logique de la Psychologie (Paris: Revue de Syntese).
- (1952): Fundamentals of Concept Formation in Empirical Science (Intern. Encycl. of Unif. Sc. Vol. II, no. 7).
HILGARD, E. (1963): Motivation in Learning Theory (in S. Koch (Ed.): Psychology – A Study of a Science. Vol. V).
HINDE, R. A. (1956): Ethological Models and the Concept of 'Drive' (Brit. Journ. Phil. Sc. 1956, 6, pp. 321–31).
HULL, C. L. (1963): Principles of Behavior (N.Y.: Appleton).
- (1952): A Behavior System (New Haven: Yale Univ. Press).
- (1962): Psychology of the Scientist: IV. Passage from the 'Idea Books' of Clark L. Hull (Percept. & Motor Skills, 1962, 15, (3) pp. 807–882).
HUNT, McV. (1965): Incentive Motivation and its Role in Psychological Development (in David Levine (Ed.): Nebraska Symposium on Motivation. Lincoln: Nebr. Univ. Press).
HUTTEN, E. (1956): The Language of Modern Physics. (London).
HYMAN, R. (1964): The Nature of Psychological Inquiry (N.Y.: Prentice-Hall).
IRWIN, F. W. (1971): Intentional Behavior and Motivation – A Cognitive Theory (Philadelphia: Lippincott).

JONES, E. (1964): The Life and Work of Sigmund Freud (Harmondsworth: Penguin Books).
JØRGENSEN, J. (1935): Filosofiske Forelæsninger (Copenhagen: Munksgaard).
- (1941): Psykologi på Biologisk Grundlag (Copenhagen: Munksgaard).
- (1949): Remarks Concerning the Concept of Mind and the Problem of Other People's Mind (Theoria, 1949, 15, pp. 116–127).
- (1955): Hvad er Psykologi? (Copenhagen: Munksgaard).
- (1956): Sandhed, Virkelighed og Fysikkens Metode (Copenhagen: Munksgaard).

KAILA, E. (1939): Den Mänskliga Kundskapen (Stockholm: Natur og Kultur).
- (1942): Psykikalismus und Phänomenalismus (Theoria, 1942), 8, pp. 85–125).
- (1944): Tankens Oro (Stockholm: Natur og Kultur.
- (1948): Personligheten Psykologi (Copenhagen: Nyt Nordisk Forlag).
KANTOR, J. R. (1953): The Logic of Modern Science (Bloomington: Principia Press).
- (1958): Interbehavioral Psychology (Indiana: Principia Press).
KAPLAN, A. (1964): The Conduct of Inquiry (San Franzisco: Chandler).
KOCH, S. (1941): Logical Character of Motivation Concept (Psych. Review, Vol. 48, 1941, pp. 15–37, 127–154).
- (1951): Theoretical Psychology 1950: An Overview (Psych. Review 1951, 58, pp.   ).
- (1959–63): Psychology – A Study of a Science (N.Y.: McGraw-Hill, Vol. I–VI).

Konorski, J. (1948): Conditioned Reflexes and Neuron Organization (Cambridge: Cambridge Univ. Press).
- (1963): On the Mechanism of Instrumental Conditioning (Proceedings of the 17th International Congress of Psychology, Washington).
- (1967): Integrative Activity of the Brain (Chicago: Univ. of Chicago Press).
Krech, D. (1951): Cognition and Motivation in Psychological Theory (in W. Dennes et al.: Current Trends in Psychology. Pittsburg).
- and G. S. Klein (Eds.) (1952): Theoretical Models and Personality Theory (London, Cambridge: Duke Univ. Press).
Kriedl, P. H. (1949): Differential Interest Patterns of Psychologists (Unpubl. Doct. Dissert. Univ. of Minnesota).
Kuhn, Th. S. (1962): The Structure of Scientific Revolutions (Chicago and London: Chicago Univ. Press).
Lehman, H. (1962): The Creative Production Rates of Present Versus Past Generations of Scientists (Journal of Gerontology, 1962, 17, pp. 409–417).
Lesche, C. (1960): A Metascientific Study of Psychosomatic Theories (Copenhagen: Munksgaard).
Lewin, K. (1936): Principles of Topological Psychology (N.Y.: McGraw-Hill).
- (1938): The Conceptual Repsentation and the Measurement of Psychological Forces (Durham: Duke Univ. Press).
Lewis, C. J. (1946): An Analysis of Knowledge and Valuation (Paul Carus Clectures 7, serie 1945. Open Court Publishing Co., La Salle, Illinois).
Littman, R. A. and E. Rosen (1950): Molar and Molecular (Psych. Review 1950), 57, pp. 58–65).
Lockman, R. F. (1962): Characteristics of APA Members in the 1962 'National Scientific Register' (American Psychologis 1962), 17 (10), pp. 789–792).
Logan, A. (1960): Incentive (New Haven: Yale Univ. Press).
Luria, A. R. (1966): Human Brain and Psychological Processes (N.Y.: Harper and Row).
Lynn, R. (1966): Attention, Arousal and Orientation Reaction (Oxford: Pergamon Press).
MacCorquodale, K. and P. E. Meehl (1948): On a Distinction Between Hypothetical Constructs and Intervening Variables (Psychol. Review, 1948, 55, pp. 97–107).
Madsen, K. B. (1968): Theories of Motivation (Copenhagen: Munksgaard, 4th ed.).
- (1973): Theories of Motivation (in Benjamin B. Wolman (Ed.): Handbook of General Psychology (Englewood-Cliffs: Prentice-Hall).
Mandler, G. and W. Kessen (1959): The Language of Psychology (N.Y.: Wiley).
Marx, M. H. (1951): Intervening Variable or Hypothetical Construct (Psych. Review 1951, 58, pp. 235–47).
McClelland, D. C. (1951): Personality (N.Y.: Dryden Press).
- (Ed.) (1955): Studies in Motivation (N.Y.: Appleton).
- (1961): The Achieving Society (Princeton, N.Y.: Von Nostrand).
- J. W. Atkinson, A. Russel, Clark and L. Lowell (1953): The Achievement Motive (N.Y.: Appleton).
- and D. G. Winter (1969): Motivating Economic Achievement (N.Y.: The Free Press).
McDougall, W. (1908): An Introduction to Social Psychology (London: Methuen. The 1960 ed. is used here).
- (1932): The Energies of Men (London: Methuen).
Maslow, A. H. (1954): Motivation and Personality (N.Y.: Harper).
- (1966): The Psychology of Science (N.Y.: Harper).
Mill, J. S. (1843): A System of Logic.
Miller, G. A., E. Galantier and K. H. Pribram (1960): Plans and the Structure of Behavior (N.Y.: Holt, Rinehart and Winston).

MILLER, N. E. (1941): An Experimental Investigation of Acquired Drives (Psychol. Bull. 1941, 38, pp. 534–535).
- (1944): Experimental Studies in Conflict (in J. McV. Hunt (Ed.): Personality and the Behavior Disorders. N.Y.: Ronald).
- (1948): Studies of Fear as an Acquirable Drive (Journ. of Experimental Psych. 1948, 38, pp. 89–101).
- (1951): Lernable Drives and Rewards (in S. S. Stevens (Ed.): Handbook of Experimental Psychology. N.Y.: Wiley).
- (1957): Experiments on Motivation (Science, 1957, 126, pp. 1271–1278).
- (1959): Liberalization of Basic S-R-Concepts: Extention to Conflict-behavior, Motivation, and Social Learning (in S. Koch (Ed.): Psychology – A Study of a Science. Vol. II. N.Y.: McGraw-Hill).
- (1963): Some Reflections of the Law of Effect Produce a New Alternative to Drive Reduction (in M. R. Jones (Ed.): Nebraska Symposium on Motivation. Lincoln: Nebr. Univ. Press).
- (1965): Chemical Coding of Behavior in the Brain (Science, 1965, 148, pp. 328–338).
- (1967): Behavioral and Physiological Techniques (Handbook of Physiology, U.S.A. 1967).
- (1969): Learning of Visceral and Glandular Responses (Science, 1969, 163, pp. 434–445).
- and J. Dollard (1941): Social Learning and Imitation (New Haven: Yale Univ. Press).
MISIAK, HENRY and Virginia Sexton (1966): History of Psychology (N.Y.: Grune and Stratton).
MOORE, T. V. (1948): The Driving Forces of Human Nature (N.Y.: Grune and Stratton).
MORGAN, D. N. (1953): Creativity Today. A Constructive Analytical Review of Certain Philosophical and Psychological Work (Journ. of Aesthetics & Art Criticism 1953, 12, pp. 1–24).
MOWRER, O. H. (1950): Learning Theory and Personality Dynamics (N.Y.: Ronald Press).
- (1952): Motivation (Annual Review of Psych. 1952, Vol. 3).
- (1960): Learning Theory and Behavior (N.Y. and London: Wiley).
- (1960): Learning Theory and the Symbolic Processes (N.Y. and London: Wiley).
MURPHY, G. (1951): Historical Introduction to Modern Psychology (N.Y.: Harcourt).
MURRAY, EDW. J. (1965): Sleep, Dreams, and Arousal (N.Y.: Appleton).
MURRAY, H. A. et al. (1938): Explorations in Personality (Oxford: Oxford Univ. Press).
NAGEL, E. (1953): Teleological Explanations and Teleological Systems (in Feigl and Brodbeck :Readings in the Philosophy of Science. N.Y.: Appleton).
- (1961): The Structure of Science. Problems in the Logic of Scientific Explanation (London: Routledge and Kegan Paul).
NESS, A. (1936): Erkenntnis und Wissenschaftliches Verhalten. (Ed. by The Norwedish Academy of Science. Oslo).
- (1962): Science as Behavior (Oslo: Universitetsforlaget).
NEURATH, O., N. Bohr, I. Dewey, B. Russel, R. Carnap, C. W. Morris: Encyclopodia and Unified Science (Int. Enc. Unif. Sc. Vol. I, no. 1).
NUTTIN, J. (1968): Reward and Punishment in Human Learning (N.Y.: Academic Press).
PELZ, D. C. (1958): Social Factors in the Motivation of Engineers and Scientists (School Science and Mathematics, 1958, 58, pp. 417–429).
- (1964): Freedom in Research (International Science and Technique, 1964, 31, pp. 54–66).
PETERS, R. S. (Ed.) (1953): Brett's History of Psychology (London: Allen & Unwin).
POLANYI, M. (1958): Personal Knowledge (London: R. Kegan and Paul).
POPPER, K. R. (1965): The Logic of Scientific Discovery (N.Y.: Harper and Row).
- (1972): "Conjectures and Refutations" (4thed.) London.
POSTMAN, L. (Ed.) (1962): Psychology in the Making (N.Y.: Knopf).
PRATT, C. C. (1940): The Logic of Modern Psychology (N.Y.: MacMillan).
PRIBRAM, K. H. (1962): Interrelations of Psychology in the Neurological Disciplines (in S.

Koch (Ed.): Psychology – A Study of a Science. Vol. IV. (N.Y.: McGraw-Hill).
- (1965): Proposals for a Structural Pragmatism: Some Neuropsychological Considerations of Problems in Philosophy (in B. B. Wolman (Ed.): Scientific Psychology. N.Y.: Basic Books).
- (1969): Brain and Behavior (Penguin Modern Books. 4 Vol.).
- (1969): Unpublished Paper. The Second Banff Conference in Theoretical Psychology).
- (1971): The Language of the Brain (Englewood-Cliffs: Prentice Hall).

RADNITZKY, G. (1968): Contemporary Schools of Metascience (Göteborg, Sweden: Scandinavian Univ. Books. 2. ed. 1970).

RAPAPORT, D. (1959): The Structure of Psychoanalytic Theory: A Systematic Attempt (in S. Koch (Ed.): Psychology: – A Study of a Science. Vol. III. N.Y. McGraw-Hill).
- (1960): On the Psychoanalytic Theory of Motivation (in M. R. Jones (Ed.): Nebraska Symposium on Motivation. Lincoln: Nebr. Univ. Press).

RASMUSSEN, E. TRANEKJÆR (1956): Bevidsthedsliv og Erkendelse. (Copenhagen: Munksgaard).

RAZRAN, G. (1965): Russian Psychologist'S Psychology and American Experimental Psychology: A Historical and a Systematic Collation and a Look into the Future (Psychol. Bull. 1965, Vol. 63, pp. 42–64).

REICHENBACK, H. (1957): The Rise og Scientific Philosophy (Los Angeles: Univ. of California Press).

REVENTLOW, I. (1970): Studier af komplicerede psykobiologiske fænomener (Copenhagen: Munksgaard).

ROE, A. (1953): The Makkng of a Scientist (N.Y.: Dodd-Mead).

ROSENTHAL, R. (1963): On the Social Psychology of the Psychological Experiment (American Scientist 1963, 51, pp. 268–283).

ROYCE, J. R. (1973): The Present Situation in Theoretical Psychology (in Benjamin B. Wolman (Ed.): Handbook of General Psychology (Englewood-Cliffs: Prentice-Hall).

RUSSEL, B. (1922): The Analysis of Mind (London).
- (1927): Our Knowledge of the External World.
- (1940): An Inquiry into Meaning and Truth (London: Allen).
- (1948): Human Knowledge. (London: Allen).

RYLE, G. (1949): The Concept of Mind (London: Penguin).

SCHACHTER, S. (1959): The Psychology of Affiliation (Stanford: Stanford Univ. Press).

SCHULTZ, D. P. (1965): Sensory Restriction: Effects on Behavior (N.Y.: Academic Press).

SCRIVEN, M. (1964): Views of Human Nature (in Wann (Ed.): Behaviorism and Phenomenology (Chicago: Univ. of Chicago Press).

SMEDSLUND, J. (1951): Studies in Psychological Theory (Oslo).

SMITH, F. V. (1960): Explanation of Human Behavior (London: Constable).

SOKOLOV, E. N. (1960): Neural Models and the Orienting Reflex (in M. A. Brazier (Ed.): The Central Nervous System and Behavior N.Y.: Macy).
- (1963): Perception and the Conditioned Reflex (Oxford: Pergamon Press).

SPENCE, K. W. (1944): The Nature of Theory Construction in Contemporary Psychology (Psych. Review 1944, 41, pp. 47–68).
- (1948): The Methods and Postulates of 'Behaviorism' (Psych. Review 1948, 55, pp. 67–78).
- (1951): Theoretical Interpretations of Learning (In Stevens et al.: Handbook of Experimental Psychology. N.Y.: Wiley).
- (1960): Behavior Theory and Learning (Englewood-Cliffs: Prentice-Hall).
- and Janet Taylor Spence (Eds.): The Psychology of Learning and Motivation (N.Y. and London: Academic Press).

STEVENS, S. S. (1935): The Operational Basis of Psychology (American Psych. 1935, 47, pp. 323–330).

- (1935): The Operational Definition of Psychological Concepts (Psych. Review 1935, 42, pp. 517–527).
- (1939): Psychology and the Science of Science (Psych. Bull. 1939, 36, pp. 221–263).

STONE, P. et al (1966): The General Inquirer. A Computer Approach to Content Analysis (Mass.: The M.I.T. Press).

TEGEN, E. (1949): Amerikansk Psykologi (Stockholm: Tiden).

THOMAE, H. (Ed.) (1965): Allgemeine Psychologie II: Motivation (Göttingen: Hogrefe's Verlag für Psychologie).

TINBERGEN, N. (1951): The Study of Instinct (N.Y.: Oxford Univ. Press).

TOLMAN, E. C. (1932): Purposive Behavior in Animals and Men (N.Y.: Appleton).
- (1951): A Psychological Model (in T. Parson and E. A. Shills (Eds.): Toward a General Theory of Action. Cambridge, Mass.: Harvard Univ. Press).
- (1951): Operational Behaviorism and the Current Trends in Psychology. (In Collected Papers. Los Angeles: Univ. of Calif. Press).
- (1959): Principles of Behavior (in S. Koch (Ed.) Psychology – A Study of a Science. Vol. II. N.Y.: McGraw-Hill).

TOULMIN, S. (1953): The Philosophy of Science (London: Hutchinson).

TURNER, M. B. (1967): Philosophy and the Science of Behavior (N.Y.: Appleton).

TÖRNEBOHM H. (1955): Discourse Analysis (Theoria 1955, 21, pp. 42–54).
- (1957): Fysik och Filosofi (Gothenburg: Univ.)
- (1962): A Logical Analysis of the Theory of Relativity (Stockholm: Almquist).

VALPOLA, V. and P. Tørnudd (1963): Vetenskapeligt Samarbete och Inter-disciplinära Problem (Helsinki: Nordisk Sommeruniversitet).

WATSON, I. R. (1963): The Great Psychologists: From Aristotle to Freud (N.Y.: Lippincott).

WOLMAN, BENJAMIN B. (1960): Contemporary Theories and Systems in Psychology (N.Y.: Harper).
- (Ed.) (1973): Handbook of General Psychology (Englewood-Cliffs: Prentice-Hall).

WOODGER, J. H. (1939): The Technique of Theory Construction (Int. Encycl. Unif. Sci. Vol. II (5)).

WOODWORTH, R. S. (1918): Dynamic Psychology (N.Y.: Colombia Univ. Press).
- (1958): Dynamics of Behavior (N.Y.: Holt, Rinehart and Winston).
- and Mary Sheehan (1964): Contemporary Schools of Psychology (N.Y.: Ronald. 3rd. ed.).

WRIGHT, G. H.: Den Logiska Empirismen (Stockholm: Natur och Kultur).

YOUNG, P. T. (1936): Motivation of Behavior (N.Y.: Wiley).
- (1941): The Experimental Analysis of Appetite (Psych. Bull. 1941, 38, pp. 129–164).
- (1961): Motivation and Emotion (N.Y.: Wiley).

Index

Abduction: 245
A combined model: 427
Ability traits (Cattell): 247
Abstract D-levels of the theories: 431–432
Abstract descriptive terms: 431
Ach, N.: 85
Act (Irwin): 339, 346
Action: 437
Actions: 436
Activating variables (Brown): 202
Activation (Duffy): 98
Affective arousal: 84
Affective states (Atkinson): 281
Affiliation (Schachter): 385
Allport, G. W.: 90, 289, 395, 423
Analogies: 65
Analytical philosophy: 45
Analyzer (Luria): 353
Anokhin, P. K.: 123, 352
Anticipation-invigoration mechanism (AIM): 378
Antidrive units (Konorski): 135
Anti-theoretical: 13
Anxiety (Eysenck): 330
Apel, K. O.: 395, 437
Appley, M. H.: 377, 413
Arousal (Berlyne): 118
Arousal level (Bindra): 106
Aspiration (Atkinson): 285
Atkinson, J. W.: 268, 367, 378, 382, 423
Atkinson and Hull, a comparison: 274
Atkinson's and Birch's theory: chapter 14
Atkinson's and Birch's diagram: 282
Atkinson's original theory: 270
Attitudes (Cattell): 248, 252, 254
Attitudes towards theories: 13

Basic hypotheses of motivation: 426
Basic structure of life (Bühler): 322

Behavior acts: 435
Behavior-primacy theory: 214
Behavioral approach (Brown): 199
Behavioral data-language: 50
Behavioristic, phenomenological (Reventlow): 362
Berkowitz, L.: 375
Berkowitz's theory: 375–377
Berlyne, D. E.: 27, 84, 115, 328, 348, 350, 367, 372, 374, 380, 419, 432
Berlyne's theory: chapter 6
Berlyne's theory; diagram: 119
Bernard, C.: 420
Bindra, D.: 59, 83, 104, 346, 367, 436
Bindra's theory: chapter 5
Bindra's theory; diagram: 106
Birch, D.: 268, 367
Blood chemistry (Bindra): 106
Bolles, R. C.: 83, 314
Bolles's theory: 314–318
Boredom (Berlyne): 122
Boredom Drive (Fowler): 348
Boring, E. G.: 21, 26
Brain-model (Konorski): 130
Brown, J. S.: 83, 348, 353, 417
Brown's theory: chapter 10
Brown's theory; diagram: 201
Bühler, Charlotte: 90, 289
Bühler's theory: 318–327

Calculation of H. Q.: 454
Calculus: 38
Canalization learning (Nuttin): 355, 356, 357
Cannon, W. B.: 420
Categories of motivation (classification scheme): 428
Cattell, R. B.: 89, 243, 327, 362, 367, 429, 432, 441
Cattell and Hull, a comparison: 266, 267

Cattell's H-terms (Classification): 258
Cattell's theory: chapter 13
Cattell's theory; diagram: 249
Central motive state (Bindra): 114
Change-incentive-motivation (Fowler): 348
Chosen act (Irwin): 346
Christiansen, J. Thanning: 358, 364
Classifications of motivational variables: 414
Clinical method (Maslow): 295
Cofer, C. N.: 378, 413
Cofer and Appley's theory: 377
Cognitive elements (Festinger): 226
Cognitive model: 424
Cognitive status of theories: 398
Collative variables: 374
Collative variables (Berlyne): 126
Combined classification scheme: 412
Comparative-physiological criterion: 416
Comparative study: part III
Competence (Pribram): 158
Complex functional system (Luria): 352, 372
Complexity (Berlyne): 125
Complexity of hypotheses: 56
Complexity of hypotheses; classification scheme: 429
Computer-assisted analysis: 71, 453–456
Computer-assisted instruction: 456
Computer simulation programs: 65
Conception of man; classification scheme: 393
Conceptions of science: 394–395
Conceptions of science; classification scheme: 396
Conceptual conflicts (Berlyne): 125
Conceptual nervous system: 397
Concrete D-levels of the theories: 432
Concrete vs abstract meaning (Maslow): 294
Conflict (Festinger): 241
Conflict theory (Miller): 178
Constructive theories: 398
Consummatory forces (Atkinson): 277
Consummatory reflexes (Konorski): 147
Content analysis: 453
Continuum of abstraction: 42
Conventionalism: 397
Coping acts (Maslow): 299, 309
Correlation between H. Q. and $H/_D$: 449
Covering-law-explanation: 40
Creative expansion (Bühler): 323

Criteria for definition of primary motives: 416
Cue Criteria: 416
Cue-stimulus (Miller): 192
Curiosity (Fowler): 317
Curiosity (Konorski): 140
Curiosity behavior (Berlyne): 118
Cybernetic models: 398

Darwin: 78, 79
Data: 35, 59
Data language: 49, 50, 400–401
Data language; classification scheme: 401
Decision (Festinger): 237, 241
Deductive explanations: 37
Deductive systems: 37, 64
Defensive scientists (Maslow): 293
Definitions of motivational terms: 413
Descriptive strata of the theories: chapter 19
Descriptive stratum: 35, 59
Descriptive theories: 66
Descriptive units: 61
Descriptive units; classification scheme: 439
Descriptive units of theories: 397
Determinism: 57
Development of achievement motivation (Heckhausen): 380
Diagnostic rules (Irwin): 342, 343
Diagram-making (Konorski): 131
Dialectical-critical ideals of science: 395
Dialectical reversal: 396
Dialectical synthesis: 350
Dimensions of personality (Eysenck): 329
Dimensions of theories (Cattell): 244
Directive variables: 53
Disposition and function terms; classification schemes: 408, 409
Disposition variables: 52
Dissonance (Festinger): 225
Dreams: 383
Drive (Brown): 200
Drive$_{1, 2, 3}$ (Berlyne): 118
Drive and antidrive (Konorski): 135
Drive-stimulus (Miller): 192
»Drive x Habit« theory: 271
Dollard, J. et al.: 375, 381
Dualistic theories: 44, 45
Duffy, E.: 95, 330, 367
Duffy's theory: chapter 4
Duffy's theory; diagram: 97
Dynamic cross-roads (Cattell): 262, 263

Dynamic, directive and vector terms; classification schemes: 410, 411
Dynamic lattice (Cattell): 248
Dynamic traits (Cattell): 247
Dynamic variables: 53
Dysthymics: 335

Eclectics: 13
Emotional stability (Eysenck): 329
Emotional stability traits: 335
Empirical determinism (Bolles): 315
Empirical hypotheses: 55
Empirical law of effect: 194
Empirical law of effect (Bolles): 317
Empiricism: 390, 391, 453
Engram (Cattell): 251
Energizing variables (Brown): 202
Epistemic behavior (Berlyne): 126
Epistemological classification of theories: 65, 67
Epistemological properties: 443, 444
Epistemological propositions: 389
Epistemology: 17
Ergic drives (Cattell): 247, 249
Ergic tension level (Cattell): 251
Eros: 85
Ethological method: 363
Ethology: 358
Eupsychian principle (Maslow): 297
Existentialistic philosophy: 58
Existentialist philosophy: 319
Expectancies (Irwin): 339
»Expectancy x Value« theory: 271-378
Epectation (Atkinson): 271
Explanation: 36
Explanations, types of: 37
Explanatory power: 71, 415
Explanatory propositions: 36
Explanatory sketches: 37, 64
Explanatory terms: 36
Explanatory theories: 66
Exploratory behavior (Berlyne): 126
Exploratory behavior (Fowler): 347, 349
Exploratory behavior (Sokolov): 372
Expressive behavior (Maslow): 299, 309
Extraversion (Eysenck): 329
Extraversive traits: 335
Eysenck, H. J.: 89, 327, 453
Eysenck Personality Inventory: 336
Eysenck's theory: 327-337
Eysenck's theory; diagram: 334

Factor analysis: 327, 351
Factor analytic approach: 245
Farber, L. F.: 417
Fear of failure (Heckhausen): 379, 382
Fear-Relief System (Konorski): 135
Feather, N. T.: 268, 284
Festinger, Leon: 223, 424
Festinger's theory: chapter 12
Festinger's theory; diagram: 229
Field-theory: 56, 85
Fleischer, Anne V.: 347
Force of resistance (Atkinson): 278
Forced compliance (Festinger): 238
Formal properties of models: 65
Formal properties of theories: 440-443
Fowler, H.: 347, 372, 419
Fowler's theory: 347-349
Freud, S.: 84, 384, 397, 420, 423
Freud-Lewin-Murray tradition: 93
Frustration-Aggression hypothesis: 375
Frustration interpretation of incentive motivation: 419
Frustration theory (Brown): 206
Function variables: 52
Functional autonomy: 89
Functional relationships: 37, 54, 56
Functional relationships; classification scheme: 430

Galton, Francis: 246
General activating drive (Brown): 202
General and differential psychology: 329
General Inquirer: 453
General metascientific theory: 390, 391
Geography of science: 23
Go mechanism (Miller): 180
Go mechanisms (Pribram): 159
Goal: 436
Goal (Bindra): 110
Goal-directed (Bindra): 110
Goal-directed activities: 105
Goal-directed behavior: 59, 435, 436
Goal Inventory (Bühler): 323
Goal Setting (Bühler): 321
Goldstein, Kurt: 296, 320
Gravsholdt, Jutta: 350, 372
Greenwald, A. G.: 354

Habermas, J.: 294, 395
Habit (Brown): 200
Habit strength (Bindra): 106

468 · Index

»Habit x Drive« theory: 378
Habituation (Knorski): 140
Hall, C. S.: 384
Hanson, N. R.: 40, 245
Harlow, H. F.: 422
Hartman, H.: 320
Hartnack, J.: 401, 437
H/D ratio: 447
Hebb, D. O.: 83, 104, 120, 121, 298, 423
Heckhausen, H.: 379, 382
Heckhausen's theory: 379–380
Hedonic arousal: 84
Hedonistic conception of motivation: 88
Hempel, C. G.: 39
H-H hypotheses: 55
Heider, F.: 424
Hermeneutic-humanistic ideals of science: 394
Heuristic: 39
Hierarchy hypotheses (Maslow): 298, 307
Higher-level-language: 13
Highly organized motives (Luria): 353
Hilgard, E. R.: 26
Historical-biographical method (Bühler): 321
Historical explanations: 40
Historical introduction: chapter 3
Historical survey (diagram): 91
History of psychology: 21
History of science: 20
Holistic-dynamic view (Maslow): 241
Homeostatic model: 420
H. Q.: 69, 70
Hope of success (Heckhausen): 379, 382
H.-R.-hypotheses: 55
Hull, C. L.: 81
Hull and Atkinson, a comparison: 274
Hull and Cattell, a comparison: 266, 267
Hull's formula: 82, 266, 348, 423
Humanistic approach: 437
Humanistic conception of man (Nuttín): 355
Humanistic indeterminism: 58
Humanistic model: 423
Humanistic philosophy of man: 320
Humanistic principle (Maslow): 297
Humanistic psychology: 58, 319
Hunger-Satiation System (Knorski): 134
Hypotheses of motivation: 420–429
Hypotheses of the theories: 420–430
Hypotheses Quotient: 69, 70

Hypotheses Quotients: 445
Hypothesis: 37, 54
Hypothetical constructs: 36, 46, 49
Hypothetical strata of the theories: chapter 18
Hypothetical stratum: 36, 51
Hypothetical terms: 404–419
Hypothetical variable: 47, 49
Hysterics: 335

Ideals of science: 395
Idiographic: 89
Idiographic vs. nomothetic: 395
Images of Achievement (Pribram): 153, 161, 163
Images of Events (Pribram): 153, 160, 163
Incentive (Bindra): 110
Incentive (Logan): 381
Incentive model: 422
Incentive theory of motivation (Bolles): 317
Incentive value (Atkinson): 271
Incorporation (Nuttín): 357
Indeterminism: 57
Induction model of memory: 157
Inductive-hypothetico-deductive method (Cattell): 245
Inductive-statistical explanations: 39
Inhibitory force (Atkinson): 278
Innate Releasing Mechanisms (IRM): 80, 260, 364
Instigating forces (Atkinson): 277
Instinct theories: 78–80
Instrumentalist view of science: 397
Integrated interests (Cattell): 253
Integrating self (Bühler): 323
Integrative neo-associationism (Berlyne): 116
Integrative theorists: 13
Intensity (Duffy): 101
Intent (Bühler): 322
Intention: 437
Intentional acts: 338, 346
Intentional behavior: 337
Interpretation of the H. Q.: 446
Interpreting theories: 66
Intervening variables: 47, 49, 436
Intrinsic motivation: 424
Introversion (Eysenck): 329
Introversion-Extraversion: 453
Intuitionism: 453
Invigoration (Cofer and Appley): 378

IRM (Innate Releasing Mechanisms): 80
Irwin, F. W.: 337
Irwin's concepts: 340
Irwin's theory: 337–347
Irwin's theory; diagram: 345

Jørgensen, Svend: 70, 431, 453, 455

Koch, S.: 26, 32, 386
Konorski, J.: 129, 328, 350, 367, 372, 382, 397
Konorski's theory: chapter 5
Konorski's theory; diagram: 138
Kuhn, Th.: 28, 32, 245, 415

Lashley, K.: 83
Law of effect: 423, 432
Law of reinforcement (Bolles): 317
Laws: 36, 54
Laws in the theories: 432
Laws of the life-cycle (Bühler): 325
Learned drives (Miller): 182
Lesche, C.: 19, 395, 437
Levels of abstraction: 59
Lewin, K.: 85, 397, 423, 424, 435
Liberal S-R theory: 174
Life-cycle structure (Bühler): 324
Life record data (Cattell): 264
Logan, F. A.: 381
Logan's theory: 381
Logical structure of theories: 455
London, I. D.: 269
Lorenz, K.: 80
Lower and higher needs (Maslow): 302
Luria, A. R.: 349, 372
Luria's theory: 349–354
Lynn, R.: 373

McClelland, D.: 87, 268, 379, 423
MacCorquodate, K.: 47
McDougal, W.: 79, 376, 436
Marcuse, H.: 396
Mathematical model: 38
Maudsley Personality Inventory: 336
Marx, K.: 350
Massarik, F.: 319
Maslow, A. H.: 90, 289, 426
Maslow's theory: chapter 15
Maslow's theory; diagram: 300
Mathematical theores: 64
May, Rollo: 289

Mechanistic theories: 56
Mediated learned drives (Miller): 183
Meehl, P. E.: 47
Mentalistic surplus meaning: 46
Metamotivation: 425
Metaphorism: 68
Metaphorism (intuitionism): 391
Metapsychology: 25
Metascience: 17
Metascience; model: 29
Metascientific paradigms: 402, 452
Metascientific patterns of preference: 402
Metascientific psychology: 24, 25
Metastrata of the theories: chapter 17
Metastratum: 41, 42
Metatheoretical propositions: 41, 46, 394 399
Metatheoretical propositions; classification scheme: 398
Metatheoretical psychology: 19
Metatheory: 18, 31
Methodological propositions: 41, 49
Methodological propositions: 399–403
Methodology: 18
Methods in psychology: 399
M-H-D-ratio: 447
M-H-D-ratio; classification scheme: 448
Micromolar theory (Logan): 381
Miller, N. E.: 47, 83, 174, 348, 353, 376, 415, 417, 432
Miller's theory: chapter 9
Miller's theory; diagram: 181
Mind-body problem: 392
Model: 38, 65
Model-explanations: 38
Models of motivation (Bindra): 113
Models of motivation; diagram: 421
Models in the model: 373
Molar: 429
Molar behavior: 401, 435
Molar theories: 62
Molecular: 439
Molecular behavior: 401, 435
Molecular theories: 62
Monistic theories: 44, 45
Monitor Images (Pribram): 153, 160, 163
Mono-theorists: 13
Moore, Th. V.: 423
Morgan, C. T.: 413
Motivated behavior: 435
Motive (Atkinson): 271

Motivational component factors (Cattell): 252, 253
Motivational systems: 415
Motivational terms, definitions: 413
Motivation (Atkinson): 271
Mowrer, O. H.: 83, 380, 381, 417
Mowrer's theory: 381–382
M-theories: 66, 67
Multi-dimensional hypotheses: 56
Multi-level conception of scientific discourses: 438
Multi-level structuralism (Pribram): 152
Multivariate experimental method: 246
Multivariate method: 362
Murray, H. E.: 86, 383, 383–385

Nagel, E.: 397
Naturalistic conception of man: 79
Naturalistic ideal of science: 394
Naturalistic theory: 437
Need (Nuttín): 356
Need satisfactions (Bühler): 323
Need system (Maslow): 301
Negaction tendency (Atkinson): 278
Ness, A.: 19
Nest behavior (stickleback): 364, 365, 366
Neuronal model (Sokolov): 372
Neuroses (Miller): 184
Neuroticism (Eysenck): 329
Neurotics: 335
Neutral surplus meaning: 40
Nomothetic: 89
Novelty (Berlyne): 125
Nuttín, J. R.: 354
Nuttín's theory: 354–358,

Objective test (Cattell): 247
Objective test data (Cattell): 264
One-dimensional hypotheses: 56
Operational definitions: 36
Operationel definitions: 431
Orientation reaction (Sokolov): 372
Orienting reflex (Sokolov): 372, 373
Outcome (Irwin): 339, 346
Oxford philosophy: 401

Pathologies of cognition (Maslow): 293
Patterns of preferences: 451–453
Pavlov-Hebb-tradition: 93
Pelz, C. C.: 22
Perceptual deprivation: 370

Persistence (Atkinson): 285
Personality syndrome (Maslow): 303
Phenomenological behaviorism: 362
Phenomenological data language: 50
Phenomenological propositions: 41, 42, 389–394
Philosophy of man: 290, 393
Philosophy of psychology: 19
Philosophy of science: 17
Philosophy of values: 290
Physiological criterion: 416
Physiological surplus meaning: 46
Piaget, J.: 245, 424
Pleasure principle: 423
Pluralistic view of science (Maslow): 292
Poincaré, H.: 397
Polanyi, M.: 173
Positive Reinforcing Mechanism (PRM): 106
Preciseness of representation: 64
Preciseness of representation; classification scheme: 441
Prediction: 38
Preference (Irwin): 339
Preferred methods; classification scheme: 400
Preservative drives (Konorski): 137
Pribram, K.: 328, 350, 372, 424, 437
Pribram's theory: chapter 8
Pribram's theory; diagram: 155
Primary motives; classifications: 417
Primary motives; definitions: 416
Principle of economy: 415
Principle of parsimony: 176, 224
PRM (positive reinforcing mechanism): 206
Probalistic theories: 58
Probality (Atkinson): 271, 285
Processes, States, Changes (Cattell): 256
Propensity (McDougall): 79
Properties of the models; classification scheme: 443
Protective drives (Konorski): 137
Protective reflexes (Konorski): 147
Protocol sentences: 35, 39
Pseudo-explanatory approach 414
Psychanalysis as a hermeneutic and naturalistic science: 396
Psycho-epistemological profile: 453
Psycho-epistemological theory (Royce): 391
Psychogenic needs (Murray): 87

Psychological conception of science (Maslow): 292
Psychological terms: 51
Psychological theory; diagram: 63
Psychology of psychology: 22
Psychology of science: 21
Psychopathological criterion: 417
Psychopaths: 335
Psychosomatic theories; classification scheme: 392
Psychosomatics: 335
Psychotics: 335
Purposive behavior: 59, 436

Questionnaire data (Cattell): 264

$R = f(S, O)$: 247
Radnitzky, G.: 395, 401, 437
Rapaport, D.: 84
Rationalism: 390, 391, 453
Reaction variables: 47, 61
Realist view of science: 397
Reinforcer (Bindra): 106, 110
Relational theory of needs (Nuttín): 355
Responsiveness (Duffy): 99
Retroflex (Woodworth): 220
Reventlow, I.: 358
Reventlow's theory: 358–367
Reventlow's theory; diagram: 364
RNA in memory (Pribram): 166
Rogers, C.: 289
Royce, J.: 68, 390, 453
R-R-laws: 432
R-R-relationships: 335
R-variables: 61

S- and R-variables; classification scheme: 433, 434
SAO system (Irwin): 338
Schachter, S.: 385
Schachter's theory: 385
Science (definition): 30
Scientific text: 43
Scientific theory: 43
Screen (Pribram): 157
School performance (Atkinson): 286
Schultz, D. P.: 367
Schultz's theory: 367–371
Secondary motivation: 417
Self-actualizing people (Maslow): 310, 311
Self-limiting adaptation (Bühler): 323

Sensitization function (Woodworth): 218
Sensitization-invigoration mechanism (SIM): 378
Sensoristasis (Schultz): 367, 368
Sensory cues (Bindra): 106
Sensory deprivation: 370
Sensory restriction: 370
Sentiments (Cattell): 247, 251
Signal reflexes (Luria): 353
Simulation: 38, 65
Simultaneous synthesis (Luria): 352
Situation, act, outcome: 339
Sleep motivation: 383
Skinner, B. F.: 83, 397, 435
Skousen, Th.: 454
Social psychology of science: 22
Social support (Festinger): 239
Sociology of psychology: 23
Sociology of science: 22
Sokolov, Y. N.: 328, 331, 367, 372
Sokolov's model: 373
Sources of drive (Brown): 204
Soviet conception of Man: 351
Soviet psychology: 350
Spearman, C.: 246
Spectator knowledge (Maslow): 293
Speculative philosophical approach: 414
Spence, K. W.: 55, 82, 423
Stop mechanisms (Pribram): 159
Strata of a theory: 35
Strata of psychological theories: 42
Strong vs. weak theories: 328
Structural Pragmatism (Pribram): 150
Subjective behaviorism (Pribram): 152
Success and failure (Atkinson): 286
Successive synthesis (Luria): 352
Surplus meaning: 36, 49, 52
Surplus meaning of H-terms; Classification schemes: 405, 406
Symbolized theories: 64
Syndrome analysis: 351
Systematic formulations: 32
Systematic metascience: 23
Systematic organization; classification scheme: 441
Systematic organization of theories: 62
Systematic theories: 37, 64
Systematological computer program: 71
Systematological Questionnaire: 72–77
Systematology; chapter 2: 18
Systematology; definition: 32

Taostic vs. controlling science (Maslow): 294
Task tension (Nuttín): 356
TAT: 87
Taxonomy of theories (Cattell): 244
Teleological explanations: 39
Temperamental traits (Cattell): 247
Tendency (Atkinson): 271
t/e-ratio: 69
Test Anxiety Questionnaire: 285
Thanatos: 85
The General Inquirer: 286
Thematic Apperception Test: 87
Theoretical hypotheses: 55
Theories as Wholes: chapter 20
Theories of knowledge; classification scheme: 391
Theory; definition: 33, 34
Theory-empiry-ratio: 69, 445, 446
Thing-language: 50
Thomae, H.: 26, 385, 416
Thomae's metatheory: 385
Thorndike, E. L.: 423
Thorndike-Hull-tradition: 93
Thought and action (Atkinson): 280
Three-dimensional models: 65
Tinbergen, N.: 80, 361, 363
Tolman, E. C.: 81, 346, 397, 401, 424, 435, 436
TOTE (Pribram): 155, 160, 170
TOTE-TO BE (Pribram): 172
Transformation concepts (Bindra): 105
Turner, Merle B.: 397
Two-dimensional models: 65
Two-factor theory of learning: 382
Type I, conditioned response (Konorski): 145

Type II, conditioned response (Konorski): 146
Types of explanation: 398
Types of explanation; classification scheme: 399
Types of theories: 443
Types of theories; classification scheme: 444
Törnebohm, H.: 19, 32

Uhrenholdt, Gorm: 354
Uncertainty (Berlyne): 125
Unconscious motivation (Maslow): 297
Unified theory of motivation: 378
Unintegrated interests (Cattell): 253
Units of description: 61
Univariate method: 246, 362
Upholding of internal order (Bühler): 323

Watson, J. B.: 435
Weak vs. strong theories: 328
Vector variables: 53
Verbal analogies: 65
Verbal theories: 64
Winter, D. G.: 379
Visceral brain (Eysenck): 330
Viscerogenic needs (Murray): 87
Vocational preferance (Atkinson): 286
Voluntary behavior (Luria): 353
Woodworth, R. S.: 80, 211, 424, 435
Woodworth's theory: chapter 11
Woodworth's theory; diagram: 215
World of science: 29

Yale group: 381
Young, P. T.: 84, 422

Modern theories of motivation:

4